THE PAPERS OF

WOODROW WILSON

VOLUME 52

SPONSORED BY THE WOODROW WILSON
FOUNDATION
AND PRINCETON UNIVERSITY

THE PAPERS OF

WOODROW
WILSON

CONTENTS AND INDEX, VOLUMES 40-49, 51

Volume 52 · 1916-1918

PRINCETON, NEW JERSEY

PRINCETON UNIVERSITY PRESS

1987

Printed in the United States of America
by Princeton University Press
Princeton, New Jersey

CONTENTS

Explanatory Note, ix

Contents

  Wilson Materials

    Addresses, statements, and press releases, 3
    Political correspondence, reports, and memoranda
      From Wilson, 7
      To Wilson, 26
    Diplomatic notes
      By Wilson and from Wilson, 48
      To Wilson, 49
    Correspondence, reports, memoranda, and aide-mémoire about
      diplomatic affairs
      By Wilson and from Wilson, 50
      To Wilson, 57
    Correspondence, reports, and memoranda about military and
      naval affairs
      By Wilson and from Wilson, 69
      To Wilson, 71
    Personal correspondence
      From Wilson, 74
      To Wilson, 78
    Interviews, 81
    Press Conferences, 82
    News Reports, 82
    Writings, 83

  Collateral Materials

    Political correspondence, reports, memoranda, and aide-
      mémoire, 83
    Diplomatic correspondence, reports, memoranda, and aide-
      mémoire, 91
    Correspondence, reports, and memoranda on military and
      naval affairs, 112
    Personal correspondence, 118
    Diaries, 118

Illustrations, 123

Indexes by volume, 125

Index, 127

EXPLANATORY NOTE

T HE eleven volumes covered by this cumulative table of contents and index begin with the last few months of American
neutrality and end on the very eve of the Armistice. Thus they con-
stitute the "Wartime Volumes" of *The Papers of Woodrow Wilson*.
During this cataclysmic era, the United States is drawn into the war
by the actions of Germany and thus participates in the first major
foreign war in its history. Thereby, the American people, as does
their President, face challenges unlike any they have ever experi-
enced before. As Wilson's stature as a war leader grows, so does his
importance as a leader of the western powers. Moreover, looking beyond the conflict to the return of peace, he begins to plan for a new
international order.

Although each of these volumes has its own table of contents and
index, Volume 52 brings all these together in one place: consolidated, integrated, and arranged in alphabetical, topical, and chronological order. Here we have sought to provide the reader and re-
searcher with a convenient and detailed guide to the subjects,
events, and personalities which fill these volumes.

We have not included Volume 50, *The Complete Press Conferences, 1913-1919*, because it covers an earlier period, 1913-1915,
and to have integrated its index in the present volume would have
served only to confuse rather than to edify.

The Table of Contents is divided into two main sections: Wilson
Materials and Collateral Materials. Together, they list, under special
editorial headings and in alphabetical or chronological order, all the
items printed in Volumes 40-49 and Volume 51. Correspondence,
reports, memoranda, or aide-mémoire by Wilson and to Wilson are
arranged alphabetically under separate categories, depending upon
whether the subject matter is primarily political, diplomatic, or personal. Wilson's public addresses, statements, diplomatic notes,
press conferences, interviews with him, or news reports about him
are arranged chronologically under the relevant heading. Collateral
correspondence, reports, memoranda, or aide-mémoire follow the
same arrangement as that described for the Wilson Materials. Illustrations are listed separately.

The index includes all persons, places, and subjects mentioned in
the text and footnotes. All books, articles, pamphlets, and poems are
indexed by author and title. Book titles and plays appear in italics;
quotation marks are omitted for articles, editorials, and poems.
Newspapers are listed under the city of publication; magazines are

listed under their titles, with places of publication added in parentheses. Page references to footnotes which carry a comma between the page number and the "n" cite both the text and the footnote, thus: "186,n2." Absence of the comma indicates reference to the footnote only, thus: "354n1." In both cases, the page number refers to the page on which the textual reference occurs.

This index supersedes the individual indexes of Volumes 40-49 and Volume 51: it corrects errors and omissions discovered since their publication. *Subjects* are indexed selectively, not exhaustively; this is not intended to be a concordance to Wilson's writings and statements.

Phyllis Marchand prepared the indexes of Volumes 40-49 and 51. The consolidation, arrangement, and typing of the Table of Contents was done by Susannah Jones Link and reviewed by David W. Hirst. Anne Cipriano Venzon consolidated the individual volume indexes and prepared the typescript. All major entries were checked for accuracy by Fredrick Aandahl. All index entries were reviewed by the Editor, Manfred F. Boemeke, and David W. Hirst. However, from the beginning to the end, the Senior Associate Editor had chief responsibility for and worked unflaggingly on this volume. I join the entire staff in congratulating him on a superb achievement.

THE EDITOR

Princeton, New Jersey
July 31, 1986

THE PAPERS OF
WOODROW WILSON
VOLUME 52

CONTENTS
FOR VOLUMES 40–49, 51

WILSON MATERIALS

Addresses, statements, and press releases

Remarks upon giving the signal to light the Statue of Liberty, Dec. 2, 1916, **40:** 119

After-dinner remarks celebrating the illumination of the Statue of Liberty, Dec. 2, 1916, **40:** 119

Annual messages on the State of the Union, Dec. 5, 1916, **40:** 155; Dec. 4, 1917, **45:** 194

Remarks to a Social Security Conference, Dec. 8, 1916, **40:** 188

After-dinner remarks to the Gridiron Club, Dec. 9, 1916, **40:** 193; Feb. 17, 1917, **41:** 240; Dec. 8, 1917, **45:** 238

Remarks to a woman suffrage delegation, Jan. 9, 1917, **40:** 427

A memorial tribute to Admiral Dewey, Jan. 16, 1917, **40:** 491

An address to the Senate, Jan. 22, 1917, **40:** 533

Remarks to the Maryland League for National Defense, Jan. 25, 1917, **41:** 10

Veto messages, Jan. 29, 1917, **41:** 52; July 1, 1918, **48:** 471; July 11, 1918, **48:** 589; July 12, 1918, **48:** 595

An address to a joint session of Congress, Feb. 3, 1917, **41:** 108

A statement reassuring foreign depositors of the safety of their accounts, Feb. 8, 1917, **41:** 157

An address to a joint session of Congress, Feb. 26, 1917, **41:** 283

An unpublished statement about plans to filibuster legislation in the House and Senate, Feb. 26, 1917, **41:** 287

A statement on filibustering in the Senate ("a little group of willful men"), March 4, 1917, **41:** 318

The Second Inaugural Address, March 5, 1917, **41:** 332

A proclamation calling a special session of Congress, March 21, 1917, **41:** 446

A draft of a resolution declaring the existence of a state of war with Germany, April 1, 1917, **41:** 516

The war message to Congress, April 2, 1917, **41:** 519

A statement on legislation for the increase of army and navy forces, April 6, 1917, **41:** 550

Drafts of an Executive Order establishing the War Trade Committee, April 10, 1917, **42:** 49; April 21, 1917, **42:** 118

A press release about the creation of the Committee on Public Information, April 14, 1917, **42:** 59

An appeal to the American people, April 15, 1917, **42:** 71

A proclamation about the penalties for disloyalty and treason, April 16, 1917, **42:** 77

A news report about remarks at the reception of Ignacio Bonillas, April 17, 1917, **42:** 79

A draft of a proclamation about registration under the Selective Service Act, May 1, 1917, **42:** 180

Remarks to a conference of state councils of national defense, May 2, 1917, **42:** 185

A statement announcing the creation of the Red Cross War Council, May 10, 1917, **42:** 258

Remarks at the dedication of the Red Cross building, May 12, 1917, **42:** 281

Remarks to the Labor Committee of the Council of National Defense, May 15, 1917, **42:** 296

A statement on the limited objectives of censorship, May 17, 1917, **42:** 304

A statement objecting to the organization of volunteer army divisions, May 18, 1917, **42:** 324

A statement on the Lever bill, May 19, 1917, **42:** 344

A proclamation establishing Red Cross Week, May 25, 1917, **42:** 391

A Memorial Day address at Arlington Cemetery, May 30, 1917, **42:** 422

A statement to a conference on classical studies at Princeton University, June 2, 1917, **42:** 439

Remarks to the twenty-seventh annual reunion of Confederate veterans in Washington, June 5, 1917, **42:** 451

A Flag Day address, June 14, 1917, **42:** 498

Remarks to the National Service Commission of the Presbyterian Church, June 19, 1917, **42:** 536

An emended draft of the Executive Order establishing the Exports Council, June 22, 1917, **42:** 558

A statement explaining the responsibilities of the Exports Council, June 26, 1917, **43:** 14

A greeting to the new Russian ambassador, July 5, 1917, **43:** 100

An emended statement on the purposes of exports controls, July 8, 1917, **43:** 122

An Executive Order defining the authority of the United States Shipping Board Emergency Fleet Corporation, July 11, 1917, **43:** 144

A statement to the American people, July 12, 1917, **43:** 151

A statement to soldiers and sailors about the Bible, July 23, 1917, **43:** 244

A press release about the resignations of George Washington Goethals and William Denman, July 24, 1917, **43:** 260

A message to the soldiers of the National Army, Aug. 7, 1917, **43:** 380; Sept. 4, 1917, **44:** 142

An address to the officers of the Atlantic Fleet, Aug. 11, 1917, **43:** 427

A press release on the scale of prices for bituminous coal, Aug. 21, 1917, **44:** 3

A statement on the price of wheat, Aug. 30, 1917, **44:** 89

Memorandum on the appointment of the President's Mediation Commission, Sept. 18, 1917, **44:** 214

A statement on the price of copper, Sept. 20, 1917, **44:** 223

A statement of appreciation for the work of the Sixty-fifth Congress, Oct. 6, 1917, **44:** 317

A proclamation designating Oct. 28 as a day of prayer, Oct. 18, 1917, **44:** 399

A reply in support of a delegation from the New York State Woman Suffrage party, Oct. 25, 1917, **44:** 441

A statement on the need for food conservation, Oct. 25, 1917, **44:** 443

A Thanksgiving proclamation, Nov. 7, 1917, **44:** 525

An appeal to the American people to assist local and district selective service boards and registrants under the new regulations, Nov. 8, 1917, **44:** 533

An appeal to the American people to join the Red Cross, Nov. 9, 1917, **44:** 555

An address in Buffalo to the American Federation of Labor, Nov. 12, 1917, **45:** 11

Lessons of the War, Dec. 3, 1917, **45:** 187

A proclamation on the takeover of the railroads, Dec. 26, 1917, **45:** 358

A proposed statement on the progress of the war effort (draft), Dec. 31, 1917, **45:** 407

An address to a joint session of Congress regarding federal control of the railways, Jan. 4, 1918, **45:** 448

The Fourteen Points Address: first drafts, Jan. 5, 1918, **45:** 476; shorthand draft, Jan. 6, 1918, **45:** 493; transcript of the shorthand draft, Jan. 6, 1918, **45:** 506; final draft, Jan. 7, 1918, **45:** 519; Address to a joint session of Congress, Jan. 8, 1918, **45:** 534

A reply to an address by James Duval Phelan, Jan. 10, 1918, **45:** 560

A proclamation concerning various measures to assure the conservation of food, Jan. 17, 1918, **46:** 19

A statement on the fuel order, Jan. 18, 1918, **46:** 25

A statement on the observance of the Sabbath in the army and the navy, Jan. 20, 1918, **46:** 41

A press release in reply to Senator Chamberlain's address alleging inefficiency in governmental bureaus and departments, Jan. 21, 1918, **46:** 55

A statement approving a maximum price for copper, Jan. 21, 1918, **46:** 59

A message to a farmers' conference, Jan. 31, 1918, **46:** 174

The Four Points Address: outline, Feb. 8, 1918, **46:** 273; draft, Feb. 8, 1918, **46:** 274; revised draft, Feb. 8-10, 1918, **46:** 291; Address to a joint session of Congress, Feb. 11, 1918, **46:** 318

Remarks to farmers' representatives, Feb. 8, 1918, **46:** 281

A statement announcing a guaranteed price for wheat, Feb. 24, 1918, **46:** 430

A draft of an address in response to the Reichstag speech by Count von Hertling, March 1, 1918, **46:** 496

A message to the Fourth All-Russia Congress of Soviets, March 11, 1918, **46:** 598

Remarks to representatives of livestock growers, March 13, 1918, **47:** 3

An address in Baltimore on the first anniversary of America's entry into the war, April 6, 1918, **47:** 267

A proclamation establishing the National War Labor Board, April 8, 1918, **47:** 282

Remarks to foreign correspondents, April 8, 1918, **47:** 284

A press release about a conference with friends of Liberia, April 8, 1918, **47:** 289

An appeal to the American people for additional support of the Red Cross, May 4, 1918, **47:** 515

A proclamation making May 30, 1918, a day of public humiliation, prayer, and fasting, May 11, 1918, **47:** 598

A message to the Italian people on the anniversary of Italy's entry into the war, May 11, 1918, **47:** 600

An address in New York on behalf of the American Red Cross, May 18, 1918, **48:** 53

A message to various ethnic societies, May 23, 1918, **48:** 117

An address to a joint session of Congress, May 27, 1918, **48:** 162

An unpublished statement about General Leonard Wood, May 28, 1918, **48:** 173

An Executive Order establishing the War Industries Board as a separate governmental agency, May 28, 1918, **48:** 176

Remarks to Mexican editors, June 7, 1918, **48:** 255

A platform for the Indiana Democratic party, June 15, 1918, **48:** 318

Remarks to a delegation from the United States Employment Service, June 15, 1918, **48:** 320

An appeal to employers and workers on behalf of the United States Employment Service, June 17, 1918, **48:** 333

A message to teachers, June 28, 1918, **48:** 455

An address at Mount Vernon about war objectives, July 4, 1918, **48:** 514

A press release on the action of the United States and Japan in Siberia, July 19, 1918 (draft), **49:** 39; Aug. 3, 1918, **49:** 170

A statement on lynchings and mob violence, July 26, 1918, **49:** 97

A statement on the Fourth Liberty Loan, July 26, 1918, **49:** 99

A statement urging increased coal production, July 31, 1918, **49:** 144

A proclamation requesting the granting of rate increases to transit companies, Aug. 14, 1918 (draft), **49:** 252; Sept. 6, 1918, **49:** 458

An addendum to a registration-day proclamation, Aug. 27, 1918, **49:** 358

A memorandum fixing a guaranteed price on next year's wheat crop, Aug. 29, 1918, **49:** 391

A statement extending *de facto* recognition to the Czechoslovak National Council, Aug. 30, 1918 (draft), **49:** 405; Sept. 2, 1918, **49:** 415

A statement on various courts-martial, Aug. 31, 1918, **49:** 400

A Labor Day message, Sept. 2, 1918, **49:** 414

A statement on Sunday School education, Sept. 3, 1918, **49:** 422

A statement on the cancellation of a western speaking tour, Sept. 9, 1918, **49:** 490

A statement condemning the Red Terror, Sept. 18, 1918 (draft), **51:** 62; Sept. 20, 1918, **51:** 78

A preamble to a proclamation designating Oct. 12, 1918, as Liberty Day, Sept. 19, 1918, **51:** 75

An address in the Metropolitan Opera House, Sept. 27, 1918, **51:** 127

A statement promoting the Fourth Liberty Loan, Sept. 28, 1918, **51:** 146

An address to the Senate on behalf of the woman suffrage amendment, Sept. 30, 1918, **51:** 158

Remarks to a group of American blacks, Oct. 1, 1918, **51:** 168

Remarks to a group of suffragists, Oct. 3, 1918, **51:** 190

An appeal to voters for the election of a Democratic Congress: draft by Joseph Patrick Tumulty, Oct. 11, 1918, **51:** 304; fragment of first draft, Oct. 13, 1918, **51:** 317; second draft, Oct. 15, 1918, **51:** 343; third draft, Oct. 17, 1918, **51:** 353; final draft, Oct. 19, 1918, **51:** 381

An unpublished statement on the establishment of a Conference of National Labor Adjustment Agencies, Oct. 17, 1918, **51:** 368

An appeal to the peoples of the constituent nations of Austria-Hungary, Nov. 5, 1918, **51:** 603

Political correspondence, reports, and memoranda

From Wilson to

William Charles Adamson, Dec. 5, 1916, **40:** 163; Dec. 12, 1916, **40:** 218; Jan. 25, 1917, **41:** 13; Jan. 29, 1917, **41:** 54; April 11, 1917, **42:** 34; June 27, 1917, **43:** 20; June 29, 1917, **43:** 39; Sept. 1, 1917, **44:** 116; March 29, 1918, **47:** 191

Jane Addams, Nov. 23, 1916, **40:** 46; Dec. 27, 1916, **40:** 335; Dec. 28, 1916, **40:** 343; Jan. 15, 1918, **45:** 593

Harry Clay Adler, Oct. 29, 1918, **51:** 482

Archibald Stevens Alexander, July 20, 1910, **51:** 649

Joshua Willis Alexander, Jan. 3, 1917, **40:** 387; Feb. 8, 1918, **46:** 282; Feb. 12, 1918, **46:** 329

The American Alliance for Labor and Democracy, June 10, 1918, **48:** 275

George Weston Anderson,, Dec. 11, 1917, **45:** 267

A draft of a bill authorizing the arming of American merchant vessels, Feb. 24, 1917, **41:** 279

Henry Fountain Ashurst, July 9, 1917, **43:** 131; April 16, 1918, **47:** 349

George Babbitt, Oct. 22, 1918, **51:** 404

John Miller Baer, Feb. 18, 1918, **46:** 370

David Baird, July 31, 1918, **49:** 139

Bernard Nadal Baker, Jan. 26, 1917, **41:** 21

Newton Diehl Baker

1916

Nov. 20, 1916, **40:** 3; Nov. 22, 1916 (2), **40:** 37; Dec. 26, 1916 (2), **40:** 330

January–June 1917

Jan. 4, 1917 (2), **40:** 405, 406; Jan. 13, 1917, **40:** 464; Jan. 16, 1917, **40:** 492; Jan. 23, 1917, **40:** 551; Feb. 13, 1917, **41:** 209; March 31, 1917, **41:** 509; April 4, 1917, **41:** 542; April 11, 1917 (3), **42:** 34; April 16, 1917, **42:** 75; April 26, 1917, **42:** 135; May 3, 1917 (3), **42:** 201; May 5, 1917, **42:** 221; May 8, 1917, **42:** 242; May 14, 1917, **42:** 292; June 13, 1917, **42:** 495; June 25, 1917 (2), **43:** 4, 5; June 29, 1917, **43:** 41

July–December 1917

July 3, 1917, **43:** 78; July 5, 1917 (2), **43:** 102; July 12, 1917, **43:** 156; July 17, 1917 (2), **43:** 192, 193; July 18, 1917, **43:** 203; Aug. 8, 1917, **43:** 391; Aug. 16, 1917 (3), **43:** 489, 492; Aug. 20, 1917, **43:** 535; Aug. 21, 1917 (2), **44:** 8, 10; Aug. 27, 1917, **44:** 62; Aug. 29, 1917, **44:** 81; Sept. 1, 1917, **44:** 108; Sept. 18, 1917, **44:** 212; Sept. 19, 1917, **44:** 216; Sept. 20, 1917, **44:** 224; Sept. 21, 1917 (2), **44:** 231, 232; Sept. 25, 1917, **44:** 248; Oct. 2, 1917, **44:** 293; Oct. 13, 1917, **44:** 372; Oct. 15, 1917, **44:** 382; Oct. 20, 1917, **44:** 412; Oct. 26, 1917, **44:** 449; Nov. 1, 1917, **44:** 482; Nov. 3, 1917, **44:** 498; Nov. 5, 1917, **44:** 512; Nov. 6, 1917 (2), **44:** 515; Nov. 8, 1917 (2), **44:** 533, 535; Nov. 10, 1917, **44:** 571; Nov. 12, 1917, **45:** 25; Nov. 15, 1917, **45:** 51; Nov 19, 1917, **45:** 75; Nov. 20, 1917, **45:** 92; Dec. 7, 1917, **45:** 230; Dec. 24, 1917, **45:** 349

1918

Jan. 9, 1918 (2), **45:** 546, 547; Jan. 15, 1918, **45:** 594; Jan. 16, 1918, **46:** 3; Jan. 17, 1918, **46:** 13; Feb. 1, 1918, **46:** 206; Feb. 18, 1918, **46:** 369; Feb. 19, 1918, **46:** 385; Feb. 25, 1918, **46:** 446; May 1, 1918, **47:** 478; May 7, 1918, **47:** 545; May 8, 1918, **47:** 554; May 9, 1918, **47:** 577; May 13, 1918, **48:** 3; May 22, 1918, **48:** 115; May 31, 1918, **48:** 208; June 3, 1918, **48:** 230; June 12, 1918, **48:** 290; June 19, 1918 (2), **48:** 357; July 15, 1918, **48:** 609; July 24, 1918, **49:** 71; July 26, 1918, **49:** 101; July 30, 1918, **49:** 129; Aug. 2, 1918, **49:** 158; Aug. 6, 1918, **49:** 185; Aug. 12, 1918, **49:** 236; Aug. 13, 1918, **49:** 242; Aug. 20, 1918, **49:** 294; Aug. 23, 1918, **49:** 334; Aug. 24, 1918, **49:** 347; Aug. 26, 1918, **49:** 350; Aug. 27, 1918, **49:** 358; Aug. 28, 1918, **49:** 368

John Hollis Bankhead, Jan. 26, 1917, **41:** 23; Jan. 11, 1918, **45:** 568; Jan. 26, 1918, **46:** 103

John Hollis Bankhead, Jr., May 16, 1918, **48:** 30

James Alfred Bardin, May 9, 1918, **47:** 579

Bernard Mannes Baruch, May 8, 1917, **42:** 244; May 16, 1917, **42:** 301; Aug. 27, 1917, **44:** 64; Sept. 25, 1917, **44:** 247; Jan. 19, 1918, **46:** 36; Feb. 12, 1918, **46:** 330; March 4, 1918, **46:** 520; March 12,

1918, **46:** 607; March 16, 1918, **47:** 43; March 27, 1918, **47:** 159; May 24, 1918 (2), **48:** 139; May 28, 1918, **48:** 176; June 3, 1918, **48:** 228; July 1, 1918, **48:** 474; July 15, 1918, **48:** 611; July 29, 1918, **49:** 121

Elizabeth Merrill Bass, May 4, 1917, **42:** 214; Dec. 8, 1917, **45:** 242; Jan. 9, 1918, **45:** 545; Jan. 22, 1918, **46:** 67; May 22, 1918, **48:** 116; June 20, 1918, **48:** 365

Harrison Leroy Beach, July 24, 1918, **49:** 73

John Crepps Wickliffe Beckham, Sept. 19, 1918, **51:** 76

John H. Beckmeyer, April 18, 1918, **47:** 359

Martin Behrman, Aug. 13, 1918, **49:** 240

George Lewis Bell, Aug. 22, 1917, **44:** 27

Thomas Montgomery Bell, July 19, 1917, **43:** 210

Christie Benet, Sept. 18, 1918, **51:** 59; Sept. 26, 1918, **51:** 122

Jacques A. Berst, June 4, 1917, **42:** 447; Aug. 11, 1917, **43:** 431; Aug. 21, 1917, **44:** 13

Samuel Reading Bertron, Dec. 5, 1916, **40:** 167; Oct. 5, 1917, **44:** 309; Oct. 11, 1917, **44:** 359; Dec. 29, 1917, **45:** 389; Jan. 11, 1918, **45:** 569; April 18, 1918, **47:** 359; July 24, 1918, **49:** 72

Julio Betancourt, Dec. 27, 1916, **40:** 334

Anita Eugénie McCormick Blaine, April 22, 1918, **47:** 394; May 1, 1918 (2), **47:** 477

William Thomas Bland, Aug. 20, 1918, **49:** 295

Rudolph Blankenburg, March 14, 1918, **47:** 19

Frank C. Blied, Oct. 6, 1917, **44:** 318

Edward William Bok, June 21, 1918, **48:** 382

William Edgar Borah, Oct. 17, 1918, **51:** 356

Gutzon Borglum, Dec. 5, 1917, **45:** 214; Jan. 2, 1918, **45:** 427; Jan. 23, 1918, **46:** 82; Jan. 29, 1918, **46:** 150; Feb. 1, 1918, **46:** 205; March 15, 1918, **47:** 41; March 19, 1918, **47:** 67; March 28, 1918, **47:** 174; March 29, 1918, **47:** 193; April 4, 1918, **47:** 247; April 5, 1918, **47:** 259; April 11, 1918, **47:** 313; April 15, 1918, **47:** 344

William Patterson Borland, June 18, 1917, **42:** 531

Charles W. Boyle, E. J. Stack, and John O'Connell, Sept. 23, 1917, **44:** 243

Thomas W. Brahany, Jan. 8, 1916, **40:** 423; May 21, 1918, **48:** 95

Theodore Brent, July 25, 1917, **43:** 272

Arthur Brisbane, April 25, 1917, **42:** 129; Aug. 10, 1917, **43:** 416; Sept. 24, 1917, **44:** 245; Jan. 26, 1918, **46:** 102

Robert Somers Brookings, Dec. 11, 1916, **40:** 215; March 4, 1918, **46:** 523; March 12, 1918, **46:** 607; March 25, 1918 (2), **47:** 138; March 28, 1918, **47:** 173; April 22, 1918, **47:** 395; April 27, 1918, **47:** 450; May 3, 1918, **47:** 502; July 3, 1918, **48:** 489

Herbert Bruce Brougham, Dec. 15, 1916, **40:** 243; Oct. 30, 1917, **44:** 473

Edward Thomas Brown, March 29, 1918, **47:** 192

Louis Brownlow, March 15, 1918, **47:** 38; March 19, 1918, **47:** 66; Aug. 22, 1918, **49:** 314; Sept. 18, 1918, **51:** 61

Martin Grove Brumbaugh, June 4, 1917, **42:** 446

William Jennings Bryan, Nov. 30, 1916, **40:** 108; Dec. 27, 1916, **40:** 333; Dec. 29, 1916, **40:** 354; Feb. 2, 1917, **41:** 94; April 7, 1917, **42:** 4

William Christian Bullitt, Sept. 30, 1918, **51:** 162

John Burke, Aug. 30, 1917, **44:** 88

Albert Sidney Burleson, Nov. 27, 1916, **40:** 89; Feb. 9, 1917, **41:** 179; Feb. 27, 1917, **41:** 294; July 13, 1917, **43:** 164; July 19, 1917, **43:** 212; Aug. 7, 1917 (2), **43:** 381, 382; Aug. 27, 1917, **44:** 62; Sept. 4, 1917, **44:** 147; Sept. 24, 1917, **44:** 245; Oct. 4, 1917, **44:** 301; Oct. 11, 1917, **44:** 358; Oct. 13, 1917, **44:** 371; Oct. 18, 1917, **44:** 396; Oct. 23, 1917, **44:** 428; Oct. 30, 1917, **44:** 472; Dec. 8, 1917, **45:** 242; Jan. 19, 1918 (2), **46:** 37, 38; March 13, 1918, **47:** 8; March 30, 1918, **47:** 209; April 19, 1918, **47:** 372; May 1, 1918, **47:** 477; May 4, 1918, **47:** 516; May 8, 1918, **47:** 560; Aug. 1, 1918, **49:** 146; Aug. 3, 1918, **49:** 174; Sept. 16, 1918, **51:** 12; Oct. 29, 1918, **51:** 483

John Lawson Burnett, Jan. 23, 1917, **40:** 549

Otto H. Butz, April 12, 1918, **47:** 324

James Francis Byrnes, Aug. 22, 1918, **49:** 315

James Hall Caine, Oct. 29, 1918, **51:** 482

Charles Pope Caldwell, April 27, 1917, **42:** 144; Jan. 29, 1918, **46:** 148

Anthony Caminetti, March 26, 1917, **41:** 469

Ella E. Martin Caminetti, March 22, 1917, **41:** 453

Thomas Edward Campbell, July 12, 1917, **43:** 158

W. A. Campbell, Nov. 14, 1917, **45:** 46

Ezekiel Samuel Candler, Jr., May 8, 1917, **42:** 243

James Cannon, Jr., June 29, 1917, **43:** 42; July 3, 1917, **43:** 84

Arthur Capper, July 8, 1917, **43:** 123; July 8, 1918, **48:** 556; Aug. 13, 1918, **49:** 241

Washington Lee Capps, July 25, 1917, **43:** 271; Nov. 23, 1917, **45:** 103

Andrew Carnegie, Jan. 24, 1917, **41:** 5

Waddill Catchings, Aug. 21, 1917, **44:** 15; Jan. 18, 1918, **46:** 30

Carrie Clinton Lane Chapman Catt, Jan. 25, 1917, **41:** 13; May 8, 1917 (2), **42:** 241; Oct. 13, 1917, **44:** 372; June 13, 1918, **48:** 303; Sept. 18, 1918, **51:** 58; Sept. 30, 1918, **51:** 161

Thomas Lincoln Chadbourne, Jr., Aug. 30, 1917, **44:** 91; Sept. 1, 1917, **44:** 119

George Earle Chamberlain, Aug. 8, 1917, **43:** 393; Jan. 11, 1918, **45:** 566; Jan. 20, 1918, **46:** 49

William Lea Chambers, Dec. 21, 1916, **40:** 312; Oct. 26, 1917, **44:** 448; Feb. 26, 1918, **46:** 448

John Wilbur Chapman, Dec. 19, 1917, **45:** 330

Edwin Barfield Chappell, Aug. 22, 1918, **49:** 317

William Edwin Chilton, July 2, 1917, **43:** 69
Champ Clark, Nov. 16, 1917, **45:** 70; Jan 24, 1918, **46:** 90; June 12, 1918, **48:** 294
John Hessin Clarke, Dec. 21, 1916, **40:** 312; April 3, 1917, **41:** 536
Grosvenor Blaine Clarkson, March 26, 1918, **47:** 143, 527; May 8, 1918, **47:** 561
Frank Irving Cobb, May 23, 1917, **42:** 376; June 1, 1917, **42:** 433; Sept. 26, 1917, **44:** 265; Sept. 28, 1917, **44:** 274; Nov. 30, 1917, **45:** 161; Dec. 8, 1917, **45:** 241; Jan. 17, 1918, **46:** 17; Feb. 7, 1918, **46:** 264
William Frederick (Buffalo Bill) Cody, Nov. 20, 1916, **40:** 4
Howard Earle Coffin, April 20, 1918, **47:** 383; May 6, 1918, **47:** 537
John Sanford Cohen, March 7, 1918, **46:** 563; April 10, 1918, **47:** 312
Bainbridge Colby, Dec. 5, 1916, **40:** 162; July 25, 1917, **43:** 271; March 25, 1918, **47:** 137; Sept. 16, 1918, **51:** 14
Robert Bruce Coleman and Thomas Samuel Hawes, Aug. 29, 1917, **44:** 82; Sept. 4, 1917, **44:** 145
William Byron Colver, July 20, 1917, **43:** 221; Sept. 6, 1918, **49:** 460; Sept. 23, 1918, **51:** 92
Edwin Grant Conklin, Feb. 16, 1917, **41:** 235
Waldo Lincoln Cook, March 22, 1917, **41:** 450
Mortimer Elwyn Cooley, Jan. 18, 1918, **46:** 29
Edward Prentiss Costigan, May 31, 1918, **48:** 208
William Riley Crabtree, Feb. 28, 1917, **41:** 299
Charles Richard Crane, Nov. 22, 1916, **40:** 37; Jan. 16, 1917, **40:** 492; Jan. 23, 1917, **40:** 548; May 1, 1918, **47:** 478
George Creel
  1917
  May 14, 1917 (2), **42:** 290, 291; May 17, 1917, **42:** 304; June 25, 1917, **43:** 3; Aug. 10, 1917, **43:** 415; Sept. 4, 1917, **44:** 142; Sept. 25, 1917, **44:** 248; Sept. 27, 1917, **44:** 270; Oct. 27, 1917, **44:** 452; Nov. 5, 1917, **44:** 511; Nov. 20, 1917, **45:** 87; Nov. 23, 1917, **45:** 103; Nov. 30, 1917, **45:** 162; Dec. 8, 1917, **45:** 241; Dec. 10, 1917, **45:** 257; Dec. 24, 1917, **45:** 348; Dec. 29, 1917, **45:** 387
  1918
  Jan. 14, 1918 (2), **45:** 580; Jan. 16, 1918, **46:** 3; Feb. 18, 1918, **46:** 369; Feb. 22, 1918, **46:** 413; Feb. 28, 1918, **46:** 491; March 25, 1918, **47:** 134; March 30, 1918, **47:** 207; April 1, 1918, **47:** 215; April 15, 1918, **47:** 341; May 10, 1918, **47:** 586; May 24, 1918, **48:** 140; June 18, 1918, **48:** 346; June 26, 1918, **48:** 440; July 21, 1918, **49:** 51; July 31, 1918, **49:** 137; Aug. 2, 1918, **49:** 159; Aug. 3, 1918, **49:** 172; Aug. 8, 1918, **49:** 216; Sept. 4, 1918, **49:** 432; Sept. 30, 1918, **51:** 162
Herbert David Croly, Jan. 25, 1917, **41:** 13; Oct. 22, 1917, **44:** 420
Oscar Terry Crosby, July 2, 1918, **48:** 482
Enoch Herbert Crowder, Sept. 11, 1918, **49:** 514

Benedict Crowell, March 4, 1918, **46:** 525; March 5, 1918, **46:** 546; March 8, 1918, **46:** 573; March 15, 1918, **47:** 38; March 19, 1918, **47:** 66; April 5, 1918, **47:** 259; April 9, 1918 (2), **47:** 299, 300.

Charles Allen Culberson, May 14, 1917, **42:** 289

Homer Stillé Cummings, Oct. 24, 1918, **51:** 425; Nov. 5, 1918, **51:** 592

Minnie Fisher Cunningham, March 26, 1918, **47:** 144

Charles Curtis, Jan. 17, 1918, **46:** 16

Juliana Stevens Cuyler, Dec. 7, 1917, **45:** 232

Richard Heath Dabney, Aug. 13, 1917, **43:** 437

Thomas H. Daniel, Aug. 14, 1918, **49:** 246

Josephus Daniels, Jan. 11, 1917, **40:** 443; April 12, 1917, **42:** 43; May 16, 1917, **42:** 301; June 4, 1917, **42:** 446; June 22, 1917, **42:** 559; July 12, 1917, **43:** 156; Aug. 27, 1917, **44:** 60; Nov. 28, 1917, **45:** 148; Feb. 4, 1918, **46:** 238; Feb. 8, 1918, **46:** 286; March 7, 1918, **46:** 564; March 12, 1918, **46:** 607; March 21, 1918, **47:** 95; April 24, 1918, **47:** 412; July 24, 1918, **49:** 70; July 26, 1918, **49:** 105; July 31, 1918, **49:** 139; Sept. 6, 1918, **49:** 461; Sept. 25, 1918, **51:** 110; Oct. 4, 1918, **51:** 214

Winthrop More Daniels, Dec. 19, 1916, **40:** 279; Oct. 19, 1917, **44:** 400; Oct. 20, 1917, **44:** 413; Oct. 23, 1917, **44:** 428; Oct. 24, 1917, **44:** 434; Feb. 4, 1918, **46:** 238; March 29, 1918, **47:** 187; Aug. 2, 1918, **49:** 159; Aug. 7, 1918, **49:** 204; Aug. 10, 1918, **49:** 232; Aug. 30, 1918, **49:** 389; Sept. 6, 1918, **49:** 460; Sept. 23, 1918, **51:** 92; Oct. 1, 1918, **51:** 173; Oct. 7, 1918, **51:** 258

Clarence Seward Darrow, Aug. 9, 1917, **43:** 400

James L. Davidson, June 14, 1917, **42:** 504

Joseph Edward Davies, March 18, 1918, **47:** 52; April 12, 1918, **47:** 326

Felix Cordova Davila, May 13, 1918, **48:** 3

Ellen Duane Davis, Sept. 23, 1918, **51:** 93

Henry Pomeroy Davison, May 9, 1917, **42:** 251; June 3, 1918, **48:** 231

Kate Trubee Davison, March 4, 1918, **46:** 526

Perl D. Decker, Aug. 31, 1918, **49:** 402

Democrats of New Jersey, March 20, 1918, **47:** 82

William Denman, April 4, 1917, **41:** 542; July 3, 1917, **43:** 84; July 11, 1917, **43:** 144; July 18, 1917, **43:** 206; July 19, 1917, **43:** 211; July 24, 1917 (3), **43:** 257, 258, 259; July 25, 1917, **43:** 270

Collins Denny, May 4, 1917, **42:** 213

Stanley Hubert Dent, Jr., May 11, 1917, **42:** 274

Brice P. Disque, March 2, 1918, **46:** 510

Thomas Dixon, Jr., Jan. 25, 1917, **41:** 12

Alexander Monroe Dockery, Aug. 9, 1918, **49:** 224; Sept. 21, 1918, **51:** 85

Cleveland Hoadley Dodge, April 4, 1917, **41:** 542; Oct. 29, 1918, **51:** 486

John H. Donlin, Nov. 13, 1917, **45:** 41
J. L. Donnelly, Aug. 14, 1917, **43:** 461
William Henry Donner, May 14, 1917, **42:** 293
Garrett Droppers, Dec. 12, 1916, **40:** 219
Fred Thomas Dubois, Aug. 1, 1918, **49:** 147
Frank Duffy, April 15, 1918, **47:** 343
Maude Edwin Dunaway, March 9, 1918, **46:** 583
Jessie Kennedy Dyer, Sept. 20, 1918, **51:** 80
Leonidas Carstarphen Dyer, July 28, 1917, **43:** 299; Aug. 1, 1917,
    43: 336

Walter Evans Edge, Jan. 15, 1918, **45:** 592
Richard Hathaway Edmonds, Oct. 5, 1917, **44:** 308
Thomas Francis Egan, July 26, 1918, **49:** 103
Charles William Eliot, Nov. 27, 1916, **40:** 89; Jan. 29, 1917, **41:** 55;
    March 31, 1917, **41:** 510; April 7, 1917, **42:** 4; April 11, 1917, **42:**
    35; July 24, 1917, **43:** 261; July 27, 1917, **43:** 292; Nov. 2, 1918,
    51: 551; Nov. 8, 1918, **51:** 637
Howard Elliott, Dec. 28, 1917, **45:** 371

John Henry Fahey, Jan. 26, 1918, **46:** 103
John Cardinal Farley, Aug. 21, 1917, **44:** 12
Scott Ferris, Sept. 4, 1917, **44:** 145; April 24, 1918, **47:** 415; May 20,
    1918, **48:** 74; May 28, 1918, **48:** 177; Aug. 21, 1918, **49:** 304; Aug.
    27, 1918, **49:** 357; Sept. 10, 1918, **49:** 510; Sept. 17, 1918 (3), **51:**
    27; Oct. 1, 1918, **51:** 171; Nov. 7, 1918, **51:** 620
Edward Albert Filene, Sept. 7, 1918, **49:** 472; Nov. 2, 1918, **51:** 552
John Joseph Fitzgerald, March 2, 1917, **41:** 309; Sept. 4, 1917, **44:**
    147; Sept. 7, 1917, **44:** 161; Jan. 2, 1918, **45:** 422
William Bowyer Fleming, Jan. 25, 1917, **41:** 15; April 9, 1918, **47:**
    301
Duncan Upshaw Fletcher, Feb. 13, 1917, **41:** 209; Feb. 16, 1917, **41:**
    236
Joseph Wingate Folk, Aug. 8, 1918, **49:** 216
Henry Jones Ford, Jan. 23, 1918, **46:** 83
Rudolph Forster, Aug. 17, 1917, **43:** 505; Nov. 7, 1917, **44:** 526
John Franklin Fort, May 4, 1917, **42:** 212; July 2, 1917, **43:** 70; July
    14, 1917, **43:** 176; Aug. 9, 1917, **43:** 400; Aug. 21, 1917, **44:** 13
Raymond Blaine Fosdick, April 2, 1918, **47:** 222; Sept. 3, 1918, **49:**
    425; Sept. 30, 1918, **51:** 162
The Four Minute Men, Nov. 4, 1917, **44:** 505
John Fox, Sept. 1, 1917, **44:** 118
Joseph Irwin France, March 31, 1917, **41:** 510; July 11, 1917, **43:**
    146; Feb. 14, 1918, **46:** 343
Hugh Frayne, March 4, 1918, **46:** 523
Lynn Joseph Frazier, Jan. 23, 1917, **40:** 549
Joseph Sherman Frelinghuysen, Jan. 19, 1918, **46:** 36
Hollis Burke Frissell, Dec. 20, 1916, **40:** 293

Antoinette Funk, June 19, 1918, **48:** 361
Andrew Furuseth, Nov. 5, 1918, **51:** 593

Sterling Galt, April 1, 1918, **47:** 217
Helen Hamilton Gardener, May 14, 1917, **42:** 293; June 18, 1918,
    48: 347; June 24, 1918, **48:** 404; Aug. 21, 1918, **49:** 304; Oct. 10,
    1918, **51:** 294
William Gwynn Gardiner, Nov. 10, 1917, **44:** 562
Frederick Dozier Gardner, Aug. 13, 1917, **43:** 437
Harry Augustus Garfield, March 26, 1917, **41:** 468; April 11, 1917,
    42: 35; May 5, 1917, **42:** 222; Sept. 4, 1917, **44:** 144; Oct. 25, 1917,
    44: 444; Oct. 27, 1917, **44:** 453; Dec. 1, 1917, **45:** 176; Dec. 6, 1917,
    45: 221; Jan. 18, 1918, **46:** 28; March 11, 1918, **46:** 599; April 24,
    1918, **47:** 413; May 16, 1918, **48:** 31; July 15, 1918, **48:** 612; July
    18, 1918, **49:** 3; Aug. 3, 1918, **49:** 173
John Nance Garner, May 10, 1917, **42:** 260
Elbert Henry Gary, Oct. 1, 1918, **51:** 172
John Palmer Gavit, Nov. 27, 1916, **40:** 91; Jan. 29, 1917, **41:** 55
James Cardinal Gibbons, April 27, 1917, **42:** 145; Oct. 9, 1917, **44:**
    343
Washington Gladden, April 11, 1917, **42:** 35
Carter Glass, April 9, 1917, **42:** 21
Franklin Potts Glass, May 28, 1918, **48:** 177; July 31, 1918, **49:** 138;
    Aug. 9, 1918, **49:** 224
George Washington Goethals, July 11, 1917, **43:** 145; July 19,
    1917, **43:** 211; July 24, 1917, **43:** 259; July 25, 1917, **43:** 270; Jan.
    26, 1918, **46:** 105
Samuel Gompers, Dec. 6, 1916, **40:** 177; Dec. 11, 1916, **40:** 213;
    April 26, 1917, **42:** 134; June 13, 1917, **42:** 497; July 21, 1917, **43:**
    238; Aug. 8, 1917, **43:** 393; Aug. 27, 1917, **44:** 60; Aug. 31, 1917
    (draft), **44:** 95; Aug. 31, 1917, **44:** 101; Dec. 12, 1917, **45:** 276; Dec.
    24, 1917 (2), **45:** 348, 349; March 30, 1918, **47:** 207; May 9, 1918,
    47: 577; May 20, 1918, **48:** 74; June 10, 1918, **48:** 275; June 24,
    1918, **48:** 404; July 24, 1918, **49:** 73; Aug. 2, 1918, **49:** 158; Aug.
    6, 1918, **49:** 185; Aug. 8, 1918, **49:** 212
Thomas Pryor Gore, May 17, 1917, **42:** 314
Patrick Emmet Gorman, Oct. 4, 1918, **51:** 214
Charles Ashford Greathouse , Feb. 8, 1918, **46:** 285
Thomas Watt Gregory
    1917
    Feb. 19, 1917, **41:** 247; April 26, 1917, **42:** 134; June 4, 1917, **42:**
    446; June 20, 1917, **42:** 546; June 25, 1917, **43:** 5; June 28, 1917,
    43: 33; July 3, 1917, **43:** 86; July 7, 1917 (2), **43:** 116, 117; July
    11, 1917, **43:** 146; July 12, 1917, **43:** 154; July 13, 1917, **43:** 161;
    July 16, 1917, **43:** 187; July 23, 1917, **43:** 247; Aug. 17, 1917 (2),
    43: 503, 504; Aug. 27, 1917, **44:** 60; Aug. 30, 1917, **44:** 90; Sept.
    24, 1917, **44:** 246; Sept. 25, 1917, **44:** 247; Sept. 26, 1917, **44:** 265;
    Oct. 2, 1917, **44:** 290; Oct. 10, 1917, **44:** 347; Oct. 19, 1917, **44:**

405; Oct. 29, 1917, **44:** 463; Nov. 1, 1917, **44:** 480; Nov. 3, 1917, **44:** 497; Nov. 5, 1917, **44:** 512; Nov. 13, 1917, **45:** 39; Nov. 20, 1917, **45:** 92; Nov. 22, 1917, **45:** 95; Dec. 6, 1917, **45:** 223; Dec. 11, 1917, **45:** 268
1918
Jan. 10, 1918, **45:** 562; Jan. 26, 1918, **46:** 104; Jan. 28, 1918, **46:** 119; Feb. 27, 1918, **46:** 469; March 25, 1918, **47:** 136; April 1, 1918, **47:** 219; April 3, 1918 (2), **47:** 232; April 24, 1918, **47:** 414; May 10, 1918, **47:** 587; May 29, 1918, **48:** 193; May 31, 1918, **48:** 209; June 1, 1918 (3), **48:** 220; June 5, 1918, **48:** 241; June 12, 1918, **48:** 290; June 24, 1918, **48:** 405; June 26, 1918, **48:** 438; July 15, 1918, **48:** 612; Aug. 14, 1918, **49:** 247; Aug. 27, 1918, **49:** 357; Sept. 5, 1918, **49:** 451; Oct. 1, 1918 (2), **51:** 171, 172; Oct. 4, 1918, **51:** 211; Oct. 7, 1918, **51:** 257
Solomon Bulkley Griffin, May 3, 1918, **47:** 499
Don Niko Gršković, Dec. 5, 1916, **40:** 165
George Wilkins Guthrie, Dec. 11, 1916, **40:** 216; Feb. 27, 1917, **41:** 295

Leon Samuel Haas, June 4, 1918, **48:** 237
Matthew Hale, Dec. 5, 1916, **40:** 166; Oct. 2, 1917 (2), **44:** 292; Nov. 30, 1917, **45:** 160
Henry Clay Hall, May 4, 1917, **42:** 213; July 28, 1917, **43:** 300
Henry Noble Hall, Aug. 21, 1917, **44:** 12
Charles Sumner Hamlin, July 29, 1918, **49:** 118; Aug. 1, 1918, **49:** 148; Aug. 20, 1918, **49:** 295
George P. Hampton, Aug. 21, 1918, **49:** 304; Sept. 5, 1918, **49:** 452; Sept. 11, 1918, **49:** 515
William Procter Gould Harding, Nov. 26, 1916, **40:** 77; Nov. 27, 1916, **40:** 88; Dec. 11, 1917, **45:** 266; July 15, 1918, **48:** 611; July 18, 1918, **49:** 4; July 24, 1918, **49:** 73; Sept. 7, 1918, **49:** 472; Sept. 10, 1918, **49:** 511; Sept. 16, 1918, **51:** 12
Joseph Wright Harriman, Sept. 18, 1917, **44:** 212; Sept. 21, 1917, **44:** 231; Oct. 11, 1917, **44:** 360
Emerson Columbus Harrington, June 6, 1918, **48:** 248
William Julius Harris, Feb. 7, 1917, **41:** 146; Feb. 26, 1917, **41:** 288; March 2, 1917, **41:** 309; Feb. 13, 1918, **46:** 335; Sept. 6, 1918, **49:** 461
Francis Burton Harrison, Dec. 1, 1916, **40:** 112
Thomas Samuel Hawes, Oct. 8, 1917, **44:** 328
Pompey Long Hawkins, Jan 13, 1918, **45:** 579
Mary Garrett Hay, Nov. 8, 1917, **44:** 537
Frank J. Hayes, Jan. 8, 1918, **45:** 540; Aug. 8, 1918, **49:** 216
James Thomas Heflin, May 18, 1917, **42:** 326; May 22, 1917, **42:** 370; June 13, 1917, **42:** 497; July 2, 1917, **43:** 71
Guy Tresillian Helvering, April 19, 1917, **42:** 97
Francis Joseph Heney, Dec. 5, 1916, **40:** 166; Aug. 8, 1918, **49:** 215
Charles O'Connor Hennessy, Oct. 26, 1918, **51:** 452

John Grier Hibben, Jan. 11, 1918, **45:** 568

Henry Lee Higginson, July 3, 1917, **43:** 85; July 26, 1917, **43:** 282; Aug. 1, 1917, **43:** 338; Oct. 25, 1917, **44:** 444; Nov. 15, 1917, **45:** 53

Walker Downer Hines, Aug. 6, 1918, **49:** 186

Gilbert Monell Hitchcock, March 31, 1917, **41:** 510; July 11, 1918, **48:** 591; Oct. 22, 1918, **51:** 405

William Pettus Hobby, Nov. 30, 1917, **45:** 161

Hale Holden, Dec. 31, 1917, **45:** 403

Henry French Hollis, Feb. 17, 1917, **41:** 241; Feb. 21, 1917, **41:** 262; April 24, 1918, **47:** 414

Hamilton Holt, Feb. 27, 1918, **46:** 469; Aug. 24, 1918, **49:** 347

Richard Hooker, Feb. 27, 1917, **41:** 295; June 5, 1918, **48:** 242

Herbert Clark Hoover

1917

June 12, 1917, **42:** 485; June 13, 1917, **42:** 494; July 19, 1917, **43:** 210; Aug. 16, 1917, **43:** 493; Aug. 24, 1917, **44:** 38; Sept. 4, 1917, **44:** 146; Sept. 7, 1917, **44:** 160; Nov. 19, 1917, **45:** 74; Nov. 20, 1917 (2), **45:** 91; Nov. 27, 1917, **45:** 128; Nov. 30, 1917, **45:** 163; Dec. 10, 1917, **45:** 256

1918

Feb. 18, 1918, **46:** 368; Feb. 19, 1918 (2), **46:** 386; Feb. 21, 1918, **46:** 407; March 5, 1918, **46:** 546; March 8, 1918, **46:** 572; March 25, 1918, **47:** 137; March 27, 1918, **47:** 158; March 29, 1918, **47:** 192; April 2, 1918, **47:** 225; April 4, 1918, **47:** 246; May 8, 1918, **47:** 558; May 20, 1918, **48:** 75; May 28, 1918, **48:** 178; Aug. 27, 1918, **49:** 356; Aug. 28, 1918, **49:** 368; Sept. 2, 1918, **49:** 419; Sept. 3, 1918, **49:** 424; Sept. 10, 1918 (3), **49:** 509, 510; Sept. 20, 1918 (2), **51:** 80

Charlotte Everett Wise Hopkins, Feb. 1, 1918, **46:** 206; March 18, 1918, **47:** 53

John Appleton Haven Hopkins, Dec. 5, 1916, **40:** 166

Edward Mandell House, May 7, 1917, **42:** 235; July 29, 1917, **43:** 313; Sept. 17, 1917, **44:** 203; Feb. 25, 1918, **46:** 445

David Franklin Houston, Feb. 3, 1917, **41:** 112; Nov. 19, 1917, **45:** 76; Feb. 13, 1918, **46:** 335; March 4, 1918, **46:** 522; March 14, 1918, **47:** 20; March 29, 1918, **47:** 188; April 2, 1918, **47:** 222; July 26, 1918, **49:** 101; Sept. 5, 1918, **49:** 451

William Cannon Houston, Dec. 20, 1916, **40:** 292

William Schley Howard, April 12, 1918, **47:** 325; April 20, 1918, **47:** 382

Frederic Clemson Howe, Dec. 20, 1917, **45:** 334

Clark Howell, Aug. 7, 1918 (2), **49:** 205

George Huddleston, Aug. 12, 1918, **49:** 236

Charles Evans Hughes, Nov. 23, 1916, **40:** 46; May 8, 1918 (2), **47:** 553, 554; May 11, 1918, **47:** 603; May 13, 1918, **48:** 3; May 17, 1918, **48:** 45; Nov. 7, 1918, **51:** 618

Cordell Hull, May 16, 1918, **48:** 27

George Wylie Paul Hunt, July 2, 1917, **43:** 72; July 3, 1917, **43:** 87; Dec. 31, 1917, **45:** 403; March 11, 1918, **46:** 598; March 29, 1918, **47:** 187

Edward Nash Hurley, Dec. 19, 1916, **40:** 278; Jan. 10, 1917, **40:** 427; Feb. 2, 1917, **41:** 93; July 25, 1917, **43:** 270; Aug. 21, 1917, **44:** 13; Sept. 18, 1917, **44:** 211; Oct. 26, 1917, **44:** 449; Nov. 14, 1917, **45:** 46; Jan. 26, 1918, **46:** 101; Feb. 12, 1918, **46:** 329; March 2, 1918, **46:** 510; March 5, 1918, **46:** 546; March 13, 1918, **47:** 5; May 3, 1918, **47:** 500; May 24, 1918, **48:** 140; Sept. 16, 1918, **51:** 13; Nov. 6, 1918, **51:** 605

Paul Oscar Husting, May 3, 1917, **42:** 200; July 7, 1917, **43:** 117

William Levi Hutcheson, Feb. 17, 1918, **46:** 366

Camille Hart Irvine, Nov. 5, 1917, **44:** 513

Frank Watterson Jackson, Oct. 2, 1918, **51:** 180

Ollie Murray James, Sept. 5, 1917, **44:** 154; Jan. 23, 1918, **46:** 82; Jan. 26, 1918, **46:** 101; Feb 18, 1918, **46:** 368; June 24, 1918, **48:** 404

Charles Francis Jenkins, Sept. 27, 1917, **44:** 269

George Sibley Johns, April 25, 1917, **42:** 130

Ben Johnson, March 29, 1918, **47:** 192; Aug. 3, 1918, **49:** 174

Jesse Holman Jones, May 13, 1918, **48:** 6; May 22, 1918, **48:** 116

Rufus Matthew Jones, Aug. 28, 1917, **44:** 75

Thomas Davies Jones, Jan. 26, 1917, **41:** 24; Feb. 2, 1917, **41:** 93; Feb. 13, 1917, **41:** 208; July 27, 1917, **43:** 291; Aug. 2, 1917, **43:** 347; Dec. 27, 1917, **45:** 367

Julius Kahn, July 25, 1917, **43:** 272

Edward Keating, July 1, 1918, **48:** 474; Oct. 25, 1918 (draft), **51:** 461; Oct. 29, 1918, **51:** 482

John Reese Kenly, Nov. 24, 1917, **45:** 118; Nov. 26, 1917, **45:** 126; Nov. 27, 1917, **45:** 129; Nov. 30, 1917, **45:** 162

J. R. Kennamer, Sept. 4, 1917, **44:** 144

Mitchell Kennerley, Oct. 1, 1917, **44:** 287

William Kent, Dec. 11, 1916, **40:** 214; Dec. 20, 1916 (2), **40:** 290; Jan. 23, 1917 (2), **40:** 548, 561; Feb. 13, 1917, **41:** 208; July 17, 1917, **43:** 193; Feb. 28, 1918, **46:** 493; March 5, 1918, **46:** 547; May 1, 1918, **47:** 475; May 22, 1918, **48:** 116; Sept. 30, 1918, **51:** 161; Oct. 7, 1918, **51:** 257; Oct. 9, 1918, **51:** 281; Oct. 21, 1918, **51:** 393

William Squire Kenyon, March 14, 1918, **47:** 19

Edward John King, Aug. 2, 1917, **43:** 347

Claude Kitchin, Dec. 20, 1916, **40:** 293; April 10, 1917, **42:** 27; Jan. 17, 1918, **46:** 15; July 26, 1918, **49:** 105; Aug. 2, 1918, **49:** 163

John George David Knight, Aug. 8, 1918, **49:** 215

Ben La Fayette, Oct. 25, 1918, **51:** 444

Polk Lafoon, Oct. 10, 1918, **51:** 295

Thomas William Lamont, Oct. 18, 1918, **51:** 372; Nov. 4, 1918, **51:** 576

George Mason La Monte, Oct. 22, 1918, **51:** 403; Oct. 26, 1918, **51:** 451; Nov. 8, 1918, **51:** 640

Francis Griswold Landon, Dec. 5, 1916, **40:** 165

Franklin Knight Lane, Dec. 11, 1916, **40:** 214; Dec. 19, 1916, **40:** 278; Jan. 30, 1917, **41:** 69; May 5, 1917, **42:** 221; June 18, 1917, **42:** 533; June 29, 1917, **43:** 43; July 3, 1917, **43:** 84; Aug. 7, 1917, **43:** 385; Oct. 4, 1917, **44:** 301; Nov. 5, 1917, **44:** 512; Dec. 19, 1917, **45:** 329; Dec. 31, 1917, **45:** 402; Jan. 3, 1918, **45:** 433; Jan. 26, 1918, **46:** 101; Feb. 25, 1918, **46:** 439; March 14, 1918, **47:** 20; May 14, 1918, **48:** 11; Oct. 4, 1918, **51:** 213

Harry Lane, Jan. 3, 1917, **40:** 387; Feb. 9, 1917, **41:** 179

Robert Lansing, Dec. 3, 1916 (3), **40:** 129; Jan. 3, 1917, **40:** 385; Jan. 12, 1917, **40:** 447; Jan. 31, 1917 (4), **41:** 70; Feb. 6, 1917, **41:** 132; May 3, 1917, **42:** 195; May 7, 1917, **42:** 236; Aug. 16, 1917, **43:** 493; Sept. 4, 1917, **44:** 143; Nov. 24, 1917, **45:** 115; Feb. 7, 1918, **46:** 265; Feb. 20, 1918, **46:** 393; March 12, 1918, **46:** 606; Aug. 21, 1918, **49:** 305; Sept. 3, 1918, **49:** 424; Sept. 13, 1918, **49:** 540

David Lawrence, May 25, 1917, **42:** 395; Jan. 29, 1918, **46:** 152; April 9, 1918, **47:** 301

Victor Fremont Lawson, Aug. 7, 1918, **49:** 203

Elisha Lee, March 17, 1917, **41:** 420

William J. Lee, July 6, 1917, **43:** 109

Russell Cornell Leffingwell, Aug. 2, 1918, **49:** 163

Asbury Francis Lever, May 16, 1917, **42:** 301; July 23, 1917, **43:** 245; Feb. 18, 1918, **46:** 368; June 7, 1918 (draft), **48:** 259; June 9, 1918, **48:** 272

David John Lewis, July 8, 1918, **48:** 556; July 16, 1918, **48:** 628

James Hamilton Lewis, Jan. 27, 1917, **41:** 37; June 9, 1917, **42:** 467; July 13, 1918, **48:** 603

Horace Mather Lippincott, April 24, 1918, **47:** 415

Walter Lippmann, Feb. 7, 1917, **41:** 146; April 7, 1917, **42:** 4; June 16, 1917, **42:** 528

Ernest Lister, Aug. 16, 1917, **43:** 494; Aug. 21, 1917, **44:** 15

Deborah Knox Livingston, Sept. 4, 1917, **44:** 144

Thomas Francis Logan, April 15, 1918, **47:** 343; Nov. 8, 1918, **51:** 640

Breckinridge Long, Nov. 20, 1917, **45:** 86; Dec. 19, 1917, **45:** 329

J. Weller Long, Oct. 4, 1918, **51:** 212

James Revell Lord, Oct. 4, 1918, **51:** 214

George Horace Lorimer, April 9, 1918, **47:** 301

Robert Scott Lovett, Aug. 17, 1917, **43:** 504; Sept. 20, 1917, **44:** 223; Dec. 17, 1917, **45:** 314; Jan. 21, 1918, **46:** 52; Jan. 22, 1918, **46:** 68; Feb. 13, 1918, **46:** 336; Feb. 28, 1918, **46:** 491; March 4, 1918, **46:** 524

Edward George Lowry, June 13, 1917, **42:** 497

Simon Julius Lubin, April 12, 1918, **47:** 325

William Gibbs McAdoo
1916–1917
Dec. 21, 1916, **40:** 313; Jan. 25, 1917, **41:** 16; Feb. 24, 1917, **41:** 279; March 28, 1917, **41:** 485; May 11, 1917, **42:** 274; June 16, 1917, **42:** 527; June 25, 1917, **43:** 6; July 29, 1917, **43:** 314; Aug. 1, 1917, **43:** 337; Aug. 7, 1917, **43:** 385; Nov. 15, 1917, **45:** 51; Nov. 19, 1917, **45:** 74; Nov. 20, 1917, **45:** 91; Dec. 13, 1917, **45:** 283; Dec. 26, 1917, **45:** 362; Dec. 31, 1917 (2), **45:** 401
1918
Jan. 10, 1918, **45:** 561; Jan. 16, 1918, **46:** 3; Feb. 20, 1918, **46:** 394; Feb. 22, 1918, **46:** 413; Feb. 26, 1918 (2), **46:** 446, 448; Feb. 27, 1918, **46:** 469; Feb. 28, 1918, **46:** 490; March 4, 1918, **46:** 524; March 13, 1918, **47:** 6; March 28, 1918, **47:** 172; July 26, 1918, **49:** 103; Aug. 29, 1918, **49:** 375; Sept. 7, 1918, **49:** 472; Sept. 13, 1918, **49:** 541; Oct. 5, 1918, **51:** 228
Charles Williston McAlpin, Dec. 12, 1916, **40:** 219
Charles Raymond Macauley, Nov. 5, 1917, **44:** 512
Maurice McAuliffe, Sept. 3, 1918, **49:** 427
Cyrus Hall McCormick, Jr., May 1, 1917, **42:** 178; May 3, 1917, **42:** 203
Vance Criswell McCormick, Dec. 5, 1916, **40:** 163; May 19, 1917, **42:** 347; July 2, 1917, **43:** 71; March 18, 1918, **47:** 53
William Leonard McEwan, May 17, 1917, **42:** 313
Charles Stedman Macfarland, Feb. 2, 1917, **41:** 93
Grenville Stanley Macfarland, Oct. 1, 1917, **44:** 286; Oct 18, 1917, **44:** 397; Sept. 19, 1918, **51:** 76; Oct. 3, 1918, **51:** 193
John Thomas McGraw, Nov. 1, 1918, **51:** 540
John Avery McIlhenny, April 7, 1917, **42:** 3; Dec. 21, 1917, **45:** 337
Clarence Hungerford Mackay, June 11, 1918, **48:** 282; June 13, 1918, **48:** 301
Kenneth Douglas McKellar, July 6, 1917, **43:** 107; July 9, 1917, **43:** 131; July 13, 1917, **43:** 163; June 27, 1918, **48:** 444
Alexander Jeffrey McKelway, Dec. 20, 1917, **45:** 333
Edward Beale McLean, July 12, 1917, **43:** 154; March 4, 1918, **46:** 525; April 8, 1918, **47:** 292; Oct. 26, 1918, **51:** 452; Oct. 29, 1918, **51:** 485
Macmillan and Company, April 9, 1917, **42:** 21
Myron S. McNeil, Aug. 5, 1918, **49:** 180
Valentine Everit Macy, Sept. 18, 1918, **51:** 59; Oct. 3, 1918, **51:** 194; Oct. 22, 1918, **51:** 406
Zachary Taylor Malaby, Oct. 28, 1918, **51:** 477
Dudley Field Malone, Sept. 12, 1917, **44:** 190
John J. Mangan, Nov. 12, 1917, **45:** 18
Franc Mangum, Jan. 19, 1918, **46:** 38
Richard Irvine Manning, Oct. 10, 1918, **51:** 294; Oct. 18, 1918, **51:** 375
Thomas Riley Marshall, Dec. 15, 1916, **40:** 243; March 15, 1918, **47:** 40; May 8, 1918, **47:** 560
Daniel Hoffman Martin, April 18, 1918, **47:** 360

George Brown Martin, Oct. 9, 1918, **51:** 281; Oct. 10, 1918, **51:** 294

Thomas Staples Martin, July 13, 1917, **43:** 162; Sept. 1, 1917, **44:** 117; Sept. 5, 1917, **44:** 154; Sept. 14, 1917, **44:** 199; Sept. 28, 1917, **44:** 273; May 14, 1918, **48:** 10; July 5, 1918, **48:** 526; July 6, 1918, **48:** 534

Royal Meeker, Nov. 28, 1917, **45:** 149; March 21, 1918, **47:** 95; Aug. 30, 1918, **49:** 389

Members of District Lodge No. 55 and other striking workers, Sept. 13, 1918, **49:** 539

Edwin Thomas Meredith, Oct. 2, 1917, **44:** 291

William Penn Metcalf, Oct. 28, 1918, **51:** 478

Eugene Meyer, Jr., May 9, 1918, **47:** 579

E. L. Miley, Oct. 21, 1918, **51:** 395

Andrew Jackson Montague, Jan. 11, 1918, **45:** 567

Joseph Hampton Moore, March 7, 1918, **46:** 562

John Pierpont Morgan, Jr., April 7, 1917, **42:** 6

William Fellowes Morgan, April 1, 1918, **47:** 218

Henry Morgenthau, June 14, 1918, **48:** 311

Roland Sletor Morris, Aug. 2, 1917, **43:** 347

Frank Morrison, Sept. 20, 1918, **51:** 81; Sept. 26, 1918, **51:** 122

Robert Russa Moton, Dec. 12, 1916, **40:** 218; March 16, 1917, **41:** 414; July 9, 1917, **43:** 132; June 18, 1918, **48:** 346; Aug. 2, 1918, **49:** 166; Sept. 13, 1918, **49:** 541

John R. Mott, Feb. 3, 1917, **41:** 113; Nov. 9, 1917, **44:** 551; Nov. 8, 1918, **51:** 636

Charles Allen Munn, Jan. 29, 1918, **46:** 151

The National Conference Committee of the Railways, March 16, 1917, **41:** 414

The workmen and executive staff of the New York Shipbuilding Company, May 3, 1918, **47:** 500

Francis Griffith Newlands, Dec. 19, 1916, **40:** 278; Jan. 25, 1917, **41:** 14; Jan. 26, 1917, **41:** 21; Feb. 8, 1917, **41:** 160; Feb. 17, 1917, **41:** 241

Oliver Peck Newman, Dec. 5, 1916, **40:** 167

Lucius William Nieman, Oct. 23, 1917, **44:** 429

John Frost Nugent, Oct. 2, 1918, **51:** 180

Adolph Simon Ochs, Nov. 20, 1916, **40:** 4

William Bacon Oliver, April 2, 1918, **47:** 223

Richard Olney, Jan. 26, 1917, **41:** 23

Lucretia Thatcher Osborn, July 23, 1917, **43:** 247

Lee Slater Overman, March 21, 1918, **47:** 94; March 22, 1918, **47:** 109; April 16, 1918, **47:** 350; April 20, 1918, **47:** 381; April 22, 1918, **47:** 394; Oct. 5, 1918, **51:** 227

Robert Latham Owen, July 23, 1917, **43:** 246; Aug. 3, 1917, **43:** 357; Feb. 1, 1918, **46:** 206; July 23, 1918, **49:** 61; Sept. 7, 1918, **49:** 471; Sept. 11, 1918, **49:** 515; Sept. 19, 1918, **51:** 76

Helena de Rosen Paderewska, May 9, 1918, **47:** 576
Ignace Jan Paderewski, Jan. 11, 1918, **45:** 569
Arthur Wilson Page, Aug. 16, 1917, **43:** 493
Charles R. Page, Nov. 5, 1918, **51:** 593
Walter Hines Page, Aug. 24, 1918, **49:** 346
Alexander Mitchell Palmer, March 31, 1917, **41:** 510; June 3, 1918,
    48: 228; Sept. 4, 1918, **49:** 432; Oct. 21, 1918, **51:** 395
Edgar Palmer, Sept. 22, 1917, **44:** 238
Maud May Wood Park, Nov. 27, 1917, **45:** 129
George Foster Peabody, Feb. 27, 1917, **41:** 296; Dec. 6, 1917, **45:**
    225; Jan. 11, 1918, **45:** 570; Jan. 21, 1918, **46:** 52; Aug. 7, 1918,
    49: 204; Sept. 18, 1918, **51:** 57
James Duval Phelan, March 22, 1917, **41:** 454; Aug. 8, 1917, **43:**
    392
William Phillips, Jan. 16, 1917, **40:** 492; April 4, 1917, **41:** 542;
    Dec. 6, 1917, **45:** 221
Mary Pickford, April 9, 1918, **47:** 301
Amos Richards Eno Pinchot, July 13, 1917, **43:** 164; July 17, 1917,
    43: 193
Key Pittman, Feb. 21, 1917, **41:** 261; March 28, 1917, **41:** 485; June
    25, 1917, **43:** 5; Sept. 10, 1918, **49:** 511; Sept. 18, 1918, **51:** 59;
    Nov. 7, 1918, **51:** 620
Miles Poindexter, Jan. 27, 1917, **41:** 37; July 18, 1917, **43:** 202
Frank Lyon Polk, June 9, 1917, **42:** 467; June 16, 1917, **42:** 527
Atlee Pomerene, Jan. 29, 1917, **41:** 55; March 25, 1918, **47:** 139;
    July 6, 1918, **48:** 534
Allen Bartlit Pond, July 17, 1917, **43:** 193; Sept. 26, 1917, **44:** 265
Louis Freeland Post, Nov. 20, 1916, **40:** 3; July 6, 1917, **43:** 108;
    Sept. 17, 1917, **44:** 205; Nov. 30, 1917, **45:** 162; Feb. 11, 1918, **46:**
    324
Elizabeth Herndon Potter, March 8, 1918, **46:** 573
Edward William Pou, April 13, 1917, **42:** 52; May 14, 1917, **42:** 293;
    May 21, 1917, **42:** 357; May 1, 1918, **47:** 474; May 3, 1918, **47:**
    501; Sept. 3, 1918, **49:** 425
Joseph Morris Price, Dec. 11, 1916, **40:** 215
Ralph Pulitzer, Nov. 20, 1916, **40:** 3; Feb. 18, 1918, **46:** 370; Oct. 10,
    1918, **51:** 293

Manuel Castro Quesada, Dec. 27, 1916, **40:** 333
Manuel Luis Quezon, Dec. 1, 1916, **40:** 112

Henry Thomas Rainey, May 23, 1918, **48:** 119
William Harryman Rapley, May 1, 1918, **47:** 476
Caroline Seaman Read, May 17, 1918, **48:** 46
Lord Reading, April 15, 1918, **47:** 343
William Cox Redfield, Dec. 21, 1916, **40:** 305; May 10, 1917 (2), **42:**
    260; July 6, 1917, **43:** 108; July 7, 1917, **43:** 116; July 26, 1917,
    43: 281; Aug. 21, 1917 (2), **44:** 11; Oct. 29, 1917, **44:** 464; Dec. 10,
    1917, **45:** 256; Aug. 7, 1918, **49:** 205

Verner Zevola Reed, Nov. 26, 1917, **45:** 122
Paul Samuel Reinsch, Dec. 27, 1916, **40:** 335
The Remington Arms Company, Sept. 17, 1918, **51:** 24
Robert Goodwyn Rhett, Sept. 4, 1917, **44:** 148; Dec. 12, 1917, **45:**
    276
Dee Richardson, July 25, 1917, **43:** 272
Edgar Rickard, July 16, 1918, **48:** 629; July 26, 1918, **49:** 104
Allen W. Ricker, Aug. 7, 1917, **43:** 386
Joseph Taylor Robinson, Feb. 6, 1918, **46:** 258; May 11, 1918, **47:**
    602
Milton Andrew Romjue, Jan. 26, 1918, **46:** 102
Franklin Delano Roosevelt, Oct. 5, 1917, **44:** 310
Elihu Root, April 7, 1917, **42:** 6
Robert Kilburn Root, May 14, 1917, **42:** 291
Julius Rosenwald, March 7, 1918, **46:** 563
Leo Stanton Rowe, May 31, 1918, **48:** 209
John Dennis Ryan, May 3, 1918, **47:** 501

Willard Saulsbury, June 25, 1917, **43:** 4; May 29, 1918, **48:** 192;
    June 4, 1918, **48:** 238; Sept. 5, 1918, **49:** 450
Jessie Woodrow Wilson Sayre, May 3, 1918, **47:** 502
John Nevin Sayre, May 1, 1917, **42:** 179
Jacob Henry Schiff, Nov. 22, 1917, **45:** 100
Emmett Jay Scott, July 31, 1918, **49:** 139
Frank Augustus Scott, Oct. 29, 1917, **44:** 464
James George Scripps, Sept. 18, 1918, **51:** 60
Samuel Seabury, Jan. 25, 1917, **41:** 12
Louis Seibold, June 27, 1917, **43:** 23; July 5, 1917, **43:** 102
The Senate and the House of Representatives, Jan. 17, 1917, **40:**
    506; Aug. 22, 1918, **49:** 310
John Franklin Shafroth, Jan. 3, 1917, **40:** 386; March 14, 1917, **41:**
    403; May 29, 1918, **48:** 193
Isaac M. Shaine, Oct. 24, 1918, **51:** 424
William Graves Sharp, Sept. 13, 1918, **49:** 543
Albert Shaw, Dec. 5, 1916, **40:** 165; April 28, 1917, **42:** 153; Sept.
    28, 1917, **44:** 273; Dec. 10, 1917, **45:** 257; April 22, 1918, **47:** 395
Anna Howard Shaw, May 16, 1918, **48:** 28; May 22, 1918, **48:** 117;
    May 28, 1918, **48:** 174; May 31, 1918, **48:** 209; June 1, 1918 (2),
    48: 221, 222; June 6, 1918, **48:** 250
Morris Sheppard, March 15, 1918, **47:** 39; March 22, 1918, **47:** 106;
    May 28, 1918, **48:** 175; June 26, 1918, **48:** 440
Joseph Swagar Sherley, May 11, 1918, **47:** 600; May 24, 1918, **48:**
    137
John Knight Shields, June 20, 1918, **48:** 371; June 26, 1918, **48:**
    440
Jouett Shouse, Feb. 27, 1917, **41:** 296; Aug. 27, 1917, **44:** 61; Sept.
    5, 1917, **44:** 153; Oct. 9, 1917, **44:** 343; June 10, 1918, **48:** 279;
    Aug. 22, 1918, **49:** 315

CONTENTS   23

Furnifold McLendel Simmons, May 27, 1918, **48:** 167; May 28, 1918, **48:** 175
Thetus Willrette Sims, Dec. 31, 1917, **45:** 403; June 28, 1918, **48:** 458; July 6, 1918, **48:** 533; Aug. 22, 1918, **49:** 317; Aug. 26, 1918, **49:** 351; Sept. 21, 1918, **51:** 86
George H. Slater, March 26, 1918, **47:** 144
John Humphrey Small, Jan. 24, 1918, **46:** 90; Aug. 27, 1918, **49:** 356
Edward Parson Smith, Oct. 28, 1918, **51:** 477
Howard Alexander Smith, Feb. 7, 1918, **46:** 265
Marcus Aurelius Smith, July 9, 1917, **43:** 128
Roland Cotton Smith, Dec. 29, 1916, **40:** 354; Jan. 5, 1917, **40:** 412
Douglas Smithe, Feb. 24, 1918, **46:** 433
Bertrand Hollis Snell, March 20, 1918, **47:** 85
Homer Peter Snyder, July 1, 1918, **48:** 475
Rudolph Spreckels, Dec. 21, 1916, **40:** 312
Augustus Owsley Stanley, Aug. 30, 1918, **49:** 388; Sept. 12, 1918, **49:** 529
Lincoln Steffens, Jan. 15, 1918, **45:** 593
William Dennison Stephens, May 11, 1917, **42:** 270; Aug. 7, 1917, **43:** 386; Jan. 22, 1918, **46:** 74; March 27, 1918, **47:** 160; June 4, 1918, **48:** 237
Edward Riley Stettinius, April 12, 1918, **47:** 325
Samuel Vernon Stewart, Oct. 4, 1918, **51:** 213
William Joel Stone, Jan. 3, 1917, **40:** 385
Daisy Allen Story, March 2, 1917, **41:** 310
Claude Augustus Swanson, Feb. 15, 1917, **41:** 234
Herbert Bayard Swope, Jan. 14, 1918, **45:** 581; Jan. 22, 1918, **46:** 75; Feb. 23, 1918, **46:** 423; March 21, 1918, **47:** 93; March 27, 1918, **47:** 159; April 18, 1918, **47:** 358; July 3, 1918, **48:** 492

William Howard Taft, May 10, 1917, **42:** 261; Aug. 8, 1917, **43:** 393
William Howard Taft and Francis Patrick Walsh, July 9, 1918, **48:** 567
Ida Minerva Tarbell, Dec. 28, 1916, **40:** 343; Jan. 3, 1917, **40:** 384; May 1, 1918, **47:** 476; May 23, 1918, **48:** 120
Frank William Taussig, Nov. 23, 1917, **45:** 104; March 30, 1918, **47:** 208; April 3, 1918, **47:** 233
Teachers and school officers, Aug. 23, 1917, **44:** 32
Harry Bates Thayer, April 24, 1918, **47:** 415
Charles Spalding Thomas, March 7, 1918, **46:** 563; March 11, 1918, **46:** 599; March 13, 1918, **47:** 7; March 15, 1918, **47:** 37; May 6, 1918, **47:** 535
Samuel Huston Thompson, Jr., Jan. 16, 1917, **40:** 493; June 28, 1917, **43:** 33; May 8, 1918, **47:** 559
A message for Benjamin Ryan Tillman about voting on the Jones amendment, June 25, 1918, **48:** 428
George Holden Tinkham, May 3, 1917, **42:** 202

Arthur Charles Townley, March 29, 1918 (draft), **47:** 193
Park Trammell, Sept. 26, 1918, **51:** 123
Martin Travieso, Jr., Nov. 29, 1916, **40:** 97
Joseph Patrick Tumulty
  1916
  Nov. 22, 1916, **40:** 35; Dec. 5, 1916, **40:** 154
  January–June 1917
  Jan. 27, 1917, **41:** 37; Feb. 20, 1917, **41:** 257; April 7, 1917, **42:** 8;
  April 20, 1917, **42:** 108; April 24, 1917, **42:** 123; April 28, 1917,
  42: 153; May 31, 1917, **42:** 427; June 6, 1917, **42:** 458; June 13,
  1917, **42:** 495; June 14, 1917 (2), **42:** 505, 506; June 18, 1917, **42:**
  532
  July–December 1917
  July 3, 1917, **43:** 86; July 5, 1917, **43:**103; July 6, 1917, **43:** 106;
  July 9, 1917, **43:** 128; July 11, 1917, **43:** 146; July 14, 1917, **43:**
  176; July 20, 1917, **43:** 222; July 21, 1917, **43:** 239; July 30, 1917,
  43: 318; Aug. 1, 1917, **43:** 343; Aug. 2, 1917, **43:** 345; Aug. 24,
  1917, **44:** 40; Aug. 28, 1917, **44:** 77; Sept. 17, 1917 (2), **44:** 206,
  207; Sept. 21, 1917 (2), **44:** 231, 232; Sept. 23, 1917, **44:** 242; Sept.
  28, 1917, **44:** 273; Sept. 29, 1917, **44:** 279; Oct. 1, 1917, **44:** 287;
  Oct. 4, 1917, **44:** 302; Oct. 12, 1917 (2), **44:** 364, 365; Oct. 15,
  1917, **44:** 384; Oct. 25, 1917, **44:** 384; Oct. 25, 1917, **44:** 445; Oct.
  27, 1917, **44:** 453; Oct. 30, 1917, **44:** 467; Nov. 2, 1917, **44:** 490;
  Nov. 8, 1917, **44:** 536; Nov. 10, 1917, **44:** 559; Nov. 13, 1917 (2),
  45: 40; Nov. 14, 1917, **45:** 46; Nov. 15, 1917, **45:** 53; Nov. 16, 1917,
  45: 69; Dec. 6, 1917, **45:** 221; Dec. 10, 1917, **45:** 262, Dec. 12, 1917,
  45: 275; Dec. 17, 1917, **45:** 314; Dec. 18, 1917 (2), **45:** 318, 320;
  Dec. 22, 1917, **45:** 344; Dec. 28, 1917, **45:** 371; Dec. 30, 1917, **45:**
  397
  January–June 1918
  Jan. 23, 1918 (3), **46:** 79, 84; Jan. 28, 1918, **46:** 119; Jan. 29, 1918,
  46: 150; Jan. 31, 1918, **46:** 194; Feb. 6, 1918, **46:** 256; Feb. 21,
  1918, **46:** 406; March 11, 1918, **46:** 601; March 12, 1918, **46:** 608;
  March 29, 1918, **47:** 193; April 5, 1918, **47:** 260; April 10, 1918
  (3), **47:** 275, 311; April 9, 1918 (2), **47:** 276, 279; April 8, 1918, **47:**
  293; April 19, 1918, **47:** 352; April 25, 1918, **47:** 437; May 9, 1918
  (2), **47:** 572, 578; May 10, 1918 (2), **47:** 587, 588; May 16, 1918,
  48: 24; May 22, 1918, **48:** 115; May 23, 1918 (2), **48:** 118, 119; May
  27, 1918, **48:** 166; June 3, 1918, **48:** 230; June 4, 1918, **48:** 237;
  June 5, 1918, **48:** 241; June 13, 1918, **48:** 302; June 14, 1918, **48:**
  311; June 17, 1918, **48:** 335; June 18, 1918, **48:** 345; June 19,
  1918, **48:** 356; June 20, 1918, **48:** 370; June 22, 1918, **48:** 392
  July–October 1918
  July 5, 1918, **48:** 526; July 10, 1918, **48:** 578; July 12, 1918, **48:**
  597; July 16, 1918, **48:** 628; July 17, 1918, **48:** 643; Aug. 2, 1918
  (3), **49:** 164, 165; Aug. 3, 1918, **49:** 172; Aug. 8, 1918, **49:** 211;
  Aug. 9, 1918, **49:** 222; Aug. 13, 1918, **49:** 240; Aug. 22, 1918, **49:**
  314; Aug. 27, 1918, **49:** 360; Sept. 2, 1918, **49:** 419; Sept. 5, 1918

(2), **49:** 449, 450; Sept. 6, 1918 (3), **49:** 455, 458, 460; Sept. 13, 1918, **49:** 541; Sept. 16, 1918, **51:** 15; Sept. 18, 1918, **51:** 55; Sept. 23, 1918, **51:** 91; Sept. 25, 1918, **51:** 111; Oct. 3, 1918, **51:** 191; Oct. 17, 1918, **51:** 353

Theodore Newton Vail, April 24, 1918, **47:** 414
Arthur Hendrick Vandenberg, Dec. 3, 1917, **45:** 188
Charles Richard Van Hise, Jan. 15, 1918, **45:** 593; Aug. 13, 1918, **49:** 241
Ambrose White Vernon, Dec. 11, 1916, **40:** 215
Alexander Theodore Vogelsang, May 20, 1918, **48:** 78

Robert Ferdinand Wagner, May 18, 1917, **42:** 327
Lillian D. Wald, Dec. 5, 1916, **40:** 163; April 28, 1917, **42:** 153
John Milton Waldron, April 19, 1917, **42:** 98; May 21, 1917, **42:** 357
Leslie E. Wallace, Oct. 18, 1918, **51:** 375
William English Walling, May 14, 1917, **42:** 291
Francis Patrick Walsh, April 1, 1918, **47:** 219; April 2, 1918, **47:** 223; Nov. 2, 1918, **51:** 553
Thomas James Walsh, Jan. 24, 1917, **41:** 5; May 19, 1917, **42:** 346; June 29, 1917, **43:** 43; May 9, 1918, **47:** 580
Paul Moritz Warburg, Aug. 9, 1918, **49:** 222
Charles Warren, Feb. 13, 1918, **46:** 335
John Thomas Watkins, June 3, 1918, **48:** 229
Edwin Yates Webb, May 22, 1917, **42:** 369
John Wingate Weeks, Aug. 14, 1917, **43:** 461
Herbert Welsh, May 8, 1918, **47:** 559
John Wesley Wescott, Sept. 4, 1918, **49:** 432; Oct. 2, 1918, **51:** 179
Harry Andrew Wheeler, Oct. 5, 1918, **51:** 229
Andrew Dickson White, May 3, 1917, **42:** 200
Edward Douglass White, March 2, 1917, **41:** 310
The White House staff, Sept. 28, 1917, **44:** 274; July 17, 1918 (2), **48:** 643, 645
Vira Boarman Whitehouse, Aug. 14, 1917, **43:** 462; Aug. 27, 1917 (2), **44:** 61, 62; Nov. 8, 1917, **44:** 537
Charles Seymour Whitman, Jan. 18, 1918, **46:** 24
Whom It May Concern (for Roy Wilson Howard), Jan. 29, 1918, **46:** 153
William Royal Wilder, Feb. 9, 1917, **41:** 180
Louis Wiley, July 23, 1917, **43:** 246; July 27, 1917, **43:** 291
Xenophon Pierce Wilfley, Oct. 18, 1918, **51:** 374
Daniel Willard, Nov. 19, 1917, **45:** 75; Nov. 20, 1917, **45:** 92; Dec. 8, 1917, **45:** 244; Dec. 22, 1917, **45:** 344; Jan. 17, 1918, **46:** 15
John Sharp Williams, Dec. 8, 1916, **40:** 190; Dec. 28, 1916, **40:** 344; April 7, 1917, **42:** 5; May 4, 1917, **42:** 213; June 29, 1917, **43:** 78; Aug. 2, 1917, **43:** 344; Sept. 1, 1917, **44:** 117; Jan. 26, 1918, **46:** 104; Feb. 6, 1918, **46:** 257; May 8, 1918, **47:** 561; July 8, 1918, **48:** 558

John Skelton Williams, Dec. 11, 1916, **40:** 214; May 28, 1917, **42:** 411; Oct. 23, 1917, **44:** 428; July 24, 1918, **49:** 72; Aug. 1, 1918, **49:** 148

William Franklin Willoughby, Jan. 23, 1917, **40:** 549

Joseph R. Wilson, Jr., Nov. 19, 1917, **45:** 77; March 13, 1918, **47:** 6; March 15, 1918, **47:** 37

Luther Barton Wilson, May 10, 1917, **42:** 259

William Bauchop Wilson
1917
Feb. 20, 1917, **41:** 258; March 22, 1917, **41:** 450; June 25, 1917 (2), **43:** 3, 4; Aug. 13, 1917, **43:** 437; Sept. 12, 1917, **44:** 191; Sept. 19, 1917, **44:** 216; Oct. 23, 1917, **44:** 429; Nov. 1, 1917, **44:** 483; Nov. 7, 1917, **44:** 526; Nov. 23, 1917, **45:** 103; Nov. 27, 1917, **45:** 129; Dec. 8, 1917, **45:** 244
1918
Jan. 22, 1918, **46:** 74; Jan. 29, 1918, **46:** 149; Jan. 31, 1918 (2), **46:** 179; March 2, 1918, **46:** 509; March 9, 1918, **46:** 582; March 29, 1918 (2), **47:** 188; April 8, 1918, **47:** 292; May 6, 1918, **47:** 537; May 8, 1918, **47:** 557; June 1, 1918, **48:** 219; June 6, 1918, **48:** 248; July 18, 1918, **49:** 3; July 24, 1918, **49:** 72; July 26, 1918, **49:** 104; Aug. 1, 1918 (2), **49:** 147, 148; Aug. 2, 1918, **49:** 166; Aug. 6, 1918, **49:** 186; Aug. 8, 1918, **49:** 211; Aug. 28, 1918, **49:** 367; Sept. 3, 1918, **49:** 424; Oct. 9, 1918 (2), **51:** 280

Stephen Samuel Wise, Feb. 13, 1917, **41:** 209; Jan. 11, 1918, **45:** 567

Robert G. Withers, Oct. 26, 1918, **51:** 453

Josiah Oliver Wolcott, May 9, 1918, **47:** 577; Sept. 27, 1918, **51:** 133; Oct. 1, 1918, **51:** 171

The delegates to the first annual conference of the Woman's Committee of the Council of National Defense, May 1, 1918, **47:** 476

Edward Augustus Woods, Nov. 8, 1918, **51:** 639

Robert Wickliffe Woolley, April 8, 1918, **47:** 291; April 27, 1918, **47:** 449

Edward H. Wright, Aug. 21, 1917, **43:** 507

Theodore Wright, Nov. 22, 1916, **40:** 35

Arthur Yager, Nov. 27, 1916, **40:** 90; April 1, 1917, **41:** 515

To Wilson from
Lawrence Fraser Abbott, Sept. 12, 1918, **51:** 15

William Charles Adamson, Dec. 6, 1916, **40:** 182; Jan. 26, 1917, **41:** 29; Jan. 29, 1917, **41:** 53; July 31, 1918, **49:** 143

Jane Addams, Jan. 14, 1918, **45:** 586

Joshua Willis Alexander, Jan. 5, 1917, **40:** 417; Feb. 16, 1917, **41:** 236

Brent Dow Allinson, March 26, 1918, **47:** 154

A committee of the American Federation of Labor, Aug. 13, 1918, **49:** 244

A resolution by the American Federation of Labor demanding the
  takeover of the telegraph companies, June 14, 1918, **48:** 313
George Weston Anderson, Dec. 10, 1917, **45:** 265
William Albert Ashbrook, Aug. 17, 1918, **49:** 277
Henry Fountain Ashurst, July 6, 1917, **43:** 113; Aug. 29, 1917, **44:**
  86

John Miller Baer, Feb. 7, 1918, **46:** 270
David Baird, Aug. 5, 1918, **49:** 182
Bernard Nadal Baker, Jan. 25, 1917, **41:** 16
George Luis Baker, Sept. 24, 1917, **44:** 247
Newton Diehl Baker
  1916
  Nov. 20, 1916, **40:** 7; Nov. 22, 1916, **40:** 42; Nov. 27, 1916, **40:** 91;
  Dec. 26, 1916, **40:** 327
  January–May 1917
  Jan. 10, 1917, **40:** 438; Jan. 12, 1917 (2), **40:** 455, 456; Feb. 8,
  1917, **41:** 169; Feb. 12, 1917, **41:** 206; Feb. 23, 1917, **41:** 278;
  March 6, 1917, **41:** 345; March 7, 1917, **41:** 353; March 16, 1917,
  41: 417; March 29, 1917, **41:** 500; March 30, 1917, **41:** 505; April
  3, 1917, **41:** 541; April 12, 1917, **42:** 47; April 18, 1917, **42:** 91;
  April 30, 1917, **42:** 166; May 1, 1917, **42:** 179; May 4, 1917, **42:**
  217; May 5, 1917, **42:** 227; May 9, 1917, **42:** 251; May 11, 1917 (2),
  42: 279; May 17, 1917, **42:** 321; May 18, 1917, **42:** 342
  June–August 1917
  June 13, 1917, **42:** 498; June 15, 1917, **42:** 522; June 18, 1917, **42:**
  533; June 26, 1917, **43:** 16; June 27, 1917, **43:** 25; June 30, 1917,
  43: 59; July 3, 1917 (2), **43:** 90, 92; July 6, 1917, **43:** 113; July 7,
  1917, **43:** 118; July 14, 1917 (2), **43:** 177; July 23, 1917, **43:** 248;
  July 30, 1917, **43:** 324; Aug. 1, 1917, **43:** 341; Aug. 9, 1917, **43:**
  413; Aug. 13, 1917, **43:** 454; Aug. 17, 1917, **43:** 506; Aug. 18, 1917
  (3), **43:** 514, 515; Aug. 20, 1917, **43:** 534; Aug. 17, 1917, **44:** 8;
  Aug. 22, 1917, **44:** 29; Aug. 24, 1917, **44:** 41; Aug. 25, 1917, **44:**
  50; Aug. 27, 1917, **44:** 74; Aug. 28, 1917, **44:** 77
  September–December 1917
  Sept. 1, 1917, **44:** 120; Sept. 2, 1917, **44:** 123; Sept. 4, 1917, **44:**
  150; Sept. 6, 1917, **44:** 157; Sept. 7, 1917, **44:** 161; Sept. 19, 1917
  (2), **44:** 219, 221; Sept. 20, 1917 (2), **44:** 225; Sept. 21, 1917, **44:**
  232; Sept. 22, 1917, **44:** 239; Oct. 1, 1917, **44:** 288; Oct. 9, 1917,
  44: 344; Oct. 18, 1917, **44:** 398; Oct. 22, 1917, **44:** 421; Oct. 26,
  1917, **44:** 450; Oct. 28, 1917, **44:** 461; Nov. 2, 1917, **44:** 493; Nov.
  3, 1917 (3), **44:** 501, 502, 503; Nov. 6, 1917, **44:** 522; Nov. 10,
  1917, **44:** 562; Nov. 12, 1917, **45:** 29; Nov. 17, 1917, **45:** 71; Nov.
  30, 1917, **45:** 172; Dec. 9, 1917, **45:** 254; Dec. 10, 1917, **45:** 265;
  Dec. 12, 1917, **45:** 279; Dec. 25, 1917, **45:** 355
  January–May 1918
  Jan. 2, 1918, **45:** 426; Jan. 11, 1918, **45:** 570; Jan. 13, 1918, **45:**
  579; Jan. 14, 1918, **45:** 583; Jan. 21, 1918 (2), **46:** 56, 57; Jan. 24,

1918, **46:** 91; Feb. 1, 1918 (3), **46:** 208, 209, 215; Feb. 2, 1918, **46:** 215; Feb. 3, 1918, **46:** 229; Feb. 5, 1918, **46:** 252; Feb. 23, 1918 (2), **46:** 427, 428; May 3, 1918, **47:** 509; May 6, 1918, **47:** 541; May 10, 1918, **47:** 588; May 11, 1918, **47:** 613; May 15, 1918, **48:** 15; May 16, 1918, **48:** 35; May 25, 1918, **48:** 151

June–October 1918

June 1, 1918, **48:** 221; June 11, 1918, **48:** 285; June 15, 1918, **48:** 321; June 17, 1918, **48:** 336; July 1, 1918, **48:** 475; July 14, 1918, **48:** 607; July 16, 1918, **48:** 637; July 22, 1918, **49:** 56; July 23, 1918, **49:** 66; July 28, 1918, **49:** 117; Aug. 14, 1918, **49:** 252; Aug. 20, 1918, **49:** 296; Aug. 22, 1918, **49:** 328; Aug. 24, 1918 (2), **49:** 349; Aug. 29, 1918 (2), **49:** 384, 386; Aug. 30, 1918, **49:** 394; Oct. 26, 1918, **51:** 455

A memorandum by Newton Diehl Baker on the government of the Danish West Indies, Jan. 3, 1917, **40:** 401

A memorandum for the President by Newton Diehl Baker on the powers of the War Industries Board, Aug. 9, 1917, **43:** 489

Emily Greene Balch, March 5, 1917, **41:** 340

Roger Nash Baldwin, Jan. 31, 1918, **46:** 196; Feb. 27, 1918, **46:** 481

John Hollis Bankhead, Jan. 31, 1917, **41:** 82

James Alfred Bardin, May 1, 1918, **47:** 578

Wharton Barker, March 12, 1918, **46:** 611

Frank Coe Barnes, Oct. 8, 1917, **44:** 364

Bernard Mannes Baruch, May 11, 1917, **42:** 279; May 15, 1917, **42:** 298; May 30, 1917, **42:** 424; June 4, 1917, **42:** 447; June 19, 1917, **42:** 538; July 11, 1917, **43:** 148; Aug. 27, 1917, **44:** 73; Sept. 26, 1917, **44:** 268; Jan. 18, 1918, **46:** 33; Feb. 5, 1918, **46:** 251; Feb. 8, 1918, **46:** 288; March 4, 1918, **46:** 527; March 5, 1918, **46:** 550; March 28, 1918, **47:** 180; April 4, 1918, **47:** 255; May 28, 1918 (2), **48:** 188, 189; June 24, 1918, **48:** 405; July 13, 1918, **48:** 606; Aug. 2, 1918, **49:** 170; Nov. 6, 1918, **51:** 610

Elizabeth Merrill Bass, May 3, 1917, **42:** 208; Dec. 7, 1917, **45:** 242; Dec. 12, 1917, **45:** 277; Dec. 21, 1917, **45:** 338; Jan. 8, 1918, **45:** 542; Jan. 21, 1918, **46:** 59; May 21, 1918, **48:** 110; June 3, 1918, **48:** 233; June 19, 1918, **48:** 363

John Crepps Wickliffe Beckham, May 9, 1918, **47:** 580

George Lewis Bell, Aug. 16, 1917 (2), **43:** 494; Aug. 29, 1917, **44:** 86; May 1, 1918, **47:** 479

Jefferson Bell, March 11, 1918, **46:** 604

Thomas Montgomery Bell, July 16, 1917, **43:** 190

Christie Benet, Sept. 30, 1918, **51:** 167

Herman Bernstein, March 23, 1917, **41:** 457

Jacques A. Berst, Aug. 16, 1917, **43:** 501

Samuel Reading Bertron, Oct. 8, 1917, **44:** 335; Dec. 28, 1917, **45:** 373; April 17, 1918, **47:** 354; July 22, 1918, **49:** 54

Anita Eugénie McCormick Blaine, April 21, 1918, **47:** 391; April 26, 1918, **47:** 447

William Thomas Bland, Aug. 12, 1918, **49:** 239
Edward William Bok, June 19, 1918, **48:** 361
Gutzon Borglum, Dec. 10, 1917, **45:** 266; Dec. 12, 1917, **45:** 280; Dec. 25, 1917, **45:** 356; Jan. 5, 1918, **45:** 492; Jan. 24, 1918, **46:** 94; Jan. 21, 1918, **46:** 94; Jan. 26, 1918, **46:** 106; Feb. 24, 1918, **46:** 433; March 27, 1918, **47:** 169; March 28, 1918, **47:** 181; April 3, 1918, **47:** 234; April 8, 1918, **47:** 296; April 10, 1918, **47:** 313; April 13, 1918, **47:** 335; April 16, 1918, **47:** 352; May 3, 1918, **47:** 511; May 13, 1918, **48:** 10
William Patterson Borland, June 16, 1917, **42:** 528
Charles M. Bottomley, Sept. 23, 1917, **44:** 244
William Bouck and others, June 10, 1918, **48:** 291
Charles W. Boyle, Sept. 25, 1917, **44:** 263
Thomas W. Brahany, Jan. 6, 1917, **40:** 420
Howard Allen Bridgman, Nov. 20, 1917, **45:** 94
Arthur Brisbane, April 20, 1917, **42:** 107; Dec. 18, 1917, **45:** 320
Minnie Bronson, Dec. 22, 1917, **45:** 345
Robert Somers Brookings, Dec. 20, 1916, **40:** 303; March 11, 1918, **46:** 603; March 22, 1918 (2), **47:** 117, 118; March 27, 1918 (2), **47:** 167, 168; April 20, 1918, **47:** 383; April 26, 1918, **47:** 444; May 2, 1918, **47:** 494; May 6, 1918, **47:** 538; June 22, 1918, **48:** 392; July 2, 1918, **48:** 487; July 8, 1918, **48:** 563; Sept. 21, 1918, **51:** 90; Oct. 4, 1918, **51:** 218; Oct. 9, 1918, **51:** 285
Herbert Bruce Brougham, Dec. 21, 1916, **40:** 315; Dec. 27, 1916, **40:** 337; Dec. 30, 1916, **40:** 371; Oct. 27, 1917, **44:** 459; Oct. 31, 1917, **44:** 478
Louis Brownlow, March 18, 1918, **47:** 58; Aug. 22, 1918, **49:** 313
Martin Grove Brumbaugh, June 1, 1917, **42:** 434
William Jennings Bryan, Jan. 26, 1917, **41:** 29; April 6, 1917, **41:** 556
William Christian Bullitt, Sept. 27, 1918, **51:** 136
Albert Sidney Burleson, Feb. 27, 1917, **41:** 294; April 9, 1917, **42:** 22; May 3, 1917, **42:** 195; May 18, 1917, **42:** 343; July 16, 1917, **43:** 187; Aug. 6, 1917, **43:** 373; Aug. 8, 1917 (2), **43:** 394, 396; Oct. 9, 1917, **44:** 344; Oct. 16, 1917, **44:** 389; April 5, 1918, **47:** 264; May 10, 1918, **47:** 596; Sept. 17, 1918, **51:** 28; Oct. 30, 1918, **51:** 520
John Lawson Burnett, Jan. 20, 1917, **40:** 531
Joseph Alfred Arner Burnquist, Feb. 26, 1918, **46:** 463

Charles Pope Caldwell, April 19, 1917, **42:** 103; Jan. 28, 1918, **46:** 147
James C. Caldwell and Christian H. Wendt, March 31, 1918, **47:** 216
Ella E. Martin Caminetti, March 24, 1917, **41:** 465
Thomas Edward Campbell, July 12, 1917, **43:** 157
W. A. Campbell, Nov. 13, 1917, **45:** 44

James Cannon, Jr., May 28, 1918, **48:** 190

James Cannon, Jr., and others, June 29, 1917, **43:** 52; June 30, 1917, **43:** 64

Arthur Capper, July 6, 1917, **43:** 112; Oct. 23, 1917, **44:** 432; July 2, 1918, **48:** 486; Aug. 10, 1918, **49:** 232

Washington Lee Capps, Nov. 24, 1917, **45:** 117

Newcomb Carlton, June 17, 1918, **48:** 337

Andrew Carnegie, Jan. 23, 1917, **40:** 560

Waddill Catchings, Aug. 17, 1917, **43:** 511; Jan. 18, 1918, **46:** 29

Carrie Clinton Lane Chapman Catt, May 7, 1917, **42:** 237; Oct. 16, 1917, **44:** 391; June 13, 1918, **48:** 304; Sept. 18, 1918, **51:** 58; Sept. 29, 1918, **51:** 155

A proposal by the Chamber of Commerce of the United States for the establishment of a department of supplies, Nov. 15, 1917, **45:** 61

George Earle Chamberlain, May 12, 1917, **42:** 285; Jan. 21, 1918, **46:** 53

William Lea Chambers, Dec. 20, 1916, **40:** 303; Aug. 20, 1917, **43:** 530; Oct. 23, 1917, **44:** 430; Oct. 27, 1917, **44:** 458; Nov. 12, 1917, **45:** 25; Nov. 14, 1917, **45:** 49; Feb. 23, 1918, **46:** 446; April 26, 1918, **47:** 446

John Wilbur Chapman, Dec. 17, 1917, **45:** 315

Champ Clark, Nov. 15, 1917, **45:** 58; Jan. 23, 1918, **46:** 85

Francis Edward Clark, Sept. 28, 1918, **51:** 149

John Hessin Clarke, Dec. 21, 1916, **40:** 311; April 3, 1917, **41:** 536

Grosvenor Blaine Clarkson, March 22, 1918, **47:** 110; May 5, 1918, **47:** 526

Memoranda by Grosvenor Blaine Clarkson about the future functions of the Council of National Defense, March 22, 1918, **47:** 110; May 6, 1918, **47:** 527

Frank Irving Cobb, May 22, 1917, **42:** 371; Oct. 1, 1917, **44:** 288; Nov. 27, 1917, **45:** 135; Jan. 17, 1918, **46:** 16

Howard Earle Coffin, April 18, 1918, **47:** 361; May 4, 1918, **47:** 521

George M. Cohan, Jan. 17, 1918, **46:** 28

Bainbridge Colby, Dec. 12, 1916, **40:** 221; July 28, 1917, **43:** 310; March 26, 1918, **47:** 148; Sept. 13, 1918, **49:** 547

Robert Bruce Coleman and Thomas Samuel Hawes, Aug. 31, 1917, **44:** 106

William Byron Colver, June 25, 1917 (2), **43:** 6, 7; Feb. 26, 1918, **46:** 462; March 18, 1918, **47:** 54; Aug. 28, 1918, **49:** 372; Sept. 9, 1918, **49:** 504; Sept. 21, 1918, **51:** 90; Oct. 24, 1918, **51:** 441

William Byron Colver and others, July 3, 1918, **48:** 507; June 28, 1918, **49:** 130

John Rogers Commons, March 21, 1917, **41:** 448

Edwin Grant Conklin, Feb. 14, 1917, **41:** 230

Waldo Lincoln Cook, March 28, 1917, **41:** 495

John Gardner Coolidge, Dec. 1, 1916, **40:** 116

John Paul Cooper, May 4, 1918, **47:** 520

John Jacob Cornwell, June 30, 1917, **43:** 59
Alfred B. Cosey, Aug. 9, 1917, **43:** 412
Edward Prentiss Costigan, May 29, 1918, **48:** 197
Frederic René Coudert, April 23, 1917, **42:** 122
Winfield F. Cozart and others, Jan. 7, 1918, **45:** 546
Charles Richard Crane, Nov. 20, 1916, **40:** 9; Jan. 23, 1917, **40:** 559;
    April 29, 1918, **47:** 466; Sept. 4, 1918, **49:** 443
George Creel
    1917
    Aug. 15, 1917, **43:** 477; Aug. 24, 1917, **44:** 49; Sept. 26, 1917, **44:**
    267; Oct. 22, 1917, **44:** 424; Oct. 25, 1917, **44:** 446; Nov. 4, 1917,
    44: 504; Nov. 9, 1917, **44:** 551; Nov. 28, 1917 (3), **45:** 152, 153;
    Dec. 8, 1917, **45:** 246; Dec. 21, 1917, **45:** 339; Dec. 22, 1917, **45:**
    344; Dec. 31, 1917, **45:** 407
    1918
    Jan. 29, 1918, **46:** 160; Feb. 19, 1918, **46:** 386; Feb. 21, 1918, **46:**
    410; Feb. 26, 1918 (3), **46:** 458, 459, 460; March 27, 1918, **47:** 169;
    April 2, 1918, **47:** 226; May 9, 1918, **47:** 581; June 17, 1918, **48:**
    341; June 25, 1918, **48:** 428; July 5, 1918, **48:** 528; July 19, 1918,
    49: 23; Aug. 2, 1918, **49:** 168; Aug. 6, 1918, **49:** 200; Sept. 12,
    1918, **49:** 536; Sept. 18, 1918, **51:** 64; Sept. 25, 1918 (2), **51:** 117,
    118; Sept. 26, 1918, **51:** 124; Oct. 1, 1918, **51:** 175; Nov. 8, 1918,
    51: 645
Herbert David Croly, Jan. 23, 1917, **40:** 559; Oct. 19, 1917, **44:** 408
Benedict Crowell, March 9, 1918, **46:** 584; April 8, 1918, **47:** 296;
    April 12, 1918, **47:** 328
Charles Allen Culberson, May 15, 1917, **42:** 299
Homer Stillé Cummings, Oct. 22, 1918, **51:** 408; Nov. 4, 1918, **51:**
    588; Nov. 7, 1918, **51:** 627
A memorandum by Homer Stillé Cummings on Wilson's appeal to
    voters, Oct. 18, 1918, **51:** 380
A memorandum by Homer Stillé Cummings about the senatorial
    situation, Nov. 4, 1918, **51:** 589
A memorandum by Homer Stillé Cummings about the result of the
    congressional election, Nov. 7, 1918, **51:** 628
Charles Curtis and Daniel Read Anthony, Jr., Jan. 11, 1918, **46:** 13
Lloyd Walley Curtis, Jan. 23, 1917, **40:** 562
Juliana Stevens Cuyler, Dec. 4, 1917, **45:** 231

Richard Heath Dabney, Nov. 23, 1916, **40:** 61; Aug. 9, 1917, **43:** 415
Josephus Daniels
    1917
    Jan. 2, 1917, **40:** 382; Jan. 16, 1917, **40:** 490; Jan. 18, 1917, **40:**
    523; Feb. 26, 1917, **41:** 293; March 8, 1917, **41:** 361; March 14,
    1917, **41:** 407; April 6, 1917, **41:** 555; April 11, 1917, **42:** 39; June
    20, 1917, **42:** 547; July 12, 1917, **43:** 155; Aug. 6, 1917, **43:** 373;
    Aug. 25, 1917, **44:** 54; Sept. 13, 1917, **44:** 198; Nov. 10, 1917, **44:**
    571; Nov. 30, 1917 (2), **45:** 170

1918
Jan. 3, 1918, **45:** 448; Jan. 26, 1918, **46:** 105; Feb. 2, 1918, **46:** 217;
Feb. 12, 1918, **46:** 330; March 11, 1918, **46:** 602; March 23, 1918,
47: 123; March 26, 1918, **47:** 153; April 20, 1918, **47:** 413; Sept. 9,
1918, **49:** 498; Sept. 25, 1918, **51:** 110; Sept. 26, 1918, **51:** 123;
Oct. 3, 1918, **51:** 207
A memorandum by Josephus Daniels on the governorship of the
Danish West Indies, March 8, 1917, **41:** 362
Winthrop More Daniels, Dec. 16, 1916, **40:** 255; Oct. 19, 1917, **44:**
406; Oct. 23, 1917, **44:** 429; March 27, 1918, **47:** 166; Aug. 5,
1918, **49:** 183; Aug. 14, 1918, **49:** 252; Sept. 2, 1918, **49:** 420; Oct.
5, 1918, **51:** 247
James L. Davidson, June 6, 1917, **42:** 460
Joseph Edward Davies, March 12, 1918, **46:** 609
Felix Cordova Davila, May 10, 1918, **48:** 4
Ellen Duane Davis, Sept. 20, 1918, **51:** 82
John William Davis, Sept. 13, 1917, **44:** 192
Henry Pomeroy Davison, May 29, 1918, **48:** 199; June 3, 1918, **48:**
234
Perl D. Decker, Aug. 28, 1918, **49:** 370
William Denman, June 29, 1917, **43:** 50; July 5, 1917, **43:** 105; July
18, 1917 (2), **43:** 204, 205; July 23, 1917, **43:** 249; July 24, 1917
(3), **43:** 258, 261
James Hardy Dillard, June 28, 1918, **48:** 462
Frederick Dixon, Nov. 4, 1918, **51:** 579
Alexander Monroe Dockery, Aug. 10, 1918, **49:** 235; Sept. 20, 1918,
51: 82
Cleveland Hoadley Dodge, April 3, 1917, **41:** 539; May 11, 1917, **42:**
280; Oct. 24, 1918, **51:** 443
J. L. Donnelly and Thomas A. French, Aug. 6, 1917, **43:** 373
William Henry Donner, May 5, 1917, **42:** 242; May 16, 1917, **42:**
304
William Truman Drury, April 6, 1918, **47:** 274
Fred Thomas Dubois, Aug. 1, 1918, **49:** 145
Leonidas Carstarphen Dyer, July 20, 1917, **43:** 222; July 26, 1917,
43: 284; July 30, 1917, **43:** 323; July 23, 1918, **49:** 61

Joe Henry Eagle, Aug. 24, 1917, **44:** 63
James Stanislaus Easby-Smith, Jan. 13, 1917, **40:** 466
Max Eastman, Sept. 28, 1917, **44:** 274
Max Eastman and others, July 12, 1917, **43:** 165
Walter Evans Edge, Jan. 12, 1918, **45:** 573
A resolution by a conference of black newspaper editors, June 21,
1918, **48:** 529
Richard Hathaway Edmonds, Oct. 4, 1917, **44:** 305
Charles William Eliot, Jan. 11, 1917, **40:** 443; March 27, 1917, **41:**
480; April 3, 1917, **41:** 540; April 8, 1917, **42:** 19; April 14, 1917

(2), **42:** 76; July 20, 1917, **43:** 232; July 26, 1917, **43:** 282; Nov. 5, 1918, **51:** 599

Howard Elliott, Dec. 27, 1917, **45:** 367

John Henry Fahey, Jan. 24, 1918, **46:** 92

John Cardinal Farley, Aug. 15, 1917, **43:** 492

A petition by the Federal Board of Farm Organizations, Feb. 8, 1918, **46:** 279

Scott Ferris, Sept. 2, 1917, **44:** 121; April 23, 1918, **47:** 402; May 16, 1918, **48:** 42; May 27, 1918, **48:** 170; June 27, 1918, **48:** 452; July 9, 1918, **48:** 576; Aug. 26, 1918, **49:** 355; Sept. 14, 1918, **51:** 6; Sept. 27, 1918, **51:** 138; Oct. 12, 1918, **51:** 312

Edward Albert Filene, Sept. 4, 1918, **49:** 444

Henry Burchard Fine, Aug. 10, 1918, **49:** 242

Irving Fisher, May 17, 1917, **42:** 323

Ludvik J. Fisher, Dec. 5, 1917, **45:** 223

John Joseph Fitzgerald, Sept. 6, 1917, **44:** 158

William Bowyer Fleming, Jan. 24, 1917, **41:** 5; Jan. 5, 1917, **41:** 6; April 8, 1918, **47:** 295

Duncan Upshaw Fletcher, Feb. 14, 1917, **41:** 230; May 11, 1918, **47:** 609

Joseph Wingate Folk, Aug. 7, 1918, **49:** 210

Henry Jones Ford, Jan. 21, 1918, **46:** 62; Jan. 26, 1918, **46:** 108

Rudolph Forster, Nov. 5, 1917, **44:** 527

A memorandum by Rudolph Forster on the investigation of William Bayard Hale by the Secret Service, Oct. 31, 1917, **44:** 481

John Franklin Fort, May 3, 1917, **42:** 205; June 30, 1917, **43:** 61; July 13, 1917, **43:** 167; Aug. 8, 1917, **43:** 397; Aug. 18, 1917, **43:** 519; July 30, 1918, **49:** 129

Raymond Blaine Fosdick, Aug. 15, 1917, **43:** 478; April 1, 1918, **47:** 220; Sept. 27, 1918, **51:** 136; Oct. 2, 1918, **51:** 185

A memorandum by Raymond Blaine Fosdick about the "negro problem" at Newport News, Sept. 27, 1918, **51:** 136

John Fox, Aug. 29, 1917, **44:** 85; Sept. 4, 1917, **44:** 152

Joseph Irwin France, March 28, 1917, **41:** 488; Feb. 11, 1918, **46:** 325

Hollis Burke Frissell, Dec. 12, 1916, **40:** 221

Antoinette Funk, June 17, 1918, **48:** 342

Andrew Furuseth, Nov. 4, 1918, **51:** 587

Helen Hamilton Gardener, May 10, 1917, **42:** 269; June 10, 1917, **42:** 474; July 19, 1917, **43:** 214; June 17, 1918, **48:** 340; June 23, 1918, **48:** 400; Aug. 16, 1918, **49:** 268; Oct. 9, 1918, **51:** 288

William Gwynn Gardiner, Nov. 9, 1917, **44:** 559

Frederick Dozier Gardner, Sept. 4, 1918, **49:** 444

Harry Augustus Garfield, Jan. 23, 1917, **40:** 560; March 6, 1917, **41:** 344; March 17, 1917, **41:** 423; March 28, 1917, **41:** 487; May

4, 1917, **42:** 214; Oct. 26, 1917, **44:** 450; Nov. 30, 1917, **45:** 173; Dec. 5, 1917, **45:** 215; Jan. 18, 1918, **46:** 30; Jan. 19, 1918, **46:** 41; March 20, 1918, **47:** 89; April 23, 1918, **47:** 404; May 15, 1918, **48:** 22; July 16, 1918, **48:** 638; July 17, 1918, **48:** 646; Sept. 16, 1918, **51:** 19; Sept. 25, 1918, **51:** 116; Sept. 27, 1918, **51:** 138

A memorandum by Harry Augustus Garfield on the railroad fuel question, May 15, 1918, **48:** 22

Elbert Henry Gary, Sept. 28, 1918, **51:** 150

Roy James Gaston, April 5, 1918, **47:** 260

John Palmer Gavit, Nov. 22, 1916, **40:** 40; Jan. 26, 1917, **41:** 32; March 25, 1917, **41:** 467

James Cardinal Gibbons, Oct. 6, 1917, **44:** 320

Carter Glass, April 6, 1917, **41:** 555

Franklin Potts Glass, June 11, 1917, **42:** 496; Aug. 11, 1917, **43:** 433; May 24, 1918, **48:** 148; Aug. 13, 1918, **49:** 245

Marguerite Godham, Aug. 1, 1917, **43:** 341

George Washington Goethals, July 20, 1917, **43:** 233

Samuel Gompers, Dec. 4, 1916, **40:** 146; Dec. 5, 1916, **40:** 174; March 14, 1917, **41:** 407; April 20, 1917, **42:** 135; June 12, 1917, **42:** 488; June 27, 1917, **43:** 20; July 20, 1917, **43:** 230; July 25, 1917, **43:** 278; Aug. 2, 1917, **43:** 352; Aug. 10, 1917, **43:** 416; Aug. 18, 1917, **43:** 513; Aug. 24, 1917, **44:** 47; Sept. 21, 1917, **44:** 233; Nov. 20, 1917, **45:** 94; Nov. 27, 1917, **45:** 141; Dec. 11, 1917, **45:** 269; Dec. 14, 1917 (2), **45:** 295, 298; May 6, 1918, **47:** 543; May 23, 1918, **48:** 130; June 13, 1918, **48:** 309; June 14, 1918, **48:** 313; June 18, 1918, **48:** 349; June 17, 1918, **48:** 438; July 19, 1918, **49:** 23; July 30, 1918, **49:** 135; Aug. 14, 1918, **49:** 255

A memorandum by Samuel Gompers on the commutation of sentences, Dec. 5, 1916, **40:** 175

Thomas Pryor Gore, May 23, 1917, **42:** 382

Patrick Emmet Gorman, Sept. 28, 1918, **51:** 149

Samuel Jordan Graham, Dec. 15, 1916, **40:** 244

William Green, Aug. 1, 1917, **43:** 340; Aug. 2, 1917, **43:** 352

William Green and others, Aug. 4, 1917, **43:** 368

James Edgar Gregg, Oct. 1, 1918, **51:** 176

Thomas Watt Gregory

1917

Feb. 26, 1917, **41:** 288; April 20, 1917, **42:** 113; June 14, 1917, **42:** 509; June 30, 1917, **43:** 54; July 19, 1917, **43:** 215; July 22, 1917, **43:** 243; July 27, 1917 (3), **43:** 297, 298, 315; Aug. 21, 1917, **44:** 17; Aug. 22, 1917, **44:** 31; Sept. 4, 1917 (2), **44:** 151, 152; Oct. 5, 1917, **44:** 313; Oct. 6, 1917, **44:** 323; Oct. 20, 1917, **44:** 415; Nov. 2, 1917, **44:** 492; Nov. 3, 1917, **44:** 504; Nov. 5, 1917, **44:** 514; Nov. 9, 1917, **44:** 552; Nov. 12, 1917, **45:** 28; Nov. 28, 1917, **45:** 154; Dec. 28, 1917, **45:** 374

1918

Jan. 20, 1918, **46:** 50; Jan. 25, 1918, **46:** 97; Feb. 7, 1918, **46:** 283; March 6, 1918, **46:** 560; March 24, 1918, **47:** 135; March 28, 1918

(2), **47**: 173, 179; May 11, 1918 (2), **47**: 603, 604; May 14, 1918, **48**: 12; June 1, 1918, **48**: 222; June 6, 1918, **48**: 251; June 15, 1918, **48**: 322; June 25, 1918, **48**: 422; July 24, 1918, **49**: 79; Aug. 21, 1918, **49**: 306; Sept. 9, 1918, **49**: 499; Sept. 13, 1918, **51**: 13; Sept. 18, 1918, **51**: 68; Oct. 8, 1918, **51**: 270; Oct. 12, 1918, **51**: 310; Oct. 18, 1918, **51**: 376

A memorandum by Thomas Watt Gregory about a bill proposing the establishment of a military war zone in the United States, Feb. 7, 1918, **46**: 283

Don Niko Gršković, Nov. 29, 1916, **40**: 104

Leon Samuel Haas, June 18, 1918, **48**: 352

Matthew Hale, Sept. 7, 1917, **44**: 165; May 6, 1918, **47**: 540

William Bayard Hale, April 6, 1918, **47**: 275

Henry Clay Hall, July 27, 1917, **43**: 296

Henry Noble Hall, Aug. 15, 1917, **43**: 476

John William Hamilton, March 12, 1918, **46**: 612

Peter Joseph Hamilton, May 15, 1918, **48**: 17; May 17, 1918, **48**: 48

Charles Sumner Hamlin, Oct. 22, 1917, **44**: 423; July 29, 1918, **49**: 119

George P. Hampton, Aug. 19, 1918, **49**: 289; Sept. 3, 1918, **49**: 430; Sept. 9, 1918, **49**: 499

Norman Hapgood, Dec. 5, 1916, **40**: 173

William Procter Gould Harding, Nov. 27, 1916, **40**: 87; July 12, 1918, **48**: 597; July 17, 1918, **48**: 646; July 20, 1918, **49**: 47; Sept. 9, 1918, **49**: 503

A memorandum by William Procter Gould Harding about the cotton situation, July 20, 1918, **49**: 47

John Marshall Harlan, April 6, 1918, **47**: 274

William Julius Harris, Feb. 12, 1917, **41**: 205; Feb. 12, 1918, **46**: 330; July 27, 1918, **49**: 114; Sept. 11, 1918, **49**: 528

William Harrison and others, Oct. 1, 1918, **51**: 191

Mary Garrett Hay, Nov. 7, 1917, **44**: 532

Frank J. Hayes and others, Nov. 1, 1918, **51**: 545

William Dudley Haywood, July 30, 1917, **43**: 325

William Dudley Haywood and others, May 8, 1918, **47**: 573

James Thomas Heflin, May 17, 1917, **42**: 323; June 28, 1917, **43**: 36

Guy Tresillian Helvering, April 19, 1917, **42**: 96

Francis Joseph Heney, Dec. 30, 1916, **40**: 370

Henry Lee Higginson, June 29, 1917, **43**: 52; July 23, 1917, **43**: 251; July 30, 1917, **43**: 337; Oct. 22, 1917, **44**: 425; Nov. 13, 1917, **45**: 44

Philip Hiss, Jan. 25, 1918, **46**: 98

Gibert Monell Hitchcock, March 29, 1917, **41**: 498; Oct. 23, 1918, **51**: 423

Daniel Webster Hoan, Oct. 4, 1917, **44**: 339

William Pettus Hobby, Nov. 18, 1917, **45**: 76; Dec. 8, 1917, **45**: 253

Frank Norton Hoffstot, June 14, 1917, **42**: 540

Hale Holden, Dec. 28, 1917, **45:** 373

Henry French Hollis, Feb. 19, 1917, **41:** 251; April 22, 1918, **47:** 399

Lydia Wickliffe Holmes, June 18, 1918, **48:** 352; Oct. 31, 1918, **51:** 537

Hamilton Holt, Feb. 20, 1918, **46:** 460; Aug. 17, 1918, **49:** 277

Edith Houghton Hooker, April 26, 1917, **42:** 138

Herbert Clark Hoover

1917

May 31, 1917, **42:** 430; June 12, 1917, **42:** 480; June 15, 1917 (2), **42:** 522, 532; June 29, 1917, **43:** 48; June 30, 1917, **43:** 56; July 7, 1917, **43:** 117; July 12, 1917, **43:** 160; July 18, 1917, **43:** 207; Aug. 1, 1917, **43:** 339; Aug. 23, 1917, **44:** 36; Aug. 27, 1917, **44:** 72; Aug. 31, 1917, **44:** 107; Nov. 15, 1917, **45:** 58; Nov. 19, 1917 (2), **45:** 83, 85; Nov. 23, 1917, **45:** 113; Nov. 24, 1917, **45:** 115; Nov. 26, 1917, **45:** 124; Dec. 1, 1917 (3), **45:** 178, 179; Dec. 6, 1917, **45:** 228; Dec. 23, 1917, **45:** 347

1918

Jan. 17, 1918, **46:** 19; Jan. 28, 1918 (2), **46:** 125, 126; Feb. 9, 1918, **46:** 304; Feb. 14, 1918, **46:** 345; Feb. 19, 1918, **46:** 394; Feb. 20, 1918, **46:** 401; Feb 21, 1918, **46:** 409; Feb. 26, 1918, **46:** 461; March 1, 1918, **46:** 501; March 7, 1918, **46:** 565; March 22, 1918, **47:** 120; March 26, 1918 (2), **47:** 149; April 1, 1918, **47:** 221; April 8, 1918, **47:** 293; May 13, 1918, **48:** 7; May 21, 1918, **48:** 107; May 27, 1918, **48:** 169; June 14, 1918, **48:** 313; July 2, 1918, **48:** 484; July 8, 1918, **48:** 562; July 10, 1918, **48:** 580; Aug. 26, 1918 (2), **49:** 352, 354; Aug. 27, 1918, **49:** 362; Aug. 30, 1918, **49:** 391; Sept 6, 1918, **49:** 464; Sept. 9, 1918, **49:** 498; Sept. 11, 1918, **49:** 522; Sept. 13, 1918, **49:** 550; Sept. 16, 1918, **51:** 18; Sept. 18, 1918, **51:** 70; Sept. 21, 1918, **51:** 88; Sept. 26, 1918, **51:** 126; Oct. 17, 1918, **51:** 357; Oct. 21, 1918, **51:** 397

A memorandum by Herbert Clark Hoover on the necessity for food legislation, June 12, 1917, **42:** 481

A memorandum by Herbert Clark Hoover on the organization of community controls, June 12, 1917, **42:** 483

A memorandum by Herbert Clark Hoover on the organization of voluntary conservation, June 12, 1917, **42:** 484

A memorandum by Herbert Clark Hoover on the proposed governmental operation of the meat-packing plants, May 21, 1918, **48:** 108

A memorandum by Herbert Clark Hoover about the administration's opposition to the closing of breweries, May 27, 1918, **48:** 166

Herbert Clark Hoover and others, April 4, 1917, **41:** 543

A report to the President by Herbert Clark Hoover and others on the meat-packing industry, May 11, 1918, **48:** 7

A schedule by Herbert Clark Hoover of the export of food to Europe, Sept. 21, 1918, **51:** 89

Alison Low Turnbull Hopkins, July 20, 1917, **43:** 235

Charlotte Everett Wise Hopkins, Jan. 31, 1918, **46:** 195
John Appleton Haven Hopkins, July 18, 1917, **43:** 213
Edward Mandell House
  1916
  Dec. 8, 1916, **40:** 192; Dec. 29, 1916, **40:** 359; Dec. 31, 1916, **40:**
  374
  1917
  Jan. 5, 1917, **40:** 413; Jan. 22, 1917, **40:** 539; Jan. 30, 1917, **41:**
  69; March 1, 1917, **41:** 308; March 15, 1917, **41:** 411; April 4,
  1917, **41:** 543; April 6, 1917, **41:** 554; May 4, 1917, **42:** 220; May
  6, 1917, **42:** 233; May 8, 1917, **42:** 248; June 14, 1917, **42:** 520;
  June 21, 1917 (2), **42:** 553, 554; July 2, 1917, **43:** 76; July 13,
  1917, **43:** 167; July 21, 1917, **43:** 242; July 24, 1917, **43:** 265; July
  26, 1917, **43:** 283; Aug. 10, 1917, **43:** 424; Sept. 19, 1917, **44:** 221;
  Sept. 21, 1917, **44:** 246
  1918
  Jan. 10, 1918, **45:** 564; Feb. 6, 1918, **46:** 259; Feb. 16, 1918, **46:**
  361; Feb. 17, 1918, **46:** 367; May 5, 1918, **47:** 525; May 7, 1918,
  47: 546; May 9, 1918, **47:** 584; May 24, 1918, **48:** 143; July 6,
  1918, **48:** 541; Aug. 24, 1918, **49:** 348; Aug. 25, 1918, **49:** 350
David Franklin Houston, May 14, 1917, **42:** 294; Nov. 23, 1917, **45:**
  105; Nov. 30, 1917, **45:** 168; March 1, 1918, **46:** 503; March 28,
  1918, **47:** 177; May 10, 1918, **47:** 589; June 12, 1918, **48:** 298; July
  26, 1918, **49:** 99; Sept. 4, 1918 (2), **48:** 439, 440
William Cannon Houston, Dec. 21, 1916, **40:** 315
Frederic Clemson Howe, Dec. 15, 1917, **45:** 309
A memorandum by Frederic Clemson Howe on nationalization of
  the railroads, Dec. 13, 1917, **45:** 283
Clark Howell, July 24, 1918, **49:** 80; Aug. 12, 1918, **49:** 237
George Huddleston, Aug. 10, 1918, **49:** 236
James Alexander Hudson and William Hirth, March 20, 1918, **47:**
  90
Charles Evans Hughes, Nov. 22, 1916, **40:** 38; May 15, 1918, **48:** 15
Cordell Hull, May 15, 1918, **48:** 19
George Wylie Paul Hunt, July 2, 1917, **43:** 72; July 4, 1917, **43:** 98;
  Sept 1, 1917, **44:** 134; Sept. 3, 1917, **44:** 134; March 22, 1918, **47:**
  115; April 15, 1918, **47:** 347
George Wylie Paul Hunt and John McBride, July 13, 1917, **43:** 171
Richard Melancthon Hurd, March 25, 1918, **47:** 141
Edward Nash Hurley, Nov. 23, 1916, **40:** 58; Dec. 16, 1916, **40:** 250;
  Jan. 6, 1917, **40:** 419; Jan. 18, 1917, **40:** 519; Jan. 31, 1917 (2), **41:**
  84; Sept. 21, 1917, **44:** 234; Oct. 17, 1917, **44:** 394; Oct. 29, 1917,
  44: 466; Nov. 13, 1917, **45:** 42; Dec. 17, 1917, **45:** 314; Jan. 28,
  1918, **46:** 123; Feb. 13, 1918, **46:** 338; Feb. 16, 1918, **46:** 362; Feb.
  18, 1918, **46:** 378; March 1, 1918, **46:** 503; March 12, 1918, **46:**
  610; March 19, 1918, **47:** 73; April 3, 1918, **47:** 233; April 13,
  1918, **47:** 336; Sept. 7, 1918, **49:** 474
Paul Oscar Husting, April 27, 1917, **42:** 146

William Levi Hutcheson, Feb. 16, 1918, **46:** 364; Feb. 17, 1918, **46:** 367

William Moulton Ingraham, Oct. 25, 1917, **44:** 446
W. I. Irvine and Paul Hanna, Aug. 4, 1917, **43:** 383
Eugene Semmes Ives, June 29, 1917, **43:** 53

Charles Samuel Jackson, July 24, 1917, **43:** 266
Melancthon Williams Jacobus, March 4, 1917, **41:** 320; April 5, 1917, **41:** 548
Ollie Murray James, Sept. 4, 1917, **44:** 151
Ben Johnson, April 4, 1918, **47:** 255; May 28, 1918, **48:** 190; Aug. 2, 1918, **49:** 169
Jesse Holman Jones, May 11, 1918, **47:** 604; May 15, 1918, **48:** 16; May 18, 1918, **48:** 59
Richard Lloyd Jones, Sept. 28, 1918, **51:** 148
Thomas Davies Jones, Jan. 29, 1917, **41:** 58; July 30, 1917, **43:** 325; Nov. 24, 1917, **45:** 116; Dec. 24, 1917, **45:** 350
David Starr Jordan, May 23, 1917, **42:** 382; Feb. 11, 1918, **46:** 326

Julius Kahn, July 27, 1917, **43:** 299
Otto Hermann Kahn, April 6, 1917, **42:** 7
John Reese Kenly, Nov. 26, 1917, **45:** 125; Nov 28, 1917, **45:** 155
Elizabeth Thacher Kent, May 8, 1918, **47:** 572
William Kent, Dec. 8, 1916, **40:** 192; Dec. 19, 1916, **40:** 287; Jan. 19, 1917, **40:** 526; Jan. 23, 1917, **40:** 561; Jan. 26, 1917, **41:** 31; Feb. 12, 1917, **41:** 207; July 16, 1917, **43:** 190; Aug. 11, 1917, **43:** 432; Aug. 16, 1917, **43:** 495; Dec. 14, 1917 (2), **45:** 299, 302; Dec. 20, 1917, **45:** 335; Dec. 28, 1917, **45:** 379; Jan. 31, 1918, **46:** 195; Feb. 28, 1918, **46:** 492; March 12, 1918, **46:** 614; March 16, 1918, **47:** 45; April 22, 1918, **47:** 399; May 20, 1918, **48:** 93; June 3, 1918, **48:** 235; Aug. 29, 1918, **49:** 384; Sept. 9, 1918, **49:** 505; Sept. 16, 1918, **51:** 20; Sept. 26, 1918, **51:** 125; Sept. 28, 1918, **51:** 147; Oct. 3, 1918, **51:** 203; Oct. 5, 1918, **51:** 249; Oct. 9, 1918, **51:** 287; Oct. 30, 1918, **51:** 520
William Squire Kenyon, March 9, 1918, **46:** 588
Claude Kitchin, Dec. 22, 1916, **40:** 318; July 29, 1918, **49:** 124
S. J. Konenkamp, June 15, 1918, **48:** 329
Louis Kopelin, Dec. 4, 1917, **45:** 203
Arthur Bernard Krock, Sept. 7, 1918, **49:** 480

George B. LaBarre, May 14, 1918, **48:** 11
Polk Lafoon, Oct. 7, 1918, **51:** 259
Thomas William Lamont, Oct. 11, 1918, **51:** 296; Oct. 31, 1918, **51:** 530
George Mason La Monte, Oct. 4, 1918, **51:** 210; Nov. 6, 1918, **51:** 606
Franklin Knight Lane, Dec. 9, 1916 (2), **40:** 205, 206; Dec. 17, 1916,

40: 263; Jan. 8, 1917, **40:** 424; Jan. 23, 1917, **40:** 560; Jan. 25, 1917, **41:** 19; May 4, 1917, **42:** 218; June 28, 1917, **43:** 36; July 2, 1917, **43:** 73; Aug. 4, 1917, **43:** 367; Aug. 8, 1917, **43:** 399; Oct. 2, 1917, **44:** 293; Nov. 3, 1917, **44:** 498; Nov. 30, 1917, **45:** 171; Dec. 31, 1917, **45:** 406; Jan. 4, 1918, **45:** 453; March 12, 1918, **46:** 608; March 13, 1918, **47:** 10; March 14, 1918, **47:** 30; March 26, 1918, **47:** 148; May 11, 1918, **47:** 610; Oct. 3, 1918, **51:** 206; Oct. 7, 1918, **51:** 259

Memoranda by Franklin Knight Lane about discussions at cabinet, Oct. 23, 1918, **51:** 413; Nov. 1, 1918, **51:** 548; Nov. 5, 1918, **51:** 604

A suggestion by Franklin Knight Lane for a water power bill, Dec. 9, 1916, **40:** 207

Harry Lane, Feb. 12, 1917, **41:** 207

Robert Lansing, Dec. 1, 1916, **40:** 113; Dec. 2, 1916, **40:** 122; Jan. 6, 1917, **40:** 419; Feb. 14, 1917, **41:** 225; Feb. 23, 1917, **41:** 277; April 8, 1917, **42:** 16; April 21, 1917, **42:** 117; June 3, 1917, **42:** 444; June 9, 1917, **42:** 469; Nov. 1, 1917, **44:** 483; Dec. 1, 1917, **45:** 177; Feb. 9, 1918, **46:** 298; Feb. 21, 1918, **46:** 408; June 14, 1918, **48:** 312; Sept. 3, 1918, **49:** 423; Sept. 28, 1918, **51:** 147

Robert Lansing and others, April 13, 1917, **42:** 55

Samuel Lavit, Sept. 6, 1918, **49:** 465; Sept. 17, 1918, **51:** 24

David Lawrence, May 24, 1917, **42:** 386; April 8, 1918, **47:** 295

Elisha Lee, March 16, 1917, **41:** 415

Asbury Francis Lever, July 21, 1917, **43:** 242; June 8, 1918, **48:** 268

David John Lewis, July 15, 1918, **48:** 623

James Hamilton Lewis, Jan. 26, 1917, **41:** 33; Dec. 13, 1917, **45:** 319

Charles August Lindbergh, Aug. 27, 1917, **44:** 108

Washington Ellsworth Lindsey, July 13, 1917, **43:** 170

Walter Lippmann, Feb. 6, 1917, **41:** 134; April 3, 1917, **41:** 537; June 15, 1917, **42:** 525; Oct. 8, 1917, **44:** 333

Ernest Lister, Aug. 18, 1917, **44:** 14

Louis Paul Lochner, Aug. 28, 1917, **44:** 78

Thomas Francis Logan, April 13, 1918, **47:** 342

Breckinridge Long, Nov. 19, 1917, **45:** 87

A memorandum by Breckinridge Long on the establishment of a censorship board, Nov. 19, 1917, **45:** 88

James Revell Lord and Samuel McCune Lindsay, Sept. 30, 1918, **51:** 165

George Horace Lorimer, April 15, 1918, **47:** 348

Robert Scott Lovett, Sept. 19, 1917, **44:** 222; Dec. 15, 1917, **45:** 311; Jan. 19, 1918, **46:** 39; Jan. 21, 1918, **46:** 85; Feb. 27, 1918, **46:** 476

Edward George Lowry, June 12, 1917, **42:** 486

Simon Julius Lubin, March 29, 1918, **47:** 194

William Gibbs McAdoo
1916
Dec. 28, 1916, **40:** 347

1917

March 9, 1917 (2), **41:** 379; March 28, 1917, **41:** 485; March 29, 1917, **41:** 500; April 3, 1917, **41:** 541; April 10, 1917, **42:** 25; May 11, 1917, **42:** 278; May 12, 1917, **42:** 285; May 14, 1917, **42:** 294; May 16, 1917 (2), **42:** 302, 303; June 2, 1917, **42:** 440; June 5, 1917, **42:** 455; June 23, 1917, **42:** 565; July 3, 1917, **43:** 93; July 9, 1917, **43:** 133; July 10, 1917 (2), **43:** 136, 139; July 16, 1917, **43:** 189; July 18, 1917, **43:** 203; July 30, 1917 (2), **43:** 319, 320; Aug. 15, 1917, **43:** 478; Aug. 22, 1917, **44:** 29; Aug. 30, 1917, **44:** 92; Sept. 17, 1917, **44:** 208; Sept. 25, 1917, **44:** 257; Oct. 6, 1917, **44:** 323; Nov. 12, 1917, **45:** 26; Nov. 22, 1917, **45:** 101; Dec. 6, 1917, **45:** 225; Dec. 14, 1917, **45:** 287; Dec. 15, 1917 (2), **45:** 304, 306; Dec. 16, 1917, **45:** 313

1918

Jan. 14, 1918, **45:** 587; Jan. 17, 1918 (2), **46:** 17; Jan. 27, 1918, **46:** 111; Feb. 5, 1918, **46:** 252; Feb. 23, 1918, **46:** 424; Feb. 25, 1918 (2), **46:** 442, 443; Feb. 27, 1918, **46:** 477, 478; March 1, 1918, **46:** 506; May 3, 1918, **47:** 506; May 8, 1918, **47:** 561; May 14, 1918, **48:** 12; May 20, 1918 (2), **48:** 80, 81; May 23, 1918 (2), **48:** 121, 128; May 24, 1918, **48:** 148; May 27, 1918 (2), **48:** 168; July 25, 1918 (2), **49:** 84, 85; Aug. 8, 1918, **49:** 218; Aug. 27, 1918 (2), **49:** 361; Aug. 28, 1918, **49:** 372; Aug. 29, 1918 (2), **49:** 377, 379; Aug. 30, 1918, **49:** 393; Aug. 31, 1918, **49:** 405; Sept. 18, 1918, **51:** 65; Oct. 3, 1918, **51:** 204; Oct. 4, 1918, **51:** 217; Oct. 9, 1918, **51:** 285; Oct. 25, 1918, **51:** 446; Oct. 26, 1918, **51:** 461

John McCarthy and others, July 27, 1917, **43:** 299

Charles Raymond Macauley, Nov. 2, 1917, **44:** 494

Cyrus Hall McCormick, Jr., April 22, 1917, **42:** 167

Vance Criswell McCormick, June 28, 1917, **43:** 34; March 22, 1918, **47:** 120; Oct. 9, 1918, **51:** 287

Edwin T. McCoy, May 10, 1918, **47:** 597

Grenville Stanley Macfarland, Sept. 28, 1917, **44:** 275; Oct. 4, 1917, **44:** 307; Oct. 12, 1917, **44:** 366; Oct. 20, 1917, **44:** 416; Dec. 11, 1917, **45:** 270; Sept. 16, 1918, **51:** 19

John Avery McIlhenny and Charles Mills Galloway, April 5, 1917, **41:** 547

John Avery McIlhenny and others, April 5, 1917, **41:** 546; Dec. 20, 1917, **45:** 336

Clarence Hungerford Mackay, June 12, 1918, **48:** 298

Kenneth Douglas McKellar, July 7, 1917, **43:** 120; July 11, 1917, **43:** 148; July 20, 1917, **43:** 234; June 22, 1918, **48:** 395

Alexander Jeffrey McKelway, Dec. 19, 1917, **45:** 331; Dec. 22, 1917, **45:** 346; March 13, 1918, **47:** 15

Thomas Deitz McKeown, Aug. 11, 1917, **43:** 434

Edward Beale McLean, July 14, 1917, **43:** 182; March 4, 1918, **46:** 527; April 4, 1918, **47:** 256; Oct. 27, 1918, **51:** 464

Gavin McNab, June 15, 1917, **42:** 525; Sept. 23, 1917, **44:** 243

John Aldus McSparran, March 11, 1918, **46:** 602

John Aldus McSparran and others, Sept. 25, 1917, **44:** 258

Valentine Everit Macy, Sept. 20, 1917, **44:** 226; Sept. 25, 1917, **44:** 256; Aug. 20, 1918, **49:** 298; Sept. 17, 1918, **51:** 32; Sept. 20, 1918, **51:** 83; Oct. 3, 1918, **51:** 194; Oct. 21, 1918, **51:** 396; Oct. 23, 1918 (2), **51:** 422, 423

Dudley Field Malone, Sept. 7, 1917, **44:** 167; Sept. 15, 1917, **44:** 200

Richard Irvine Manning, Oct. 14, 1918, **51:** 337

Hudson Snowden Marshall, Edward Hubbard Wells, and Gavin McNab, April 12, 1918, **47:** 328

Thomas Riley Marshall, Dec. 13, 1916, **40:** 230; March 18, 1918, **47:** 57; May 7, 1918, **47:** 547

Thomas Staples Martin, Sept. 4, 1917, **44:** 150; Sept. 29, 1917, **44:** 279

Henry Lowndes Maury, Sept. 25, 1917, **44:** 259

Royal Meeker, Nov. 27, 1917, **45:** 132; Nov. 28, 1917, **45:** 150; Dec. 1, 1917, **45:** 183; March 14, 1918, **47:** 28; Aug. 29, 1918, **49:** 375

Cleveland Langston Moffett, Aug. 16, 1917, **43:** 499

Thomas Joseph Mooney, April 29, 1918, **47:** 467

John Denis Joseph Moore, Aug. 17, 1917, **43:** 509

Joseph Hampton Moore, March 6, 1918, **46:** 561

Henry Morgenthau, June 11, 1918, **48:** 284; June 18, 1918, **48:** 350

Emery T. Morris and others, March 5, 1918, **46:** 550

A memorial to the President by Emery T. Morris and others, April 20, 1917, **42:** 113

Roland Sletor Morris, July 31, 1917, **43:** 333

Frank Morrison, Sept. 25, 1918, **51:** 120

Robert Russa Moton, Dec. 4, 1916, **40:** 153; March 15, 1917, **41:** 412; July 7, 1917, **43:** 119; Feb. 27, 1918, **46:** 480; June 15, 1918, **48:** 323; June 24, 1918, **48:** 416; July 27, 1918, **49:** 113; Sept. 11, 1918, **49:** 522

Fred William Mueller, April 13, 1918, **47:** 337

Henry Lee Myers and James Duval Phelan, Feb. 23, 1917, **41:** 278

A petition by the New York branch of the National Association for the Advancement of Colored People, Feb. 19, 1918, **46:** 383

National Association of Manufacturers, Jan. 17, 1918, **46:** 18

A memorandum by the National Civil Liberties Bureau about the pending trial of leaders of the Industrial Workers of the World, Feb. 27, 1918, **46:** 481

A memorandum and petition from the Committee of the Negro Silent Protest Parade on lynching and mob violence, Aug. 1, 1917, **43:** 342

Keith Neville, May 28, 1918, **48:** 191

Francis Griffith Newlands, Dec. 15, 1916, **40:** 246; Jan. 25, 1917, **41:** 20; Feb. 7, 1917, **41:** 156; Feb. 11, 1917, **41:** 197; Feb. 16, 1917, **41:** 238; June 7, 1917, **42:** 462

Edward Nockels and others, Dec. 4, 1916, **40:** 176

A. H. Nowaka, Aug. 21, 1917, **44:** 344

George Francis O'Shaunessy, Jan. 6, 1918, **45:** 518
Lee Slater Overman, March 22, 1918, **47:** 109; April 26, 1918, **47:** 446; May 21, 1918, **48:** 110; Oct. 4, 1918, **51:** 216
Robert Latham Owen, Aug. 2, 1917, **43:** 348; Jan. 8, 1918, **45:** 541; July 3, 1918, **48:** 506; July 18, 1918, **49:** 6; Sept. 20, 1918, **51:** 83; Sept. 28, 1918, **51:** 148; Oct. 24, 1918, **51:** 439

Arthur Wilson Page, Aug. 14, 1917, **43:** 465
Charles R. Page, Nov. 6, 1918, **51:** 610
A statement by Thomas Walker Page and Charles John Brand on the stabilization of the cotton industry, Nov. 6, 1918, **51:** 611
Walter Hines Page, Aug. 1, 1918, **49:** 155
A memorandum by Walter Hines Page on Herbert Clark Hoover and Irwin Boyle Laughlin, Dec. 30, 1916, **40:** 369
Alexander Mitchell Palmer, Oct. 25, 1918, **51:** 445
Frank Park, Aug. 20, 1917, **43:** 539
Maud May Wood Park, Nov. 30, 1917, **45:** 169
Alice Paul, Jan. 1, 1917, **40:** 379
George Foster Peabody, Dec. 4, 1917, **45:** 203; Jan. 19, 1918, **46:** 40; July 29, 1918, **49:** 125; Aug. 4, 1918, **49:** 179, Oct. 31, 1918, **51:** 534
John Joseph Pershing, Oct. 8, 1917, **44:** 328
Andrew James Peters, Nov. 7, 1918, **51:** 624
James Duval Phelan, Aug. 6, 1917, **43:** 372
An address to the President by James Duval Phelan, Jan. 10, 1918, **45:** 559
William Phillips, Jan. 12, 1917, **40:** 457; April 3, 1917, **41:** 539
Amos Richards Eno Pinchot, July 25, 1917, **43:** 276; May 24, 1918, **48:** 146
Henry Means Pindell, Feb. 12, 1918, **46:** 331
Lucius Eugene Pinkham, Aug. 17, 1917, **43:** 505
Key Pittman, Feb. 17, 1917, **41:** 246; March 27, 1917, **41:** 478; June 22, 1917, **42:** 562; Sept. 7, 1918, **49:** 481; Sept. 17, 1918, **51:** 30; Nov. 6, 1918, **51:** 611
Miles Poindexter, July 17, 1917, **43:** 200
Frank Lyon Polk, June 12, 1917, **42:** 489
Atlee Pomerene, March 21, 1918, **47:** 95; May 11, 1918, **47:** 608; July 6, 1918, **48:** 535; Oct. 1, 1918, **51:** 176
Allen Bartlit Pond, July 13, 1917, **43:** 168; Sept. 21, 1917, **44:** 236
Louis Freeland Post, July 5, 1917, **43:** 104; Nov. 15, 1917, **45:** 60; Nov. 27, 1917, **45:** 130; Dec. 1, 1917, **45:** 182; Dec. 10, 1917, **45:** 258; Feb. 8, 1918, **46:** 289
Elizabeth Herndon Potter, March 21, 1918, **47:** 104
Edward William Pou, May 17, 1917, **42:** 320; May 19, 1917, **42:** 349; Aug. 31, 1918, **49:** 406; Oct. 11, 1918, **51:** 299
A memorandum by the President's Mediation Commission on interference with the draft law in Bisbee, Nov. 6, 1917, **44:** 521
A memorandum by the President's Mediation Commission about

the streetcar controversy in Minneapolis and St. Paul, March 29, 1918, **47:** 189

Report of the President's Mediation Commission, Jan. 9, 1918, **46:** 128

A report by the President's Mediation Commission on the Mooney case, Jan. 16, 1918, **46:** 68

Price indices for foodstuffs, 1913-1919, Oct. 17, 1918, **51:** 358

The Prohibition National Committee, Jan. 8, 1918, **45:** 541

Ralph Pulitzer, Feb. 15, 1918, **46:** 351

An address to the President by the Rev. Wallace Radcliffe, June 19, 1917, **42:** 535

Jeannette Rankin, Aug. 1, 1917, **43:** 339; Dec. 18, 1917, **45:** 321

Caroline Seaman Read, May 3, 1918, **48:** 28

Lord Reading, April 13, 1918, **47:** 334

William Cox Redfield, Nov. 28, 1916, **40:** 95; Dec. 20, 1916, **40:** 290; Dec. 30, 1916, **40:** 366; March 15, 1917, **41:** 409; May 9, 1917 (2), **42:** 256, 257; July 6, 1917, **43:** 109; July 28, 1917 (2), **43:** 310, 312; July 27, 1917, **43:** 311; Aug. 18, 1917 (2), **43:** 518; Aug. 22, 1917, **44:** 27; Oct. 27, 1917, **44:** 458; Dec. 8, 1917, **45:** 246; Feb. 9, 1918, **46:** 309; March 13, 1918, **47:** 9; April 11, 1918, **47:** 321; Aug. 8, 1918, **49:** 218; Oct. 4, 1918, **51:** 217

Verner Zevola Reed, Nov. 25, 1917, **45:** 121; Dec. 24, 1917, **45:** 350

Robert Goodwyn Rhett, Nov. 15, 1917, **45:** 61; Dec. 14, 1917, **45:** 299

Edgar Rickard, July 26, 1918, **49:** 104

Allen W. Ricker, Aug. 3, 1917, **43:** 382; Aug. 9, 1917, **43:** 413; May 15, 1918, **48:** 16

Joseph Taylor Robinson, May 13, 1918, **48:** 9

Walter Stowell Rogers, April 6, 1918, **47:** 276

Milton Andrew Romjue, Jan. 25, 1918, **46:** 100

Franklin Delano Roosevelt, Oct. 4, 1917, **44:** 302; Feb. 16, 1918, **46:** 363; July 8, 1918, **48:** 563

John Dennis Ryan, May 2, 1918, **47:** 494

Adolph Joseph Sabath, June 20, 1918, **48:** 376

Willard Saulsbury, June 23, 1917, **42:** 567; May 28, 1918, **48:** 193; June 8, 1918, **48:** 269

William Lawrence Saunders, Sept. 5, 1918, **49:** 455

John Nevin Sayre, April 27, 1917, **42:** 159; Sept. 19, 1918, **51:** 77

Joseph Schick, July 29, 1918, **49:** 165

Marguerite de Witt Schlumberger and others, Feb. 1, 1918, **48:** 25

Emmett Jay Scott, June 26, 1918, **48:** 529

Louis Seibold, July 3, 1917, **43:** 95

Anne Leddell Seward, July 2, 1915, **40:** 565

John Franklin Shafroth, March 16, 1917, **41:** 417; May 28, 1918, **48:** 189

Albert Shaw, Dec. 1, 1916, **40:** 117; April 27, 1917, **42:** 150; Dec. 8, 1917, **45:** 247; April 20, 1918, **47:** 385

Anna Howard Shaw, May 21, 1918, **48:** 111; May 27, 1918, **48:** 169; May 29, 1918, **48:** 198

Lucius Elmer Sheppard and others, March 7, 1917, **41:** 352

Morris Sheppard, March 20, 1918, **47:** 88; May 26, 1918, **48:** 161; June 24, 1918, **48:** 413

John Knight Shields, June 25, 1918, **48:** 427

John R. Shillady, July 25, 1918, **49:** 88

Jouett Shouse, Aug. 25, 1917, **44:** 53; June 7, 1918, **48:** 263; Aug. 21, 1918, **49:** 308; Nov. 7, 1918, **51:** 623

Furnifold McLendel Simmons, May 25, 1918, **48:** 153; May 27, 1918, **48:** 168; July 30, 1918, **49:** 134

Thetus Willrette Sims, Dec. 29, 1917, **45:** 391; June 28, 1918, **48:** 457; July 6, 1918, **48:** 532; Aug. 22, 1918, **49:** 329; Sept. 21, 1918, **51:** 90

Upton Beall Sinclair, Oct. 22, 1917, **44:** 467; May 18, 1918, **48:** 59; July 9, 1918, **48:** 610; Aug. 7, 1918, 49: 207

George H. Slater, March 21, 1918, **47:** 104

John Albert Sleicher, April 16, 1918, **47:** 352

John Humphrey Small, June 18, 1918, **48:** 350; Aug. 23, 1918, **49:** 344

Hoke Smith, July 12, 1917, **43:** 162

Marcus Aurelius Smith, July 8, 1917, **43:** 127

Roland Cotton Smith, Jan. 2, 1917, **40:** 383

Bertrand Hollis Snell, March 19, 1918, **47:** 72

John Spargo, Nov. 1, 1917, **44:** 491; Nov. 14, 1917, **45:** 50; Jan. 8, 1918, **45:** 542

Augustus Owsley Stanley, Sept. 7, 1918, **49:** 481

Julius Stephens and J. L. Jarrett, July 8, 1917, **43:** 128

Richard Stephens and W. R. Davis, Sept. 8, 1917, **44:** 172

William Dennison Stephens, May 11, 1917, **42:** 279; Jan. 30, 1918, **46:** 170; March 30-31, 1918, **47:** 210; June 5, 1918, **48:** 247

Edward Riley Stettinius, April 11, 1918, **47:** 321

Raymond Bartlett Stevens, Oct. 5, 1917, **44:** 313

Henry Lewis Stimson, April 17, 1917, **42:** 83

William Joel Stone, Jan. 2, 1917, **40:** 385; Jan. 8, 1917, **40:** 424; Jan. 25, 1917, **41:** 19

Moorfield Storey and others, Feb. 13, 1917, **41:** 217

Charles Lee Swem, Aug. 4, 1917, **43:** 368; Dec. 10, 1917, **45:** 262

Herbert Bayard Swope, July 31, 1917, **43:** 334; Feb. 22, 1918, **46:** 416; July 2, 1918, **48:** 486

William Howard Taft, May 14, 1917, **42:** 295; Aug. 8, 1917, **43:** 399; April 9, 1918, **47:** 302

Ida Minerva Tarbell, Dec. 30, 1916, **40:** 372; May 18, 1918, **48:** 57

Frank William Taussig, Nov. 22, 1917, **45:** 101; Nov. 26, 1917, **45:** 127; April 2, 1918, **47:** 224; April 4, 1918, **47:** 255

Edward Thomas Taylor, April 27, 1918, **47:** 451
Charles Spalding Thomas, March 9, 1918, **46:** 600; March 12, 1918, **46:** 610; March 14, 1918, **47:** 33
Samuel Huston Thompson, Jr., Jan. 15, 1917, **40:** 490; May 6, 1918, **47:** 539
William Howard Thompson, March 13, 1918, **47:** 8
Benjamin Ryan Tillman, Jan. 6, 1917, **40:** 420; July 17, 1917, **43:** 198; May 10, 1918, **47:** 597
George Carroll Todd, Nov. 29, 1916, **40:** 102; Sept. 6, 1918, **49:** 463
Helen Todd, Aug. 18, 1917, **43:** 536
Robert Henry Todd, March 2, 1917, **41:** 312
Arthur Charles Townley, Sept. 10, 1917 (2), **44:** 182; March 20, 1918, **47:** 87
Park Trammell, May 16, 1918, **48:** 43; Sept. 30, 1918, **51:** 165
Joseph Patrick Tumulty
  1916
  Nov. 28, 1916, **40:** 96
  1917
  Jan. 13, 1917, **40:** 465; March 16, 1917, **41:** 414; March 24, 1917, **41:** 462; April 7, 1917, **42:** 6; April 20, 1917, **42:** 106; May 8, 1917, **42:** 245; May 31, 1917 (2), **42:** 427; June 6, 1917 (2), **42:** 458, 459; June 26, 1917, **43:** 19; July 5, 1917, **43:** 104; July 10, 1917, **43:** 139; July 11, 1917, **43:** 145; July 12, 1917, **43:** 156; Aug. 1, 1917, **43:** 342; Aug. 3, 1917, **43:** 359; Aug. 8, 1917, **43:** 393; Sept. 17, 1917, **44:** 208; Sept. 23, 1917, **44:** 242; Sept. 27, 1917, **44:** 271; Oct. 15, 1917, **44:** 383; Dec. 7, 1917, **45:** 232; Dec. 12, 1917, **45:** 277; Dec. 15, 1917, **45:** 306
  January–June 1918
  Jan. 3, 1918, **45:** 435; Jan. 8, 1918, **45:** 541; Jan. 23, 1918 (2), **46:** 83, 84; Jan. 31, 1918, **46:** 194; Feb. 7, 1918, **46:** 269; March 7, 1918, **46:** 565; March 12, 1918, **46:** 608; March 14, 1918, **47:** 34; March 15, 1918, **47:** 42; April 4, 1918, **47:** 253; April 22, 1918 (2), **47:** 396; April 25, 1918, **47:** 436; May 3, 1918, **47:** 508; May 7, 1918, **47:** 547; May 8, 1918, **47:** 571; May 10, 1918, **47:** 587; May 16, 1918, **48:** 32; May 23, 1918 (2), **48:** 118, 128; June 7, 1918, **48:** 261; June 18, 1918, **48:** 347; June 20, 1918, **48:** 370; June 27, 1918, **48:** 444
  July–November 1918
  July 5, 1918 (2), **48:** 526; July 11, 1918, **48:** 591; July 20, 1918, **49:** 51; July 26, 1918, **49:** 105; Aug. 2, 1918, **49:** 162; Aug. 7, 1918, **49:** 210; Aug. 9, 1918, **49:** 223; Aug. 28, 1918, **49:** 369; Aug. 29, 1918, **49:** 381; Sept. 4, 1918 (2), **49:** 438, 439; Sept. 5, 1918, **49:** 451; Sept. 6, 1918, **49:** 457; Sept. 7, 1918, **49:** 476; Sept. 13, 1918, **49:** 540; Sept. 18, 1918, **51:** 63; Sept. 23, 1918, **51:** 111; Sept. 25, 1918, **51:** 117; Oct. 9, 1918, **51:** 283; Oct. 24, 1918, **51:** 437; Oct. 26, 1918, **51:** 460; Oct. 31, 1918, **51:** 537; Nov. 2, 1918, **51:** 552; Nov. 3, 1918, **51:** 572
A draft by Joseph Patrick Tumulty of a statement on labor disputes, June 7, 1918, **48:** 261

A memorandum for the President by Joseph Patrick Tumulty on the railroad priorities bill, June 14, 1917, **42:** 505

Suggestions by Joseph Patrick Tumulty for Wilson's message to Congress, Nov. 30, 1917, **45:** 164

A resolution by the Union Française pour le Suffrage des Femmes, Feb. 1, 1918, **48:** 25

The Faculty of the University of Wisconsin, Jan. 14, 1918, **45:** 586

Theodore Newton Vail, April 22, 1918, **47:** 400

Charles Richard Van Hise, Nov. 27, 1917, **45:** 142; Jan. 14, 1918, **45:** 586

Ambrose White Vernon, Dec. 1, 1916, **40:** 116

Oswald Garrison Villard, Sept. 17, 1918, **51:** 56

Alexander Theodore Vogelsang, May 23, 1918, **48:** 129

Alice Hay Wadsworth, July 23, 1917, **43:** 250

Lillian D. Wald, Dec. 2, 1916, **40:** 121; April 21, 1917, **42:** 118; Jan. 8, 1918, **45:** 541

Lillian D. Wald and others, Jan. 24, 1917, **41:** 7; April 16, 1917, **42:** 118; Aug. 10, 1917, **43:** 420

John Milton Waldron, April 12, 1917, **42:** 49

John Milton Waldron and Thomas Montgomery Gregory, May 11, 1917, **42:** 321

A memorandum for the President by John Milton Waldron and John MacMurray on blacks as voters, May 25, 1918, **48:** 155

Amelia Himes Walker, July 22, 1917, **43:** 243

William English Walling, July 3, 1917, **43:** 103

Francis Patrick Walsh, March 30, 1918, **47:** 212; June 20, 1918, **48:** 374; July 15, 1918, **48:** 623; Oct. 30, 1918, **51:** 522

Thomas James Walsh, Jan. 18, 1917, **40:** 522; June 22, 1917, **42:** 561; July 2, 1917, **43:** 75; May 6, 1918, **47:** 541; July 25, 1918, **49:** 90

Paul Moritz Warburg, May 27, 1918, **48:** 171; Aug. 10, 1918, **49:** 236

Alice Edith Binsse Warren, March 13, 1917, **41:** 399

Ben Webb and others, July 23, 1917, **43:** 253

Edwin Yates Webb, May 15, 1917, **42:** 298

A memorandum for the President by Louis Brandeis Wehle on the adjustment of labor disputes in the production of munitions and supplies, Nov. 11, 1917, **45:** 7

Harry Andrew Wheeler and Elliot Hersey Goodwin, Oct. 3, 1918, **51:** 207

Harry Covington Wheeler, Oct. 31, 1917, **44:** 479; Nov. 6, 1917, **44:** 523

Andrew Dickson White, April 26, 1917, **42:** 139

John Philip White, May 23, 1917, **42:** 459

John Philip White and William Green, Dec. 11, 1916, **40:** 217

The White House staff, Dec. 19, 1916, **40:** 287; Feb. 15, 1917, **41:** 234; Aug. 13, 1917, **43:** 455; Aug. 20, 1917, **43:** 535; Nov. 9, 1917, **44:** 554; Nov. 30, 1917, **45:** 167; Jan. 23, 1918, **46:** 84; Feb. 25, 1918, **46:** 443; March 12, 1918, **46:** 614; July 17, 1918, **48:** 645; Aug. 10, 1918, **49:** 235; Sept. 14, 1918, **51:** 5; Oct. 2, 1918, **51:** 181

A memorandum for the President by the White House staff on the Lever bill, June 16, 1917, **42:** 529

A memorandum by the White House staff about an appointment with suffrage leaders, Nov. 6, 1917, **44:** 523

Vira Boarman Whitehouse, Aug. 28, 1917, **44:** 79; Oct. 8, 1917, **44:** 335; Nov. 7, 1917, **44:** 533

An address to the President by Vira Boarman Whitehouse, Oct. 25, 1917, **44:** 440

Brand Whitlock, April 8, 1917, **42:** 20

Charles Seymour Whitman, Jan. 17, 1918, **46:** 19

Louis Bernard Whitney, July 12, 1917, **43:** 158

Edmond A. Whittier, May 15, 1918, **48:** 17

Louis Wiley, July 31, 1917, **43:** 333

Daniel Willard, Nov. 19, 1917, **45:** 77; Dec. 7, 1917, **45:** 233; Dec. 22, 1917, **45:** 342; Jan. 11, 1918, **45:** 600; Jan. 21, 1918, **46:** 61

Dixon C. Williams, April 3, 1918, **47:** 235

John Sharp Williams, Dec. 9, 1916, **40:** 201; Dec. 22, 1916, **40:** 318; June 30, 1917, **43:** 79; Aug. 4, 1917, **43:** 368; Sept. 5, 1917, **44:** 155; Feb. 8, 1918, **46:** 287

John Skelton Williams, Dec. 6, 1916, **40:** 181; Dec. 9, 1916, **40:** 202; May 25, 1917, **42:** 401; Oct. 22, 1917, **44:** 422; April 23, 1918, **47:** 405; April 24, 1918, **47:** 418; May 1, 1918, **47:** 488; July 31, 1918, **49:** 143

A memorandum by John Skelton Williams on the railroad fuel question, April 23, 1918, **47:** 407

A memorandum by John Skelton Williams on the Second Liberty Loan, Oct. 18, 1917, **44:** 400

William Franklin Willoughby, Jan. 16, 1917, **40:** 497

Emil Carl Wilm, May 4, 1918, **47:** 518

Clarence True Wilson, March 2, 1917, **41:** 311

Frederick J. Wilson, Feb. 18, 1918, **46:** 380

Joseph R. Wilson, Jr., March 14, 1918, **47:** 33

William Bauchop Wilson
1916
Nov. 29, 1916, **40:** 97; Dec. 20, 1916, **40:** 295
1917
Feb. 19, 1917, **41:** 253; March 21, 1917, **41:** 446; Feb. 2, 1917, **41:** 447; June 9, 1917 (2), **42:** 471, 473; June 22, 1917, **42:** 562; June 26, 1917, **43:** 16; July 26, 1917, **43:** 292; Aug. 17, 1917, **43:** 506; Aug. 31, 1917, **44:** 103; Sept. 18, 1917, **44:** 213; Sept. 22, 1917, **44:** 241; Sept. 29, 1917, **44:** 290; Oct. 22, 1917, **44:** 424; Oct. 31, 1917, **44:** 478; Nov. 6, 1917, **44:** 515; Nov. 22, 1917, **45:** 95; Nov. 26, 1917, **45:** 126; Nov. 27, 1917, **45:** 134; Dec. 7, 1917, **45:** 234; Dec. 14, 1917, **45:** 295; Dec. 19, 1917, **45:** 331

January–May 1918
Jan. 22, 1918, **46:** 68; Jan. 26, 1918, **46:** 106; Jan. 28, 1918 (2), **46:** 127, 151; Jan. 30, 1918 (2), **46:** 170, 171; Feb. 2, 1918, **46:** 218; March 1, 1918, **46:** 509; March 8, 1918, **46:** 578; March 28, 1918, **47:** 180; April 4, 1918, **47:** 247; April 6, 1918 (2), **47:** 272; April 5, 1918, **47:** 291; April 29, 1918, **47:** 461; May 7, 1918, **47:** 557; May 16, 1918, **48:** 43; May 24, 1918, **48:** 150
June–October 1918
June 1, 1918, **48:** 222; June 8, 1918, **48:** 270; June 10, 1918, **48:** 281; June 22, 1918, **48:** 393; July 7, 1918, **48:** 546; July 11, 1918, **48:** 594; July 22, 1918, **49:** 53; July 25, 1918, **49:** 89; July 30, 1918, **49:** 132; Aug. 5, 1918 (2), **49:** 181; Aug. 7, 1918, **49:** 206; Aug. 14, 1918, **49:** 251; Sept. 6, 1918 (2), **49:** 463, 464; Sept. 11, 1918, **49:** 519; Oct. 7, 1918, **51:** 260; Oct. 8, 1918, **51:** 270; Oct. 17, 1918, **51:** 361
A draft by William Bauchop Wilson of a proclamation about the appointment of the National War Labor Board, April 2, 1918, **47:** 247
William Bauchop Wilson and others, Nov. 6, 1917, **44:** 516
Stephen Samuel Wise, Feb. 9, 1917, **41:** 180
Josiah Oliver Wolcott, Oct. 1, 1918, **51:** 177
Simon Wolf, June 11, 1917, **42:** 506
A resolution by the Woman's Committee of the Council of National Defense, May 15, 1918, **48:** 170
A resolution by the state representatives of the Woman's Committee of the Council of National Defense, May 13-15, 1918, **48:** 198
The National Board of the Woman's Peace Party, Jan. 14, 1918, **45:** 586
Levi Hollingsworth Wood and others, Sept. 26, 1917, **44:** 266
Robert Wickliffe Woolley, March 30, 1918, **47:** 210; April 25, 1918, **47:** 425; April 29, 1918, **47:** 467; Oct. 22, 1918, **51:** 409
Robert Wickliffe Woolley and Matthew Hale, April 19, 1918, **47:** 376; April 21, 1918, **47:** 391
A memorandum by Robert Wickliffe Woolley and Matthew Hale about the labor situation, April 19, 1918, **47:** 377
Edward H. Wright and others, Aug. 7, 1917, **43:** 392
C. Wyatt and Clem Wessel, Sept. 23, 1917, **44:** 242

Arthur Yager, Nov. 23, 1916, **40:** 57; Feb. 23, 1917, **41:** 278
Teodoro Yangco and Jaime C. de Veyra, March 5, 1917, **41:** 345
Allyn Abbott Young, Nov. 27, 1917, **45:** 141

Diplomatic notes

By Wilson and from Wilson to
A prolegomenon to a peace note, Nov. 25, 1916, **40:** 67
A note to the belligerents asking for a statement of war aims: first draft, Nov. 25, 1916, **40:** 70; first redraft, Dec. 9, 1916, **40:** 197; comments by Robert Lansing on the first redraft, Dec. 10, 1916,

40: 210; second redraft, Dec. 17, 1916, **40:** 256; comments by Robert Lansing on the second redraft, Dec. 17, 1916, **40:** 260; note as sent, Dec. 18, 1916, **40:** 273

A note verbale to the German government protesting against the deportation of Belgian civilians: suggestions, Nov. 26, 1916, **40:** 83; Nov. 28, 1916, **40:** 94-95; note as sent, Nov. 29, 1916, **40:** 106.

A draft of a note to the Entente Powers in reply to the peace overture by the Central Powers, Dec. 13, 1916, **40:** 222

A draft of a note to the Central Powers in reply to their peace overture, Dec. 13, 1916, **40:** 226

A note to all neutral countries about the severance of diplomatic relations with Germany, Feb. 3, 1917, **41:** 116

Suggestions for a reply to the Swiss proposal for a conference of neutrals, Feb. 9, 1917, **41:** 173

A note to the Mexican government about a united peace action by the neutrals, March 14, 1917, **41:** 404

Alfonso XIII, Feb. 28, 1918 (draft), **46:** 486

Charles I, March 5, 1918, **46:** 551

A note to the Japanese government on the proposed intervention in Siberia, March 4, 1918, **46:** 531; March 5, 1918, **46:** 545

A reply to the note of the Austro-Hungarian government of Sept. 16, 1918, Sept. 16, 1918, **51:** 10 (draft), 11

A reply to the note of the Austro-Hungarian government of Oct. 7, 1918, Oct. 19, 1918, **51:** 383

A note to the French government on the postponement of peace negotiations with Bulgaria, Oct. 2, 1918, **51:** 187

A reply to the note of the German government of Oct. 6, 1918: first draft, Oct. 7, 1918, **51:** 255; second draft, Oct. 8, 1918, **51:** 263; penultimate draft, Oct. 8, 1918, **51:** 264; final draft, Oct. 8, 1918, **51:** 268

A reply to the note of the German government of Oct. 12, 1918, Oct. 14, 1918, **51:** 333

A reply to the note of the German government of Oct. 20, 1918: tentative drafts by Robert Lansing, Oct. 21, 1918 (2), **51:** 400, 401; Oct. 22, 1918, **51:** 401; draft by Newton Diehl Baker, Oct. 22, 1918, **51:** 413; final Wilson draft, Oct. 23, 1918, **51:** 417

To Wilson from

A note from the Belgian government about the deportation of Belgian civilians, Nov. 25, 1916, **40:** 83

A note from the Belgian government, Dec. 12, 1916, **40:** 220

A peace note by the Central Powers, Dec. 12, 1916, **40:** 231

A note from the Swiss Federal Council, Dec. 23, 1916, **40:** 325

A note from the German government in reply to Wilson's peace note, Dec. 26, 1916, **40:** 331

A note from the Allies in reply to Wilson's peace note, Jan. 10, 1917, **40:** 439

A note by the German government announcing the inauguration of unrestricted submarine warfare, Jan. 31, 1917, **41:** 76

A note by the German government defining the blockade zones around Great Britain, France, and Italy, Jan. 31, 1917, **41:** 77

A note by the Swiss government on a conference of neutrals, Feb. 2, 1917, **41:** 105

A note by the Swiss government reaffirming Switzerland's strict neutrality, Feb. 10, 1917, **41:** 193

A note by the Swiss government about Germany's willingness to continue negotiations with the United States, Feb. 11, 1917, **41:** 204

Alfonso XIII, Feb. 25, 1918, **46:** 440

Charles I, Feb. 18, 1918, **46:** 397; Feb. 25, 1918, **46:** 440

Notes from the Austro-Hungarian government: Oct. 7, 1918, **51:** 259; Oct. 29, 1918, **51:** 505

A note from the Bulgarian government, Sept. 27, 1918, **51:** 154

Notes from the German government: Oct. 6, 1918, **51:** 253; Oct. 12, 1918, **51:** 317; Oct. 20, 1918, **51:** 402

A memorandum by the German government supplementing its note of Oct. 20, 1918, Oct. 27, 1918, **51:** 518

Correspondence, reports, memoranda, and aide-mémoire about diplomatic affairs

By Wilson and from Wilson to

Albert, King of the Belgians, Jan. 18, 1917 (draft), **40:** 518; Nov. 15, 1917, **45:** 50; May 25, 1918, **48:** 151

The Allied governments, Oct. 23, 1918, **51:** 416

Ambassadors of the United States at London, Paris, and Rome, Oct. 23, 1917, **44:** 427

The American embassy, Petrograd, June 9, 1917, **42:** 466

A draft of instructions to American representatives delivering the peace overtures of the Central Powers, Dec. 15, 1916, **40:** 242

American representatives in the belligerent countries, Dec. 23, 1916, **40:** 325

Newton Diehl Baker, Dec. 3, 1916, **40:** 130; Dec. 26, 1916, **40:** 330; May 8, 1917, **42:** 242; May 21, 1917, **42:** 357; Aug. 22, 1917, **44:** 27; Oct. 29, 1917, **44:** 463; Oct. 30, 1917, **44:** 467; Jan. 31, 1918, **46:** 179; Nov. 7, 1918, **51:** 617

Arthur James Balfour, May 19, 1917, **42:** 346; Oct. 7, 1917, **44:** 325

Colville Adrian de Rune Barclay, Jan. 16, 1918, **46:** 4

Bases of Peace, Feb. 8, 1917, **41:** 160 (draft); Feb. 9, 1917, **41:** 173 (redraft)

Perry Belden, March 17, 1917, **41:** 420

A note to Benedict XV, Aug. 16, 1917, **43:** 487 (notes for a reply); Aug. 23, 1917, **44:** 33 (draft); Aug. 27, 1917, **44:** 57

Benedict XV, Oct. 17, 1918, **51:** 355

Samuel Reading Bertron, March 16, 1918, **47:** 43; March 30, 1918, **47:** 208; June 25, 1918, **48:** 422

Julio Betancourt, Jan. 25, 1917, **41:** 14; March 22, 1917, **41:** 450

Anita McCormick Blaine, Feb. 3, 1917, **41:** 113

The Most Reverend John Bonzano, Oct. 17, 1918, **51:** 355

Wenceslao Braz Pereira Gomes, June 2, 1917, **42:** 440; July 8, 1918, **48:** 550

Herbert Bruce Brougham, Sept. 29, 1917, **44:** 279

William Jennings Bryan, Jan. 22, 1918, **46:** 67; July 18, 1918, **49:** 3; July 23, 1918, **49:** 60

A memorandum on possible peace negotiations with Bulgaria, Oct. 1, 1918, **51:** 170

Albert Sidney Burleson, Feb. 23, 1918, **46:** 422

Venustiano Carranza, July 8, 1918, **48:** 551

Carrie Clinton Lane Chapman Catt, May 8, 1917, **42:** 241

Charles Francis Joseph, Nov. 22, 1916, **40:** 34

An aide-mémoire about the correspondence with Emperor Charles, March 1, 1918, **46:** 508

Frank Clark, Nov. 13, 1917, **45:** 39

John Hessin Clarke, Sept. 4, 1917, **44:** 146

Georges Clemenceau, April 8, 1918, **47:** 291

Gilbert Fairchild Close, Oct. 28, 1918, **51:** 475

Frank Irving Cobb, Sept. 1, 1917, **44:** 118; Sept. 12, 1917, **44:** 190

Bainbridge Colby, Dec. 26, 1917, **45:** 363; March 16, 1918, **47:** 43; March 25, 1918, **47:** 137; Oct. 26, 1918, **51:** 453

Lincoln Colcord, Dec. 6, 1917, **45:** 222; Feb. 4, 1918, **46:** 239; July 9, 1918, **48:** 568

Constantine, Jan. 26, 1917, **41:** 34

Charles Richard Crane, June 11, 1918, **48:** 283; June 28, 1918, **48:** 457; July 11, 1918, **48:** 590; July 29, 1918, **49:** 122

George Creel, May 14, 1917, **42:** 290; May 18, 1917, **42:** 326; Sept. 4, 1917 (2), **44:** 142, 143; Oct. 24, 1917, **44:** 435; Nov. 10, 1917, **44:** 557; Dec. 29, 1917, **45:** 387; Jan. 2, 1918, **45:** 422; Feb. 21, 1918, **46:** 407; July 15, 1918, **48:** 612; July 16, 1918 (2), **48:** 629, 630; Oct. 10, 1918, **51:** 294

Benedict Crowell, March 6, 1918, **46:** 554; March 10, 1918, **46:** 595

Richard Heath Dabney, April 3, 1917, **41:** 537

Josephus Daniels, Feb. 8, 1917, **41:** 159; Nov. 8, 1917, **44:** 537; Jan. 20, 1918, **46:** 49; Aug. 1, 1918, **49:** 149

Henry Pomeroy Davison, Dec. 2, 1916, **40:** 121; Feb. 22, 1918, **46:** 414

The Duke of Devonshire, Dec. 7, 1917, **45:** 230

Cleveland Hoadley Dodge, Dec. 5, 1917, **45:** 215

Michael Francis Doyle, Aug. 17, 1917, **43:** 505

Max Eastman, Sept. 18, 1917, **44:** 210

Maurice Francis Egan, May 16, 1918, **48:** 31

Charles William Eliot, Nov. 22, 1916, **40:** 38; Jan. 21, 1918, **46:** 53

Abram Isaac Elkus, Aug. 24, 1917, **44:** 40

Edward Albert Filene, Jan. 30, 1917, **41:** 68; Jan. 17, 1918, **46:** 14
Henry Burchard Fine, May 14, 1917, **42:** 292
Henry Prather Fletcher, April 21, 1917, **42:** 116
Felix Frankfurter, June 11, 1917, **42:** 475
A reply to questions by the French government about the conduct
   of the war and the conclusion of peace, Aug. 7, 1917, **43:** 388

Harry Augustus Garfield, Oct. 31, 1917, **44:** 478; Nov. 3, 1917, **44:**
   498
John Palmer Gavit, Nov. 22, 1916, **40:** 36; Dec. 5, 1916, **40:** 164
George V, April 6, 1918, **47:** 271; June 16, 1918, **48:** 366
James Cardinal Gibbons, Dec. 20, 1917, **45:** 334; Oct. 18, 1918, **51:**
   374
Braxton Davenport Gibson, May 5, 1917, **42:** 221
Samuel Gompers, Aug. 7, 1917, **43:** 383; Aug. 17, 1917, **43:** 505;
   Jan. 19, 1918, **46:** 37; Jan. 21, 1918, **46:** 53; May 7, 1918, **47:** 545

Charles Sumner Hamlin, Feb. 15, 1917, **41:** 233
Russell Benjamin Harrison, Aug. 14, 1918, **49:** 247
George Davis Herron, July 1, 1918, **48:** 473
Henry French Hollis, Oct. 30, 1918, **51:** 510; Nov. 5, 1918, **51:** 593
Hamilton Holt, Jan. 17, 1918, **46:** 14
Herbert Clark Hoover, Jan. 23, 1918, **46:** 79; June 14, 1918, **48:**
   310; Oct. 26, 1918 (draft), **51:** 458; Nov. 7, 1918, **51:** 618
Edward Mandell House
   1916
   Nov. 21, 1916, **40:** 20; Nov. 24, 1916, **40:** 62; Nov. 25, 1916, **40:**
   74; Dec. 3, 1916, **40:** 131; Dec. 5, 1916, **40:** 160; Dec. 8, 1916, **40:**
   189; Dec. 19, 1916, **40:** 276; Dec. 28, 1916, **40:** 343
   1917
   Jan. 16, 1917, **40:** 491; Jan. 17, 1917, **40:** 507; Jan. 19, 1917, **40:**
   524; Jan. 24, 1917, **41:** 3; Feb. 6, 1917, **41:** 134; Feb. 7, 1917, **41:**
   137; Feb. 12, 1917, **41:** 201; Feb. 26, 1917, **41:** 288; April 9, 1917,
   42: 20; April 10, 1917, **42:** 24; April 12, 1917, **42:** 45; June 1, 1917
   (2), **42:** 432, 433; June 15, 1917, **42:** 520; July 21, 1917, **43:** 237;
   Aug. 16, 1917, **43:** 488; Aug. 23, 1917, **44:** 33; Sept. 2, 1917, **44:**
   120; Sept. 19, 1917, **44:** 216; Sept. 24, 1917, **44:** 244; Oct. 7, 1917,
   44: 324; Oct. 13, 1917 (2), **44:** 371; Oct. 16, 1917, **44:** 388; Oct. 25,
   1917, **44:** 446; Oct. 26, 1917, **44:** 448; Nov. 16, 1917, **45:** 69; Nov.
   19, 1917, **45:** 83; Dec. 1, 1917, **45:** 176; Dec. 3, 1917, **45:** 187
   1918
   Jan. 2, 1918, **45:** 421; Jan. 30, 1918, **46:** 169; Jan. 31, 1918, **46:**
   178; March 20, 1918, **47:** 85; March 22, 1918, **47:** 105; May 6,
   1918, **47:** 534; July 8, 1918, **48:** 549; Aug. 31, 1918, **49:** 402; Sept.
   7, 1918, **49:** 466; Oct. 5, 1918, **51:** 226; Oct. 28, 1918 (2), **51:** 473;
   Oct. 29, 1918, **51:** 504; Oct. 30, 1918 (2), **51:** 511, 513; Oct. 31,
   1918, **51:** 533; Nov. 1, 1918, **51:** 541; Nov. 4, 1918 (2), **51:** 575;
   Nov. 7, 1918 (2), **51:** 617

Roy Wilson Howard, Jan. 2, 1917, **40**: 381; Jan. 5, 1917, **40**: 413; Jan. 16, 1918, **46**: 4
Frederic Clemson Howe, June 5, 1918, **48**: 241
Mary Eloise Hoyt, March 25, 1918, **47**: 139
Hsü Shih-ch'ang, Oct. 10, 1918, **51**: 292
Edward Nash Hurley, Aug. 29, 1918, **49**: 374; Sept. 9, 1918, **49**: 490
Paul Oscar Husting, May 10, 1917, **42**: 259

Viscount Kikujiro Ishii, July 9, 1918, **48**: 569

An aide-mémoire about the proposed Japanese intervention in Siberia, March 1, 1918 (draft), **46**: 498
Thomas Davies Jones, Nov. 19, 1917, **45**: 82
Jean Jules Jusserand, April 8, 1918, **47**: 290; July 1, 1918, **48**: 473; Aug. 1, 1918, **49**: 149

President Kerenskii of the National Council Assembly at Moscow, Aug. 24, 1917, **44**: 38

Thomas William Lamont, Jan. 11, 1918, **45**: 569; Jan. 31, 1918, **46**: 179
Franklin Knight Lane, Dec. 5, 1916, **40**: 161; Dec. 12, 1916, **40**: 218
Robert Lansing
  1916
  Nov. 26, 1916 (3), **40**: 80, 81, 82; Nov. 27, 1916, **40**: 88; Nov. 28, 1916, **40**: 94; Dec. 3, 1916 (2), **40**: 129, 130, Dec. 5, 1916 (2), **40**: 160, 163; Dec. 8, 1916, **40**: 189; Dec. 9, 1916, **40**: 197; Dec. 15, 1916, **40**: 241; Dec. 17, 1916, **40**: 256; Dec. 18, 1916, **40**: 272; Dec. 19, 1916, **40**: 276; Dec. 21, 1916 (2), **40**: 306, 307; Dec. 23, 1916, **40**: 324
  January–March 1917
  Jan. 4, 1917, **40**: 405; Jan. 5, 1917, **40**: 411; Jan. 11, 1917 (2), **40**: 442; Jan. 23, 1917 (2), **40**: 547, 549; Jan. 24, 1917 (2), **41**: 4; Jan. 27, 1917, **41**: 36; Jan. 31, 1917 (3), **41**: 70, 71; Feb. 6, 1917 (2), **41**: 131; Feb. 7, 1917 (2), **41**: 138, 145; Feb. 9, 1917 (3), **41**: 172, 175, 179; Feb. 10, 1917, **41**: 186; Feb. 12, 1917, **41**: 204; Feb. 14, 1917, **41**: 218; Feb. 15, 1917, **41**: 232; Feb. 19, 1917, **41**: 247; Feb. 20, 1917 (2), **41**: 257, 258; Feb. 28, 1917 (2), **41**: 299, 301; March 3, 1917, **41**: 313; March 14, 1917, **41**: 404; March 27, 1917 (4), **41**: 475, 476, 477
  April–June 1917
  April 1, 1917, **41**: 516; April 6, 1917, **41**: 552; April 8, 1917, **42**: 14; April 10, 1917, **42**: 24; April 11, 1917, **42**: 38; April 12, 1917 (3), **42**: 43, 44; April 13, 1917 (2), **42**: 53, 54; April 19, 1917 (3), **42**: 94, 95; April 20, 1917 (2), **42**: 105, 106; May 1, 1917, **42**: 176; May 3, 1917, **42**: 196; May 5, 1917, **42**: 222; May 7, 1917, **42**: 239; May 10, 1917 (3), **42**: 258, 262; May 11, 1917 (2), **42**: 271, 274; May 14, 1917, **42**: 289; May 22, 1917, **42**: 368; May 23, 1917, **42**:

376; May 25, 1917, **42**: 392; May 28, 1917, **42**: 410; June 1, 1917, **42**: 434; June 2, 1917, **42**: 439; June 13, 1917, **42**: 491; June 29, 1917 (2), **43**: 39, 40

July–December 1917

July 3, 1917, **43**: 80; Aug. 7, 1917, **43**: 384; Aug. 14, 1917 (3), **43**: 459, 460; Aug. 21, 1917, **44**: 3; Aug. 24, 1917, **44**: 38; Aug. 30, 1917, **44**: 90; Sept. 17, 1917, **44**: 207; Sept. 18, 1917 (2), **44**: 211; Sept. 26, 1917, **44**: 264; Oct. 6, 1917, **44**: 318; Oct. 11, 1917, **44**: 358; Oct. 20, 1917, **44**: 411; Oct. 22, 1917, **44**: 417; Oct. 24, 1917, **44**: 433; Oct. 25, 1917, **44**: 445; Nov. 3, 1917, **44**: 496; Nov. 5, 1917, **44**: 510; Nov. 7, 1917, **44**: 530; Nov. 28, 1917, **45**: 148; Dec. 8, 1917, **45**: 243; Dec. 12, 1917, **45**: 274; Dec. 29, 1917, **45**: 388; Dec. 31, 1917, **45**: 401

January–June 1918

Jan. 1, 1918 (3), **45**: 415, 417; Jan. 17, 1918, **46**: 14; Jan. 20, 1918 (3), **46**: 45, 46, 47; Jan. 21, 1918, **46**: 65; Jan. 24, 1918, **46**: 88; Jan. 29, 1918 (2), **46**: 149; Feb. 4, 1918 (6), **46**: 232, 233, 235, 236; Feb. 13, 1918 (2), **46**: 334; Feb. 16, 1918 (4), **46**: 357, 358, 360; Feb. 20, 1918, **46**: 393; Feb. 21, 1918, **46**: 406; March 16, 1918, **47**: 44; March 22, 1918, **47**: 106; March 28, 1918, **47**: 173; April 3, 1918, **47**: 231; April 4, 1918 (3), **47**: 241, 246; April 11, 1918, **47**: 315; April 18, 1918 (3), **47**: 357, 358; April 20, 1918, **47**: 380; May 1, 1918 (2), **47**: 474; May 8, 1918, **47**: 555; May 20, 1918 (2), **48**: 71, 72; May 24, 1918, **48**: 136; June 6, 1918 (2), **48**: 247; June 17, 1918 (2), **48**: 335; June 19, 1918, **48**: 358; June 21, 1918 (2), **48**: 382; June 26, 1918, **48**: 435; June 28, 1918 (3), **48**: 456, 457

July–November 1918

July 1, 1918, **48**: 473; July 3, 1918, **48**: 489; July 4, 1918, **48**: 517; July 8, 1918 (3), **48**: 551, 552; Aug. 14, 1918 (3), **49**: 248, 250; Aug. 22, 1918 (4), **49**: 310, 312, 313; Aug. 23, 1918 (2), **49**: 332, 333; Aug. 24, 1918 (2), **49**: 346; Aug. 29, 1918, **49**: 373; Sept. 2, 1918 (2), **49**: 415, 417; Sept. 5, 1918 (4), **49**: 446, 447, 448; Sept. 12, 1918, **49**: 529; Sept. 16, 1918, **51**: 10; Sept. 17, 1918 (3), **51**: 25, 26; Sept. 18, 1918, **51**: 50; Sept. 19, 1918, **51**: 75; Sept. 20, 1918 (3), **51**: 78; Sept. 23, 1918 (2), **51**: 91; Sept. 30, 1918, **51**: 161; Oct. 23, 1918, **51**: 416; Oct. 29, 1918, **51**: 481; Nov. 4. 1918, **51**: 576; Nov. 5, 1918, **51**: 592; Nov. 7, 1918, **51**: 618; Nov. 8, 1918, **51**: 634

David Lawrence, Jan. 23, 1917, **40**: 550; Jan. 30, 1917, **41**: 69; Oct. 5, 1917, **44**: 309

A covenant of a league of nations, Sept. 7, 1918, **49**: 467

James Hamilton Lewis, July 24, 1918, **49**: 74

Walter Lippmann, Feb. 3, 1917, **41**: 113

David Lloyd George, Jan. 2, 1918, **45**: 421

Meyer London, May 1, 1917, **42**: 179

Breckinridge Long, May 7, 1917, **42**: 236; March 14, 1918, **47**: 18

Abbott Lawrence Lowell, Aug. 21, 1917, **44**: 12; July 11, 1918, **48**: 590

Walter Lowrie, Sept. 25, 1917, **44**: 249

Citizens of Lyon, July 20, 1918, **49**: 37

William Gibbs McAdoo, Dec. 26, 1917, **45:** 362; Jan. 9, 1918, **45:** 546; Feb. 11, 1918, **46:** 324; Feb. 20, 1918, **46:** 393; Feb. 23, 1918, **46:** 423; Sept. 6, 1918, **49:** 462
Charles Raymond Macauley, May 16, 1918, **48:** 29
Cyrus Hall McCormick, Jr., April 27, 1917, **42:** 143
Vance Criswell McCormick, Oct. 17, 1917, **44:** 392
Grenville Stanley Macfarland, July 1, 1918, **48:** 474
William Douglas Mackenzie, May 25, 1917, **42:** 395
Benton McMillin, Dec. 5, 1916, **40:** 164
Theodore Marburg, March 8, 1918, **46:** 572; May 6, 1918, **47:** 535; Aug. 8, 1918, **49:** 214
Thomas Staples Martin, March 21, 1918, **47:** 94
Thomas Garrigue Masaryk, July 22, 1918, **49:** 53; Aug. 7, 1918, **49:** 203; Sept. 10, 1918, **49:** 511; Oct. 21, 1918, **51:** 395
Carlos Meléndez, July 29, 1918, **49:** 118
Mario García Menocal, April 12, 1917, **42:** 51
Désiré-Joseph Cardinal Mercier, July 2, 1917, **43:** 75; July 5, 1917, **43:** 101
Sidney Edward Mezes, Nov. 12, 1917, **45:** 17
William Fellowes Morgan, July 1, 1918, **48:** 472
Henry Morgenthau, Nov. 27, 1917, **45:** 128
John R. Mott, Aug. 22, 1917, **44:** 27; July 29, 1918, **49:** 123

Vittorio Emanuele Orlando, Nov. 5, 1917, **44:** 510
Robert Latham Owen, Jan. 24, 1918, **46:** 88

Walter Hines Page, Dec. 16, 1916, **40:** 250; Feb. 8, 1917, **41:** 158; April 10, 1917, **42:** 24; Sept. 24, 1917, **44:** 245
Lady Mary Fiske Stevens Paget, Dec. 6, 1916, **40:** 178
Nikola P. Pašić, July 29, 1918, **49:** 126
James Duval Phelan, July 1, 1918, **48:** 471
William Phillips, May 4, 1918, **47:** 516
Raymond Poincaré, April 5, 1918, **47:** 258; June 13, 1918, **48:** 301; Sept. 16, 1918, **51:** 11
Frank Lyon Polk, March 17, 1917, **41:** 420; July 9, 1917, **43:** 132; Aug. 2, 1917 (2), **43:** 344, 345; Aug. 7, 1917, **43:** 381; Aug. 10, 1917, **43:** 416; Nov. 13, 1917, **45:** 40; Jan. 19, 1918, **46:** 34; Jan. 23, 1918, **46:** 83; Jan. 28, 1918, **46:** 117; March 10, 1918 (4), **46:** 592, 594, 595; March 15, 1918, **47:** 36; June 10, 1918 (3), **48:** 276; July 15, 1918 (2), **48:** 609; July 17, 1918, **48:** 639; July 18, 1918, **49:** 4; July 22, 1918, **49:** 53; July 26, 1918, **49:** 101; July 29, 1918, **49:** 118; Aug. 2, 1918, **49:** 166; Aug. 3, 1918 (2), **49:** 174, 175; Aug. 8, 1918, **49:** 212; Aug. 10, 1918, **49:** 231
Theodore Hazeltine Price, May 10, 1917, **42:** 259
The Prime Ministers of Great Britain, France, and Italy, Oct. 23, 1917, **44:** 427

Chevalier Willem Louis Frederik Christiaan van Rappard, Jan. 26, 1917, **41:** 22

Lord Reading, May 9, 1918, **47:** 580; June 20, 1918, **48:** 365; July 8, 1918, **48:** 550; July 24, 1918, **49:** 70

William Cox Redfield, Aug. 21, 1917, **44:** 10; Oct. 11, 1917, **44:** 359; June 13, 1918, **48:** 303

Paul Ritter, Feb. 12, 1917, **41:** 204

Elihu Root, June 26, 1917, **43:** 15; June 27, 1917, **43:** 15

Leo Stanton Rowe, June 10, 1918, **48:** 278

Charles Edward Russell, May 10, 1917, **42:** 262; Nov. 10, 1917, **44:** 558; July 3, 1918, **48:** 492

The Provisional Government of Russia, May 22, 1917, **42:** 365

A note verbale to the Provisional Russian Government about the American High Commission, May 18, 1917, **42:** 368

Aide-mémoire about military intervention in Siberia, July 16, 1918 (draft), **48:** 624; July 17, 1918, **48:** 640

Furnifold McLendel Simmons, Oct. 28, 1918, **51:** 476

Edgar Grant Sisson, Oct. 24, 1917, **44:** 435

Sir Cecil Arthur Spring Rice, June 23, 1917, **42:** 564; Dec. 11, 1917, **45:** 267

John Frank Stevens, Aug. 14, 1917, **43:** 459

William Joel Stone, Feb. 17, 1917, **41:** 240; Feb. 21, 1917, **41:** 261

Pleasant Alexander Stovall, Dec. 19, 1916, **40:** 277

John St. Loe Strachey, April 5, 1918, **47:** 258

Herbert Bayard Swope, April 2, 1918, **47:** 224

André Tardieu, Aug. 7, 1917, **43:** 385

Frank William Taussig, Nov. 9, 1917, **44:** 545

William Boyce Thompson, Oct. 24, 1917, **44:** 435

Joseph Patrick Tumulty, Jan. 30, 1917, **41:** 68; May 5, 1917 (2), **42:** 222, 223; July 30, 1917, **43:** 318; Feb. 23, 1918, **46:** 422; April 25, 1918, **47:** 420; May 10, 1918, **47:** 561; May 11, 1918, **47:** 600; June 27, 1918, **48:** 444; July 16, 1918, **48:** 627; July 19, 1918, **49:** 20

The Right Reverend Arsène E. Vehouni, Dec. 21, 1916, **40:** 311

Eleuthérios Vénisélos, April 6, 1918, **47:** 271

Vittorio Emanuele III, Dec. 11, 1917, **45:** 267; April 7, 1918, **47:** 280; Nov. 4, 1918, **51:** 576

A memorandum on various war measures, Nov. 20, 1917, **45:** 86

Sherman Leland Whipple, Oct. 26, 1918, **51:** 451; Oct. 29, 1918, **51:** 485

Brand Whitlock, Feb. 15, 1917, **41:** 234

William Royal Wilder, April 26, 1917, **42:** 134

Charles Turner Williams, July 3, 1918, **48:** 493

John Sharp Williams, Dec. 5, 1916, **40:** 168; Feb. 18, 1918, **46:** 369

Stephen Samuel Wise, April 12, 1917, **42:** 44; April 28, 1917, **42:** 152; Aug. 27, 1918 (draft), **49:** 364; Aug. 31, 1918, **49:** 403

Samuel Isett Woodbridge, Aug. 21, 1917, **44:** 7
Hiram Woods, Jr., Dec. 28, 1916, **40:** 344

Yoshihito, March 14, 1917, **41:** 403

To Wilson from
James Francis Abbott, July 10, 1918, **48:** 581
A memorandum by James Francis Abbott on Japanese interven-
tion in Siberia, July 10, 1918, **48:** 581
Albert, King of the Belgians, Nov. 11, 1916, **40:** 171
Alexander of Serbia, Oct. 24, 1917, **44:** 436
The Allied governments, Oct. 30, 1918, **51:** 515
A memorandum by Norman Angell on peace strategy, Nov. 20,
1916, **40:** 10
Prince Arthur of Connaught, May 25, 1918, **48:** 154
Gordon Auchincloss, Jan. 31, 1918, **46:** 183; Feb. 3, 1918, **46:** 221;
Feb. 7, 1918, **46:** 265; March 5, 1918, **46:** 549; March 7, 1918, **46:**
567; Aug. 3, 1918, **49:** 177; Aug. 31, 1918, **49:** 408; Sept. 30, 1918,
51: 164

Warren Worth Bailey, Feb. 3, 1917, **41:** 115
Newton Diehl Baker
1916
Nov. 29, 1916, **40:** 100; Nov. 30, 1916, **40:** 109; Dec. 2, 1916, **40:**
123; Dec. 9, 1916, **40:** 202
1917
Jan. 18, 1917, **40:** 522; Feb. 7, 1917, **41:** 152; March 31, 1917, **41:**
511; April 5, 1917, **41:** 545; April 14, 1917, **42:** 60; May 5, 1917,
42: 225; May 14, 1917, **42:** 295; May 19, 1917, **42:** 352; May 28,
1917 (2), **42:** 411; May 31, 1917, **42:** 431; July 24, 1917, **43:** 262;
Aug. 9, 1917, **43:** 414; Aug. 13, 1917 (2), **43:** 454, 455; Aug. 20,
1917, **43:** 532; Oct. 5, 1917, **44:** 312; Oct. 8, 1917, **44:** 332; Nov.
23, 1917, **45:** 104; Dec. 26, 1917, **45:** 364
1918
Feb. 26, 1918, **46:** 452; Aug. 12, 1918, **49:** 238; Sept. 15, 1918, **51:**
17; Oct. 24, 1918 (2), **51:** 425, 433; Oct. 31, 1918, **51:** 525; Nov. 1,
1918, **51:** 544; Nov. 2, 1918, **51:** 553; Nov. 3, 1918, **51:** 570; Nov.
4, 1918, **51:** 583; Nov. 5, 1918 (2), **51:** 595, 596; Nov. 6, 1918, **51:**
607
Arthur James Balfour, May 18, 1917, **42:** 327; Jan. 2, 1918, **45:** 430;
Jan. 31, 1918, **46:** 180; March 18, 1918, **47:** 61
Colville Adrian de Rune Barclay, Jan. 13, 1918, **45:** 578
Bernard Mannes Baruch, Oct. 23, 1918, **51:** 419
Benedict XV, Jan. 26, 1917, **41:** 34; translation, 34; Oct. 10, 1918,
51: 296; Nov. 8, 1918, **51:** 641
An appeal to the belligerents by Benedict XV, Aug. 13, 1917, **43:**
438; Aug. 1, 1917, **43:** 485
Samuel Reading Bertron, Nov. 27, 1916, **40:** 92; Dec. 6, 1916, **40:**
184; Dec. 12, 1917, **45:** 282; June 24, 1918, **48:** 414

Julio Betancourt, Jan. 24, 1917, **41:** 8; March 6, 1917, **41:** 344;
    March 24, 1917, **41:** 465; May 8, 1918, **47:** 572
The Most Reverend John Bonzano, Oct. 11, 1918, **51:** 296
Sir Robert Laird Borden, May 21, 1917, **42:** 360
Wenceslao Braz Pereira Gomes, June 14, 1917, **42:** 548
The British Embassy, Aug. 5, 1917, **43:** 369; Jan. 5, 1918, **45:** 486
Sydney Brooks, April 20, 1917, **42:** 112
Herbert Bruce Brougham, Sept. 28, 1917, **44:** 275
William Jennings Bryan, Dec. 21, 1916, **40:** 314; Jan. 15, 1918, **45:**
    599, July 17, 1918, **48:** 645; July 19, 1918, **49:** 21
James Viscount Bryce, Dec. 22, 1916, **40:** 316
William Christian Bullitt, Dec. 7, 1917, **45:** 235

Manuel Estrada Cabrera, April 10, 1917, **42:** 46
Venustiano Carranza, June 29, 1917, **43:** 39
Carrie Clinton Lane Chapman Catt, May 4, 1917, **42:** 215
Charles I, March 23, 1918, **47:** 124
Charles Francis Joseph, Nov. 22, 1916, **40:** 34
Georgii Vasil'evich Chicherin, Oct. 29, 1918, **51:** 508; Nov. 2, 1918,
    51: 555
Georges Clemenceau, Dec. 21, 1917, **45:** 337; April 6, 1918, **47:** 277
Georges Clemenceau, David Lloyd George, and Vittorio Orlando,
    Feb. 2, 1918, **46:** 213
Frank Irving Cobb, Aug. 27, 1917, **44:** 74; Sept. 5, 1917, **44:** 154
A memorandum by Frank Irving Cobb on the diplomatic situation,
    Nov. 6, 1918, **51:** 613
Bainbridge Colby, March 15, 1918, **47:** 42; March 22, 1918, **47:** 119;
    March 26, 1918, **47:** 147; Oct. 24, 1918, **51:** 440
Lincoln Ross Colcord, Dec. 3, 1917, **45:** 191; Dec. 8, 1917, **45:** 250;
    Jan. 27, 1918, **46:** 113; July 7, 1918, **48:** 546; July 9, 1918, **48:** 576
Constantine, Dec. 16/29, 1916, **40:** 453
Charles Richard Crane, March 28, 1917, **41:** 493; June 21, 1917,
    43: 13; May 8, 1918, **47:** 561; June 9, 1918, **48:** 273; June 27,
    1918, **48:** 450; July 2, 1918, **48:** 485; July 9, 1918, **48:** 570; July
    23, 1918, **49:** 62; Aug. 1, 1918, **49:** 154
Richard Crane, July 27, 1917, **43:** 298; May 7, 1918, **47:** 548; May
    11, 1918, **47:** 610
George Creel, May 10, 1917, **42:** 267; May 17, 1917, **42:** 320; Aug.
    20, 1917, **43:** 526; Oct. 12, 1917, **44:** 367; Oct. 24, 1917, **44:** 434;
    Oct. 6, 1917, **44:** 450; Dec. 27, 1917, **45:** 367; Dec. 31, 1917, **45:**
    407; Jan. 15, 1918, **45:** 596; Feb. 27, 1918, **46:** 479; Feb. 28, 1918,
    46: 495; May 2, 1918, **47:** 492; May 4, 1918, **47:** 521; July 15,
    1918, **48:** 613; Sept. 25, 1918, **51:** 118; Oct. 9, 1918, **51:** 282
A memorandum by George Creel about the establishment of an
    American Bureau of Public Information in Europe, Jan. 31,
    1918, **46:** 200
John Daniel Crimmins, April 28, 1917, **42:** 219
Benedict Crowell, March 5, 1918, **46:** 532; March 13, 1918, **47:** 12;
    Sept. 17, 1918, **51:** 33

Richard Heath Dabney, April 1, 1917, **41:** 516

Domicio da Gama, June 25, 1917, **43:** 11

Josephus Daniels, Feb. 2, 1917, **41:** 94; Feb. 7, 1917, **41:** 149; Nov. 7, 1917, **44:** 532; Jan. 21, 1918, **46:** 59; March 27, 1918, **47:** 162; June 24, 1918, **48:** 410

Henry Pomeroy Davison, Nov. 25, 1916, **40:** 75; Feb. 21, 1918, **46:** 408

Alexander N. Debskí and Bronislaw D. Kulakowski, Aug. 8, 1917, **44:** 6; Feb. 18, 1918, **46:** 402

The Duke of Devonshire, Dec. 8, 1917, **45:** 253; Jan. 15, 1918, **45:** 598

Roman Dmowskí, Oct. 18, 1918, **51:** 447

Cleveland Hoadley Dodge, Dec. 2, 1917, **45:** 185

Michael Francis Doyle, Aug. 15, 1917, **43:** 472

James Taylor Du Bois, Feb. 26, 1917, **41:** 293

James Duncan, May 7, 1917, **42:** 263

Max Eastman, Sept. 8, 1917, **44:** 169

An address to the President by Max Eastman, Feb. 28, 1917, **41:** 305

Charles William Eliot, Nov. 21, 1916, **40:** 27; Jan. 17, 1918, **46:** 22

Abram Isaac Elkus, Aug. 23, 1917, **44:** 37

Charles Ferguson, Jan. 22, 1917, **40:** 540

Edward Albert Filene, Jan. 16, 1918, **46:** 5; Jan. 21, 1918, **46:** 62

Henry Burchard Fine, May 12, 1917, **42:** 287

Ferdinand Foch, April 1, 1918, **47:** 219

John Franklin Fort, Feb. 19, 1917, **41:** 255

The Fourth All-Russian Congress of Soviets, March 15, 1918, **47:** 79

David Rowland Francis, Jan. 3, 1917, **45:** 433

Felix Frankfurter, June 12, 1917, **42:** 486

Arthur Hugh Frazier, March 16, 1918, **47:** 59; March 19, 1918, **47:** 74; March 18, 1918, **47:** 86

Harry Augustus Garfield, Feb. 2, 1917, **41:** 101; Oct. 30, 1917, **44:** 474; Nov. 30, 1917, **45:** 173; June 12, 1918, **48:** 296

A memorandum by Harry Augustus Garfield about the proposed inter-Allied super board, June 12, 1918, **48:** 296

A memorandum by Harry Augustus Garfield on the Russian situation, June 12, 1918, **48:** 297

A memorandum by Harry Augustus Garfield on responding to Germany's declaration of unrestricted submarine warfare, Feb. 2, 1917, **41:** 101

John Palmer Gavit, Nov. 21, 1916, **40:** 29; Dec. 2, 1916, **40:** 124

George V, April 5, 1918, **47:** 265; May 10, 1918, **47:** 596; July 24, 1918, **49:** 69

James Cardinal Gibbons, Dec. 19, 1917, **45:** 330; Oct. 12, 1918, **51:** 309; Oct. 22, 1918, **51:** 410; Nov. 5, 1918, **51:** 600

Peter Golden, May 4, 1918, **47:** 520

Samuel Gompers, May 10, 1917, **42:** 265; Aug. 13, 1917, **43:** 449; Jan. 17, 1918, **46:** 21; Jan. 19, 1918, **46:** 39; Feb. 9, 1918, **46:** 310; April 16, 1918, **47:** 351; July 19, 1918, **49:** 23; July 18, 1918, **49:** 25; Nov. 7, 1918, **51:** 621

Samuel Gompers and others, Nov. 5, 1918, **51:** 643

Matthew Hale, March 28, 1917, **41:** 490

Charles Sumner Hamlin, Feb. 14, 1917, **41:** 231

Norman Hapgood, Jan. 29, 1917, **41:** 56

George Davis Herron, May 31, 1918, **48:** 210; July 6, 1918, **48:** 538

Morris Hillquit, May 10, 1917, **42:** 268

Henry French Hollis, Oct. 2, 1918, **51:** 182; Oct. 6, 1918, **51:** 255; Oct. 11, 1918, **51:** 298; Oct. 13, 1918, **51:** 319; Oct. 23, 1918, **51:** 421

Hamilton Holt, July 12, 1918, **48:** 627

Herbert Clark Hoover, May 17, 1918, **48:** 46; May 20, 1918, **48:** 80; June 13, 1918, **48:** 308; June 29, 1918, **48:** 466; Oct. 24, 1918, **51:** 437; Oct. 26, 1918, **51:** 457; Nov. 2, 1918, **51:** 577; Nov. 7, 1918, **51:** 634

Edward Mandell House

1916

Nov. 20, 1916, **40:** 4; Nov. 21, 1916, **40:** 29; Nov. 22, 1916, **40:** 39; Nov. 23, 1916, **40:** 60; Nov. 25, 1916, **40:** 74; Nov. 30, 1916, **40:** 110; Dec. 3, 1916 (2), **40:** 132, 133; Dec. 4, 1916, **40:** 137; Dec. 5, 1916, **40:** 172; Dec. 6, 1916, **40:** 178; Dec. 7, 1916, **40:** 185; Dec. 9, 1916, **40:** 201; Dec. 10, 1916, **40:** 212; Dec. 14, 1916, **40:** 233; Dec. 17, 1916, **40:** 262; Dec. 20, 1916, **40:** 293; Dec. 27, 1916, **40:** 337; Dec. 28, 1916, **40:** 345; Dec. 29, 1916, **40:** 359

January–February 1917

Jan. 13, 1917, **40:** 464; Jan. 15, 1917, **40:** 477; Jan. 16, 1917, **40:** 493; Jan. 17, 1917, **40:** 508; Jan. 18, 1917, **40:** 516; Jan. 19, 1917, **40:** 525; Jan. 20, 1917, **40:** 526; Jan. 22, 1917, **40:** 540; Jan. 23, 1917, **40:** 558; Jan. 25, 1917, **41:** 17; Jan. 26, 1917 (2), **41:** 24, 26; Jan. 27, 1917, **41:** 39; Feb. 2, 1917, **41:** 95; Feb. 4, 1917, **41:** 117; Feb. 5, 1917, **41:** 127; Feb. 7, 1917, **41:** 149; Feb. 8, 1917, **41:** 164; Feb. 10, 1917, **41:** 190; Feb. 11, 1917, **41:** 196; Feb. 13, 1917, **41:** 214; Feb. 14, 1917, **41:** 226; Feb. 19, 1917, **41:** 250; Feb. 26, 1917, **41:** 292; Feb. 27, 1917, **41:** 296

March–May 1917

March 9, 1917, **41:** 373; March 16, 1917, **41:** 418; March 17, 1917, **41:** 422; March 19, 1917, **41:** 428; March 25, 1917, **41:** 466; March 29, 1917, **41:** 501; March 30, 1917, **41:** 501; April 5, 1917, **41:** 544; April 8, 1917, **42:** 18; April 9, 1917, **42:** 22; April 10, 1917, **42:** 29; April 13, 1917, **42:** 58; April 17, 1917, **42:** 80; April 20, 1917, **42:** 110; April 22, 1917, **42:** 120; May 2, 1917, **42:** 194; May 11, 1917, **42:** 275; May 13, 1917, **42:** 288; May 20, 1917, **42:** 354; May 22, 1917, **42:** 372; May 24, 1917, **42:** 388; May 30, 1917, **42:** 425; May 31, 1917, **42:** 428

June–August 1917
June 5, 1917, **42:** 456; June 7, 1917, **42:** 461; June 12, 1917, **42:** 487; June 15, 1917, **42:** 523; June 17, 1917, **42:** 530; June 19, 1917, **42:** 542; June 27, 1917, **43:** 24; June 29, 1917, **43:** 44; July 8, 1917, **43:** 123; July 11, 1917, **43:** 147; July 17, 1917, **43:** 194; July 19, 1917, **43:** 219; July 20, 1917, **43:** 223; July 23, 1917, **43:** 248; July 25, 1917, **43:** 274; Aug. 4, 1917 (2), **43:** 364, 365; Aug. 9, 1917 (3), **43:** 400, 409, 411; Aug. 10, 1917, **43:** 425; Aug. 13, 1917, **43:** 451; Aug. 15, 1917, **43:** 471; Aug. 16, 1917, **43:** 497; Aug. 17, 1917, **43:** 508; Aug. 19, 1917, **43:** 522; Aug. 21, 1917, **44:** 16; Aug. 22, 1917 (2), **44:** 30, 31; Aug. 24, 1917, **44:** 40; Aug. 25, 1917, **44:** 49; Aug. 27, 1917, **44:** 69; Aug. 29, 1917, **44:** 83; Aug. 31, 1917, **44:** 105

September–December 1917
Sept. 4, 1917, **44:** 149; Sept. 7, 1917, **44:** 164; Sept. 18, 1917, **44:** 213; Sept. 20, 1917, **44:** 226; Sept. 24, 1917, **44:** 246; Sept. 29, 1917, **44:** 284; Oct. 3, 1917, **44:** 298; Oct. 5, 1917, **44:** 310; Oct. 7, 1917, **44:** 324; Oct. 15, 1917, **44:** 385; Oct. 16, 1917, **44:** 390; Oct. 17, 1917, **44:** 392; Oct. 27, 1917, **44:** 454; Oct. 28, 1917, **44:** 462; Nov. 9, 1917 (2), **44:** 545, 546; Nov. 11, 1917 (2), **45:** 3; Nov. 14, 1917 (2), **45:** 47; Nov. 15, 1917, **45:** 54; Nov. 16, 1917, **45:** 70; Nov. 18, 1917 (2), **45:** 73, 74, 82; Nov. 20, 1917, **45:** 93; Nov. 23, 1917, **45:** 112; Nov. 26, 1917, **45:** 122; Nov. 28, 1917 (3), **45:** 151; Nov. 29, 1917 (2), **45:** 156, 157; Nov. 30, 1917, **45:** 166; Dec. 1, 1917, **45:** 177; Dec. 2, 1917, **45:** 184; Dec. 3, 1917, **45:** 188; Dec. 7, 1917, **45:** 232

January–June 1918
Jan. 31, 1918, **46:** 181; Feb. 1, 1918, **46:** 207; Feb. 2, 1918, **46:** 214; Feb. 3, 1918, **46:** 221; Feb. 5, 1918, **46:** 250; Feb. 15, 1918, **46:** 350; March 3, 1918 (3), **46:** 516, 518; March 6, 1918, **46:** 555; March 8, 1918, **46:** 574; March 10, 1918, **46:** 597; March 13, 1918, **47:** 11; March 21, 1918, **47:** 101; March 23, 1918, **47:** 122; April 21, 1918, **47:** 391; April 24, 1918, **47:** 417; April 26, 1918, **47:** 441; April 29, 1918, **47:** 465; April 30, 1918, **47:** 468; May 3, 1918, **47:** 503; May 20, 1918, **48:** 79; May 25, 1918, **48:** 152; June 4, 1918, **48:** 240; June 11, 1918, **48:** 283; June 13, 1918, **48:** 306; June 21, 1918, **48:** 390; June 23, 1918, **48:** 400; June 25, 1918, **48:** 424

July–November 1918
July 6, 1918, **48:** 540; July 8, 1918, **48:** 561; July 11, 1918, **48:** 592; July 14, 1918, **48:** 608; July 16, 1918, **48:** 630; Aug. 9, 1918, **49:** 225; Sept. 3, 1918, **49:** 428; Sept. 18, 1918, **51:** 64; Sept. 25, 1918, **51:** 116; Sept. 30, 1918, **51:** 164; Oct. 6, 1918 (2), **51:** 254; Oct. 16, 1918, **51:** 346; Oct. 22, 1918, **51:** 406; Oct. 27, 1918 (2), **51:** 406; Oct. 27, 1918 (2), **51:** 462, 463; Oct. 28, 1918, **51:** 473; Oct. 29, 1918 (3), **51:** 495, 504; Oct. 30, 1918 (6), **51:** 511, 514, 515, 517; Oct. 31, 1918 (3), **51:** 523, 531, 534; Nov. 1, 1918 (3), **51:** 541, 542; Nov. 2, 1918 (3), **51:** 562; Nov. 3, 1918 (2), **51:** 568, 569; Nov. 4, 1918 (2), **51:** 580, 582; Nov. 5, 1918 (2), **51:** 594, 595; Nov. 6, 1918, **51:** 606; Nov. 8, 1918 (2) **51:** 637, 638

A memorandum by Edward Mandell House on the appointment of an American chairman of the Inter-Allied Council, Oct. 5, 1917, **44:** 312

A draft by Edward Mandell House of a covenant of a league of nations, July 16, 1918, **48:** 632

A list by Edward Mandell House of suggested advisers to an American peace commission, Oct. 22, 1918, **51:** 407

David Franklin Houston, March 30, 1917, **41:** 503

Roy Wilson Howard, Jan. 5, 1917, **40:** 412; Jan. 12, 1918, **45:** 597

A memorandum by Frederic Clemson Howe on the background of the war, Oct. 30, 1917, **44:** 474

Hsü Shih-ch'ang, Oct. 13, 1918, **51:** 318

Edward Nash Hurley, Sept. 17, 1917, **44:** 209; Sept. 7, 1918, **49:** 473

Paul Oscar Husting, May 9, 1917, **42:** 253

Viscount Kikujiro Ishii, July 9, 1918, **48:** 569

Jeremiah Whipple Jenks, April 14, 1917, **42:** 60

Francis Johnson, Jan. 6, 1917, **41:** 36

Thomas Davies Jones, Nov. 19, 1917 (2), **45:** 78, 80

Jean Jules Jusserand, July 4, 1917, **43:** 99; Feb. 2, 1918, **46:** 213; March 13, 1918, **47:** 14; June 30, 1918, **48:** 469; July 29, 1918, **49:** 123; Sept. 9, 1918, **49:** 497

William Williams Keen, Oct. 13, 1918, **51:** 324

William Kent, July 22, 1918, **49:** 54

President Kerenskii of the National Council Assembly at Moscow, Aug. 30, 1917, **44:** 91

Thomas William Lamont, Jan. 9, 1918, **45:** 547; Jan. 29, 1918, **46:** 160

Franklin Knight Lane, Dec. 1, 1916, **40:** 114; Dec. 9, 1916, **40:** 204; Dec. 20, 1916, **40:** 297; Aug. 10, 1917, **43:** 424; Dec. 3, 1917, **45:** 193

Franklin Knight Lane and others, Jan. 3, 1917, **40:** 390; Jan. 15, 1917 (2), **40:** 478, 479

Robert Lansing
1916
Nov. 21, 1916, **40:** 24; Nov. 22, 1916, **40:** 38; Nov. 23, 1916 (2), **40:** 46, 48; Nov. 22, 1916, **40:** 82; Dec. 1, 1916, **40:** 112; Dec. 4, 1916 (2), **40:** 140, 141; Dec. 5, 1916, **40:** 170; Dec. 6, 1916, **40:** 180; Dec. 7, 1916, **40:** 184; Dec. 8, 1916, **40:** 190; Dec. 10, 1916, **40:** 209; Dec. 11, 1916, **40:** 216; Dec. 12, 1916, **40:** 220; Dec. 13, 1916, **40:** 229; Dec. 14, 1916, **40:** 230; Dec. 17, 1916, **40:** 259; Dec. 19, 1916, **40:** 279; Dec. 20, 1916, **40:** 298; Dec. 21, 1916, **40:** 313; Dec. 24, 1916, **40:** 326; Dec. 29, 1916, **40:** 358
January–February 1917
Jan. 3, 1917, **40:** 388; Jan. 5, 1917, **40:** 409; Jan. 10, 1917, **40:** 428; Jan. 12, 1917 (2), **40:** 447, 453; Jan. 15, 1917, **40:** 478; Jan. 17,

1917 (2), **40:** 509, 512; Jan. 18, 1917 (2), **40:** 518, 519; Jan. 23, 1917 (4), **40:** 552, 554, 556, 557; Jan. 25, 1917, **41:** 18; Jan. 26, 1917, **41:** 27; Jan. 27, 1917, **41:** 37; Jan. 31, 1917, **41:** 71; Feb. 2, 1917 (2), **41:** 96, 99; Feb. 5, 1917, **41:** 126; Feb. 7, 1917, **41:** 139; Feb. 8, 1917, **41:** 160; Feb. 10, 1917 (2), **41:** 185; Feb. 12, 1917, **41:** 201; Feb. 13, 1917, **41:** 210; Feb. 14, 1917, **41:** 224; Feb. 17, 1917, **41:** 242; Feb. 19, 1917 (2), **41:** 248, 249; Feb. 21, 1917, **41:** 267; Feb. 22, 1917, **41:** 268; Feb. 23, 1917, **41:** 273

March–April 1917
March 3, 1917, **41:** 312; March 7, 1917 (3), **41:** 350, 352; March 8, 1917, **41:** 360; March 12, 1917, **41:** 391; March 14, 1917, **41:** 404; March 15, 1917, **41:** 408; March 16, 1917 (2), **41:** 415, 418; March 17, 1917, **41:** 421; March 19, 1917 (2), **41:** 425, 427; March 23, 1917, **41:** 456; March 26, 1917 (2), **41:** 471, 472; March 27, 1917, **41:** 476; March 30, 1917, **41:** 502; April 5, 1917, **41:** 544; April 6, 1917, **41:** 553; April 8, 1917 (2), **42:** 14, 18; April 11, 1917 (2), **42:** 36, 37; April 12, 1917 (3), **42:** 45, 46, 53; April 17, 1917, **42:** 81; April 18, 1917, **42:** 92; April 19, 1917 (2), **42:** 99, 101; April 20, 1917 (2), **42:** 108, 109; April 25, 1917, **42:** 130; April 30, 1917 (4), **42:** 163, 164, 165

May–August 1917
May 3, 1917 (2), **42:** 203, 204; May 4, 1917, **42:** 216; May 5, 1917, **42:** 224; May 7, 1917 (2), **42:** 238, 239; May 9, 1917, **42:** 252, May 10, 1917 (2), **42:** 264, 271; May 12, 1917, **42:** 284; May 17, 1917 (3), **42:** 314, 315, 318; May 19, 1917 (2), **42:** 350, 368; May 21, 1917 (2), **42:** 358, 360; May 23, 1917, **42:** 377; May 25, 1917, **42:** 396; May 28, 1917, **42:** 417; June 5, 1917, **42:** 453; June 8, 1917, **42:** 463; June 14, 1917, **42:** 507; June 21, 1917, **42:** 552; June 25, 1917, **43:** 7; June 30, 1917, **43:** 55; July 2, 1917, **43:** 74; July 3, 1917, **43:** 94; July 5, 1917, **43:** 106; Aug. 9, 1917, **43:** 413; Aug. 13, 1917 (3), **43:** 438, 439, 442; Aug. 15, 1917, **43:** 473; Aug. 20, 1917 (2), **43:** 523, 525; Aug. 21, 1917 (2), **44:** 18, 22; Aug. 27, 1917 (2), **44:** 65, 66; Aug. 29, 1917 (2), **44:** 84

September–December 1917
Sept. 10, 1917 (2), **44:** 179, 180; Sept. 11, 1917, **44:** 187; Sept. 19, 1917, **44:** 222; Sept. 25, 1917, **44:** 249; Oct. 3, 1917, **44:** 297; Oct. 8, 1917, **44:** 331; Oct. 10, 1917, **44:** 347; Oct. 20, 1917, **44:** 413; Oct. 25, 1917, **44:** 445; Oct. 27, 1917, **44:** 453; Nov. 5, 1917, **44:** 513; Nov. 7, 1917, **44:** 530; Nov. 12, 1917, **45:** 30; Nov. 15, 1917, **45:** 55; Nov. 22, 1917, **45:** 96; Nov. 30, 1917, **45:** 166; Dec. 10, 1917, **45:** 263; Dec. 12, 1917, **45:** 274; Dec. 13, 1917, **45:** 286; Dec. 15, 1917, **45:** 307; Dec. 24, 1917, **45:** 349; Dec. 25, 1917, **45:** 354; Dec. 26, 1917, **45:** 364; Dec. 27, 1917, **45:** 368; Dec. 31, 1917, **45:** 405

January–March 1918
Jan. 2, 1918, **45:** 427; Jan. 10, 1918, **45:** 562; Jan. 16, 1918, **46:** 7; Jan. 25, 1918, **46:** 96; Jan. 27, 1918, **46:** 110; Jan. 28, 1918, **46:** 120; Feb. 9, 1918 (3), **46:** 299, 301; Feb. 13, 1918, **46:** 338; Feb. 14, 1918, **46:** 344; Feb. 15, 1918, **46:** 349; Feb. 16, 1918 (2), **46:** 357,

358; Feb. 18, 1918 (3), **46:** 372, 373, 375; Feb. 19, 1918, **46:** 387; Feb. 20, 1918, **46:** 395; Feb. 22, 1918, **46:** 415; Feb. 23, 1918, **46:** 424; Feb. 26, 1918 (2), **46:** 450, 451; Feb. 27, 1918, **46:** 474; Feb. 28, 1918, **46:** 493; March 1, 1918, **46:** 499; March 15, 1918, **47:** 44; March 18, 1918, **47:** 55; March 19, 1918, **47:** 67; March 21, 1918, **47:** 96; March 22, 1918, **47:** 108; March 24, 1918, **47:** 131; March 25, 1918, **47:** 140; March 27, 1918, **47:** 163; March 30, 1918, **47:** 210

April–May 1918
April 1, 1918, **47:** 219; April 2, 1918, **47:** 225; April 5, 1918, **47:** 257; April 11, 1918, **47:** 317; April 12, 1918, **47:** 327; April 15, 1918, **47:** 344; April 18, 1918, **47:** 360; April 22, 1918, **47:** 397; April 24, 1918, **47:** 416; April 25, 1918 (3), **47:** 426, 430, 432; April 27, 1918 (2), **47:** 450, 451; April 29, 1918, **47:** 459; May 2, 1918, **47:** 490; May 8, 1918, **47:** 568; May 10, 1918 (2), **47:** 589, 591; May 11, 1918 (2), **47:** 605, 608; May 16, 1918, **48:** 37; May 19, 1918, **48:** 63; May 20, 1918, **48:** 79; May 21, 1918 (4), **48:** 96, 97, 99; May 24, 1918, **48:** 141; May 28, 1918, **48:** 183; May 29, 1918 (2), **48:** 194, 195

June–August 1918
June 3, 1918, **48:** 236; June 4, 1918, **48:** 238; June 13, 1918, **48:** 305; June 19, 1918, **48:** 359; June 20, 1918 (2), **48:** 371, 374; June 23, 1918, **48:** 398; June 24, 1918, **48:** 406; June 27, 1918 (2), **48:** 447, 448; June 28, 1918, **48:** 461; June 29, 1918 (2), **48:** 464, 465; July 3, 1918, **48:** 518; July 8, 1918 (2), **48:** 559, 560; July 9, 1918, **48:** 574; July 10, 1918, **48:** 579; Aug. 19, 1918, **49:** 287; Aug. 22, 1918 (2), **49:** 320, 323; Aug. 24, 1918, **49:** 348; Aug. 29, 1918 (2), **49:** 382, 383; Aug. 30, 1918, **49:** 396; Aug. 31, 1918, **49:** 404

September–November 1918
Sept. 4, 1918 (3), **49:** 434, 435, 436; Sept. 5, 1918, **49:** 446; Sept. 9, 1918, **49:** 491; Sept. 11, 1918, **49:** 515; Sept. 13, 1918 (2), **49:** 544, 545; Sept. 14, 1918, **51:** 3; Sept. 16, 1918 (2), **51:** 17, 18; Sept. 17, 1918, **51:** 31; Sept. 18, 1918, **51:** 61; Sept. 19, 1918, **51:** 76; Sept. 21, 1918 (4), **51:** 86, 87; Sept. 23, 1918, **51:** 93; Sept. 24, 1918, **51:** 95; Sept. 27, 1918 (3), **51:** 133, 135; Sept. 30, 1918 (2), **51:** 162, 163; Oct. 1, 1918, **51:** 173; Oct. 4, 1918, **51:** 215; Oct. 5, 1918 (2), **51:** 229, 246; Oct. 7, 1918, **51:** 258; Oct. 8, 1918, **51:** 269; Oct. 14, 1918, **51:** 334; Oct. 15, 1918, **51:** 345; Oct. 19, 1918, **51:** 386; Oct. 25, 1918, **51:** 446; Oct. 26, 1918 (2), **51:** 456, 457; Oct. 29, 1918, **51:** 506; Oct. 30, 1918, **51:** 518; Oct. 31, 1918 (3), **51:** 526, 527, 528; Nov. 1, 1918, **51:** 542; Nov. 5, 1918, **51:** 598; Nov. 7, 1918, **51:** 622; Nov. 8, 1918, **51:** 642

Memoranda by Robert Lansing: on the peace note of the Central Powers, Dec. 14, 1916, **40:** 234; on the reply by the Spanish government to Wilson's note to the belligerents, Dec. 31, 1916, **40:** 378; on Germany's declaration of unrestricted submarine warfare, Feb. 1, 1917, **41:** 96; on the Bases of Peace, Feb. 7, 1917, **41:** 160, 162; on the peace appeal by Benedict XV, Aug. 19, 1917, **44:**

18; on the preparatory work for the peace conference, Sept. 15, 1917, **44:** 217; about conferences with Viscount Ishii, Sept. 6, 1917, **44:** 249; Sept. 22, 1917, **44:** 253; Oct. 8, 1917, **44:** 340; Oct. 10, 1917, **44:** 356; Oct. 12, 1917, **44:** 367; Oct. 13, 1917, **44:** 376; Oct. 20, 1917, **44:** 413; Oct. 22, 1917, **44:** 418; on the open door policy toward China, Oct. 20, 1917 (draft), **44:** 415; Oct. 22, 1917, **44:** 418; Oct. 20, 1917 (redraft), **44:** 419; on the recognition of a Russian government, Jan. 10, 1918, **45:** 563; about the nationalities in the Austro-Hungarian Empire, June 24, 1918, **48:** 435; on a conference with Viscount Ishii about intervention in Siberia, July 8, 1918, **48:** 559; about the Bulgarian armistice, Oct. 1, 1918, **51:** 169

David Lawrence, Jan. 23, 1917, **40:** 550; Jan. 27, 1917, **41:** 40; March 31, 1917, **41:** 512; Oct. 3, 1917, **44:** 299; Oct. 6, 1917, **44:** 321; Oct. 13, 1918, **51:** 320

Russell Cornell Leffingwell, July 11, 1918, **48:** 593

Walter Lippmann, Jan. 31, 1917, **41:** 83; March 11, 1917, **41:** 388

A memorandum by Walter Lippmann on the policy of the United States vis-à-vis Germany and Great Britain, March 11, 1917, **41:** 389

A memorandum by Walter Lippmann and Frank Irving Cobb on the Fourteen Points, Oct. 29, 1918, **51:** 495

The Lithuanian National Council, May 2, 1918, **47:** 492

David Lloyd George, Sept. 3, 1917, **44:** 125; Oct. 11, 1917, **44:** 362; Dec. 31, 1917, **45:** 405

David Lloyd George and the British War Cabinet, June 28, 1918, **48:** 463

Meyer London, April 28, 1917, **42:** 154

Breckinridge Long, June 25, 1917, **43:** 12; March 4, 1918, **46:** 527

A memorandum by Breckinridge Long about the situation in Russia and Siberia, March 4, 1918, **46:** 527

Abbott Lawrence Lowell, Aug. 18, 1917, **43:** 513; July 10, 1918, **48:** 586

Walter Lowrie, Sept. 2, 1917, **44:** 123

William Gibbs McAdoo, March 31, 1917, **41:** 514; April 17, 1917, **42:** 80; Sept. 13, 1917, **44:** 195; Sept. 29, 1917, **44:** 280; Nov. 15, 1917, **45:** 54; Dec. 8, 1917, **45:** 245; Dec. 24, 1917, **45:** 351; Jan. 2, 1918, **45:** 424; Jan. 7, 1918, **45:** 532; Jan. 14, 1918, **45:** 588; Jan. 17, 1918, **46:** 65; Jan. 22, 1918, **46:** 75; Feb. 18, 1918 (2), **46:** 379; Feb. 21, 1918, **46:** 409; Oct. 27, 1918 (2), **51:** 465, 467; Oct. 26, 1918 (2), **51:** 465, 468

Cyrus Hall McCormick, Jr., April 30, 1917, **42:** 166

Vance Criswell McCormick, Oct. 19, 1917, **44:** 411; Oct. 24, 1917, **44:** 437; Dec. 21, 1917, **45:** 339; June 15, 1918, **48:** 324

A memorandum by Vance Criswell McCormick and others on the proposed inter-Allied super board, June 15, 1918, **48:** 325 (draft), 328

James Ramsay MacDonald and others, May 29, 1917, **42:** 420
Grenville Stanley Macfarland, June 27, 1918, **48:** 449
William Douglas Mackenzie, May 23, 1917, **42:** 393
Theodore Marburg, March 5, 1918, **46:** 549; May 3, 1918, **47:** 507;
    Aug. 6, 1918, **49:** 201
A memorandum by Theodore Marburg suggesting the immediate
    establishment of a rudimentary league of nations, Aug. 6, 1918,
    49: 202
Marie of Rumania, July 3, 1917, **43:** 95
Louis Marshall, May 4, 1918, **47:** 555; Nov. 7, 1918, **51:** 625
Thomas Garrigue Masaryk, July 20, 1918, **49:** 44; Aug. 5, 1918, **49:**
    185; Sept. 7, 1918, **49:** 485
Mario García Menocal, March 5, 1917, **41:** 339
Désiré-Joseph Cardinal Mercier, Feb. 9, 1917, **43:** 40; Oct. 17,
    1918, **51:** 370
Sidney Edward Mezes, Nov. 9, 1917, **44:** 549
A memorandum by Sidney Edward Mezes on subjects to be dealt
    with by The Inquiry, Nov. 9, 1917, **44:** 550
A memorandum by Sidney Edward Mezes, David Hunter Miller,
    and Walter Lippmann on the war aims and peace terms of the
    United States, Jan. 4, 1918, **45:** 459
Henry Morgenthau, June 7, 1917, **42:** 462; Nov. 26, 1917, **45:** 122
Ira Nelson Morris, Sept. 3, 1918, **49:** 437
John R. Mott, Aug. 21, 1917, **44:** 15; Aug. 30, 1917, **44:** 94; March
    11, 1918, **46:** 604; July 24, 1918, **49:** 77

Waclaw Jósef Niemojowski, Jan. 31, 1917, **41:** 139

Friedrich Oederlin, Oct. 6, 1918, **51:** 252
Rollo Ogden, Feb. 22, 1918, **46:** 417
Vittorio Emanuele Orlando, Nov. 1, 1917, **44:** 511
Robert Latham Owen, Jan. 22, 1918, **46:** 89; July 5, 1918, **48:** 530

Ignace Jan Paderewski, Oct. 4, 1917, **44:** 303
Thomas Nelson Page, Jan. 22, 1917, **41:** 221; June 27, 1917, **43:** 27;
    Oct. 2, 1917, **44:** 295; Nov. 4, 1917, **44:** 506; Jan. 29, 1918, **46:**
    155; Feb. 26, 1918, **46:** 454; July 23, 1918, **49:** 63; Nov. 5, 1918,
    51: 600
Walter Hines Page, Nov. 24, 1916, **40:** 63; Dec. 29, 1916, **40:** 355;
    Dec. 30, 1916, **40:** 366; Jan. 20, 1917, **40:** 531; Feb. 3, 1917, **41:**
    115; Feb. 4, 1917, **41:** 116; Feb. 6, 1917, **41:** 136; Feb. 11, 1917,
    41: 211; Feb. 20, 1917, **41:** 260; Feb. 21, 1917, **41:** 262; Feb. 22,
    1917, **41:** 270; Feb. 24, 1917, **41:** 280; March 5, 1917 (2), **41:** 336,
    337; March 9, 1917, **41:** 372; March 28, 1917, **41:** 494; April 3,
    1917, **41:** 538; April 17, 1917, **42:** 93; April 18, 1917, **42:** 93; June
    28, 1917, **43:** 34; June 29, 1917, **43:** 46; July 6, 1917 (2), **43:** 113,
    132; July 20, 1917, **43:** 223; Aug. 2, 1917, **43:** 347; Sept. 3, 1917,
    44: 130; Aug. 31, 1917, **44:** 140; Sept. 10, 1917, **44:** 181; Oct. 6,

1917, **44:** 318; Oct. 8, 1917, **44:** 329; Oct. 13, 1917, **44:** 388; Oct. 19, 1917, **44:** 412; Nov. 23, 1917, **45:** 148; Feb. 20, 1918 (2), **46:** 397, 400; Feb. 27, 1918, **46:** 473; March 28, 1918, **47:** 176

Lady Mary Fiske Stevens Paget, March 20, 1917, **41:** 494
George Foster Peabody, Aug. 29, 1917, **44:** 83
Frederic Courtland Penfield, March 13, 1917, **41:** 398
James Duval Phelan, June 29, 1918, **48:** 466
August Philips, March 20, 1918, **47:** 87
William Phillips, June 1, 1917, **42:** 434; Sept. 3, 1917, **44:** 139; Sept. 5, 1917, **44:** 156; May 3, 1918, **47:** 506; June 4, 1918, **48:** 239; June 6, 1918, **48:** 250; Sept. 29, 1918, **51:** 154
Gertrude Minturn Pinchot, Jan. 5, 1917, **40:** 418
Sir Horace Plunkett, May 8, 1918, **47:** 575
Michael M. Podolsky, May 4, 1917, **42:** 218
Raymond Poincaré, March 3, 1917, **41:** 314, translation, 314; April 4, 1918, **47:** 257
Frank Lyon Polk
  1917
  March 10, 1917 (2), **41:** 382, 384; July 9, 1917, **43:** 133; July 12, 1917 (2), **43:** 159, 160; July 18, 1917 (2), **43:** 206; July 25, 1917, **43:** 273; July 28, 1917, **43:** 300; July 27, 1917, **43:** 346; Aug. 4, 1917, **43:** 362; Aug. 6, 1917, **43:** 378
  1918
  Jan. 19, 1918, **46:** 34; Jan. 22, 1918, **46:** 78; Jan. 24, 1918, **46:** 118; Jan. 29, 1918, **46:** 153; March 2, 1918, **46:** 510, March 5, 1918, **46:** 547; March 6, 1918, **46:** 554; March 8, 1918 (2), **46:** 574, 580; March 9, 1918 (2), **46:** 584, 585; March 12, 1918, **46:** 615; March 14, 1918 (2), **47:** 20, 24; June 7, 1918, **48:** 262; June 8, 1918, **48:** 264; June 6, 1918, **48:** 277; July 15, 1918 (2), **48:** 621; July 16, 1918, **48:** 637; July 18, 1918 (2), **49:** 5; July 19, 1918, **49:** 21; July 20, 1918 (3), **49:** 37, 41, 42; July 24, 1918 (2), **49:** 75, 77; July 26, 1918, **49:** 107; July 31, 1918 (2), **49:** 140, 142; Aug. 1, 1918, **49:** 153; Aug. 2, 1918 (2), **49:** 168, 213; Aug. 3, 1918 (2), **49:** 175, 176; Aug. 6, 1918, **49:** 187; Aug. 9, 1918, **49:** 228; Oct. 1, 1918, **51:** 175
A memorandum by Frank Lyon Polk on the proposed Japanese intervention in Siberia, March 5, 1918, **46:** 544
Theodore Hazeltine Price, May 9, 1917, **42:** 255

Lord Reading, Oct. 15, 1917, **44:** 385; Feb. 27, 1918, **46:** 470; April 5, 1918, **47:** 265; June 28, 1918, **48:** 463; July 3, 1918 (2), **48:** 493, 501; July 24, 1918, **49:** 69
William Cox Redfield, Oct. 8, 1917, **44:** 337; June 8, 1918, **48:** 269
Paul Samuel Reinsch, Jan. 10, 1917, **40:** 436; Feb. 14, 1917, **41:** 229; Feb. 12, 1918, **46:** 331; Aug. 31, 1918, **49:** 406
A memorandum by Edward Alsworth Ross about a program of aid to Russia, July 9, 1918, **48:** 570
Charles Edward Russell, May 11, 1917, **42:** 280; Nov. 7, 1917, **44:** 557; June 20, 1918, **48:** 375

William Graves Sharp, Jan. 15, 1917, **40:** 481; Jan. 21, 1917, **40:** 532; May 5, 1917, **42:** 227; June 30, 1917, **43:** 57; Aug. 24, 1917, **44:** 43; Aug. 27, 1917, **44:** 75; Aug. 31, 1917, **44:** 103; Sept. 16, 1918, **51:** 21

Albert Shaw, Feb. 6, 1917, **41:** 135

George Jan Sosnowski, April 7, 1917, **42:** 11; June 5, 1917, **42:** 491; Aug. 8, 1917, **44:** 4; Jan. 11, 1918, **45:** 575

Sir Cecil Arthur Spring Rice, April 20, 1917, **42:** 112; Dec. 9, 1917, **45:** 255; Dec. 29, 1917, **45:** 392

Pleasant Alexander Stovall, Dec. 7, 1917, **45:** 235

John St. Loe Strachey, March 12, 1918, **46:** 617; Oct. 25, 1918, **51:** 444

Sun Yat-sen, June 8, 1917, **42:** 466; June 9, 1917, **42:** 468

Herbert Bayard Swope, Oct. 9, 1918, **51:** 284

André Tardieu, Aug. 3, 1917, **43:** 358

Frank William Taussig, Nov. 8, 1917, **44:** 541; Jan. 3, 1918, **45:** 440

A memorandum by Frank William Taussig on the future commercial policy of the United States, Nov. 8, 1917, **44:** 542

William Boyce Thompson, Jan. 3, 1918, **45:** 441; Jan. 31, 1918, **46:** 193

A memorandum by William Boyce Thompson on the situation in Russia, Jan. 3, 1918, **45:** 442

Charles Philips Trevelyan, Nov. 23, 1916, **40:** 178

Joseph Patrick Tumulty, Nov. 20, 1916, **40:** 7; Nov. 21, 1916, **40:** 24; Dec. 21, 1916, **40:** 306; April 20, 1917, **42:** 111; May 5, 1917, **42:** 223; May 8, 1917, **42:** 244; May 21, 1917 (2), **42:** 360, 363; June 6, 1917, **42:** 458; Aug. 2, 1917, **43:** 351; Nov. 30, 1917, **45:** 163; Dec. 14, 1917, **45:** 288; Jan. 3, 1918, **45:** 436; June 27, 1918, **48:** 444; Oct. 8, 1918 (2), **51:** 265, 266; Oct. 14, 1918, **51:** 329

A memorandum by Joseph Patrick Tumulty on John Daniel Crimmins, May 4, 1917, **42:** 219

A memorandum by Joseph Patrick Tumulty on the Russian situation, June 12, 1918, **48:** 299

The Right Reverend Arsène E. Vehouni, Nov. 29, 1916, **40:** 105

Eleuthérios Vénisélos, April 5, 1918, **47:** 263

Vittorio Emanuele III, Dec. 10, 1917, **45:** 262; April 6, 1918, **47:** 278

Lillian D. Wald, Feb. 8, 1917, **41:** 168

William English Walling, May 10, 1917, **42:** 267; May 21, 1917, **42:** 364

Sherman Leland Whipple, Oct. 24, 1918, **51:** 439; Oct. 29, 1918, **51:** 484

The White House staff, Jan. 14, 1918, **45:** 582; March 23, 1918, **47:** 123; Aug. 9, 1918, **49:** 225; Sept. 4, 1918, **49:** 436

Mary Bird Whiteway, Sept. 6, 1917, **44:** 159

Brand Whitlock, Jan. 20, 1917, **40:** 530

Frederick Wallingford Whitridge and others, Nov. 25, 1916, **40:** 88
Karl H. von Wiegand, Dec. 31, 1916, **40:** 375
William Royal Wilder, April 19, 1917, **42:** 104; Jan. 12, 1918, **45:** 574; Feb. 20, 1918, **46:** 401
Charles Turner Williams, July 1, 1918, **48:** 477
John Sharp Williams, Dec. 5, 1916, **40:** 168; Feb. 3, 1917, **41:** 107
William Bauchop Wilson, April 30, 1917, **42:** 165; May 3, 1917, **42:** 197; May 9, 1917, **42:** 252; June 23, 1917, **42:** 566
Stephen Samuel Wise, April 11, 1917, **42:** 41; April 24, 1917, **42:** 124; Aug. 27, 1918, **49:** 363
A memorandum by Sir William Wiseman and Colonel House about relations between the United States and Great Britain, March 6, 1917, **41:** 347

Yoshihito, March 10, 1917, **41:** 382

Baron Erich Zwiedinek, Dec. 1, 1916, **40:** 113

Correspondence, reports, and memoranda about military and naval affairs

By Wilson and from Wilson to
Gordon Auchincloss, March 27, 1918, **47:** 158

Newton Diehl Baker
1917
March 23, 1917, **41:** 455; March 27, 1917, **41:** 478; March 28, 1917, **41:** 486; March 31, 1917, **41:** 507; April 3, 1917, **41:** 537; April 11, 1917, **42:** 33; May 3, 1917 (2), **42:** 201, 202; May 10, 1917, **42:** 263; May 23, 1917, **42:** 377; June 21, 1917, **42:** 552; June 26, 1917, **43:** 16; Aug. 7, 1917, **43:** 380; Sept. 22, 1917, **44:** 239; Nov. 19, 1917, **45:** 75; Nov. 30, 1917, **45:** 160; Dec. 5, 1917, **45:** 208; Dec. 27, 1917, **45:** 366
1918
Jan. 2, 1918, **45:** 421; Jan. 20, 1918, **46:** 42; Feb. 4, 1918, **46:** 236; Feb. 22, 1918 (2), **46:** 414; March 29, 1918, **47:** 186; May 1, 1918, **47:** 478; May 3, 1918, **47:** 501; May 4, 1918, **47:** 516; May 6, 1918, **47:** 535; May 13, 1918 (2), **48:** 4, 5; May 20, 1918, **48:** 73; May 24, 1918, **48:** 136; May 28, 1918, **48:** 177; June 7, 1918, **48:** 261; June 19, 1918, **48:** 357; June 24, 1918, **48:** 403; July 2, 1918, **48:** 482; Aug. 9, 1918, **49:** 224; Aug. 24, 1918, **49:** 347; Aug. 27, 1918, **49:** 359; Aug. 31, 1918 (2), **49:** 399, 400; Oct. 18, 1918, **51:** 372; Oct. 21, 1918 (2), **51:** 396; Oct. 22, 1918, **51:** 405
Bernard Mannes Baruch, Sept. 17, 1918, **51:** 26
Tasker Howard Bliss, April 6, 1918, **47:** 271

Winston Churchill, Aug. 3, 1917, **43:** 358; Nov. 12, 1917, **45:** 24
Benedict Crowell, March 7, 1918, **46:** 562; March 22, 1918, **47:** 107;

April 16, 1918, **47:** 349; Sept. 5, 1918, **49:** 449; Sept. 13, 1918 (2), **49:** 542; Oct. 5, 1918, **51:** 228
Charles Allen Culberson, April 21, 1917, **42:** 116

Josephus Daniels, March 12, 1917, **41:** 391; March 24, 1917, **41:** 461; May 14, 1917, **42:** 292; June 19, 1917, **42:** 538; July 2, 1917, **43:** 71; July 3, 1917 (2), **43:** 79, 88; Aug. 2, 1917, **43:** 344; Nov. 12, 1917, **45:** 18; Nov. 15, 1917, **45:** 52; Dec. 6, 1917, **45:** 223; April 8, 1918, **47:** 290; June 10, 1918, **48:** 280; Oct. 2, 1918, **51:** 179; Oct. 9, 1918, **51:** 281
William Denman, April 26, 1917, **42:** 133

Abram Isaac Elkus, Nov. 15, 1917, **45:** 51

Ferdinand Foch, March 29, 1918, **47:** 186; May 28, 1918, **48:** 178

John Palmer Gavit, Jan. 2, 1918, **45:** 423
George Washington Goethals, April 11, 1917, **42:** 32; April 27, 1917, **42:** 145

Sir Douglas Haig, March 25, 1918, **47:** 134
Edward Mandell House, March 27, 1918, **47:** 158
Jean Jules Jusserand, June 12, 1918, **48:** 295; June 25, 1918, **48:** 421

Robert Lansing, Feb. 15, 1917, **41:** 232; April 8, 1917, **42:** 13; May 20, 1918, **48:** 73; Aug. 22, 1918, **49:** 312; Sept. 2, 1918 (2), **49:** 416, 417; Sept. 3, 1918, **49:** 423; Sept. 5, 1918, **49:** 447; Sept. 26, 1918, **51:** 121; Oct. 2, 1918 (2), **51:** 178

Peyton Conway March, Sept. 18, 1918, **51:** 51; Oct. 4, 1918, **51:** 211
Mark Allison Matthews, Sept. 16, 1918, **51:** 16
John R. Mott, Aug. 30, 1918, **49:** 390
William Benjamin Munson, April 22, 1918, **47:** 395

Naval terms of an armistice, Oct. 28, 1918, **51:** 474

John Joseph Pershing, Dec. 27, 1917, **45:** 366; March 28, 1918, **47:** 172; July 24, 1918, **49:** 74; Sept. 14, 1918, **51:** 3
William Phillips, Sept. 4, 1917, **44:** 147
Raymond Poincaré, Jan. 8, 1918, **45:** 539

William Cox Redfield, May 21, 1917, **42:** 358
Franklin Delano Roosevelt, Oct. 30, 1917, **44:** 473
Theodore Roosevelt, May 19, 1917, **42:** 346

William Sowden Sims, July 3, 1917 (2), **43:** 79, 88; Aug. 2, 1918, **49:** 158

John Humphrey Small, April 19, 1917, **42:** 98
The Student Army Training Corps, Oct. 1, 1918, **51:** 168

Joseph Patrick Tumulty, Oct. 1, 1918, **51:** 170

To Wilson from
Newton Diehl Baker
1917
Jan. 24, 1917, **41:** 15; Feb. 3, 1917, **41:** 114; Feb. 7, 1917 (2), **41:** 151, 153; Feb. 16, 1917, **41:** 236; March 26, 1917, **41:** 469; March 28, 1917, **41:** 486; March 31, 1917, **41:** 511; April 2, 1917, **41:** 527; April 11, 1917, **42:** 33; April 13, 1917 (2), **42:** 56, 58; May 2, 1917 (2), **42:** 191, 194; May 8, 1917, **42:** 249; May 27, 1917, **42:** 405; June 19, 1917, **42:** 541; June 20, 1917, **42:** 549; July 3, 1917, **43:** 89; Aug. 12, 1917, **43:** 435; Aug. 25, 1917, **44:** 51; Sept. 22, 1917, **44:** 239; Oct. 11, 1917, **44:** 361; Nov. 8, 1917, **44:** 538; Nov. 11, 1917, **45:** 4; Nov. 14, 1917, **45:** 49; Nov. 23, 1917, **45:** 107, Nov. 29, 1917, **45:** 157; Dec. 11, 1917, **45:** 268; Dec. 18, 1917, **45:** 328; Dec. 19, 1917, **45:** 331; Dec. 26, 1917, **45:** 363
January–April 1918
Jan. 2, 1918, **45:** 425; Jan. 3, 1918, **45:** 438; Jan. 4, 1918, **45:** 452; Jan. 5, 1918 (2), **45:** 489, 491; Jan. 11, 1918, **45:** 571; Jan. 14, 1918, **45:** 582; Jan. 15, 1918, **45:** 594; Jan. 16, 1918, **46:** 8; Jan. 19, 1918, **46:** 43; Feb. 1, 1918, **46:** 210; Feb. 4, 1918, **46:** 239; Feb. 6, 1918, **46:** 259; Feb. 13, 1918, **46:** 337; Feb. 20, 1918, **46:** 400; March 12, 1918, **46:** 612; March 27, 1918 (2), **47:** 160, 166; March 28, 1918 (2), **47:** 174, 175; March 30, 1918, **47:** 209; April 5, 1918 (2), **47:** 261, 262; April 19, 1918, **47:** 372; April 25, 1918, **47:** 421; April 29, 1918 (2), **47:** 455, 458
May–July 1918
May 1, 1918 (2), **47:** 480, 486; May 2, 1918, **47:** 491; May 4, 1918 (2), **47:** 517, 518; May 8, 1918 (2), **47:** 563, 566; May 10, 1918, **47:** 595; May 11, 1918, **47:** 611; **48:** 5; May 16, 1918, **48:** 32; May 17, 1918 (2), **48:** 49, 73; May 28, 1918, **48:** 178; June 5, 1918, **48:** 243; June 8, 1918, **48:** 265; June 13, 1918, **48:** 307; June 20, 1918, **48:** 367; June 21, 1918, **48:** 383; July 1, 1918, **48:** 476; July 2, 1918 (2), **48:** 83, 483; July 6, 1918, **48:** 536; July 7, 1918, **48:** 544; July 9, 1918, **48:** 568; July 14, 1918, **48:** 607; July 20, 1918, **49:** 43; July 21, 1918, **49:** 52
August–November 1918
Aug. 1, 1918, **49:** 156; Aug. 8, 1918, **49:** 217; Aug. 17, 1918, **49:** 276; Aug. 22, 1918, **49:** 324; Aug. 23, 1918, **49:** 335; Aug. 26, 1918, **49:** 354; Aug. 29, 1918, **49:** 387; Aug. 30, 1918, **49:** 395; Sept. 23, 1918, **51:** 94; Oct. 17, 1918, **51:** 356; Oct. 19, 1918 (2), **51:** 383, 385; Oct. 22, 1918, **51:** 404; Oct. 26, 1918, **51:** 453; Oct. 28, 1918, **51:** 471; Nov. 6, 1918, **51:** 608

Winston Churchill, Aug. 2, 1917, **43:** 354; Oct. 22, 1917, **45:** 19
Georges Clemenceau, Dec. 15, 1917, **45:** 302

Georges Clemenceau, David Lloyd George, and Vittorio Emanuele Orlando, June 2, 1918, **48:** 226

Sir Richard Frederick Crawford, June 25, 1917, **43:** 9; June 29, 1917, **43:** 45

Enoch Herbert Crowder, Oct. 5, 1918, **51:** 250

Benedict Crowell, March 6, 1918 (2), **46:** 558, 560; March 19, 1918, **47:** 72; March 22, 1918, **47:** 107; March 26, 1918, **47:** 144; April 15, 1918, **47:** 348; April 16, 1918, **47:** 349; Sept. 8, 1918, **49:** 487; Sept. 17, 1918, **51:** 33; Oct. 8, 1918, **51:** 271

Josephus Daniels, Feb. 10, 1917 (2), **41:** 188, 189; March 8, 1917, **41:** 363; March 9, 1917 (2), **41:** 369, 376; March 11, 1917, **41:** 387; March 12, 1917, **41:** 391; March 20, 1917, **41:** 432; April 10, 1917, **42:** 27; April 23, 1917, **42:** 121; June 18, 1917, **42:** 534; July 3, 1917, **43:** 87; July 6, 1917, **43:** 112; July 14, 1917, **43:** 178; July 28, 1917 (2), **43:** 302, 305; Dec. 3, 1917, **45:** 189; Dec. 5, 1917, **45:** 215; Jan. 31, 1918, **46:** 194; March 27, 1918, **47:** 161; April 5, 1918, **47:** 263; June 10, 1918, **48:** 279; July 5, 1918, **48:** 527; July 31, 1918, **49:** 142; Sept. 26, 1918, **51:** 124

William Denman, June 21, 1917, **42:** 555

Abram Isaac Elkus, Nov. 14, 1917, **45:** 52

Ferdinand Foch, June 27, 1918, **48:** 445

Arthur Hugh Frazier, March 19, 1918, **47:** 73

George Washington Goethals, April 19, 1917, **42:** 102; June 11, 1917, **42:** 475; June 15, 1917, **42:** 523; July 2, 1917, **43:** 72

Memoranda by George Washington Goethals on the shipbuilding program, May 6, 1917, **42:** 234; May 8, 1917, **42:** 249

Thomas Watt Gregory, Sept. 1, 1917, **44:** 119

Sir Douglas Haig, March 27, 1918, **47:** 160

Edward Mandell House, March 11, 1917, **41:** 388; March 24, 1918, **47:** 131; April 9, 1918, **47:** 302; April 25, 1918, **47:** 433; May 12, 1918, **47:** 616; June 3, 1918, **48:** 231; Sept. 3, 1918, **49:** 429

Jean Jules Jusserand, June 12, 1918, **48:** 294; June 24, 1918, **48:** 415

Robert Lansing, Feb. 10, 1917, **41:** 187; Feb. 14, 1917, **41:** 232; Feb. 22, 1917, **41:** 263; March 6, 1917, **41:** 341; March 9, 1917, **41:** 368; April 7, 1917, **42:** 9; April 10, 1917, **42:** 28; May 21, 1918, **48:** 104; May 31, 1918, **48:** 206; June 28, 1918, **48:** 458; Aug. 18, 1918, **49:** 282; Aug. 28, 1918, **49:** 369; Aug. 31, 1918, **49:** 403; Sept. 4, 1918, **49:** 433; Sept. 11, 1918, **49:** 517; Sept. 13, 1918, **49:** 543; Sept. 24, 1918, **51:** 97

Breckinridge Long, Sept. 7, 1918, **49:** 479

Peyton Conway March, July 3, 1918, **48:** 503; Sept. 12, 1918, **49:** 529; Oct. 3, 1918, **51:** 195
A memorandum by Peyton Conway March about a military campaign in Siberia, June 24, 1918, **48:** 419
Thomas Garrigue Masaryk, Aug. 6, 1918, **49:** 194
A memorandum by Basil Miles on the military situation in Siberia, May 21, 1918, **48:** 104
William Benjamin Munson, April 17, 1918, **47:** 354

Walter Hines Page, June 20, 1917, **42:** 546; June 26, 1917, **43:** 18; June 27, 1917, **43:** 26; July 13, 1917, **43:** 171; Aug. 14, 1917, **43:** 463
John Joseph Pershing, June 27, 1918, **48:** 451; Sept. 18, 1918, **51:** 61
William Phillips, May 23, 1917, **42:** 378; July 28, 1917, **43:** 302
Raymond Poincaré, Dec. 28, 1917, **45:** 372; Sept. 13, 1918, **49:** 547
Frank Lyon Polk, July 27, 1917, **43:** 293; March 14, 1918, **47:** 26; Aug. 1, 1918, **49:** 150
A memorandum by William Veazie Pratt about the proposed naval terms for an armistice, Oct. 29, 1918, **51:** 487

William Cox Redfield, May 19, 1917, **42:** 348
Franklin Delano Roosevelt, June 5, 1917, **42:** 457; Oct. 29, 1917, **44:** 464
A memorandum by Franklin Delano Roosevelt about antisubmarine measures in the English Channel and the North Sea, Oct. 29, 1917, **44:** 465
A memorandum by Franklin Delano Roosevelt about the naval terms of an armistice, Oct. 29, 1918, **51:** 486
Theodore Roosevelt, May 18, 1917, **42:** 324

William Graves Sharp, Dec. 15, 1917, **45:** 302
William Sowden Sims, July 11, 1917, **43:** 179; July 13, 1918, **48:** 604
Sir Cecil Arthur Spring Rice, July 10, 1917, **43:** 140; Aug. 6, 1917, **43:** 374
Teofil A. Starzynski, Feb. 27, 1917, **41:** 508
Teofil A. Starzynski and others, Feb. 19, 1917, **41:** 507

Joseph Patrick Tumulty, Dec. 29, 1917, **45:** 390

A memorandum by the War Council about the shortage of tonnage, March 26, 1918, **47:** 145
The White House staff, June 4, 1917, **42:** 449

Personal correspondence

From Wilson to
Lyman Abbott, April 12, 1911, **42:** 570; Aug. 31, 1912, **42:** 570
Herbert Adams, Oct. 10, 1917, **44:** 347
Alvey Augustus Adee, Aug. 1, 1918, **49:** 149
The Council of the American Philosophical Society, March 13, 1918, **47:** 4
Stockton Axson, April 12, 1918, **47:** 326

Newton Diehl Baker, Aug. 29, 1917, **44:** 82; May 16, 1918, **48:** 30
Benjamin Franklin Battin, Aug. 23, 1917, **44:** 36
Eleanor Orbison Beach, Aug. 22, 1918, **49:** 318
Frank D. Beattys, July 3, 1917, **43:** 85
Paul Lendrum Blakely, Dec. 17, 1907, **51:** 649
Maria Leont'evna Frolkova Bochkareva, July 1, 1918, **48:** 475
Edward William Bok, Jan. 26, 1917, **41:** 22; May 3, 1917, **42:** 202
Helen Woodrow Bones, Feb. 26, 1918, **46:** 449
James Oscar Boyd, Jan. 11, 1918, **45:** 570
Robert Bridges, Jan. 2, 1918, **45:** 423; Feb. 4, 1918, **46:** 239; Feb. 18, 1918, **46:** 371; May 24, 1918, **48:** 141; Nov. 8, 1918, **51:** 640
Robert Seymour Bridges, May 25, 1917, **42:** 392; Sept. 6, 1918, **49:** 462
William Harlowe Briggs, Oct. 1, 1918, **51:** 172
Marrette Applegate Broussard, April 15, 1918, **47:** 341
Jessie Woodrow Bones Brower, Aug. 1, 1917, **43:** 338
Curtis Brown, March 25, 1918, **47:** 139
James Viscount Bryce, Oct. 18, 1918, **51:** 375
Edward Rogers Bushnell, Sept. 1, 1904, **42:** 569
Witter Bynner, Dec. 10, 1917, **45:** 258

Kate Benedict Freeman Carter, Nov. 13, 1917, **45:** 41
William Lea Chambers, Feb. 11, 1918, **46:** 325
Caroline Dutcher Sterling Choate, May 16, 1917, **42:** 302
Grosvenor Blaine Clarkson, Oct. 29, 1918, **51:** 485
M. Clemmons, Nov. 27, 1917, **45:** 130
Gilbert Fairchild Close, July 18, 1918, **49:** 4
Annie Wilson Howe Cothran Compton, July 29, 1917, **43:** 317; July 22, 1917, **43:** 318
Edward Samuel Corwin, Aug. 30, 1918, **49:** 390
Annie Wilson Howe Cothran, Nov. 30, 1916, **40:** 108; March 26, 1917, **41:** 469
George Creel, May 23, 1918, **48:** 120

Richard Heath Dabney, Nov. 27, 1916, **40:** 90
Addie Worth Bagley Daniels, Dec. 29, 1917, **45:** 389
Edward Parker Davis, March 22, 1917, **41:** 452; Oct. 1, 1917, **44:** 287; Oct. 5, 1917, **44:** 310; April 23, 1918, **47:** 401; Sept. 6, 1918, **49:** 462; Oct. 26, 1918, **51:** 452

Ellen-Duane Gillespie Davis, Feb. 13, 1918, **46:** 336
John Lionberger Davis, Jan. 18, 1918, **46:** 28
George Parmly Day, Dec. 26, 1917, **45:** 362; Jan. 8, 1918, **45:** 540
The Duke of Devonshire, Jan. 21, 1918, **46:** 51; Feb. 14, 1918, **46:**
    343
George Dewey, Dec. 26, 1916, **40:** 327
Cleveland Hoadley Dodge, Jan. 25, 1917, **41:** 11; Feb. 6, 1917, **41:**
    133; May 25, 1917, **42:** 396; Sept. 1, 1917, **44:** 119; Jan. 14, 1918,
    45: 581; April 16, 1918, **47:** 350; May 23, 1918, **48:** 121; Oct. 2,
    1918, **51:** 180
Robert Langton Douglas, June 20, 1917, **42:** 545
Robert James Drummond, Aug. 20, 1918, **49:** 295
Nelson C. Durand, Feb. 5, 1917, **41:** 126

Henry Burchard Fine, April 20, 1918, **47:** 383
Ferdinand Foch, Nov. 4, 1918, **51:** 578
Mrs. F. C. Foley, Feb. 21, 1918, **46:** 407
Henry Ford, Oct. 9, 1918, **51:** 280
Frank Foxcroft, Feb. 6, 1917, **41:** 133
Hans Froelicher, May 6, 1918, **47:** 536
Eda Blankart Funston, Feb. 20, 1917, **41:** 259

Harry Augustus Garfield, Dec. 27, 1916, **40:** 334; March 13, 1918,
    47: 8; Sept. 6, 1918, **49:** 461
John Palmer Gavit, July 30, 1918, **49:** 128
George Gladden, July 3, 1918, **48:** 491
Washington Gladden, March 14, 1918, **47:** 19
Mary Owen Graham, Oct. 29, 1918, **51:** 486
Ferris Greenslet, Nov. 7, 1918, **51:** 621
Solomon Bulkley Griffin, Oct. 18, 1918, **51:** 376
William Westley Guth, May 6, 1918, **47:** 537

Ruth Preble Hall, Jan. 25, 1917, **41:** 15
William Judson Hampton, Sept. 15, 1917, **44:** 199
The Right Reverend Alfred Harding, March 25, 1918, **47:** 137
George McLean Harper, Jan. 8, 1903, **43:** 540; Dec. 20, 1917, **45:**
    334
Harper & Brothers, July 2, 1918, **48:** 482
Charles Homer Haskins, Jan. 30, 1918, **46:** 169
Azel Washburn Hazen, Sept. 5, 1917, **44:** 154
Ripley Hitchcock, April 9, 1918, **47:** 302
Henry French Hollis, Oct. 24, 1918, **51:** 425
Herbert Clark Hoover, Nov. 4, 1918, **51:** 578
Houghton, Mifflin & Company, March 15, 1918, **47:** 41
Edward Mandell House, Jan. 1, 1917, **40:** 379; March 26, 1917, **41:**
    468; Sept. 23, 1917, **44:** 242; Oct. 8, 1917, **44:** 328; Oct. 28, 1917,
    44: 461; Dec. 16, 1917, **45:** 313; Feb. 26, 1918, **46:** 448
David Franklin Houston, Sept. 17, 1917, **44:** 207

Émile Lucien Hovelaque, Jan. 26, 1918, **46:** 100
George Howe III, Feb. 13, 1917, **41:** 210; Feb. 20, 1917, **41:** 259
James Wilson Howe, Sept. 17, 1918, **51:** 27
William Dean Howells, March 2, 1917, **41:** 311
Margaret Hughes Hughes, Jan. 30, 1918, **46:** 169
Allen Schoolcraft Hulbert, Aug. 29, 1917, **44:** 82
Jean Pierre Husting and Mary Magdelena Juneau Husting, Oct. 22, 1917, **44:** 421
William DeWitt Hyde, March 29, 1910, **42:** 570

William Mann Irvine, April 27, 1918, **47:** 450

Melancthon Williams Jacobus, April 7, 1917, **42:** 6
Ollie Murray James, Oct. 12, 1917, **44:** 365
Ruth Thomas James, Aug. 28, 1918, **49:** 368
Frank Latimer Janeway, Feb. 8, 1918, **46:** 286
Claude Motley Jones, April 19, 1918, **47:** 372
David Benton Jones, Dec. 7, 1917, **45:** 230
John Henry Jowett, April 25, 1918, **47:** 420
Jean Jules Jusserand, July 3, 1918, **48:** 491

William Lacy Kenly, July 16, 1918, **48:** 628
Eleanor Smith Kent, Oct. 30, 1917, **44:** 474
Araminta Cooper Kern, Aug. 18, 1917, **43:** 512
Claude Kitchin, April 10, 1917, **42:** 27

Franklin Knight Lane, Dec. 5, 1916, **40:** 162
The Most Reverend Cosmo Gordon Lang, March 20, 1918, **47:** 84
Eleanor Foster Lansing, May 20, 1918, **48:** 78
Robert Lansing, March 7, 1907, **45:** 602; March 20, 1918, **47:** 85; May 16, 1918, **48:** 27; Oct. 1, 1918, **51:** 171
David Lawrence, March 13, 1918, **47:** 4; March 15, 1918, **47:** 39
Richard Ludwig Enno Littmann, Feb. 1, 1906, **47:** 623; July 10, 1909, **47:** 623; Aug. 26, 1909, **47:** 624; Nov. 9, 1911, **47:** 624
Thomas Francis Logan, Feb. 20, 1917, **41:** 259
Walter Lowrie, Jan. 26, 1918, **46:** 105

William Gibbs McAdoo, May 6, 1918, **47:** 533
James Gray McAllister, July 29, 1918, **49:** 122
Harvey MacCauley, Nov. 4, 1918, **51:** 578
Rhoda Isabel McDonald, Jan. 16, 1918, **46:** 5
Ruth Smith McKelway, April 18, 1918, **47:** 359
Lucius Hopkins Miller, Dec. 5, 1916, **40:** 169
Olive Child Mitchel, July 9, 1918, **48:** 568
Florence Crowe Mitchell, Dec. 31, 1917, **45:** 404
Frank Gardner Moore, Jan. 28, 1918, **46:** 119

The Institution of Naval Architects of Great Britain, March 19, 1918, **47:** 67

The Norman Foster Company, May 1, 1918, **47:** 479
Percival Chandler Norris, Dec. 5, 1916, **40:** 169

The Most Reverend Thomas O'Gorman, Oct. 3, 1918, **51:** 191
Frederick Law Olmsted, Jr., Sept. 11, 1918, **49:** 513
Agnes Thomas Olney, April 9, 1917, **42:** 22

Walter Hines Page, March 20, 1918, **47:** 85; Oct. 17, 1918, **51:** 356
George Foster Peabody, Aug. 28, 1917, **44:** 77
William Phillips, June 6, 1918, **48:** 249; July 10, 1918, **48:** 579
Frank Lyon Polk, March 13, 1918, **47:** 5; June 26, 1918, **48:** 441
Ambrose Preece, March 22, 1917, **41:** 451

John Herbert Quick, Sept. 11, 1918, **49:** 514

Jeannette Rankin, Dec. 26, 1917, **45:** 363
Lord Reading, March 25, 1918, **47:** 138
James B. Regan, Nov. 13, 1917, **45:** 41
Edith Gittings Reid, March 10, 1918, **46:** 596
Harry Fielding Reid, April 11, 1917, **42:** 36
Melvin A. Rice, Dec. 6, 1916, **40:** 177
William Henry Roberts, Dec. 14, 1917, **45:** 286
Flora Lois Robinson, Dec. 5, 1917, **45:** 214
Edith Kermit Carow Roosevelt, Feb. 8, 1918, **46:** 287
Theodore Roosevelt, July 20, 1918, **49:** 37
Georges Roth, April 25, 1918, **47:** 421
Charles Edward Russell, Dec. 28, 1917, **45:** 371

Louis de Sadeleer, April 12, 1918, **47:** 324
John Singer Sargent, July 18, 1917, **43:** 203; Oct. 11, 1917, **44:** 360;
    Oct. 15, 1917, **44:** 383; Nov. 8, 1917, **44:** 536
Francis Bowes Sayre, April 7, 1917, **42:** 5; June 22, 1917, **42:** 559;
    June 30, 1917, **43:** 53
Jessie Woodrow Wilson Sayre, June 22, 1917, **42:** 560; July 21,
    1917, **43:** 240; Aug. 27, 1917, **44:** 64; May 6, 1918, **47:** 536; May
    13, 1918, **48:** 6; Aug. 2, 1918, **49:** 167; Aug. 22, 1918, **49:** 318
Charles Scribner, Feb. 8, 1918, **46:** 285
Fred Loring Seely, Sept. 3, 1918, **49:** 427
Edwin Robert Anderson Seligman, Dec. 8, 1917, **45:** 244
Anna Howard Shaw, Jan. 23, 1917, **40:** 548
Edward Wright Sheldon, March 22, 1917, **41:** 452; Oct. 19, 1917,
    44: 406; May 23, 1918, **48:** 120
Arthur Everett Shipley, April 22, 1918, **47:** 396; June 6, 1918, **48:**
    250
Bella Wilson Shope, Dec. 5, 1916, **40:** 170
Kate Drayton Mayrant Simons, Aug. 21, 1918, **49:** 305
Lucy Marshall Smith, Jan. 14, 1918, **45:** 581; Feb. 18, 1918, **46:** 371
Lucy Marshall Smith and Mary Randolph Smith, Dec. 27, 1916,
    40: 336

Jessie Eldridge Southwick, Aug. 26, 1918, **49:** 351
James Sprunt, April 19, 1917, **42:** 99
John Dalziel Sprunt, May 3, 1917, **42:** 203
Emily Contee Lewis Stevens, March 9, 1918, **46:** 583
Sarah Louise Winston Stone, April 16, 1918, **47:** 350

André Tardieu, Nov. 4, 1918, **51:** 577
James Henry Taylor, Nov. 14, 1917, **45:** 46; March 9, 1918, **46:** 582
Samuel Huston Thompson, Jr., Nov. 30, 1917, **45:** 163
Sallie Starke Tillman, July 3, 1918, **48:** 492
Joseph Patrick Tumulty, July 10, 1917, **43:** 136; Feb. 7, 1918, **46:** 264; Aug. 2, 1918, **49:** 165; Sept. 16, 1918, **51:** 14; Oct. 29, 1918, **51:** 485

An Unnamed Person, Oct. 22, 1918, **51:** 406

Hamilton Vreeland, Jr., Aug. 14, 1917, **43:** 462

Charles Doolittle Walcott, Feb. 27, 1918, **46:** 468; March 2, 1918, **46:** 509
Bernhardt Wall, July 8, 1918, **48:** 557
Thomas James Walsh, Aug. 27, 1917, **44:** 64; Aug. 31, 1917, **44:** 102
John Howell Westcott, Dec. 29, 1916, **40:** 355
The White House staff, March 19, 1918, **47:** 67
John Sharp Williams, July 8, 1918, **48:** 557
Joseph R. Wilson, Jr., Nov. 27, 1916, **40:** 90; July 23, 1917, **43:** 247
Margaret Woodrow Wilson, April 16, 1917, **42:** 77; Sept. 26, 1917, **44:** 266
Smith W. Wilson, March 20, 1907, **43:** 540
William Bauchop Wilson, Dec. 28, 1917, **45:** 370
R. H. Windsor, Aug. 30, 1918, **49:** 391
William Winter, Dec. 27, 1916, **40:** 335
Felexiana Shepherd Baker Woodrow, Nov. 27, 1916, **40:** 91; Dec. 31, 1917, **45:** 404; June 3, 1918, **48:** 231
James Woodrow, Feb. 9, 1917, **41:** 180
Edwin Augustus Woods, May 20, 1918, **48:** 78
Hiram Woods, Jr., Dec. 31, 1917, **45:** 404
Ethel Morgan Lyle Wyatt, July 29, 1918, **49:** 123
Laura Isabelle Moore Wylie, Dec. 5, 1916, **40:** 169

To Wilson from
Herbert Adams, Oct. 8, 1917, **44:** 340
Alvey Augustus Adee, Aug. 2, 1918, **49:** 170
The Viscount of Alte, May 27, 1918, **48:** 173

Newton Diehl Baker, Aug. 12, 1918, **49:** 238
Eleanor Orbison Beach, Aug. 14, 1918, **49:** 257
Martha Berry, Nov. 19, 1914, **40:** 565

Edward William Bok, May 1, 1917, **42:** 182

Hester Drayton Boylston, Sept. 26, 1917, **44:** 268

Robert Bridges, Dec. 19, 1916, **40:** 289; March 7, 1917, **41:** 354; Dec. 31, 1917, **45:** 410; Feb. 2, 1918, **46:** 218; May 21, 1918, **48:** 111; July 8, 1918, **48:** 564

Robert Seymour Bridges, May 3, 1917, **42:** 209

Robert Seymour Bridges, "To the United States of America, May 1, 1917" (poem), May 1, 1917, **42:** 209

Curtis Brown, March 9, 1918, **46:** 589

William Lea Chambers, Feb. 10, 1918, **46:** 314

Grosvenor Blaine Clarkson, Oct. 26, 1918, **51:** 459

Gilbert Fairchild Close, July 22, 1918, **49:** 56

Annie Wilson Howe Cothran, Nov. 27, 1916, **40:** 93; Dec. 2, 1916, **40:** 127; March 23, 1917, **41:** 457; July 20, 1917, **43:** 236

Charles Richard Crane, Aug. 20, 1918, **49:** 298

Edward Parker Davis, Sept. 29, 1917, **44:** 285; Oct. 29, 1918, **51:** 508

Edward Parker Davis, "Woodrow Wilson, President, March 5, 1917" (poem), March 17, 1917, **41:** 452

George Parmly Day, Dec. 24, 1917, **45:** 352; Jan. 4, 1918, **45:** 453

George Dewey, Dec. 27, 1916, **40:** 338

Cleveland Hoadley Dodge, Dec. 27, 1916, **40:** 338; Jan. 24, 1917, **41:** 6; Feb. 5, 1917, **41:** 128; Feb. 8, 1917, **41:** 170; March 5, 1917, **41:** 339; May 23, 1917, **42:** 384; Aug. 30, 1917, **44:** 93; Dec. 8, 1917, **45:** 254; May 20, 1918, **48:** 94; Sept. 28, 1918, **51:** 151

Robert Langton Douglas, May 24, 1917, **42:** 390; May 26, 1917, **42:** 403

Edward Graham Elliott, Oct. 31, 1918, **51:** 535

Henry Burchard Fine, April 19, 1918, **47:** 380

Ferdinand Foch, Oct. 2, 1918, **51:** 181

Norman Foster, June 10, 1918, **48:** 280

Hans Froelicher, April 27, 1918, **47:** 453

Harry Augustus Garfield, Dec. 21, 1916, **40:** 314; March 14, 1918, **47:** 35; Sept. 5, 1918, **49:** 452; Oct. 22, 1918, **51:** 411

John Palmer Gavit, Dec. 29, 1917, **45:** 395; Aug. 5, 1918, **49:** 184

Ferris Greenslet, March 11, 1918, **46:** 605

Thomas Watt Gregory, Feb. 28, 1918, **46:** 496

Ruth Preble Hall, Jan. 16, 1917, **40:** 551

Harper & Brothers, July 1, 1918, **48:** 479

Frank Oscar Hellier, Jan. 17, 1917, **40:** 516; March 14, 1917, **41:** 408

Ripley Hitchcock, April 13, 1918, **47:** 336

Henry French Hollis, Oct. 2, 1918, **51:** 185
Edward Mandell House, Dec. 15, 1917, **45:** 309; July 25, 1918, **49:** 90; Sept. 9, 1918, **49:** 499; Sept. 13, 1918, **49:** 548
George Howe III, Feb. 8, 1917, **41:** 172
Allen Schoolcraft Hulbert, Aug. 16, 1917, **43:** 502

Ruth Thomas James, Oct. 3, 1918 **51:** 208
Frank Latimer Janeway, Feb. 6, 1918, **46:** 260
Caesar Augustus Rodney Janvier, July 5, 1918, **48:** 531

Franklin Knight Lane, Dec. 8, 1916, **40:** 193
Eleanor Foster Lansing, May 16, 1918, **48:** 45; May 20, 1918, **48:** 94
Robert Lansing, Nov. 15, 1917, **45:** 67

William Gibbs McAdoo, Dec. 28, 1917, **45:** 380; May 5, 1918, **47:** 533
Harvey MacCauley, Nov. 1, 1918, **51:** 547
James McGranahan, Sept. 18, 1918, **51:** 74
Chalmers Martin, March 4, 1917, **41:** 321
Jerome A. Myers, Oct. 5, 1918, **51:** 251

Alice Wilson Page, Oct. 19, 1918, **51:** 388
William Phillips, July 9, 1918, **48:** 575

John Herbert Quick, Sept. 10, 1918, **49:** 512

Lord Reading, March 22, 1918, **47:** 116; July 29, 1918, **49:** 125
William Cox Redfield, Dec. 28, 1917, **45:** 380
Melvin Augustus Rice, Dec. 5, 1916, **40:** 174
William Henry Roberts, Dec. 12, 1917, **45:** 282
Flora Lois Robinson, Nov. 29, 1917, **45:** 158
Edith Kermit Carow Roosevelt, Feb. 8, 1918, **46:** 287
Theodore Roosevelt, July 20, 1918, **49:** 50

John Singer Sargent, July 16, 1917, **43:** 191; July 21, 1917, **43:** 243; Oct. 13, 1917, **44:** 372
Francis Bowes Sayre, April 5, 1917, **41:** 549; April 29, 1917, **42:** 158; June 21, 1917, **42:** 556
Jessie Woodrow Wilson Sayre, June 20, 1917, **42:** 551; Aug. 25, 1917, **44:** 55; March 26, 1918, **47:** 154; April 21, 1918, **47:** 392; Aug. 19, 1918, **49:** 292; Aug. 29, 1918, **49:** 388
Charles Scribner, Feb. 6, 1918, **46:** 259
Edward Wright Sheldon, March 9, 1917, **41:** 380; Oct. 17, 1917, **44:** 395; Oct. 25, 1917, **44:** 447; May 19, 1918, **48:** 66
Arthur Everett Shipley, April 5, 1918, **47:** 264
Mary Randolph Smith and Lucy Marshall Smith, Dec. 28, 1916, **40:** 347
James Sprunt, April 17, 1917, **42:** 86

Samuel Huston Thompson, Jr., Dec. 9, 1917, **45:** 255
Joseph Patrick Tumulty, July 10, 1917, **43:** 135; Dec. 27, 1917, **45:** 369

Charles Doolittle Walcott, Feb. 26, 1918, **46:** 461; March 1, 1918, **46:** 502
John Howell Westcott, Dec. 28, 1916, **40:** 347
Joseph R. Wilson, Jr., Nov. 23, 1916, **40:** 62; Dec. 22, 1917, **45:** 346
Margaret Woodrow Wilson, May 18, 1918, **48:** 60
Felexiana Shepherd Baker Woodrow, Nov. 23, 1916, **40:** 62; Dec. 28, 1917, **45:** 381; May 30, 1918, **48:** 203
James Woodrow, Feb. 7, 1917, **41:** 157

Interviews

A memorandum by Louis Paul Lochner about a talk with Wilson, Feb. 1, 1917, **41:** 89
A report about an interview with delegates from American peace societies, Feb. 28, 1917, **41:** 302
A memorandum by John Howard Whitehouse about a talk with Wilson, April 14, 1917, **42:** 65
An account by an unknown person about Wilson's conference with René Viviani and Marshal Joffre, April 30, 1917, **42:** 173, translation, 175
A memorandum by Spencer Cosby about a conversation between Wilson and Marshal Joffre, May 2, 1917, **42:** 186
A description of Wilson by Émile Hovelaque, May 2, 1917, **42:** 210
A memorandum by Jacob Judah Aaron de Haas about a conversation between Wilson and Louis Dembitz Brandeis, May 6, 1917, **42:** 234
A news report about a conference between Wilson and General Pershing, May 25, 1917, **42:** 391
A memorandum by George Lewis Bell about suggestions by Wilson for a program to offset the growth of the I.W.W., July 25, 1917, **43:** 280
A news report about a talk between Wilson and John Appleton Haven Hopkins on the suffrage pickets, Aug. 13, 1917, **43:** 436
A memorandum by Edmundo E. Martínez about a talk with Wilson on Mexican-American relations, Aug. 4, 1917, **43:** 378
A memorandum by Sir Thomas Royden and James Arthur Salter about a conference with Wilson on the shipping problem, July 26, 1917, **43:** 287
A memorandum by Sir William Wiseman about an interview with Wilson, July 13, 1917, **43:** 172
A memorandum by William Emmanuel Rappard about an interview with Woodrow Wilson, Nov. 1, 1917, **44:** 484
A memorandum of an interview with William Howard Taft, Dec. 12, 1917, **45:** 272

A memorandum by Lawrence Bennett about a conversation between Wilson and Vance Criswell McCormick, Dec. 27, 1917, **45:** 366

A proposed press release by the Woman's bureau of the National Democratic Committee about a conference between Wilson and the House steering committee for the woman suffrage amendment, Jan. 23, 1918, **46:** 80

A memorandum by Sir William Wiseman about an interview with Wilson, Jan. 23, 1918, **46:** 85

An account by James Weldon Johnson about a conference with Wilson, Feb. 19, 1918, **46:** 385

A memorandum by William Howard Taft about a conference at the White House, March 29, 1918, **47:** 198

An interview with Thomas Garrigue Masaryk about Japanese intervention in Siberia, June 19, 1918, **48:** 358

Memoranda by Homer Stillé Cummings about conferences at the White House about the domestic political situation, Oct. 11, 1918, **51:** 300; Oct. 20, 1918, **51:** 389; Nov. 8, 1918, **51:** 646

A memorandum by Jean Jules Jusserand about an interview with Wilson on the question of the armistice, Oct. 11, 1918, **51:** 307

A memorandum by Thomas William Lamont about a conversation at the White House, Oct. 4, 1918, **51:** 220

A memorandum by Sir William Wiseman about a conference with Wilson on the principles of a general peace, Oct. 16, 1918, **51:** 347

Press conferences

Dec. 18, 1916, **40:** 264; Jan. 8, 1917, **40:** 421; Jan. 15, 1917, **40:** 470; Jan. 23, 1917, **40:** 543; Jan. 30, 1917, **41:** 63; *see also The Complete Press Conferences*, March 22, 1913-July 10, 1919, **50:** 3-786.

News reports

Of a conference with Henry Pomeroy Davison about Allied loans, Nov. 21, 1916, **40:** 19

About plans of woman suffragists to picket the White House, Jan. 9, 1917, **40:** 426

About a meeting with the League for National Unity, Oct. 8, 1917, **44:** 325

About Wilson's disapproval of a Senate committee's handling of the inquiry into the sugar shortage, Dec. 25, 1917, **45:** 352

A statement by the Suffrage Committee of the House of Representatives about Wilson's support of the woman suffrage amendment, Jan. 9, 1918, **45:** 545

About an appeal by union leaders for the nationalization of the meat-packing industry, Jan. 18, 1918, **46:** 25

About a conference with senators on the war cabinet bill, Feb. 1, 1918, **46:** 204

About a visit to the premiere of "Friendly Enemies," March 4, 1918, **46:** 519

About Wilson's plan for economic aid to Russia, June 26, 1918, **48:** 432

About a reception of a delegation of suffragists at the White House, Oct. 3, 1918, **51:** 189

Writings

A last will and testament, May 31, 1917, **42:** 426

A preface to William North Rice's *From Darkness to Dawn*, July 3, 1917, **43:** 85

COLLATERAL MATERIALS

Political correspondence, reports, memoranda, and aide-mémoire

A memorandum by Frederic Winthrop Allen on the establishment of a Central Purchasing Commission, July 2, 1917, **43:** 77

A declaration by the Executive Council of the A. F. of L. on a proposed international socialist conference, Oct. 25, 1917, **44:** 483

A declaration of principles by Americans of German descent, May 4, 1918, **47:** 519

A memorandum by the American Union Against Militarism on the suppression of civil liberties, Aug. 13, 1917, **43:** 421

Newton Diehl Baker to Joseph Alfred Arner Burnquist, Dec. 4, 1917, **45:** 260

Newton Diehl Baker to Grosvenor Blaine Clarkson, April 17, 1918, **47:** 528

Newton Diehl Baker to Josephus Daniels, Nov. 8, 1917, **44:** 544

Newton Diehl Baker to Walter Sherman Gifford, June 30, 1917, **43:** 60

Newton Diehl Baker to Joseph Patrick Tumulty, Nov. 28, 1917, **45:** 155

A statement by Newton Diehl Baker on the general purpose of the President's Mediation Commission, Aug. 31, 1917, **44:** 104

A statement by Newton Diehl Baker about a conference with representatives of the steel industry, July 12, 1917, **43:** 155

Roger Nash Baldwin to Edward Mandell House, Feb. 18, 1918, **46:** 382

A memorandum by Roger Nash Baldwin about suppression of the liberal and radical press, Jan. 24, 1918, **46:** 382

G. D. Barclay to Marcus Aurelius Smith, July 7, 1917, **43:** 128

Bernard Mannes Baruch to Newton Diehl Baker, Feb. 4, 1918, **46:** 252

A memorandum by Bernard Mannes Baruch on price fixing, May 28, 1917, **42:** 414

Alexander Bruce Bielaski to William M. Offley, June 12, 1917, **42:** 513

A circular letter by Alexander Bruce Bielaski about the American
    Protective League, March 22, 1917, **42:** 512
Herbert Seely Bigelow to Newton Diehl Baker, Sept. 5, 1917, **44:** 158
Robert Worth Bingham to Joseph Patrick Tumulty, Sept. 17, 1918,
    51: 49
Gutzon Borglum to Joseph Patrick Tumulty, Nov. 14, 1917, **45:** 69;
    Nov. 22, 1917, **45:** 102; Feb. 12, 1918, **46:** 332; April 3, 1918, **47:** 235
James H. Brennan to Joseph Patrick Tumulty, Oct. 4, 1917, **44:** 307
James H. Brennan to the members of the International Brotherhood
    of Electrical Workers, Oct. 3, 1917, **44:** 307
Herbert Bruce Brougham to Irwin Hood Hoover, Jan. 1, 1917, **40:** 380
William Jennings Bryan to Joseph Patrick Tumulty, March 1, 1917,
    41: 309
Albert Sidney Burleson to Joseph Patrick Tumulty, May 11, 1918,
    47: 615
A proclamation by Joseph Alfred Arner Burnquist prohibiting the
    national convention of the People's Council of America in Minne-
    sota, Aug. 28, 1917, **44:** 78
Theodore Elijah Burton to Joseph Patrick Tumulty, July 13, 1918,
    48: 644

Thomas Edward Campbell to William Bauchop Wilson, Nov. 21,
    1917, **45:** 134
Carrie Clinton Lane Chapman Catt to Joseph Patrick Tumulty, May
    14, 1918, **48:** 25; June 8, 1918, **48:** 271
John Loomis Chamberlain to Newton Diehl Baker, Oct. 9, 1917, **44:**
    345
Drafts by the Civil Service Commission of an executive order barring
    disloyal persons from government service, April 5, 1917, **41:** 546,
    547
A draft by the Civil Service Commission of an executive order au-
    thorizing the removal from governmental service of persons sus-
    pected of disloyalty, April 5, 1917, **41:** 547
Frank Irving Cobb to Edward Mandell House, July 13, 1917, **43:** 167;
    Aug. 2, 1917, **43:** 366; Dec. 21, 1917, **45:** 340
Frank Irving Cobb to Joseph Patrick Tumulty, Sept. 5, 1918, **49:** 451
Robert S. Coleman to Louis Freeland Post, Dec. 5, 1917, **45:** 260
William Byron Colver to John Franklin Fort, May 16, 1918, **48:** 75
William Byron Colver to Joseph Patrick Tumulty, Sept. 11, 1917, **44:**
    206
A memorandum for the Federal Trade Commission by William By-
    ron Colver on the meat-packing industry, May 16, 1918, **48:** 76
A public statement on censorship by the Committee on Public Infor-
    mation, May 17, 1917, **42:** 304
A report of the Conference Committee of National Labor Adjustment
    Agencies, Oct. 14, 1918, **51:** 363
A memorandum by George Creel on the establishment of a bureau of
    publicity, April 11, 1917, **42:** 39

A memorandum by Enoch Herbert Crowder about the draft provisions of the National Defense Act, Dec. 26, 1916, **40:** 329

Frederick Asbury Cullen and others to Joseph Patrick Tumulty, Feb. 13, 1918, **46:** 339

Charles Curtis to Joseph Patrick Tumulty, Jan. 12, 1918, **45:** 577

An advertisement by the Democratic National Committee calling for the election of a Democratic Congress, Nov. 3, 1918, **51:** 572

John B. Densmore to Joseph Patrick Tumulty, Dec. 4, 1916, **40:** 154

Thomas Joseph Dillon to Ashmun Norris Brown, July 24, 1917, **43:** 267

Leonidas Carstarphen Dyer to Rudolph Forster, July 26, 1917, **43:** 284

Max Eastman to William Kent, May 31, 1918, **48:** 235

C. O. Edwards to Samuel Gompers, Aug. 2, 1917, **43:** 354

Everett E. Ellinwood to Marcus Aurelius Smith, July 7, 1917, **43:** 127

A proposed statement by the Federal Reserve Board on foreign credits, Nov. 27, 1916, **40:** 78, 87 (revision)

A memorandum by Scott Ferris on the water-power bill, Aug. 22, 1918, **49:** 316

John Franklin Fort to William Byron Colver, May 16, 1918, **48:** 44

Felix Frankfurter to Newton Diehl Baker, Dec. 25, 1917, **45:** 356

Felix Frankfurter to William Bauchop Wilson, Oct. 15, 1918, **51:** 363

A memorandum by Felix Frankfurter on western labor troubles, Sept. 4, 1917, **44:** 161

Thomas A. French to Samuel Gompers, July 19, 1917 (2), **43:** 231

A draft by Thomas Gallagher of a proposed House resolution about the creation of an independent Polish state, June 14, 1918, **48:** 312

Helen Hamilton Gardener to Thomas W. Brahany, July 26, 1917, **43:** 284

Helen Hamilton Gardener to Joseph Patrick Tumulty, Jan. 10, 1918, **45:** 565; Aug. 15, 1918, **49:** 264

A memorandum by Gilson Gardner on the imprisonment of the suffrage pickets, July 17, 1917, **43:** 201

Harry Augustus Garfield to Thomas Riley Marshall, Jan. 18, 1918, **46:** 31

Harry Augustus Garfield to Charles Spalding Thomas, March 20, 1918, **47:** 89

A statement by Harry Augustus Garfield on the fuel order, Jan. 18, 1918, **46:** 31

Cyrus Garnsey, Jr., and others to Harry Augustus Garfield, March 20, 1918, **47:** 89

John Palmer Gavit to Joseph Patrick Tumulty, Oct. 25, 1918, **51:** 483

James Watson Gerard to Robert Lansing, Sept. 1, 1918, **49:** 424

Samuel Gompers to J. L. Donnelly, Aug. 9, 1917, **43:** 416

Samuel Gompers to Joseph Patrick Tumulty, Oct. 25, 1917, **44:** 448;

Nov. 9, 1917, **44:** 556; March 23, 1918, **47:** 126; Aug. 13, 1918, **49:** 246

William Green to Samuel Gompers, Aug. 1, 1917, **43:** 353

Thomas Watt Gregory to Franklin Knight Lane, Feb. 21, 1917, **41:** 289

Thomas Watt Gregory to William Gibbs McAdoo, June 12, 1917, **42:** 510; Feb. 1918, **42:** 518

Thomas Watt Gregory to Claude Augustus Swanson, Feb. 26, 1917, **41:** 290

Thomas Watt Gregory to Joseph Patrick Tumulty, July 23, 1917, **43:** 253

A memorandum by Thomas Watt Gregory about new appointments to the Federal Trade Commission, Jan. 5, 1917, **40:** 417

David Wark Griffith to Edith Bolling Galt Wilson, June 14, 1918, **48:** 313

William Bayard Hale to Rudolph Forster, Nov. 2, 1917, **44:** 527

William Bayard Hale to Joseph Patrick Tumulty, April 18, 1918, **47:** 362

Glossbrenner Wallace William Hanger to William Lea Chambers, Oct. 26, 1917, **44:** 458

Francis Burton Harrison to Newton Diehl Baker, July 28, 1917, **44:** 8; Aug. 17, 1917, **44:** 9

Francis Burton Harrison to William Moulton Ingraham, Oct. 25, 1917, **44:** 446

Jesse Richardson Hildebrand to Joseph Patrick Tumulty, April 20, 1918, **47:** 388

James Ripley Wellman Hitchcock to Edward Mandell House, March 7, 1918, **46:** 570

W. E. Holm and F. J. Perry to Samuel Gompers, July 18, 1917, **43:** 230

Henry French Hollis to Elizabeth Merrill Bass, Dec. 20, 1917, **45:** 338

Henry French Hollis to Joseph Patrick Tumulty, June 12, 1917, **42:** 495

William R. Hollister to Josephus Daniels, March 23, 1918, **47:** 129

Herbert Clark Hoover to Lord Reading, Feb. 26, 1918, **46:** 461

Herbert Clark Hoover to Joseph Patrick Tumulty, June 1, 1917, **42:** 437; Sept. 12, 1917, **44:** 191; Sept. 18, 1917, **44:** 215; Jan. 26, 1918, **46:** 109; May 27, 1918, **48:** 166

David Franklin Houston to Albert Sidney Burleson, June 7, 1918, **48:** 259

David Franklin Houston to Joseph Patrick Tumulty, April 26, 1918, **47:** 449

Edward Nash Hurley to Samuel Gompers, Sept. 21, 1917, **44:** 234

Edward Nash Hurley to Joseph Patrick Tumulty, Oct. 1, 1917, **44:** 289

A memorandum by William Hugh Johnston on the Bridgeport strike, Sept. 12, 1918, **49:** 537

CONTENTS   87

Mary Harris (Mother) Jones to Edward Mandell House, Dec. 9, 1916, **40:** 207

Frank Billings Kellogg to Herbert Clark Hoover, Sept. 18, 1918, **51:** 70
John Benjamin Kendrick to Franklin Knight Lane, Dec. 17, 1916, **40:** 263
Taylor Kennerly to Joseph Patrick Tumulty, Jan. 21, 1918, **46:** 63
A memorandum by Sir Stephenson Hamilton Kent on the labor situation, Nov. 8, 1917, **44:** 563
William Kent to Norman Hapgood, Nov. 29, 1916, **40:** 173
Hugh Leo Kerwin to Joseph Patrick Tumulty, Aug. 28, 1917, **44:** 80; Sept. 10, 1917, **44:** 183
Alexander Konta to Frank Irving Cobb, Nov. 26, 1917, **45:** 135

William Harmong Lamar to Albert Sidney Burleson, Aug. 8, 1917, **43:** 394
Franklin Knight Lane to George Whitfield Lane, March 6, 1917, **41:** 350
Franklin Knight Lane to Hoke Smith and William Joseph Sears, March 14, 1918, **47:** 30
A memorandum by Franklin Knight Lane on the congressional election campaign, Nov. 6, 1918, **51:** 616
Robert Lansing to Breckinridge Long, Jan. 8, 1917, **40:** 425
Robert Lansing to Frank Lyon Polk, Sept. 6, 1918, **49:** 465
Robert Lansing to Edward North Smith, June 12, 1917, **42:** 490
Robert Lansing to Joseph Patrick Tumulty, Oct. 18, 1917, **44:** 398; Nov. 6, 1917, **44:** 524
Asbury Francis Lever to David Franklin Houston, Aug. 20-21, 1917, **44:** 10
James Hamilton Lewis to Robert Lansing, March 12, 1917, **41:** 393
Liliuokalani to Lucius Eugene Pinkham, Aug. 17, 1917, **43:** 506
A memorandum by Walter Lippmann on the adjustment of labor disputes in private shipyards, Sept. 19, 1917, **44:** 219

William Gibbs McAdoo to Thomas Watt Gregory, June 2, 1917, **42:** 441; Jan. 5, 1918, **42:** 519
William Gibbs McAdoo to Claude Kitchin, Aug. 1, 1918, **49:** 163
William Gibbs McAdoo to Robert Lansing, Feb. 6, 1917, **41:** 132
William Gibbs McAdoo to Furnifold McLendel Simmons, May 8, 1918, **47:** 562; Oct. 3, 1918, **51:** 204
A statement by William Gibbs McAdoo on the bond bill, April 9, 1917, **42:** 25
A proposed statement by William Gibbs McAdoo on the crisis in the security markets, Dec. 14, 1917, **45:** 287
John McBride to William Bauchop Wilson, June 26, 1917 (2), **43:** 17
Frank McIntyre to Newton Diehl Baker, May 15, 1918, **48:** 35
Frank McIntyre to Francis Burton Harrison, Aug. 17, 1917, **44:** 8
Gavin McNab to Edward Mandell House, April 20, 1918, **47:** 388

Robert Malachi McWade to Louis Freeland Post, Dec. 1, 1917, **45:** 184

Victorino Mapa to Francis Burton Harrison, Aug. 17, 1917, **44:** 9

Benjamin C. Marsh to William Byron Colver, Sept. 10, 1917, **44:** 206

Royal Meeker to Joseph Patrick Tumulty, Sept. 4, 1918, **49:** 445

Edwin Thomas Meredith to Joseph Patrick Tumulty, Oct. 1, 1917, **44:** 289

A resolution by the Metal Mine Workers' Union of Butte, Montana, on the Bisbee deportations, July 25, 1917, **43:** 339

Robert Hugh Morris to Joseph Patrick Tumulty, Aug. 29, 1918, **49:** 420

Robert Russa Moton to Joseph Patrick Tumulty, July 18, 1917, **43:** 208

Resolutions by the National Consumers' League, Nov. 20, 1916, **40:** 7

James Brown Neale to Harry Augustus Garfield, July 31, 1918, **49:** 144

"A Program for Labor," *The New Republic*, April 14, 1917, **42:** 135

Lucius William Nieman to Joseph Patrick Tumulty, July 27, 1917, **43:** 319

A. H. Nowaka to Newton Diehl Baker, Oct. 9, 1917, **44:** 344

John Lord O'Brian to Thomas Watt Gregory, April 18, 1918, **47:** 363

Santiago Iglesias Pantín to Samuel Gompers, Dec. 4, 1916, **40:** 146

Maud May Wood Park to Helen Hamilton Gardener, Nov. 24, 1917, **45:** 121

James Parker to Newton Diehl Baker, Aug. 24, 1917, **44:** 41

Andrew James Peters to William Bauchop Wilson, July 24, 1917, **43:** 267

Amos Richards Eno Pinchot to Joseph Patrick Tumulty, July 14, 1917, **43:** 175

Louis Freeland Post to Charles Lee Swem, Dec. 1, 1917, **45:** 184

Louis Freeland Post to Joseph Patrick Tumulty, Nov. 24, 1917, **45:** 117; Nov. 26, 1917, **45:** 125

Louis Freeland Post to William Bauchop Wilson, Nov. 14, 1917, **45:** 60

Edward William Pou to Joseph Patrick Tumulty, April 11, 1917, **42:** 42

Percy L. Prentis to William Bauchop Wilson, July 24, 1917, **43:** 267

John White Preston to Thomas Watt Gregory, July 23, 1917, **43:** 254

John White Preston to Maurice L. Oppenheim, July 9, 1917, **43:** 254

A memorandum from William Cox Redfield suggesting appointment of a federal advisory commission on public utilities, Aug. 2, 1918, **49:** 159

James Reed to the editor of the *American Swineherd*, Aug. 15, 1917, **44:** 37

A statement by the Republican conference of the House of Representatives in support of the woman suffrage amendment, Jan. 21,
1918, **46:** 61

Allen W. Ricker to Edward Mandell House, April 25, 1918, **47:** 437;
April 30, 1918, **47:** 471

Walter Stowell Rogers to George Creel, Aug. 13, 1917, **43:** 456

Daniel Calhoun Roper to Joseph Patrick Tumulty, Sept. 3, 1918, **49:**
438

George Rublee to Edward Mandell House, Jan. 27, 1917, **41:** 45; Jan.
26, 1917, **41:** 46

Isaac K. Russell to Joseph Patrick Tumulty, Sept. 17, 1918, **51:** 49

A resolution by Willard Saulsbury about the use of American ports
by belligerent warships, Feb. 14, 1917, **41:** 226

Henry Rogers Seager to Royal Meeker, Nov. 28, 1917, **45:** 150

Louis Seibold to Joseph Patrick Tumulty, Feb. 14, 1918, **46:** 347

Two polls of senators and congressmen on the woman suffrage
amendment, July 19, 1917, **43:** 214; Jan. 21, 1918, **46:** 61

Anna Howard Shaw to Alice Edith Binsse Warren, March 9, 1917,
41: 399

John R. Shillady to Joseph Patrick Tumulty, Feb. 18, 1918, **46:** 380

Edward North Smith to Robert Lansing, June 7, 1917, **42:** 469

John J. Spurgeon to Robert Lansing, Oct. 25, 1917, **44:** 524

John J. Spurgeon to Joseph Patrick Tumulty, April 6, 1918, **47:** 278

Augustus Owsley Stanley to Joseph Patrick Tumulty, Sept. 7, 1918,
49: 486

A memorandum by Lincoln Steffens on growing class antagonisms in
the United States, Dec. 28, 1917, **45:** 381

William Joel Stone to Robert Lansing, Feb. 13, 1917, **41:** 225

Benjamin Strong to Joseph Patrick Tumulty, Oct. 9, 1917, **44:** 346;
Oct. 10, 1917, **44:** 351

A memorandum by George M. Sutton on censorship in the Post Office
Department, Aug. 15, 1917, **43:** 480

A suggestion by Claude Augustus Swanson for the settlement of the
California oil land controversy, Feb. 21, 1917, **41:** 289

Charles Lee Swem to Albert Sidney Burleson, Oct. 8, 1917, **44:** 338

Charles Lee Swem to Joseph Patrick Tumulty, May 16, 1918, **48:** 32;
July 8, 1918, **48:** 564

Charles Lee Swem to the White House staff, June 28, 1918, **48:** 463

Herbert Bayard Swope to Joseph Patrick Tumulty, March 17, 1918,
47: 51

William Howard Taft to William Bauchop Wilson, Oct. 15, 1918, **51:**
367

William Howard Taft and Francis Patrick Walsh to William
Bauchop Wilson, Sept. 10, 1918, **49:** 520

Charles Spalding Thomas to Joseph Patrick Tumulty, May 3, 1918,
47: 511

Albert Lee Thurman to William Cox Redfield, Aug. 18, 1917, **43:** 519
Worth Marion Tippy to Newton Diehl Baker, March 5, 1917, **41:** 353
Helen Todd to Rudolph Forster, Aug. 20, 1917, **43:** 536
Frank Trumbull to Edward Mandell House, July 21, 1917, **43:** 242
Joseph Patrick Tumulty to Richard Manuel Bolden, July 10, 1917, **43:** 139
Joseph Patrick Tumulty to Albert Sidney Burleson, Sept. 15, 1917, **44:** 204
Joseph Patrick Tumulty to the Just Government League of Maryland, April 24, 1917, **42:** 124
Joseph Patrick Tumulty to John Spargo, Nov. 15, 1917, **45:** 68
Joseph Patrick Tumulty to John J. Spurgeon, April 9, 1918 (draft), **47:** 279
Joseph Patrick Tumulty to Lillian D. Wald, Nov. 12, 1917, **45:** 39

Oswald Garrison Villard to Joseph Patrick Tumulty, July 20, 1917, **43:** 239; Sept. 26, 1917, **44:** 271; Sept. 17, 1918, **51:** 57; Sept. 18, 1918, **51:** 57; Sept. 20, 1918, **51:** 84; Nov. 8, 1918, **51:** 646

Thomas James Walsh to Joseph Patrick Tumulty, May 31, 1918, **48:** 217
Lester Aglar Walton to Joseph Patrick Tumulty, June 12, 1918, **48:** 302
A report by the War Labor Conference Board, March 29, 1918, **47:** 248
A memorandum by Louis Brandeis Wehle on coordinating the labor policies of the War and Navy Departments, Aug. 9, 1917, **45:** 10
Henry Middleton White and Edgar Callender Snyder to William Bauchop Wilson, Aug. 21, 1917, **44:** 50
Vira Boarman Whitehouse to Joseph Patrick Tumulty, Oct. 13, 1917, **44:** 384; Oct. 27, 1917, **44:** 460
Daniel Willard to Joseph Patrick Tumulty, Jan. 15, 1918, **45:** 600; April 25, 1918, **47:** 437
Joseph R. Wilson, Jr., to Charles Theodore Cates, Jr., March 14, 1918 (draft), **47:** 34
Philip Whitwell Wilson to the London *Daily News*, April 8, 1918, **47:** 297
William Bauchop Wilson to Newton Diehl Baker, June 22, 1917, **42:** 563
William Bauchop Wilson to Wesley Livsey Jones, Jan. 25, 1918, **46:** 107
William Bauchop Wilson to Percy L. Prentis, July 24, 1917, **43:** 267
William Bauchop Wilson to Joseph Patrick Tumulty, March 13, 1917, **41:** 402; March 15, 1917 (2), **41:** 412, 413; July 24, 1917, **43:** 266; Aug. 21, 1917, **44:** 22; Sept. 19, 1917, **44:** 223; Sept. 26, 1917, **44:** 268; Sept. 28, 1917 (2), **44:** 276, 277
A memorandum by William Bauchop Wilson about a conference on the housing problem, Jan. 30, 1918, **46:** 171

A statement by William Bauchop Wilson at the first meeting of the War Labor Conference Board, Feb. 25, 1918, **46:** 578

Robert Wickliffe Woolley to Edward Mandell House, July 14, 1917, **43:** 197

Robert Wickliffe Woolley to Joseph Patrick Tumulty, Sept. 23, 1918, **51:** 113

Peter Christopher Yorke to the Department of Justice, June 30, 1917, **43:** 216

Diplomatic correspondence, reports, memoranda, and aide-mémoire

Carl William Ackerman to Edward Mandell House, Jan. 30, 1918, **46:** 172; Feb. 4, 1918, **46:** 556; May 4, 1918, **47:** 523

Edwin Anderson Alderman to David Franklin Houston, March 22, 1917, **41:** 503

Alfonso XIII to Charles I, March 5, 1918, **47:** 177

A memorandum by the Allied governments on the correspondence between Wilson and the German government, Nov. 4, 1918, **51:** 581

A memorandum by the Allied Prime Ministers and Colonel House about the procedure for an armistice with Germany, Nov. 4, 1918, **51:** 580

A report by a commission of the American Federation of Labor on the situation in Mexico, July 18, 1918, **49:** 26

Meetings and reports of the American-Mexican Joint High Commission concerning troop withdrawal and border control, Nov. 23, 1916, **40:** 54; Nov. 22, 1916, **40:** 116; Nov. 24, 1916, **40:** 282; Dec. 18, 1916, **40:** 280; Dec. 19, 1916, **40:** 301; Jan. 15, 1917, **40:** 478

Memoranda by Chandler Parsons Anderson on the inauguration of Venustiano Carranza as President of Mexico, April 25, 1917 (2), **42:** 131, 132

D. Anderson to John Palmer Gavit, Dec. 1, 1916, **40:** 125

Count Julius Andrássy to Robert Lansing, Oct. 30, 1918, **51:** 526

A memorandum by Norman Angell on politics and military affairs, March 3, 1918, **48:** 614

A proposal by Norman Angell for a conference of the Allies as the nucleus for a postwar league of nations, Aug. 6, 1917, **43:** 401

The Argentine Foreign Ministry to Rómulo Sebastian Naón, May 17, 1917, **42:** 359

Gordon Auchincloss to Edith Bolling Galt Wilson, March 18, 1918, **47:** 59

A memorandum by Gordon Auchincloss about British opinion of the Sisson documents, Oct. 4, 1918, **51:** 246

Joseph Allen Baker to Arthur James Balfour, April 2, 1917, **41:** 532

Newton Diehl Baker to Tasker Howard Bliss, Oct. 21, 1918, **51:** 399; Nov. 1, 1918, **51:** 544

Newton Diehl Baker to David Rowland Francis, March 31, 1917, **41:** 511
Newton Diehl Baker to Frederick Funston, Nov. 28, 1916, **40:** 101
Newton Diehl Baker to Francis Burton Harrison, Feb. 7, 1917, **41:** 153
Newton Diehl Baker to William Gibbs McAdoo, Jan. 4, 1918, **45:** 532
Newton Diehl Baker to John Joseph Pershing, Nov. 1, 1918, **51:** 545; Nov. 5, 1918, **51:** 596
A statement by Newton Diehl Baker on the status of German ships in the Philippines and the Panama Canal Zone, Feb. 7, 1917, **41:** 152
Memoranda by Boris Aleksandrovich Bakhmet'ev on the conditions in Russia, Dec. 14, 1917, **45:** 288; Nov. 1, 1918, **51:** 542
Karl F. Baldwin to the Department of State, July 23, 1918, **49:** 107
Arthur James Balfour to Colville Adrian de Rune Barclay, Oct. 13, 1918 (3), **51:** 335, 336; Oct. 21, 1918, **51:** 411
Arthur James Balfour to Sir George William Buchanan, Dec. 3, 1917, **45:** 188
Arthur James Balfour to Lord Robert Cecil, May 23, 1917, **42:** 385; May 27, 1917, **42:** 428; June 3, 1917, **42:** 445
Arthur James Balfour to Count de Salis, Aug. 21, 1917, **44:** 23
Arthur James Balfour to the Foreign Office, May 23, 1917, **42:** 385
Arthur James Balfour to Sir William Conyngham Greene, March 26, 1918 (draft), **47:** 156
Arthur James Balfour to Edward Mandell House, June 28, 1917, **43:** 38; July 8, 1917, **43:** 125; July 20, 1917, **43:** 223; Aug. 22, 1917, **44:** 30; Oct. 5, 1917, **44:** 311; Oct. 6, 1917, **44:** 323; Oct. 8, 1917, **44:** 342; Oct. 11, 1917, **44:** 362; Oct. 14, 1917, **44:** 382; Oct. 15, 1917, **44:** 391; Feb. 7, 1918, **46:** 271; Feb. 27, 1918, **46:** 483; March 6, 1918, **46:** 576; March 7, 1918, **46:** 577; March 13, 1918, **47:** 11; March 22, 1918, **47:** 122; April 2, 1918, **47:** 227; April 3, 1918, **47:** 239
Arthur James Balfour to Robert Lansing, May 9, 1917, **42:** 264
Arthur James Balfour to Walter Hines Page, Aug. 16, 1917, **44:** 70
Arthur James Balfour to Lord Reading, Feb. 22, 1918, **46:** 419; Feb. 26, 1918 (2), **46:** 470, 472; March 11, 1918, **46:** 605; April 17, 1918, **47:** 355; April 18, 1918, **47:** 366; April 23, 1918, **47:** 412; May 7, 1918, **47:** 552; May 11, 1918 (2), **47:** 606, 607; May 15, 1918, **48:** 99; May 21, 1918, **48:** 114; June 20, 1918, **48:** 379; July 22, 1918 (2), **49:** 57, 58
Arthur James Balfour to Sir Cecil Arthur Spring Rice, Jan. 13, 1917, **40:** 500
Arthur James Balfour to Sir William Wiseman, June 28, 1917, **43:** 38; Oct. 5, 1917 (2), **44:** 311, 312; Oct. 6, 1917, **44:** 323; Oct. 8, 1917, **44:** 342; Oct. 14, 1917, **44:** 382; Feb. 2, 1918, **46:** 220; April 3, 1918, **47:** 239; Sept. 17, 1918, **51:** 64
A memorandum by Arthur James Balfour on the discussions of the British commission in the United States, May 24, 1917, **42:** 396
Colville Adrian de Rune Barclay to Arthur James Balfour, Sept. 13, 1918 (2), **49:** 550, 551; Oct. 19, 1918, **51:** 389

Colville Adrian de Rune Barclay to the British Foreign Office, Aug. 28, 1918, **49:** 373; Sept. 9, 1918, **49:** 508; Sept. 20, 1918, **51:** 85; Oct. 7, 1918, **51:** 263; Nov. 3, 1918, **51:** 574

Colville Adrian de Rune Barclay to Robert Lansing, July 1, 1917, **43:** 67; Aug. 3, 1918, **49:** 178

Memoranda by Colville Adrian de Rune Barclay about the proposed Japanese intervention in Siberia, Jan. 28, 1918, **46:** 154; Feb. 6, 1918, **46:** 270

Georg Barthelme to the *Kölnische Zeitung*, Feb. 5, 1917, **41:** 149

A peace program by the Bavarian government, July 5, 1918, **48:** 553

George Bell, Jr., to Frederick Funston, Nov. 30, 1916, **40:** 109

Henri Bergson to Aristide Briand, March 3, 1917, **41:** 315; translation, 316

Henri Bergson to Stéphen Jean Marie Pichon, June 26, 1918, **48:** 441; July 26, 1918, **49:** 112

A memorandum by Henri Bergson about an interview with Wilson on intervention in Siberia, July 25, 1918, **49:** 94

Count Johann Heinrich von Bernstorff to Theobald von Bethmann Hollweg, Jan. 16, 1917, **40:** 504; translation, 505; Jan. 27, 1917, **41:** 49; translation, 51

Count Johann Heinrich von Bernstorff to the German Foreign Office about the Allied decision to arm merchant vessels, Dec. 10, 1916, **40:** 452

Count Johann Heinrich von Bernstorff to the German Foreign Office, Dec. 29, 1916, **40:** 362; translation, 364

Count Johann Heinrich von Bernstorff to Edward Mandell House, Nov. 20, 1916, **40:** 39; Nov. 23, 1916, **40:** 75; Dec. 9, 1916, **40:** 212; Jan. 18, 1917, **40:** 525; Jan. 20, 1917, **40:** 528; Jan. 31, 1917, **41:** 80; Feb. 3, 1917, **41:** 117

Count Johann Heinrich von Bernstorff to Robert Lansing, Dec. 8, 1916, **40:** 191; Jan. 10, 1917, **40:** 448; Jan. 31, 1917, **41:** 74

A memorandum by Count Johann Heinrich von Bernstorff about the Allied decision to arm merchant vessels, Jan. 10, 1917, **40:** 448

Theobald von Bethmann Hollweg to Count Johann Heinrich von Bernstorff, Jan. 29, 1917, **41:** 59; translation, 61

A statement by Alexander Birkenheim about urging Allied intervention in Siberia, June 12, 1918, **48:** 359

Robert Woods Bliss to the Department of State, Sept. 27, 1918, **51:** 134; Sept. 28, 1918, **51:** 155

Tasker Howard Bliss to Newton Diehl Baker, Feb. 25, 1918, **46:** 453; Feb. 21, 1918, **47:** 12; Oct. 9, 1918, **51:** 425; Oct. 23, 1918 (2), **51:** 434, 583; Nov. 3, 1918, **51:** 571

Tasker Howard Bliss to Newton Diehl Baker and Peyton Conway March, Sept. 15, 1918, **51:** 33; Oct. 7, 1918, **51:** 261; Oct. 8, 1918, **51:** 272; Oct. 31, 1918, **51:** 544

Tasker Howard Bliss to Robert Lansing, Feb. 15, 1918, **46:** 352; May 7, 1918, **47:** 570

Tasker Howard Bliss to Robert Lansing and others, April 12, 1918, **47:** 332; Oct. 8, 1918, **51:** 272

Tasker Howard Bliss to Henry Pinckney McCain, Feb. 19, 1918, **46:** 391

Proposals by the Brazilian Government of a protocol complementary to and a new preamble to the Pan-American Treaty of guarantee, April 19, 1917, **42:** 99, 100

George Tom Molesworth Bridges to Lord Reading, June 18, 1918, **48:** 352

The British Embassy to the Department of State, Feb. 12, 1918, **46:** 333

The British Embassy at Petrograd to Sir William Wiseman, Oct. 10, 1917, **44:** 387

A memorandum by the British Foreign Office about the need for Japanese intervention in Siberia, March 29, 1918, **47:** 243; Aug. 12, 1918, **49:** 248

The British Foreign Office to Sir William Conyngham Greene, March 4, 1918, **46:** 548

The British Foreign Office to Lord Northcliffe, Aug. 14, 1917, **44:** 16

The British Foreign Office to Lord Reading, March 20, 1918, **47:** 92

The British Foreign Office to Sir Cecil Arthur Spring Rice, May 19, 1917, **42:** 354; July 30, 1917, **43:** 326

The British Foreign Office to Sir William Wiseman, Oct. 2, 1917, **44:** 298; Oct. 15, 1917, **44:** 385

A memorandum by the British Foreign Office on Allied policy in Russia, Dec. 29, 1917, **45:** 417

A memorandum by the British Foreign Office about a conference between Robert Hamilton Bruce Lockhart and Leon Trotsky, April 2, 1918, **47:** 245

A memorandum by the British Government on the Russian situation, June 8, 1917, **42:** 463

A list of American banks participating in secured British loans, July 13, 1917, **43:** 196

William Jennings Bryan to Joseph Patrick Tumulty, Nov. 30, 1916, **40:** 111

James Viscount Bryce to Edward Mandell House, Jan. 14, 1917, **40:** 468; Jan. 24, 1917, **41:** 217; July 28, 1917, **43:** 498

James Viscount Bryce to Theodore Marburg, May 1, 1918, **47:** 507

Sir George William Buchanan to the Foreign Office, Aug. 5, 1917, **43:** 371; Aug. 6, 1917, **43:** 387

William Hepburn Buckler to Edward Mandell House, Nov. 24, 1916, **40:** 180; Dec. 7, 1916, **40:** 187; Dec. 22, 1916, **40:** 413; Jan. 5, 1917, **40:** 494; Feb. 23, 1917, **41:** 374; May 10, 1917, **42:** 435; Nov. 3, 1917, **44:** 546; Nov. 30, 1917, **45:** 174

A memorandum by William Hepburn Buckler about a conversation with Lord Milner, Nov. 3, 1917, **44:** 546

Arthur Bullard to George Creel, Feb. 18, 1918, **47:** 522

Arthur Bullard to Robert Lansing, May 22, 1917, **42:** 378; June 13, 1917, **42:** 508

William Christian Bullitt to Edward Mandell House, May 20, 1918, **48:** 144

Memoranda by William Christian Bullitt: Count von Hertling's
    Reichstag speech, Jan. 29, 1918, **46:** 162; the political situation in
    Germany, Jan. 31, 1918, **46:** 183; a comparison of the addresses of
    Count von Hertling and Count Czernin, Feb. 3, 1918, **46:** 222;
    strikes in Germany, Feb. 7, 1918, **46:** 266; on the proposed Japa-
    nese intervention in Siberia, March 2, 1918, **46:** 510; the political
    situation in Germany and Austria-Hungary, March 6, 1918, **46:**
    567; the Bolshevik movement in Europe, Nov. 2, 1918, **51:** 563;
    Nov. 6, 1918, **51:** 622
Richard Carlton Bundy to the Department of State, April 10, 1918
    (4), **47:** 315, 316, 317
Henry Marison Byllesby to William Gibbs McAdoo, March 31, 1917,
    41: 514

Estrada Cabrera to Joaquín Méndez, Oct. 8, 1917, **44:** 331
Luis Cabrera and others to Franklin Knight Lane and others, Dec.
    18, 1916 (2), **40:** 285, 393; Dec. 27, 1916, **40:** 394
John Kenneth Caldwell to the Department of State, July 18, 1918,
    49: 42
Jules Martin Cambon to William Graves Sharp, Jan. 5, 1918, **45:** 492
Ronald Hugh Campbell to Edward Mandell House, Jan. 2, 1918, **45:**
    430
Lord Robert Cecil to Colville Adrian de Rune Barclay, Oct. 31, 1918,
    51: 539
Lord Robert Cecil to the British Embassy, Jan. 1, 1918, **45:** 420; Oct.
    9, 1918 (3), **51:** 288, 289, 290
Lord Robert Cecil to Edward Mandell House, Sept. 4, 1917, **44:** 150;
    Feb. 16, 1918, **47:** 103; July 8, 1918, **48:** 566; July 22, 1918, **49:** 225;
    Sept. 30, 1918, **51:** 164
Lord Robert Cecil to Sir Cecil Arthur Spring Rice, June 4, 1917, **42:**
    450
Lord Robert Cecil to Sir Cecil Arthur Spring Rice and Arthur James
    Balfour, May 26, 1917, **42:** 428
Lord Robert Cecil to Sir William Wiseman, Aug. 19, 1918, **49:** 548
A resolution by the Central Committee of the Constitutional Demo-
    cratic party about Allied intervention in Russia, June 10, 1918, **48:**
    364
Charles I to Alfonso XIII, Feb. 18, 1918, **46:** 397
Georgii Vasil'evich Chicherin to David Rowland Francis, June 5,
    1918, **48:** 265
A report by the Chief Cable Censor on the outbreak of revolution in
    Germany, Nov. 6, 1918, **51:** 607
Georges Clemenceau to Jean Jules Jusserand, June 24, 1918, **48:** 416
Frank Irving Cobb to Edward Mandell House, July 17, 1917, **43:** 198;
    July 18, 1917, **43:** 219; July 26, 1917, **43:** 285; Oct. 29, 1918, **51:** 504
Frank Irving Cobb to Theodor Wolff, Aug. 8, 1917, **43:** 411
A memorandum by Frank Irving Cobb about possible attendance by
    Wilson at peace conference, Nov. 4, 1918, **51:** 590

Bainbridge Colby to William Howard Taft, March 23, 1918, **47:** 147, 199; March 14, 1918, **47:** 198

Bainbridge Colby to Joseph Patrick Tumulty, Dec. 21, 1917, **45:** 340

Lincoln Ross Colcord to Edward Mandell House, June 20, 1917, **42:** 554

Charles Richard Crane to Richard Crane, May 5, 1917, **42:** 232; July 6, 1917, **43:** 149; July 21, 1917, **43:** 298

Charles Richard Crane to Joseph Patrick Tumulty, Feb. 21, 1918, **46:** 411; March 12, 1918, **46:** 619

Richard Crane to Joseph Patrick Tumulty, July 11, 1917, **43:** 149

Sir Richard Crawford to the Foreign Office, Feb. 15, 1917, **41:** 256

George Creel to Edgar Grant Sisson, Dec. 3, 1917, **45:** 194

A proposed budget by George Creel for a news bureau in Russia, Aug. 20, 1917, **43:** 526

Herbert David Croly to Edward Mandell House, Dec. 29, 1916, **40:** 359; April 17, 1917, **42:** 89

Oscar Terry Crosby to William Gibbs McAdoo, Dec. 3, 1917, **45:** 245; Dec. 7, 1917, **45:** 245; Dec. 24, 1917, **45:** 351; Feb. 14, 1918, **46:** 359

Count Ottokar Czernin von und zu Chudenitz to Robert Lansing, Feb. 5, 1917, **41:** 129

Count Ottokar Czernin von und zu Chudenitz to Prince Karl Emil zu Fürstenberg, Feb. 18, 1918, **46:** 397; Feb. 21, 1918, **46:** 412; March 23, 1918, **47:** 124

A memorandum by Count Ottokar Czernin von und zu Chudenitz about a possible peace between Austria-Hungary and the Allies, April 3, 1918, **47:** 239

Domicio da Gama to Robert Lansing, June 14, 1917, **42:** 548

Josephus Daniels to Austin Melvin Knight, March 29, 1918, **47:** 162

Marcel Delanney to the French Foreign Ministry, June 18, 1918, **48:** 355

Frederick Dixon to Edward Mandell House, Feb. 15, 1917, **41:** 235

Henry Percival Dodge to the Department of State, March 8, 1918, **47:** 36

A memorandum by Frank Nelson Doubleday about an interview with Baron Shimpei Gotō, March 22, 1918, **48:** 461

Sir Eric Drummond to Arthur James Balfour, Nov. 15, 1917, **45:** 68

Sir Eric Drummond to Edward Mandell House, April 5, 1917, **41:** 545

Sir Eric Drummond to Sir Cecil Arthur Spring Rice, Jan. 12, 1918, **45:** 577

Sir Eric Drummond to Sir William Wiseman, June 26, 1917, **43:** 20; Jan. 30, 1918, **46:** 181; Feb. 7, 1918, **46:** 272; Feb. 22, 1918, **46:** 419; March 26, 1918, **47:** 156; April 2, 1918, **47:** 227; April 3, 1918, **47:** 239; Aug. 17, 1918, **49:** 280; Sept. 12, 1918, **49:** 537

Charles Jerome Edwards to Edward Mandell House, May 21, 1918, **48:** 153

Maurice Francis Egan to Robert Lansing, March 16, 1917, **41:** 430

Maurice Francis Egan to the New York *Evening Mail*, April 7, 1917, **42:** 22

Wilhelm August Ferdinand Ekengren to Robert Lansing, Oct. 7, 1918, **51:** 258; Oct. 29, 1918, **51:** 505; Oct. 30, 1918, **51:** 526

A memorandum by Wilhelm August Ferdinand Ekengren about a proposed conference of neutrals, Nov. 23, 1916, **40:** 47

Rafael Héctor Elizalde to Robert Lansing, Feb. 19, 1917, **41:** 249

William Thomas Ellis to Josephus Daniels, June 21, 1918, **48:** 410

Enver Pasha to Henry Morgenthau, June 7, 1917, **42:** 463

Henry Prather Fletcher to Robert Lansing, Feb. 21, 1917, **41:** 350; March 10, 1917, **41:** 392; April 10, 1917, **42:** 37; April 23, 1917, **42:** 132; Aug. 2, 1917, **43:** 384; March 13, 1918, **47:** 163; April 3, 1918, **47:** 345

David Rowland Francis to the Department of State, June 21, 1917, **43:** 13; July 6, 1917, **43:** 149; July 21, 1917, **43:** 298

David Rowland Francis to Robert Lansing, March 14, 1917, **41:** 409; April 10, 1917, **42:** 37; April 24, 1917, **42:** 273; May 11, 1917, **42:** 319; May 14, 1917, **42:** 320; Nov. 7, 1917, **44:** 532; Nov. 24, 1917, **45:** 119; Dec. 31, 1917, **45:** 411; Feb. 13, 1918, **46:** 341; Feb. 11, 1918, **46:** 358; May 11, 1918, **48:** 112; May 16, 1918, **48:** 141; June 5, 1918, **48:** 265; June 3, 1918, **48:** 277; Sept. 3, 1918, **49:** 495

Felix Frankfurter to Robert Lansing, Aug. 7, 1917, **43:** 442

Arthur Hugh Frazier to Edward Mandell House, June 1, 1917, **42:** 437; June 22, 1917, **43:** 275; Oct. 12, 1917, **44:** 462

Arthur Hugh Frazier to Robert Lansing, Feb. 16, 1917, **41:** 376; Feb. 23, 1918, **46:** 429

Arthur Hugh Frazier to Robert Lansing and Edward Mandell House, Feb. 19, 1918, **46:** 388

Arthur Hugh Frazier to William Graves Sharp, Feb. 2, 1918, **46:** 233

The French Foreign Ministry to Jean Jules Jusserand, Feb. 27, 1918, **46:** 476

A draft by the French government of a joint declaration about the creation of an independent Polish state, March 8, 1918, **46:** 587

A statement by the French Socialist minority on self-determination, May 6, 1917, **42:** 364

Frederick Funston to Newton Diehl Baker, Nov. 28, 1916, **40:** 100; Nov. 30, 1916, **40:** 109; Dec. 9, 1916, **40:** 202

Prince Karl Emil zu Fürstenberg to Count Ottokar Czernin von und zu Chudenitz, Feb. 20, 1918, **46:** 411; March 5, 1918, **46:** 551

Pietro Cardinal Gasparri to Count de Salis, Sept. 28, 1917, **44:** 348

Sir Eric Geddes to David Lloyd George, Oct. 13, 1918 (2), **51:** 325, 327

James Watson Gerard to Robert Lansing, Dec. 26, 1916, **40:** 331; Jan. 2, 1917, **40:** 383; Jan. 21, 1917, **40:** 552; Jan. 3, 1917, **40:** 554; Jan. 31, 1917, **41:** 79; Feb. 4, 1917, **41:** 137

A memorandum by James Watson Gerard about interviews with William II, June 15, 1917, **42:** 521

A note verbale by the German government on armed merchantmen, Jan. 20, 1917, **40:** 553

Samuel Gompers to Edmundo E. Martínez, Aug. 13, 1917, **43:** 449

Samuel Gompers to Joseph Patrick Tumulty, April 24, 1918, **47:** 420

William Elliott Gonzales to the Department of State, July 14, 1917, **43:** 207

Ulysses Grant-Smith to Robert Lansing, Jan. 15, 1918, **46:** 45; Jan. 17, 1918, **46:** 48

Sir William Conyngham Greene to the British Foreign Office, Oct. 5, 1917, **44:** 314; March 7, 1918, **46:** 571

Joseph Clark Grew to Robert Lansing, Nov. 17, 1916, **40:** 21; Nov. 7, 1916, **40:** 141; Dec. 1, 1916, **40:** 160; Dec. 5, 1916, **40:** 184; Dec. 8, 1916, **40:** 217; Dec. 12, 1916 (2), **40:** 231, 233; Dec. 21, 1916, **40:** 428

A memorandum by Joseph Clark Grew on the political situation in Germany, Nov. 5, 1917, **45:** 30

Viscount Grey of Fallodon to Edward Mandell House, Nov. 2, 1916, **40:** 60; Dec. 10, 1916, **40:** 212

Pearl Merrill Griffith to Robert Lansing, Feb. 21, 1917, **41:** 268

George Wilkins Guthrie to Robert Lansing, Feb. 9, 1917, **41:** 181

Jacob Judah Aaron de Haas to Robert Lansing, Feb. 27, 1918, **46:** 494

Henry Noble Hall to Lord Reading, May 19, 1918, **48:** 66

Henry Noble Hall to the London *Times*, May 9, 1918, **47:** 582; May 18, 1918, **48:** 67

Norman Hapgood to Edward Mandell House, Dec. 30, 1916, and Jan. 4, 1917 (extracts), **40:** 496; July 28, 1917, **44:** 72

Maximilian Harden to Karl H. von Wiegand, Dec. 8, 1916, **40:** 376

Samuel Northrup Harper to Richard Crane, March 16, 1917, **41:** 415

Leland Harrison to Robert Lansing, Jan. 3, 1917, **40:** 388

Emmanuel Havenith to Robert Lansing, Dec. 12, 1916, **40:** 220

A memorandum by Carlton Joseph Huntley Hayes on alternatives to a declaration of war, Feb. 8, 1917, **41:** 165

George Davis Herron to Charles Ferguson, Dec. 31, 1916, **40:** 541

George Davis Herron to William Graves Sharp, Sept. 12, 1918, **51:** 230

George Davis Herron to Pleasant Alexander Stovall, July 11, 1918, **48:** 621

George Davis Herron to Hugh Robert Wilson, July 1, 1918, **49:** 187

A memorandum by George Davis Herron about a conversation with Robert de Fiori, Sept. 10, 1918, **51:** 231

A memorandum by George Davis Herron about a conversation with Heinrich Lammasch, Feb. 3, 1918, **46:** 242

Morris Hillquit to Robert Lansing, May 10, 1917, **42:** 268

Robert MacLeod Hodgson to the British Foreign Office, Aug. 9, 1918, **49:** 249

Arthur Hoffmann to Paul Ritter, Feb. 2, 1917, **41:** 105

Thomas Beaumont Hohler to Lord Hardinge, March 23, 1917, **41:** 458

A memorandum by Thomas Beaumont Hohler about a conversation
with Colonel House on Mexican affairs, March 9, 1917, **41:** 459
Herbert Clark Hoover to Joseph Potter Cotton, Nov. 7, 1918, **51:** 635
Herbert Clark Hoover to Frederic René Coudert, Nov. 2, 1918, **51:**
554
Herbert Clark Hoover to Edward Mandell House, Feb. 13, 1917, **41:**
227
Herbert Clark Hoover to Robert Lansing, Jan. 2, 1917, **40:** 409; April
19, 1917, **42:** 109
Herbert Clark Hoover to David Lloyd George, May 16, 1918, **48:** 47
Herbert Clark Hoover to William Babcock Poland, May 16, 1918, **48:**
47
Jean Marie de Horodyski to Sir Eric Drummond, Oct. 5, 1917, **44:** 316
Jean Marie de Horodyski to Erasme Piltz, May 20, 1917, **42:** 356
Edward Mandell House to Arthur James Balfour, Aug. 24, 1917, **44:**
41; Jan. 5, 1918, **45:** 486; Feb. 24, 1918, **46:** 432; March 1, 1918, **46:**
507; March 4, 1918, **46:** 530; April 3, 1918, **47:** 238
Edward Mandell House to Count Johann Heinrich von Bernstorff,
Feb. 2, 1917, **41:** 95
Edward Mandell House to Lord Robert Cecil, June 25, 1918, **48:** 425;
Oct. 2, 1918, **51:** 188
Edward Mandell House to Frank Irving Cobb, July 15, 1917, **43:** 184;
July 19, 1917, **43:** 220
Edward Mandell House to Robert Lansing, Jan. 24, 1917, **41:** 18;
Sept. 20, 1917, **44:** 229; Nov. 28, 1917, **45:** 151; Nov. 7, 1918, **51:** 616
Edward Mandell House to David Lloyd George, Dec. 7, 1916, **40:** 185
Edward Mandell House to Aimaro Satō, May 10, 1917, **42:** 278
Edward Mandell House to Sir William Wiseman, Dec. 18, 1917, **45:**
322; Dec. 19, 1917, **45:** 332
Roy Wilson Howard to William Walter Hawkins, Oct. 31, 1918, **51:**
538
Roy Wilson Howard to Edward Mandell House, Dec. 1, 1916, **40:** 134;
Dec. 26, 1916, **40:** 345

Proceedings of the Imperial War Council, March 22, 1917, **42:** 328
A resolution by the Inter-Allied Council on War Purchases and Finance, Feb. 14, 1918, **46:** 359
A resolution by Irish Americans against the introduction of conscription in Ireland, May 4, 1918, **47:** 520
Viscount Kikujiro Ishii to Baron Shimpei Gotō, April 30, 1918, **47:**
472
Viscount Kikujiro Ishii to the Japanese Foreign Office, Nov. 1, 1918,
51: 548
Viscount Kikujiro Ishii to Robert Lansing, Oct. 8, 1917, **44:** 340; Oct.
12, 1917, **44:** 368
A memorandum by Viscount Kikujiro Ishii about a military agreement between Japan and China, March 25, 1918, **48:** 61

Jesse B. Jackson to the Department of State, Oct. 8, 1917, **44:** 337

The Japanese government to Viscount Kikujiro Ishii, June 26, 1918, **48:** 448

A memorandum by the Japanese government on its policy toward China, Oct. 27, 1917, **44:** 454

A note from the Japanese government to the Allied governments about intervention in Siberia, June 28, 1918, **48:** 495

A declaration by the Japanese government on intervention in Siberia, July 24, 1918, **49:** 75

Peter Augustus Jay to Robert Lansing, Aug. 21, 1917, **44:** 26

Thomas Davies Jones to Vance Criswell McCormick, Nov. 15, 1917, **45:** 79; Nov. 17, 1917, **45:** 81

Jonkheer Benjamin de Jong van Beek en Donk to George Davis Herron, Jan. 31, 1918, **46:** 198

William Vorhees Judson to Newton Diehl Baker, Nov. 14, 1917, **45:** 104

Memoranda by William Vorhees Judson on the situation in Russia, Feb. 26, 1918, **46:** 533; March 4, 1918, **46:** 537

Jean Jules Jusserand to Colville Adrian de Rune Barclay, Oct. 11, 1918, **51:** 307

Jean Jules Jusserand to Aristide Briand, March 3, 1917, **41:** 315; translation, 316

Jean Jules Jusserand to the Foreign Ministry, March 7, 1917, **41:** 354; translation, 356; April 14, 1917, **42:** 69; translation, 70; April 24, 1917, **42:** 127; translation, 128; May 1, 1917, **42:** 182; translation, 184; May 3, 1917, **42:** 210; translation, 212; May 15, 1917, **42:** 299; translation, 300; May 25, 1917, **42:** 402; translation, 403; July 10, 1917, **43:** 142; translation, 143; May 10, 1918, **47:** 585; June 18, 1918, **48:** 355; July 25, 1918, **49:** 91; July 29, 1918, **49:** 127; Aug. 7, 1918, **49:** 211; Sept. 20, 1918, **51:** 84; Sept. 28, 1918, **51:** 152

Jean Jules Jusserand to Robert Lansing, July 20, 1917, **43:** 274; Aug. 18, 1917, **43:** 525; March 8, 1918, **46:** 587; March 12, 1918, **47:** 21; March 14, 1918, **47:** 318; April 23, 1918, **47:** 430; May 28, 1918, **48:** 239; Sept. 28, 1918, **51:** 174

Jean Jules Jusserand to Stephen Jean Marie Pichon, Dec. 5, 1917, **45:** 219; Dec. 26, 1917, **45:** 365; Jan. 9, 1918, **45:** 550; May 29, 1918, **48:** 202; June 6, 1918, **48:** 252; June 9, 1918, **48:** 273; June 27, 1918, **48:** 446; July 26, 1918, **49:** 111; Aug. 1, 1918, **49:** 156; Aug. 12, 1918, **49:** 239; Sept. 12, 1918, **49:** 538; Oct. 3, 1918, **51:** 209

George Kennan to Robert Lansing, May 26, 1918, **48:** 183; Aug. 18, 1918, **49:** 320

George Washington Kirchwey to Robert Lansing, Feb. 12, 1917, **41:** 242

A draft by George Washington Kirchwey of a proposed message to the German government, Feb. 6, 1917, **41:** 245

Austin Melvin Knight to the Chief of Naval Operations, March 20, 1918, **47:** 92

A memorandum by Aleksandr Ivanovich Konovalov about Allied intervention in Russia, June 24, 1918, **48:** 406

Heinrich Lammasch to George Davis Herron, Jan. 31, 1918, **46:** 198
Heinrich Lammasch to Jonkheer Benjamin de Jong van Beek en Donk, March 9, 1918, **46:** 589
A proposal by Thomas William Lamont for a message to the people of Russia, March 9, 1918, **46:** 586
Baron von der Lancken-Wakenitz to Désiré-Joseph Cardinal Mercier, Oct. 17, 1918, **51:** 371
Franklin Knight Lane to George Whitfield Lane, Feb. 9, 1917, **41:** 183; Feb. 10, 1917, **41:** 195; Feb. 16, 1917, **41:** 239; Feb. 20, 1917, **41:** 260; Feb. 25, 1917, **41:** 282; April 1, 1917, **41:** 517
Franklin Knight Lane to Robert Lansing, Nov. 21, 1916 (2), **40:** 33, 48; Dec. 18, 1916, **40:** 279; Dec. 19, 1916, **40:** 298
A memorandum by Franklin Knight Lane about a cabinet discussion of Japanese intervention in Siberia, March 2, 1918, **46:** 515

Remarks by Franklin Knight Lane to the Mexican commissioners, Nov. 21, 1916, **40:** 52
A statement by Franklin Knight Lane to the Mexican commissioners about border control and the right of pursuit, Nov. 21, 1916, **40:** 115
Franklin Knight Lane and others to Luis Cabrera and others, Nov. 21, 1916, **40:** 55; Nov. 22, 1916, **40:** 56; Dec. 19, 1916, **40:** 299; Jan. 3, 1917, **40:** 397
Robert Lansing to John Jay Abbott (draft), Nov. 21, 1917, **45:** 99
Robert Lansing to all diplomatic missions of the United States in all neutral countries, Feb. 3, 1917, **41:** 116
Robert Lansing to all diplomatic missions of the United States in Allied countries, Aug. 18, 1917, **43:** 520
Robert Lansing to the American Embassy in London, Sept. 11, 1918, **49:** 516
Robert Lansing to the American legation in Jassy, Rumania, Feb. 11, 1918, **46:** 326; Feb. 21, 1918, **46:** 374; Nov. 28, 1917, **46:** 375
Robert Lansing to the American legations in Guatemala, Honduras, Nicaragua, and El Salvador, Feb. 7, 1917, **41:** 145
Robert Lansing to Boris Aleksandrovich Bakhmet'ev, Aug. 15, 1917, **43:** 475
Robert Lansing to Colville Adrian de Rune Barclay, Sept. 27, 1918, **51:** 139
Robert Lansing to Tasker Howard Bliss, Feb. 2, 1918, **46:** 219
Robert Lansing to Oscar Terry Crosby, Dec. 12, 1917, **45:** 274
Robert Lansing to Rámon P. De Negri, March 16, 1917, **41:** 404
Robert Lansing to Garrett Droppers, Jan. 26, 1917, **41:** 34
Robert Lansing to Henry Prather Fletcher, April 28, 1917, **42:** 154; Aug. 8, 1917, **43:** 384
Robert Lansing to David Rowland Francis, April 6, 1917, **41:** 552;

April 30, 1917, **42:** 176; May 22, 1917, **42:** 365; May 18, 1917, **42:** 368; May 8, 1918, **48:** 106; June 12, 1918, **48:** 277

Robert Lansing to Arthur Hugh Frazier, March 22, 1918, **47:** 108

Robert Lansing to William Elliott Gonzales, March 10, 1917, **41:** 384; April 12, 1917, **42:** 51

Robert Lansing to Elbridge Gerry Greene, June 24, 1918, **48:** 417

Robert Lansing to Joseph Clark Grew, Nov. 29, 1916, **40:** 106

Robert Lansing to Pearl Merrill Griffith, Feb. 23, 1917, **41:** 278

Robert Lansing to George Wilkins Guthrie, Feb. 9, 1917, **41:** 186

Robert Lansing to Edward Joseph Hale, Feb. 6, 1917, **41:** 146

Robert Lansing to Edward Mandell House, Dec. 1, 1916, **40:** 118; March 19, 1917, **41:** 429

Robert Lansing to Kikujiro Ishii, Sept. 25, 1917, **44:** 255; Sept. 26, 1917, **44:** 264

Robert Lansing to Jean Jules Jusserand, Oct. 1, 1918, **51:** 174

Robert Lansing to Ljubo Mihajlović, June 24, 1918, **48:** 437

Robert Lansing to J. P. Morgan and Company and others, July 9, 1918, **48:** 521

Robert Lansing to Roland Sletor Morris, March 20, 1918, **47:** 91; Sept. 9, 1918, **49:** 506; Oct. 23, 1918, **51:** 481

Robert Lansing to Friedrich Oederlin, Oct. 8, 1918, **51:** 268

Robert Lansing to Walter Hines Page, Jan. 11, 1917, **40:** 444; Feb. 5, 1917, **41:** 128; Feb. 27, 1917, **41:** 297; Aug. 27, 1917 (2), **44:** 57, 188; Dec. 13, 1917, **45:** 274; Feb. 13, 1918, **46:** 339; Feb. 18, 1918, **46:** 395; May 20, 1918, **48:** 71

Robert Lansing to Frederic Courtland Penfield, Feb. 22, 1917, **41:** 267; March 3, 1917, **41:** 313

Robert Lansing to Frank Lyon Polk, Jan. 21, 1918, **46:** 64

Robert Lansing to William Jennings Price, April 12, 1917, **42:** 51

Robert Lansing to Paul Samuel Reinsch, Dec. 4, 1916, **40:** 140; Feb. 10, 1917 (2), **41:** 187, 195; March 9, 1917, **41:** 383; March 13, 1917, **41:** 401; Nov. 5, 1917, **44:** 531

Robert Lansing to William Graves Sharp, Oct. 2, 1918, **51:** 187

Robert Lansing to Edgar Grant Sisson, Sept. 14, 1918, **51:** 3

Robert Lansing to Pleasant Alexander Stovall, Nov. 5, 1918, **51:** 603

Robert Lansing to Joseph Patrick Tumulty, Jan. 23, 1917, **40:** 562; Jan. 27, 1917, **41:** 44; June 20, 1917, **42:** 548; June 25, 1917, **43:** 13; June 19, 1918, **48:** 364; Oct. 2, 1918, **51:** 186

Robert Lansing to Charles Joseph Vopicka, May 3, 1918, **47:** 451

Robert Lansing to Hugh Robert Wilson, Feb. 15, 1918, **46:** 353

Memoranda by Robert Lansing: on Wilson's peace note, Dec. 21, 1916, **40:** 306; Dec. 22, 1916, **40:** 308; on the severance of diplomatic relations with Germany, Feb. 4, 1917, **41:** 118; about a conversation with Paul Ritter, Feb. 21, 1917, **41:** 273; on the Zimmermann telegram, March 4, 1917, **41:** 321; of a cabinet meeting on the crisis with Germany, March 20, 1917, **41:** 436; of a proposed statement to the press, March 26, 1917, **41:** 471; on a suggested list of contraband, April 19, 1917, **42:** 102; reviewing the policy of the United States with regard to Japan's interests in China, July 6, 1917, **43:** 80; a draft of a statement on the situation in Russia, Dec. 4, 1917, **45:** 205; on Heinrich Lammasch, Feb. 10, 1918, **46:** 315; a proposed message concerning a joint protest against the use of poisonous gases in warfare, Feb. 18, 1918, **46:** 395; about the Austro-Hungarian request for an armistice, Oct. 31, 1918, **51:** 527

Irwin Boyle Laughlin to the Department of State, Oct. 14, 1918, **51:** 345; Oct. 30, 1918, **51:** 528

Andrew Bonar Law to William Gibbs McAdoo, July 30, 1917, **43:** 326; Jan. 22, 1918, **46:** 76

William Hayne Leavell to Robert Lansing, April 10, 1917, **42:** 46

Shane Leslie to Joseph Patrick Tumulty, April 22, 1918, **47:** 401; April 23, 1918, **47:** 411; May 7, 1918, **47:** 552; June 12, 1918, **48:** 300

A statement by James H. Lewis on conditions in Poland, Jan. 17, 1918, **46:** 48

Walter Lippmann to Edward Mandell House, Aug. 6, 1917, **43:** 401; Oct. 17, 1917, **44:** 393

A memorandum by Walter Lippmann on a possible reply to the papal peace note, Aug. 20, 1917, **43:** 532

David Lloyd George to Sir Eric Geddes, Oct. 12, 1918, **51:** 313

David Lloyd George to Edward Mandell House, Nov. 3, 1918, **51:** 569

David Lloyd George to Lord Reading, Oct. 31, 1917, **44:** 480; Nov. 1, 1917, **44:** 496; May 18, 1918, **48:** 61; July 18, 1918, **49:** 9

Extracts of an address by David Lloyd George on British war aims and peace terms, Jan. 5, 1918, **45:** 488

A memorandum by Frank Pruit Lockhart about the appointment of Baron Shimpei Gotō, April 25, 1918, **47:** 426

Robert Hamilton Bruce Lockhart to Arthur James Balfour, May 11, 1918, **47:** 606

Robert Hamilton Bruce Lockhart to the British Foreign Office, Feb. 22, 1918, **46:** 419; April 23, 1918, **48:** 39; June 18, 1918, **48:** 380; June 20, 1918, **48:** 398

A memorandum by Robert Hamilton Bruce Lockhart and Joseph Noulens about Allied intervention in Russia, June 18, 1918, **48:** 380

Breckinridge Long to Robert Lansing, July 2, 1918, **48:** 518

A draft by Breckinridge Long of a letter for a consortium of American bankers about a loan to China, July 4, 1918, **48:** 519

A memorandum by Breckinridge Long of a conversation with John Sookine about Japanese intervention in Siberia, March 2, 1918, **46:** 513

Memoranda by Breckinridge Long and others on Japanese intervention in Siberia, Feb. 9, 1918, **46:** 302; Feb. 8, 1918, **46:** 303

Abbott Lawrence Lowell to Edward Mandell House, March 13, 1918, **47:** 102; July 5, 1918, **48:** 561

William Gibbs McAdoo to Oscar Terry Crosby, Dec. 3, 1917, **45:** 245; Jan. 5, 1918, **45:** 533

William Gibbs McAdoo to Robert Lansing, Jan. 5, 1918, **45:** 533; Jan. 17, 1918, **46:** 65

Henry Pinckney McCain to Tasker Howard Bliss, March 12, 1918, **46:** 619

Henry Pinckney McCain to Frederick Funston, Jan. 18, 1917, **40:** 522

A memorandum by Charles McCarthy on conditions in Ireland, Sept. 12, 1918, **49:** 545

Count Macchi di Cellere to Robert Lansing, Oct. 9, 1917, **44:** 348; Oct. 30, 1918, **51:** 529

Vance Criswell McCormick to Thomas Davies Jones, Nov. 14, 1917, **45:** 80

John Van Antwerp MacMurray to the Department of State, Sept. 23, 1918, **51:** 101

James Clifford McNally to Hugh Robert Wilson, Feb. 23, 1918, **46:** 428

Peyton Conway March to Tasker Howard Bliss, May 28, 1918, **48:** 182; Oct. 8, 1918, **51:** 272

Thomas Garrigue Masaryk to Robert Lansing, Sept. 23, 1918, **51:** 96; Oct. 29, 1918, **51:** 506

A memorandum by Thomas Garrigue Masaryk on the conditions of an armistice, Oct. 29, 1918, **51:** 507

A memorandum by Thomas Garrigue Masaryk about the situation in Russia, April 10, 1918, **47:** 549

Julius Meinl to Jonkheer Benjamin de Jong van Beek en Donk, Feb. 28, 1918, **46:** 581; March 4, 1918, **46:** 581

Charles Edward Merriam to George Creel, Sept. 25, 1918, **51:** 118

Charles Merz to Robert Lansing, Sept. 12, 1918, **49:** 536

Sidney Edward Mezes to Edward Mandell House, March 12, 1918, **47:** 12

Memoranda by Sidney Edward Mezes on the future elimination of trade barriers, Oct. 27, 1917 (2), **44:** 455, 456

Lioubomir Michailovitch to Robert Lansing, April 23, 1918, **47:** 416

Basil Miles to Robert Lansing, May 21, 1918, **48:** 112; Oct. 28, 1918, **51:** 478

Memoranda by Basil Miles: about the future policy of the United States toward Russia, Jan. 8, 1918, **45:** 543; on the French attitude toward intervention in Siberia, Feb. 26, 1918, **46:** 451; about the possible effect on Russian public opinion of Japanese intervention in Siberia, March 18, 1918, **47:** 68; about the dispatch of an American warship to Murmansk, April 2, 1918, **47:** 226; about the movements for autonomy in Siberia, April 22, 1918, **47:** 397

Sherman Miles to William Vorhees Judson, March 4, 1918, **46:** 540

David Hunter Miller to Edward Mandell House, Aug. 30, 1917, **44:** 105

Baron Moncheur to Baron Charles de Broqueville, Aug. 14, 1917, **43:** 465

Henry Morgenthau to Robert Lansing, July 17, 1917, **43:** 201
Ira Nelson Morris to Robert Lansing, May 27, 1918, **48:** 194
Roland Sletor Morris to the Department of State, Oct. 25, 1918, **51:** 479; Oct. 27, 1918, **51:** 481
Roland Sletor Morris to Robert Lansing, Jan. 17, 1918, **46:** 46; March 12, 1918, **46:** 620; March 19, 1918, **47:** 77; Jan. 10, 1918, **47:** 427; Jan. 22, 1918, **47:** 429
Charles Kroth Moser to the Department of State, April 20, 1918, **47:** 594
A memorandum by Viscount Ichiro Motono about Japanese intervention in Siberia, March 19, 1918, **47:** 77
John R. Mott to Ethan Theodore Colton, April 9, 1918, **47:** 304
John R. Mott to George Creel, Feb. 8, 1918, **46:** 479; Feb. 26, 1918, **46:** 495
John R. Mott to Robert Lansing, Aug. 22, 1917, **44:** 66

Fridtjof Nansen to Nils Claus Ihlen, Nov. 23, 1917, **45:** 114
Fridtjof Nansen to Thomas Davies Jones, Nov. 16, 1917, **45:** 81
Rómulo Sebastian Naón to Robert Lansing, May 17, 1917, **42:** 359
Reports by the Office of Naval Intelligence on German submarine activities, Jan. 3, 1917, **40:** 388
A memorandum by the Office of Naval Intelligence about the political situation in Britain, Nov. 30, 1917, **45:** 167
Noel Edward Noel-Buxton to William Hepburn Buckler, Jan. 4, 1917, **40:** 495
A memorandum by Noel Edward Noel-Buxton on American opinion regarding the war, Jan. 5, 1917, **40:** 415
Lord Northcliffe to Arthur James Balfour and Andrew Bonar Law, Aug. 28, 1917, **44:** 80
Lord Northcliffe to Arthur James Balfour and David Lloyd George, June 30, 1917, **43:** 66
Lord Northcliffe to Edward Mandell House, Aug. 25, 1917, **44:** 70
Lord Northcliffe to William Gibbs McAdoo, Sept. 13, 1917, **44:** 195
A note by the Norwegian government to the belligerents, Dec. 29, 1916, **40:** 359
Joseph Noulens to the French Foreign Ministry, April 23, 1918, **47:** 431

A memorandum by Thomas Power O'Connor and Richard Hazleton about charges against the Sinn Fein, May 29, 1918, **48:** 195
George Talbot Odell to Robert Lansing, Nov. 10, 1917, **45:** 55
Friedrich Oederlin to Robert Lansing, Oct. 30, 1918, **51:** 518
Constantin Onou to Robert Lansing, Aug. 3, 1917, **43:** 474

Ignace Jan Paderewski to Robert Lansing, Jan. 19, 1918, **46:** 122
Thomas Nelson Page to Robert Lansing, Dec. 29, 1916, **40:** 556; Jan. 22, 1917, **41:** 218; March 20, 1917, **41:** 433; April 20, 1917, **42:** 110; Jan. 29, 1918 (2), **46:** 178, 376; Feb. 16, 1918, **46:** 365

Walter Hines Page to the Department of State, March 16, 1918, **47:** 59; April 24, 1918, **47:** 432

Walter Hines Page to Edward Mandell House, Oct. 16, 1917, **44:** 390

Walter Hines Page to Thomas Davies Jones, Nov. 11, 1917, **45:** 78

Walter Hines Page to Robert Lansing, Dec. 15, 1916, **40:** 247; Dec. 22, 1916, **40:** 319; Dec. 26, 1916, **40:** 332; Jan. 2, 1917, **40:** 409; Jan. 5, 1917, **40:** 509; Feb. 6, 1917, **41:** 137; April 19, 1917, **42:** 109; Aug. 15, 1917, **43:** 482; Aug. 21, 1917, **44:** 23; Sept. 4, 1917, **44:** 189; Dec. 29, 1917, **45:** 417; Jan. 15, 1918, **46:** 45; Feb. 14, 1918, **46:** 359; Feb. 21, 1918, **46:** 411; Feb. 22, 1918, **46:** 418; May 10, 1918, **48:** 65; Sept. 12, 1918, **49:** 536; Sept. 15, 1918, **51:** 17

Walter Hines Page to Frank Lyon Polk, July 18, 1917, **43:** 208

Lady Mary Fiske Stevens Paget to Edward Mandell House, Dec. 3, 1916, **40:** 135

A proposal for a Pan-American Treaty, April 19, 1917, **42:** 100

Nikola Pašić to William Graves Sharp, Aug. 27, 1917, **44:** 75

A memorandum by Philip Halsey Patchin about John Foster Bass, May 12, 1917, **42:** 284

George Foster Peabody to Warren Worth Bailey, Feb. 2, 1917, **41:** 115

Frederic Courtland Penfield to Robert Lansing, Nov. 20, 1916, **40:** 23; Feb. 5, 1917, **41:** 129; Feb. 27, 1917, **41:** 297; Jan. 22, 1917, **41:** 300

John Joseph Pershing to Newton Diehl Baker, April 5, 1917, **41:** 545; July 9, 1917, **43:** 262; Nov. 4, 1918, **51:** 595

John Joseph Pershing to Frederick Funston, Dec. 9, 1916, **40:** 202

John Joseph Pershing to Hugh Lenox Scott, May 1, 1917, **42:** 225

John Joseph Pershing to the Supreme War Council, Oct. 30, 1918, **51:** 524

August Philips to Jonkheer John Loudon, March 24, 1918, **47:** 133; March 25, 1918, **47:** 142

William Phillips to Robert Lansing, May 28, 1917, **42:** 417; June 4, 1917, **42:** 454; April 16, 1918, **47:** 353; Oct. 4, 1918, **51:** 216

William Phillips to Joseph Patrick Tumulty, Dec. 27, 1916, **40:** 339

A memorandum by William Phillips on conversations between George Davis Herron and Robert de Fiori, Aug. 9, 1918, **49:** 229

Stéphen Jean Marie Pichon to Jean Jules Jusserand, July 29, 1918, **49:** 124

Sir Horace Plunkett to Arthur James Balfour, Aug. 3, 1917, **43:** 360; Sept. 17, 1917, **44:** 210

Sir Horace Plunkett to Edward Mandell House, Nov. 2, 1916, **40:** 30; Dec. 27, 1916, **40:** 339; June 1, 1917, **42:** 542; April 28, 1918, **47:** 469

Sir Horace Plunkett to Shane Leslie, May 24, 1918, **48:** 300

Frank Lyon Polk to Arthur Hugh Frazier, Feb. 5, 1918, **46:** 254

Frank Lyon Polk to Jean Jules Jusserand, Aug. 3, 1917, **43:** 359

Frank Lyon Polk to Robert Lansing, Nov. 25, 1916, **40:** 83; Feb. 10, 1917, **41:** 203; April 7, 1917, **42:** 15; May 7, 1917, **42:** 240; March 5, 1918, **46:** 550; April 2, 1918, **47:** 226

Frank Lyon Polk to Roland Sletor Morris, Jan. 20, 1918, **46:** 35; March 5, 1918, **46:** 545

Frank Lyon Polk to Walter Hines Page, July 11, 1917, **43:** 150; July 20, 1917, **43:** 236

Frank Lyon Polk to Paul Samuel Reinsch, Aug. 4, 1917, **43:** 363

Frank Lyon Polk to William Graves Sharp, July 31, 1917, **43:** 335; Aug. 4, 1917, **43:** 364

Frank Lyon Polk to Joseph Patrick Tumulty, Aug. 7, 1917, **43:** 386

A memorandum by Frank Lyon Polk about a talk with Domicio da Gama, May 17, 1917, **42:** 314

A statement by Frank Lyon Polk on an international consortium of bankers for China, July 26, 1918, **49:** 102

A memorandum by Frank Lyon Polk about a conversation with Viscount Kikujiro Ishii on intervention in Siberia, July 25, 1918, **49:** 107

DeWitt Clinton Poole, Jr., to Robert Lansing, June 12, 1918, **48:** 359

William Jennings Price to Robert Lansing, Dec. 26, 1917, **45:** 388

Chevalier Willem Louis Frederik Christiaan van Rappard to the Netherlands Foreign Ministry, Feb. 4, 1917, **41:** 125; translation, 125; Feb. 5, 1917, **41:** 130; translation, 131; Feb. 11, 1917, **41:** 200; translation, 200

Lord Reading to Arthur James Balfour, Feb. 26, 1918, **46:** 465; Feb. 27, 1918, **46:** 482; March 6, 1918, **46:** 561; March 13, 1918, **47:** 18; March 18, 1918 (2), **47:** 63; March 19, 1918, **47:** 78; March 27, 1918, **47:** 170; April 7, 1918, **47:** 281; April 25, 1918, **47:** 440; May 1, 1918, **47:** 488; May 2, 1918, **47:** 496; May 6, 1918, **47:** 544; May 12, 1918, **47:** 620; May 23, 1918 (2), **48:** 132, 134; June 16, 1918, **48:** 333; June 29, 1918, **48:** 469; July 3, 1918, **48:** 514; July 19, 1918, **49:** 36; July 23, 1918, **49:** 67; July 24, 1918, **49:** 83

Lord Reading to Arthur James Balfour and Walter Hume Long, June 2, 1918, **48:** 228

Lord Reading to the British Foreign Office, Feb. 15, 1918, **46:** 353; Feb. 19, 1918, **46:** 390; March 1, 1918, **46:** 506; April 8, 1918, **47:** 299

Lord Reading to Sir Eric Drummond, March 27, 1918, **47:** 170

Lord Reading to Jacob Judah Aaron de Haas, Feb. 27, 1918, **46:** 495

Lord Reading to David Lloyd George, July 12, 1918, **48:** 602

Lord Reading to David Lloyd George and Arthur James Balfour, July 21, 1918, **49:** 52; July 26, 1918, **49:** 110

Lord Reading to David Lloyd George and others, Nov. 2, 1917, **44:** 494

Lord Reading to William Gibbs McAdoo, July 11, 1918, **48:** 593

Lord Reading to Joseph Patrick Tumulty, May 8, 1918, **47:** 575

Lord Reading to the War Cabinet, Sept. 21, 1917, **44:** 237

Lord Reading to the War Cabinet and others, Oct. 12, 1917, **44:** 369

Lord Reading to Sir William Wiseman, Aug. 20, 1918, **49:** 302; Aug. 27, 1918, **49:** 366; Sept. 6, 1918, **49:** 466; Oct. 10, 1918, **51:** 295; Oct. 12, 1918, **51:** 313; Oct. 13, 1918, **51:** 324

Memoranda by Lord Reading about the situation in Siberia, April 1, 1918 (2), **47:** 242, 244

Paul Samuel Reinsch to the Department of State, Aug. 3, 1917, **43:**
362; April 10, 1918, **47:** 592
Paul Samuel Reinsch to Robert Lansing, Dec. 2, 1916, **40:** 128; Dec.
18, 1916, **40:** 514; Dec. 8, 1916, **40:** 563; Feb. 6, 1917 (2), **41:** 175,
176; Feb. 7, 1917, **41:** 177; Feb. 8, 1917, **41:** 178; Feb. 9, 1917, **41:**
182; Feb. 10, 1917, **41:** 195; March 12, 1917, **41:** 394; Nov. 4, 1917,
44: 510; Dec. 12, 1917, **45:** 308; Feb. 21, 1918, **46:** 499; May 16,
1918, **48:** 72; June 13, 1918, **48:** 335
A memorandum by Paul Samuel Reinsch about the financial situation of China, Aug. 14, 1918, **49:** 311
Bernard Herman Ridder to Edward Mandell House, Aug. 7, 1917, **43:**
410
Paul Ritter to Arthur Hoffmann, Dec. 22, 1916, **40:** 320; translation,
323; Dec. 28, 1916, **40:** 348; translation, 351; Jan. 12, 1917, **40:** 457;
translation, 460; Feb. 2, 1917, **41:** 102; translation, 105
A memorandum by Paul Ritter about a talk with Wilson on joint me-
diation by the neutrals, Nov. 22, 1916, **40:** 42; translation, 44
A memorandum by Malcolm Arnold Robertson on peace feelers by
the Austrian government, Nov. 3, 1917, **44:** 514
Raymond Robins to Henry Pomeroy Davison, Jan. 23, 1918, **46:** 232
Raymond Robins to Robert Lansing, July 1, 1918, **48:** 489
Elihu Root to Edward Mandell House, Aug. 16, 1918, **49:** 269
Elihu Root to Robert Lansing, May 3, 1917, **42:** 216
James A. Ruggles to the Department of State, March 12, 1918, **47:**
140
Charles Edward Russell to Robert Lansing, May 15, 1917, **42:** 350

Aimaro Satō to Edward Mandell House, May 8, 1917, **42:** 276
A memorandum by Aimaro Satō on Japanese-American relations,
May 8, 1917, **42:** 276
A memorandum by Aimaro Satō about Japan's special interests in
China, June 15, 1917, **43:** 55
A memorandum by Aimaro Satō about the situation in East Asia,
Dec. 29, 1917, **45:** 393
Albert George Schmedeman to Robert Lansing, Sept. 30, 1918, **51:**
186
Hans Frederick Arthur Schoenfeld to the Department of State, Aug.
21, 1918, **49:** 333
William Graves Sharp to Jules Martin Cambon, Aug. 6, 1917, **43:**
379; Aug. 7, 1917, **43:** 387
William Graves Sharp to the Department of State, Jan. 10, 1918, **47:**
24; May 7, 1918, **47:** 570
William Graves Sharp to Robert Lansing, Jan. 10, 1917, **40:** 439;
June 27, 1917, **43:** 29; July 17, 1917, **43:** 201; July 23, 1917, **43:** 255;
July 24, 1917, **43:** 267; Aug. 2, 1917, **43:** 355; Aug. 21, 1917, **44:** 24;
Jan. 5, 1918, **45:** 492; Feb. 2, 1918, **46:** 233; Feb. 19, 1918, **46:** 388;
Feb. 23, 1918, **46:** 429; Sept. 19, 1918, **51:** 229
Edgar Grant Sisson to George Creel, Dec. 4, 1917, **45:** 216; Jan. 13,
1918, **45:** 596

A statement by Henry Leon Slobodin about American propaganda in Russia, Aug. 24, 1917, **44:** 39

Stephen L'Hommedieu Slocum to Newton Diehl Baker, Oct. 8, 1917, **44:** 332

Henry Edward Sly to the British Foreign Office, March 18, 1918, **47:** 96; March 21, 1918, **47:** 100

Wilhelm Solf to Baron Kress von Kressenstein, Oct. 13, 1918, **51:** 345

Remarks by Baron Sidney Sonnino about the peace appeal of Benedict XV, Oct. 10, 1917, **44:** 350

Sir Cecil Arthur Spring Rice to Arthur James Balfour, Dec. 21, 1916, **40:** 316; June 28, 1917, **43:** 37; July 3, 1917 (2), **43:** 97; July 26, 1917, **43:** 285; Jan. 4, 1918 (2), **45:** 454, 458; Jan. 6, 1918, **45:** 518; Jan. 12, 1918, **45:** 578

Sir Cecil Arthur Spring Rice to Lord Robert Cecil, May 20, 1917, **42:** 355

Sir Cecil Arthur Spring Rice to the Department of State, Jan. 16, 1917, **40:** 499

Sir Cecil Arthur Spring Rice to Sir Eric Drummond, Oct. 5, 1917, **44:** 316

Sir Cecil Arthur Spring Rice to the Foreign Office, Dec. 3, 1916, **40:** 136; Dec. 15, 1916, **40:** 249; Jan. 4, 1917, **40:** 406; Jan. 14, 1917, **40:** 469; Feb. 19, 1917, **41:** 256; March 6, 1917, **41:** 349; May 14, 1917, **42:** 296; June 14, 1917, **42:** 520; July 23, 1917, **43:** 256; July 31, 1917, **43:** 335; Sept. 4, 1917, **44:** 153; Dec. 17, 1917, **45:** 316; Dec. 20, 1917, **45:** 336; Dec. 22, 1917, **45:** 347; Dec. 27, 1917 (2), **45:** 369, 370; Jan. 2, 1918, **45:** 431; Jan. 9, 1918, **45:** 549; Jan. 10, 1918, **45:** 566; Jan. 11, 1918 (2), **45:** 572

Sir Cecil Arthur Spring Rice to Robert Lansing, Sept. 3, 1917, **44:** 187

Sir Cecil Arthur Spring Rice to David Lloyd George, April 26, 1917, **42:** 140

A memorandum by Sir Cecil Arthur Spring Rice on British policy with regard to Poland, July 23, 1917, **43:** 301

A memorandum by Sir Cecil Arthur Spring Rice about a possible conference with representatives of the Russian government, Sept. 10, 1917, **44:** 179

A memorandum by Jordan Herbert Stabler on the overthrow of the government of Costa Rica, Feb. 6, 1917, **41:** 140

Pleasant Alexander Stovall to the Department of State, Sept. 27, 1918, **51:** 154; Oct. 16, 1918, **51:** 387

Pleasant Alexander Stovall to Robert Lansing, Nov. 20, 1916, **40:** 22; Feb. 10, 1917, **41:** 193; Feb. 19, 1917, **41:** 275; March 8, 1918, **46:** 580; March 9, 1918 (2), **46:** 589, 615; March 6, 1918, **46:** 594; March 11, 1918, **46:** 617; March 18, 1918, **47:** 64; March 23, 1918, **47:** 128; July 5, 1918, **48:** 552; July 11, 1918, **48:** 621; Aug. 26, 1918, **49:** 382

A memorandum by the Supreme War Council on the terms of an armistice with Germany and Austria-Hungary, Oct. 7, 1918, **51:** 261

A resolution by the Supreme War Council on the terms of an armistice with Austria-Hungary, Oct. 31, 1918, **51:** 532

A resolution by the Supreme War Council about the procedure for an armistice with Germany, Nov. 4, 1918, **51:** 581

A resolution by the Supreme War Council about the shipment of food to Austria, Turkey, and Bulgaria, Nov. 5, 1918, **51:** 595

A statement by the Supreme War Council on the addresses of Count von Hertling and Count Czernin, Feb. 2, 1918, **46:** 234

Maddin Summers to Robert Lansing, Dec. 6, 1917, **45:** 228

Raymond Edwards Swing to Edward Mandell House, May 23, 1917, **42:** 388

William Howard Taft to Bainbridge Colby, March 24, 1918, **47:** 147

A memorandum by Tokichi Tanaka on the future policy of the Allies toward Russia, March 7, 1918, **46:** 585

Ida Minerva Tarbell to Edward Mandell House, Feb. 8, 1917, **41:** 215

André Tardieu to William Gibbs McAdoo, Sept. 13, 1917, **44:** 196

André Tardieu to Alexandre Ribot, May 22, 1917, **42:** 374; translation, 375

Count Adam Tarnowski von Tarnow to Robert Lansing, March 26, 1917, **41:** 477

Mikhail Ivanovich Tereshchenko to Boris Aleksandrovich Bakhmet'ev, Aug. 21, 1917, **44:** 181

Mikhail Ivanovich Tereshchenko to Constantin Onou, May 8/21, 1917, **42:** 418

Roger Culver Tredwell to Robert Lansing, Dec. 5, 1917, **45:** 216

A declaration by Leon Trotsky on the peace negotiations at Brest-Litovsk, Dec. 31, 1917, **45:** 411

Joseph Patrick Tumulty to John Daniel Crimmins, May 5, 1917, **42:** 223

Joseph Patrick Tumulty to Robert Lansing, Jan. 26, 1917, **41:** 33

Joseph Patrick Tumulty to Frank Lyon Polk, July 29, 1918, **49:** 126

A message to the people of Russia from the United States Railway Commission, July 4, 1917, **43:** 440

Oswald Garrison Villard to Joseph Patrick Tumulty, Dec. 14, 1916, **40:** 236

René Viviani to Alexandre Ribot, May 3, 1917, **42:** 210; translation, 212; May 15, 1917, **42:** 299; translation, 300

Lillian D. Wald to Joseph Patrick Tumulty, Feb. 8, 1917, **41:** 167

William English Walling to Frank Lyon Polk, May 16, 1917, **42:** 319

William English Walling to William Bauchop Wilson, May 2, 1917, **42:** 197

A memorandum by William English Walling on possible revolutions in Western Europe, Feb. 9, 1918, **46:** 310

A memorandum by William English Walling about a statement by Henry Leon Slobodin, Aug. 24, 1917, **44:** 39

Paul Moritz Warburg to Edward Mandell House, July 15, 1917, **43:** 185

John Oliver Wardrop to the British Foreign Office, May 8, 1918, **48:** 40; May 15, 1918, **48:** 102

A memorandum by Josiah Wedgwood on peace terms, Dec. 29, 1916, **40:** 361

A White House memorandum about the situation in Costa Rica, April 3, 1918, **47:** 231

John Howard Whitehouse to Edward Mandell House, Jan. 31, 1917, **41:** 85

A memorandum by John Howard Whitehouse on the change of government in Great Britain, Dec. 7, 1916, **40:** 186

A memorandum by John Howard Whitehouse on the consequences of Germany's declaration of unrestricted submarine warfare, Jan. 31, 1917, **41:** 85

Karl von Wiegand to Edward Mandell House, Aug. 31, 1917, **44:** 105

Joseph Edward Willard to Robert Lansing, Dec. 20, 1916, **40:** 304; Jan. 26, 1917, **41:** 35

Joseph Edward Willard to Charles Stetson Wilson, Dec. 20, 1916, **40:** 304

Edward Thomas Williams to Robert Lansing, Feb. 21, 1918, **46:** 500

A memorandum by Edward Thomas Williams of a talk between Robert Lansing and Aimaro Satō, Jan. 25, 1917, **41:** 38

Memoranda by Edward Thomas Williams about a loan to China, April 12, 1917, **42:** 53; Nov. 21, 1917 (2), **45:** 97, 98

Hugh Robert Wilson to Robert Lansing, Dec. 28, 1917 (2), **45:** 384, 415; Jan. 30, 1918, **46:** 172; Jan. 31, 1918, **46:** 198; Feb. 4, 1918 (2), **46:** 241; Feb. 5, 1918, **46:** 253; Feb. 6, 1918, **46:** 261; Feb. 15, 1918, **46:** 352; Feb. 19, 1918, **46:** 388; Feb. 21, 1918, **46:** 412; ⅞ Feb. 23, 1918, **46:** 428; March 3, 1918, **46:** 592

William Bauchop Wilson to Robert Lansing, June 21, 1917, **42:** 566

Stephen Samuel Wise and Jacob Judah Aaron de Haas to Edward Mandell House, March 2, 1918, **46:** 516

Stephen Samuel Wise and others to Abraham Menahem Mendel Ussishkin and others, Jan. 10, 1918, **45:** 572

Sir William Wiseman to Arthur James Balfour, Feb. 3, 1918, **46:** 231; March 4, 1918, **46:** 530; Aug. 20, 1918, **49:** 299

Sir William Wiseman to Lord Robert Cecil, July 17, 1918, **48:** 647; July 18, 1918, **49:** 11

Sir William Wiseman to Sir Eric Drummond, June 16, 1917, **42:** 529; June 19, 1917, **42:** 543; June 20, 1917, **42:** 551; July 18, 1917, **43:** 209; Sept. 20, 1917, **44:** 230; Sept. 28, 1917, **44:** 278; Oct. 7, 1917, **44:** 325; Oct. 13, 1917, **44:** 373; Oct. 16, 1917, **44:** 391; Oct. 17, 1917, **44:** 396; Feb. 1, 1918, **46:** 213; Feb. 4, 1918, **46:** 250; Feb. 19, 1918, **46:** 389; Feb. 26, 1918, **46:** 464; Feb. 27, 1918, **46:** 485; March 1, 1918, **46:** 507; March 4, 1918, **46:** 531; March 6, 1918, **46:** 561; March 14, 1918, **47:** 35; April 5, 1918, **47:** 266; May 30, 1918, **48:** 203; June 14, 1918, **48:** 315; June 15, 1918, **48:** 331; June 30, 1918,

48: 470; July 9, 1918, **48:** 577; Aug. 27, 1918, **49:** 365; Oct. 2, 1918, **51:** 188; Oct. 5, 1918, **51:** 252; Oct. 16, 1918, **51:** 352

Sir William Wiseman to Sir Eric Drummond and Arthur James Balfour, Feb. 4, 1918, **46:** 247

Sir William Wiseman to the Foreign Office, Jan. 16, 1917, **40:** 503; Aug. 28, 1917, **44:** 80

Sir William Wiseman to Edward Mandell House, Aug. 2, 1917, **43:** 356; Aug. 9, 1917, **43:** 426; Aug. 11, 1917 (3), **43:** 451, 452, 453; Aug. 12, 1917, **43:** 453; Aug. 22, 1917, **44:** 31; Aug. 25, 1917, **44:** 56; Oct. 10, 1917, **44:** 353; Dec. 15, 1917, **45:** 311; April 25, 1918, **47:** 442; April 27, 1918, **47:** 465; May 1, 1918, **47:** 503

Sir William Wiseman to Arthur Cecil Murray, July 4, 1918, **48:** 523; Aug. 30, 1918, **49:** 397; Sept. 14, 1918, **51:** 6

Sir William Wiseman to Lord Reading, Feb. 12, 1918, **46:** 333; Aug. 15, 1918, **49:** 265; Aug. 16, 1918, **49:** 273; Aug. 20, 1918, **49:** 300; Aug. 23, 1918, **49:** 345; Aug. 27, 1918, **49:** 366; Aug. 31, 1918, **49:** 409; Sept. 5, 1918 (3), **49:** 452, 453, 454; Sept. 27, 1918, **51:** 145; Oct. 2, 1918, **51:** 188; Oct. 3, 1918, **51:** 208; Oct. 9, 1918, **51:** 290

Sir William Wiseman to Lord Reading and Sir Eric Drummond, Oct. 9, 1918, **51:** 291; Oct. 13, 1918, **51:** 328

Sir William Wiseman to Sir Cecil Arthur Spring Rice, March 6, 1917, **41:** 346

Memoranda by Sir William Wiseman about American representation on Allied councils, Oct. 10, 1917, **44:** 355; about a talk with Colonel House on an early peace conference, Jan. 26, 1917, **41:** 26; on the attitude of the United States with regard to the proposed Japanese intervention in Siberia, March 9, 1918, **46:** 590; on a league of nations, July 18, 1918, **49:** 14, June 22, 1918, **49:** 16

Arthur Zimmermann to Heinrich von Eckhardt, Jan. 19, 1917, **41:** 281

Correspondence, reports, and memoranda on military and naval affairs

Newton Diehl Baker to Tasker Howard Bliss, Jan. 21, 1918, **46:** 44; May 31, 1918, **48:** 218; June 15, 1918, **48:** 330; July 1, 1918, **48:** 481; July 9, 1918, **48:** 577; Oct. 21, 1918, **51:** 400

Newton Diehl Baker to Frederick Funston, Feb. 16, 1917, **41:** 237

Newton Diehl Baker to John Joseph Pershing, May 26, 1917, **42:** 404; Dec. 18, 1917, **45:** 328; Dec. 24, 1917, **45:** 438; May 11, 1918, **47:** 615; Oct. 27, 1918 (2), **51:** 470 (draft), 471

Newton Diehl Baker to Theodore Roosevelt, April 13, 1917, **42:** 56

Newton Diehl Baker to Teofil A. Starzynski, March 31, 1917, **41:** 511

Newton Diehl Baker to William Howard Taft, Feb. 7, 1917, **41:** 155

Newton Diehl Baker to Leonard Wood, Feb. 3, 1917, **41:** 114

A message by Newton Diehl Baker for Department Commanders on the suppression of disloyalty and violence, March 28, 1917, **41:** 487

Arthur James Balfour to Edward Mandell House, March 26, 1918, **47:** 157

Arthur James Balfour to Lord Reading, March 23, 1918, **47:** 130; May 28, 1918, **48:** 207; June 11, 1918, **48:** 285; June 20, 1918, **48:** 378; July 2, 1918 (3), **48:** 493, 494, 496; July 11, 1918, **48:** 595; July 10, 1918, **48:** 622

Arthur James Balfour to Sir Cecil Arthur Spring Rice, June 30, 1917, **43:** 65

Paul Henry Bastedo to William Sowden Sims, Sept. 9, 1917, **44:** 173

William Shepherd Benson to Josephus Daniels, Dec. 2, 1917, **45:** 190

William Shepherd Benson to Josephus Daniels and William Veazie Pratt, Oct. 29, 1918, **51:** 488

A memorandum by William Shepherd Benson about possible desperate action by the German navy, Nov. 1, 1918, **51:** 541

Robert Woods Bliss to Robert Lansing, Aug. 31, 1918, **49:** 423

Tasker Howard Bliss to Newton Diehl Baker, May 25, 1917, **42:** 408; Dec. 4, 1917, **45:** 208; Jan. 30, 1918, **46:** 211; May 1, 1918, **47:** 487; April 27, 1918, **47:** 563; May 26, 1918, **48:** 179; June 18, 1918 (2), **48:** 367, 396; June 8, 1918, **48:** 383; Aug. 7, 1918, **49:** 335; Aug. 22, 1918, **51:** 34

Tasker Howard Bliss to Newton Diehl Baker and Peyton Conway March, June 29, 1918, **48:** 481; July 12, 1918, **48:** 599; Aug. 14, 1918, **49:** 258; Aug. 18, 1918, **49:** 285

Tasker Howard Bliss to Robert Lansing and others, May 3, 1918, **47:** 512; May 29, 1918, **48:** 200; July 2, 1918, **48:** 503; July 5, 1918, **48:** 536; July 6, 1918, **48:** 545

Tasker Howard Bliss to Henry Pinckney McCain, Jan. 29, 1918, **46:** 162; Feb. 2, 1918, **46:** 220; Feb. 3, 1918, **46:** 240; March 6, 1918, **46:** 558

Tasker Howard Bliss to Peyton Conway March, March 23, 1918, **47:** 130; April 3, 1918, **47:** 237; June 23, 1918, **48:** 401; July 29, 1918, **49:** 126; Aug. 17, 1918, **49:** 279; Sept. 3, 1918, **49:** 530; Sept. 7, 1918, **51:** 52; Oct. 14, 1918, **51:** 337

The British cabinet to Edward Mandell House, Dec. 17, 1917, **45:** 316

A memorandum by the British General Staff about the need for immediate American reinforcements, April 14, 1918, **47:** 338

A memorandum by the British War Cabinet on the submarine situation, Aug. 4, 1917, **43:** 375

British War Office to Frederick Cuthbert Poole, Aug. 18, 1918, **49:** 285

William Hepburn Buckler to Edward Mandell House, May 4, 1917, **42:** 379

John Kenneth Caldwell to Robert Lansing, June 25, 1918, **48:** 428; Aug. 15, 1918, **49:** 263; Sept. 5, 1918, **49:** 494

A memorandum by the Council of National Defense on the shipping situation, Jan. 5, 1918, **45:** 490

Josephus Daniels to William Shepherd Benson, Nov. 3, 1918, **51:** 575
Josephus Daniels to Austin Melvin Knight, July 6, 1918, **48:** 543; Aug. 17, 1918, **49:** 278
Josephus Daniels to Robert Lansing, March 11, 1917, **41:** 387
A memorandum by Josephus Daniels on the conduct of American armed merchant vessels, March 13, 1917, **41:** 395
A memorandum by Edward Andrew Deeds on the history of the Liberty airplane engine, Nov. 6, 1917, **44:** 538
Lord Derby to Arthur James Balfour, March 23, 1918, **47:** 130
A memorandum by the Division of Foreign Intelligence about Walter Lippmann, Sept. 4, 1918, **49:** 433
Sir Eric Drummond to Sir William Wiseman, March 26, 1918, **47:** 157

An agreement between Ferdinand Foch, John Joseph Pershing, and Lord Milner about the transportation of American troops, June 2, 1918, **48:** 227
A memorandum by Ferdinand Foch about the need for American reinforcements, May 2, 1918, **47:** 497
A statement by Ferdinand Foch about Allied intervention in Russia, June 24, 1918, **48:** 415
David Rowland Francis to Robert Lansing, Sept. 10, 1918, **49:** 518
Philip Albright Small Franklin to Robert Lansing, Feb. 10, 1917, **41:** 187
Arthur Hugh Frazier to Edward Mandell House, April 11, 1918, **47:** 505
Arthur Hugh Frazier to Robert Lansing and Edward Mandell House, Aug. 30, 1918, **49:** 404
Arthur Hugh Frazier to William Graves Sharp, Jan. 31, 1918, **46:** 237
A proposal by the French government for intervention in Siberia, May 26, 1918, **48:** 179

Sir Eric Geddes to David Lloyd George, Aug. 29, 1917, **44:** 86
Sir Eric Geddes to Franklin Delano Roosevelt, Aug. 31, 1918, **49:** 410
A memorandum by Sir Eric Geddes about the use of sea power by a league of nations, Nov. 7, 1918, **51:** 633
Vaclav Girsa and others to Thomas Garrigue Masaryk, July 31, 1918, **49:** 219
A memorandum by George Washington Goethals on the construction of steel ships, April 25, 1917, **42:** 248
William Sidney Graves to Henry Pinckney McCain, Sept. 11, 1918, **49:** 543
William Sidney Graves to Newton Diehl Baker, Oct. 18, 1918, **51:** 384; Oct. 1, 1918, **51:** 608
William Sidney Graves to Peter Charles Harris, Oct. 25, 1918, **51:** 448
Lloyd Carpenter Griscom to John Joseph Pershing, Oct. 15, 1918, **51:** 373

Ernest Lloyd Harris to the Department of State, Aug. 13, 1918, **49:** 448

Ernest Lloyd Harris to John Van Antwerp MacMurray, Sept. 23, 1918, **51:** 101

Francis Burton Harrison to Newton Diehl Baker, June 19, 1917, **42:** 541; Nov. 14, 1917, **45:** 49

Lord Kitchener to the British troops in France and Belgium, June 21, 1917, **42:** 558

Edward Mandell House to Arthur James Balfour, March 26, 1918, **47:** 158; March 27, 1918, **47:** 170; March 29, 1918, **47:** 203

Edward Mandell House to Sir William Wiseman, April 25, 1918, **47:** 436; April 26, 1918, **47:** 444

A report by Vladimir S. Hurban on the origin of the conflict between the Bolsheviks and the Czech Legion, Aug. 6, 1918, **49:** 194; July 21, 1918, **49:** 221

Viscount Kikujiro Ishii to Robert Lansing, Aug. 17, 1918 (2), **49:** 284

A statement by Joseph Jacques Césaire Joffre on the military situation in western Europe, June 15, 1918, **48:** 332

Jean Jules Jusserand to Stéphen Jean Marie Pichon, Dec. 29, 1917 (2), **45:** 396, 397

Austin Melvin Knight to the Navy Department, March 18, 1918, **47:** 69

Austin Melvin Knight to Josephus Daniels, June 26, 1918, **48:** 459; June 29, 1918, **48:** 480; July 5, 1918, **48:** 528; July 31, 1918 (2), **49:** 150, 151; Aug. 1, 1918, **49:** 151; Aug. 15, 1918, **49:** 262; Sept. 7, 1918, **49:** 479

Memoranda by Robert Lansing: on the arming of American merchant vessels, Feb. 20, 1917, **41:** 263; March 9, 1917, **41:** 372; about the dispatch of American troops to Murmansk, June 3, 1918, **48:** 236; of a White House conference on the Siberian situation, July 6, 1918, **48:** 542; about the disposition of the American forces in Siberia and northern Russia, Sept. 27, 1918, **51:** 140

David Lloyd George to Georges Clemenceau, Aug. 2, 1918, **49:** 217

David Lloyd George to Edward Mandell House, Dec. 17, 1917, **45:** 317

David Lloyd George to Lord Reading, March 28, 1918, **47:** 181; March 29, 1918, **47:** 203; April 1, 1918, **47:** 221; April 2, 1918, **47:** 229; April 9, 1918 (2), **47:** 303, 307; April 14, 1918, **47:** 338; July 10, 1918, **48:** 587

David Lloyd George and Arthur James Balfour to Lord Reading, April 9, 1918, **47:** 305

Henry Pinckney McCain to Tasker Howard Bliss, Jan. 19, 1918, **46:** 44

John Van Antwerp MacMurray to Robert Lansing, Aug. 30, 1918, **49:** 448

Peyton Conway March to Newton Diehl Baker, June 24, 1918, **48:** 418

Peyton Conway March to Tasker Howard Bliss, April 5, 1918, **47:** 260; April 6, 1918, **47:** 279; June 24, 1918, **48:** 418; July 22, 1918, **49:** 57; July 23, 1918, **49:** 66; July 30, 1918, **49:** 136; Aug. 15, 1918, **49:** 262; Aug. 19, 1918, **49:** 293; Sept. 27, 1918, **51:** 139

Peyton Conway March to John Joseph Pershing, May 11, 1918, **47:** 615

Peyton Conway March to Joseph Patrick Tumulty, March 23, 1918, **47:** 129

An agreement between Thomas Garrigue Masaryk and General Janin on the military policy in Russia, Sept. 21, 1918, **51:** 95

A memorandum by Henry Thomas Mayo on the purpose of the Allied naval conference, Aug. 29, 1917, **44:** 87

Basil Miles to Robert Lansing, July 1, 1918, **48:** 479

George Gordon Moore to Edward Mandell House, May 17, 1917, **42:** 373

Roland Sletor Morris to Robert Lansing, Sept. 5, 1918, **49:** 493; Sept. 23, 1918, **51:** 98

Naval terms of an armistice as proposed by the Inter-Allied Naval Council, Oct. 29, 1918, **51:** 488

Walter Hines Page to Josephus Daniels, April 21, 1917, **42:** 121

Walter Hines Page to the Department of State, July 11, 1917, **43:** 179

Leigh Carlyle Palmer to Josephus Daniels, March 9, 1917, **41:** 370

John Joseph Pershing to Newton Diehl Baker, Aug. 24, 1917, **44:** 51; Nov. 13, 1917, **45:** 107; Dec. 25, 1917, **45:** 364; Jan. 2, 1918, **45:** 426; Jan. 1, 1918, **45:** 439; Jan. 8, 1918, **45:** 571; Jan. 13, 1918, **45:** 583; Jan. 14, 1918, **45:** 594; Feb. 12, 1918, **46:** 337; April 24, 1918, **47:** 456; Oct. 18, 1918, **51:** 373; Oct. 26, 1918, **51:** 454

John Joseph Pershing to Henry Pinckney McCain, Jan. 13, 1918, **46:** 8; Jan. 14, 1918, **46:** 11; Jan. 30, 1918, **46:** 196

John Joseph Pershing to Peyton Conway March, May 10, 1918, **47:** 611; Aug. 7, 1918, **49:** 217; Oct. 18, 1918, **51:** 384

John Joseph Pershing to Peyton Conway March and Newton Diehl Baker, April 29, 1918, **47:** 468; May 3, 1918, **47:** 517; May 6, 1918, **47:** 567; May 15, 1918, **48:** 32; June 4, 1918, **48:** 245

John Joseph Pershing to Sir William Robert Robertson, Jan. 14, 1918, **46:** 11

Comments by John Joseph Pershing on general officers of the United States army, Nov. 13, 1917, **45:** 111

A memorandum by John Joseph Pershing on the amalgamation of American battalions with British forces, Jan. 30, 1918, **46:** 197

Frank Lyon Polk to Walter Hines Page, March 16, 1918, **47:** 27

Frank Lyon Polk to Joseph Patrick Tumulty, Aug. 8, 1918, **49:** 219

A memorandum by William Veazie Pratt about a military and naval offensive against Turkey, Nov. 17, 1917, **45:** 72

Lord Reading to Arthur James Balfour, April 10, 1918 (2), **47:** 314, 315; May 23, 1918, **48:** 133; June 25, 1918, **48:** 429; June 27, 1918, **48:** 453; July 3, 1918, **48:** 511; July 6, 1918, **48:** 543; July 8, 1918, **48:** 565

Lord Reading to Arthur James Balfour and Lord Milner, July 24, 1918, **49:** 82

Lord Reading to Robert Lansing, Aug. 30, 1918, **49:** 418

Lord Reading to David Lloyd George, March 28, 1918, **47:** 183; March 30, 1918 (2), **47:** 213, 214; April 7, 1918, **47:** 280; April 18, 1918, **47:** 369; April 20, 1918, **47:** 386; April 21, 1918, **47:** 393

Lord Reading to David Lloyd George and Arthur James Balfour, April 4, 1918, **47:** 256; July 10, 1918, **48:** 586

Lord Reading to David Lloyd George and Lord Milner, June 22, 1918, **48:** 395

Louis Clark Richardson to Josephus Daniels, June 10, 1918, **48:** 279

A memorandum by Franklin Delano Roosevelt on the arming of American merchant vessels, Feb. 10, 1917, **41:** 189

Theodore Roosevelt to Newton Diehl Baker, March 23, 1917, **41:** 470

William Graves Sharp to Robert Lansing, May 23, 1918, **48:** 131; June 16, 1918, **48:** 332

William Graves Sharp to Robert Lansing and Edward Mandell House, Jan. 31, 1918, **46:** 237

William Sowden Sims to the Chief of Naval Operations, March 27, 1918, **47:** 161

William Sowden Sims to Josephus Daniels, April 21, 1917, **42:** 121; July 28, 1917 (2), **43:** 302, 304

V. Spacek and Vaclav Girsa to Thomas Garrigue Masaryk, July 14, 1918, **49:** 44

Sir Cecil Arthur Spring Rice to Edward Mandell House, Dec. 17, 1917, **45:** 316

Sir Cecil Arthur Spring Rice to Frank Lyon Polk, July 25, 1917, **43:** 293

Supreme War Council, a resolution about the creation of an Inter-Allied General Reserve, March 5, 1918, **46:** 558

Supreme War Council, Joint Note No. 18: Replacement and Disposition of American Forces on the Western Front, March 27, 1918, **47:** 175; Joint Note No. 20: The Situation in the Eastern Theatre, March 29, 1918, **47:** 422; Joint Note No. 31: Allied Intervention at the White Sea Ports, June 3, 1918, **48:** 287; Joint Note No. 37: Allied Military Policy, 1918-1919, Sept. 10, 1918, **51:** 195

William Howard Taft to Newton Diehl Baker, Feb. 6, 1917, **41:** 154

A memorandum by David Watson Taylor on the method of protecting merchant ships from submarine attacks, March 9, 1917, **41:** 377

Joseph Patrick Tumulty to Nick Chiles, Oct. 1, 1918, **51:** 170

A statement by Joseph Patrick Tumulty on the arming of American merchant vessels, March 9, 1917, **41:** 367

Emanuel Victor Voska to the Military Intelligence Branch of the War Department, July 17, 1918, **49:** 41

Edith Bolling Wilson to Robert Lansing, March 9, 1917, **41:** 367
Sir William Wiseman to Arthur James Balfour, March 28, 1918, **47:** 184
Sir William Wiseman to the British Foreign Office, March 28, 1918, **47:** 184
Sir William Wiseman to Sir Eric Drummond, March 26, 1918, **47:** 158; March 27, 1918, **47:** 170; March 29, 1918, **47:** 203
Sir William Wiseman to Edward Mandell House, April 24, 1918, **47:** 433; April 26, 1918, **47:** 443; April 29, 1918, **47:** 471; May 11, 1918, **47:** 616

Personal correspondence

Helen Woodrow Bones to Jessie Woodrow Wilson Sayre, Oct. 17, 1914, **40:** 572; Nov. 21, 1914, **40:** 572; Dec. 6, 1914, **40:** 573; April 12, 1915, **40:** 573; May 29, 1915, **40:** 574; March 8, 1916, **40:** 575; July 9, 1916, **40:** 575; April 27, 1917, **42:** 151
Edward Thomas Brown to Mary Celestine Mitchell Brown, Dec. 7, 1917, **45:** 236
Frances Mitchell Froelicher to Jessie Woodrow Wilson Sayre, April 26, 1918, **47:** 454
Cary Travers Grayson to the Norman Foster Company, May 29, 1918, **48:** 201
Jessie Woodrow Wilson Sayre to Edith Bolling Galt Wilson, April 28, 1918, **47:** 454
Frank Thilly to Joseph Patrick Tumulty, July 7, 1917, **43:** 135
Joseph Patrick Tumulty to the Norman Foster Company, Sept. 25, 1918, **51:** 120
Ellen Axson Wilson to Jessie Woodrow Wilson (Sayre), Dec. 12, 1906, **40:** 566; April 12, 1907, **40:** 566; Oct. 2, 1907, **40:** 567; Oct. 19, 1907, **40:** 568; Dec. 14, 1907, **40:** 569; Jan. 14, 1908, **40:** 570; May 8, 1910, **40:** 571; Dec. 19, 1913, **40:** 571; Feb. 20, 1914, **40:** 571

Diaries

Chandler Parsons Anderson, March 8, 1917, **41:** 365; March 10, 1917, **41:** 385
Henry Fountain Ashurst, Dec. 2, 1916, **40:** 128; Oct. 14, 1918, **51:** 338
Thomas W. Brahany, March 4, 1917, **41:** 327; March 7, 1917, **41:** 357; March 8, 1917, **41:** 364; March 9, 1917, **41:** 381; March 17, 1917, **41:** 424; March 19, 1917, **41:** 431; March 20, 1917, **41:** 445; March 21, 1917, **41:** 448; March 26, 1917, **41:** 473; March 30, 1917, **41:** 506; March 31, 1917, **41:** 515; April 2, 1917, **41:** 531; April 5, 1917, **41:** 549; April 6, 1917, **41:** 557; April 7, 1917, **42:** 13; April 9, 1917, **42:** 23; April 10, 1917, **42:** 31; April 14, 1917, **42:** 64; April 15, 1917, **42:** 71; April 16, 1917, **42:** 77; April 17, 1917, **42:** 91; April 18, 1917, **42:**

93; April 22, 1917, **42**: 121; April 23, 1917, **42**: 123; April 24, 1917, **42**: 125; April 25, 1917, **42**: 132

Josephus Daniels

February–June 1917
Feb. 27, 1917, **41**: 298; March 4, 1917, **41**: 331; March 6, 1917, **41**: 346; March 8, 1917, **41**: 364; March 9, 1917, **41**: 381; March 12, 1917, **41**: 395; March 13, 1917, **41**: 403; March 19, 1917, **41**: 430; March 20, 1917, **41**: 444; March 22, 1917, **41**: 455; March 23, 1917, **41**: 461; March 24, 1917, **41**: 466; March 26, 1917, **41**: 473; March 27, 1917, **41**: 484; March 28, 1917, **41**: 496; March 30, 1917, **41**: 506; April 2, 1917, **41**: 530; April 3, 1917, **41**: 541; April 6, 1917, **41**: 556; April 9, 1917, **42**: 23; April 12, 1917, **42**: 52; April 13, 1917, **42**: 58; April 17, 1917, **42**: 90; April 30, 1917, **42**: 168; May 4, 1917, **42**: 220; May 11, 1917, **42**: 281; May 18, 1917, **42**: 343; May 22, 1917, **42**: 374; May 28, 1917, **42**: 419; June 15, 1917, **42**: 526

July–December 1917
July 6, 1917, **43**: 115; July 7, 1917, **43**: 122; July 10, 1917, **43**: 142; July 13, 1917, **43**: 174; July 16, 1917, **43**: 191; July 20, 1917, **43**: 237; July 23, 1917, **43**: 257; Aug. 1, 1917, **43**: 336; Aug. 3, 1917, **43**: 361; Aug. 6, 1917, **43**: 380; Aug. 7, 1917, **43**: 389; Aug. 14, 1917, **43**: 470; Aug. 16, 1917, **43**: 503; Aug. 17, 1917, **43**: 512; Aug. 24, 1917, **44**: 49; Aug. 28, 1917, **44**: 80; Aug. 31, 1917, **44**: 107; Sept. 18, 1917, **44**: 216; Sept. 21, 1917, **44**: 237; Sept. 25, 1917, **44**: 263; Sept. 28, 1917, **44**: 278; Oct. 2, 1917, **44**: 296; Oct. 9, 1917, **44**: 346; Oct. 12, 1917, **44**: 370; Oct. 15, 1917, **44**: 387; Oct. 16, 1917, **44**: 392; Oct. 19, 1917, **44**: 411; Oct. 26, 1917, **44**: 452; Oct. 28, 1917, **44**: 463; Oct. 30, 1917, **44**: 477; Nov. 2, 1917, **44**: 495; Nov. 9, 1917, **44**: 556; Nov. 10, 1917, **44**: 571; Nov. 20, 1917, **45**: 95; Nov. 26, 1917, **45**: 127; Nov. 27, 1917, **45**: 147; Nov. 30, 1917, **45**: 176; Dec. 4, 1917, **45**: 207; Dec. 7, 1917, **45**: 237; Dec. 11, 1917, **45**: 271; Dec. 21, 1917, **45**: 341

January–March 1918
Jan. 1, 1918, **45**: 420; Jan. 3, 1918, **45**: 448; Jan. 4, 1918, **45**: 474; Jan. 9, 1918, **45**: 559; Jan. 11, 1918, **45**: 573; Jan. 15, 1918, **45**: 601; Jan. 16, 1918, **46**: 12; Jan. 18, 1918, **46**: 33; Jan. 19, 1918, **46**: 41; Jan. 21, 1918, **46**: 67; Jan. 22, 1918, **46**: 78; Jan. 31, 1918, **46**: 203; Feb. 1, 1918, **46**: 212; Feb. 8, 1918, **46**: 297; Feb. 24, 1918, **46**: 438; Feb. 26, 1918, **46**: 468; March 1, 1918, **46**: 508; March 5, 1918, **46**: 553; March 8, 1918, **46**: 581; March 12, 1918, **46**: 620; March 19, 1918, **47**: 82; March 20, 1918, **47**: 92; March 27, 1918, **47**: 171; March 29, 1918, **47**: 206

April–July 1918
April 2, 1918, **47**: 231; April 3, 1918, **47**: 241; April 12, 1918, **47**: 334; April 15, 1918, **47**: 348; April 16, 1918, **47**: 353; May 14, 1918, **48**: 14; May 16, 1918, **48**: 45; May 27, 1918, **48**: 173; May 28, 1918, **48**: 192; June 5, 1918, **48**: 247; June 18, 1918, **48**: 356; June 25, 1918, **48**: 432; July 2, 1918, **48**: 488; July 6, 1918, **48**: 544; July 9, 1918, **48**: 578; July 23, 1918, **49**: 69; July 24, 1918, **49**: 83; July 29, 1918, **49**: 128; July 30, 1918, **49**: 137; July 31, 1918, **49**: 145

August–November 1918
Aug. 1, 1918, **49:** 157; Aug. 8, 1918, **49:** 221; Aug. 9, 1918, **49:** 230; Aug. 13, 1918, **49:** 246; Aug. 14, 1918, **49:** 258; Sept. 3, 1918, **49:** 431; Sept. 10, 1918, **49:** 513; Oct. 8, 1918, **51:** 275; Oct. 14, 1918, **51:** 328; Oct. 15, 1918, **51:** 344; Oct. 16, 1918, **51:** 347; Oct. 17, 1918, **51:** 372; Oct. 21, 1918, **51:** 403; Oct. 22, 1918, **51:** 412; Oct. 23, 1918, **51:** 416; Nov. 3, 1918, **51:** 575; Nov. 4, 1918, **51:** 592; Nov. 5, 1918, **51:** 604; Nov. 6, 1918, **51:** 615

Charles Sumner Hamlin, Nov. 25, 1916, **40:** 76; Nov. 27, 1916, **40:** 87; Nov. 30, 1916, **40:** 112

Edward Mandell House
1916
Nov. 26, 1916, **40:** 84; Nov. 28, 1916, **40:** 96; Dec. 14, 1916, **40:** 237; Dec. 20, 1916, **40:** 304; Dec. 23, 1916, **40:** 326

January–June 1917
Jan. 3, 1917, **40:** 402; Jan. 4, 1917, **40:** 407; Jan. 5, 1917, **40:** 418; Jan. 11, 1917, **40:** 445; Jan. 12, 1917, **40:** 462; Feb. 1, 1917, **41:** 86; March 3, 1917, **41:** 317; March 4, 1917, **41:** 331; March 5, 1917, **41:** 340; March 22, 1917, **41:** 454; March 25, 1917, **41:** 468; March 27, 1917, **41:** 482; March 28, 1917, **41:** 496; April 2, 1917, **41:** 528; April 26, 1917, **42:** 142; April 28, 1917, **42:** 155; April 29, 1917, **42:** 160; April 30, 1917, **42:** 168; June 15, 1917, **42:** 527

July–December 1917
July 4, 1917, **43:** 99; July 14, 1917, **43:** 183; July 26, 1917, **43:** 290; Aug. 7, 1917, **43:** 390; Aug. 15, 1917, **43:** 485; Aug. 18, 1917, **43:** 521; Sept. 3, 1917, **44:** 141; Sept. 5, 1917, **44:** 157; Sept. 9, 1917, **44:** 175; Sept. 10, 1917, **44:** 184; Sept. 16, 1917, **44:** 200; Oct. 13, 1917, **44:** 378; Oct. 22, 1917, **44:** 426; Oct. 23, 1917, **44:** 433; Oct. 24, 1917, **44:** 437; Dec. 17, 1917, **45:** 317; Dec. 18, 1917, **45:** 323; Dec. 19, 1917, **45:** 332; Dec. 4, 1917, **45:** 333; Dec. 30, 1917, **45:** 397

January–April 1918
Jan. 4, 1918, **45:** 458; Jan. 9, 1918, **45:** 550; Jan. 17, 1918, **46:** 23; Jan. 27, 1918, **46:** 114; Jan. 29, 1918, **46:** 167; Feb. 8, 1918, **46:** 290; Feb. 9, 1918, **46:** 313; Feb. 10, 1918, **46:** 316; Feb. 11, 1918, **46:** 327; Feb. 23, 1918, **46:** 429; Feb. 24, 1918, **46:** 435; Feb. 25, 1918, **46:** 444; Feb. 26, 1918, **46:** 467; Feb. 27, 1918, **46:** 485; Feb. 28, 1918, **46:** 487; March 3, 1918, **46:** 519; March 4, 1918, **46:** 532; March 5, 1918, **46:** 553; March 28, 1918, **47:** 185; March 29, 1918, **47:** 206; March 30, 1918, **47:** 215; March 31, 1918, **47:** 215; April 9, 1918, **47:** 307; April 10, 1918, **47:** 313; April 11, 1918, **47:** 323

May–October 1918
May 2, 1918, **47:** 498; May 9, 1918, **47:** 585; May 17, 1918, **48:** 50; May 18, 1918, **48:** 62; May 19, 1918, **48:** 69; May 20, 1918, **48:** 94; May 23, 1918, **48:** 135; June 11, 1918, **48:** 288; June 13, 1918, **48:** 310; June 14, 1918, **48:** 317; June 20, 1918, **48:** 381; June 21, 1918, **48:** 391; June 27, 1918, **48:** 454; July 25, 1918, **49:** 96; Aug. 15, 1918, **49:** 265; Aug. 16, 1918, **49:** 275; Aug. 17, 1918, **49:** 281; Aug. 18, 1918, **49:** 286; Aug. 19, 1918, **49:** 293; Aug. 20, 1918, **49:** 303;

Sept. 8, 1918, **49:** 488; Sept. 9, 1918, **49:** 508; Sept. 16, 1918, **51:** 23; Sept. 24, 1918, **51:** 102; Sept. 27, 1918, **51:** 142; Sept. 28, 1918, **51:** 145; Oct. 9, 1918, **51:** 275; Oct. 13, 1918, **51:** 314; Oct. 15, 1918, **51:** 340

Breckinridge Long, Jan. 30, 1917, **41:** 70

William Phillips, April 24, 1917, **42:** 127; May 5, 1917, **42:** 232; July 20, 1918, **49:** 51; July 25, 1918, **49:** 97; Aug. 3, 1918, **49:** 178; Aug. 14, 1918, **49:** 261; Sept. 27, 1918, **51:** 141

Frank Lyon Polk, March 11, 1918, **46:** 597; July 16, 1918, **48:** 639

ILLUSTRATIONS

Illustrations appear in the center section of each volume

WOODROW WILSON

The happy warrior, **40**
Taking the oath for a second time, **41**
Delivering the second Inaugural, **41**
The return to the White House, **41**
Delivering the War Message, **41**
Leading the parade in honor of the men drafted in the District of Columbia, **42**
A moment of relaxation, **43**
The Red Cross War Council, **44**
Reviewing the troops at Fort Myer, Virginia, **45**
The first versions of the Fourteen Points, **45**
The shorthand draft of the Fourteen Points, **45**
Wilson's transcript of his shorthand draft, **45**
The final draft of the Fourteen Points Address, **45**
Marching in the Red Cross Parade in New York, May 18, 1918, **46**
Portrait by John Singer Sargent (frontispiece), **47**
The War Cabinet, **47**
Speaking at Mount Vernon, July 4, 1918, **48**
Etching by Bernhardt Wall, **48**
Christening the *Quistconck* at Hog Island, August 5, 1918, **49**
Marching in the Fourth Liberty Loan Parade in New York, **51**

COLLATERAL

General Pershing arriving in Boulogne, France, June 13, 1917, **42**
Arthur James Balfour and Robert Lansing, **42**
Admiral William S. Sims, **42**
George Creel, **42**
Stockton Axson, **42**
Raymond B. Fosdick, **42**
Alexander F. Kerensky, **42**
David Lloyd George, **43**
Sir William Wiseman, **43**
Gen. Tasker H. Bliss in France, **43**
Samuel Gompers, **43**
The Council of National Defense and the Advisory Commission, **43**
The Women's Committee of the Council of National Defense, **43**
The Secretary of War draws the first draft number, July 20, 1917, **43**
Myrtle Hill Cemetery, Rome, Georgia, **44**

Secretary Baker with his civilian staff, **44**
Major General Peyton C. March, **44**
Harry A. Garfield, **44**
Edward N. Hurley, **44**
Lincoln Steffens, **44**
Max Eastman, **44**
Leon Trotsky, **45**
V. I. Lenin, **45**
Aboard the U.S.S. *Mayflower* (Secretary Daniels, Ambassador Satō, Viscount Ishii, Secretary Lansing), **45**
Lord Reading, **46**
William B. Wilson, **46**
General Enoch H. Crowder, **46**
General Pershing and Secretary Baker in Bordeaux, **46**
Count Ottokar Czernin von und zu Chudenitz, **46**
Count Georg F. von Hertling, **46**
The Russian Commission, **46**
In the frontline trenches of the Rainbow Division, March 1918, **47**
Marshal Ferdinand Foch, **47**
Alfred Milner, 1st Viscount Milner, **47**
David Franklin Houston, **47**
Gutzon Borglum, **47**
The National War Labor Board, **47**
Carrie Clinton Lane Chapman Catt, **47**
David Rowland Francis, **48**
DeWitt Clinton Poole, Jr., **48**
John Kenneth Caldwell, **48**
Austin Melvin Knight, **48**
Thomas Garrigue Masaryk, **48**
U.S.S. *Brooklyn* arriving in Golden Horn Bay, Vladivostok, **48**
The Senate Committee on Military Affairs, **49**
John F. Stevens, **49**
Major General Leonard Wood, **49**
Sir Eric Drummond, **49**
General William S. Graves; General Rudolf Gajda, **49**
General Grigorii Mikhailovich Semenov, **49**
Vice Consul L. S. Gray and Consul General Ernest L. Harris, **49**
Prince Maximilian von Baden, **51**
Wilhelm Solf, **51**
General Maurice Janin, **51**
Herbert Hoover, **51**
John William Davis, **51**
William Graves Sharp, **51**
Pleasant Alexander Stovall, **51**
Thomas Nelson Page, **51**
Theodore Roosevelt, **51**
Henry Cabot Lodge, **51**
Thomas William Lamont, **51**

INDEXES BY VOLUME

40: 577
41: 559
42: 573
43: 543
44: 573
45: 603

46: 623
47: 625
48: 649
49: 553
51: 651

INDEX FOR VOLUMES 40–49, 51

A. Barton Hepburn: His Life and Service to His Time (Bishop), **48:** 582n1

Abancourt, France, **48:** 389

Abangarez gold field, Costa Rica, **46:** 450

Abbeville, France; meeting of Supreme War Council at, **47:** 497-98, 517, 535, 567, 595, 615, 618; **48:** 32,n3, 34, 386; German attacks on, **48:** 389

Abbott, Grace, **51:** 181-82,n1,4

Abbott, James Francis, **48:** 450,n2, 451, n3, 457, 485, 581-85

Abbott, John Jay, **41:** 383,n1; **42:** 54; **45:** 99-100; **48:** 518,n1

Abbott, Lawrence Fraser, **47:** 16,n3; **51:** 15-16

Abbott, Lyman, **42:** 570-71; **47:** 16,n3

Abbott, Robert Sengstacke, **43:** 392n1

Abdul-Hamid II (of Turkey), **40:** 501,n1

Abraham and Straus, **51:** 644n2

Abrogation of Treaty with Norway and Sweden of 1827 by Resolution of the Senate (L. H. Woolsey), **45:** 177n1

Abusing Free Speech (Bryan), **44:** 54n1

Abyssinian Baptist Church of New York, **43:** 412n2

Académie des Sciences Morales et Politiques of the Institut de France, **48:** 27n1

Academy of Arts and Letters: *see* American Academy of Arts and Letters

Acid Test (New York *Sun*), **46:** 574n1

Acid Test of Our Democracy (Thomas), **51:** 12n2

Ackerman, Carl William, **41:** 240n2; **45:** 385,n3; **46:** 172-73, 215, 352-53, 555, 556-57; **47:** 523-25

"Across the Flood" Addresses at the Dinner in Honor of the Earl of Reading at the Lotos Club, New York, March 27th, 1918, **47:** 185n1

Activities of the Committee on Public Information, **45:** 580,n1

Adamic, Louis, **40:** 176n1

Adams, Herbert, **44:** 340, 347

Adams, John, **41:** 302, 303, 307; **42:** 245, 246,n5

Adams, John Quincy, **44:** 110, 115, 116

Adams, Samuel Hopkins, **44:** 301n1

Adamson, William Charles, **40:** 421-22,n2; **42:** 34, 218n1, 221, 290n2, 299; **43:** 20, 39, 111n4; **44:** 92, 116-17; **47:** 191,n1; **49:** 143; and Redfield exchange on pensions, **40:** 95,n1, 163, 182-83, 218; and railroad legislation, **41:** 13-14,n2, 29-31, 53-54, 54, 66, 156, 157, 258; and water-power legislation, **41:**

19-20, 23; and export restrictions, **42:** 224,n2

Adamson Act (Eight-Hour Act), **40:** 7-8, 92, 246n2, 265, 266-67, 303, 422n3; **41:** 352n1, 413, 430n2, 432; **42:** 218n1, 221; **45:** 225n1

Adamson railway mediation bill, **40:** 421-22,n2

Adamson water-power bill, **40:** 207; **41:** 19-20; Sherley amendment to, **51:** 525,n2; *see also* conservation legislation

Adana, Turkey, **45:** 52

Addams, Jane, **40:** 46, 335, 343-44; **41:** 302, 303-304,n3; **42:** 118-19,n1, 208, 214; **45:** 586, 593

Address of President Wilson . . . May 18, 1918, **48:** 57n

Address of President Wilson to the American Federation of Labor Convention, **45:** 17n

Address of President Wilson to the Officers of the Atlantic Fleet, **43:** 431n

Adee, Alvey Augustus, **49:** 149, 170

Adee, Ellen Skeel (Mrs. David Graham), **49:** 149,n1

Adler, Harry Clay, **51:** 482-83,n1

Adler, Viktor, **51:** 564,n4, 566

Admiral of the New Empire: The Life and Career of George Dewey (Spector), **44:** 296n1

Admiral Sims and the Modern American Navy (Morison), **42:** 82n1

Admiral Spaun, S.M.S., **51:** 492

Admirals, Generals, and American Foreign Policy, 1898-1914 (Challener), **51:** 718n5

Ador, Gustave, **43:** 28,n1; **51:** 249,n9

Adriance, Walter Maxwell, **42:** 570,n3

Aehrenthal, Alois Lexa, Count von, **41:** 56n2

Aeolian Company of New York, **44:** 77n1

Aerial Estimate Cut 40 Per Cent (Swope), **47:** 52n3

Aero Club of America, **47:** 293,n1

Afghanistan, **47:** 244, 334, 366, 423, 424

Africa, **42:** 389n4; **48:** 27

African Methodist Episcopal Church, **41:** 218n1; **46:** 614,n1,2; **51:** 168n1, 193n1

Against Service Abroad (*Milwaukee Journal*), **43:** 319,n1

Against the Specter of a Dragon: The Campaign for American Military Preparedness, 1914-1917 (Finnegan), **40:** 267n1

agricultural appropriations bills: and

agricultural appropriations bills (*cont.*)
Gore amendment, **48:** 42,n1, 74; and prohibition, **48:** 161,n2, 166; **51:** 28,n2, 105; WW on, **48:** 260; and Jones amendment, **48:** 428n2; WW vetoes because of wheat section, **48:** 595-97

Agricultural Discontent in the Middle West, 1900-1938 (Saloutos and Hicks), **49:** 441n7

agriculture, **44:** 36, 37; **45:** 58-60, 181; WW on importance of during war, **42:** 73-74; and food-production bills, **42:** 294,n1; H. Hoover on grain crisis, **43:** 117-18; **46:** 304-309; **47:** 120-21,n1; farmers and draft exemption, **44:** 53, 61, 72-73, 150, 240-41, 258, 269-70,n3, 343n1; **45:** 181, 584; **46:** 428n1, 446; prices and price fixing, **44:** 88,n1, 89, 191-92; **47:** 117; **51:** 118n1, 126-27,n1,2; and livestock industry, **44:** 160,n1; **45:** 85; **46:** 505; **47:** 149-53; request for agricultural labor in France, **44:** 461-62, 467; and brewing industry, **45:** 83-84; WW's message to farmers' conference, **46:** 174-78; and farmers' petition, **46:** 279-81, 281-82, 335-36; WW's statement on wheat prices, **46:** 430-32; WW on cultivating war gardens, **46:** 439; and Pennsylvania farmers, **46:** 602,n1; and Baer bill, **47:** 20,n1, 72, 85; and farmers and Nonpartisan League in Minnesota, **47:** 87-88, 178-79, 236; and western grain exchanges, **47:** 158-59,n1; A. F. Lever and House of Reps. Committee on, **48:** 259-60; and Indiana Democratic platform, **48:** 319; breakup of Washington State Grange meeting at Walla Walla, **48:** 291-94; and aid to drought-stricken farmers, **49:** 90-91, 99-100, 101; *see also* farmers and farming

Agriculture, Committee on (House of Reps.), **42:** 301n2; **45:** 300, 301, 335n1; **47:** 178,n2; **49:** 476n1; A. F. Lever and, **48:** 259-60, 272

Agriculture, Department of, **40:** 28, 521; **41:** 84-85, 148, 206; **42:** 136, 344, 383, 430, 437n1; **46:** 175-76, 432, 478, 614; **47:** 46, 88n1, 193-94, 449; **48:** 8, 219-20,n1, 298, 344; **49:** 53n1, 101, 386, 440; **51:** 357; and drought crisis in Texas, **45:** 76-77, 106, 161; and Federal Power Commission, **45:** 168,n1

Agriculture and Forestry, Committee on (Senate), **42:** 301n2, 529, 532; **43:** 48n1, 120; **47:** 8; **48:** 428n1

Agudath Achim Congregation, Harlem, **51:** 424n1

Aguilar, Cándido, **41:** 350-51,n3, 392,n1; **47:** 164

Aguilar, Francisco, **41:** 142-43

Ahumada, Chihuahua, Mexico: *see* Villa Ahumada

Air Nitrates Corporation of Sheffield, Ala., **47:** 462

Aircraft International Standardization Board, **47:** 293n1

Aircraft Production Board, **42:** 549; **44:** 538n2; **45:** 155, 280-81, 314n1, 357; **46:** 57, 94n1, 208-209, 229; **47:** 112, 396. 400; **49:** 349, 350; and G. Borglum charges against, **47:** 41n1; A. Landon on, **47:** 322n4; and Marshall-Wells-McNab preliminary report on, **47:** 331, 332; H. Coffin resigns as chairman of, **47:** 361-62, 383; and H. B. Thayer resignation, **47:** 414, 415; J. D. Ryan appointed head of, **47:** 437, 494, 501, 526

aircraft program (U.S.), **42:** 530-31, 549-50, 552; **47:** 39, 386; **51:** 15-16,n1, 38, 618,n1; and Liberty airplane engine, **44:** 538-41; and G. Borglum, **45:** 69-70, 102, 155, 214, 280-81, 314, 356-58, 397, 426-47; **46:** 57, 82, 94-95,n1, 106, 206, 332, 433-34; **47:** 41,n2, 67, 169-70, 234-35, 235, 259, 296-97, 344, 521, 535-36, 541, 541-42, 545, 546, 554, 580, 587n1, 603; N. D. Baker on, **45:** 155-56, 331, 426-27; B. Fiske on, **45:** 387n1; and copper industry, **46:** 128; and lumber industry, **46:** 138; and Marshall-Wells-McNab report, **47:** 41,n2, 193, 259, 293,n1, 328-32, 335-36,n1, 508-509, 509-10, 545,n1, 554: and H. B. Swope's articles on, **47:** 51-52,n1,3; and false optimism, **47:** 207,n1; and Senate investigation, **47:** 303, 321-22,n1,4; J. D. Ryan on, **47:** 526; D. Lawrence's disclosures about Borglum, **47:** 587,n1, 587-88; C. E. Hughes agrees to assist in investigation of, **48:** 3, 15, 45-46, 50,n1; and Senate Military Affairs Committee, **48:** 10n1; military separated from Signal Corps, **48:** 73-74

Airplane Scandal (*The Outlook*), **51:** 15,n1

Aishton, Richard Henry, **47:** 418-19,n1

Aitchison, Clyde Bruce, **51:** 248,n5

Aitken, William Maxwell: *see* Beaverbrook, William Maxwell Aitken, 1st Baron

Aix-les-Bains, France, **49:** 65

Ajo, Arizona, **43:** 157

Alabama, **48:** 553; Birmingham suggested for training camp site, **42:** 496, 522; coal mines in, **42:** 460-61, 473, 504; **47:** 410; coal mining situation in, **43:** 368, 433-34, 437, 506, 511; **44:** 15, 80, 144n1; **45:** 269, 276; **46:** 29-30, 103,n2; politics in, **49:** 138,n1, 236,n1, 245,n2; **51:** 632

Alabama claims, **41:** 303

Alabama Coal Operators Association, **42:** 460-61, 473; **45:** 269, 568n1; **46:** 103n2

Alaska, **43:** 385n1; and general leasing bill, **45:** 376

Alaska general fisheries bill, **40:** 290-92,n1, 292, 293, 305-306, 315, 318-19, 366, 387, 417-18; **41:** 179, 207, 209,n1, 230, 236

Alaskan Packers' Association, **40:** 291n2

Albania, **40:** 28; **44:** 546, 547; **45:** 470; **51:** 43, 274, 501, 503

Albert, France, **47:** 162; **48:** 332

Albert I (of Belgium), **40:** 405; **42:** 172; **43:** 469; **45:** 50; **48:** 151; and deportation issue, **40:** 26, 171-72, 518-19, 547-48

Albert, Heinrich, **43:** 133n1

Alcedo, S. S., **44:** 532n1

alcohol: *see* prohibition

Alcohol: Its Relation to Human Efficiency and Longevity (Fisk), **42:** 323n2

Alderman, Edwin Anderson, **40:** 444; **41:** 503-505

Aldrich-Vreeland Act, and emergency currency limits, **51:** 538,n8-9

Alekseev, Mikhail Vasil'evich, **45:** 228-29,n2, 264; **46:** 341, 411n1; **47:** 549,n2

Alexander (of Serbia), **44:** 436-37; **47:** 36,n2

Alexander I (of Russia), **46:** 618

Alexander II (of Russia), **42:** 329

Alexander III (of Russia), **51:** 567

Alexander, Archibald Stevens, **51:** 649-50

Alexander, Joshua Willis, **46:** 150, 151, 171, 282, 283, 329-30; and Alaskan general fisheries bill, **40:** 291, 319, 366, 387, 417-18; **41:** 209n1, 230, 236

Alexander, Magnus Washington, **47:** 272,n1

Alexander, Moses, **43:** 494; **44:** 81,n1; **47:** 194; **49:** 145n2

Alexander, Thomas Mathew, **51:** 113,n2, 115

Alexander Anderson, S. S., **44:** 159

Alexander Sprunt and Son, **42:** 203n1

Alexandra Fedorovna (Empress of Russia), **41:** 416

Alfieri, Vittorio, **46:** 454,n1, 455, 456, 559,n3

Alfonso XIII (of Spain), **40:** 405; **41:** 35, 40; **47:** 124, 140, 176-77,n1; and Austria-Hungary's peace moves, **46:** 397, 400, 418, 432, 435, 440-42, 467n1, 473,n1, 483, 484, 486-87

Alfonso XIII, S. S., **42:** 438

Algeciras Conference, **44:** 476

Alien and Sedition Acts (1798), **42:** 245, 246

Alien Property Act, **49:** 432

Alien Property Custodian, **48:** 228n1; and Busch case, **51:** 395n1, 445, 469

Alien Property Custodian Creates a Selling Organization to Dispose of All German-Owned Corporations (Official Bulletin), **49:** 432n1

Aliens and Dissenters: Federal Suppression of Radicals, 1903-1933 (Preston), **44:** 17n1

aliens in the United States, **45:** 200n1, 224, 268-69, 271; **46:** 206, 213, 284, 604; **47:** 275-76, 325-26, 360-61, 362-63, 363-65, 380-81; and Miller case, **46:** 97-98, 119; and employment, **44:** 493, 498; and conscription, **45:** 177n1

All Want Peace: Why Not Have It Now? (Butler), **40:** 24n1

Alleged Divulgence of President's Note to Belligerent Powers: Hearings Before the Committee on Rules, House of Representatives, Sixty-Fourth Congress, Second Session, **40:** 349n11

Allemagne et les Problèmes de la Paix pendant la Première Guerre Mondiale: Documents extraits des archives de l'Office allemand des Affaires étrangères (Scherer and Grunewald, eds.), **40:** 504n1; **41:** 49n1

Allen, Benjamin Shannon, **51:** 113-16,n1

Allen, Frederic Winthrop, **43:** 76,n1, 77-78, 338,n1

Allenby, Edmund Henry Hynman, **46:** 471,n2

Allentown, Pa., **45:** 364

alley legislation, **47:** 53, 192-93,n2, 255,n1

Alliance of Poles in America, Cleveland, **44:** 33

Alliance of Polish Singers, **44:** 303

Allied Action in Russia Urgent (Williams), **49:** 93n1

Allied councils, *see for example*: Inter-Allied Embargo Council; Inter-Allied Naval Council; Inter-Allied Council on War Purchases and Finance; Supreme War Council; Inter-Allied Food Council

Allied Maritime Transport Council, **48:** 233n1; **49:** 418; **51:** 94, 223n6, 638

Allied Military Council at Vladivostok, **51:** 25, 86n1

Allied Naval Council: *see* Inter-Allied Naval Council

Allied Purchasing Commission, **46:** 111, 112, 217, 394; **48:** 145n3

Allies, **43:** 173, 174; **51:** 8; tonnage problems, **43:** 45, 140-42; **45:** 489; **51:** 94-95; and British financial crisis, **43:** 67; and Asia Minor, **43:** 355-56: N. Angell memorandum on diplomatic strategy of, **43:** 401-409; differences among, **43:** 464; **44:** 462-63; **48:** 605; and Pope's peace appeal, **43:** 520; **44:** 24-25; G. J. Sosnowski on, **44:** 4-6; Lloyd George on war plans of, **44:** 125-30; H. F. Bouillon on plan for, **44:** 141,n1; and Russia, **44:** 179, 180; **45:** 166n1, 184-85, 411-14, 417-19; **46:** 45-46,n3; W. H. Page on peace terms of, **44:** 329-31; and woman suffrage, **44:** 441; H. Hoover on food supplies and, **44:** 443-44, 544n1; **46:** 565n1; **48:** 466-68; and Brest-Litovsk peace proposals, **45:** 384n2, 432,n1, 436-37; assets in peace negotiations, **45:** 462-65; and Poland, **46:** 48, 120; and speeches of G. Hertling and O. Czernin, **46:** 234; and proposed "white list" and financial blockade, **46:** 423n1; A. J. Balfour on Austria-Hungary's peace moves, **46:** 473-74; E. M. House on WW's reply to Charles I and, **46:** 507; and Inter-Allied General Reserve, **46:** 558-60; and Socialists and peace terms, **47:** 75; and cereal supplies, **47:** 120,n1; and Austria-Hungary, **47:** 122-23; **48:** 447-48; House on building morale of **47:** 131; **48:** 400; request for U.S. troops

Allies (*cont.*)
and brigading issue, **47:** 204, 213-14,n1, 214,n1, 230, 260-61, 338-41, 497-98, 618-19; **48:** 226; objectives in eastern theater, **47:** 423-24; and Rumania, **47:** 474n2; and question of U.S. war declaration against Bulgaria and Turkey, **47:** 490-91,n2; **48:** 79-80; **49:** 365,n1,2, 537; C. Ackerman on U.S. confidence in, **47:** 524-25; T. Masaryk on Russia and, **47:** 549-52; and the Netherlands, **47:** 564-65; and proposed Russian relief commission, **48:** 315-16; **49:** 177; and Czech legion, **48:** 428-29, 496-97; **49:** 46, 220, 263,n1; and league of nations, **49:** 202-203, 428-29; and Britain's appointment of High Commissioner to Siberia, **49:** 250n1; and T. H. Bliss' plan for ending war in 1919, **49:** 259-61, 276-77, 336-44; and proposal for inter-Allied civilian board on Russia, **49:** 323,n1, 332,n2; Sweden and, **49:** 437-38; Bliss on, **51:** 40-45; 46-47, 427-28; Czechs' plea for assistance from, **51:** 51n2; and U.S. food program, **51:** 89; WW on U.S. military policy and, **51:** 121-22; and Bulgaria, **51:** 145, 163; and conduct of operations in various theaters of war, **51:** 195-203; and consultation on peace terms, **51:** 254, 289,n1, 307-309, 411-12, 413, 414-15, 416-17, 427-29, 514-17; and Polish National Army, **51:** 447-48; and Turkey, **51:** 456; and acceptance of WW's peace terms, **51:** 580-82; and delegates to peace conference, **51:** 606-607; *see also* Russia: *intervention in*; Supreme War Council; World War—strategic plans; *see also* under names of individual countries

Allies and the Holy See (London *Times*), **49:** 189n4

Allies and the Russian Revolution (Warth), **49:** 11n4

Allies Reported Eager to Send Aid to Russia . . . Fear that We May Act Too Late Oppresses Allies (*New York Times*), **49:** 93n1

Allinson, Brent Dow, **47:** 154-55,n1

Allport, James H., **47:** 89

All-Russian Provisional Government, **51:** 102n1

All-Russian Tanners' Union, **49:** 321

All-Russian Union of Cooperative Societies, **48:** 359

All-Russian Union of Zemstvos, **43:** 455,n3

Alma-Tadema, Lawrence, **42:** 545,n7

Almossava, S.M.S., **51:** 493

Along This Way: The Autobiography of James Weldon Johnson, **46:** 384n, 385n1

Alpine, John R., **51:** 523,n2

Alsace: *see* Alsace-Lorraine

Alsace-Lorraine, **40:** 16, 68, 69, 186n1, 307n1, 404, 435, 501, 504n1; **41:** 26n1, 62, 80, 217, 315n2, 356, 464; **42:** 155, 156, 198, 341-42, 382, 385, 389n4, 444n1, 456; **43:** 246n1, 276, 277, 407n4, 445, 468, 471, 496; **44:** 21, 24, 44, 218, 319, 329, 330, 379, 477; **45:** 3, 4, 176, 207, 220, 222n1, 232, 365, 412, 416, 418, 441, 466, 467; **46:** 87, 113, 113n2, 163, 185, 187, 190, 244, 253, 275, 290, 292, 312, 428; **47:** 202, 239, 240, 430, 589n1; **48:** 153, 214, 215, 553, 554; **49:** 111, 123, 229-30, 398-99; **51:** 21n1, 47, 106n7, 156n2, 232, 236, 240, 244, 255n1, 262, 265n1, 269,n1, 273, 277n7, 331, 335, 339, 351, 385, 411, 412, 454, 463, 470, 472, 500; mentioned in Inquiry memorandum, **45:** 468-69, 473-74; and Fourteen Points, **45:** 477-78, 484, 514, 527, 537, 550, 552, 557, 595, 599; and British war aims, **45:** 487n2; G. Hertling's and O. Czernin's views on, **46:** 224

Alsberg, Carl Lucas, **45:** 84,n1

Alsberg, Henry Garfield, **42:** 316,n1

Alschuler, Samuel, **47:** 425,n2, 426

Alston, Beilby Francis, **40:** 514,n1; **41:** 176,n6, 178,n1, 187

Alte, José Francisco da Horta Machada da Franca, Viscount of, **48:** 173,n1

Alvarado, Salvador, **44:** 331n3

Alvarez, Salvador, **49:** 34

Amalgamated Association of Street and Electric Railway Employees of America, **47:** 207,n1

Amalgamated Clothing Workers of America, **44:** 162, 164,n2

Amalgamated Copper Company, **46:** 111

Amateur Diplomacy Abroad (Dell), **48:** 482n3

Ambassador Henry Morgenthau's Special Mission of 1917 (Yale), **42:** 317n3

Ambassador Morgenthau's Story, **45:** 128n1; **48:** 284n1

America and the Fight for Irish Freedom, 1866-1922 (Tansill), **48:** 118n1

America and the Future (Gardiner), **40:** 35,n3

America and the Revolution (*Springfield, Mass., Republican*), **41:** 451n2

America Now in "League to Enforce Peace" (Shaw), **42:** 151,n1

American Alliance for Labor and Democracy, **44:** 47-48,n1, 60, 95, 101, 166,n3, 467n1; **48:** 275-76

American Association for Labor Legislation, **51:** 165

American Association of Commerce and Trade of Berlin, **40:** 463n1

American Association of University Professors, **45:** 141n1,2

American Belgian Relief Society, **43:** 40n1

American Bible Society, **44:** 85, 118, 152

American Civil Liberties Union, **47:** 155n3

American Consecration Hymn, **44:** 266,n1

American Cotton Oil Company, **47:** 557n4

American Defense Society, **43**: 499, 510; **44**: 410; **46**: 459n1; **47**: 141-42; **51**: 147n1, 161, 162, 175

American Economic Cooperation with Russia (Robins), **48**: 489,n1

American Educational Association, **46**: 29

American Electric Railway Association, **49**: 251

American Exchange National Bank, N.Y., **43**: 196

American Expeditionary Forces, **47**: 172,n1; **49**: 512n1; **51**: 61, 139-41, 188; and U.S. propaganda in Russia, **46**: 200-201; *see also* United States Army

American Federation of Labor, **40**: 146, 266; **42**: 165n1, 198, 471; **43**: 25n2, 230, 266, 267, 352, 353, 393, 417; **44**: 47, 242, 302n1, 314; **45**: 7, 41n1,2, 258n2, 383; **46**: 21n2, 26, 134, 135, 356n6, 362n2, 364, 578; **47**: 106, 272, 282, 351, 461-62, 558; **49**: 24, 25, 78, 159, 181, 232,n2, 450n1; F. Frankfurter on I.W.W. and, **44**: 161-64; national convention of, **44**: 398,n1, 412, 500, 556, 562; and WW statement on eight-hour day, **44**: 421-22,n1; declines Russian request for international conference of socialists and workingmen, **44**: 483, 483-84; WW addresses national convention, **45**: 11-17, 47, 50, 68, 70, 101,n1, 104; and resolution on housing for war contract workers, **45**: 141; adopts resolution supporting WW, **45**: 298, 348-49; WW sends message to, **48**: 275, 309; on government takeover of telegraph companies, **48**: 313, 349; and Mooney case, **48**: 404; **49**: 244; and resolution on detective agencies, **48**: 438-39,n1; and proposed commission for Porto Rico, **49**: 136, 297; and draft legislation, **49**: 256

American Federation of Labor Commission to Mexico, **49**: 24, 25; report of, **49**: 26-36

American Financing of World War I (Gilbert), **43**: 350n2

American flag, **43**: 429-30; **47**: 364n4; WW on, **42**: 498-99

American Friends of Russian Freedom, **43**: 175n2

American Friends Service Committee, **43**: 492n1; **44**: 267n3

American Fruit Company, **41**: 145

American Geographical Society, **46**: 23n2

American Group of the Four-Power Consortium (proposed), **45**: 98-100; **48**: 371-74, 519-20, 522; **49**: 77, 102-103

American Group of the Six-Power Consortium, **40**: 512-13, 514-15; **45**: 97, 98-99; **48**: 371, 373

American Historical Review, **40**: 349n11; **44**: 296n1

American-Hungarian Loyalty League, **45**: 241n1

American Indians: and oil lands, **47**: 10

American Industries, **47**: 127

American Institute of International Law, **40**: 546n2, 547n3

American International Corporation, **40**: 513; **41**: 394; **42**: 63,n5; **46**: 124n2; **48**: 372-73

American International Shipbuilding Corporation, **51**: 13-14

American Intervention in Russia: The North Russian Expedition, 1918-1919 (Long), **49**: 516n1

American Iron and Steel Institute, **42**: 556n3; **43**: 155, 156

American Jewish Committee, **46**: 525n1; **47**: 555; **51**: 644; on rights of Polish Jews, **51**: 625-27

American-Jewish Joint Distribution Committee, **47**: 44, 555; **48**: 98n6

American Journal of International Law, **44**: 43n3; **45**: 603n1

American Labor Legislation Review, **43**: 418n1

American Labor Mission: *see* American Federation of Labor Commission to Mexico

American Library Association, **44**: 68; **49**: 425-26; **51**: 621,n1, 636

American Line, **41**: 187, 189, 364, 436

American National Conference Committee, **43**: 481: *see also* People's Council of America

American National Live Stock Association, **51**: 212n2

American National Red Cross, **40**: 133, 135, 513; **41**: 39, 113n2, 556; **42**: 77n1, 162, 248; **43**: 264; **44**: 74, 75, 445n1, 554-55,n1; **45**: 187,n1, 194, 330, 446; **46**: 121, 159, 485,n1, 489, 570, 596n2; **47**: 155, 388, 476n2,5, 502n1, 604-605, 613-14, 620; **48**: 221; **49**: 128, 176, 383, 385, 387, 518n5, 543; **51**: 4,n3, 593, 618; War Council of, **42**: 251, 251-52,n2, 258, 280-81; and W. H. Taft, **42**: 261, 295-96; WW's remarks at dedication of building of, **42**: 281-83, 323-24, 326, 349, 357; WW proclaims Red Cross Week, **42**: 391; **47**: 515-16; alleged discrimination in, **43**: 86n1,2,3; R. H. Dabney on, **43**: 415; and Queen Liliuokalani, **43**: 505, 506; and profits from WW's *History* . . . , **47**: 302, 336; and war fund drive, **48**: 6, 16, 53-57, 59, 94, 116, 119n1, 199,n1,2, 231; and Porto Rico, **48**: 35-36; Mrs. Lansing asks WW for contribution, **48**: 45; WW's address in New York on behalf of, **48**: 53-57, 66, 120, 256-57; WW contributes to, **48**: 78; WW refuses to appear at a Sunday meeting, **48**: 119,n1; WW and aid to Belgium and, **48**: 151; and "White House wool," **48**: 191,n3, 475; and Blue Devils, **48**: 307n1

American Neutral Conference Committee, **40**: 124n1

American News Company, **48**: 187n4

American Newspaper Publishers' Association, **48**: 148n1, 149

American Opinion and the Irish Ques-

American Opinion (cont.)
  tion, 1910-23: A Study in Opinion and Policy (Carroll), **48:** 118n1
American Patriotic League, **46:** 459n1
American Peace Movement and Social Reform, 1898-1918 (Marchand), **43:** 175n3, 512n1
American Peace Society, **41:** 243, 244
American Philosophical Society, **47:** 4,n1
American Protective League, **49:** 501, 502; W. G. McAdoo's condemnation of T. W. Gregory's defense of, **42:** 440, 441-43,n3, 446, 509-18
American Radiator Company, **46:** 91; **47:** 322n4, 557n4; **48:** 484n1
American Red Cross: *see* American National Red Cross
American Red Cross Commission to Italy, **44:** 295,n1, 296
American Red Cross Commission to Russia, **44:** 367n2; **46:** 232n1, 233n2,3, 300, 479; **48:** 142n4, 234; **49:** 529n1
American Red Cross Commission to Switzerland, **48:** 250-51,n2
American Red Cross Mission to Rumania, **48:** 303n1, 477
American Relief Clearing House, **41:** 113n3
American Republics Corporation of Delaware, **43:** 99n1
American Review of Reviews, **42:** 151,n1; **46:** 218n2; **47:** 385,n2,4
American Revolution, **42:** 440, 443
American Russian League, **51:** 644
American-Russian Relations, 1781-1947 (Williams), **46:** 232n1
American Security League, **44:** 410
American Shipbuilding Company, **42:** 477
American Ships Damaged or Destroyed by German Submarines, **41:** 502n1
American-Slavic legion, **51:** 178,n1,2
American Socialist, **43:** 165; **44:** 471
American Society for Judicial Settlement of International Disputes, **41:** 250,n3
American Society of Equity, **49:** 291, 441,n7; **51:** 212n1
American Society of Mechanical Engineers, **40:** 315n1
American Sugar Refining Company, **45:** 344n1
American Taxation: Its History as a Social Force in Democracy (Ratner), **43:** 350n2
American Telephone and Telegraph Company, **43:** 60n1; **51:** 523n1
American Union Against Militarism, **40:** 121; **41:** 7-8, 305n1; **43:** 175n1, 395, 481; **44:** 192-93, 266n2; memorandum on suppression of civil rights, **43:** 420-24
American University, Washington, D.C., **45:** 455n2; **46:** 612n1
American University of Beirut, **41:** 128n1; **45:** 185n1
American War Publicity League in France, **45:** 329n2

American Woman's Club of Shanghai, **44:** 8
American Zionism from Herzl to the Holocaust (Urofsky), **49:** 363n2
Americanism (Lansing), **40:** 276-77,n1, 557-58,n1
Americanism for the World (Wilson), **40:** 445n1
America's Answer (film), **49:** 512n2
America's Siberian Adventure, 1918-1920 (Graves), **49:** 543n1; **51:** 8n2
America's Threatened Fronts (*Springfield, Mass., Republican*), **41:** 451n2
Americus, Ga., *Times-Recorder*, **46:** 38n1
Ames, Mrs., **46:** 429,n3
Ames, Charles Wilberforce, **45:** 259,n4; **46:** 348,n3, 369, 386
Amidon, Beulah, **44:** 111, 114
Amidon, Charles Fremont, **44:** 111,n3
Amiens, France, **47:** 161, 162, 166, 181, 204, 339, 498; **48:** 332
Amoy, China, **49:** 213
Amur Railway, **46:** 47, 302, 340, 470; **47:** 71, 245, 592; **48:** 105; **51:** 479
Amur River, **49:** 283
Anaconda, Mont., **44:** 259-63
Anaconda Copper Mining Company, **43:** 341; **44:** 260-61; **45:** 322
Anatolia, **42:** 157; **51:** 503
Anatoly, Bishop of Tomsk, **44:** 69,n2
Ancient Order of Gleaners, **51:** 212n2
Anderson, Alden, **47:** 196-97,n5
Anderson, Chandler Parsons, **41:** 365-67, 385-87; **42:** 131,n1; **46:** 269
Anderson, Rev. D., **40:** 124,n1, 125-27, 164
Anderson, Edwin Hatfield, **41:** 380,n1
Anderson, George Weston, **40:** 104, 244n1; **44:** 152,n1, 422-23,n1; **45:** 265-66,n1, 267; **49:** 422,n1
Anderson, Henry Watkins, **48:** 303,n1
Anderson, John M., **51:** 212,n2
Anderson, Kenneth, **42:** 379
Anderson, Louis Bernard, **43:** 392,n1
Anderson, Sydney, **44:** 379,n1
Anderson, William Alexander, **47:** 16, n6
Andover Theological Seminary, **42:** 292n2
Andrássy, Count Julius (Andrássy von Czik-Szent-Király und Krasznahorka), **51:** 526,n1, 526-27
Andrews, Frank, **46:** 429,n1
Andrews, James W., **51:** 4,n3, 18n1
Andrews, R. McCants, **42:** 116
Angell, Norman, **40:** 10-19; **42:** 89-90, 422; **48:** 629; memorandum on Allied diplomatic strategy, **43:** 401-409; on league of nations, **48:** 613, 617-18; on political conditions of Allied success, **48:** 614-21
Anglo-American relations: *see* Great Britain and the United States
Anglo-French Conference, Dec. 26, 1916, **40:** 439n1
Anglo-Soviet Relations, 1917-1921: Intervention and the War (Ullman), **45:**

189n1, 544n6; **47:** 245n3; **49:** 518n4; **51:** 4n2

Anheuser-Busch Brewing Association, **51:** 395n1

Annals of the American Academy of Political and Social Sciences, **43:** 454n1; **49:** 441n8

Annapolis: *see* United States Naval Academy

Annual Reports of the Navy Department for the Fiscal Year 1917, **41:** 298n1

Annual Reports of the Secretary of the Navy for the Fiscal Year 1918, **47:** 223n2

Anschuetz, Carl, **43:** 324n2

Answer, The (New York *Sun*), **51:** 279,n9

Antachan, Manchuria, **51:** 479,n1

Anthony, Daniel Read, Jr., **42:** 85,n2; **46:** 13, 16

Anthony, Susan Brownell, **44:** 168

anthracite coal, **40:** 102-103

Anti-Imperialist League, **46:** 257n1

antilynching campaign, **46:** 380-81, 385,n1, 550; **49:** 89, 97-98, 113-14

antiprofiteering rent bill, **48:** 190, 192-93, 193, 222, 238

Anti-Saloon League of America, **42:** 259n1; **43:** 42n1,2, 52,n1, 64,n1, 84; **48:** 350-51

Anti-Saloon League of New Jersey, **51:** 547n1

antisubmarine craft, **43:** 209n1

antitrust legislation, **40:** 103-104; *see also* Clayton Antitrust Act; Federal Trade Commission Act; Sherman Antitrust Act

antitrust suits, **46:** 297,n2

Antwerp, Belgium, **43:** 466,n2

Apache Indians, **41:** 467

Appeal to Reason (Girard, Kan.), **43:** 165; **45:** 203,n1

Appleton, William Archibald, **46:** 21,n1,2, 356n6

Appropriations Committee (House of Reps.), **40:** 251; **42:** 478, 479; **43:** 234; **44:** 28; **47:** 38, 58, 600, 602; **48:** 119n2, 137, 139, 140, 189, 335n1; **49:** 233, 315; **51:** 138

Appropriations Committee (Senate), **43:** 233; **48:** 119n2

Arabia, **45:** 471, 487n2; **51:** 503, 514

Arabia incident, **40:** 75, 95, 107, 190, 191, 212, 272, 307n1 430, 432

Arcade Auditorium, Washington, D.C., **42:** 451n1

Archangel (Arkhangelsk), Russia, **43:** 249; **47:** 355, 367, 513n7; **48:** 262; **49:** 285, 312n1; **51:** 31, 32, 141; General Poole's interference in affairs of, **49:** 496, 508; intervention in : *see* Russia—Murmansk and Archangel, intervention in

Archangel-Vologda-Ekaterinburg Railroad, **49:** 285; **51:** 52

Archbishop of York: *see* Long, Cosmo Gordon

Archinard, Louis, **43:** 426,n1

Areopagitica (WW's draft of speech), **40:** 445n1

Argentina, **41:** 249n1, 499; **42:** 15, 314, 315, 358-60; **44:** 215n2; **47:** 120; ambassador to, **40:** 463,n2; and proposed conference of American nations, **42:** 358-60, 376; and Germany, **44:** 131, 140,n3, 164,n1, 181; and wheat, **45:** 59, 69, 74, 86; **46:** 305, 307

Arguments Advanced For and Against Compulsory Control of the Steel Industry (memorandum), **51:** 285,n1

Arizona, **42:** 563; **46:** 128, 129-34, 573; **47:** 194, 347, 597-98; and Bisbee deportations, **45:** 134-35; gubernatorial contest in, **45:** 403,n1; labor disturbances and copper mine strike in, **43:** 3, 53,n1, 98, 104, 104-105, 113,n1, 127, 128, 131, 157, 157-58, 158-59, 170, 171, 222n1, 230-31, 239, 253, 339-40, 352, 353, 373, 416-17, 461; **44:** 17, 86,n1, 134-39, 172, 223, 424-25, 478, 479, 483, 516-20, 521-22; and alien labor, **49:** 33-34; politics in, **49:** 404,n1,2, 632

Arizona State Federation of Labor, **43:** 373, 416-17

Arkansas, **46:** 252-53; **47:** 441; and woman suffrage, **45:** 169,n1; politics in, **51:** 632

Arkansas College, **49:** 305

Arlington National Cemetery: WW's address on Memorial Day at, **42:** 422-23

Armed Merchantmen (Lansing), **41:** 71,n1

armed neutrality: *see* World War—maintenance of United States neutrality

Armed Progressive: General Leonard Wood (Lane), **48:** 173n1

armed ship bill, **41:** 278-80,n1, 294,n1, 323, 331; approved by House but debated by Senate, **41:** 317-18,n1, 324, 327, 328, 329, 350; and Zimmermann telegram, **41:** 324, 325; WW angry at senators who filibustered, **41:** 332; WW seeks support of Congress, **41:** 367

Armées Français dans la Grande Guerre, **51:** 200n3

Armenia and Armenians, **40:** 25, 65, 311, 317, 318, 414n1, 440, 469, 501; **41:** 217, 220n4; **42:** 157, 316, 332; **43:** 346, 355, 439, 485; **44:** 21, 37, 387; **45:** 419, 462, 471, 487n2, 553; **46:** 154, 182, 190; **47:** 44, 244, 424; **48:** 79n1; **49:** 20,n2; **51:** 503, 642; massacre of, **48:** 132, 284, 311; **51:** 62

Armenian Apostolic Church, **40:** 105n1; sends framed parchment of appreciation to WW, **40:** 105-106,n1

Armenian National Union of America, **49:** 20n1

Armenian Relief Commission, **41:** 113n3

Armin and Tupper Mortgage Loan Company, **43:** 200n2

Armistice 1918 (Rudin), **51:** 621n1

armor-plate factory, **42:** 23

Armour, Barbara: *see* Lowrie, Barbara Armour

Armour, George Allison, **46:** 105n1
Armour, Harriette Foote (Mrs. George Allison), **46:** 105n1
Armour, Jonathan Ogden, **42:** 301n1; **45:** 179,n1,2; **48:** 77
Armour and Company, **42:** 301n1; **46:** 28, 111, 462,n3; **49:** 498,n1; **51:** 92n1
Armour Institute of Technology, **45:** 143n4
Armstrong, Anne, **40:** 570,n5
Army (U.S.): *see* United States Army
Army Appropriations Act (1916), **41:** 151, 329; **42:** 290, 408; **43:** 7n1
Army Appropriations Act (1918), **49:** 185n1
army bill: *see* Selective Service bill
Army Reorganization Act (1916); and "joker" clause, **40:** 121-22,n1, 163; and nitrate plant provision, **40:** 272, 456-57,n1, 545; and draft provisions, **40:** 327-30, 330
Army War College, **42:** 33, 39, 56, 191, 550n1; **43:** 92; **45:** 4-6, 474-75; **46:** 43; statue of Frederick the Great removed from, **48:** 192
Arnett, Emmet W., **44:** 231n1
Arnold, Benedict, **41:** 455
Arnold, George Stanleigh, **51:** 125,n1, 172, 204, 376, 377, 378
Arnold, Henry Harley, **47:** 518n1
Arnold Toynbee House, N.Y., **48:** 311n1
Arraga, Mr., **51:** 76n1
Arras, France, **47:** 238, 262; **48:** 332
Art and Craft of Judging: The Decisions of Judge Learned Hand (Shanks, ed.), **43:** 165n2
Arthur, Prince (William Patrick Albert), *see* Connaught, Duke of
Arthur Henderson: A Biography (Hamilton), **49:** 11n4
As Bad As Ever (*New York Times*), **42:** 245n3
As to the Overman Bill (*American Review of Reviews*), **47:** 385,n4
Asahi (Japanese flagship), **49:** 150
Asbury Park Evening Press, **51:** 552n8
Ascherson, Charles S., **46:** 88; **48:** 525,n3
Ashbrook, William Albert, **49:** 277-78,n1
Ashe, John E., **43:** 480,n3
Asheville, N. C., *Citizen*, **51:** 482n1
Ashley, James Mitchell, Jr., **49:** 510,n2
Ashurst, Henry Fountain, **40:** 96, 111n1, 128-29, 523; **43:** 113, 131; **44:** 86,n1; **46:** 598; **47:** 116, 349,n1; and woman suffrage, **45:** 278, 338; **51:** 58; and peace terms, **51:** 277,n7, 338-40, 391, 403, 414
Asia Minor, **40:** 361; **43:** 255, 335, 355, 388, 471; **44:** 476; **45:** 13, 176; **46:** 240; Greeks in, **51:** 180-81,n1
Asker, C. A., **51:** 18n2
Asleep at the Switch (*Newark Evening News*), **47:** 253, 254,n4
Aspinwall, Iowa, **44:** 452
Asquith, Herbert Henry, **40:** 32, 172, 186, 187, 201, 319, 333, 366; **41:** 535; **43:**

404; **44:** 202, 441; **45:** 548; **46:** 351n3; **47:** 298; **48:** 555n7, 615
Associated Newspapers, Ltd., **42:** 446n2
Associated Oil Company, **40:** 205
Associated Polish Press, **47:** 576n2
Associated Press, **40:** 29, 122, 123, 217, 346, 432, 462; **41:** 274,n2, 308,n1,2, 323, 324, 432; **43:** 333; **44:** 164, 170; **46:** 348n1; **47:** 51, 380, 519; **48:** 142,n5; **49:** 5,n1
Association for an Equitable Federal Income Tax, **46:** 15n1
Association of Colleges and Preparatory Schools of the Middle States, **51:** 649
Association of Collegiate Alumnae, **48:** 345,n5
Association of Poles in America, **44:** 303
Association of Polish Clergy in America, **44:** 303
Association of Railroad Organizations, **41:** 54
Astor, Nancy Witcher Langhorne Shaw (Mrs. Waldorf), **45:** 325,n2
Astor, Waldorf, **45:** 325
Astor Hotel, N.Y., **45:** 598n2; **46:** 49n1
Astor Trust Company, N.Y., **43:** 196
Astrakhan, Russia, **51:** 153,n2
Aswell, James Benjamin, **48:** 457,n1, 458n1
At Close Quarters: A Sidelight on Anglo-American Diplomatic Relations (Murray), **48:** 523n1
At the Eleventh Hour: A Memorandum on the Military Situation (Masaryk), **41:** 56n1
Atkins, Arthur Kennedy, **47:** 518n1
Atlanta, Ga., **41:** 455n1
Atlanta, Birmingham and Atlantic Railroad Company, **45:** 401n1
Atlanta Constitution, **40:** 153,n1, 414n3; **47:** 192n1, 325n1, 382,n1; **48:** 323,n1; and Georgia's senatorial race, **49:** 81, 82, 114, 115, 116, 237,n1
Atlanta Georgian, **49:** 427n1
Atlanta Journal, **44:** 257n1; **46:** 563n1,2; **47:** 192n2; and Georgia's senatorial race, **49:** 114, 115, 116, 369-70
Atlanta *Southern Ruralist*, **44:** 257n1
Atlanta University, **42:** 321, 322n1
Atlantic City, N.J., **40:** 55; **50:** 267n8
Atlantic Coast Line, **44:** 459; **45:** 117-18, 125-26, 129-30, 155, 162, 184,n3
Atlantic Coast Shipbuilders' Association, **46:** 610
Atlantic Monthly, **43:** 247n2; **44:** 178n5; **45:** 423; **49:** 350,n3; **51:** 221,n5
Attitude of the United States toward Mexico . . ., **48:** 259n
Attucks, Crispus, **46:** 550
Auchincloss, Charles Crooke, **49:** 286,n2
Auchincloss, Gordon, **40:** 491; **41:** 149, 501,n1; **42:** 433; **43:** 183,n1,2, 486; **44:** 105, 157, 184, 378, 380, 426; **45:** 309, 317, 333, 397-98, 399, 400; **46:** 85, 183, 221, 265, 290, 316, 328, 380, 429, 437, 467, 487, 488,n1, 490, 510n1, 532, 549,

553, 567; **47:** 59, 85, 102, 122, 158, 308, 310, 313, 584, 585; **48:** 71,n2, 95, 135, 152, 238n1, 289, 306, 310, 317; **49:** 140, 177, 265, 267, 286n2, 294, 304, 348n1, 397, 408-409, 409, 465, 489, 508; **51:** 23, 104, 107, 142, 143, 146, 164, 275, 342, 505n1; rejected for military service, **48:** 541,n1

Auchincloss, Janet House (Mrs. Gordon), **42:** 433; **44:** 426, 439; **45:** 317-18, 332, 397-98, 398, 399, 400; **46:** 168, 290, 316, 327, 328, 467-68; **47:** 185, 215; **49:** 265, 267, 294

Auchincloss, Louise, **44:** 378, 426, 439; **45:** 317,n1, 398, 400; **46:** 290, 316, 328; **49:** 294

Auchincloss, Samuel Sloan, **43:** 183,n2; **45:** 399

Auchincloss Brothers, N.Y., **43:** 183n2

Augusta, Ga., *The Jeffersonian*, **43:** 165, 389n1

Aurora, Mo., **49:** 169n1

Austin, J. C., **51:** 168n1

Australia, **41:** 213; **42:** 109; **44:** 213, 215n2; **48:** 27, 228; **49:** 217; **51:** 614; and wheat, **45:** 69, 74, 86; railroads in, **45:** 310; proposed visit to U.S. by Prime Minister of, **49:** 408-409, 409, 466

Austria-Hungary, **40:** 21, 23-24, 30n1, 204, 231, 250, 317, 318, 446n2, 477; **41:** 39, 40, 149, 211, 217, 464; **42:** 68, 340, 362, 425, 433, 501; **43:** 236, 255, 388, 406, 468, 471, 525; **44:** 200, 201, 547; **45:** 13, 14, 38, 186, 197, 247-48, 313, 553n2, 559; **46:** 249, 261, 268, 292, 352, 369,n1; **47:** 205; **48:** 136, 497; **49:** 193, 287-88, 404; **51:** 266, 388, 548, 595, 638; death of Francis Joseph, **40:** 34; and food shortages, **40:** 485, 488; **41:** 164, 300-301; and H. Friedjung trial, **41:** 56n2; fears of dismemberment, **41:** 75, 76, 81, 159, 357; **42:** 65-66; the Vatican and, **41:** 219-20; and peace moves and Great Britain, **41:** 211-14, 260, 262, 267-68, 270-73; **44:** 513-14; **45:** 430-31; **46:** 271-72, 473, 483-84, 574, 577; **47:** 11, 122-23, 239-41; W. E. Walling on, **42:** 198; G. J. Sosnowski on, **42:** 492-93; and Poles and Poland, **44:** 5; **49:** 382; Pope's peace appeal and, **44:** 19-20, 25, 26, 43, 76, 348-51; forces advancing into Italy, **44:** 506-509; peace moves by, **45:** 55-57; **51:** 10-11n1,3, 23; talk of separate peace, **45:** 151; Italy on U.S. war declaration against, **45:** 262-63; and Brest-Litovsk peace conference, **45:** 384n2, 411-12, 413; J. Meinl on peace terms of, **45:** 416; and British war aims statement, **45:** 487n2; and comparison of G. Hertling's and O. Czernin's responses, **46:** 162-68, 172-73, 189-93, 222-29; and Italy, **46:** 199-200; **48:** 96-97; **51:** 119, 529-30; and peace moves and Germany, **46:** 589-90; and Siberia, **47:** 97, 398-99, 466; Balkans and, **47:** 417, 451,n3, 474,n1; and Six-

tus letter, **47:** 589,n1; and woman suffrage, **48:** 304; issue of self-determination and minorities in, **48:** 435-37, 437-38,n2, 447-48, 456,n1, 530-31; and Bolsheviks, **51:** 96n2, 564-65, 567, 623; and proposed treatment of captured aviators, **51:** 174-75; and naval terms, **51:** 487, 488, 492-94; T. Masaryk on Czechs and, **51:** 506-507; Allies draw up terms, **51:** 531-32, 541, 544, 562; and appeal for moderation to liberated nations of, **51:** 553, 603-604; signs armistice with Italy, **51:** 576,n1; requests her troops remain in Ukraine, **51:** 616-17, 617

Austria-Hungary and the United States, WW hopes to maintain diplomatic relations, **41:** 88-89, 95, 129-30,n1,2, 158-59, 185; and exchange of peace prospects, **41:** 297-98, 312, 313, 398-99, 421-22; breakdown in relations, **41:** 476, 477, 477-78, 525-26; **42:** 23; Balfour, House, and WW on peace terms and, **42:** 128-29, 141, 142n1, 156, 288, 329, 332-33, 334, 354, 456; R. L. Owen's peace-terms resolution, **42:** 444,n1; advocates of declaring war, **44:** 295, 296; **45:** 135-40, 163-64,n1, 199-200; U.S. declares war against, **45:** 224,n1, 359; proclamation on Austro-Hungarian citizens in U.S., **45:** 268-69,n1; American press on peace offer of, **45:** 436-37; and Inquiry memorandum, **45:** 461, 463, 466-67, 471; and Fourteen Points, **45:** 481-82, 485, 514, 527, 537; **46:** 78, 83, 115n1; and Lammasch-Herron exchange on peace moves, **46:** 198-200,n2, 242-47, 261-63, 315, 388, 412-13, 483-84, 580,n1; **47:** 24-26, 64n2; Von Wiegand on peace moves and, **46:** 350n1; and possible postwar U.S. financial aid to, **46:** 353; Charles I's message to WW, **46:** 418, 424, 432, 435, 440-42; WW's reply, **46:** 486-87, 507-508, 551-53; C. Ackerman on situation in, **46:** 556-57; W. C. Bullitt on situation in, **46:** 567-69; Charles I answers WW on peace terms, **47:** 124-26; R. Lansing on defining U.S. policy toward, **47:** 589-91; W. Wiseman and WW discuss, **48:** 205-206; A. M. Palmer on definition of "enemy" and alien property seizure, **48:** 228n1; and U.S. declaration recognizing Czechs, **49:** 287-88, 405, 416; WW on liberals in, **49:** 399; editorials on peace proposals of, **51:** 106,n7; peace note to WW and WW's reply, **51:** 258-59, 282-83, 348-49, 374, 383, 391, 395; and naval terms, **51:** 487, 488, 492-94; replies to WW's note, **51:** 505-506, 526-27; U.S. will submit peace negotiation request to Allies, **51:** 527

Austrian Americans, **42:** 68; **43:** 86n2,3

Austrian Peace Overture (*New York Times*), **51:** 106n7

Autobiography of George Dewey, Admiral of the Navy, **44:** 296,n1
Avanceña, Ramon, **44:** 8n1
Avanti: see Rome *Avanti*
aviation program: *see* aircraft program
Ávila, Fidel, **50:** 388n1
Axson, Edward William, brother of EAW, **40:** 565
Axson, Stockton (Isaac Stockton Keith Axson II), brother of EAW, **40:** 336, 566, 570; **42:** 88; **46:** 209, 371, 488, 489; **47:** 326-27; **48:** 455n1; **49:** 543; photograph: *illustration section,* 42
Azk (The Nation, Boston), **49:** 20n2

Babbit, George, **51:** 404,n1
Babcock and Wilcox Company, **47:** 41n2
Babst, Earl D., **45:** 344n1
Bach, Johann Sebastian, **49:** 360n2
Bachmač, Battle of, **49:** 195
Bacon, Robert, **40:** 89; **41:** 224,n2; **45:** 332n1; **48:** 606,n3; **51:** 147n1
Badell, Mr., **41:** 269
Badger, Charles Johnston, **41:** 377, 432n1,2
Baer, John Miller, **44:** 112,n4, 153n1; **46:** 270,n1, 370; **47:** 20n1, 352n2,3
Baer bill, **47:** 20n1, 72, 85, 178,n2
Baghdad, **45:** 459-60
Baghdad Railway, **44:** 476, 477; **45:** 13, 419
Bagley, David Worth, **45:** 238,n2
Bagley, James J., **44:** 79
Bagusa, S.M.S., **51:** 493
Baikal, Lake, Siberia, **49:** 151, 152, 220, 221, 262,n1, 283, 285; **51:** 449
Bailey, Herbert, **42:** 361,n2, 363,n1
Bailey, Thomas Andrew, **44:** 296n1
Bailey, Warren Worth, **41:** 115
Baird, David; and woman suffrage, **49:** 139-40, 182-83; **51:** 58, 452
Baker, Mrs. Abbey Scott, **42:** 237n4
Baker, Bernard Nadal, resigns from Shipping Board, **41:** 16, 21, 66
Baker, Elizabeth Leopold (Mrs. Newton Diehl), **42:** 281n1; **47:** 397, 398
Baker, Emelia Jane Stubbs (Mrs. Alfred Brittin), **45:** 231,n4
Baker, George Fisher, Jr., **44:** 295,n1; **49:** 233
Baker, George Luis, **44:** 247, 268
Baker, James Marion, **46:** 31,n1
Baker, Joseph Allen, **41:** 532-36,n1; **45:** 184
Baker, Newton Diehl, **40:** 3, 57, 173, 207, 330, 551; **41:** 15-16, 83, 88, 198, 245, 278, 345, 353, 474, 476, 484, 496, 545-46; **42:** 33,n1, 37, 44, 90, 135, 166, 176, 185,n1, 191, 213n2, 225, 281n1, 292, 343, 350, 374, 377, 391,n1, 495, 496, 498, 530, 533, 563-64; **43:** 4, 5, 61, 102, 110, 116, 121, 122, 156, 203, 248,n1, 257, 262, 262-65, 380, 388n1, 391, 414, 435, 454, 486, 492, 512, 532; **44:** 10, 14, 27, 29, 41, 50, 61, 62, 77, 81, 108, 157-58, 198, 212, 216, 231, 232, 239, 246, 248, 277, 332,n1, 372, 379, 380, 381, 393, 412, 448,n1, 449, 461, 467, 493, 495, 498, 512, 515, 533, 538, 544, 556, 562-63, 571; **45:** 8, 10-11, 25, 69, 75, 102n1, 104, 107, 148n1, 160, 168, 208, 230, 265, 272, 299, 301, 323, 325, 328, 342, 349, 363, 364, 366, 390n1, 407, 421-22, 425, 448, 451, 474, 546, 547, 570-71, 571, 573, 582, 594, 601; **46:** 3, 8, 12, 13, 23, 24, 26, 30, 42, 92, 93, 94, 111,n3, 112, 151n2, 179, 205, 206, 210, 212, 219n5, 239, 257, 259, 297, 337, 369, 375, 385, 406n1, 438, 444n2, 452, 482; **47:** 12-14, 15n2, 40n3, 72, 157, 170, 338, 348, 358, 440, 465, 478, 499, 528, 577; **48:** 3-4, 4, 32, 54-55, 115, 130, 178, 200-201, 205, 253, 261, 295, 354, 357, 383, 403, 432, 434, 439, 444, 469n1, 479, 481, 536, 542, 544, 568, 599, 607, 609; **49:** 38, 41n1, 51, 71n1, 135, 145, 179, 179,n2, 181, 185, 207, 209, 217, 221, 224, 235n1, 236, 238, 242, 246, 258-61, 265, 285-86, 320,n1, 347, 363, 368, 378; **51:** 15n1, 78, 110, 152, 228, 255, 261, 287n1, 302, 328, 341, 347, 372, 383, 396, 399-400, 403, 412, 425, 433, 453, 570, 583, 592, 595, 604, 605,n1, 607, 616

and labor laws for women and children, **40:** 7, 37, 42, 91-92; on Mexico, **40:** 100, 101, 109, 123, 130, 202, 522; on National Defense (Army Reorganization) Act, **40:** 327-29; on Danish West Indies, **40:** 401-402, 405, 424; and governmental ownership of telephones and telegraphs in District of Columbia, **40:** 438, 492; on Howland's proposed history of the war, **40:** 455-56, 464; on hydroelectric power, **40:** 456-57; orders J. J. Pershing to begin troop withdrawal from Mexico, **41:** 40n1; and war preparations, **41:** 114, 151-52, 152-53, 153, 155-56, 169-70, 226n1; on arming merchant ships, **41:** 184, 331; on W. B. Colver as Trade Commission appointee, **41:** 206, 209; on renewal of Mexican border raids, **41:** 236-37,n1; on Philippine vice-governorship, **41:** 417-18, 505, 509; advocates war declaration, **41:** 439; and increase in army, **41:** 455,n1; 500-501,n1; on General Wood, **41:** 455,n2, 461; **48:** 173n1, 189, 192; and T. Roosevelt on raising a volunteer division, **41:** 469,n1, 469-71, 478; **42:** 56, 56-57; and newspaper censorship, **41:** 474n2, 530, 556; E. M. House on, **41:** 483; **42:** 158; **44:** 176, 246; on overt incidents of disloyalty, **41:** 486-87, 487; suggested for British ambassadorship, **41:** 497; on recreation and leisure in army, **41:** 505-506, 509, 527-28, 537; and Polish-American desire to form a military unit, **41:** 507, 511-12; **42:** 60, 352-53, 357, 431-32; and Trans-Siberian Railway, **41:** 511; on WW's war message, **41:** 541, 542; on Council of National Defense, **42:** 47-49, 498; **43:** 59-61, 90, 102, 113, 177, 192; on Committee on Public Information, **42:** 55, 59, 71; on volunteer system in Civil War, **42:** 58; on postwar army, **42:** 75, 91-92; prepares and revises proclamations on draft, **42:** 179-82, 201, 342; **49:** 349-50, 358; meets with General G.T.M. Bridges, **42:** 191-92; on sending expeditionary force to France, **42:** 192, 194, 249-51, 263-64; on T. E. Burton, **42:** 217, 221; against special foreign legions in U.S., **42:** 227; and steel situation, **42:** 242, 279; **43:** 155-56; on Red Cross War Council, **42:** 251-52; on Cuba, **42:** 295; on training camps for Negroes, **42:** 321, 322; **43:** 391-92, 506-507; on Pershing's command authority and duties in Europe, **42:** 404-405; on strategy and training, **42:** 405-406, 408-10; **44:** 239, 361,n1; **45:** 4-6; on building cantonments, **42:** 406-407; on centralized purchasing and price fixing, **42:** 411,n1, 411-13, 419; **43:** 41,n1, 59-61, 90-92; against training camp in Birmingham, **42:** 522; on Philippine army division, **42:** 541-42, **43:** 16; on plan for Allied air supremacy, **42:** 549-50, 552; and Dockery-Young affair, **43:** 4, 16, 78, 118; on War Industries Board, **43:** 25-26, 177, 341, 413-14, 489, 515; **46:** 91-92, 215-17, 252, 427; on German ships in U.S. ports, **43:** 89; on H. L. Stimson as military attaché in London, **43:** 92, 102; and war-risk insurance, **43:** 94; and Arizona copper-mining situation, **43:** 156, 158; on strikes, **43:** 177; **44:** 225; **45:** 258-62, 279; and sweet potatoes on army menu, **43:** 324-25; and draft exemptions, **43:** 515-17, 534, 535; **44:** 123, 150, 239-41; **45:** 254-55, 583-86, 594; **46:** 428n1, 446; **48:** 151-52,n1; **49:** 294-95, 328-29, 386-87

on New York's Irish National Guard regiment, **43:** 514; on appointments to Philippine Supreme Court, **44:** 8,n1, 8-9; on French request for use of army, **44:** 51, 312; on conscientious objectors, **44:** 74, 221,n1, 288-89, 293, 370-71; **49:** 56; on Houston racial clash, **44:** 77-78; **45:** 577, 579-80; **49:** 324-28, 347, 399-402; and President's Mediation Commission, **44:** 103-104, 120, 161; on need for unity among Allies, **44:** 197; and Lippmann memorandum on shipbuilding labor, **44:** 219-21, 224; and Polish army, **44:** 316; on arrest of I.W.W. in Spokane, **44:** 344-45; WW asks to speak on Liberty Loan, **44:** 382-83; on American Federation of Labor conference, **44:** 398; on WW not making statement on eight-hour day, **44:** 421-22; and resignation of F. A. Scott, **44:** 450; on Pershing-Pétain friction, **44:** 463; and

housing of war-contract workers, **44:** 448, 482; **46:** 150, 151, 171; on shipping situation, **44:** 501; **45:** 489-91; **51:** 94-95; on coordination of New York port facilities, **44:** 502-503; on Jewish troops at Camp Upton, **44:** 503-504; **45:** 157; on E. H. Crowder's foreword to new army regulations, **44:** 522, 533; and cancellation of Army-Navy game, **44:** 535, 571; **45:** 29-30; on Philippine shipbuilding offer, **45:** 49-50; and public-health concerns in war industries and training camps, **45:** 51, 91, 92, 452-53, 491-92; **46:** 209-10; D. Willard as War Industries Board chairman, **45:** 71-72; on aircraft program, **45:** 155-56, 331, 426-27; on legislation Congress should consider, **45:** 172-73; on military program for 1918, **45:** 268; on meatpackers' labor settlement, **45:** 355; and proclamation for takeover of railroads, **45:** 359, 361; on American troops in France, **45:** 438, 438-39; on General Bliss as representative to Supreme War Council, **45:** 532-33; and W. G. McAdoo on O. T. Crosby, **45:** 588-90; charges against War Department and response, **46:** 40n1, 41, 147-48,n1, 153; on British request for troops, **46:** 43-44, 44-45, 236-37; WW supportive of, **46:** 56, 148; willing to resign, **46:** 56-57; and G. Borglum, **46:** 57-58, 208-209, 229-30, 433,n1,2; and peace commission, **46:** 116; talk of as presidential candidate, **46:** 116; meets with WW and W. Wiseman, **46:** 247-49; makes inspection tour abroad, **46:** 248-49, 400-401, 414, 429-30, 487-88,n1, 612; **47:** 261; J. S. Williams' praise of, **46:** 288; and E. N. Hurley, **46:** 338; WW authorizes to decide immediate military questions, **47:** 158, 183, 186-87; reports on military situation in France, **47:** 160-61, 166, 261-62, 611; supports Supreme War Council's resolution regarding U.S. troops, **47:** 174-76, 176, 213,n1, 262-63, 271, 280, 305, 306; on F. Foch as Supreme Commander, **47:** 209; and WW on Allied troop requests, and U.S. plan, **47:** 306, 314, 369-70, 372-76, 386-87, 393-94; and issue of intervention in Russia, **47:** 333, 421-24, 491-92; **48:** 330-31, 367, 577; and General Bliss' rank, **47:** 458-59; request for truck gardens at training camps, **47:** 478n1; opposes death penalty in certain court-martial cases, **47:** 480-86, 516; on General Pershing's new plan for troop disposition, **47:** 455, 517, 535, 563, 566, 585, 615-16, 618; on sending troops to Italy, **47:** 486-87, 501; and YM-YWCA work abroad, **47:** 502, 613-14; **48:** 6; on aircraft investigation, **47:** 509-10, 541, 545, 554, 588; and Liberty airplane engine, **47:** 518; on not enlarging Pershing's power to enforce death

Baker, Newton Diehl (*cont.*)
penalty, **48:** 5-6; on Porto Rico, **48:** 15-16, 35, 75, 637-38; **49:** 158, 252, 296-98, 334, 394; gives WW inscribed *Frontiers of Freedom*, **48:** 30,n1,2

on German and American aircraft, **48:** 49-50; on separation from Signal Corps of military aircraft program, **48:** 73; on Major Freeman case, **48:** 136,n1, 177; and religious discrimination by YWCA, **48:** 208, 221-22,n1, 230; answers Bliss' questions, **48:** 218-19; on importance of independent U.S. army divisions, **48:** 243-45; on House's suggestions for military reorganization in France, **48:** 265-68; on Council of National Defense and reconstruction studies, **48:** 285, 290, 336-37, 357; and statistics on troop shipments, **48:** 307, 476-77, 482; **51:** 404-405, 405; on importance of Woman's Committee of Council of National Defense, **48:** 321-22, 357-58; and government takeover of telegraph system, **48:** 458n1, 488; on lynching of and unrest among Negroes, **48:** 475-76, 607; on number of Allied soldiers on western front, **48:** 483; on plans for Czech troops, **48:** 483-84; concern over U.S. commitment of supplies for France, **48:** 543-44; on forces for Murmansk expedition, **49:** 43-44, 52; on commissioning J. S. Sargent to paint war picture, **49:** 66, 101; on universal military service, **49:** 117-18, 129; on army poll of three cardinal sins, **49:** 156; on classification of Russia as a belligerent, **49:** 238-39, 247; suggested as peace conference representative, **49:** 267; on Bliss' suggestion for concerted Allied effort to win war, **49:** 276-77; and water-power legislation, **49:** 289, 316, 329-32, 344, 356, 357; goes to Europe to secure Allied tonnage agreement, **49:** 335,n1, 354, 416, 417, 419; on reorganization of Aircraft Production Board, **49:** 349, 350-51; on YMCA security clearance for passports, **49:** 359-60, 387, 390, 395-96; on joint drive for agencies engaged in war work, **49:** 384-85; and W. Lippmann, **49:** 429, 487-88; **51:** 9; McAdoo on, **49:** 489; and slacker raids, **49:** 500; and W. S. Graves, **51:** 8,n2, 356-57; against sending additional troops to Russia, **51:** 17, 33, 608; and peace conference plans, **51:** 316, 341, 346; on Sir H. Wilson, **51:** 385, 386; on reasons for slow progress on Pershing's front, **51:** 385-86; draft of reply to German note, **51:** 413, 414; on T. Roosevelt's peace terms, **51:** 455; advises Pershing on peace negotiations, **51:** 470-72; and Pershing's letter to Supreme War Council about peace terms, **51:** 525-26, 544, 545, 596-98, 617-18;

suggests antirevolutionary statement be made to Austria-Hungary, **51:** 553; photograph: *illustration section*, **43; 44; 46**

Baker, Paul, **47:** 574
Baker, Purley Albert, **43:** 52,n1, 65
Baker, Ray Stannard, **40:** 374; **43:** 41n1; **45:** 93n3; **46:** 147n2, 194n1; **48:** 347n1
Bakhmeteff, George, **41:** 455; **42:** 236-37, 381n9
Bakhmet'ev, Boris Aleksandrovich, **43:** 37,n1, 38, 95, 175n2, 248, 473, 475-76, 522; **44:** 22, 180, 446; **45:** 252, 253, 282, 283, 288-95, 336; **46:** 66, 387, 513-15, 518, 519; **47:** 397, 398; **48:** 274, 364, 374, 382, 454, 570; **49:** 396,n1; **51:** 481n2, 542-43; WW greets as new ambassador, **43:** 100-101,n1
Balaton, S.M.S., **51:** 492
Balch, Emily Greene, **41:** 455; **44:** 79
Baldwin, George Johnson, **51:** 14,n2
Baldwin, Karl F., **49:** 107,n1
Baldwin, Roger Nash, **43:** 175n1, 176, 420; **44:** 266-67; **47:** 155; **51:** 534,n1; and I.W.W. and industrial unrest, **46:** 196, 481-82; on censorship, **46:** 382-83
Baldwin Wallace College, **46:** 612
Balfour, Arthur James, **40:** 30, 201, 212, 307n1, 316, 341,n1, 358, 439n1, 452, 499, 517, 524; **41:** 26n1, 115, 136, 214, 219, 273, 532-36; **42:** 67, 133, 274, 281,n1, 317, 354, 456, 527, 542, 552, 555, 556; **43:** 37-38, 44, 94-95, 97-98, 133, 150, 172, 206, 223, 230, 285-87, 347, 356,n1, 360-61, 369-70, 386; **44:** 5, 23, 25, 56, 69, 70, 80, 130-31, 150, 203, 210, 311, 325, 362-64, 369, 375, 382, 494, 545; **45:** 3, 68, 166n1, 173n1, 313, 323, 430, 445, 454-57, 486, 518, 556, 578; **46:** 4, 85, 231-32, 247-49, 334, 408, 413, 468, 482, 487, 490; **47:** 11, 18, 63, 130-31, 184-85, 238, 256, 281-82, 305-306, 310, 314-15, 334-35, 417, 433, 440, 544, 582, 620-22; **48:** 61-62, 114, 132-35, 228, 285-86, 333, 381, 448n1, 453-54, 469, 511-14, 543-44, 565-66, 586, 627; **49:** 36-37, 52, 67-69, 82-83, 83, 110-11, 168, 177, 178, 550; **51:** 10,n6, 230, 295, 325, 327n1, 352, 389, 446

Count Bernstorff on, **40:** 213; reply to WW's peace note, **40:** 500-503; and Zimmermann telegram, **41:** 280, 281, 297, 332, 325; and requisitioning ships, **41:** 337; **43:** 70-72; and proposed mission to U.S., **41:** 544-45, 553, 553-54; **42:** 18, 20, 22, 69, 82-83, 91, 93; and Irish Home Rule, **42:** 111, 223,n2; **47:** 227; meetings with E. M. House, WW and R. Lansing, **42:** 120, 123, 140-41, 142n1, 142-43, 155, 170-73, 288; receptions for, **42:** 121, 123, 125-26, 127; J. J. Jusserand meets with, **42:** 128-29; on export restrictions, **42:** 224; delivers speech to House of Reps., **42:** 232, 288; on European situation, **42:** 264-65;

sends WW texts of some British secret treaties with Allies, **42:** 327,n1, 346; memorandum on foreign policy, **42:** 328-42; and Polish Army, **42:** 372, 385-86, 431; **43:** 426; on WW's message to Russian provisional government, **42:** 385; W. D. Mackenzie on, **42:** 394-95; memorandum on British mission to U.S., **42:** 396-401; on Lord Northcliffe, **42:** 428,n1,2, 445-46, 461; and British financial crisis, **43:** 34, 38-39, 46, 47, 66-67, 67, 68, 69; proposes naval agreements, **43:** 113-14, 123, 125-26; and Pope's peace appeal, **43:** 451, 453, 488, 521; **44:** 30; on Japan, **43:** 464-65; and WW's reply to Pope, **44:** 41; on an American chairman for Inter-Allied Council, **44:** 312; and reply to German peace offer through Spain, **44:** 318-20, 342; on Zionist movement and Palestine, **44:** 323-24; **45:** 149,n2; on House mission, **44:** 391; on Russia and separate peace terms, **45:** 188-89,n1; on Fourteen Points Address, **45:** 577,n1, 578; on Italy's claims under Treaty of London, **46:** 180-81; advocates Japanese intervention in Siberia, **46:** 220-21, 470-71, 530, 561, 574, 576-77, 605-606; on Austria-Hungary's peace moves, **46:** 271-72, 432, 435, 473, 483-84, 507, 577; **47:** 122-23, 239-41; on political statement by Supreme War Council, **46:** 419; and Allied intervention in Russia, **47:** 60, 61, 61-63, 170-71, 239, 355-57, 366-69, 412, 436,n1, 488-90, 496, 605, 606-608; **48:** 99-102, 112, 378-79, 390, 493-94, 496, 622; on proposed international Socialist conference, **47:** 75, 76; on use of U.S. Army divisions, **47:** 156, 157, 170; on situation in Mexico, **47:** 552-53; **49:** 299-300, 303; urges WW to send troops to Murmansk, **48:** 207-208; and Phillimore Committee, **48:** 501,n1; on F. Foch's responsibilities, **48:** 595; on WW's decision to send troops to Siberia, **49:** 57-58; on WW's aide-mémoire on Russian situation, **49:** 58-60, on Bulgaria, **51:** 64; and Sisson Papers, **51:** 246-47, 352; on peace terms, **51:** 335-36, 411-12, 484, 511, 512, 513, 571, 594, 638; photograph: *illustration section*, 42

Balfour Declaration, **45:** 149n2; **46:** 493; **49:** 364, 403

Balfour Declaration (Stein), **45:** 149n2

Balkan states, **40:** 15, 232, 307n1, 435, 446n4; **41:** 159; **42:** 310, 433, 500, 501; **43:** 25, 269, 439, 485, 487, 523; **44:** 20, 34, 57, 149, 476, 477, 547; **45:** 6, 13, 123, 197, 324, 416; **46:** 167, 320, 486, 487, 552; **47:** 451n3; **48:** 457n1, 481n1, 497, 545, 554; **49:** 229, 339, 436n1; **51:** 40, 41, 43, 45, 47, 119, 151, 155, 163, 164, 169, 170, 180, 187, 199-200, 427, 501, 502, 584; Treaty of Bucharest and Inquiry Memorandum, **45:** 469-70; and

Fourteen Points, **45:** 479-80, 484-85, 507, 514, 520, 528, 534, 538

Ballou, Charles Clarendon, **48:** 157,n3; **49:** 179n2

Baltic, S.S., **42:** 379

Baltic Sea, **51:** 490

Baltic states, **46:** 186, 228, 275, 292, 533; **48:** 490; **51:** 623

Baltimore, Md., **45:** 150n1; WW's address in, **47:** 267-70, 295-96, 308, 335, 343

Baltimore, Charles W., **46:** 384,n2; **49:** 324,n2

Baltimore and Ohio Railroad, **41:** 402; **44:** 459; **47:** 488; D. Willard and, **45:** 600-601; **46:** 15, 17

Baltimore Platform: *see* Democratic Platform, 1912

Baltimore *Sun*, **43:** 133n1; **45:** 437

Bamberger, Simon, **47:** 194

Bang, Jacob Peter, **42:** 394,n5

Bank of China, **40:** 563

Bank of England, **43:** 227

Bank of Manhattan Company, **43:** 196

Bank of New York, **43:** 196

Banker and the Nation (Wilson), **41:** 67n5

Bankers Trust Company of New York, **43:** 196

Bankhead, John Hollis, **40:** 287, 424,n1, 523; **46:** 29, 103,n2; **47:** 610; **48:** 31; **50:** 688,n5; and water-power legislation, **41:** 19, 20, 23, 82-83; and woman suffrage, **45:** 278, 339; **51:** 58; and Alabama coal-mining situation, **45:** 568

Bankhead, John Hollis, Jr., **45:** 568,n1; **46:** 103n2; **48:** 30-31

Bankhead Coal Company, **46:** 103n2

banking: foreign securities held by national banks, **40:** 181-82,n1, 214; WW allays fears concerning bank accounts of enemy subjects, **41:** 132, 157-58; and "white list" proposal, **46:** 423n1

Banking and Currency, Committee on (House of Reps.), **40:** 476n4

Banking and Currency, Committee on (Senate), **40:** 476n4

Banking and Currency Problem in the United States, **49:** 168n2

Banks, Charlie, **49:** 399-400

Barbash, Samuel, **45:** 572,n2

Barbeau, Arthur E., **48:** 157n4, 160n6

Barbee, Richard, **46:** 520

Barber, Benjamin Russell, **42:** 393,n1

Barclay, Colville Adrian de Rune, **41:** 458,n1; **43:** 67-69, 140n2; **44:** 230n1; **45:** 578-79; **46:** 4, 154-55, 181, 270-71, 395, 547, 548; **48:** 525; **49:** 178, 354, 417; **51:** 7, 8,n4, 24n1, 85, 139, 188, 246, 263, 291, 295, 307-309, 335, 389, 411-12, 456, 539, 574-75; on Czechs in Siberia, **49:** 373; on Gen. F. C. Poole's interference in Archangel, **49:** 508; on T. Masaryk's concern over Anglo-American relations and Russia, **49:** 550-51

Barclay, G. D., **43:** 127,n2, 128

Bardin, James Alfred, **47:** 578-79,n1, 579

Barker, Wharton, **46:** 611
Barkley, Alben William, **43:** 42n2
Barkley amendment to Lever bill, **43:** 42,n2, 84n1
barley, **46:** 306
Barnard, George Grey, **44:** 536,n1
Barnes, Earl Bryant, **43:** 165n2
Barnes, Frank Coe, **44:** 364-65,n1
Barnes, George, **46:** 21
Barnes, George Nicoll, **51:** 327,n1
Barnes, John Earl B., **48:** 146n1
Barnes, Julius Howland, **42:** 483,n1, 484; **48:** 306,n1, 580; **49:** 354,n1
Barnes, Lee, **48:** 292,n3
Barnes-Ames Company, N.Y., **42:** 483n1; **48:** 306n1
Barnett, George, **48:** 279,n4
Barquero, Aguilar, **47:** 231n1
Barrère, Camille Eugène Pierre, **46:** 158,n1, 178
Barrett, Alva Pearl, **49:** 137n3
Barrett, Charles Simon, **44:** 258-59,n2; **49:** 440,n2, 441
Barrett, James J., **45:** 44,n1, 60
Barrett, John, **42:** 281,n1; **43:** 11
Barry, Thomas Henry, **41:** 486,n1; **44:** 177,n3
Barrymore, John, **46:** 264,n1
Barthelme, Georg, **41:** 149-51,n1, 242, 243, 244, 274, 275
Bartlett, George True, **45:** 111,n10
Bartlett, Ruhl Jacob, **41:** 250n3
Barton, Arthur James, **43:** 52,n1, 65
Barton, Bruce, **48:** 362,n2
Barton, James Levi, **45:** 185,n3
Baruch, Annie Griffen (Mrs. Bernard Mannes), **41:** 358,n2
Baruch, Bernard Mannes, **40:** 60: **41:** 69, 358; **42:** 23, 161; **43:** 155; **44:** 64, 73, 208, 233, 247, 268; **45:** 43, 398; **46:** 23, 327, 444n2, 476, 477, 524, 550, 610; **47:** 43, 51, 111, 143, 208, 255, 292, 436, 445, 527, 558-59,n1; **48:** 62, 139, 228, 247, 562, 606-607, 611; **49:** 145, 147, 225, 230, 258, 278, 435, 550; **51:** 26, 64, 87, 104n4, 372, 605,n1, 615, 638; and alleged peace note leak to Wall Street, **40:** 349n11; and New York district attorneyship, **42:** 244, 279-80; on price controls and a centralized purchasing agency, **42:** 298, 301, 374, 411,n1, 412, 413, 414-17, 419, 424, 447-49, 538-39; **46:** 251,n1, 288-89, 330; and Central Purchasing Commission, **43:** 76, 137, 189; on Council of National Defense reorganization, **43:** 148, 156,n1, 177; and War Industries Board, **43:** 192,n1, 341n1; **46:** 17, 91-92, 105-106, 112, 168, 205, 215-17, 238, 252, 269, 438,n1, 443, 448, 520-22, 527; **48:** 189, 474; on H. A. Garfield's fuel proclamation, **46:** 33, 36; and plan to acquire newspaper, **46:** 36,n1, 113n1; and W. G. McAdoo's plan for discouraging industrial development in eastern U.S., **47:** 159,n1, 180; and railroad fuel question, **47:** 407,

408, 409; WW establishes War Industries Board, **48:** 176; on checking war activities in government departments, **48:** 188,n1; on coordination of Allied nonmilitary activities, **48:** 324-29; on water-power bill, **48:** 405; and hydroelectric plant project in Seattle, **49:** 120, 121-22, 170; and supplies for Czechs, **49:** 417, 434, 446, 446n1, 492, 529; and C. A. Lindbergh appointment, **49:** 536,n1; and cotton prices, **51:** 5n1, 610, 611; and peace conference, **51:** 407; on German note, **51:** 416; on economic equality of opportunity and peace terms, **51:** 419-20
Basis of a Durable Peace (Butler), **40:** 24n1
Basler National Zeitung, **40:** 22
Bass, Elizabeth Merrill (Mrs. George), **42:** 208-209,n1, 214; **45:** 242, 242-43, 277, 338-39, 542, 545; **46:** 59-61, 67-68; **51:** 304; and woman suffrage, **48:** 110-11, 116, 233-34, 363-64, 365
Bass, John Foster, **42:** 252,n1,3, 258, 284-85, 289
Bass, Robert Perkins, **42:** 284
Basserman, Ernst, **40:** 433,n6
Bastedo, Paul Henry, **44:** 173-75
Bates, James Leonard, **40:** 561n2; **50:** 775n9
Battin, Benjamin Franklin, **43:** 36
Battin, Sarah Ellen Williams (Mrs. Benjamin Franklin), **44:** 36n1
Baucus, Joseph D., **44:** 504
Bauer, Stephen, **49:** 187, 192, 193
Baum, Jacob, **44:** 483; **45:** 252
Baumer Films, Inc., of N.Y., **51:** 14n1
Bautzen, Saxony, **46:** 189,n6, 192, 193
Bavaria, **42:** 425; **43:** 548n2; **46:** 165, 245; and peace moves, **48:** 552-55,n1,8, 621; **49:** 228, 229-30, 231; **51:** 230, 231
Bay State trolley system, **49:** 422
Bayern, S.M.S., **51:** 490
Bayly, Lewis, **44:** 346n1
Bayonne, France, **47:** 230
Bazoilles, France, **43:** 443
Beach, Cyprian Woodbridge, **49:** 257,n5, 318
Beach, Eleanor Orbison (Mrs. Sylvester Woodbridge), **49:** 257,n1, 318
Beach, Harrison Leroy, **49:** 73,n1, 137,n2
Beach, John Staats, **48:** 395,n1
Beach, Mary Hollingsworth, **49:** 257,n5, 318
Beach, Sylvester Woodbridge, **49:** 257, 318
Beach, Sylvia Woodbridge, **49:** 257,n5, 318
Beard, Charles Austin, **44:** 366n2
Beard, Mary Ritter (Mrs. Charles Austin), **45:** 40n1
Beatty, Bessie, **46:** 519,n1
Beatty, David, **44:** 87,n2
Beattys, Frank D., **43:** 85,n1
Beauvais, France, **47:** 238; **48:** 389
Beauvais Agreement, **48:** 387,n7; **49:** 126

Beaver, Daniel Roy, **43**: 25n1; **44**: 158n1; **45**: 390n1; **46**: 444n2; **48**: 32n4, 173n1; **49**: 335n1

Beaverbrook, William Maxwell Aitken, 1st Baron, **46**: 351n3

Bebel, August, **49**: 209

Beck, James Montgomery, **40**: 89, 237; **45**: 270, 596,n1; **46**: 3

Becker, Alfred Le Roy, **44**: 528,n1

Beckham, John Crepps Wickliffe, **46**: 61; **47**: 580-81; **49**: 480; **51**: 63, 76; and woman suffrage, **45**: 278, 279n1, 338, 339; **51**: 58

Beckmeyer, John H., **47**: 359,n1

Bedford, Alfred Cotton, **42**: 548,n1

Bee, Carlos, **49**: 137,n3; **51**: 616,n2

beef trust, **47**: 50,n1

Beernaert, Auguste, **42**: 255n1

Beers, Burton F., **43**: 57n1; **44**: 454n1

Beethoven, Ludwig van, **49**: 360n2

Behrman, Martin, **49**: 240,n1; **51**: 537,n3

Belasco Theater, Washington, D.C., **42**: 64; **46**: 264n1; **47**: 414n1; **49**: 23, 512n1

Belavin, Vasilii Ivanovich: *see* Tikhon

Belden, Perry, **41**: 420,n2

Belgian Congo, **43**: 225

Belgian deportations, **40**: 24-27, 27-28, 30, 88-89, 92, 106-107, 112-13, 138, 168, 180, 184, 220, 344,n1, 384, 422, 469, 555; WW on, **40**: 38, 83, 83-84, 89, 94-95, 168, 411-12; news leaks on protest note, **40**: 122-23, 130; Albert asks WW to protest, **40**: 171-72; Belgian government sends note on, **40**: 180,n1; J. C. Grew on Bethmann Hollweg's views on, **40**: 184-85, 429, 430, 431; H. Hoover on, **40**: 409-11; WW responds to Albert's plea for public protest, **40**: 518-19, 547-48

Belgian Relief Commission: *see* Commission for Relief of Belgium

Belgium, **40**: 15, 65, 161, 231, 239, 317, 414n1, 440, 502; **41**: 234, 520; **42**: 382, 425, 433, 502; **43**: 74, 140n2, 464; **45**: 24, 197, 207, 412, 416, 466, 573; **46**: 253, 312, 365, 418; **47**: 269, 293-94, 513n6; **48**: 608; **51**: 438, 567, 605; and peace terms, **40**: 13, 16, 21n1, 22, 69, 234, 240, 248, 307n1, 318, 340, 341, 383n1, 404, 435, 441, 446n4, 477, 507n1, 530-31, 554; **41**: 25, 26n1, 62, 74-75, 80-81, 138; **42**: 155, 338-39, 354, 385, 389n4, 425n1, 444n1; **43**: 291n1, 439, 465-66, 484, 498, 523-24; **45**: 35; **48**: 153, 214, 215, 553; **49**: 111, 123, 229; **51**: 47, 48, 106n7, 156n2, 236,n6, 237, 239, 256, 262, 263, 264, 267, 269n1, 273, 274, 282, 420, 454, 455, 463, 491, 499-500, 557, 558, 569, 570; atrocities in, **42**: 427; **51**: 135; suggests consortium of Allies, **43**: 7-8; acknowledges U.S. aid, **43**: 40-41, 74-75, 101-102; and British financial crisis, **43**: 68; and financial assistance from U.S. and Britain, **43**: 225; Baron Moncheur interview with WW on, **43**: 465-69;

B. Whitlock's writings on, **43**: 493; **44**: 84-85, 450n1; and Pope's appeal, **44**: 19, 20, 21, 24, 44, 319, 329, 330, 351, 379; requests for loans by, **44**: 281-82; British military strategy in, **44**: 332-33,n1; WW reaffirms support for, **45**: 50; railroads in, **45**: 310; and Inquiry memorandum on, **45**: 468, 473; and Fourteen Points, **45**: 476, 484, 513-14, 526, 537, 550, 552, 599; and British war aims, **45**: 487n2; P. Scheidemann on, **46**: 113n2; comments on G. Hertling's and O. Czernin's views on, **46**: 164, 165, 166, 186, 186-87, 189, 190, 223, 227-28, 277, 428; Charles I on, **46**: 399, 442; WW on, **46**: 295, 322, 487, 552; and woman suffrage, **48**: 24n2, 25-26; and league of nations, **49**: 19, 467; and the Vatican, **49**: 189; H. F. Hollis meets with Albert, **51**: 184; Germans to evacuate, **51**: 370-71,n2, 371-72,n1; and relief and postwar reconstruction, **51**: 397-99, 457-59, 461-62, 605, 618-20; and peace conference plans, **51**: 607; German plan to destroy coal mines in, **51**: 577

Belgium (Whitlock), **43**: 493n1

Belgium: A Personal Narrative (Whitlock), **43**: 493n1

Belgrade, Yugoslavia, **40**: 204

Beliaev, Mikhail Alekseevich, **41**: 416,n5

Belin, Emile Eugène, **47**: 571,n1; **51**: 38, 203, 586,n3

Belknap, Charles, Jr., **41**: 474n2

Belknap, Reginald Rowan, **42**: 457,n1

Bell, Bernard Iddings, **44**: 302n1

Bell, Edward Price, **44**: 181-82, 245; **51**: 345,n1

Bell, George, Jr., **40**: 100, 101, 109-10; **41**: 486; **43**: 158n1; **51**: 39

Bell, George Lewis, **43**: 222,n1, 237n2, 248, 280-81, 494, 495, 505; **44**: 17, 27, 86; **47**: 194,n2, 197, 232-33, 325, 479

Bell, James Ford, **42**: 483-84,n2

Bell, James Franklin, **44**: 503,n1, 513; **45**: 111,n11

Bell, Jefferson, **46**: 604,n1

Bell, Josephine, **43**: 165n2

Bell, Theodore Arlington, **51**: 213,n1, 259-60

Bell, Thomas Montgomery, **43**: 190-91,n1, 210; **51**: 5

Bell Telephone Company, **44**: 518-19; **47**: 400

Belmont, Alva Erskine Smith Vanderbilt (Mrs. Oliver Hazard Perry), **41**: 400,n1

Belmont, Percy, **51**: 147n1

Benckendorff, Count Alexander Constantinovich, **42**: 327n1

Bendheim, Charles, **44**: 277-78

Benedict XV, **40**: 231, 339; **41**: 39, 219, 434,n2; **46**: 244-46, 261, 262, 365, 438; **47**: 63n1; **51**: 283, 309, 355, 374, 410, 600, 641-42; and clergy in Mexico, **41**: 33, 34, 44-45; peace appeal by, **43**: 438-39, 482-85; WW on appeal, **43**: 487-88,

Benedict XV (cont.)
488; comments on appeal by, **43**: 451,
453, 471, 472, 496, 508, 513, 521,n1,
523-24, 525, 532-34; **44**: 12, 18-22, 23-
24, 24-26, 26, 37, 43-46, 76, 84,n1; British reaction, **44**: 30; WW's reply to, **44**:
33-36, 56-59; comments on WW's reply,
44: 40-41, 49-50, 83, 83-84, 93, 94, 103,
105, 105-106, 130-31, 149, 153, 155,
157, 169-70, 181, 184,n3, 295-96, 390-
91, 393-94, 468, 469; WW on his reply
to, **44**: 119, 120, 146; concern for starv-
ing Serbians and Syrians, **45**: 330;
G. D. Herron on, **49**: 189-90, 191-93;
urges WW to consider armistice request, **51**: 296
Benedict, Crystal Eastman: see Eastman,
Crystal
Benedikt, Heinrich, **46**: 198n1,3
Beneš, Eduard, **49**: 287n1; **51**: 580
Benet, Christie; and woman suffrage, **51**:
30,n1, 31, 58, 59, 110, 122-23, 133, 156,
167-68, 294, 375
Benham, Edith, **40**: 551, 552; **42**: 160,n1,
210n1; **45**: 267
Bennett, Lawrence, **45**: 366,n2
Bennett, William Mason, **44**: 333n1,
556n2; **45**: 157
Bennion, Harden, **43**: 17,n5
Benson, Allan Louis, **42**: 148n1, 198, 199;
43: 171n1
Benson, William Shepherd, **40**: 82; **41**:
94, 243, 298, 364, 369, 370, 371, 377,
403; **43**: 89,n2,3, 179, 345, 503; **44**: 371,
382, 433, 463; **45**: 127, 223, 323, 327,
365; **46**: 194, 203, 444, 621; **47**: 327,
348, 353; **48**: 479, 542, 544; **49**: 346; **51**:
341, 403, 407, 541, 562, 575; on Inter-
Allied Naval Conference, **45**: 189, 190-
91; on naval terms, **51**: 488-95
Benz, Wolfgang, **48**: 213n8
Berg, Lieutenant von, **48**: 607,n1
Berger, Victor Luitpold, **42**: 198,n5, 199,
253, 254; **43**: 190,n1, 193; **44**: 79, 245,
272; **45**: 345-46; **47**: 326n1, 439
Bergholz, Leo Allen, **40**: 142-43,n1
Bergson, Henri, **41**: 315,n1,2,3; urges
U.S. intervention in Russia, **48**:
317,n2, 414; confers with Wilson, 441-
43,n1, 447; **49**: 94-95, 112-13
Bering River coal field, **43**: 36, 37, 43
Berkman, Alexander, **43**: 165n2; **44**:
274n1, 290,n1; **45**: 382
Berlin, Treaty of (1878), **44**: 476; **51**: 625-
26
Berlin, University of, **42**: 389n2
Berlin Deutscher Reichsanzeiger, **45**:
384n2
Berlin Germania, **46**: 163
Berlin Norddeutsche Allgemeine Zei-
tung, **48**: 213n8
Berlin Tägliche Rundschau, **46**: 191-92
Berlin Vörwarts, **43**: 405,n1; **46**: 164, 166,
184, 187, 192, 225, 226, 227, 567
Berlin Vossische Zeitung, **51**: 565
Berlin Die Zukunft, **43**: 246n1

Berliner Lokalanzeiger, **51**: 265n1
Berliner Tageblatt, **43**: 184, 220, 238, 274,
285, 366, 411-12; **46**: 163, 165-66, 187,
192, 227, 254n6, 267, 569; **48**: 213n8
Bermuda, **46**: 438; **50**: 177
Bern Freie Zeitung, **48**: 213n8
Bernabé, Luis Polo de: see Polo de Ber-
nabé, Luis
Bernard, John Henry, Archbishop of
Dublin, **42**: 403,n2
Bernard, Sam (Barnett), **46**: 519-20
Bernardsville, N.J., **41**: 257n1
Bernhardi, Friedrich Adam Julius von,
40: 487,n6,7
Bernstein, Eduard, **42**: 197,n3
Bernstein, Herman, **41**: 457; **42**: 363,n3;
48: 410,n2
Bernstorff, Johann Heinrich von, **40**: 5-6,
20, 39-40, 60, 111, 133, 173, 343, 345,
349n8, 408, 555,n4; **41**: 190, 196, 203,
245; **42**: 11, 23, 389; **44**: 237, 412n3,
528n2; **48**: 63n1, 65; **49**: 351n2; on Marina and Arabia incidents, **40**: 75, 191-
92; E. M. House on, **40**: 139; on deportation issue, **40**: 212-13; on Anglo-Ger-
man relations, **40**: 213; and E. M.
House and German reply, **40**: 337, 362-
65, 447-78, 504-506, 508, 517, 525-26,
528-29; R. Lansing on, **40**: 445; on Germany's unrestricted submarine campaign, **40**: 447, 448-52; **41**: 59-63,n1,2,
74-76, 80-82, 87, 95, 110, 118-20, 183;
secret negotiations with E. M. House,
41: 3, 17, 18, 24-26, 26,n1, 40-50, 69,
95; advises delay in unrestricted submarine campaign, **41**: 52; and U.S. decision to send home, **41**: 87-88,n1, 95,
99, 106, 111, 116, 122-24, 125, 195n1,
214, 292-93; farewell to E. M. House,
41: 117, 117-18; and break in diplomatic relations, **41**: 118-20, 243-44; attempts to keep peace between Germany and U.S., **41**: 274, 275; and
Zimmermann telegram, **41**: 280, 322-
23, 326; and V. Carranza peace proposal, **41**: 429, 430
Berres, Albert Julius, **44**: 227,n1, 234; **46**:
362,n2
Berry, John H., **40**: 176,n1
Berry, Martha, **40**: 565,n1
Berry School, Mount Berry, Ga., **40**: 565
Bersaglieri, **44**: 507,n2
Berson, Stanislaw, **46**: 49,n2
Berst, Jacques A., **42**: 447,n1, 467,n1,
489; **43**: 431-32, 501-502; **44**: 13
Bertelli, Charles Filippo, **43**: 133,n1
Berthelot, Henri Mathias, **48**: 352-
53,n1,3, 420, 441n1; **51**: 587
Berthelot, Philippe Joseph-Louis, **40**:
439n1
Bertrand, Francisco, **41**: 143,n18
Bertron, Samuel Reading, **40**: 89, 92-93,
167, 184; **41**: 468; **43**: 409; **44**: 309, 335-
37, 359; **45**: 288, 389, 569; **46**: 519; **47**:
10, 20, 43, 208,n2, 354-55, 359; **48**: 414-
15,n1, 422; **50**: xivn16; and Russian

Commission, **42:** 45,n2,3, 81, 95, 143,n1, 216, 239, 262; on Russian situation, **45:** 282-83,n1; congratulates WW on railroad proclamation, **45:** 373; and public utilities, **49:** 54, 72, 406

Beshlin, Earl Hanley, **44:** 153n1

Bessarabia, **46:** 420n2, 568; **47:** 450, 474; **51:** 502

Bestor, Arthur Eugene, **44:** 248,n2; **47:** 235,n1, 236

Betancourt, Julio, **40:** 334; **41:** 8-10, 14-15, 344-45, 450, 465; on Colombian treaty, **47:** 572-73,n1

Bethlehem Steel Corporation, **47:** 385n6

Bethmann Hollweg, Theobald von, **40:** 21,n1, 24n1, 94-95, 106, 160, 161, 204, 217, 218, 229n1, 378, 434, 504-506, 555; **41:** 25-26, 26n1, 49-52, 96,n1, 388n1, **42:** 361, 389,n4; **43:** 185,n1, 404; **44:** 44, 140n3; **45:** 30, 173n1; **46:** 163; **47:** 524n1; **48:** 213n8; **51:** 331; and W. B. Hale interview, **40:** 39-40; J. C. Grew on, **40:** 184-85, 428-36; and German peace offer, **40:** 231-32, 233; **50:** 753n2; D. Lloyd George on, **40:** 342n4, 356; on Allied reply, **40:** 383-84; and decision to begin unrestricted submarine warfare, **40:** 529n1; **41:** 59-63,n1,2; reveals peace terms to J. W. Gerard, **41:** 137-38

Bevans, Charles I., **51:** 576n1

Beveridge, Albert Jeremiah, **43:** 276-77

Bey, Achmed Nessimy, **45:** 384n2

Beyens, Eugene van, **43:** 466,n3

Bianchi, Riccardo, **46:** 545,n1

Bi-Centennial Celebration in Paris (*Louisiana Historical Quarterly*), **46:** 100n1

Bickett, Thomas Walter, **40:** 443,n2; **51:** 328-29,n2

Biddle, John, **40:** 551,n5; **45:** 109,n6, 110, 439,n1; **46:** 196,n1, 452, 562n1

Bielaski, Alexander Bruce, **40:** 466-67; **42:** 17,n1, 272n10, 512,n2, 517; **44:** 574,n1; **45:** 153,n4; **48:** 322,n1

Bielskis, Julius J., **47:** 494n1

Bierer, Bion Barnett, **51:** 79,n1

Bigelow, Herbert S., **44:** 157-58,n1

Bill to Authorize the President to further mobilize the Federal forces and to increase temporarily the Military Establishment of the United States, **46:** 325,n1, 343

Billings, Edmund, **43:** 290

Billings, Warren K., **44:** 290n1; **46:** 69, 69-70, 70, 70-71

Billington, Monroe Lee, **43:** 48n1, 393n1

Billy, Edouard de, **51:** 465

Biltmore Hotel, N.Y., **41:** 418n1, 430n2

Bingham, Robert Worth, **49:** 268,n1; and woman suffrage, **51:** 49

Binghamton, N.Y., **42:** 470

Biography of a Progressive: Franklin K. Lane, 1864-1921 (Olson), **43:** 385n1; **51:** 103n3

Birkenheim, Alexander, **48:** 359

Birmingham, Ala., **42:** 496, 522; **44:** 15,

144n1; and proposed coal strike in, **43:** 433-34, 437

Birmingham News, **43:** 434n1; **48:** 148n1; **49:** 224n2, 236n1, 245,n1

Birmingham Terminal Company, **45:** 269n1

Birth of a Nation, **46:** 550; **47:** 388,n2,3

Birth of the German Republic, 1871-1918 (Rosenberg), **43:** 185n1; **51:** 253n2

Bisbee, Ariz., **43:** 157, 158n1, 158-59, 230, 231, 253, 326, 336, 339, 373, 418; **44:** 134, 135, 138, 478, 479, 515-16; **45:** 95, 134-35; **46:** 144,n1, 146; deportations, **44:** 516-20, 521-22; **47:** 115-16, 166-67, 187, 597-98

Bishop, Bennett, **44:** 79

Bishop, Farnham, **42:** 554n1

Bishop, Joseph Bucklin, **42:** 554n1; **48:** 582n1

Bishop Cannon's Own Story: Life as I Have Seen It (Watson, ed.), **43:** 65n1

Bismarck-Schönhausen, Otto Eduard Leopold von, **40:** 416; **45:** 436; **48:** 630; **51:** 330n3

Bissing, Moritz Ferdinand von, **40:** 384

Bissolati, Leonida (Bissolati-Bergamaschi), **47:** 59,n1, 74, 75

Bjorkman, Edwin August, **46:** 458,n1

Black, William Murray, **42:** 192,n2

Black Jack: The Life and Times of John J. Pershing (Vandiver), **43:** 32n6

Blackstone (Va.) College for Girls, **43:** 42n1

Blackwood's Magazine, **42:** 381n7

Blagoveshchensk, Russia, **47:** 68-69,n2, 99, 101, 242; **49:** 152; **51:** 609

Blaine, Anita Eugènie McCormick (Mrs. Emmons), **41:** 113-14,n1; **47:** 391-92, 394, 447-49, 477

Blair, Clinton Ledyard, **40:** 569,n7

Blakely, Paul Lendrum, **51:** 649

Blanchet, Louis, **48:** 39n1

Bland, William Thomas, **49:** 224,n3, 239, 295; **51:** 82, 85

Bland, William Thomas, Jr., **49:** 239,n1

Blankenburg, Rudolph, **47:** 19

Blankenhorn, Heber, **49:** 402n3, 434, 487, 488

Blasewitz, Germany, **40:** 144

Blatch, Harriet Eaton Stanton (Mrs. William Henry), **40:** 426,n1

Blatchford, Richard Milford, **45:** 111,n15; **48:** 417n5

Blease, Coleman Livingston, **44:** 10,n1; **48:** 260n2; **49:** 246-47,n4, 369n2

Blied, Frank C., **44:** 318,n1

Bliss, Cornelius Newton, **42:** 252,n2

Bliss, Robert Woods, **49:** 404,n1, 423; **51:** 134,n4, 141, 142, 155

Bliss, Tasker Howard, **40:** 3; **42:** 406, 408-10; **43:** 248n1, 435; **44:** 52, 312, 332n1, 361n1, 371, 382, 461, 462, 463; **45:** 4, 111, 113, 151, 156, 268, 323, 396, 438, 490, 532, 539; **46:** 9, 86, 196, 439; **47:** 18, 131, 158, 170, 174-76, 314; **48:** 50, 266, 330-31, 396, 418, 448n1, 481, 566,

Bliss, Tasker Howard (*cont.*)
577; **49:** 57, 66-67, 136-37, 285-86, 293, 336-44; **51:** 17, 52-55, 139, 203, 272, 290, 399, 407, 462,n2, 544, 562, 583-87; appointed Chief of Staff, **44:** 232n1; and Supreme War Council, **45:** 47, 54, 69, 93,n2, 317, 364, 532, 533; **46:** 211-12, 212, 240-41, 254-55, 391-92, 453-54; on war plans for 1918, **45:** 208-13; W. G. McAdoo on O. T. Crosby and, **45:** 588-89, and British request for U.S. troops, **46:** 42, 43, 44, 162, 210-12, 220, on Japanese intervention in Siberia, **46:** 213, 215, 219-20, 236, 248, 250, 352, 391-92, 392, 590; **47:** 81, 332-34, 421, 422, 491-92; and Inter-Allied General Reserve, **46:** 241, 558-60, 595-96, 619; on Supreme War Council's resolution on U.S. troop disposition, **47:** 12-14, 238, 260-61, 262-63, 271, 279, 280, 306, 512-14, 563-64; and requisitioning of Dutch ships, **47:** 26, 27; on U.S. troops in Italy, **47:** 107,n1, 130, 486-97; on F. Foch as military coordinator, **47:** 237-38; relinquishes Chief of Staff but retains rank of General, **47:** 458-59; on situation between the Netherlands and Germany, **47:** 564-66; on declaration of war against Turkey and Bulgaria, **47:** 568, 570-71; and J. J. Pershing, **47:** 616; on Supreme War Council and Russian intervention, **48:** 179-81, 200-201, 218-19, 383-90, 503-506, 506, 545-46; on Murmansk and Archangel expeditions, **48:** 367-70, 401-403, 536-38, 599-602; **49:** 43, 44, 529-32; clarifies term "supreme command," **49:** 126-27; on ending war in 1919, **49:** 258-61, 276, 277, 336-44; and 80-division program, **49:** 258, 262, 279-80, 354; on Russian officers serving with Allied troops, **49:** 335-36; on importance of fighting on western front, **49:** 532; on Italy, **49:** 533-35; on not sending additional troops to Russia, **51:** 33; reviews military situation and necessity for unity of command and objectives, **51:** 34-49; on peace terms, **51:** 261-62, 272-75, 291-92, 295, 425-33, 434-36, 571; on joint note on Russia not being official, **51:** 337-38; on league of nations, **51:** 430-31, 432-33; photograph: *illustration section*, **43**
Block Island, **46:** 213n2
Blockade Council: *see* Inter-Allied Embargo Council
Blocksom, Augustus Perry, **45:** 111,n1
Blue, Rupert, **42:** 311,n4; **45:** 26-27,n1, 51, 91
Blue, Victor, **46:** 213,n2
Blue Devils, **48:** 307,n1
Blum, John Morton, **40:** 349n11; **45:** 18n2, 93n3; **46:** 332n1, 406n1
Blumenthal, Daniel, **43:** 276
Blythe, James E., **47:** 236,n4

Blythe, Samuel George, **42:** 126; **46:** 367, 438, 575,n3; **48:** 604; **49:** 158
Boardman, Mabel Thorp, **47:** 199,n1
Bochkareva, Maria Leont'evna Frolkova, **48:** 469,n1, 473, 475
Boggs, Lily G. (Mrs. J. L.), **49:** 305,n1
Bogota, Treaty of (1914): *see* Colombia and the United States
Bohemia and Bohemians, **41:** 56-57, 211, 212, 260, 267; **42:** 156, 334, 335, 501; **44:** 387; **45:** 237, 271, 412, 553n2; **46:** 198n2; **47:** 549-51; **48:** 435, 436, 485, 530-31, 591; **51:** 565, 580, 638, 639; in Russia, **42:** 464
Bohemian Americans, **45:** 224; **47:** 300n2, 561, 576
Bohemian National Alliance of America, **45:** 223-24,n2
Böhm, Clara, **40:** 174
Bohn, Frank, **51:** 330n3, 331
Boissevain, Inez Milholland (Mrs. Eugen Jan), **40:** 379,n1, 421, 426; **43:** 175n4
Bok, Edward William, **41:** 22,n1; **42:** 182, 202; **48:** 361, 382-83
Bolden, Richard Manuel, **43:** 106,n1, 139
Bolivia, **42:** 359
Bolling, Bertha, sister of EBW, **46:** 371,n1; **51:** 108
Bolling, John Randolph, brother of EBW, **46:** 489,n1
Bolling, Richard Wilmer, **40:** 459,n3, 462
Bolling, Sallie White (Mrs. William Holcombe), mother of EBW, **41:** 288; **46:** 327
Bolo, Paul Marie (Bolo Pasha, Paul), **44:** 528,n2
Bologna, University of, **47:** 85,n2
Bolsheviki and the American Aid to Russia (Novosseloff), **49:** 321,n3
Bolsheviks, **44:** 180n2, 496,n4, 532; **45:** 216-17,n4, 228-29, 271, 288, 336, 347, 368, 370, 420, 432n1, 464, 474, 487, 543; **46:** 88, 182, 185, 187,n3, 191, 215, 229, 232-33, 233, 341-34, 392, 407n1, 419, 452, 513, 535, 539,n1, 576; **47:** 60, 69, 92n1, 97, 239, 242, 245, 299, 318, 319, 333, 397, 398, 412, 424, 459, 473, 489, 496, 503, 504, 586, 594, 605, 606, 607, 608; **48:** 38n1, 40, 96,n1,3, 99-102, 102-104, 142, 144-45, 241n1, 247, 274, 316, 365, 409, 449, 454, 493, 587-88, 609n1; **49:** 9, 40n1, 44, 45-46, 74,n1, 150, 151, 152, 175n1, 220, 262n1, 479, 495-96, 508, 532; **51:** 18n1,2, 95n2, 101, 604; L. Colcord on, **45:** 191, 192-93, 222n1, 251; R. Lansing on, **45:** 205-207, 263-65, 427-30, 562-64; **46:** 45-46,n3, 299-300, 358-59; WW on, **45:** 220, 417; **46:** 360, 485; and peace negotiations at Brest Litovsk and L. Trotsky's declaration, **45:** 384n2, 411-14; W. B. Thompson on, **45:** 443, 444; WW on Trotsky's declaration, **45:** 455-56, 458; W. R. Wilder on, **45:** 574-75; G. J. Sosnowski on, **45:** 575-76; and Fourteen

Points address, **46:** 22,n1; S. Gompers on, **46:** 39; Constituent Assembly broken up by, **46:** 46n3, 53; and Poland, **46:** 48; and question of recognition, **46:** 89, 333-34, 389, 419-21, 485; W. E. Walling on, **46:** 310-12; and Sisson Documents, **46:** 341,n1, 372,n1,3; **51:** 4,n2, 18; mission to Sweden of, **46:** 341,n2; and Joffre document, **46:** 372,n3; H. Williams on, **46:** 411n1; S. Strunsky on, **46:** 422n1; and treaty with Germany, **46:** 471n3, 543, 576; and killing of Japanese nationals, **47:** 68n2, 316,n3; R.H.B. Lockhart on favorable attitude of toward Allies, **47:** 245-46; indications of hostility toward U.S., **47:** 544; T. G. Masaryk on, **47:** 549; **51:** 96,n2; and Semenov's advance, **48:** 104-106; comments and observations on, **48:** 112-14, 131-32, 179-80, 181, 183-85, 194-95, 202,n1, 299-300, 410n2, 411, 528, 548, 570-73; plan to send representatives to Washington, **48:** 264-65, 276; U.S. policy in event of collapse of government of, **48:** 276, 277-78; and Czech troops, **48:** 398, 480, 494; **49:** 194-99; W. Wiseman on American public opinion toward, **48:** 470; A. J. Balfour on waning power of, **48:** 497-98; and the Red Terror, **51:** 61n1, 97-98, 542-43;
W. C. Bullitt on European movement of, **51:** 563-68, 622; petition urges WW to make statement against Red Terror, **51:** 643-44

Bolsheviks and the Czechoslovak Legion: Origin of Their Armed Conflict, March-May 1918 (Fic), **48:** 335n1; **49:** 45n3

Bolsheviks and the World War: The Origin of the Third International (Gankin and Fisher), **46:** 457n3

Bolton, Guy, **51:** 314n1

Bon, Ferdinand Jean Jacques de, **48:** 385,n4

Bonaparte, Charles Joseph, **51:** 147n1

Bonaparte, Napoleon: *see* Napoleon I

Bonar Law, Andrew, **41:** 214; **44:** 80,n1, 202; **45:** 93n4, 245; **46:** 359; **51:** 298, 571; on British food crisis and U.S. Treasury, **46:** 75,n1, 76-78

bond bill: *see* War Loan Act

Bones, Helen Woodrow, **40:** 94, 128; **41:** 358, 380, 452, 531, 557; **42:** 125, 151-52, 153-54, 160, 161, 171, 426; **43:** 241, 247, 318, 338; **44:** 65,n1; **46:** 115, 167, 371, 449,n1; **47:** 392, 506; **48:** 313n1; **49:** 167, 319; **51:** 77, 316; letters to Jessie (1914-16), **40:** 572-76; on friendship with EBG, **40:** 574; WW attempts to find job for, **51:** 640-41

Bonillas, Ignacio, **40:** 50, 51, 54, 55, 56, 280, 285-87, 393-94, 394-97; **42:** 79-80,n1; **43:** 154, 378-79, 381

Bonzano, Archbishop Giovanni, **41:** 45n1; **44:** 184n3; **51:** 296, 355

Book Cliffs coal field, **43:** 73

Bookwalter-Ball Printing Company, **46:** 285n1

Boone, William D., **49:** 327, 328

Booth and Company, **46:** 317n4

Booth Fisheries, **40:** 291n2

Bopp, Franz, **43:** 217,n4,5

Borah, William Edgar, **41:** 11n1; **42:** 106, 107; **43:** 216, 432, 433,n2; **45:** 582; **46:** 606n1; **47:** 381n2; **48:** 487n1; **49:** 145-46,n2, 147; **51:** 330,n2, 331, 356; and woman suffrage, **51:** 58

Bordeaux, France, **42:** 228; **43:** 443; **45:** 108

Borden, Sir Robert (Laird), **42:** 334, 338, 360; **44:** 441; **49:** 437-38

Borgesius, H. Goeman, **46:** 615n4

Borglum, Gutzon, **45:** 155-56, 214, 266, 314n1, 397, 492; **46:** 332; **48:** 10; and aircraft program, **45:** 69-70, 102, 280-81, 356-58, 426-27, 427; **46:** 82, 94-95,n1, 106, 150, 205, 206, 433; N. D. Baker and, **46:** 57-58, 208-209, 229-30, 433; WW on, **46:** 445; charges against Aircraft Board lead to investigation and report, **47:** 41,n1, 51,n1, 67, 169-70, 174, 181, 193, 234-35, 235, 247, 259, 296-97, 313, 335-36,n1, 344, 352, 508-509, 509-10,n1, 511, 511-12, 535-36, 546, 554, 588; D. Lawrence's article about, **47:** 587,n1, 587-88; photograph: *illustration section,* **47**

Borglum Charged with Using Confidence of the President to Promote Aero Company (Lawrence), **47:** 587,n1

Boris, Prince of Bulgaria, **51:** 141,n1

Borland, William Patterson, **41:** 84,n1, 85; **42:** 528-29, 531-32; **48:** 444n1; **49:** 224,n4, 239

Borsarelli de Rifreddo, Marquis Luigi, **49:** 64,n2

Boselli, Paolo, **42:** 110,n1; **44:** 427

Bosnia, **41:** 212; **42:** 156, 333, 334; **45:** 412; **46:** 244

Bosporus, **40:** 446n4, 494, 495-96; **44:** 387

Boston, Mass., **43:** 422; **49:** 501; and street railways, **51:** 20

Boston, University of, **47:** 518n1

Boston and Maine Railroad, **44:** 152,n1, 183, 205, 425

Boston *Christian Science Monitor,* **43:** 14, 150,n3; **47:** 509; **48:** 393n2; **51:** 579-80

Boston *Congregationalist and Advance,* **45:** 371n1

Boston Daily Globe, **42:** 246,n4

Boston Elevated Trolley System, **49:** 422

Boston Evening Transcript, **42:** 523

Boston Globe, **44:** 204, 246n1; **45:** 437; **48:** 149

Boston Herald, **42:** 523

Boston Jewish Advocate, **42:** 234n1

Boston Journal, **44:** 246n1

Boston *Living Age,* **40:** 336n1

Boston peace parade, **44:** 192-93, 194n4
Boston Post, **44:** 204; **51:** 552n1
Bottomley, Charles M., **44:** 244
Bouck, William, **48:** 294; **49:** 79-80; **51:** 212,n2, 249,n2, 257, 310-12, 393-94, 520
Bouillon, Henri Franklin, **44:** 141,n1,2
Boulogne, France, **42:** 188; **46:** 389
Bourgeois, Léon Victor Auguste, **43:** 446,n4; **48:** 613,n1, 627; **49:** 226n2
Bourgois, Gaston, **47:** 101,n6
Bourke, Dermot Robert Wyndham: *see* Mayo, 7th Earl of
Bourne, Francis Cardinal, **44:** 330,n1
Bow, Washington, **51:** 249n2
Bowdoin College, **42:** 570,n1
Bowerman, Charles William, **42:** 266,n1; **49:** 24
Bowlby, Harry Laity, **47:** 311,n1
Bowles, George H., **44:** 259
Bowman, Isaiah, **46:** 23,n2; **51:** 408
Box, George G., **48:** 594,n2
Boxer Rebellion, **41:** 176, 177
Boyd, James Oscar, **45:** 570,n1
Boyden, Roland William, **48:** 77,n1; **49:** 443
Boyden, William Cowper, **48:** 77n1
Boy-Ed, Karl, **41:** 506
Boykin, Julia Fulton Sharp Williams (Mrs. Thomas Reeves), **48:** 557n1
Boyle, Charles W., **44:** 243, 263
Boyle, Emmet Derby, **44:** 81,n1; **47:** 194
Boyle, G. E., **43:** 340
Boyle, Joseph Whiteside, **48:** 100,n2
Boylston, Hester Drayton (Mrs. J. Reid), **44:** 268,n1
Brachet, Albert, **41:** 230,n1, 235
Bracken, Leonidas Locke, **46:** 492,n1
Brackett, Cyrus Fogg, **40:** 255,n1, 279
Brackett, Edgar Truman, **49:** 106,n3
Bradley, John Jewsbury, **47:** 380,n1
Brady, James Henry, **49:** 145n2; **51:** 180n1
Brady, James Hezekiah, **46:** 61,n2; death of, **46:** 204,n1
Brady, Matthew I., **42:** 272,n7
Brady, William Augustus, **47:** 311,n1
Bragdon, Henry Wilkinson, **46:** 508n1
Brahany, Lucy Cahill (Mrs. Thomas W.), **41:** 331,n1, 358
Brahany, Thomas W., **40:** 420-21,n1, 423; **41:** 327-31, 357-59, 364-65, 381-82, 424-25, 431-32, 445, 448-49, 473-75, 506-507, 515, 531-32, 549-50, 557-58; **42:** 13, 23, 64, 71, 77, 91, 93-94, 121, 237; **43:** 272n1, 284-85; **48:** 95; on WW's meeting with T. Roosevelt, **42:** 31; on receptions for French and British missions, **42:** 123, 125-26, 132-33
Brahms, Johannes, **49:** 360n2
Brailsford, Henry Noel, **41:** 375,n6
Braisted, William Clarence, **40:** 523,n2; **42:** 311
Braisted, William Reynolds, **42:** 59n2
Brand, Charles Hillyer, **44:** 40,n1
Brand, Charles John, **51:** 610,n1

Brandegee, Frank Bosworth, **41:** 20; **47:** 381n2, 416n2, 584; **49:** 310n1; and woman suffrage, **51:** 58
Brandeis, Louis Dembitz, **40:** 315,n1; **41:** 48, 49; **42:** 81, 195, 204, 234, 235, 462,n1, 533; **43:** 159n2, 189; **44:** 164, 261, 299n1,2; **45:** 7,n1; **46:** 482, 585, 610; **47:** 210, 212, 557; **48:** 145; **49:** 422; **51:** 125; and Hitchman case, **46:** 297n1; on N. D. Baker's inspection tour, **46:** 429-30; recommended for Director General of Labor, **47:** 377, 425-26, 449, 467, **51:** 125
Brandeis The Adjuster and Private-Life Judge (Hard), **40:** 315n1
Brandeis The Conservative Or A 'Dangerous Radical'? (Hard), **40:** 315n1
Brannan, Eunice Dana (Mrs. John Winters), **40:** 379,n2; **43:** 201n1
Bratenahl, George Carl Fitch, **46:** 435,n1,2
Braz Pereira Gomes, Wenceslao, **42:** 15,n1, 314,n1, 489, 548-49; **48:** 550-51
Brazil, **41:** 9, 249n1; **42:** 359; and Pan-American Pact, **42:** 14, 15, 44, 45, 54, 80, 94, 99, 105; and decision to enter war, **42:** 265,n4, 314, 314-15, 439-40,n1, 548-49
Brazil and the United States, **43:** 11-12,n1; **44:** 176,n2, 543; **48:** 550-51
Breckinridge, Clifton Rodes, **42:** 393,n2
Breckinridge, James Carson, **46:** 45,n1
Bremse, S.M.S., **53:** 490
Brennan, James H., **44:** 307, 307-308
Breshko-Breshkovskaya, Ekaterina Konstantinova (Babushka), **44:** 39,n3; **45:** 194
Breslau, S.M.S., **42:** 316; **49:** 411n1
Breslich, Arthur Louis, **46:** 612,n4
Bresnan, Maurice, **46:** 574
Brest, France, **42:** 301; **46:** 8n1, 12; **47:** 230
Brest-Litovsk: peace negotiations at, **45:** 384,n2, 400, 411-14, 432n1, 436, 595n2,3; **46:** 186, 190, 191n11, 193 341n4,5, 471n3; **47:** 269; mentioned in Fourteen Points Address, **45:** 506, 519-21, 534, 535; and Trotsky's no war—no peace, **46:** 341n5; Treaty of, **46:** 585, 585-86,n1, 598n1; **48:** 240, 364, 379, 409, 410n2, 497, 571, 576-77; **49:** 63,n1, 185n1, 238, 247, 496; **51:** 129, 164, 170, 187, 236n6, 239, 244, 258, 267,n3, 415, 499
Brest-Litovsk: The Forgotten Peace, March 1918 (Wheeler-Bennett), **45:** 595n2; **46:** 341n4,5, 471n3
brewing industry, **44:** 107, 146; **46:** 306-307; **47:** 88, 106-107; **48:** 166-67, 175, 209,n1, 247, 484, 485; **49:** 550,n1; **51:** 28-30; grain restrictions on, **45:** 83-84, 91, 113, 228
Briand, Aristide, **40:** 346,n2, 496; **41:** 315-17,n2; **43:** 58; **44:** 427, 548; **47:** 551
Brick Presbyterian Church of New York, **46:** 260,n1, 286

Bricker, William R., **47:** 559,n2
Bridat, Mr., **41:** 351,n1
Brides, Robert T., **40:** 89,n1
Bridge to France (Hurley), **44:** 148n1, 395n; **46:** 444n2; **47:** 385n6
Bridgeport, Conn.: labor situation in, **49:** 465,n2,3, 519, 520-22, 537, 539, 547; **51:** 14, 19, 24, 49-50
Bridges, George Tom Molesworth, **42:** 125,n1, 133, 191-93, 194, 201, 202, 209, 372, 409, 530; **47:** 386; **48:** 352-54
Bridges, Henry Wilson, **46:** 218,n2, 239
Bridges, John Miller, **46:** 218,n2
Bridges, Robert, **40:** 289,n1; **41:** 354; **45:** 410-11, 423, 575; **46:** 218-19, 239, 371,n1; **48:** 111-12, 141, 564; **51:** 640-41
Bridges, Robert Seymour, **42:** 209-10,n1, 392; **46:** 219,n4; **49:** 462-63
Bridgman, Howard Allen, **45:** 94, 371n1
Briey-Longwy district, France, **46:** 167
Briggs, Albert M., **42:** 511,n1, 512, 513, 518,n5
Briggs, Mitchell Pirie, **40:** 540n1; **48:** 555n6
Briggs, Otis, **47:** 190,n2
Briggs, William Harlowe, **48:** 120, **51:** 172-73,n1,2
Brigham, William D., **42:** 115; **46:** 550
Brisbane, Arthur, **42:** 106,n1, 106-107, 129,n1; **43:** 318,n1, 416,n1; **44:** 245; **45:** 40n1, 320-21; on T. Roosevelt, **46:** 102n1
Bristol, England, **43:** 308
British-American relations: see Great Britain and the United States
British-American Relations, 1917-1918: The Role of Sir William Wiseman (Fowler), **40:** 262n1; **43:** 24n1, 278n2
British-American Tobacco Company, **48:** 372
British Labor Mission, **46:** 356n6
British Responses to President Wilson's Peace Efforts, 1914-1917 (Oxman), **40:** 307n1
British Women's Army Auxiliary Corps, **49:** 546n1
Brizon, Pierre, **48:** 211,n2
Brno (Brünn) Austria *Lidove Noviny* (*People's Newspaper*), **51:** 506n1
Broadway Auditorium, Buffalo, N.Y., **45:** 11n1
Brochner, Jessie, **42:** 394n5
Brockdorff-Rantzau, Count Ulrich von, **43:** 186,n5
Brockner, Fletcher Sims, **42:** 557,n2; **49:** 78,n4
Brockton, Mass., **49:** 133
Bronson, Minnie, **45:** 345-46,n1
Bronx, N.Y., **49:** 502
Brookings, Robert Somers, **40:** 9,n2, 215-16, 303, 443n1, 444; **41:** 55n1; **43:** 25, 192,n1, 341n1; **47:** 117-18, 118-19, 138, 383-84; and reorganization of War Industries Board, **46:** 523, 603, 607; and steel and iron prices, **47:** 167-68, 183; **48:** 392-93; **51:** 90-91, 285-86,n1; on cot-

ton prices, **47:** 168-69, 173, 395; **48:** 563; and wool prices, **47:** 383-84, 395, 444-45, 450; and leather prices, **47:** 383-84, 395; on "Liberty garments," **47:** 494-96, 502, 538-39; on copper prices, **48:** 487-88, 489; on prices and price fixing, **51:** 218-20
Brookings Institution, **40:** 443n1
Brookings Institution: A Fifty-Year History (Saunders), **40:** 443n1
Brooklyn, N.Y., **49:** 502
Brooklyn, U.S.S., **46:** 34, 47; **49:** 150, 262, 479
Brooklyn Eagle; on prohibition, **49:** 477
Brooks, Sydney, **40:** 233-34, 276, 494,n1; **41:** 468; **42:** 111, 112
Broomstick Apologists (T. Roosevelt), **44:** 394n1
Broomstick Preparedness (T. Roosevelt), **44:** 394n1
Brophy, W. H., **43:** 104n1
Broqueville, Charles de, **43:** 465,n1
Brotherhood of Locomotive Engineers, **45:** 26
Brotherhood of Locomotive Firemen and Engineers, **45:** 26
Brotherhood of Railway Clerks, **45:** 184
Brotherhood of Railroad Trainmen, **45:** 26; **47:** 447
Brougham, Herbert Bruce, **40:** 243,n1, 315, 337-38, 371-72, 374, 380-81, 402; **41:** 191; **46:** 36,n1, 113; **47:** 279n2; and controversy over article on House mission, **44:** 275-76,n2, 279, 459-60, 473, 478-79, 524
Broussard, Marrette Applegate (Mrs. Robert Foligny), **47:** 341
Broussard, Robert Foligny, **46:** 61,n1; and woman suffrage, **45:** 278, 339; death of, **47:** 341n1; **48:** 233n1
Browder, Robert Paul, **42:** 418n2
Brower, Jessie Woodrow Bones (Mrs. Abraham Thew H.), first cousin of WW, **40:** 574,n1; **43:** 338
Brower, Marion McGraw Bones (Mrs. Abraham Thew), **44:** 65n1
Brown, Mr., **44:** 55,n3
Brown, Arthur Judson, **45:** 185,n3
Brown, Ashmun Norris, **43:** 267,n4
Brown, C. C., **51:** 92n1
Brown, Curtis, **46:** 589,n1; **47:** 139
Brown, Demetra Vaka (Mrs. Kenneth), **47:** 308,n2
Brown, Edward Thomas, first cousin of EAW, **40:** 572,n1; **45:** 236-37; **47:** 192, 503; **49:** 237
Brown, Fred W., **43:** 231
Brown, George Martin: and woman suffrage, **51:** 281
Brown, Harvey Winfield, **49:** 104,n2, 132, 133
Brown, Lathrop, **41:** 518
Brown, Marjorie, **48:** 60
Brown, Mary Celestine Mitchell (Mrs. Edward Thomas), **45:** 236-37; **47:** 503; **48:** 60

Brown Brothers, **45:** 332
Brown University, **42:** 322n1
Browne, Louis Edgar, **48:** 142,n4, 143, 299-300,n1
Browning, Frederick Henry, **43:** 209-10,n2
Browning, Montague Edward, **42:** 121,n1; **44:** 452,n1
Browning, William John, **51:** 179n3
Brownlow, Louis, **43:** 201n1; **44:** 453; **46:** 37n1; **47:** 38,n1, 58, 66, 596; **49:** 313-14, 314; **51:** 61
Brownsville, Tex., **50:** 714n3
Bruère, Henry, **40:** 115; **51:** 68,n2
Bruges, Belgium, **44:** 332
Brumbaugh, Clement Laird, **42:** 21n1; **43:** 21
Brumbaugh, Martin Grove, **42:** 434,n1, 446; **48:** 445,n2
Brummer, S.M.S., **51:** 490
Brundage, Edward Jackson, **43:** 297,n2, 300
Bruner, Ben Lone, **51:** 49,n1
Brunschvicg, Cécile Kahn (Mrs. Léon), **48:** 26
Brusher, Joseph Stanislaus, **43:** 216n1
Brusilov, Aleksei Alekseevich, **42:** 287,n3; **43:** 460n1; **45:** 228, 264
Brussels, Belgium, mentioned as site for peace conference, **51:** 371n2, 473
Brussels, University of, **41:** 230
Bryan, Mary Elizabeth Baird (Mrs. William Jennings), **40:** 129n2, 333, 355
Bryan, William Jennings, **40:** 41, 63, 111, 173, 354-55; **41:** 115, 197, 242, 243,n1, 244-45, 443; **42:** 4, 77, 277; **43:** 55, 56, 81; **44:** 54,n1, 60-61,n1; **46:** 67, 117; **48:** 645; A. G. Gardiner on, **40:** 35n3; desires appointment to peace mission, **40:** 85,n1, 131-32, 137-38; **46:** 115, 116; WW and dinner honoring, **40:** 85-86,n1, 96, 128-29, 167; WW thanks for encouragement during campaign, **40:** 108; congratulates WW on peace note, **40:** 314, 333; on WW's Peace without Victory speech, **41:** 29, 94; opposes diplomatic break with Germany, **41:** 235; on Napoleon and peace, **41:** 309; offers his services in wartime, **41:** 556; on Fourteen Points Address, **45:** 599-600; and Costa Rica, **48:** 645; **49:** 3, 5, 21-23, 60-61, 431
Bryce, James Viscount, **40:** 568; **41:** 217, 270; **42:** 255; **43:** 497, 498-99; **44:** 132; **45:** 68; **46:** 549,n1, 572, 574-75; **47:** 103, 200; **51:** 375, 422; on WW's peace note, **440:** 316-18, 319, 413-14, 446,n2, 489; on Allied reply, **40:** 468-69; on a league of nations, **47:** 507-508, 535
Bryce, Elizabeth M. A., Lady Bryce, **41:** 270
Brylinski, R., **47:** 318,n2
Bryn, Helmer Halvorsen, **45:** 115,n3
Bryn Mawr College, **46:** 508n1; **47:** 454n1
Buchan, John, **43:** 361,n2; **45:** 445
Buchanan, Sir George William, **42:**

337,n2, 436; **43:** 369,n1, 371, 372, 386, 387; **44:** 180; **45:** 370; **49:** 11n4; withdrawn from Russian ambassadorship, **45:** 418, 447
Buchanan, James Paul, **50:** 451,n7, 452
Bucharest, Treaty of (1916), **45:** 469, 470, 479, 554; **46:** 373,n1; **51:** 129, 164, 170, 187, 239, 244, 258, 267, 499
Buckler, William Hepburn, **40:** 140, 178, 180, 187, 293, 413-14, 446,n4, 493, 494-95, 495-96; **41:** 374-75; **42:** 379-81, 435-37; **44:** 149, 546, 546-49; **45:** 174-75; **47:** 86; **51:** 10
Buckmaster, 1st Baron (Stanley Owen Buckmaster), **45:** 175,n1
Buckner, Emory Roy, **47:** 558,n6
Bucks County (Pa.) Historical Society Papers, **44:** 199n
Budapest, **51:** 565
Budd, Britton Ihrie, **49:** 211n1, 251
Buell, Raymond Leslie, **48:** 417n3,5
Buena Vista Hills oil reserve, **40:** 206,n3, 560n1
Buenos Aires *Razon*, **50:** 734,n2
Buffalo, N.Y., **44:** 566; **47:** 446; **50:** 745n9; **51:** 248; WW's address to American Federation of Labor in, **45:** 11-17
Buffalo, U.S.S., **42:** 281,n2; **43:** 414n1
Buffalo Bill: *see* Cody, William Frederick
Buffum, Frank Washburn, **48:** 294,n2
Bugšeg, Vilim, **51:** 562,n1
Bukhedu, Manchuria, **51:** 479,n1
Bukovina, **43:** 523
Bulgaria, **40:** 231, 239, 250, 477, 496, 554n1; **41:** 75, 138, 300, 464; **42:** 142n1, 156, 198, 317, 334, 340, 436, 456, 501; **43:** 236, 406; **44:** 45, 239n1, 295, 476, 547, 548; **45:** 123, 186, 200, 249, 416; **46:** 172, 173, 277, 295, 483, 556, 568; **49:** 365, 399, 404, 416, 436; **51:** 151, 152, 183, 266; and Brest-Litovsk peace conference, **45:** 384n2, 411-12, 576; and Inquiry memorandum, **45:** 461, 463-64, 466, 469-70; and Fourteen Points, **45:** 554; and talk of separate peace, **46:** 235,n1; **48:** 457n1; and issue of U.S. war declaration against, **47:** 416-17,n2, 490-91,n2, 570-71; **48:** 70, 79-80,n1; **49:** 282,n3, 365,n1,2, 447, 537, 538; suggestion that U.S. threaten, **51:** 64, 105; surrender and peace negotiations, **51:** 133-34, 141-42, 142-44, 145, 146, 154, 154-55, 155, 162-63, 163-64, 169, 170, 183, 187, 254, 292, 455n1, 502; W. C. Bullitt on Bolshevism and, **51:** 563,n1,2; food and supplies made available to, **51:** 595
Bulgarian Americans, **43:** 86n2,3
Bullard, Arthur (pseud. Albert Edwards), **42:** 254,n3,5, 267,n1, 289, 290-91, 377, 378, 410, 507, 508-509; **45:** 217; **47:** 521, 522
Bullard, Frederic Lauriston, **44:** 536n1
Bullard, Ralph E., **46:** 256n1
Bulletin of the United States Bureau of Labor Statistics, **44:** 220n1

Bullitt, William Christian, **44**: 298, 459,n2, 473, 478-79, 524-25; **45**: 235; **46**: 36n1, 221, 265, 532n1; **48**: 144-45; on G. Hertling's address, **46**: 162-67; on political situation in Germany and Austria-Hungary, **46**: 183-93, 567-69; compares Hertling's and Czernin's addresses, **46**: 222-29; on strikes in Germany, **46**: 266-68; calls for protest against Japan's intervention in Siberia, **46**: 510-13,n1; on WW's speech in Metropolitan Opera House, **51**: 136, 162; on Bolshevik movement, **51**: 563-68, 622-23

Bülow, Bernhard Heinrich Martin Karl, Prince von, **45**: 33, 415,n4; **46**: 253n2; **49**: 193

Bundy, Richard Carlton, **47**: 315-16,n3, 317

Bunting, Samuel J., **47**: 155

Bureau for Conscientious Objectors, **43**: 175n1

Bureau of: *see* under the latter part of the names, such as, Foreign and Domestic Commerce, Bureau of

Burián von Rajecz, Count Stefan, **41**: 300; **51**: 154, 267

Burke, Edmund, **44**: 416; **47**: 288, 298

Burke, Edward Lathrop, **46**: 614,n1

Burke, John, **44**: 88,n1; **48**: 628n1

Burleigh, George William, **40**: 35,n3

Burleson, Albert Sidney, **40**: 89-90, 173, 292, 366, 426; **41**: 88, 123, 179-80, 323, 332, 381, 382, 454, 461, 484, 506-507, 518, 556; **42**: 374; **43**: 164, 165n2, 212, 272, 276, 312, 313, 336n1, 381, 389; **44**: 62, 147, 204-205, 221, 245, 263, 289, 301-302, 379, 380, 452; **45**: 95, 104, 147, 148n1, 242, 272, 342; **46**: 37, 38, 63, 117, 422, 508,n2, 515, 554, 581,n1, 621; **47**: 8, 94,n1, 206, 209, 372, 477, 516, 560; **48**: 259, 356, 432, 532, **49**: 137, 146, 147, 174, 316, 431, 438,n2; **51**: 12, 103, 300, 548, 616, 646; and armed-ship bill, **41**: 279, 294,n1, 331; J. P. Tumulty on, **41**: 382; advocates war declaration, **41**: 442, 443, 444, 445; and espionage bill, **42**: 22, 245n2; on censorship, **42**: 195-96; **43**: 187-88; **51**: 55,n1, 483, 520-21; on deficiency appropriation bill, **42**: 343; and Trading with the Enemy Act, **43**: 317; on Sassman case, **43**: 373-74; and People's Council, **43**: 383, 394, 512; on *Pearson's Magazine* complaint, **43**: 396-97; M. Eastman on *Masses* case and, **44**: 171; on war revenue bill and postal rate increase, **44**: 257,n1; comments on censorship position of, **44**: 271-72, 338-40, 344, 358,n1, 366n1, 371-72, 389-90, 393, 393-94, 396-97,n2, 397, 408, 416, 420, 428,n1, 469-70, 472, 472-73; WW on, **45**: 555-56; E. M. House on, **46**: 327; on Crowder bill, **47**: 264-65; on T. R. Marshall's request for child welfare, **47**: 596; on airmail service, **47**: 615; and

Indiana Democratic platform, **48**: 319n1,2; on government takeover of telegraph system, **48**: 458n1, on reply to German peace note, **51**: 412, 414

Burleson Tells Newspapers What They May Not Say (*New York Times*), **44**: 366n1

Burling, Edward Burnham, **41**: 48,n1, 93, 208; **43**: 49,n3, 56

Burlingham, Charles Culp, **42**: 118-19,n1

Burnett, John Lawson, **40**: 531, 549; **43**: 191,n2

Burnett immigration bill (1917), **40**: 267-68,n2,3, 531, 544, 549; Wilson's veto of, **41**: 52-53; *see also* immigration legislation

Burnham, H. W., **51**: 396n1

Burning of Jim McIlherron: An N.A.A.C.P. Investigation (White), **49**: 88n3

Burnquist, Joseph Alfred Arner, **43**: 512n1; **44**: 78; **45**: 258,n1, 259-62, 279; **46**: 463-64; **47**: 189,n1, 190, 236, 237, 273

Burnside, R. H., **48**: 52,n3

Burton, Harry Payne, **42**: 446-47,n1,2

Burton, Pomeroy, **42**: 446-47,n2

Burton, Theodore Elijah, **42**: 217, 221; **48**: 643, 644-45,n1

Burtsev, Vladimir L'vovich, **46**: 372,n1; **48**: 194-95

Buryats, **48**: 105,n1

Busch, Lilly Anheuser (Mrs. Adolphus), **51**: 395,n1, 445-46,n2

Bush, Charles Cortland, **43**: 434n2

Bush, Irving Ter, **44**: 503,n3

Bush Terminal Company, N.Y., **44**: 503,n3

Bushnell, Edward Rogers, **42**: 569,n1

business, **44**: 335-37, 359, 360, 398; S. J. Graham on economic conditions of, **40**: 244-46; E. N. Hurley on cost accounting and, **40**: 250-55; W. Kent on Trade Commission and, **41**: 207-208; Chamber of Commerce proposal and, **45**: 61-67; reaction to H. A. Garfield's coal proclamation, **46**: 18; F. B. Kellogg on proposed License Act, **51**: 70-73

Business Chronicle of the Pacific Northwest, **49**: 296-97,n1,2

Butler, John T., **40**: 176,n1

Butler, Nicholas Murray (*pseud.* Cosmos), **40**: 24n1, 30,n2, 35; **41**: 250, 251; **43**: 11, **49**: 12

Butler, Rush Clark, **49**: 314n1

Butte, Mont., **42**: 564; **44**: 259-63; **45**: 321-22; **46**: 144n1; **49**: 134; labor problems in, **43**: 17, 18, 299, 339, 341, 345, 494

Butterfield, John L., **43**: 509,n2

Buttrick, Wallace, **45**: 272

Butz, Otto, **47**: 324,n1

Buxton, Charles Roden, **42**: 422,n1

Buxton, Noel (Noel-Buxton, Noel Edward), **40**: 139, 178; **41**: 374,n2, 375; **42**: 422n2, 436-37; **44**: 320; on peace terms, **40**: 361n1, 446,n3, 494, 495-96; speech

Buxton, Noel (*cont.*)
on American support of Britain, **40:** 414,n1; memorandum on American opinion of the war, **40:** 415-16
Buzzards Bay, Mass., **51:** 345
By Way of Interpretation: What Was the Consideration? (*Business Chronicle of the Pacific Northwest*), **49:** 295-96,n1,2
Byars, Winfield Scott, **46:** 254,n1
Bychov, Russia, **46:** 403
Byllesby, Henry Marison, **41:** 514,n1; **47:** 335-36,n2
Bynner, Witter, **45:** 258,n1
Byoir, Carl, **49:** 24,n3, 25,n1, 26
Byrnes, James Francis, **49:** 315
Byrns, Joseph Wellington, **49:** 317,n2

Cabell, DeRosey Carroll, **43:** 4,n4
Cabrera, Luis, **40:** 49-50, 53, 54, 55, 56, 280, 281, 282, 285-87, 393-94, 394-97; R. Lansing on, **40:** 114-15
Cachin, Marcel, **43:** 30,n3; **47:** 75,n3
Cadorna, Luigi, **44:** 480,n1, 508, 509; **45:** 48; **46:** 79, 241, 558n2
Caffey, Francis Gordon, **42:** 244,n1,2; **48:** 59,n1,2, 251; **51:** 534
Cahan, Abraham, **43:** 175
Caillaux, Joseph, **43:** 444,n2, 445
Caine, James Hall, **51:** 482,n1
Caine, Thomas Henry Hall (Hall Caine), **43:** 351-52,n1,2
Caine Has No Hope of Punitive Peace (Caine), **43:** 351,n2
Cairo, Egypt, **43:** 159,n3, 206
Calais, France, **42:** 188; **43:** 7
Calder, William Musgrave, **40:** 196,n4; **43:** 7; **45:** 582; **51:** 390,n1
Calderwood, Willis Greenleaf, **51:** 390,n1
Caldwell, Anne, **48:** 52,n3
Caldwell, Charles Pope, **42:** 103-104,n1,2, 144; **46:** 147-48, 148
Caldwell, James C., **47:** 216-17,n1
Caldwell, John Kenneth, **46:** 33,n2, 338,n1, 555,n2; **47:** 72n3, 544,n2; **48:** 39,n1, 428-29; **49:** 43, 176, 262,n1, 282, 494-95
Caledonia, S. S., **40:** 450
Calhoun Commercial Club of Minneapolis, **51:** 91n1
California, **44:** 17, 167, 242, 243, 290,n1, 294; **46:** 478; and 1916 presidential election, **40:** 129; and oil lands, **41:** 65, 247, 288-92; **42:** 525-26, 533, 547; and Mooney case, **42:** 270,n2, 271-72, 273; **46:** 68-74, 170; **47:** 160,n1, 210; and labor problems, **43:** 222n1, 248n1, 281, 386; and oil strikes, **45:** 121, 126, 129; **46:** 128, 134-35; I.W.W. activities in, **47:** 194, 196; and oil bill, **47:** 452; politics in, **51:** 213, 259-60, 477,n1,2, 632; and Theodora Pollak case, **51:** 125n1
California, University of, **43:** 216n1
California and Hawaiian Sugar Refining Company, **45:** 344n1, 354
California State Commission of Immigration and Housing, **43:** 222n1; **47:** 194n1, 198
California State Railroad Commission, **49:** 252n1
California's Cross-Filing Nightmare: The 1918 Gubernatorial Election (Melendy), **51:** 213n1
Calkins, John Uberto, **49:** 120,n7
Call, Arthur Deerin, **41:** 244
Calle, Benjamin T., **40:** 89,n1
Calloway, Alfred Woodward, **47:** 409,n4, 410
Calonder, Felix Ludwig, **46:** 556,n2, 592, 594; **51:** 240,n10
Calumet and Arizona Mining Company, **44:** 515, 518
Camaguey, Cuba, **41:** 268n1
Camalier, Renah F., **49:** 106,n2
Cambon, Jules Martin, **43:** 57,n2, 255, 256, 268, 355, 356, 379, 387-89,n1; **44:** 24, 25
Cambon, Paul, **40:** 439n1; **42:** 265,n5, 327n1; **44:** 318,n1, 319; **45:** 492
Cambrai, France, **45:** 174, 175, 312; **47:** 505
Cambridge University, **47:** 421n1; **48:** 249,n1, 250; WW receives honorary degree from, **47:** 85,n1, 264,n1, 396
Cambridge Springs, Pa., **41:** 508
Cameron, Henry Clay, **43:** 155,n1
Cameron House (Wash., D.C.), **44:** 108, 109, 112, 113
Caminetti, Anthony, **41:** 246, 261, 453-54, 454, 469; **51:** 69,n3
Caminetti, Ella E. Martin (Mrs. Anthony), **41:** 246, 261, 453-54, 454, 465, 469
Caminetti, Farley Drew, **41:** 246,n1, 261, 453-54, 454
Camp Bowie, Texas, **45:** 390,n2,4
Camp Cody, N.M., **45:** 111n1
Camp Dix, N.J., **47:** 478
Camp Dodge, Ia., **45:** 111n9; **48:** 136n1
Camp Doniphan, Okla., **45:** 390,n2,4; **46:** 209,n4
Camp Epidemics Laid to Want of Winter Equipment (*New York Times*), **45:** 390n4
Camp Funston, Kan., **45:** 111n12; **48:** 189
Camp Grant, Ill., **49:** 179,n2
Camp Jackson, S.C., **44:** 10; **45:** 111n14
Camp Lewis, Wash., **45:** 111n8
Camp Logan, Texas, **44:** 41n1, 42,n2
Camp Meade, Md., **44:** 288-89, 293; **47:** 186, 220, 222
Camp Merritt, N.J., **45:** 452
Camp Mills, N.Y., **45:** 452
Camp Sevier, S.C., **45:** 109n5
Camp Sheridan, Ala., **45:** 107n1
Camp Upton, N.Y., **44:** 503-504; **45:** 157
Campaigns for Progressivism and Peace (Link): *see* Wilson: Campaigns for Progressivism and Peace, 1916-1917
Campbell, Guy Edgar, **45:** 275n1
Campbell, Peter J., **51:** 120, 149

Campbell, Philip Pitt, **49**: 309,n3
Campbell, Ronald Hugh, **45**: 430-31,n1
Campbell, Thomas Edward, **43**: 53,n2, 157, 157-58; **44**: 517, 519, 520; **45**: 134-35, 403n1; **46**: 598; **47**: 598
Campbell, W. A., **45**: 44, 46, 60
Can We Help Russia (Kennan), **48**: 183,n1
Canada, **40**: 19n1, 239; **41**: 126, 131, 347-48, 388, 419; **42**: 109, 360, 403, 508; **43**: 229, 257, 296, 365-66; **45**: 209, 211, 549n1, 598; **46**: 51-52, 212, 304-305; **47**: 120n1; **49**: 437-38; **51**: 614; and proposed Polish army, **42**: 352-53, 372, 431; and wheat, **45**: 59; explosion in Halifax, **45**: 230,n1, 253
Canada and the United States, **44**: 280-81, 504,n1, 511, 543; and woman suffrage, **48**: 27, 272; and wheat, **48**: 593, 597; Duke of Connaught visits U.S., **48**: 144, 154, 365
Cañas, Alberto F., **45**: 388n2
Candler, Ezekiel Samuel, Jr., **42**: 243,n1,3
Canepa, Giuseppe, **47**: 77,n4
Cannes, Rafael, **45**: 388
Cannon, James, Jr., **47**: 94,n1; **48**: 190-91; on Lever bill and prohibition, **43**: 42,n1, 52, 64-65,n1, 84
Cannon, Joseph D., **41**: 302,n2, 304; **44**: 79
Cannon, Joseph Gurney, **46**: 602
Canova, Leon Joseph, **41**: 141
Cantacuzene, Prince Michael, **46**: 45,n2
Cantigny, Battle of, **49**: 74
Canton, China, **49**: 213; **51**: 550n5
Cantonment Adjustment Board, **45**: 11; **49**: 367
Capelle, Eduard von, **40**: 463n1; **45**: 33,n9
Capello, Luigi Attilio, **44**: 506,n1, 507, 508
Caperton, William Banks, **47**: 327, 353
Capital Issues Committee (of War Finance Corp.); and Seattle hydroelectric plant, **49**: 6, 118n1, 119n2, 120, 121-22, 143, 148, 296n2
Capital Issues Committee and War Finance Corporation (Willoughby), **46**: 442n1
Capmany, Rafael Zubáran: *see* Zubáran Capmany, Rafael
Caporetto, Italy, **44**: 506
Capper, Arthur, **42**: 85,n2; **43**: 123; **44**: 432; **48**: 486-87, 556; **49**: 232-34,n1, 241; on East St. Louis race riot, **43**: 112
Capps, Washington Lee, **44**: 220, 226, 228,n4,5, 233, 235; replaces G. W. Goethals, **43**: 260,n2, 270, 271, 286; resigns from Emergency Fleet Corp., **45**: 103, 117
Captains and Cabinets: Anglo-American Naval Relations, 1917-1918 (Trask), **43**: 236n1; **51**: 474n1
Caraway, Thaddeus Horatius, **45**: 169,n1
Cardeza, Thomas D. M., **41**: 164,n3, 185

Carl Anschuetz Says Selph Made Himself Obnoxious at Inn (St. Louis *Globe-Democrat*), **43**: 323-24,n2
Carlile, William Buford, **41**: 208,n1
Carlton, Newcomb, **48**: 281,n3, 282-83,n1, 337-40, 349-50, 393-94, 556n2
Carmack, Jesse, **49**: 139n1
Carnegie, Andrew, **40**: 560; **41**: 5, 168; **48**: 192
Carnegie Endowment for International Peace, **41**: 55,n1, 250,n2; **46**: 110n1; **47**: 384
Carnegie Hall, N.Y., **43**: 175n2, 421; **44**: 346, 351, 382; **48**: 6,n2
Carnegie Steel Corporation, **41**: 407
Carolia (Karelia), **48**: 285n3
Carpenter, Herbert L. **46**: 89,n1; **51**: 644
Carpenter, The (Indianapolis), **47**: 343n1
Carpenters' Union: *see* United Brotherhood of Carpenters and Joiners of America
Carrancistas, **40**: 203
Carranza, Venustiano, **40**: 50, 51, 55, 56, 114; **41**: 34, 43, 44, 143, 459, 546; **42**: 38, 79, 80n1, 92, 95, 116; **43**: 39-40, 378-79, 381, 384,n1, 449, 505; **46**: 354-55,n2,3; **47**: 351,n1, 552; **48**: 134-35, 255, 279n5, 551; **49**: 27, 28, 29, 32, 32-33, 34, 35, 73, 137, 141, 153, 280,n1, 300; **51**: 68; and Legal Peace party, **40**: 110n4; refuses to ratify American proposal, **40**: 280, 285-86, 297, 299-301, 391, 393-94; proposal of peace conference and U.S. response, **41**: 249n1, 351, 391, 392; 404-406; and Zimmermann telegram, **41**: 288, 297, 392,n1; C. P. Anderson on recognition of, **41**: 365, 366, 385, 386; J. H. Bernstorff on peace note of, **41**: 429, 430; and U.S. representative at inauguration, **42**: 130-32, 132, 154-55; H. P. Fletcher on war policy of, **47**: 163-66
Carranza Has Made Terms with Wilson (Fox), **46**: 355,n4
Carroll, Francis M., **48**: 118n1
Carry, Edward Francis, **44**: 227,n2, 228, 234
Carso region, **47**: 125-26,n3
Carson, Edward Henry, **40**: 133, 452,n1; **41**: 196, 375; **42**: 330,n1; **43**: 19,n1; **44**: 202; **45**: 20, 445; **46**: 161
Carter, Jesse Benedict, **45**: 41,n1
Carter, Kate Benedict Freeman (Mrs. Jesse Benedict), **45**: 41,n1
Carter, William Samuel, **41**: 29, 251,n1, 353, 420,n1; **49**: 85,n1
Caruso, Enrico; and Liberty Loan campaign, **51**: 251-52,n2
Caruso's Caricatures (Sisca, ed.), **51**: 251n2
Carver, Clifford Nickels, **40**: 5, 20, 178
Cary, William Joseph, **41**: 327,n1
Caryll, Ivan, **48**: 52n3; **51**: 314n1
Casa del Obrero Mundial, **49**: 33
Case, George Bowan, **46**: 485,n1

Case, U. S., **48**: 294
Case of Austria-Hungary (Hard), **44**: 472,n6
Case for the Bolsheviki (Reed), **48**: 144n1
Case of Thomas J. Mooney and Warren K. Billings: Abstract and Analysis of Record before Governor Young of California (Hunt), **42**: 272n8
Casement, Sir Roger, **43**: 499, 509
Cashman, Thomas E., **49**: 172n1
Castro Quesada, Augustine, **45**: 388
Castro Quesada, Manuel, **40**: 333-34,n1; **41**: 140, 142, 143, 248,n1; **45**: 388, 389, 405, 406; **47**: 231n1
Catchings, Waddill, **43**: 511; **44**: 15; **46**: 29-30, 30
Cates, Charles Theodore, Jr., **47**: 6,n2, 33, 37
Cathedral of St. Peter and St. Paul, Washington, D.C., **46**: 435,n1
Catherine the Great (of Russia), **41**: 166; **42**: 335
Catholic Church: *see* Roman Catholic Church
Catholic Church Extension Society of the United States, **46**: 406n1
Catholic War Council, **49**: 385
Catt, Carrie Clinton Lane Chapman (Mrs. George William), **41**: 13; **42**: 215-16, 237, 241, 269, 270, 425; **43**: 214-15,n1, 284, 285; **44**: 372, 391, 523,n1, 551, 556n3; **46**: 608; **47**: 547, 571-72; **49**: 264; **51**: 30, 58, 82, 155-57, 161, 189, 190; and woman suffrage, **48**: 24,n1, 111, 271-72, 279, 303-304,n1, 304, 340, 363, 365; photograph: *illustration section*, **47**
Cattell, James McKeen, **44**: 355n2; **46**: 458n3
Cattell, Owen, **46**: 458,n3
cattle industry, **45**: 76-77, 105-106, 161; **46**: 125-26, 308, 386,n1, 503-505, 547, 565n1, 588, 614; **47**: 3-4, 45-51, 90-91
Caucasians, **46**: 420, 421
Caucasus, **45**: 418, 419; **51**: 262, 274, 499
Cavell, Edith Louisa, **40**: 440; **51**: 326
Cavendish, Evelyn Emily Mary Petty-Fitzmaurice, Duchess of Devonshire, **46**: 51,n2, 52
Cavendish, Victor Christian William, Duke of Devonshire, **41**: 126-27; **45**: 230, 253, 549,n1, 598,n1,2; **46**: 51-52, 343,n2; and woman suffrage, **46**: 80-81
Cecil, Lord Robert (Edgar Algernon Robert Gascoyne-), 1st Viscount Cecil of Chelwood (1864-1958), **40**: 307n1, 332-33, 359, 439n1, 452; **41**: 348n3; **42**: 335, 339,n5, 342, 354, 355, 385, 433, 445; **44**: 56, 74, 149-50, 164, 186, 203, 230, 388; **45**: 74, 82, 351, 420, 430n2; **47**: 11, 103-104; **48**: 425-26, 561; **49**: 11, 437; **51**: 164, 188, 288-90, 298, 539-40; on Germany and peace terms, **42**: 389n4, 425,n1; on Anglo-American naval cooperation, **42**: 450-51; on Polish army, **44**: 189; on public opinion and delay

concerning Siberian decision, **48**: 566-67; on league of nations, **49**: 225-28, 548-49
Cecil, James Edward Hubert Gascoyne-, 4th Marquess of Salisbury, **41**: 271
Cecil, Robert Arthur Talbot Gascoyne-, 3rd Marquess of Salisbury (1830-1903), **40**: 213
Cecil Hotel, London, **40**: 60n1
Cederbaum, Henryk Stanislaw, **46**: 48, 49n2
Cellere, Count Vincenzo Macchi di, **43**: 12,n1; **44**: 84, 348; **45**: 592; **46**: 86, 149, 361n1, 390, 415, 565n1; **47**: 525; **48**: 112, 253, 356, 561, 574, 575; **49**: 136, 142, 312-13, 369,n1; **51**: 135, 389; and Turkey, **51**: 456; on negotiations with Austria-Hungary and Germany, **51**: 529-30
censorship, **41**: 135, 474,n2, 530, 555, 556; **42**: 22n1, 23, 55, 90, 246,n4, 343, 433n1; **44**: 49, 358,n1, 366,n1,2, 371-72, 393, 396-97,n2, 405,n1; **45**: 89, 153, 387n1; **48**: 13, 146-47,n1,3; and Creel memorandum on a publicity department, **42**: 39-41; R. Lansing on Mexico and, **42**: 92-93; J. P. Tumulty on, **42**: 106-107, 245-46,n1,2,3; and newspapers, **42**: 106-108, 386-87; L. D. Wald on, **42**: 118-19, 153; WW on, **42**: 129, 153, 376-77; **44**: 397, 420, 472-73; and mails, **42**: 163, 195-96; and Committee on Public Information, **42**: 304-13; G. B. M. Harvey on, **42**: 371n1; comments on, **43**: 96, 193, 246, 276-77, 333, 366; and suspension of mailing privileges of *The Masses* and other publications, **43**: 164, 164-65,n1,2, 175-76, 176, 187-88; and German-American newspapers, **43**: 243, 247,n2; and *Pearson's Magazine*, **43**: 382, 383, 396-97, 413; and Post Office Department, **43**, 480-82; M. Eastman on, **44**: 171-72; and Trading with the Enemy and Espionage Acts, **44**: 266,n1, 389-90; W. Lippmann on, **44**: 393-94; H. Croly on, **44**: 408-10; and New York *Call*, **44**: 428,n1; and U. Sinclair, **44**: 469-72; J. Spargo on, **44**: 491-92; R. N. Baldwin on, **46**: 382-83; and *The World Tomorrow*, **51**: 12,n1,2,3, 77; and *The Outlook*, **51**: 15-16; and O. G. Villard, **51**: 55,n1, 84; J. P. Gavit on, **51**: 483; A. S. Burleson defends his stand on, **51**: 520-21; *see also* Committee on Public Information; espionage bill; Burleson, Albert Sidney; Post Office Department
censorship bills, **42**: 39,n1, 43, 371n1; *see also* espionage bill
Censorship Blunder (*New York Journal of Commerce and Commercial Bulletin*), **42**: 245n3
Censorship to Suit Sensationalists (*Philadelphia Record*), **42**: 245n3
Central America, **41**: 241; **42**: 309, 356-58; **49**: 431; **50**: 230; overthrow of Costa

Rican government, **41:** 140-44, 145, 146
Central Committee of Negro College Men, **42:** 321-22,n1
Central National Bank, Philadelphia, **43:** 197
Central Organization for a Durable Peace, **41:** 92; **46:** 198n3
Central Polish Agency, **42:** 454
Central Powers, **45:** 14; **46:** 198n2; **47:** 239, 491n2; **49:** 189-90; and Brest-Litovsk peace conference, **45:** 384n2, 411-12, 433-35; and peace moves, **45:** 432n1; and Fourteen Points, **45:** 506-11, 519-20, 534-35; and "white list" of Allies, **46:** 423n1; and suffrage, **48:** 272; and peace note, **51:** 263, 277,n5; and Bulgaria, **51:** 133; and Supreme War Council note on military policy, **51:** 199, 201; *see also* under the names of the individual countries
Central Presbyterian Church of Washington, **46:** 582n1
Central Purchasing Agency, **42:** 424, 447-49, 524-25, 538-39
Central Relief Committee, **47:** 555
Central States Conference on Rail and Water Transportation (Evansville, Ind.), **40:** 246n2
Central Trust Company, N.Y., **43:** 196
Century Magazine, **47:** 4n1
Century of Struggle: The Woman's Rights Movement in the United States (Flexner), **45:** 565n3
Cermak, Bohumir, **49:** 45n3
Cerretti, Bonaventura Archbishop, **43:** 472-73,n1; **51:** 282-83,n2, 641
Céspedes y Quesada, Carlos Manuel de, **41:** 472,n1
Chadbourne, Thomas Lincoln, Jr., **42:** 449,n1; **44:** 91,n1, 119; **48:** 145,n4
Chaikovskii, Nikolai Vasil'evich, **49:** 496,n10, 518n4
Chalantun, Manchuria, **51:** 479,n1
Challenge to American Freedoms: World War I and the Rise of the American Civil Liberties Union (Johnson), **43:** 175n1; **44:** 266n2
Challenging Years: The Autobiography of Stephen Wise, **49:** 363n1
Chalmers, Humphrey, **40:** 127
Chamäleon, S.M.S., **51:** 492
Chamber of Commerce of the United States, **41:** 154; **42:** 180; **44:** 143n1, 148-49,n1; **45:** 265, 299, 601; **47:** 147; **50:** 34n15, 649,n8; proposal for creation of War Supplies Department, **45:** 61-67, 276; and referendum on postwar economic boycott of Germany, **46:** 5-7,n1, 7-8, 14-15; and Chamberlain bill, **46:** 92, 103-104; emergency fund of, **51:** 92,n1; on postwar reconstruction plans, **51:** 207-208, 229
Chamberlain, George Earle, **40:** 267,n1, 475; **41:** 481,n2; **42:** 76, 146, 274n1, 285; **44:** 215n2, 361n1; **45:** 4, 566-67;

46: 40n1, 82-83, 85, 92-93, 204-205, 264; **47:** 381n2; **48:** 10n1, 51, 241; **49:** 117, 129; **51:** 392,n3; and Lever bill, **43:** 48n1, 49, 339, 393n1; and woman suffrage, **45:** 278, 338; and water-power legislation, **45:** 301; and army supply hearings, **45:** 390n1; attacks military system, **46:** 49,n1, 53-55; WW's reply, **46:** 55-56, 63n1, 67, 204-205; T. Roosevelt on, **46:** 63; and Chamber of Commerce bill, **46:** 92-93; responds to WW in Senate, **46:** 101,n1, 209,n1; O. M. James on, **46:** 101,n1, 368n1; N. D. Baker responds to charges by, **46:** 147n1; J. S. Williams on, **46:** 257n2; editorials against, **46:** 264,n2; photograph: *illustration section,* **48**
Chamberlain, John Loomis, **44:** 344-45,n4; **46:** 209,n5; **49:** 324,n4
Chamberlain, (Joseph) Austen, **42:** 340
Chamberlain bills, *see* Chamberlain, George Earle
Chamberlin, William Henry, **42:** 218n2, 418n1; **43:** 474n1; **44:** 180n3, 216n1; **46:** 421n3; **49:** 63n1; **51:** 4n2, 100n2, 102n1
Chambers, Edward, **48:** 484n1
Chambers, Ernest John, **42:** 508,n2
Chambers, James Julius, **47:** 16,n3
Chambers, Louise Lanier, **46:** 314,n1, 325
Chambers, William Lea, **40:** 303, 312; **42:** 279n1, 304,n1; **43:** 530-32; **44:** 22, 23, 82, 90, 198, 328; **45:** 25-26, 49; **47:** 446-47,n1; on railroads and need for mediation, **44:** 430-31, 448-49, 458-59; **46:** 446-48, 448; and daughter's death, **46:** 314, 325
Chambrun, Marquis de (Charles Louis Antoine Pierre Gilbert Pineton), **42:** 169
Chamorro Vargas, Emiliano, **41:** 143,n16, 144; **45:** 388,n4
Chandler and Company, N.Y., **41:** 142, 144
Changsha, China, **49:** 213
Chang Tsung-hsiang, **41:** 181,n1
Chaplin, Charles, **47:** 302n2
Chaplin, Georgi Ermolaevich, **49:** 518,n4
Chapman, John Wilbur, **42:** 535,n3; **45:** 315, 330
Chappell, Edwin Barfield, **49:** 317,n1
Chappelle, William David, **46:** 614n2
Chapultepec, Mex., **47:** 474, 475n2
Character of Democracy in the United States (Wilson), **49:** 129, 184
Charles I (Charles Francis Joseph of Austria), **40:** 34: **41:** 211, 300, 398; **42:** 492,n1; **44:** 43; **45:** 56, 57, 164n1; **47:** 26,n2, 177,n1, 590; **48:** 205; **49:** 195; and H. Lammasch and peace moves, **46:** 198,n2, 199, 200, 242-47, 253, 261-63, 315-16, 388, 483, 580n1, 581, 589-90; note for WW intercepted by Britain, **46:** 271, 397-99, 400, 412, 432, 435; sends message to WW on peace terms, **46:** 440-42, 467,n1, 473,n1, 483; WW's

Charles I (*cont.*)
   reply to, **46:** 486-87, 488, 551-53; and Vatican, **46:** 488; E. M. House on WW's reply to, **46:** 507-508; answers WW on peace terms, **47:** 124-26; and Sixtus letter, **47:** 589n1; **48:** 435; meets with William II, **48:** 114,n2
Charles E. Merriam and the Study of Politics (Karl), **40:** 489n2
Charles Scribner's Sons, **46:** 259-60, 449
Charleston, S.C., **41:** 455,n1,2, 484,n1; **42:** 477
Charleston, W. Va., **42:** 23
Charleston (S.C.) *News and Courier*, **49:** 246n2
Charlottesville, Va., **41:** 516
Chase, Benjamin Franklin, **41:** 140,n6
Chase, Samuel (1741-1811), **46:** 33
Chase, Stuart, **49:** 132
Chase, William Calvin, **51:** 193n1
Chase National Bank, N.Y., **43:** 196; **48:** 519,n1
chasseurs alpins: *see* Blue Devils
Château Thierry, France, **48:** 245, 332
Chatfield, E. Charles, **47:** 326n1
Chatham and Phoenix National Bank, N.Y., **43:** 196
Chattanooga Daily Times, **51:** 482n1
Chaumont, France, **47:** 160; **48:** 265
Chautauqua Institution, **44:** 248
Chefoo, China, **49:** 213
Cheliabinsk (Chelyabinsk), Russia, **46:** 391, 392, 471, 548; **47:** 424, 504; **48:** 180, 505
Chelm (Kholm), Poland, **46:** 403
Chemnitz, Germany, **46:** 266
Chemnitzer Volksstimme, **46:** 164, 193
Chemung, S.S., **40:** 191
Ch'en Chin-t'ao, **40:** 512,n2, 513,n3; **41:** 175,n5, 176, 177
Chenault, Henry L., **49:** 399-400
Chengchiatun (Chengkiatun), Manchuria, **43:** 83,n3
Chéradame, André, **42:** 394,n4; **45:** 410,n1, 423; **47:** 112,n1
Chernov, Viktor Mikhailovich, **42:** 418n1, 419,n3; **46:** 232,n1; **49:** 495,n4
Cherrington, Ernest Hurst, **43:** 65,n1
Chesapeake, U.S.S. **42:** 29n1
Chesapeake and Ohio Railroad, **43:** 242
Chester, Pa., **45:** 132
Chester Shipbuilding Company, **42:** 477
Chestnut, C., **47:** 574
Chestnut Hill, Mass., **49:** 276
Chevalley, Abel, **49:** 333n2
Chewelah, Wash., **43:** 200,n3
Chicago, Ill., **43:** 422; **44:** 47n1, 236, 293-94, 301; **49:** 501; and postmastership, **41:** 208,n1; and meatpacking investigation, **46:** 141, 195n1; German Americans in, **47:** 324; Labor Day invitation to WW, **49:** 168, 173, 212; and railroad wage discrepancies in, **49:** 186,n2, 206-207, 211,n1, 251; and street railways, **51:** 20
Chicago, University of, **40:** 489n1; **41:**

415n1, 466; **42:** 216; **46:** 518; **47:** 558n6; **51:** 109,n10, 118n1
Chicago *Abendpost*, **44:** 236
Chicago Board of Trade, **40:** 102
Chicago, Burlington and Quincy Railroad Company, **45:** 373n1
Chicago *Daily News*, **41:** 79; **42:** 252, 258, 284, 288; **45:** 437; **46:** 114; **47:** 509; **48:** 62n1, 142, 143, 299n1; **49:** 203n1; **51:** 408n5
Chicago Daily Tribune, **47:** 324n2, 436-37,n1; **48:** 242n1
Chicago Defender, **43:** 119n1, 392n1
Chicago Elevated Railroad Company, **49:** 186,n2, 206-207, 211,n1, 251
Chicago Federation of Labor, **46:** 26
Chicago Great Western Railroad, **43:** 249n1
Chicago Herald, **49:** 434n1
Chicago *Illinois Idea*, **43:** 392n1
Chicago Nipple Manufacturing Company, **47:** 226n1
Chicago, North Shore and Milwaukee Railroad, **49:** 211,n1
Chicago *People's Counselor*, **44:** 323n1
Chicago *Tribune*, **41:** 208n1
Chicherin, Georgii Vasil'evich, **46:** 300n7; **47:** 245,n1, 367,n3; **48:** 40,n1, 106n4, 113, 265; **49:** 198, 495,n5; **51:** 4n2, 508-10, 555-61
Chief Russian Danger (Schelking), **49:** 93n1
Chihuahua state, Mex., **40:** 54, 203, 282, 283, 302, 399, 479
Chihuahua, Chihuahua, Mex., **40:** 100n1, 123, 203; fall of, **40:** 109
Child, Richard Washburn, **43:** 365; **46:** 316, 519; **47:** 15,n2, 16
child labor, **45:** 331, 334; **49:** 23,n1; and Porto Rico, **40:** 152; A. J. McKelway on, **47:** 17; legislation regarding, **51:** 165-67, 181-82,n4, 214; *see also* Keating-Owen child labor bill
Child Welfare, Bureau of (proposed for Washington, D.C.), **47:** 596, 602-603,n1; **48:** 9
children and child welfare; W. B. Wilson on, **47:** 188; and T. R. Marshall's requests concerning, **47:** 547-48, 560, 596; WW on, **47:** 602
Children's Bureau (Dept. of Labor), **47:** 180, 188, 547; **48:** 463n1; **51:** 166, 181n1
Children's-Year Campaign, **48:** 463n1
Chile, **41:** 249n1; **42:** 15, 52, 314, 359; **49:** 29; death of ambassador from, **47:** 418n2
Chiles, Nick, **45:** 577,n2; **51:** 170,n1
Chilton, William Edwin, **43:** 33,n1, 54, 69-70; **51:** 538,n3
China, **45:** 336; **47:** 71, 98, 99, 460; and Japan, **42:** 244, 331; **43:** 7-8, 55-56, 58, 80-83, 268; **48:** 61, 441n1, 442, 462; and internal discord, **42:** 466, 468,n1; and Chengchiatun affair, **43:** 83,n3; intends to declare war on Germany, **43:**

362-63, 363-64; W. S. Rogers on, **43:** 457; and Trans-Siberian Railway, **46:** 340, 528-30; and secret treaty between Japan and Russia, **46:** 539n1; and Czech forces in Siberia, **48:** 560, 609n1; Soviet forces encroach on, **49:** 284; and railway contact with Russia, **51:** 478, 479-80

China and the United States, **40:** 335, 416, 436-38; **42:** 59,n2, 275; **44:** 8; and U.S. loan, **40:** 128, 130, 140-41, 160, 512-13, 514-15, 563; **41:** 383, 394; **42:** 53, 53-54; **44:** 282; **45:** 96-97, 97-100; **48:** 371-74, 382, 517-23; **49:** 102-103, 311, 348; and Japan, **41:** 38-39, 394, 494; supports U.S. break with Germany, **41:** 175-79, 181-82, 182-83, 185-86, 186, 187, 195, 229-30,n1, 382, 383-84, 394, 401-402; C. R. Crane on, **41:** 493-94; J. W. Jenks on, **42:** 60-64; and Grand Canal project, **42:** 63,n5; Ishii Mission and open-door policy, **44:** 251-52, 253-55, 255-56, 264,n2, 315, 340-42, 356-57, 367-69, 376-78, 413-15, 417-20, 454, 510, 530, 531,n2; proposal to send Chinese troops to Europe, **45:** 307-308; and plan for international commission to China, **46:** 331,n2, 499, 500-501, 595; and U.S. policy toward Russia, **48:** 639-43; and proposed internationalization of settlements, **49:** 213-14,n3; P. S. Reinsch on completion of railway in China, **49:** 406-407; and request to use Harbin as W. S. Graves' headquarters, **51:** 121, 140, 549; WW's congratulations to new president, **51:** 292-93, 318-19; Japan suggests joint action regarding China, **51:** 457,n1,2, 550

China Merchants Steamship Company, **49:** 214

Chinda, Viscount Sutemi, **42:** 277; **43:** 55, 81; **44:** 318,n1; **46:** 574,n2; **47:** 156,n3; **48:** 447,n2, 448n1

Chinese Eastern Railway, **46:** 47, 302, 340, 344n1,2, 387; **47:** 71, 99,n6, 398, 592; **48:** 72n2, 106, 609n1; **49:** 46, 283, 396,n1; **51:** 99, 100, 384, 449, 478-81,n1

Chinese Engineering and Mining Company, **49:** 214

Chin-t'ao Ch'en, **42:** 277

Chita, Russia, **47:** 99; **48:** 105, 459; **49:** 151, 198, 220, 221, 262n1, 282, 283, 493; **51:** 384, 449, 479

Choate, Caroline Dutcher Sterling (Mrs. Joseph Hodges), **42:** 302

Choate, Joseph Hodges, **40:** 89; **42:** 255; death of, **42:** 302,n1

Chocheprat, Paul Louis Albert, **42:** 169,n1, 185; **44:** 465

Choice Before Us (Dickinson), **43:** 409

Chrislock, Carl Henry, **45:** 258n2; **46:** 348n1

Christ College, Cambridge, **47:** 264n1

Christian X (of Denmark), **45:** 114,n2

Christian, James R., **46:** 564n1

Christian Work (New York), **51:** 644

Christiania, Norway, **40:** 47; **41:** 40; **45:** 78, 79, 81, 114,n2; **49:** 333

Christie, Robert A., **46:** 356n5

Christliche Apologete (Cincinnati), **46:** 613,n5; **47:** 337n1

Chronicle of a Generation: An Autobiography (Fosdick), **47:** 220n1

Chronicles of America, **45:** 352, 362-63, 453, 540-41

Church of God, **44:** 216,n1

Church of the Redeemer, Paterson, N.J., **45:** 570n1

Church Peace Union of America, **41:** 302n2

Churchill, Marlborough, **49:** 387,n1, 390, 395; **51:** 316

Churchill, Winston (American novelist), **43:** 354,n1,2,3, 358; **45:** 19-24, 24-25

Churchill, Winston Leonard Spencer, **41:** 375; **42:** 436; **44:** 239n1; **45:** 209,n2

Ciceria, Croatia, **47:** 125,n3

Cincinnati, O., **44:** 536n1

Cincinnati Enquirer, **47:** 310; **51:** 464

Citizen Soldiers: The Plattsburgh Training Camp Movement, 1913-1920 (Clifford), **40:** 267n1

Citizens' Alliance (Minneapolis), **47:** 190

Citizens Savings and Trust Company, Cleveland, **43:** 196

citizenship, **43:** 281; and civil service, **44:** 493, 498

Citta de Messina, S.S., **40:** 449

City of Memphis, S.S., **41:** 425,n1, 431, 436

City of Violence (Reed), **48:** 147n4

Ciudad Juárez, Chihuahua, Mex., **40:** 100, 109, 110, 130, 203

Cividale de Friuli, Italy, **44:** 506, 508

Civil Liberties Bureau: *see* National Civil Liberties Bureau

Civil Liberties Dead (New York *Nation*), **51:** 55n1

civil rights, **43:** 510

civil service, **40:** 28, 182-83, 218; **44:** 493; discrimination against Negroes in, **48:** 158-59; retirement bill, **48:** 395,n1, 444, 474n1

Civil Service Act, **40:** 97; **45:** 177

Civil Service Commission, **41:** 546-48; **42:** 3; **45:** 177, 336; **47:** 601; **48:** 138

Civil Service Reform Association, **40:** 89

civil service retirement bill, *see* civil service

Civil War (U.S.), **42:** 28, 58, 180, 281, 282, 451; **43:** 115n2, 246, 350; **44:** 115, 156; **45:** 428; **47:** 349n1; **48:** 55, 232; **49:** 246

Clabaugh, Hinton Graves, **44:** 236,n2

Clancey, Eugene A., **40:** 176, 176-77,n1; **43:** 513n1,2; **47:** 179n3

Claparède, Alfred de, **40:** 231,n2

Clapp, Emma C., **41:** 557

Clapp, Moses Edwin, **41:** 11n1

Clark, Champ (James Beauchamp), **42:** 94, 269, 270; **45:** 58, 70; **46:** 85, 90; **48:** 294; **49:** 145n1

Clark, Francis Edward, **51:** 149,n1
Clark, Frank, **41:** 179-80; **45:** 39,n1; **46:** 443n1
Clark, James Woodrow, **48:** 203,n2
Clark, Mary Charlotte Woodrow (Mrs. Melton), **48:** 203,n1
Clark, Norman H., **46:** 144n1
Clark, Truman R., **48:** 203,n3
Clark, Walter, **47:** 557,n2
Clark, Washington Augustus, **48:** 203,n3
Clark, William Andrews, **44:** 261,n4
Clark University, **45:** 281n1
Clarke, James Paul, **40:** 532n1;
Clarke, John Hessin, **40:** 311, 312; **41:** 536, 536-37; **42:** 217, 221, 240; **44:** 146; **46:** 297n1
Clarke, Joseph I. C., **49:** 93n1
Clarke, Breckinridge and Caffey (New York law firm), **42:** 244n1
Clarkson, Grosvenor Blaine, **46:** 151n2; on Council of National Defense, **47:** 110-15, 143, 526-33; on postwar reconstruction program, **47:** 526-33, 561; on electing Democrats to Congress, **51:** 459-60, 485-86
Clarkson, James Sullivan, **51:** 459,n1
Claxton, Philander Priestly, **44:** 32,n1; **46:** 608; and teaching of German language, **46:** 459,n1, 491
Clay, Henry, **42:** 28; **43:** 160n1
Clay, Samuel H., **46:** 218n2
Clayton, Charles T., **49:** 53,n2
Clayton Antitrust Act, **41:** 238n1; and Hitchman case, **46:** 297; *see also* antitrust legislation, Sherman Antitrust Act
Cleary, William B., **43:** 171
Clemenceau, Georges, **41:** 376; **45:** 54n1, 108n2, 122, 151, 156, 166n1, 176, 209n1, 222n1, 337, 418, 421, 432n1, 438, 571; **46:** 10, 233-35, 268n3, 439, 496; **47:** 74; **48:** 47, 62, 131, 205, 211, 245, 283, 295, 356, 383, 384n3, 389, 421n1, 441n1, 546; **49:** 124, 149, 217-18, 293, 428; **51:** 34, 36, 41, 78, 235n4, 465; on Supreme War Council, **45:** 113; on France's need for tankers and gasoline, **45:** 302-303; J. J. Pershing and, **45:** 332n1, 583; T. H. Bliss on, **47:** 14; and issue of intervention in Russia, **47:** 59, 60, 86; **48:** 288, 355, 416, 448,n1; on Socialists and peace terms, **47:** 75, 76; and F. Foch, **47:** 160, 238, 349; cables WW on first anniversary of U.S. entry into war, **47:** 277-78; WW replies, **47:** 290, 291, 309,n6; and Sixtus letter, **47:** 589,n1; and Allied request for more U.S. troops, **48:** 226-27, 243, 246, 252; and question of U.S. troop disposition, **47:** 512, 517, 566, 567, 568, 595, 617, 618; and request for additional troops to Russia, **51:** 17, 33, 426; W. G. Sharp on, **51:** 21n1; and peace negotiations, **51:** 182, 183, 261, 272n1, 272-73, 290, 291-92, 407, 422, 427, 428, 429, 462,n2, 511,n1, 512, 513, 515-17, 523, 532, 542,

562, 568, 569, 571, 580, 582, 594; and strife with V. E. Orlando, **51:** 388
Clemens, Samuel Langhorne, **44:** 124n2
Clement, Charles Maxwell, **45:** 111,n3
Clemmons, M., **45:** 130,n1, 147
Clemo, J. L., **44:** 144n1
Clerk, George Russell, **45:** 445,n3
Clermont, France, **48:** 388n9
Cleveland, Frederick Albert, **40:** 498n1; **47:** 385,n1,2, 395, 446
Cleveland, (Steven) Grover, **44:** 85
Cleveland, O., **49:** 134
Cleveland, Cincinnati and St. Louis Railway Company, **46:** 447,n1
Cleveland *Hrvatski Svijet*, **40:** 104n1
Cleveland *Socialist News*, **43:** 165
Cleveland *Szabadsag*, **45:** 139, 140
Clifford, John Gary, **40:** 267n1
Clifton, Ariz., **43:** 157; **44:** 172, 223, 425, 478, 483
Clinedinst Studio, Washington, D.C., **45:** 371n1
Clinton Falls Nursery Company of Owatonna, Minn., **49:** 172n1
Close, Gilbert Fairchild, **47:** 4; **49:** 4,n1,2, 56, 457; **51:** 63, 463n1, 475
closed shop, **46:** 136, 356n5, 362, 363
Closing of the Public Domain: Disposal and Reservation Policies, 1900-50 (Peffer), **40:** 192n1
Clothier, Isaac Hallowell, **41:** 302n2
clothing industry: *see* garment industry
Clover Leaf Publications, St. Paul, Minn., **41:** 206n1
Clyne, Charles Francis, **47:** 135,n3
Coahuila state, Mex., **40:** 203
coal and coal industry, **42:** 205-208; **44:** 13; investigation of, **42:** 205, 212, 213; and prices, **42:** 229, 401, 534, 561; **44:** 13,n1, 29, 336-37, 403, 450-52, 453,n1; **45:** 176n1; **46:** 599, 600-601, 610,n2; **47:** 7, 33, 37, 89-90; and railroad unions, **42:** 242; and Council of National Defense, **42:** 459n1, 471-73; problems in Alabama, **42:** 460-61, 504-505; **43:** 368, 433-34; **44:** 15, 80, 144n1; **45:** 269-70, 276, 568n1; **46:** 29-30, 30; comments and issues regarding price fixing, **43:** 6,n1, 7,n1, 33n1, 41,n1, 54, 59, 60-61, 61-64, 69-70, 70, 75-76, 102, 251, 397-99,n1, 520; problems in West Virginia, **43:** 33,n1, 54, 59, 385; F. K. Lane on purchase and development of coal fields, **43:** 36-37, 43, 73-74, 84, 367, 385, 399; and draft exemptions, **45:** 547n1, 584; and D. Willard, **46:** 15; and transport to Northeast, **47:** 66, 82; and railroad fuel issue, **47:** 241, 405-11, 418, 498-99; **48:** 22-24, 51-52, 81-93; W. G. McAdoo on profits in, **48:** 88-90; H. A. Garfield on, **48:** 148,n1, 646-47,n1; W. B. Wilson on, **49:** 3, 53-54, 148; proclamation on increased production, **49:** 144-45, 173,n1; Lloyd George's concern over European coal crisis, **49:** 217-18; J. J. Jusserand on U.S. supplying Al-

lies, **49:** 239-40; WW's personal fuel conservation, **49:** 240; prices and consumption figures, **49:** 290; and general leasing bill, **49:** 483-84; H. A. Garfield on anthracite coal strike, **51:** 19, 545-47; and relationship with Fuel Administration, **51:** 111-12,n3, 113-15, 116n1, 138; German plan to destroy Belgian coal mines, **51:** 577

coal conservation order: negative comments on, **46:** 12,n1, 16, 18, 19, 23-24; WW on, **46:** 25, 26, 33, 36; and New York theaters, **46:** 28,n1, 41; and Hitchcock resolution, **46,** 31,n2; H. A. Garfield defends his action, **46:** 31-33; B. M. Baruch praises, **46:** 33

Coal Impasse Persists: The Government May Interpose (*Birmingham News*), **43:** 434n1

Coal Operators Answer Editorial in News' Columns (*Birmingham News*), **43:** 434n1

Coal Production, Committee on, **47:** 112

Coast and Geodetic Survey: *see* United States Coast and Geodetic Survey

Coast Guard: *see* United States Coast Guard

Coates, David C., **47:** 254n1

Cobb, Frank Irving, **40:** 337; **42:** 552; **43:** 167; **44:** 74, 118, 154-55, 190, 265, 274, 288; **45:** 135, 161, 241; **46:** 264, 367, 438; **47:** 303, 584; **48:** 51, 149; **49:** 275, 348, 402,n1; **51:** 407, 595; and censorship controversy and G. Creel, **42:** 371, 376-77, 433,n1; **43:** 366-67; and idea of *World* and *Tageblatt* serving as editorial forum, **43:** 184, 198, 219-20, 274-75, 285, 366, 411-12; on WW working with sympathetic Republicans, **45:** 340-41; on H. A. Garfield's coal order, **46:** 16, 17; on New York slacker raids, **49:** 451; on WW's Fourteen Points, **51:** 495-504; on WW directing peace conference from Washington, **51:** 590-91; on Britain and freedom of the seas, **51:** 613-14; on division among American people on WW's goals, **51:** 615

Cobb, Margaret Hubbard Ayer (Mrs. Frank Irving), **49:** 348,n2

Coblenz, Germany, **51:** 463

Cochin, Denys Pierre Augustin Marie, **40:** 486,n2, 532

Cochise County, Ariz., **44:** 517

Cochran, William E., **43:** 480,n2

Cockran, William Bourke, **49:** 23,n1; **51:** 592

Cody, William Frederick (Buffalo Bill), **40:** 4

Coffey, Reuben Burton, **43:** 182,n2

Coffin, Charles Albert, **41:** 113,n2,3

Coffin, Howard Earle, **42:** 449, 531; **45:** 69, 155, 314n1; **46:** 94n1, 209; **47:** 41n1, 169, 322; resigns from Aircraft Board, **47:** 361-62, 383; urges aircraft investigation, **47:** 521, 537

Coffman, Edward M., **51:** 3n1

Cohalan, Daniel Florence, **44:** 265, 274, 288; **48:** 63n1, 64,n2

Cohan, George M(ichael), **46:** 28,n1

Cohen, John Sanford, **46:** 563-64,n1; **47:** 192,n2, 312,n2; **49:** 114, 115, 116, 369-70

Cok, Ivan, **51:** 562n1

Colby, Bainbridge, **40:** 162, 221, 539; **42:** 45n3; **45:** 339, 340, 362, 363; **46:** 23; **49:** 350, 547; **51:** 14, 276, 440-41, 453; and appointment to Shipping Board, **43:** 260, 271, 310; and W. H. Taft and League to Enforce Peace, **47:** 42, 43, 85, 119,n3, 123, 137, 147, 147-48, 198-99; and Wisconsin campaign, **47:** 120, 137, 148

Colby, Nathalie Sedgwick (Mrs. Bainbridge), **40:** 221,n1

Colcord, Lincoln Ross, **40:** 371-72,n1,2, 374,n1, 380-81,n1,2,3, 402; **41:** 191,n2, 250,n1; **42:** 553, 554, 555; **44:** 275n1; **45:** 235; **46:** 36,n1, 113-14, 169, 181, 239; **47:** 279n2; **48:** 568; on Russian situation, **45:** 191-93, 222n1, 250-53; **48:** 546-49, 576-77

Cole, Felix, **49:** 518n5

Cole, George D. H., **46:** 435n3

Coleman, Robert Bruce, **44:** 82,n1, 106, 145, 328

Coleman, Robert S., **45:** 259,n3, 260-62

Collazo, Domingo, **49:** 136

Collected Works (Lenin), **46:** 310n1

College of the City of New York, **44:** 226, 541

College of William and Mary, **47:** 289n2

Collegiate Anti-Militarism League, **46:** 458n3; **47:** 154n1

Collier, Babe, **49:** 327-28, 400

Collier, Constance, **46:** 264n1

Collier, William, **47:** 414n1

Colliers, **43:** 198; **46:** 519; **47:** 15,n2, 40,n3

Cologne, Germany, **46:** 266; **51:** 463; and cease fire on Feast of Corpus Christi, **49:** 189, 190

Cologne Gazette, see kölnische Zeitung

Cologne *Volkszeitung*, **49:** 124

Colombia, **42:** 82, 359

Colombia and the United States, **40:** 116, 550; **41:** 261, 411, 450; and ratification of Treaty of Bogotá, **41:** 8-10, 14-15, 27-28, 240-41, 293-94,n1, 345, 393n1, 420-21,n1,2, 425, 465, 513; R. Lansing drafts new treaty, **41:** 456,n1; J. Betancourt urges treaty passage, **47:** 572-73

Colón, Panama, **41:** 152; **48:** 417,n3,5

Colorado, **43:** 73-74, 222n1; **46:** 478; **49:** 104, 166; and initiative, referendum, and recall, **41:** 403, 417n1; and coal prices, **46:** 599, 600-601, 610,n2; **47:** 7, 33, 37, 89-90; and I.W.W. in, **47:** 194; and oil bill, **47:** 451, 452; politics in, **51:** 312, 589, 632, 645,n1

Colorado Fuel and Iron Company, **46:** 600-601,n1

Colt, LeBaron Bradford, **51:** 537n1

Colt, Samuel Sloan, **45:** 399,n3

Colton, Ethan Theodore, **46:** 479,n2; **47:** 304-305,n1; **49:** 78,n3

Columbia, S.C., **44:** 10

Columbia, S.S., **42:** 133

Columbia Trust Company, N.Y., **43:** 196

Columbia University, **41:** 164, 230; **42:** 111n4, 322n1; **43:** 462n1; **44:** 366,n2; **45:** 92n2, 154n3; **46:** 119n1, 458n3; **47:** 323; **49:** 12; **51:** 165n1

Columbia University Press, **41:** 22n1

Columbus, N. Mex., **40:** 55, 101, 282, 284, 302; **41:** 41; **43:** 157, 158n1, 170, 326; **44:** 134, 135, 138, 518, 522; **47:** 164

Colver, William Byron, **41:** 206,n1,2, 209; **42:** 448; **43:** 6,n1, 7,n1, 221; **44:** 13, 206,n1; **46:** 462-63; **47:** 54-55, 466; **51:** 92,n1; on meat-packing situation, **48:** 44, 75-77, 107-10, 507-10; **49:** 130-32, 372, 431, 460-61, 504-505; **51:** 90, 441-43

Coming Nation (Chicago?), **42:** 254

commerce, **42:** 49; **43:** 20; **44:** 455-57, 541-44; and WW's statement on exports control, **43:** 14-15; and priority items, **42:** 289-90, 298-99, 299; **43:** 504; F. B. Kellogg on proposed License Act, **51:** 70-73

Commerce, Department of, **40:** 521; **42:** 117, 118, 256-57, 437n1, 559, 567; **43:** 90, 93; **44:** 28, 502; **48:** 336, 465-66; and War Trade Committee, **42:** 29n1, 49; and T. D. Jones, **43:** 291, 325; and trading with the enemy bill, **43:** 311, 312, 315, 316, 321-22

Commerce and the Mailed Fist (H. S. Houston), **48:** 29n1

Commerce Committee (Senate), **40:** 421n2; **41:** 238,n1

Commerce Reports, **43:** 110,n3

Commercial Economy Board (of the Council of National Defense), **47:** 114

Commercial National Bank of Raleigh, N.C., **44:** 571n1

Commercial Telegraphers' Union, **48:** 281,n1

Commercial Trust Company, Philadelphia, **43:** 197

Commission for Relief in Belgium, **40:** 25, 92, 369, 418n1, 540; **41:** 113n3, 214n2, 543; **42:** 110-11; **43:** 358,n1; **47:** 293-94; **48:** 46-48; **51:** 586, 635; to continue its responsibilities, **51:** 397-99, 605, 618-20

Commission of Fine Arts, **49:** 513

Commission of the American Federation of Labor: *see* American Federation of Labor Commission to Mexico

Commission on Efficiency and Economy (1911-1912), **40:** 498n1

Commission on relief in Russia (proposed): comments on plans, **48:** 204, 303, 305, 306-307,n2, 310, 315-16, 317, 390-91, 429-31, 432-34, 453, 454, 469, 490, 513, 514, 544, 549, 578, 643; **49:** 63, 77-79, 93, 123, 128, 172, 177, 281, 304, 320-23, 332n2, 346-47, 366, 407-

408, 507; H. C. Hoover suggested for, **48:** 607, 611

Commission on Training Camp Activities, **43:** 478-79; **47:** 220n1, 311n2; **48:** 208n1; **51:** 185

Committee of 100 Citizens on the War, **42:** 321-22

Committee on Public Information, **42:** 268, 269, 275n2, 291, 508; **43:** 3,n1, 146, 168,n2, 333,n1, 529; **44:** 148,n1, 248,n1, 270n1, 434n2; **45:** 86, 153, 241n1, 353, 580,n1; **46:** 68, 200-203, 257, 458n1; **47:** 194n1, 235n1, 276n1, 311n1, 600; **48:** 51, 117, 375n1; **49:** 24,n3, 89, 391, 434, 437, 474,n1, 487, 488, 503n1, 512n1; **51:** 3-4, 118n1, 603n1; establishment of, **42:** 39-41, 55,n1, 59, 71; and G. Creel's guidelines to the press, **42:** 304-13; and Four Minute Men, **44:** 248n1, 505n2, 505-506; Division of Pictures, **47:** 207,n1; and efforts in Russia, **47:** 522,n3,5,6; WW on, **47:** 602; **48:** 138-39, 140; proposed investigation of, **48:** 148-49, 177-78

Committee on the League of Nations (Phillimore Committee), **48:** 501,n1

Common Sense (London), **40:** 126, 494

Commoner, The (Lincoln, Neb.), **40:** 131,n1, 137-38; **44:** 54,n1, 60-61

Commons, John Rogers, **41:** 448

Comparative Prices on What the Farmer Buys and Sells (Committee on Public Information), **51:** 118n1

Compiègne, France, **48:** 332

Compilation of the Messages and Papers of the Presidents, 1789-1897 (Richardson, ed.), **45:** 250,n3

Complete Report of the Chairman of the Committee on Public Information, 1917, 1918, 1919, **47:** 522n3,5

Compton, Annie Wilson Howe Cothran (Mrs. Frank E.), **44:** 55

Compton, Frank E., **43:** 236,n1, 241, 317

Compton, J. T., **48:** 294

compulsory work laws, **48:** 248-49,n1, 270,n1

Condition of the Steel Industry for the Last Quarter of the Year 1918, both as regards Volume of Production and Price, **51:** 285,n1

Cone, Hutchinson Ingham, **43:** 182,n2

Conference on Democratic Financing of the War, **46:** 15n1

Conference of National Labor Adjustment Agencies: *see* National Labor Adjustment Agencies

Confidential Memorandum in re: The Two Statements Which I Issued to the Press on December 21, 1916 (Lansing), **40:** 307n1

Conger, Seymour Beach, **40:** 432,n4, 433

Congo Reform Association, **42:** 422n2

Congress (U.S.): *see* United States Congress

Congress of Oppressed Races of Austria-Hungary, **48:** 437n3

Congress of Vienna, **51:** 323
Congressional Government (Wilson), **46:** 63n1, 449, 605; **47:** 41, 385; **51:** 621
Congressional Record, 64th Congress, **40:** 103n2, 290n1, 291n2; **41:** 11n1, 197n1, 318n1, 324n2
Congressional Record, 65th Congress, **42:** 106n2, 144n1, 245n2, 302n1, 321n1, 462,n3; **43:** 42n1, 48n1, 71n1, 84n1, 121, 160n1, 162n1,3, 222n2, 237n1, 242n1, 313, 344n1, 393n1, 415n1, 455n1, 481n5; **44:** 166n3, 343n1; **45:** 244n1, 391n1, 433n1, 565n3, 601n1; **46:** 31n1, 40n1, 63n2, 101n1, 105n2, 147n1, 209n1, 257n2, 281n, 368n1, 606n1, 620n1; **47:** 29n1, 35n2, 94n1, 178n2, 255n1, 349n1, 416n2, 446n1, 573n1, 584n2, 610n1; **48:** 10n1, 42n1, 45n1, 50n1, 161n2, 165n, 190n1, 429n1, 433n1, 444n1, 457n1, 458n1, 487n1, 532n1, 534n1, 535n1, 556n2, 579n1, 623n1; **49:** 62n2,3, 310n1, 330n4, 476n1,3; **51:** 6n2, 156n2, 189n1, 217n1, 277n7, 391-92, 478n1; and publication of Federal Trade Commission's meat-packing report, **51:** 90,n1
Congressional Union for Woman Suffrage, **41:** 329, 330, 440, 401; **42:** 237; **44:** 551,n1
Conklin, Edwin Grant, **41:** 230-31, 235-36
Conley, Louis D., **43:** 514,n2
Conley Foil Company of New York, **43:** 514n2
Connaught, Duke of (Prince Arthur William Patrick Albert), **47:** 442, 596; **48:** 144, 154, 365
Connecticut: politics in, **51:** 632
Connecticut State Grange, **44:** 259
Conner, Valerie Jean, **46:** 578n1; **49:** 53n1, 223n1, 540n1
Connolly, Louise, **51:** 211,n2
Conrad, Joseph, **44:** 82,n1
'Conscience' of Russia Against a Separate Peace (Bernstein), **42:** 363n3
conscientious objectors, **42:** 159, 179,n2; **43:** 5,n1, 175,n1; **44:** 29n1, 74, 75, 193, 216, 221,n1, 225, 288-89, 293, 370-71; **45:** 94, 601; **47:** 72-73,n1, 154-55,n1,2, 391-92, 394, 448; **49:** 542-43,n1; U. Sinclair on, **48:** 610-11; **49:** 207-209; N. D. Baker on, **49:** 56; T. W. Gregory defends Espionage Act, **49:** 306-308
conscription: British proposals in Ireland, **47:** 182; 204, 227-28, 238, 266-67,n1, 401n2, 412, 432-33, 442, 457-58, 466, 469-71, 520, 582, 620, **48:** 300,n2,3; and Civil War (U.S.) figures, **42:** 59; *see* Selective Service
Conscription of Income (Sprague), **41:** 448,n2
Consecrated Thunderbolt: Father Yorke of San Francisco (Brusher), **43:** 216n1
conservation, **48:** 319; **49:** 289-92; H. Hoover on, **45:** 181; and national forests, **47:** 589,n1,2

Constantine I (of Greece), **40:** 453-55, 486; **41:** 34-35, 375,n5; **44:** 43,n3; **46:** 581,n1
Constantinople, **41:** 26n1, 219, 220, 221, 464; **42:** 157, 172, 316, 318, 403; **43:** 471; **44:** 239,n1, 387, 547; **45:** 416, 461; **51:** 156n2, 163, 503, 564
Constitution (U.S.): *see* United States Constitution
Constitution Hall, Washington, D.C., **42:** 281n1
Constitutional Government in the United States (Wilson), **41:** 22,n1; **42:** 69n2
Constitutional History of Georgia (Saye), **49:** 114n1
Constitutional Politics in the Progressive Era: Child Labor and the Law (Wood), **49:** 23n1
Contemporary Review (London), **43:** 497
Continental and Commercial Trust and Savings Bank of Chicago, **40:** 128, 512, 514; **41:** 383n1; **42:** 54; **43:** 196; **45:** 99; **48:** 372, 518n1, 519n1
Continental Hall, Washington, D.C., **40:** 188n1
Continental Piston Ring Company, **42:** 137
Conty, Alexander Robert, **41:** 178,n1; **43:** 363n6, 364
Convention Hall, Washington, D.C., **41:** 515
Cook, Jeff, **47:** 481-84,n1, 516
Cook, Morris Llewllyn, **51:** 92,n1, 248
Cook, Waldo Lincoln, **41:** 450-51,n1, 495
Cooley, Mortimer Elwyn, **46:** 29,n1
Cooley, Philip A., **40:** 176,n1
Cooley, Stoughton, **43:** 175
Coolidge, (John) Calvin, **44:** 292n2; **51:** 624n1
Coolidge, Clara Amory (Mrs. Thomas Jefferson), **44:** 176,n1; **48:** 391,n1; **49:** 265,n1, 275, 281, 294
Coolidge, Helen Granger Stevens (Mrs. John Gardner), **43:** 31,n4
Coolidge, John Gardner, **40:** 116,n1
Coolidge, Louis Arthur, **46:** 362,n3
Coolidge, Thomas Jefferson, Jr., **44:** 176n1
Coolidge, William Henry, **49:** 267,n5
Cooper, Henry Allen, **41:** 327,n1; **45:** 582
Cooper, John Milton, Jr., **49:** 155n1
Cooper, John Paul, **47:** 520-21,n1
Cooper, Roswell D., **49:** 441,n5
Cooper Union, N.Y., **43:** 421; **44:** 458
Coordination at the Top (Harvey), **47:** 15,n1
Copenhagen, Denmark, **44:** 154, 155
copper industry, **43:** 72, 251-52, 341; and prices, **44:** 64; **46:** 58-59, 68; **48:** 487-88, 489; strike in Montana, **44:** 107, 259-63; Arizona strike and settlement, **44:** 134-39, 172, 424-25, 429, 478, 515-16; and agreement with War Industries Board, **44:** 222, 223-24; report on Bisbee deportations, **44:** 516-20, 521-22; and President's Mediation Commission report, **46:** 128, 129-34

Copper Queen Consolidated Mining Company, **44:** 515, 518
Copper River Railroad, Ala., **43:** 36-37
Copper Trust, **46:** 111
Corbett, Julian Stafford, **48:** 501n1
Cordova, Alaska, **43:** 37
Corfu, **42:** 331; **47:** 514; **51:** 562
corn, **46:** 305-306, 307, 504; and prices, **47:** 90-91; and export program, **51:** 89
Corn Exchange Bank, N.Y., **43:** 196
Corn Exchange Bank, Philadelphia, **43:** 197
Corn Exchange National Bank, Chicago, **43:** 196
Cornell University, **43:** 135; **45:** 92n2, 141n1
Cornell University Medical School, **48:** 441n1
Cornish, Johnston, **45:** 559,n1
Cornish, N.H., **40:** 572,n2, 574,n1
Cornwall, Henry Bedinger, **46:** 553,n1
Cornwell, John Jacob, **43:** 59,n1
Corona (yacht), **42:** 385
corrupt practices bill, **40:** 41, 158
Corvey, Prince Maximilian von Ratibor und, **44:** 320,n3
Corwin, Edward Henry Lewinski, **46:** 404,n7
Corwin, Edward Samuel, **49:** 390,n1
Cosby, Spencer, **42:** 186,n1
Cosey, Alfred B., **43:** 412,n1,2,3
Cosmopolitan Trust Company, Boston, **45:** 160n1
Cosmos: *see* Butler, Nicholas Murray
Cosmos Club, **42:** 65
Cossacks, **45:** 229, 263, 322, 418, 419; **46:** 154, 420, 421,n3, 590; **47:** 100, 242, 318, 593; **48:** 105, 184, 185; **49:** 152
cost accounting, **40:** 250-55, 268-69, 278
cost of living, **47:** 117, 118, 151, 384; **51:** 365-66, 369; investigation of, **40:** 244,n1, 264, 519, 547; **44:** 569; **45:** 132,n2, 183
Costa Rica, **40:** 334; **41:** 67,n6, 257,n1,2; **42:** 359; **43:** 160n1; **44:** 232,n1; **46:** 450; **47:** 231,n1, **48:** 645; J. H. Stabler memorandum on overthrow of government, **41:** 139, 140-44; WW will not recognize government of, **41:** 145, 146, 248, 386; political situation in, **45:** 388-89, 405-406, 417; W. J. Bryan and issue of recognition, **49:** 3, 5-6, 21-23, 60-61, 431
Costa Rica Union Mining Company, **46:** 450
Costello, Stephen V., **43:** 253,n2
Costigan, Edward Prentiss, **41:** 380; and *Masses* trial, **48:** 197-98,n1, 208, 251
Cothran, Annie Wilson Howe, niece of WW, **40:** 93-94, 108-109, 127-28; **41:** 259, 457-58, 469; divorce final, **41:** 458; engagement and marriage of, **43:** 236, 241,n2, 317,n1, 318; *see also* Compton, Annie Wilson Howe Cothran
Cothran, Josephine, **40:** 93, 94, 108, 128, 336; **43:** 241, 317
Cotten, Lyman Atkinson, **43:** 182,n2

Cotton, Joseph Potter, **43:** 49,n4; **51:** 634,n1
cotton, **44:** 40; **48:** 563, 643, 644-45, 646; **51:** 5,n1, 220, 372, 610,n1, 611; and Lever bill, **43:** 190-91, 210; and prices, **46:** 83-84, 84, **47:** 118, 138, 168-69, 173, 395, 495; **49:** 4, 47-50, 73-74, 278, 461
Cottonwood County, Minn., **47:** 235n3
Cottrelly, Mathilde, **46:** 520
Coudert, Frederic René, **42:** 83n1, 122; **51:** 554-55,n1, 578
Coudert Brothers, **41:** 418
Council of National Defense, **41:** 169-70, 226n1, 239, 484, 518, 542, 553, 554; **42:** 3, 31, 34, 47, 48, 52, 142, 168,n1, 212, 242, 266, 279, 286, 289-90, 293, 323, 412, 424, 533, 548, 549; **43:** 21, 50, 93, 94, 113, 222n1; **44:** 14, 23, 248, 398, 502; **45:** 45, 61, 570; **46:** 105, 427; **47:** 9, 353n2, 463, 464, 558n6, 601; **48:** 138, 338n2, 342n1, 444n1; **49:** 281; **51:** 165n1, 460, 646; and railroad crisis, **41:** 414, 415, 424, 430n2; labor and, **42:** 135-38; WW's remarks to labor committee of, **42:** 296-98,n1; and United Mine Workers, **42:** 459, 549-60,n1, 471-73; plan for committee reorganization of, **42:** 498; **43:** 107-108, 120, 131, 148,n1, 148-49, 163-64, 167, 177, 192, 341, 345; and shipbuilding, **42:** 524; and War Industries Board, **43:** 25, 26, 156n1, 341; **48:** 176; and price fixing, **43:** 41,n1, 59-61, 62, 90-92, 102, 490; **45:** 234, 244; and Central Purchasing Commission, **43:** 319,n1; on labor and standards of living during war, **43:** 511n1; and plans for labor commission, **44:** 81, 103-104; resignation of Advisory Commission members due to conflict of interest, **44:** 238,n1; and housing for war workers, **44:** 279,n1, 448,n1; **45:** 141, 349,n2; **46:** 67, 98n1, 195n1; and labor report, **44:** 498-501; and prohibition, **45:** 40n1; and health conditions in war industries, **45:** 51, 91; and shipping situation, **45:** 489-91; and vocational rehabilitation, **47:** 95, 123-24, 153; G. B. Clarkson on, **47:** 110-15, 526-33; WW on, **47:** 143; Woman's Committee of, **47:** 180, 188, 476; **48:** 28,n1, 46, 111, 117, 169-70, 198-99, 208n1, 221, 250, 345-46,n2; and Twin City Rapid Transit strike, **47:** 189, 190, 273; I. M. Tarbell on Woman's Committee, **48:** 57-58,n1; reconstruction studies and, **48:** 285, 290, 336-37, 357; and Washington State Grange meeting, **48:** 290; N. D. Baker and WW on importance of Woman's Committee, **48:** 321-22, 357-58; photographs: *illustration section,* **43**
Courland (Kurland), **45:** 289, 412, 416, 433; **46:** 165, 189, 568; **47:** 555-56; **48:** 97-98; **51:** 415, 498
Course of American History (Wilson), **49:** 165n1

court-martial bill, **47:** 381,n2

Courtrai, Belgium, **51:** 421

Covington, James Henry, **43:** 361,n2, 386, 494, 495, 505; **44:** 86, 191; **47:** 557

Coward, Jacob Meyer, **46:** 211,n2

Cozart, Winfield F., **45:** 547,n2

C.P.I.: *see* Committee on Public Information

Crabtree, William Riley, **41:** 299,n1; **42:** 138n1, 139

Crafton, Allen, **47:** 540n1

Cram, Mathilda de, **45:** 217,n5

Crane, Charles Richard, **40:** 492, 548, 559-60; **41:** 48, 56n1, 415-16, 461, 466, 468, 493-94, 505; **42:** 161, 267, 275n2, 289; **45:** 398; **46:** 411, 422, 619; **48:** 273, 283, 353, 357,n2, 450-51, 457, 570, 581, 590; **49:** 41n1, 62-63, 122, 154, 298,n1, 443; and D. F. Houston, **40:** 9, 37, 173; on WW's peace note, **40:** 489; and appointment to Russian Commission, **42:** 43-44, 45,n3, 81, 95, 126, 168, 262; on situation in Russia, **42:** 232; **43:** 13-14, 149-50, 298-99; on Nonpartisan League, **47:** 466, 478; and T. Masaryk, **47:** 548, 561, 610; on Slavs, **48:** 485-86

Crane, Cornelia W. Smith (Mrs. Charles Richard), **40:** 489, 560; **41:** 468; **45:** 398; **49:** 62, 154, 443

Crane, Ellen Douglas Bruce (Mrs. Richard), **45:** 398,n2

Crane, Frank, **43:** 175,n2

Crane, John Oliver, **49:** 443,n3

Crane, Richard, **42:** 232; **43:** 149, 149-50, 298-99; **45:** 398; **46:** 452,n1, 550; **47:** 548, 561n1, 610-11

Cranford, Clifton, **45:** 238n2

Cravath, Paul Drennan, **45:** 351,n2; **49:** 361,n1; **51:** 184

Craven, Hermon Wilson, **41:** 546,n2; **45:** 336, 337

Crawford, Harriet Ann, **48:** 293n5; **49:** 249n2

Crawford, Richard A., **40:** 136; **41:** 256, 257, 418,n1

Crawford, Richard Frederick, **42:** 142n1, 445; **43:** 44, 67, 97, 140, 141, 224; **46:** 75; on British tonnage, **43:** 9-11, 45-46

Creasy, William T. (Farmer Creasy), **49:** 440,n2, 441

Creel, Blanche Lyon Bates (Mrs. George), **45:** 345,n3

Creel, Frances Virginia, **45:** 345,n3

Creel, George, **40:** 315,n1, 374; **41:** 191; **42:** 90, 289, 301, 320, 326, 396; **43:** 3, 145, 146, 168n2, 415, 456-59,n2, 536; **44:** 49, 62,n1, 66, 142, 248, 270-71,n1, 367,n2, 424, 446, 452, 504-505, 511, 551, 557; **45:** 86, 87, 103, 123, 152, 162, 167,n1, 216, 241,n1, 327, 407, 443, 562, 580, 596; **46:** 3, 67, 150, 151n2, 160, 233,n67, 367, 407, 460, 491; **47:** 207, 276,n3, 492; **48:** 120, 140, 440, 612, 630; **49:** 24, 51, 53, 137-38, 159, 168-69, 172-73, 216, 432-33, 434, 437, 487; **51:** 118, 162, 175, 282-83, 294, 408

and appointment to head Committee on Public Information, **42:** 23, 39, 43, 52, 55n1, 59, 71; memorandum on creation of a publicity department, **42:** 39-41; on A. Bullard, **42:** 267, 290-91, 378; WW on salary of, **42:** 291; and guidelines to the press, **42:** 304-13, 386,n1, 387; F. I. Cobb on, **43:** 366; and B. Whitlock on Belgium, **43:** 477-78, **44:** 450n1; on Root Commission to Russia, **43:** 526-30; draft of letter to S. Gompers, **44:** 95-100,n1; on Mooney case, **44:** 267; **49:** 23; on information campaign in Russia, **44:** 434, 435; **45:** 194, 367-68, 387; on criticism of term "Our Allies," **45:** 246, 257; and railroads, **45:** 309; denies S. Washburn's tour request, **45:** 339, 348; on sugar investigation, **45:** 344-45; and censorship blunder, **45:** 387,n1; statement on war progress, **45:** 407, 407-10, 422, 435,n1,2; on establishing a Public Information Bureau in Europe, **46:** 200-203; and Nonpartisan League, **46:** 369, 386-87; **47:** 215-16, 226, 235, 260, 521,n1,2; on cabling WW's addresses, **46:** 410-11, 413; on Swedish Americans who failed to register for the draft, **46:** 458-59, 469, 560; **47:** 134, 135, 136, 169; and issue of teaching German language, **46:** 459; advocates sending money to J. R. Mott, **46:** 479, 495; and foreign correspondents, **47:** 284,n1, 297; on U.S. preparedness, **47:** 334,n1; and support of, **47:** 341-42, 343; WW on, **47:** 341, 343, 602; suppresses H. N. Hall's telegram on Ireland, **47:** 581, 586; statement about Congress, **48:** 11-12,n2, 17, 45,n1, 51; and proposed investigation of CPI, **48:** 148-49, 177-78; on conference of Negro editors and concerns of, **48:** 341-42, 346, 528-29, 530; on WW's Fourth of July speech, **48:** 428; on N. Angell's plan for league of nations, **48:** 613-14, 629; on use of foreign languages, **49:** 200-201; on C. A. Lindbergh appointment, **49:** 536; **51:** 64-65; and Sisson Documents, **51:** 104-105, 252; on suffrage amendment as war necessity, **51:** 117-18; on WW's speech at Metropolitan Opera House, **51:** 124; on repairing election defeat, **51:** 645-46; photograph: *illustration section,* **42**

Creel, George Bates, **45:** 345,n3

Crewe-Milnes, Robert Offley Ashburton, Marquess of Crewe, **40:** 449, 449-50

Crimean War, **42:** 329

Crimmins, John Daniel, **42:** 219-20, 222, 223

Cripps, Charles Alfred, 1st Baron Parmoor, **41:** 375,n8; **42:** 436,n5

Crisis, The (New York), **43:** 412n2; **49:** 88n3

Crisp, Charles Robert, **45:** 307

Croatia and Croats, **40:** 104-105; **41:**

Croatia and Croats (*cont.*)
56n2; **45:** 461; **46:** 244; **49:** 126n1
Croly, Herbert David, **40:** 359-60, 423,
539, 559; **41:** 13, 389; **42:** 89-90, 118-
19,n1, 120; on censorship, **44:** 408-10,
420
Cromie, Francis Newton Allen, **51:** 4n2
Crompton, David Henry, **46:** 317,n4, 328
Crompton, Lillian Sheridan (Mrs. David
Henry), **46:** 317,n4, 328
Cromwell, Oliver, **46:** 156
Cronholm, Folke, **44:** 140n3
Crosby, Oscar Terry, **40:** 386n1, 471,n2;
43: 335-36; **44:** 411; **45:** 69, 274, 362,
445, 532, 533; **46:** 76, 379-80, 554-55;
47: 173-74,n1, 443; **48:** 233, 331, 482;
49: 361; and inter-Allied councils, **45:**
245-46, 424-25, 590-91; on Italian crisis, **45:** 351; WW on, **45:** 546; **46:** 324,
327; W. G. McAdoo on, **45:** 588-92; in-
structed not to participate in political
decisions of Inter-Allied Council, **46:**
359-60, 360, 393, 409, 415, 465
Crow, Edmund Burwell, **44:** 571,n1
*Crowded Years: The Reminiscences of
William G. McAdoo*, **43:** 385n1
Crowder, Enoch Herbert, **40:** 329-30; **41:**
384, 385, 500; **42:** 284; **43:** 534; **44:**
29,n1, 61, 123; **45:** 255; **46:** 428n1, 430;
48: 74; **51:** 579; and foreword to new
regulations for exemption boards, **44:**
522, 533-35; and industrial mobilization, **47:** 264n1, 296n1, 300; and Freeman case, **48:** 136n1, 177n1; and classification of belligerent nations, **49:**
185n1, 238, 247-48; and Houston race
riot of 1917, **49:** 325,n5, 326, 400; and
draft and exemptions, **49:** 349, 358,
386, 509, 514, 541,n1; on farmers and
draft exemptions, **51:** 250-51; photograph: *illustration section*, **46**
Crowder industrial manpower bill, **47:**
264-65,n1, 296n1, 300
Crowe, Sir Eyre, **48:** 501n1
Crowell, Benedict, **46:** 430, 525, 535-
36,n1, 546-47, 554, 558, 560, 562, 573,
584, 595-96; **47:** 12, 38-39, 51, 66, 72,
107, 144, 171, 259, 293, 328, 348, 349,
509; **49:** 449, 517, 522, 542-43; **51:** 33,
170,n1, 228; and industrial mobilization, **47:** 296, 299-300; and Herink
case, **47:** 300,n1; on training camp en-
tertainment on Sundays, **47:** 311n1; on
W. Lippmann and propaganda abroad,
49: 487-88; on selection of men for commissions, **51:** 271-72; and army absentee voting, **51:** 287,n1
Crowther, Samuel, **51:** 280n1
Crozier, William, **44:** 493; **45:** 390,n1
Csepel, S.M.S., **51:** 492
Cuba: declares war against Germany, **42:**
41,n1, 51,n1; and Mexico, **48:** 238n1;
and Costa Rica, **49:** 6
Cuba, Kan., **47:** 300,n1,2
Cuba and the United States, **40:** 66; **44:**
456, 543; and German influence, **41:**

117, 131-32,n3; and rebellion in, **41:**
268-69,n1, 278-79,n1, 298-99,n1, 339,
384-85, 423; **42:** 295n1; **43:** 207; and
U. S. war declaration, **41:** 472-73, 476,
496; and Cuban military mission, **42:**
295,n1; and U.S. Army in, **43:** 206-207;
and U.S. loan, **44:** 282; and wheat, **45:**
59; and sugar, **45:** 115-16, 163,n1, 178,
352, 354; **46:** 501-502
Cudahy, Edward Aloysius, **45:** 179n2; **46:**
28
Cudahy and Company, **46:** 28; **48:** 508
Cuff, Robert Dennis George, **42:** 168n1;
43: 25n1; 148n1; **44:** 238n1
Culberson, Charles Allen, **42:** 22, 113,
116-17, 289-90, 299, 462n2; **46:** 61; and
woman suffrage, **45:** 278, 338, 339
Culbertson, William Smith, **41:** 380
Culebra Cut: *see* Gaillard Cut
Cullen, Frederick Asbury, **43:** 412,n2; **46:**
339,n1, 383n1
Cullinan, Joseph Stephen, **43:** 99,n1
Cumming, C. K., **48:** 142n6
Cummings, Homer Stillé, **51:** 353, 425,
537, 588-90, 592; meets with WW on
Democratic politics and congressional
elections, **51:** 300-304, 389-93, 409,
627-33, 646-48; suffragists meet with,
51: 304; on draft of WW's appeal to vot-
ers, **51:** 380-81,n1, 389-93; on German
reply to WW's note, **51:** 408-409
Cummins, Albert Baird, **41:** 11n1, 20,
318n1, 328; **42:** 245n2, 505
Cummins, Herbert Ashley Cunard, **47:**
552,n1
Cunard Lines, **41:** 373n1; **43:** 366
Cunningham, Minnie Fisher (Mrs. Bev-
erly Jean), **47:** 144,n1
Curley, James Michael, **46:** 550
Current History (New York), **49:** 242n1
Current Opinion (New York), **41:** 529,n2
Curtis, Charles, **45:** 577,n1,2,4; **46:** 13,
16; **48:** 591-92
Curtis, Cyrus Hermann Kotzchmar, **40:**
243,n2, 337, 371; **44:** 478; **47:** 279,n4
Curtis, Lloyd Walley, **40:** 562,n1
Curtis Manufacturing Company, **43:** 349
Curtis Publishing Company, Phila., **40:**
243n2, 374; **47:** 279n4
Curtiss, Glenn Hammond, **45:** 357n2
Curtiss Aeroplane and Motor Company,
45: 357n2; **47:** 396
Curzon, George Nathaniel, 1st Marquess
of Kedleston, **40:** 414; **41:** 196, 214, 271;
42: 435; **44:** 202, 386; **48:** 613
Curzon, Grace Elvina Trillia Hinds Dug-
gan, Lady Curzon, **41:** 271,n1
Cusachs, Carlos Valérien, **46:** 50,n1, 59,
67, 79
Cushing, Catherine Chisholm, **46:** 314n2
Cushing, Harvey Williams, **41:** 482n3
customs: and embarkation rules, **45:** 561-
62, 587-88; and search for explosives
aboard ships, **46:** 3-4, 17-18, 51
Customs Administrative Act; **47:** 533
Customs Service, N.Y., **47:** 191n1

Cutting, Robert Fulton, **40:** 89,n1, 444
Cuyler, Juliana Stevens (Mrs. John Potter), **45:** 230, 231,n1, 232
Cuyler, Richard Mathä, **45:** 231n5
Cuxhaven, Germany, **51:** 464
Czartoryski, Prince Witold, **42:** 544,n4
Czech Legion, **48:** 106, 218-19, 285n3, 330, 335-36,n1, 358n1, 367-69, 380, 396, 397, 398, 399, 401-403; **49:** 10-11, 41-42, 45n3, 53, 58, 97, 179, 219-20, 278; **51:** 8, 84-85n1, 85, 91, 98-102, 188, 481n1, 481; requests aid from Allies, **48:** 428-29, 587, 603; possible use as guards for Russian Commission, **48:** 453-54, 469; Admiral Knight on, **48:** 458, 459-60, 479-80, 480-81; **49:** 150-53; N. D. Baker on ammunition for, **48:** 483; occupation of Vladivostok by, **48:** 494, 544; **49:** 40n1, 45-46; and Supreme War Council's resolution on Allied intervention, **48:** 496-97, 499, 500, 504; Reading, Wiseman, and WW meet on, **48:** 512, 513, 514, 523-24; Britain sends aid to, **48:** 512, 513, 545, 622; Admiral Knight needs instructions regarding, **48:** 528; and U.S. plan to aid, **48:** 542-53; **49:** 75, 76, 109; asks aid of Japan, **48:** 559-60, 578; and China, **48:** 609n1; WW and aid to, **48:** 625-27, 641-42; U.S. policy regarding, **49:** 36, 52, 171-72; and Japan's proposal, **49:** 175-76; need for clothing and supplies, **49:** 176-77, 262,n1, 322-23, 383, 417, 434-35, 446,n1, 446, 448-49, 479, 491, 491-93, 494-95, 529,n1, 544; T. Masaryk thanks WW for aid, **49:** 185; V. Hurban's report on, **49:** 194-200; British concern leads to request for more U.S. and Japanese troops, **49:** 248; possibility of Japanese sending more troops to aid, **49:** 282-84, 345; instructions to F. C. Poole regarding, **49:** 285-86; Reading's concern about, **49:** 302-303; C. A. de R. Barclay on, **49:** 373; WW on westward movement of, **49:** 448; reports of military success of, **49:** 479, 493, 494, 544; WW on not forming an eastern front with, **51:** 25, 50-51; T. Masaryk on, **51:** 86-87, 96n2; R. Lansing on Red Terror and, **51:** 97-98; and U.S. military policy, **51:** 121, 140-41; and Supreme War Council's note on military policy, **51:** 201; concern over WW's policy, **51:** 209-10,n3; G. V. Chicherin on, **51:** 509-10, 555-56, 557
Czechoslovak National Council, **48:** 459, 493, 497; **49:** 44n2, 45n3, 219, 262n1; **51:** 50n1, 395, 506; U.S. recognition of as *de facto* government, **49:** 287,n1, 288, 313, 404-405, 415-16, 434, 485, 492, 511-12
Czechs and Czechoslovakia, **45:** 224, 461, 463; **47:** 333, 590; **51:** 47, 118-19, 156n2, 326, 374, 383, 395, 501, 505, 541, 565,n5; in Russia, **42:** 464; **47:** 513-14,n7, 551-52, 565; and issue of self-de-

termination, **48:** 96, 212, 213, 436, 437,n2,3, 500, 530-31, 591
Czernin, von und zu Chudenitz, Count Ottokar, **41:** 129-30,n1, 297-98, 300, 312, 313, 398-99, 421-22, 476, 478; **44:** 351,n2, 513-14; **45:** 56, 173n1, 382n2, 432n1, 436,n1, 440, 595; **46:** 199, 312, 567, 581,n2, 589; **47:** 11, 122, 123, 124; address of commented on and compared to G. Hertling's, **46:** 110n1, 115,n1,2, 163, 164, 165, 167, 172, 183, 185, 185-86, 186-87, 189, 191, 222-29, 243, 277-78, 483, 592, 593; report of cabling address in advance to WW, **46:** 191-92; talk of WW's reply to, **46:** 167-68, 249, 262, 268; A. J. Balfour on, **46:** 271-72; mentioned in WW's Four Points address, **46:** 273, 274, 277, 291, 295-96, 319-20, 322; and Charles I's peace moves, **46:** 397, 400, 411-12, 418, 473n1, 551-53; on Britain's peace proposal, **47:** 239-41; and Sixtus letter, **47:** 589n1; photograph: *illustration section*, **46**

Da Gama, Domicio da: *see* Gama, Domicio da
Da Vinci, Leonardo, **45:** 358
Dabney, Richard Heath, **40:** 61-62, 90; **41:** 516-17, 537; **43:** 415,n2, 437; **44:** 260,n2, 263
Daily Coal Digest, **51:** 114
Dalmatia, **40:** 446n4; **42:** 156, 333; **44:** 21; **46:** 244; **51:** 388
Dalziel, Henry, **40:** 126
Damnable Question: A Study in Anglo-Irish Relations (Dangerfield), **48:** 300n2
Dana, Henry Wadsworth Longfellow, **44:** 79, 366n2
Dancy, Robert R., **40:** 516,n2; **41:** 408
Dandl, Otto von, **48:** 552,n2
Danger of Junkerism Drawing U.S. Into War (Colcord), **41:** 191,n2
Danger of U.S.-German Break Lies Behind the Peace Moves of the Kaiser and President (Hall), **40:** 406n1
Dangerfield, George, **48:** 300n2
Daniel, Edward W., **46:** 339,n3
Daniel, Thomas H., **49:** 246-47,n1
Daniels, Addie Worth Bagley (Mrs. Josephus), **41:** 530,n2; **42:** 281n1; **45:** 238n2, 389
Daniels, Frederick, **45:** 547,n2
Daniels, Jonathan Worth, **41:** 530,n3
Daniels, Josephus, **40:** 263; **41:** 94, 149-51, 159, 189, 243, 282, 329, 331, 367, 431, 432, 455, 461, 461-62, 466, 476, 484, 496, 506, 518, 530, 541, 555, 556; **42:** 23, 37, 52, 58-59,n2, 63, 77, 82n1, 168, 220, 281, 301, 323, 343, 348, 374, 446-47,n1,2, 449, 457, 526; **43:** 61, 71-72, 79, 115-16, 122, 142, 155, 156, 174-75, 178, 191-92, 237, 244n1, 257, 302-305, 336, 341,n2, 344, 358,n1, 361-62, 373, 380, 389, 427n1, 428, 463n1, 486,

Daniels, Josephus (*cont.*)
512; **44:** 49, 54, 60-61, 80-81, 107, 198,
216, 219, 227, 237, 263, 278, 296,
346,n1, 370-71, 381, 387-88, 392, 411,
452, 463, 482, 495, 501, 515, 532, 537,
544, 556, 571; **45:** 11, 18, 52, 127-28,
148, 169, 189, 215, 223, 299, 326, 474-
75; **46:** 12-13, 30, 34, 41, 49-50, 59, 67,
91, 151n2, 203, 215, 238, 351, 406n1,
438-39, 444n2, 564; **47:** 92, 161, 162,
348; **48:** 14, 45, 190, 192, 247, 253,
347n1, 356, 410, 432, 439, 488, 527-28,
542, 544, 578; **49:** 4,n1, 69, 70-71, 83-
84, 84, 85, 106, 128, 139, 142, 149, 181,
221, 225, 230-31, 258, 267, 438, 461,
513; **51:** 110, 124, 179, 214, 302, 328-29,
341, 344-45, 347, 403, 552, 575, 592,
604, 624
as possible presidential candidate, **40:**
173; discusses preparedness with E. M.
House, **40:** 238, 239; on naval oil reserves, **40:** 382-83, 420, 545, 560,
561n2; **41:** 65, 248, 289,n1, 290, 291;
42: 526, 533n1, 547-48, 559-61; **49:** 291;
and Grayson's promotion to rear admiral, **40:** 402, 443,n1, 463, 523; on Admiral Dewey's death, **40:** 490-91; on
arming merchant ships, **41:** 188, 293,
346, 363-64, 364, 369-72, 376-77, 381,
387, 387-88, 391,n1, 395-98, 403; on
rise in steel prices, **41:** 407; on Danish
West Indies, **41:** 361-62, 362-63; on
WW's desire to protect U.S. shipping,
41: 430-31; advocates war declaration,
41: 442, 443, 444-45; WW visits office,
41: 473; and censorship, **41:** 474,n2,
530, 556; **42:** 22n1, 39, 43, 90-91; House
recommends replacement of, **41:** 483;
on German interned ships, **42:** 27-
28,n1, 292; **43:** 89; and Committee on
Public Information, **42:** 55, 59, 71; on
sending destroyers abroad, **42:** 121;
and prohibition order, **42:** 123, 526,n3;
and price fixing, **42:** 374, 411,n1, 419-
20, 534-35, 538; **46:** 602-603, 607; and
coal prices, **43:** 63; on convoys, **43:** 87,
88, 112; and war-risk insurance, **43:** 94;
on plan for limiting German submarine warfare, **43:** 305-10; and Mare Island explosion and investigation, **43:**
470; on WW's views of naval campaign,
43: 503; on plan to mine North Sea, **44:**
477-78; and cancellation of Army-
Navy game, **44:** 571; **45:** 29-30; and diary on cabinet meetings, **45:** 95, 147,
176, 207, 237, 271-72, 341-42, 448, 573,
601-602; **46:** 33-34, 78-79, 79, 212-13,
297, 468, 508-509, 553-54, 581-82, 620-
21; **47:** 82, 206, 231, 334, 353; **49:** 137,
246, 431; **51:** 275, 412; on legislation
Congress should consider, **45:** 170-71;
on governmental ownership of railroads, **45:** 170-71; and general leasing
bill and oil reserves, **45:** 374, 375, 420-
21, 448, 454n1, 559; on Vladivostok situation, **46:** 33-34; **48:** 543; **49:** 278; on

B. M. Baruch on War Industries Board
position, **46:** 105-106, 217-18; and
housing crisis, **46:** 150, 151, 171; and
Admiral Sims' British appointment,
46: 194; and F. L. Janeway's chaplaincy, **46:** 260, 286, 330; on vocational
rehabilitation, **47:** 95, 123, 153; and
J. E. Davies' Wisconsin campaign, **47:**
129,n2; on War Cabinet meetings, **47:**
171-72, 241; **49:** 145; **51:** 372, 416, 615;
and decision to send ship to Mur-
mansk, **47:** 246, 263, 290; and Twin
City Rapid Transit strike, **47:** 273; and
oil prices and Standard Oil's finances,
47: 412-13; on WW's tax message, **48:**
173; on sending Marines to Galveston,
48: 279-80, 280; and government takeover of telegraph system, **48:** 458n1;
and wages and shipbuilding industry,
49: 105, 147; on Michigan's senatorial
race, **49:** 498; on meat-packing industry, **49:** 509n1; and Murmansk Region
Council resolution, **51:** 79,n1; and
woman suffrage, **51:** 110, 123; on
Z. Weaver's reelection, **51:** 207; and
hospital construction, **51:** 281-82; photograph: *illustration section,* 45
Daniels, Josephus, Jr., **40:** 443,n3
Daniels, Roger, **50:** 23n8, 41n7, 41n10
Daniels, Winthrop More, **40:** 255, 279; **44:**
400, 413, 428, 434; **46:** 238; **47:** 166-67,
187; on railroad rates, **44:** 406-407,
429-30; and transit companies, **49:** 158,
183-84, 204, 218, 222, 223, 232, 252-55,
389, 420-22, 457, 458, 460; **51:** 247-48,
250; and Federal Utilities Advisory
Board, **51:** 92, 173
Danish West Indies, **40:** 385, 385-86, 401-
402, 405,n1, 424; **41:** 361-62, 362-63,
381, 427-28, 475-76, 485, 485-86, 500
Danube, S.M.S., **51:** 492
Danube Commission, **40:** 496
Danube River, **51:** 493
Danville, Va., *Register,* **47:** 17n10
Danzig (Dantzig), **42:** 155, 156, 335-36;
44: 317; **45:** 220; **46:** 266
Dardenelles, **40:** 495-96; **41:** 25, 219,
220,n4, 221; **42:** 317, 318, 373; **44:** 21,
387, 477; **45:** 416, 514, 528, 538; **46:**
224; **51:** 503
Darlington, Frederick, **49:** 120,n3, 121
Darrow, Clarence Seward, **43:** 400, 432;
48: 93
Darstellung der Vorgänge vor Manila
von Mai bis August 1898 (Diederichs),
44: 296n1
Dartmouth College, **46:** 260
Daughters of Confederate Veterans, **42:**
451n1
Daughters of the American Revolution,
41: 180, 234; **46:** 526
David, Eduard, **46:** 189,n5, 191, 227
David, Ferdinand, **44:** 461,n2
David, Ross, **40:** 94, 108
David, Mrs. Ross, **48:** 60

Davidson, James L., **42:** 460-61, 473, 504-505
Davidson College, **48:** 203
Davies, Hywel, **44:** 163n1; **47:** 557; **48:** 43
Davies, John Thomas, **41:** 501,n1
Davies, Joseph, and British military mission, **42:** 266n1
Davies, Joseph Edward, **41:** 46; **44:** 13; **49:** 407, 456; **51:** 616; and meat-packing investigation, **46:** 462, 463; resigns from Federal Trade Commission, **46:** 566,n5, 609; **47:** 8,n1, 52-53; and Wisconsin senatorial campaign, **47:** 40-41, 129, 148, 326,n1, 390n2
Davila, Felix Cordova, **48:** 3, 4
Davis, A. C., **46:** 281,n1, 282
Davis, Anna Norwood Hallowell (Mrs. Horace Andrew), **47:** 155n3
Davis, Arthur Newton, **47:** 499-500,n1
Davis, Charles Talcott, **44:** 258-59,n2
Davis, Edward Parker, **40:** 94, 128; **47:** 401; **49:** 292, 318, 462; **51:** 83, 452-53, 508; poem on WW's inauguration, **41:** 452-53,n1; and poem of admiration for WW, **44:** 285-86, 287, 310
Davis, Ellen-Duane Gillespie (Mrs. Edward Parker), **46:** 336; **47:** 401; **51:** 82-83, 93
Davis, Ellen Graham Bassell (Mrs. John William), **49:** 348,n2
Davis, Jefferson, **42:** 168; **44:** 156
Davis, John Lionberger, **46:** 28,n1
Davis, John William, **44:** 151,n1, 192-94; **48:** 142; **49:** 241n1; as ambassador to Great Britain, **49:** 348; **51:** 22, 107, 276, 328
Davis, Jerome, **48:** 142
Davis, Norman Hezekiah, **51:** 184,n4
Davis, Royal, **43:** 175
Davis, W. R., **44:** 172-73, 223
Davison, Henry Pomeroy, **40:** 19-20,n1, 75-76, 76,n2, 121; **46:** 209, 232, 408-409, 414, 485, 489; **47:** 613; **49:** 128,n1; **51:** 605,n1; and Red Cross, **42:** 162, 248, 251-52,n2; **48:** 16, 53,n1, 119n1, 141, 199, 231, 234,n1, 250-51; talk of as Republican presidential candidate, **48:** 51
Davison, Kate Trubee (Mrs. Henry Pomeroy), **46:** 526,n1; **48:** 28
Dawson, Claude Ivan, **42:** 271,n1
Dawson, Francis Warrington, **48:** 332,n1
Day, Charles, **51:** 36,n6
Day, George Parmly, **45:** 352,n1, 362-63, 453, 540-41
Day, William Rufus, **41:** 120, 536,n1
Dayton, Arthur Gordon, **40:** 217,n1
Dayton-Wright Airplane Company, **45:** 357,n2
D. C. Heath and Company, **51:** 536
De Chair, Dudley Rawson Stratford, **42:** 220,n1, 348,n3; **43:** 307,n2; **44:** 465
De Fiori, Robert: see Fiori, Robert de
De Haas, Jacob Judah Aaron, **42:** 234-35,n1
De Negri, Ramón P., **41:** 249n1
De Valera, Eamon, **48:** 67n3

De Ville, Jean Baptiste (John B. Deville), **43:** 40,n1, 41, 74, 75, 101
De Vreese, Godefroid, **40:** 530
Deaf Ear for the People's Council: Their Pacific Program Would Leave the World a Prey to Prussianism (Dabney), **43:** 415,n2
Dealing with Lynch Law (Atlanta Constitution), **48:** 323,n1
Debs, Eugene Victor, **42:** 198; **44:** 79; **45:** 318, 319; **47:** 471-72; **49:** 208, 306; **51:** 560
Debskĭ, Alesander (Alexander Dembskí), **44:** 6-7,n1; **46:** 402-405
Decision to Intervene (Kennan), **44:** 483n1; **47:** 68n2, 281n1, 319n6; **48:** 96n2, 113n3, 142n6,8, 335n1, 489n1; **51:** 4n2
Decker, Benton Clark, **46:** 50,n1; **47:** 139n1
Decker, Perl D., **49:** 370-71, 402-403
Declaration of Independence, **48:** 117; **49:** 270
Declaration of London, 1909, **41:** 166, 303
Declaration of Paris, 1856, **41:** 166
Declare Principles, Is Barker's Appeal (W. Barker), **46:** 611,n1
Decline of Socialism in America, 1912-1925 (Weinstein), **42:** 148n1
Decoration Day, **42:** 313n2
Deeds, Edward Andrew, **44:** 538,n2, 538-41; **45:** 357n2; **47:** 296-97, 396; G. Borglum's charges against, **46:** 94n1, 230
Deere and Company, **46:** 229n3
Defence of the Realm Act, Great Britain, **42:** 384
deficiency appropriation bill, **42:** 343; and oversight committee, **44:** 117-18, 147, 158-59
Degras, Jane, **45:** 119n1; **46:** 341n5; **51:** 509n1
DeHavilland Model No. 9 (airplane), **45:** 357,n1; **51:** 587
DeKalb, S.S., **42:** 236
DeLacey, Lawrence, **43:** 217n5
Delafield, Francis, **43:** 361,n1
DeLancy, William C., **42:** 565
Delaney, John Joseph, **46:** 566,n4
Delanney (Delaney), Marcel-François, **48:** 283,n1,2, 288-89, 352, 353, 355, 505n2
Delano, Frederic Adrian, **40:** 77; **51:** 443
Delaware, **42:** 568; politics in, **51:** 28, 589, 632
Delaware and Hudson Company, **46:** 578n2
Delaware, Lackawanna and Western Railroad Co., **40:** 103; **41:** 412
Delbrück, Clemens, **40:** 416
Delbrück, Hans Gottlieb Leopold, **42:** 389,n2, 389-90
Delcassé, Théophile, **40:** 65
Delco Ignition System, **46:** 94n1
Dell, Floyd, **49:** 208,n2, 306
Dell, Robert, **48:** 482n3
Delme-Radcliffe, Charles, **48:** 601,n6

Demange-aux-eaux, France, **43**: 443
Dembskí, Alexander: *see* Debskí, Alesander
Democracy and the Party Movement in Prewar Japan: The Failure of the First Attempt (Scalapino), **47**: 427n3; **48**: 462n2
Democratic Editorial Association of Indiana, **46**: 285
Democratic National Committee, **40**: 230; **41**: 359; **45**: 122-23; **51**: 300-301, 588; and women, **46**: 68; G. McNab on Wisconsin election and, **47**: 389-90,n2
Democratic party, **42**: 208n1, 474; **43**: 35, 71; **44**: 153,n1; **46**: 566, 602; W. H. Page on, **40**: 53; and woman suffrage, **40**: 379n1, 427; **41**: 299; **44**: 167, 442; **45**: 242-43, 277, 278-79, 338-39; **46**: 80-81, 573, 608; **47**: 34, 572; **48**: 263-64, 271, 363, 404; **51**: 30-31, 133, 158, 189n1; prospective candidates for 1920 election, **40**: 173; WW on supporting platform of, **40**: 471, 472, 473; and peace promises, **41**: 304; and Chamberlain bills, **46**: 204-205; WW and E. M. House discuss, **46**: 436; J. P. Tumulty on effect of prohibition legislation on, **49**: 477-78; and Randall amendment, **51**: 28; Tumulty on WW's endorsement of candidates, **51**: 63; importance of reelection of Democratic Congress, **51**: 225, 293,n1, 299-300, 459-60; and Senate debate on peace terms, **51**: 277n7; WW's appeal for a Democratic Congress (Oct. 1918), **51**: 304-306, 317-18, 343-44, 353-55, 381-82; newspaper advertisement urging return to Congress of, **51**: 572-74; H. S. Cummings on election of 1918, **51**: 588-90, 627-33; C. W. Eliot on, **51**: 599-600; results of congressional election of 1918, **51**: 604,n1; for Democratic primary and general election campaigns in 1918, *see* Democratic party listed by states
Democratic party in Alabama, **49**: 138,n1, 236,n1, 245,n2
Democratic party in Arizona, **51**: 604,n1
Democratic party in California, **40**: 129; **51**: 213,n1, 259-60, 477,n1,2
Democratic party in Colorado, **51**: 312, 589-90
Democratic party in Georgia, **47**: 191, 312, 325,n1, 382,n1; senatorial campaign of 1918, **49**: 80-82, 114-16, 143, 205-206, 237,n1, 369,n1, 528,n1
Democratic party in Idaho, **49**: 147; **51**: 180,n1
Democratic party in Illinois, **48**: 603-604
Democratic party in Indiana, **48**: 318-20,n1
Democratic party in Kansas, **49**: 308-309, 315-16; **51**: 375
Democratic party in Kentucky, **49**: 480; **51**: 120, 149-50, 214-15, 395, 589
Democratic party in Maryland, **47**: 217n1
Democratic party in Massachusetts, **44**: 204-205, 221-22, 292,n2, 292-93,n1; **51**: 624
Democratic party in Michigan; senatorial campaign of 1918 in, **49**: 84n1, 438-39,n3, 461, 498
Democratic party in Minnesota, **47**: 54-57,n1, 237; **51**: 301, 302, 390,n1
Democratic party in Mississippi, **47**: 209; **49**: 180, 369n2
Democratic party in Missouri, **48**: 115,n1,2; **49**: 210, 224,n1,2,3,4, 235,n1, 239, 370-71, 444-45; **51**: 82,n2, 85, 612
Democratic party in Montana, **49**: 449n1; **51**: 213, 302, 612
Democratic party in Nebraska, **51**: 477,n2
Democratic party in Nevada, **51**: 453, 612
Democratic party in New Hampshire, **51**: 537,n2, 589
Democratic party in New Jersey, **49**: 455; **51**: 179,n3, 283,n1,2, 403-404, 606n2; WW's letter on reorganization, **47**: 82-84, 253-54; senatorial campaign of 1918 in, **49**: 210,n1,2, 211-12,n1
Democratic party in New Mexico, **51**: 612
Democratic party in New York, **46**: 565-66,n1; **49**: 103; **51**: 535,n2,3; gubernatorial campaign of 1918 in, **49**: 105-106,n1, 157,n1, 465
Democratic party in North Carolina, **51**: 207, 482
Democratic party in Ohio, **49**: 510n2
Democratic party in Oklahoma, **51**: 444,n1
Democratic party in Pennsylvania, **46**: 611
Democratic party in Rhode Island, **51**: 537,n1
Democratic party in South Carolina; and senatorial campaign of 1918 in, **48**: 259-60,n2, 268n1
Democratic party in Tennessee, **47**: 6,n2, 6-7, 34, 37; **51**: 482-83,n3
Democratic party in Texas, **49**: 73,n3, 137n3; **51**: 616
Democratic party in West Virginia, **51**: 437, 537-38,n3,4, 540
Democratic party in Wisconsin, **41**: 360; **47**: 129,n2, 137, 148, 326,n1, 388-90,n1
Democratic presidential campaign of 1916, **40**: 425n1; congratulatory messages and replies, **40**: 3, 4, 37,n1, 38, 46, 61-62, 62, 90, 91, 97, 108, 112, 117, 162,n1, 166, 166-67,n1, 167, 169, 170, 216, 219, 333-34, 334, 335; H. Plunkett on, **40**: 30-33; C. E. Hughes' concession, **40**: 38, 46, 90; A. G. Gardiner on, **40**: 192; WW on, **40**: 193-94, 219; and Indiana, **40**: 230, 243; for Wilson's addresses, *see* Table of Contents, Wilson Woodrow, addresses, etc., Vol. 39.
Denison, Tex., War Council, **47**: 345n1
Denison University, **40**: 330n1
Denman, William, **41**: 16n1, 542; **42**: 127, 133-34, 250, 398, 399; **43**: 109, 122, 155, 249, 486; **44**: 80, 71; **51**: 378,n2; and

bunkering agreements, **41:** 418, 418-19,n1; and Goethals controversy, **42:** 235, 248-49, 553-54,n1,2, 555-56, 567,n1; **43:** 50-51,n5, 84-85, 198-99, 204-205,n1, 211, 249-50, 257,n1, 265, 270, 285-86; and Executive Order on shipbuilding and requisitioning ships, **43:** 51,n5, 89, 144, 206; on steel costs, **43:** 105-106; resignation of, **43:** 257-58, 258-59, 259, 261, 270, 272; attacked by Hearst newspapers, **43:** 258; G. McNab on, **43:** 265

Denmark, **42:** 339, 342; **43:** 10, **45:** 74, 79, 80, 81, 82, 114n1, 310; **51:** 623; and conference of neutrals, **40:** 46-48, 81n1; reply to WW's peace note, **40:** 358; sale of ships to Great Britain, **41:** 337-38; suggestions for minister to, **48:** 143-44

Denning, William Ira, **43:** 373-74,n2

Dennis, Charles Henry, **51:** 408,n5

Denny, Collins, **42:** 213

Densmore, John B., **40:** 154,n1

Dent, Stanley Hubert, Jr., **42:** 23,n1, 91, 94, 274; **47:** 329-30

Dentler, Clarence Eugene, **44:** 344-45,n1, 372

Denton, Frances B., **49:** 303,n1

Denver and Rio Grande Railroad, **43:** 73; **46:** 448

Denver Post, **41:** 417n1

Department of: *see* under latter part of the name, such as State, Department of

Depew, Chauncy Mitchell, **40:** 119n1

Derber, Peter (Petr Iakovlevich Derber), **47:** 398,n3, 593,n3

Derby, 17th Earl of (Edward George Villiers Stanley), **40:** 75n1; **47:** 130-31,n1; **49:** 535,n4

Derfflinger, S.M.S., **51:** 490

Dernburg, Bernhard Jakob Ludwig, **42:** 389

Des Moines, Ia., **42:** 83, 84; **43:** 16

Des Moines *Iowa State Register*, **51:** 459n1

Des Moines, Ia., *Successful Farming*, **44:** 289n1

Desaris, Marguerite, **48:** 26

Descent into Darkness: The Destruction of the Roman Catholic Church in Russia, 1917-1923 (Zatko), **40:** 407n2

Desplas, Georges, **42:** 300,n1, 301

D'Estournelles de Constant, Paul-Henri Benjamin Balluat, **42:** 255,n1

Desvernine y Galdos, Pablo, **41:** 472,n3

Deutsche Bank, **46:** 254n5; **48:** 213n8

Deutsche Revolution und Wilson-Frieden (Schwabe), **48:** 555n6; **51:** 253n2

Deutsche Verfassungsgeschichte seit 1789, Band V: Weltkrieg, Revolution und Reichserneuerung, 1914-1919 (Huber), **51:** 253n2

Deutschland, Diaz und die mexikanische Revolution: Die Deutsche Politik in Mexiko, 1870-1920 (Katz), **41:** 327n5

Development of the League of Nations Idea: Documents and Correspondence of Theodore Marburg (Latané, ed.), **46:** 549n1,2; **47:** 202n5, 507n1

Developments Growing out of the alleged Leak in peace proposals (*Commercial and Financial Chronicle*), **41:** 107

Devonshire, Duchess of: *see* Cavendish, Evelyn Emily Mary Petty-Fitzmaurice

Devonshire, Duke of: *see* Cavendish, Victor Christian William

Devoy, John, **41:** 347,n1; **48:** 63n1, 64,n2

DeVries, William Levering, **46:** 435,n2

Dewey, George, **44:** 296n1, 387; **47:** 290n1; WW's birthday greetings to, **40:** 327, 338; death of, **40:** 490-91; WW's tribute to, **40:** 506-507

Dewey, John, **43:** 175; **44:** 393

Dewey, Mildred McLean Hazen (Mrs. George), **44:** 296,n1, 387

Dewey and the Germans at Manila Bay (Bailey), **44:** 296n1

DeWoody, Charles Frederick, **49:** 451,n1

Dial, Nathaniel Barksdale, **48:** 260n2, 268n1; **49:** 247n4

Diamandi, Count Constantine J., **46:** 300,n8, 420n2; and arrest by Soviets, **46:** 300n8, 420n2

Diamant, Rudolph, **41:** 6,n1

Díaz, Armando, **46:** 558,n2, 559; **49:** 127, 335-36, 533-34; **51:** 146, 386, 517, 532, 616

Díaz, José de la Cruz Porfirio, **47:** 346

Dickerson, Edwin Stuart, **51:** 179,n3

Dickinson, Alfred James, **49:** 245n2

Dickinson, Goldsworthy Lowes, **43:** 409

Diederichs, Otto von, **44:** 296n1

Dietrichs, Mikhail Konstantinovich, **44:** 496,n3; **47:** 551,n5; **48:** 480n1, 493-94,n2; **49:** 150,n2, 151, 152, 262,n1, 282, 544; **51:** 608; superseded as commander of Czechs, **49:** 479

Diffin, Frank G., **47:** 293n1

Digest of the Proceedings of the Council of National Defense during the World War (Martin), **41:** 170n3; **43:** 148n1, 222n1

Diggs, Maury I., **41:** 246,n1, 261

Dillard, James Hardy, **47:** 289,n2; **48:** 462-63

Dillon, Daniel, **43:** 133,n2

Dillon, Thomas Joseph, **43:** 267,n5

Dilnot, Frank, **40:** 465n1

Dinwiddie, Edwin Courtland, **43:** 52,n1, 65

Diplomacy and Revolution: U.S.-Mexican Relations Under Wilson and Carranza (Gilderhus), **49:** 230n1

Diplomacy of the Great War (Bullard), **42:** 254,n5

Diplomatic History, **49:** 516n1

Disclosures from Germany (Association for Conciliation; American branch), **48:** 213n8

discrimination: and Negroes, **43:** 128-30; and U.S. Army, **51:** 170, 191-93

Disloyalty Not Tolerated in America (London *Times*), **48:** 67,n1

Disloyalty of the German-American Press (Olds), **43:** 247,n2

Disque, Brice P., **46:** 218,n2, 509

Distractions of Peace during War: The Lloyd George Government's Reaction to Woodrow Wilson, December, 1916-November, 1918 (Kernek), **45:** 430n3, 487n2; **46:** 577n3; **47:** 11n1

District National Bank of Washington, **40:** 163n2

District of Columbia: *see* Washington, D.C.

District of Columbia, Committee on (House of Reps.), **47:** 255n1, 560, 596; **48:** 190,n1

Dittmann, Wilhelm Friedrich, **46:** 267,n2

Dixon, Edna, A., **44:** 110,n2

Dixon, Frederick, **41:** 235; **51:** 579-80

Dixon, Thomas, Jr., **41:** 12

Djemel Pasha, Ahmed, **42:** 316,n2, 317

Dmowski, Roman, **41:** 56n3; **42:** 335, 337, 355,n2, 544,n1, 545; **44:** 304; **45:** 553n2; **51:** 349, 446, 447-48, 625, 626

Dobrudja, **51:** 502

Dock, Lavina, **44:** 110,n2

Dockery, Albert Bowdry, **43:** 4,n2, 16, 78, 79, 118

Dockery, Alexander Monroe, **44:** 272,n1, 344, 428n1; **49:** 224, 235; **51:** 82, 85

Dr. Muehlon's Diary, **48:** 213n8

Dodd, William Edward, **46:** 518,n1; **51:** 109

Dodge, Mr. (railroad executive), **43:** 530; **44:** 23

Dodge, Bayard, **41:** 128n1; **44:** 93,n2; **45:** 185,n1

Dodge, Cleveland Hoadley, **40:** 39, 338, 374-75; **41:** 11, 55n1, 113,n3, 339-40, 539, 542-43; **42:** 162, 248, 280-81, 384-85, 396; **44:** 93, 94, 119; **45:** 581; **47:** 350, 605; **48:** 69, 112, 121; **49:** 275, 348, 385; **51:** 151-52, 180, 316, 486, 644; and British ambassadorship, **40:** 409, 463; **41:** 133, 170-72; and club-quad controversy of 1907, **40:** 568,n5, 569; on WW's "Peace without Victory" speech, **41:** 6-7; on break with Germany, **41:** 128; on not declaring war on Turkey, **45:** 185-86, 215; on WW's State of the Union message of 1917, **45:** 254; and Red Cross, **48:** 6, 16, 53n1, 66, 94; suggestions for Federal Reserve Board, **51:** 443

Dodge, Grace Parish (Mrs. Cleveland Hoadley), **40:** 338; **41:** 172, 173; **42:** 385; **45:** 186; **48:** 94; **51:** 151, 152, 316

Dodge, Mary Williams Bliss (Mrs. Bayard), **41:** 128n1; **45:** 185

Dodge Manufacturing Company of Wisconsin, **47:** 587n1

Doerries, Reinhard, R., **43:** 217n4; **48:** 63n1

Does University Lack Patriotic Leadership? Vrooman Asks Madison: Declares Students Are Not Responsive to Loyalty Plea; Calls America's Cause in War Holy (Madison *Wisconsin State Journal*), **45:** 142,n1

Dogger Bank incident, **49:** 271,n3

Doherty, Henry Latham, **40:** 119n1

Dolci, Angelo Maria, **44:** 37,n1

Domínguez, Alfredo Robles, **49:** 280,n1, 299-300

Dominican Republic, **40:** 82; **47:** 543n1

Donald, John A., **42:** 303,n1; **43:** 50,n4

Donald, Robert, **40:** 465,n1

Donald Steamship Company, **42:** 303n1

Donges, Ralph Waldo Emerson, **49:** 183,n1, 184

Donlin, John H., **45:** 41,n1,2

Donnelly, J. L., **43:** 373, 393,n1, 416, 419, 461-62

Donner, William Henry, **42:** 243,n1, 279, 293, 304

Donner Steel Company, **42:** 243, 279, 304,n1

Donop, Colonel, **49:** 496,n9, 508

Donovan, Jerome Francis, **51:** 424,n3

Doolittle, Dudley, **42:** 21n1; **46:** 492,n4

Doran, James J., **43:** 480,n3

Doremus, Frank Ellsworth, **49:** 329,n1

Dorr, Goldthwaite Higginson, **47:** 58,n1

Dorsey, Harry Woodward, **45:** 154,n1

Dorsey, Hugh Manson, **49:** 88,n3

Doubleday, Frank Nelson, **45:** 187n1; **48:** 461n1, 461-62

Doubleday, Page and Company, **45:** 187n1; **46:** 589; **48:** 461n1

Douglas, Charles Alexander, **47:** 351,n1, 546

Douglas, J. S., **43:** 104n1

Douglas, Robert Langton, **42:** 390-91,n1, 403-404, 545

Douglas, Walter, **42:** 563; **43:** 3

Doullens agreement, **49:** 126

Dove, Heinrich, **45:** 34,n12

Dover, England, **43:** 306

Dowbor-Muśnicki, Józef, **46:** 403,n3

Dowling, Victor James, **45:** 559,n2; **48:** 466,n1

Doyle, Michael Francis, **43:** 472-73, 505

draft and draft law; *see* selective service

Drafting of the Covenant (Miller), **49:** 226n2

Draper, Mr., **47:** 68

Draper, Norman, **41:** 274,n2

Dresden, Germany, **40:** 142-43, 144

Dresden, S.M.S., **51:** 490

Dresselhuys, Hendrick Coenraad, **47:** 128,n1

Dressler, Marie, **47:** 302n2

Drew, Irving Webster, **51:** 155-56,n1

Drexel and Company, Philadelphia, **43:** 197

Droppers, Garrett, **40:** 219; **41:** 34-35

Dru, Philip, **42:** 161,n3

Drucker, H. L., **46:** 615n4

Drummond, Sir (James) Eric, **40:** 212; **41:** 544, 553; **42:** 142, 143, 155, 169, 354, 355, 355-56, 454, 456, 529-30,n1,2, 543-45, 551-52; **43:** 20, 24, 125, 209-10,n1; **44:** 57, 230, 278, 316-17, 325,

373-75, 391; **45:** 68, 577-78; **46:** 213, 247-49, 250, 272-73, 389, 419-21, 485, 507-508, 531, 561-62; **47:** 35-36, 156-57, 170, 170-71, 203, 227-28, 239-41, 266-67; **48:** 203-206, 315-16, 331, 470, 524,n2, 525, 577-78; **49:** 365; **51:** 10,n7, 188, 291, 328, 352; on Mexico and Germany, **49:** 280; on U.S. attitude toward war with Bulgaria and Turkey, **49:** 537-38; photograph: *illustration section*, 49
Drummond, Robert James, **49:** 295,n1
Drury, Theodore, **42:** 115
Drury, William Truman, **47:** 274-75,n1
Drysdale, Walter Scott, **48:** 458,n2, 459
Dublin, Ireland, **44:** 439
Dublin Municipal Gallery, Ireland, **42:** 390-91, 403
Dubofsky, Melvin, **43:** 17n4, 222n1; **44:** 17n1, 50n1, 163n1; **46:** 144n1; **47:** 574n5
Dubois, Fred Thomas, **49:** 145-46,n1, 147
DuBois, James Taylor, **41:** 293-94,n1
Du Bois, William Edward Burghardt, **41:** 218
Duesenberg, Frederick Samuel, **44:** 540-41,n5
Duff, Sir Alexander Ludovic, **51:** 315,n4, 326
Duffield, Edward Dickinson, **42:** 527,n1
Duffy, Francis Patrick, **49:** 546,n2
Duffy, Frank, **47:** 343
Duggan, Alfred, **41:** 271,n2
Dukhonin, Nikolai Nikolaevich, **45:** 119,n3, 120, 217n4
Dukla, S.M.S., **51:** 492
Dulles, Allen Welsh, **46:** 413n1
Dulles, John Foster, **49:** 435,n1
DuMaurier, George Louis Palmella Busson, **46:** 264n2
Dunaway, Maude Edwin, **46:** 583-84,n1
Duncan, James, **42:** 165,n1, 262, 263, 267, 289; **49:** 78
Dunkerque (Dunkirk), France, **42:** 188
Dunluce, Viscount (Randal Mark Kerr M'Donnell), **45:** 175,n3
Dunn, Beverly Wyly, **49:** 279,n1
Dunn, John Jacob, **44:** 184,n3
Dunn, Robert Williams, **47:** 155,n3
Dunne, Finley Peter, **43:** 198,n1; **47:** 16,n3
Durand, Edward Dana, **47:** 49,n2
Durand, Nelson C., **41:** 126,n1
Durand, Walter Y., **49:** 132
Durango state, Mex., **40:** 203
Durazzo, Albania, **48:** 553
Durman, Donald Charles, **44:** 536n1
Dutasta, Paul Eugène, **51:** 622,n2
Dvina River, Russia, **49:** 518,n2,3
Dwyer, John P., **40:** 167n1; **48:** 597,n1
Dyer, Jessie Kennedy, **51:** 80-81
Dyer, Leonidas Carstarphen, **49:** 235,n1; and East St. Louis assault and riot, **43:** 222-23,n1,2, 247, 284, 297-98, 299-300; on attacks against German Americans,

43: 323-24, 336; on lynching, **49:** 61-62,n2,3
Dyersburg, Tenn., **46:** 384
Dynamite Conspiracy Trial, **40:** 176n1; **47:** 179,n2,3, 219
Dynamite: The Story of Class Violence in America (Adamic), **40:** 176n1

Eagle, Joe Henry, **44:** 62,n1, 63-64, 77
Earle, Ralph, **41:** 189,n1
Easby, William, **40:** 466,n2
Easby-Smith, James Stanislaus, **40:** 465, 466-68
East St. Louis assault and riot, **43:** 103n1, 103-104; **46:** 384; comments on, **43:** 112, 128-29, 139, 175n2, 222-23,n2, 284, 297-98, 343, 359, 510; WW on, **43:** 116,n1, 123, 128, 146, 299-300, 412n4; Negroes protest, **43:** 128-29, 342-43
Eastman, Crystal, **43:** 420; **44:** 79
Eastman, Max, **41:** 305-308,n1; **42:** 195; **43:** 164, 165,n2, 175, 187; **44:** 79, 210-11, 274-75, 468, 470n3; **48:** 93, 116, 146,n1, 147, 197-98, 208, 220, 233, 235, 241; **49:** 208, 306; **51:** 534; on WW's reply to Pope's appeal, **44:** 169-70; on freedom of speech and of the press, **44:** 170-72; photograph: *illustration section*, 44
Ebert, Friedrich, **42:** 197,n2
Echols, William Holding, Jr., **41:** 517,n1
Eckhardt, Heinrich von, **41:** 280,n1; **44:** 140n3; **47:** 475n2
École des Sciences Politiques de Paris, **43:** 135
Economic Pressures in Anglo-American Diplomacy in Mexico, 1917-1918 (Rosenberg), **47:** 357n1
Economic World: A Weekly Chronicle of Facts, Events and Opinions (New York), **44:** 105n2
Ecuador, **41:** 9; **42:** 197,n2; and peace conference proposal, **41:** 249-50, 258,n1, 352
Eddy, Sherwood, **45:** 143,n3
Edelman, Samuel, **45:** 415,n3
Edgar, William Crowell, **42:** 481,n1
Edge, Walter Evans, **42:** 458; **45:** 573-74, 592-93; **49:** 182,n1, 183, 210; **51:** 602n2
Edinburgh, University of, **42:** 394
Edison, Thomas Alva, **41:** 126,n1,2; **47:** 354
Edmonds, Richard Hathaway, **44:** 305-306, 308
Edmonson, Elton L., **46:** 433n2
Edson, John Jay, **44:** 559,n2, 561
education: WW on, **46:** 29
Education, Committee on (House of Reps.), **47:** 29, 29n1
Education and Labor, Committee on (Senate), **47:** 29, 29n1, 610
Edward VII (of Great Britain), **40:** 213, 486
Edwards, C. O., **43:** 354

Edwards, Charles Jerome, **48:** 152,n1, 153
Edwards, George Maitland, **48:** 354,n5
Edwards, William Hanford, **40:** 74,n1
Egan, Maurice Francis, **41:** 430n2; **42:** 22, 29; **48:** 31,n1, 144
Egan, Thomas Francis, **49:** 103,n1
Egan, William H., **51:** 275,n3
Egbert, Edward H., **43:** 455,n2
Egense, John N., **46:** 564n1
Egerton, George William, **45:** 487n2; **47:** 104n1; **49:** 226n2; **51:** 327n1
Egglesfield, Henry, **40:** 347,n2
Egypt, **42:** 501; **44:** 476, 477; **45:** 412, 573; **46:** 516
Eidlitz, Otto Marc, **48:** 594,n1; **49:** 464; 475,n2; **51:** 49,n2
Eight-Hour Act: *see* Adamson Act
Eight-Hour Commission; report of, **46:** 105,n2
eight-hour day, **40:** 155, 156; **41:** 352,n1; **44:** 421-22; **45:** 234; **46:** 146; **47:** 251, 378-79; **49:** 207, 215; **51:** 361, 366, 367-68; and northwestern lumber industry, **46:** 106n1; 139-40, 218, 508-509, 509, 509-10; and Standard Oil Company, **46:** 134; and meat-packing industry, **46:** 142; and WW on suspension of in construction at St. Elizabeth's Hospital **48:** 78,n1,2, 129-30,n4, 130n4; and Borland amendment, **48:** 444-45,n1; WW's veto of bill increasing hours for governmental employees, **48:** 471
Eight Years with Wilson's Cabinet, 1913-1920 (Houston), **41:** 94n1
Eighteenth Amendment, **49:** 477,n5; S. Gompers on, **45:** 295-98
Einsiedeln, Switzerland, **49:** 193
Ekaterinburg, Russia, **48:** 505; **49:** 285; **51:** 50n1
Ekengren, Wilhelm August Ferdinand, **40:** 46-48, 81n1; and Austria-Hungary's peace negotiations, **51:** 258, 259, 505-506, 526-27
El Paso, Tex., **40:** 55, 100n1, 101, 109, 110; **42:** 260n2; **43:** 158n1
El Salvador, **41:** 143,n19, 145,n1; **44:** 331; **49:** 118
Ela, Emerson, **46:** 119,n1
election of 1916, **51:** 629; A. W. Ricker on, **47:** 437-39
election of 1918: and absentee voting for soldiers, **48:** 558,n1; **51:** 287,n1; military men as candidates, **49:** 246; J. P. Tumulty on WW's endorsement of candidates, **51:** 63; and WW's appeal to voters, **51:** 304-306, 317-18, 343-44, 353-55, 380-81, 381-82, 389, 390-91, 392-93; H. S. Cummings on, **51:** 409; G. M. Hitchcock on Republican tactics, **51:** 424; congressional results, **51:** 604,n1; WW on congressional results, **51:** 620; for specific congressional or gubernatorial: *see* under names of individual states or under candidate's

name; *see also* Democratic party and Democratic party, listed by states
election of 1920, **40:** 173, 185; **51:** 631; W. G. McAdoo on, **47:** 506n1
Electric Boat Company, **42:** 477n1
electric railways, **49:** 389n1, 421
Electric Steel Company, **46:** 124n1
Elgin Ralston Lovell Gould: A Memorial, **40:** 117,n1
Eliot, Sir Charles Norton Edgecumbe, **49:** 250n1; **51:** 8,n3
Eliot, Sir Charles William, **40:** 9, 38, 89, 215,n1; **41:** 55, 510, 540; **43:** 52, 261, 292; **44:** 185,n4; **46:** 22,n1, 53; **51:** 599-600, 637; on Belgian deportations, **40:** 27-28; on Institute for Government Research, **40:** 443-44,n4; on Swiss system of military training, **41:** 480-82; **42:** 4, 19-20, 35-36, 75, 76, 91; on labor unions, **43:** 232, 282-83; on American military training, **43:** 233; on WW's appeal to voters, **51:** 551,n1
Elizalde, Rafael Héctor, **41:** 249-50, 258,n1, 352
Elk Hills oil reserve, **40:** 205,n2
Elkins, Davis, **51:** 437,n3,4, 537,n4
Elkins, Stephen Benton, **51:** 537n4
Elkus, Abram Isaac, **42:** 316,n1; **44:** 37, 40, 299n2; **45:** 51, 52-53, 185-86, 332; **46:** 445; **49:** 537
Ellinwood, Everett E., **43:** 127,n1
Elliott, Edward Graham, **49:** 120,n6, 121; **51:** 535-36,n1,2
Elliott, Howard **42:** 45,n1, 462,n1; **44:** 425,n1; **45:** 367,n1, 371
Elliott, John Lovejoy, **44:** 266-67,n3; **47:** 155
Elliott, Stewart P., **48:** 410,n1, 410-13
Ellis, Crawford, **46:** 450
Ellis, Mark St. C., **43:** 470n3
Ellis, William Thomas, **48:** 410,n1, 410-13
Ellis Island, **41:** 541, 556; **43:** 239,n1
Elmquist, Charles E., **48:** 624
embargo, **44:** 396,n1
Embargo Council: *see* Inter-Allied Embargo Council
Embree, A. S., **43:** 253
Emden, S.M.S., **51:** 490
emergency agricultural appropriation bill, **48:** 629,n2,3
Emergency Construction Committee, **45:** 10
Emergency Fleet Corporation, U.S. Shipping Board, **42:** 234, 248, 523-25, 554n1, 555n2, 567n1; **43:** 49, 50, 51n5, 72-73, 85n2, 114-45, 205n1, 211-12; **44:** 226, 227, 228,n4,5, 233, 234-36; **45:** 7, 8, 42-43, 583, 586; **46:** 611; **47:** 145, 233,n1, 261, 558n6; **48:** 140,n1, 488n1; **49:** 53n1, 386, 475; **51:** 13-14, 261; W. L. Capps resigns from **45:** 103, 117; and housing crisis, **46:** 124,n2, 171, 443n1; and carpenters' union, **46:** 363, 364; C. M. Schwab appointed head of, **47:** 385n6, 437

Emergency Housing Act, **48:** 150-51,n1, 159-60
Emergency Peace Foundation, **41:** 231, 302n1, 515; **43:** 481; *see also* People's Council of America
emergency power bill, **51:** 86, 90
Emerson, George H., **46:** 345, 387; **48:** 106n4,5, 113; **51:** 479-80
Emerson, Haven, **42:** 323,n2
Emerson College of Oratory, **49:** 351n1
Emery, Dean, **41:** 365,n1
Emmet, Robert, **43:** 509,n4; **45:** 559-61,n1, 573
Emmitsburg, Md., *Chronicle*, **47:** 217n1
Emperor William Must Go Says Morgenthau (*New York Times Magazine*), **45:** 123n1
Empey, Arthur Guy, **48:** 356,n1
Empire in Wood: A History of the Carpenters' Union (Christie), **46:** 356n5
Empire Trust Company, N.Y., **43:** 196
Employees Association of Inland Empire, **43:** 200n6
Encyclopaedia Britannica, **42:** 393n3
Endicott, Henry Bradford, **43:** 137, 189; **44:** 183; **47:** 425,n1, 557
Endicott, Johnson and Company, **43:** 137
Enemies Within: How the Honorable Institution of Free Speech in the United States Has Fallen Into the Hands of Disloyalists (*New York Tribune*), **43:** 395n1
Enemies Within: To What Extremes of Disloyalty the Socialist Party Has Committed Itself (*New York Tribune*), **43:** 395n1
England: *see* Great Britain; Great Britain and the United States
England to India (Bridges), **49:** 463,n2
English, William Hayden, **42:** 217,n1
English Channel, **43:** 306-307; **44:** 465-67
English Positivist Committee, **42:** 381n6
English Review, **42:** 381n5
Enns, S.M.S., **51:** 493
Enos, Alanson Trask, **42:** 287,n1
Enos, Jeannette Taylor (Mrs. Alanson Trask), **42:** 287n1
Enver Pasha, **42:** 316,n2, 317, 462-63
Epstein, Klaus, **43:** 185n1; **45:** 32n3
Epstein, Lewis (Eliahu Ze'ev Halevi Lewin-Epstein), **43:** 159n2, 206; **45:** 572n1; **46:** 494,n1
Equitable Life Assurance Society of the United States, **48:** 152n1; **49:** 233
Equity Co-operative Exchange of Fargo, N.D., **51:** 212n2
Erinnerungen (Kühlmann), **48:** 555n7
Erlangen, Germany, **51:** 607
Erleigh, Viscount (Gerald Rufus Isaacs), **48:** 354,n6
Ernest, Émile: *see* Marchienne, Baron Émile Ernest de Cartier de
Erskine, Marion McGraw (Mrs. Robert), **40:** 574,n2, 575; **43:** 241,n1, 247, 338; **44:** 65,n1
Erskine, Robert, **40:** 575,n1

Erzberger, Matthias, **42:** 389; **43:** 185n1; **45:** 31, 36; **46:** 312
Erzherzog Franz Ferdinand S.M.S., **51:** 492
Esch, John Jacob; and water-power legislation, **45:** 300,n2, 335
Espionage Act, **43:** 216,n2, 423; **44:** 147,n1, 389, 416, 470n3; **45:** 561n1, 587-88; **46:** 383; **47:** 364,n4; **48:** 12-14, 146,n3, 235n1; and postal censorship, **43:** 165,n2, 187, 243, 276, 396-97, 481n5; B. Johnson on *The Menace* and, **49:** 174,n1; U. Sinclair on, **49:** 207-208; T. W. Gregory defends, **49:** 306-308; A. S. Burleson on, **51:** 521
espionage bill, **42:** 22, 106-107,n1, 129, 224,n2, 558; J. P. Tumulty on, **42:** 245-46; WW signs, **42:** 370n1
Essentials to a Food Program for Next Year (G. Pinchot), **49:** 441n8
estate taxes, **43:** 350n2
Estill Springs, Tex., **46:** 380, 384, 385n1
Estimated Shipments of Cereals (Excluding Oats) to All Allies, Table No. 1, Position on 10th December, 1917, **46:** 304,n2
Estonia, **45:** 289n1; **46:** 471n3, 568
Estrada Cabrera, Manuel, **41:** 143,n17; **42:** 16,n2, 47; **44:** 331,n1,2, 358
États-Unis et la Guerre de la Neutralité à la Croisade (Hovelaque), **42:** 210n1
Eton: A History (Hollis), **40:** 488n9
Eton College, **40:** 488,n8,9
Eugene Meyer, Jr. and Company, **42:** 81n1
Europe's New Estimates of Woodrow Wilson (*Current Opinion*), **41:** 529,n2
Evans, Edmond C., **44:** 79
Evans, Elizabeth Gardiner (Mrs. Glendower), **42:** 118-19,n1, 208, 214; **47:** 155
Evans, Henry Clay, **51:** 482-83,n3
Evans, John Morgan, **42:** 21n1
Evans, Lawrence, **42:** 317n3
Evans, Peyton Randolph, **47:** 16,n8
Evansville, Ind., **40:** 246,n2
Everett, Wash., **46:** 144n1
Everett, 1916 and After (Clark), **46:** 144n1
Every Week (New York), **48:** 362n2
Everybody's Magazine (New York), **43:** 477-78,n1, 493n1; **44:** 84; **47:** 540,n1
Evolution of the Labour Party, 1910-1924 (McKibbin), **46:** 435n3
Ewing, Lucy, **44:** 110,n2
Ewing, Robert, **51:** 537,n2
Ewing Christian College, Allahabad, India, **48:** 531n1
Ex-U.S. Minister to Colombia James T. DuBois on Colombia's Claims and Rights, **41:** 293,n1
excess profits tax, **43:** 76-77, 78, 91-92, 350n2, 491; **44:** 182, 337; **49:** 419n1; **51:** 205, 206, 219, 285n1, 286; W. G. McAdoo on, **48:** 122-23, 124, 127; W. B. Wilson on, **48:** 223; H. Hoover on, **48:** 562n1

excise taxes, **43:** 350n2
Experiment in Autobiography (H. G. Wells), **45:** 340n1
Exports Administrative Board, **43:.** 512n2, 518, 519; **44:** 11, 27-28, 119, 284-85, 356, 370; *see also* War Trade Board
exports control bill, **42:** 224,n1; **43:** 315
Exports Council, **42:** 559; **43:** 14, 34-35, 122n1, 512,n2, 518, 535; **44:** 11, 11-12
Extension Magazine (Chicago), **46:** 406n1
Eynon, William John, **48:** 95n1

Fabela, Isidro, **48:** 238n1
Fabens, Tex., **40:** 101
Fabry, Jean, **42:** 186n1, 191n1
Fahey, John Henry, **46:** 92-94, 103-104, 238
Fainsod, Merle, **42:** 199n10
Fair Play for the Government and Whole Truth for the People (Harvey), **42:** 371n1
Fairbanks, Douglas, **47:** 302n2; **51:** 485,n1
Fairchild, Charles Stebbins, **51:** 147n1
Fairhaven, Mass., **48:** 569,n1, 570
Fairley, William R., **44:** 163n1
Fairmount, Minn., **47:** 235
Falck, Edward Frederick, **44:** 77,n1
Falk, Zip S., **40:** 8,n1
Falkenhayn, Erich von, **42:** 160
Fall, Albert Bacon, **51:** 478
'Fall Muehlon'; Bürgerliche Opposition im Obrigkeitsstaat während des Ersten Weltkriegs (Benz), **48:** 213n8
Famous Players-Lasky Corporation, **48:** 313n2
Faneuil Hall, Boston, **44:** 292n2
Far Eastern Affairs, Bureau of, **43:** 458
Far Eastern Committee for the Defense of the Fatherland and the Constituent Assembly, **47:** 99,n5
Far Eastern Review (Peking), **42:** 487
Fargo, N.D., **44:** 170; **47:** 178
Fargo, N.D., *Courier-News,* **44:** 111; **47:** 178
Farley, John Cardinal, **43:** 492, 514; **44:** 12; **48:** 118n1
farm commission (proposed), **46:** 281, 336
Farm Loan Banking System, **46:** 176
Farm Loan Board, **45:** 181
Farm, Stock and Home (Minneapolis), **51:** 212n2
farmers and farming: Funk's analysis of northwestern farmers, **48:** 342-45, 361; and financial aid for seed wheat, **48:** 629,n2,3; and drought aid, **49:** 90-91, 99-100, 101; and wool prices in Ohio, **49:** 277-78; and conservation legislation, **49:** 290-91; and guarantee of wheat prices, **49:** 391-93; WW compares wheat prices to other products, **49:** 433; D. F. Houston on Federal Board of Farm Organization, **49:** 440-

42; and selective service, **51:** 212, 250-51; and Washington State Grange, **51:** 249-50, 257; *see also* agriculture
Farmers and Mechanics National Bank, Philadelphia, **43:** 197
Farmers Loan and Trust Company, N.Y., **43:** 196; **45:** 399n3
Farmers National Committee on Packing Plants and Allied Industries, **51:** 212n2
Farmers' National Committee on War Finance, **49:** 232,n1
Farmers' National Congress, **44:** 257n1
Farmers' National Headquarters, **49:** 289n1, 355; **51:** 212,n1,2
Farmers' Union, **46:** 281n1; **49:** 291
Farquhar, Arthur Briggs, **41:** 558,n3
Farrell, James Augustine, **41:** 556,n1; **42:** 248,n2, 534
Fashoda incident, **47:** 323
Father Duffy's Story: A Tale of Humor and Heroism, of Life and Death with the Fighting Sixty-Ninth, **49:** 546n2
Fatherland party (Germany), **46:** 113n2, 163,n1, 189n7, 266, 267
Favor U.S. Chain of Cotton Warehouses (New York *Journal of Commerce*), **48:** 644n2
Fay, Cyril Sigourney Webster, **48:** 114,n1
Feast of Corpus Christi: cease fire on, **49:** 189, 190
Federación Libre de Trabajadores de Puerto Rico: *see* Free Federation of Workingmen of Puerto Rico
Federal Board of Farm Organization, **46:** 281,n1; **49:** 440-41, 451
Federal Commission on Reconstruction (proposed), **51:** 216n2
Federal Council of Churches of Christ in America, **41:** 353n1; **42:** 323n2; **44:** 362
Federal Farm Loan Board, **42:** 286; **48:** 629n3; **49:** 512,n1
Federal License Act (proposed): *see* License Act
Federal Penal Code, **41:** 277
Federal Power Commission, **45:** 168,n1
Federal Reserve Act, **40:** 77, 78, 476,n4; **42:** 3, 302-303,n1,2; **45:** 325; **49:** 7
Federal Reserve Bank of New York, **41:** 69; **43:** 227; **44:** 382
Federal Reserve Bank of San Francisco, **49:** 120
Federal Reserve banks, **40:** 78-80; **42:** 302n1; **43:** 186; **49:** 504
Federal Reserve Board, **40:** 245, 476,n4; **41:** 317; **42:** 286, 302n1; **43:** 316, 321; **45:** 106; **47:** 357,n1; **49:** 118n1; warns against purchase of Allied notes, **40:** 19n1, 76-80, 87-88, 112, 136, 139; and cost accounting, **40:** 252, 253; and T. D. Jones, **41:** 24; reverses policy and approves foreign loans, **41:** 256-57, 349,n2; and War Emergency Finance Corporation, **45:** 266,n1; and P. M. Warburg, **48:** 171-73; **49:** 218,n1, 222,

236; R. L. Owen on curtailment of credit and, **49:** 6, 7; vacancies on, **49:** 275; W. P. G. Harding on interest rates and, **49:** 503-504; and Mexico and gold, **51:** 66; appointment suggestions, **51:** 443, 486

Federal Reserve System, **42:** 302; **44:** 352; and farmers, **46:** 176

Federal Sugar Refining Company, **45:** 344n1

Federal Trade Commission, **41:** 45-49, 208, 282; **42:** 205,n1, 279, 284, 534, 547; **44:** 64, 73, 223, 444,n1; **45:** 125, 179, 180, 343; **46:** 58, 600; **47:** 49-50, 153, 246,n1, 446; and cost accounting, **40:** 58, 59, 251, 252, 253, 254, 269; and cost of living inquiry, **40:** 103, 519; appointment suggestions for, **40:** 413, 490, 493; **42:** 217, 221, 347,n2; **43:** 492-93, 493, 518; E. N. Hurley resigns from, **40:** 417, 419-20, 427-28; and meat-packing investigation, **41:** 31-32, 37, 84-85, 112, 148, 205-206, 207, 288, 309, 310,n2; **46:** 195, 410, 462,n3, 463; **48:** 7-8, 44, 75-76, 507-11, 562,n1, 564,n1; **49:** 129-30, 130-32, 164,n1, 309, 372,n1, 460-61, 464, 504-505, 509n1, 522-28; **51:** 18, 80, 90,n1, 441-43; and E. Burling, **41:** 93; and W. B. Colver, **41:** 206,n1,2; nominations for, **41:** 255-56; and prices, **43:** 41, 60, 61, 62, 63, 70, 78, 90, 155, 397n1, 491, 520; and War Industries Board reorganization, **46:** 216, 521, 522,n1; W. J. Harris resigns from, **46:** 330, 335; J. E. Davies resigns from, **46:** 609; **47:** 52-53; W. H. Thompson on meat-packing investigation, **47:** 8-9; and coal costs, **47:** 90, 406, 407, 410, 419; and flour costs, **47:** 246n1; on profiteering in war industries, **48:** 487,n1; and copper prices, **48:** 488; WW thanks F. J. Heney for work on, **49:** 215; vacancies on, **49:** 275; Chamber of Commerce report on, **49:** 314-15,n1,2, 430-31, 455-57; and price fixing, **51:** 218-19

Federal Trade Commission Act, **41:** 49, 84

Federal Utilities Advisory Board (proposed), **51:** 92,n1, 173

Federal Water Power Act, 1920, **40:** 207,n1

Federation of Modern Language Teachers, **44:** 364

Federation of Women's Clubs, **48:** 233

Federation of Workers' Syndicates of the Federal District of Mexico, **49:** 29

Feigenwinter, Ernst, **49:** 188-92,n1

Felix Frankfurter and His Times: The Reform Years (Parrish), **49:** 53n1

Fellowship of Reconciliation, **42:** 160,n2; **51:** 12n1

Fels, Mary (Mrs. Joseph), **46:** 494,n2

Felton, Samuel Morse, **43:** 249,n1

Feng, Kuo-chang, **43:** 362,n2, 363

Fennemore, George M., **41:** 279n1

Ferdinand I (of Bulgaria), **46:** 235n1

Ferdinand I (of Rumania), **46:** 235,n1, 326, 373, 568; **47:** 240n1

Ferguson, Charles, **40:** 315,n1, 540-41, 541-42,n4

Ferguson, James Edward, **44:** 42,n3

Fernández, Máximo, **41:** 140,n5

Fernández Guardia, Ricardo, **43:** 160n1

Ferrara, Orestes, **41:** 384,n1, 423; **49:** 6,n3

Ferrero, Giacinto, **47:** 513,n3

Ferris, Scott, **41:** 19, 23; **44:** 121-22, 145; **47:** 82n1; **49:** 304, 309, 510; **51:** 206, 301, 312, 460,n1, 620; and grazing homestead bill, **40:** 192, 263, 290; and water-power legislation, **40:** 287, 424; **45:** 171, 172, 300, 335, 379, 380, 406, 433,n1; **48:** 452-53,n1; **49:** 289, 316, 329, 330, 344,n1, 355-56, 357; **51:** 6,n2, 27; and general leasing bill, **45:** 402,n1, 448,n1, 453, 559; **47:** 402-404, 415, 452; **48:** 170-71, 177; **49:** 482; and wheat amendment to agricultural appropriations bill, **48:** 42, 74, 576; on WW endorsing candidates, **51:** 63, 138-39, 171 39, 171

Ferris oil reserves bill, **45:** 448,n1

Ferris water-power bill, **40:** 207; **45:** 171

Fic, Victor M., **48:** 335n1; **49:** 45n3

Fickert, Charles Marron, **42:** 272n10; **46:** 69,n1

Fidelity Trust Company, Phila., **43:** 197

Field, Carter, **47:** 35n2

Field, Evelyn Marshall (Mrs. Marshall III), **48:** 63n2

Field, Sara Bard, **40:** 379, 426

Field, Woolsey Hopkins, **41:** 141,n12, 142, 143; **47:** 231,n1; **49:** 5-6,n1

Fielder, James Fairman, **47:** 82n1

Fifth Avenue Bank, N.Y., **43:** 196

Fifth Avenue Presbyterian Church, N.Y., **47:** 420n1

Fight and Hold Fast (Davis), **51:** 452,n1

Fighting Fleets: Five Months of Active Service with the American Destroyers and Their Allies in the War Zone (Paine), **48:** 604,n2

Fighting Years: Memoirs of a Liberal Editor (Villard), **51:** 55n1

Filene, Edward Albert, **41:** 68, 250; **49:** 444, 472-73; **51:** 552-53; on Chamber of Commerce's referendum on postwar economic boycott of Germany, **46:** 5-7,n2, 7-8, 14, 62

Final Report of General John J. Pershing, **47:** 166n1

Final Report of the Commission on Industrial Relations, **44:** 261-62,n5

Final Report of the United States Fuel Administrator, 1917-1919 . . . , **45:** 568n1

Final Settlement Must not Be Made Secretly (New York *Herald* [Paris Edition]), **51:** 182,n2

Finance Commitee (Senate), **43**: 491; **48**: 119n2; **51**: 108n9, 204, 206
Finch, James A., **47**: 179,n1,3, 219,n1
Findlay, Sir Mansfeldt de Cardonnel, **49**: 333,n2, 333-34
Fine, Henry Burchard, **40**: 219,n1; **41**: 287-88, 292; **44**: 146; **45**: 254; on military training at Princeton, **47**: 380, 383; on selective service and student exemption, **49**: 242-43
Fine Old Saying (*New York Times*), **42**: 556n3
Finland and Finns, **45**: 84, 418; **46**: 187, 191, 341, 471n3, 533, 568; **47**: 356, 431; **48**: 186, 285n3, 402, 490; **51**: 47, 79n1, 498
Finland, U.S.S., **41**: 187-88
Finley, John Huston, **47**: 32
Finnegan, John Patrick, **40**: 267n1
Finney, Edward Clingan, **41**: 291
Finney, John Miller Turpin, **49**: 235,n1
Finnish Americans, **44**: 262
Fiori, Robert de, **48**: 552-55,n1,6; **49**: 228,n1, 229-30, 231, 436n1; **51**: 229,n1, 230-46
Firm Rule in Ireland. An Intrique with Germany. Many Arrests (London *Times*), **48**: 67,n3
First Baptist Church of Birmingham, **49**: 245n2
First Chief Becomes President (*Springfield*, Mass., *Republican*), **41**: 451n2
First Christian Church of Hickman, Ky., **51**: 395n1
First Liberty Loan Act: *see* Liberty Loan Act, First
First National Bank, Boston, **43**: 196
First National Bank, Cincinnati, **43**: 196
First National Bank, Cleveland, **43**: 196
First National Bank, N.Y., **43**: 196; **48**: 519,n1
First National Bank, Phila., **43**: 197
First National Bank of Lakeville, Minn., **47**: 216n1
First National Bank of Mineola, Tex., **47**: 260n1
First National Fire Insurance Company, **49**: 145n1
First Presbyterian Church, Londonderry, **51**: 74n1
First Presbyterian Church of Raleigh, N.C., **44**: 571n1
First Presbyterian Church of Seattle, **51**: 16n1
First Presbyterian Church of Stamford, Conn., **49**: 420n1
First Presbyterian Church of Wilmington, N.C., **42**: 86-89, 99
First Trust and Savings Bank, Chicago, **43**: 196
Fischer, Fritz, **48**: 114n2
Fish, Frederick Perry, **51**: 523,n1
Fishback, Stanley G., **47**: 484-86, 516
Fisher, Arthur, **47**: 155,n3

Fisher, Frederick Charles, **44**: 8n1
Fisher, H. H., **46**: 457n3; **51**: 100n2, 102n1
Fisher, Irving, **43**: 52; **45**: 133; on prohibition, **42**: 323
Fisher, John Arbuthnot, 1st Baron Fisher of Kilverstone, **43**: 195-96
Fisher, Lola, **44**: 427n1
Fisher, Ludvik J., **45**: 244,n2
Fisher, Walter Lowrie, **41**: 49,n2
Fisheries, Committee on (Senate), **40**: 291, 417; **41**: 207, 230
Fisk, Eugene Lyman, **42**: 323n2
Fisk University, **42**: 321, 322n1
Fiske, Bradley Allen, **45**: 387n1
Fiske, Minnie Maddern (Mrs. Harrison Grey), **47**: 476,n4,5
Fitch, Albert Parker, **42**: 292,n2
Fite, Gilbert Courtland, **43**: 434n2, 512n1; **44**: 17n1; **47**: 276n2
Fitts, William Cochran, **46**: 380,n3
Fitzgerald, John Joseph, **40**: 264, 269; **41**: 309-10,n1; **44**: 147, 158-59, 161; **45**: 422,n2; **46**: 566
Fitzgerald, Richard, **44**: 307
Fitzpatrick, John, **46**: 26,n1, 27; **49**: 136,n1
Fitz-William, Major, **47**: 592,n1
Fiume, **47**: 125,n3; **49**: 789; **51**: 501
Five-Power Consortium, **40**: 512
Five Years of Wilson (*Atlanta Journal*), **46**: 563,n2
Flack, Thomas R., **49**: 519,n8
Flag Day: WW's address on, **42**: 374, 456, 487, 491, 497, 498-504, 520, 521, 523, 525
Flanagan, Catherine Mary, **44**: 110,n2
Flanders, **40**: 410; **44**: 332, 332-33,n1, 480; **45**: 175; **47**: 131, 460; **51**: 265, 333, 384
Flannery, J. Rogers, **46**: 443n1
Fleischman, Harry, **51**: 12n3
Fleming, Robert, **40**: 138
Fleming, William Bowyer, **41**: 5-6,n1, 15; **47**: 295-96,n1, 301
Fletcher, Duncan Upshaw, **40**: 291; **42**: 343n1; **48**: 233; and Alaska general fisheries bill, **41**: 209, 230, 236; and woman suffrage, **45**: 278, 338, 339; **46**: 61, 608; **47**: 34-35,n2, 609; and water-power legislation, **45**: 301; and housing crisis, **46**: 150, 151, 171, 443n1
Fletcher, Frank Friday, **43**: 341n1; **46**: 523,n1
Fletcher, Henry Prather, **40**: 418; **41**: 40, 41, 42, 65, 350-51,n3; **42**: 37-38, 116, 154-55, 324; **43**: 384,n1; **44**: 90,n1; **46**: 327; **49**: 26, 28, 28-29, 29, 141; and Zimmermann telegram, **41**: 288, 297, 391, 391-92; question of presence at V. Carranza's inauguration, **42**: 130-31, 132, 154-55; on Mexican-U.S. relations, **47**: 163-66, 345-47, 357
Fletcher, William Bartlett, **41**: 73n4
Fleurian, Aimé-Joseph de, **44**: 25,n2

Flexner, Eleanor, **45**: 565n3

Flint, Charles Ranlett, **42**: 261,n1, 217

Flint, Leonore, **47**: 155

Flint, Mich., **51**: 91n1

Flood, Henry De LaWarr, **40**: 405n1; **42**: 232; **45**: 582; and armed-ship bill, **41**: 280n1, 294,n1

flood-control bill, **41**: 197-98

Flores, Alfredo Gonzáles: *see* Gonzáles Flores, Alfredo

Florida: and woman suffrage, **51**: 165; politics in, **51**: 632

Florida Federation of Women's Clubs, **46**: 604n3

flour-milling industry, **48**: 487n1

Flynn, Elizabeth Gurley, **45**: 383,n2

Flynn, John William, **41**: 257,n1

Flynn, Joseph Vincent, **45**: 307,n1

Flynn, William James, **41**: 127n1, 214,n1, 215; **42**: 16, 17, 517,n4; **45**: 28, 74, 101,n1

Foch, Ferdinand, **43**: 236n1, 303,n3; **45**: 48, 157, 208; **46**: 241, 439, 453, 511, 559, 590; **47**: 107,n1, 370, 371, 385, 387, 487, 501; **48**: 33, 34, 62, 178, 201, 218, 232, 236, 245, 267-68, 285n1, 286, 353, 358n1, 383, 386, 389, 454, 481, 537,n5, 577, 600; **49**: 43, 52, 136, 260, 261, 335, 338, 339, 341, 342, 369, 533; **51**: 17, 35, 46, 146, 153, 254, 297n1, 305, 338, 388, 414, 462,n2; appointed Supreme Commander, **47**: 160,n1, 181, 182, 209, 262, 309,n6, 348, 349, 443; WW approves and sends congratulations, **47**: 183, 186; thanks WW, **47**: 219; T. H. Bliss on, **47**: 237-38; **49**: 126-27; on Supreme War Council's Abbeville agreement, **47**: 497-98, 512, 517, 563, 585, 595, 615, 618, 619; given authority over Italian troops, **47**: 513,n6; and need for U.S. troops, **48**: 226, 227, 245-46, 252; and intervention in Murmansk and Archangel, **48**: 330, 367, 396-97; and defense of Paris, **48**: 389; on German recall of troops in Russia, **48**: 415; WW requests further information on Russian intervention from, **48**: 421,n1; on Siberian intervention, **48**: 431, 445-46, 470, 496, 500, 501, 504, 505; A. J. Balfour on responsibilities of, **48**: 595; and Italian front, **49**: 336-37; exchanges photographs with WW, **51**: 181,n1, 577-78; and peace negotiations, **51**: 289n1, 434, 464, 473,n1, 511n1, 517, 532, 542, 544n1, 571, 580, 581; on military conditions for armistice, **51**: 463-64; photograph: *illustration section,* **47**

Foerster, Friedrich Wilhelm, **46**: 198,n1,2, 242, 253; **47**: 26,n3,4; **48**: 213, 555,n1; **49**: 229; **51**: 243,n11

Foley, Mrs. F. C., **46**: 407,n1

Folk, John Wingate, **46**: 238n2; **48**: 115,n1; **49**: 210, 216; senatorial contest of, **51**: 138-39, 171, 612

food, **44**: 443-44, 544,n1; WW's statement on exports control and, **43**: 14-15; WW's statement concerning neutrals and, **43**: 122-23; H. Hoover on grain supply, **45**: 58-60, 178; **46**: 304-309; and drought in Texas, **45**: 76-77, 106, 161; and Norway and exports of, **45**: 78-83; and prohibition and brewing industry, **45**: 83-85, 91, 113; conservation of, **45**: 571; problems with railroad transport of, **46**: 32, 394, 424-26, 432; and beef surplus, **46**: 125-26, 565,n1; and wheat crisis, **46**: 214, 345-47, 368, 565,n1, 572-73; and farmers' petition, **46**: 279-81; Reading meets with WW on, **46**: 356; WW on cultivating war gardens, **46**: 439; W. H. Thompson on government takeover of packing industries, **47**: 8-9, 19; W. Kent on livestock and, **47**: 45-51; comparison of clothing prices and, **49**: 375-77; H. Hoover on postwar policies, **51**: 437-38, 635, 638-39; *see also* under the individual food industry, such as meat-packing industry, and specific food product, such as wheat

Food Administration, **42**: 559; **43**: 493,n1; **44**: 36, 37, 89, 146n1, 191n1, 248, 268, 444; **45**: 42, 44, 61, 64, 65, 163n1; **46**: 380n2, 386, 614; **47**: 46, 47, 49, 601; **48**: 137, 138, 168, 175, 306, 306n1; **49**: 440n1, 476; WW on, **42**: 344-46, 485-86, 497, 531-32; H. Hoover on organization of, **42**: 430, 437,n1, 480-85; S. Gompers suggests WW address Congress on, **42**: 488-89; W. Borland on, **42**: 528-29; and Lever bill, **43**: 48-49, 160-61,n1, 208; chief counsel of, **43**: 49n2; and Texas drought and cattle industry, **45**: 76-77, 106, 161; resignations from, **45**: 85; and War Trade Board, **45**: 116-17,n1; and defining reasonable profits, **45**: 124-25, 128,n1; and C. R. Van Hise, **45**: 146-47; poster on conservation arouses criticism, **45**: 246, 256-57; and sugar investigation, **45**: 344n1; and Inter-Allied Shipping Council, **45**: 424; proclamation on food conservation, **46**: 19-21, 109,n2; W. G. McAdoo on Inter-Allied Council having representative from, **46**: 75; and British, **46**: 76-78, 79, 125-26; and grain investigation, **46**: 401, 407; and War Industries Board reorganization, **46**: 477, 521, 522,n1; D. F. Houston on, **46**: 505; F. W. Taussig and Milling Division of, **47**: 208, 224, 225, 255; and meat-packing industry, **48**: 7-8; **49**: 440; and alcohol, **48**: 167; H. Hoover to visit counterparts in Europe, **48**: 308-309, 310-11, 466-67; H. Hoover on monthly reports of, **48**: 313; and Federal Trade Commission's meat-packing report, **49**: 129-30, 130-32; R. Meeker on success of, **49**: 375-76; and price control, **49**: 389-90; and the draft, **49**: 509n1; **51**: 228,n2, 271-72;

Food Administration (*cont.*)
  H. Hoover on export program, **51:** 88-89;
  H. Hoover on price index and, **51:** 357-
  61
Food Administration Grain Corporation,
  48: 306n1
Food and Drug Act, 1906: *see* Pure Food
  and Drug Act
food and fuel control bill, **42:** 294,n2
*Food Investigation. Report of the Federal
  Trade Commission on Flour Milling
  and Jobbing,* **47:** 246n1; **48:** 507,n2
food production bill, **42:** 294,n1
Food Purchase Board, **48:** 8-9; **49:** 509n1
For a Holy War (*The Independent*), **46:**
  14n1
Forbes, Rose Dabney (Mrs. J. Malcolm),
  41: 231,n1, 233
Ford, Cornelius, **41:** 531
Ford, Edsel Bryant, **49:** 438,n1, 498
Ford, Henry, **41:** 90n2, 91, 92n4; **43:** 137,
  189; **44:** 540; **45:** 238n1; **47:** 169-70,
  396, 557; **48:** 43,n1; **51:** 612; and Mich-
  igan's senatorial campaign of 1918, **48:**
  347,n1, 356; **49:** 84,n1, 438-39,n3, 461,
  498; C. R. Crane on shipbuilding, **49:**
  443; gives hospital for government use,
  51: 280,n1
Ford, Henry Jones, **46:** 62, 83, 108-109
Ford, Richard, **51:** 377,n1
Ford Motor Company, **49:** 438n1, 439n3
Fordney, Joseph Warren, **48:** 128,n1
Foreign Affairs, Committee on (House of
  Reps.), **41:** 280,n1, 294,n1; **47:** 474; **49:**
  236n1
Foreign and Domestic Commerce, Bureau of, **43:** 110, 116-17
foreign-language   newspapers,   **44:**
  405,n1, 415, 452, 492-93; **47:** 337;
  A. Konta on Hungarian press, **45:** 139-
  40; and L. Trotsky, **45:** 147n1; on G. Hertling's address, **46:** 163-66; compares
  O. Czernin's and G. Hertling's addresses, **46:** 184-87, 191-93; on strikes
  in Germany, **46:** 267; G. Creel on use of,
  49: 200-201
foreign legions, **42:** 213n1
Foreign Policy Reports, **48:** 417n3,5
Foreign Press Association, **40:** 60n1
Foreign Relations, Committee on (Sen-
  ate), **40:** 405; **41:** 225, 280n1, 478; **42:**
  44, 562; **45:** 601n1; **47:** 416n2, 490-91;
  48: 51; and armed-ship bill, **41:** 318n1,
  328; and W. J. Stone, **41:** 359
foreign trade, **41:** 84; WW on, **40:** 158,
  158-59
forestry: *see* lumber industry
*Formation of the Soviet Union: Commu-
  nism and Nationalism, 1917-1923*
  (Pipes), **46:** 341n4; **48:** 102n1
Forster, Rudolph, **41:** 252, 261, 328, 329,
  445, 448, 449, 531, 557; **42:** 31, 133; **43:**
  104, 284, 505; **44:** 222, 514, 526-27; **45:**
  28, 29, 250; **47:** 143, 147, 527; **48:** 645;
  49: 264-65; and secret service investi-

gation of W. B. Hale, **44:** 480, 481-82,
  527-30
Fort, John Franklin, **41:** 255-56; **42:** 205-
  208, 212, 213, 279; **43:** 61-64, 70, 167-
  68, 176, 397-99, 400, 519-20; **44:** 13; **46:**
  462, 463; and meat-packing investigation, **48:** 7, 44, 75-77, 507-11; **49:** 129-
  30, 130-32, 164n1
Fort Dubuque, Ia., **42:** 321, 357
Fort Leavenworth, Ka., **45:** 18n2; **47:** 486;
  49: 56
Fort Riley, Ka., **48:** 173n1
Fort Sam Houston, Tex., **46:** 339
Fort Sill, Okla., **41:** 469n1; **48:** 160n6
Fort Washington Presbyterian Church,
  N.Y., **47:** 360n1
Fosdick, Raymond Blaine, **43:** 478-79; **45:**
  100,n1,2, 108-109; **47:** 220,n1, 222; **49:**
  156, 384-85, 425-26, 546; declines vice-
  governorship of Philippines, **41:** 417-
  18, 505, 509; and recreational program
  for the army, **41:** 509, 527-28, 537; on
  Negro problem at Newport News, Va.,
  51: 136, 162, 185
Foster, John Watson, **41:** 55n1; death of,
  45: 67,n1
Foster, Martin David, **41:** 23; and water-
  power legislation, **45:** 301, 379, 406,
  433,n1
Foster, Mary Parke McFerson (Mrs. John
  Watson), **45:** 67
Foster, Norman, **47:** 479,n1; **48:** 280
Foulois, Benjamin Delahauf, **43:** 177n1
Four Lights, N.Y., **43:** 165, 481
Four Minute Men, **44:** 248n1, 505,n2,
  505-506
Four Points Address, **47:** 582; outline and
  drafts of, **46:** 273-74, 274-79, 291-97;
  E. M. House and WW edit, **46:** 290-91;
  House on, **46:** 313, 317,n2, 318, 327; delivered to Congress, **46:** 318-24; H. Pindell on, **46:** 331; Charles I replies to, **46:**
  398-99, 440-41; WW answers Charles I
  on, **46:** 486, 508, 551-52; Switzerland
  on, **46:** 592, 593; Dutch on Germany
  and, **46:** 615, 616
four-power consortium (proposed), **48:**
  519-20; **49:** 311, 348
Fourteen Points Address: early mention
  of, **45:** 323-24, 398, 400, 458; background of and Inquiry memorandum,
  45: 459-74; drafts and transcript of, **45:**
  476-86,n1, 493-517; final draft, **45:**
  519-31; WW delivers to joint session of
  Congress, **45:** 534-39; comments on, **45:**
  541, 541-42, 542, 547, 548, 550, 559,
  564, 566, 577,n1, 578, 586, 586-87, 595,
  599; E. M. House on, **45:** 550-59; **46:**
  167, 316, 328; WW's acknowledge-
  ments, **45:** 567, 568,n2, 569, 569-70,
  570, 581, 593; **46:** 4; and Russia, **46:**
  22,n1, 574,n1; **47:** 522,n2; J. J. Jusserand on, **46:** 78, 83; Italian reaction to,
  46: 78, 96, 155-56; P. Scheidemann on,
  46: 113n2; G. Hertling's response to,

46: 110,n1; O. Czernin's response to, **46:** 115n1; comments on Hertling's and Czernin's responses and reaction in Germany and Austria-Hungary, **46:** 162-67, 183-84, 222-29, 274, 274-75, 318-19, 556; WW mentions, **46:** 486, 497, 552; and Japan, **47:** 428-29,n1, 429-30; Fourteen Points: discussed, **51:** 511, 605; WW explains to W. Wiseman, **51:** 349-52; T. Roosevelt repudiates, **51:** 455n1; Lippmann-Cobb memorandum on, **51:** 495-504, 511; G. V. Chicherin on, **51:** 508-509,n2; House on meetings with Prime Ministers on, **51:** 511-12, 568, 569; Allies take issue with freedom of the seas, **51:** 511,n1, 513, 515; newspaper advertisement, **51:** 572-74: *see also* freedom of the seas; league of nations

Fourteenth Amendment, **49:** 89

Fourth of July; WW's message to various ethnic societies for celebration of, **48:** 117; and festivities on trip to Mount Vernon, **48:** 440; WW's address at Mount Vernon, **48:** 448, 514-17, 541, 550, 564; **49:** 125

Fourth Street National Bank, Phila., **43:** 197

Fowler, Wilton B., **40:** 262n1; **43:** 24n1, 278n2

Fox, Albert Whiting, **46:** 355n4, 525-26,n2,3, 527

Fox, John, **44:** 85, 118, 152

Foxcroft, Frank, **41:** 133,n1

Frachtenberg, Leo Joachim, **45:** 92n1, 141n2, 154,n2,3

Frame-up: The Incredible Case of Tom Mooney and Warren Billings (Gentry), **42:** 270n2

France, Joseph Irwin, **41:** 488-89,n1, 510-11; **43:** 139, 146; on bill to mobilize forces, **46:** 325-26,n1, 343

France, **40:** 5, 29, 248; **41:** 77, 388; **42:** 330, 331, 382, 435, 502; **43:** 9, 65, 238, 296, 389, 464, 471, 492n1; **44:** 361n1, 379; **51:** 48, 195; peace terms and, **40:** 13, 15, 16, 186n1, 341, 388, 435, 441, 446n4, 501, 540; **41:** 25, 26n1, 80, 138, 464; **42:** 155, 157, 341-42, 354, 385, 444n1, 456; **51:** 106n7, 262, 263, 264, 273, 454, 455, 463, 614; external debts of, **40:** 76; and arming of merchant ships, **40:** 449, 452-53; war atrocities in, **40:** 482-85; **49:** 497-98; **51:** 135, 215, 216; and banking interests in Mexico, **40:** 519; **41:** 4; and food crisis, **42:** 109; and Russia, **42:** 165, 319,n1; **44:** 297; **45:** 413, 414, 419; **49:** 495,n2; and agreements with Allies, **42:** 327n1; and Polish army, **42:** 352, 432, 552; **43:** 426; **44:** 189, 304; **51:** 447-48; and plans for provisional Polish government, **42:** 544-45; Socialist party in, **42:** 364-65; A. H. Frazier on situation in, **42:** 437-38; W. G. Sharp refutes R. Swing's es-

timate of situation in, **43:** 29-32; army mutinies and morale in, **43:** 30-32,n2,5, 174, 426; **44:** 72, 94; and loans to, **43:** 46-47, 225, 227; A. J. Balfour's proposed Allied treaty and, **43:** 113-14, 126; and Turkey, **43:** 159n1; **51:** 389, 456; and effect of Russian Revolution on, **43:** 275; and Asia Minor, **43:** 355; and Vatican's peace moves, **44:** 24-26, 34, 43-46, 57; **46:** 488; and reaction to G. Michaelis' speech in Reichstag, **44:** 43-44,n6

D. Lloyd George's war plans and, **44:** 126; and recognition of Polish National Committee, **44:** 278; **46:** 120; P. D. Lochridge on military strategy in, **44:** 361n1; politics in, **45:** 54,n1, 222n1; and Norway, **45:** 78-79; and Germany's peace terms, **45:** 412, 416; and British war aims statement, **45:** 487n2; and Fourteen Points address, **46:** 158; and Italy, **46:** 180; **47:** 468; **51:** 41, 43, 135, 386-87, 387-88; and G. Hertling on, **46:** 228; and Rumania, **46:** 373-74; on publishing shipping losses, **47:** 74; Austria-Hungary on annexation desires of, **47:** 126, 239, 240; and troops in Murmansk and Archangel, **47:** 140-41; **48:** 536-37; and critical situation on front lines, **47:** 166, 175, 182, 204, 303; and Belgian relief problems, **47:** 294; and Czechoslovak army, **47:** 551-52; and Abbeville agreement, **47:** 567-68, 616-20; and proposed U.S. war declaration against Bulgaria and Turkey, **47:** 568, 570-71; and Austria-Hungary and Sixtus letter, **47:** 589,n1; J. J. Pershing on U.S. troops in, **47:** 611-12; and woman suffrage, **48:** 24n1, 25-26; Soviets demand recall of ambassador, **48:** 106; F. Foch on location of front line, **48:** 201; G. D. Herron on desire for league of nations in, **48:** 210-12; comments on maximum use of troops, **48:** 243-45, 246, 387-90; and coordination of Allied nonmilitary activities, **48:** 324-29; and combat strength on western front, **48:** 483, 568n1; and loan to China, **48:** 519-20, 521; U.S. troops to be sent to, **48:** 543; and Supreme War Council and Balkan situation, **48:** 545; claims Britain not supplying all the manpower she can, **48:** 568n1; Catholics and the Vatican and, **49:** 189, 190; and league of nations, **49:** 226,n2; and recognition of Czechs as sovereign nation, **49:** 287,n1; and Murmansk Region Council, **51:** 79,n1; W. C. Bullitt on Bolshevism in, **51:** 565-66,n8; revolutionary history of, **51:** 567; and declaration on near eastern liberated territories, **51:** 539-40,n2, 574-75; and issue of intervention in Russia: *see* Russia—Siberia, intervention in; *see also* Alsace-Lorraine; France and the United States

France-America Society, **44:** 141n1
France and the United States, **40:** 139,
226, 532-33; **41:** 354-57, 481, 502; **42:**
84; **43:** 124, 136, 181, 275-76, 304,
364n1, 465; **44:** 69, 462-63, 501-502,
546; **45:** 273, 327; **46:** 87; **48:** 54, 294-95,
317,n2, 355; **49:** 111-12, 149; **50:** 77,
122,n13, 391; **51:** 8; and Federal Reserve Board's warning against purchase of Allied notes, **40:** 19-20,n1, 87-
88, 137,n3; and Statue of Liberty, **40:**
120; and German peace proposal, **40:**
231, 234, 250; WW's peace note of Dec.
18, 1916, **40:** 273-76; R. Lansing's re-
assurances on peace note, **40:** 307n1;
Anglo-French conference and reply to
WW's note, **40:** 439n1, 439-41,n1; W. G.
Sharp on reaction to WW's note, **40:**
481-82, 488-89; and China, **40:** 515; **45:**
98; **49:** 102-103; and interests in Mexico, **40:** 519; R. Poincaré congratulates
WW, **41:** 314; and Bergson mission, **41:**
315-17,n2; and financial and military
needs, **41:** 336-37, 428; **42:** 69-71; and
public opinion on U.S.-German break,
41: 376; and loans, **41:** 479, 517, 518;
44: 281; and Viviani-Joffre mission to
U.S., **41:** 553-54; **42:** 14, 18,n1, 20,n1,2,
120, 123, 127, 132-33; and possible exchange of military missions, **42:** 33,n1;
J. J. Jusserand on British mission and,
42: 128; WW's meetings with mission,
42: 173-76, 182-85, 186-91, 210-12,
300; discussions on sending U.S. expeditionary force to France, **42:** 186-91,
192, 194, 202, 249-51, 300, 325, 373-74,
407, 408-10; **44:** 237, 312; talk of an
American commission to France, **42:**
227-31; and A. Tardieu's mission to
U.S., **42:** 229,n1,2, 374-76, 445; and
Jusserand on WW's absence from reception for French mission, **42:** 233;
R. Viviani on success of French mission, **42:** 299-301; public opinion to-
wards U.S., **43:** 32; and convoys, **43:** 87;
greetings to U.S. on Fourth of July, **43:**
99; WW and reinstatement of Hearst
correspondents in, **43:** 132-33; and inter-Allied Paris conference of July
1917, **43:** 208-209, 236-37,n1, 255-56,
267-70; J. J. Pershing meets with
H. Pétain, **43:** 262-65; and French proposal for a league of nations, **43:** 273,
274, 359-60; State Department on hostile attitude of French ambassador in
China, **43:** 363,n6, 364; F. Frankfurter
report on policies and morale in, **43:**
442-48; Jusserand on answer to Pope's
appeal, **43:** 525; and WW's reply to
Pope, **44:** 40-41; H. F. Bouillon's plan
for inter-parliamentary conference, **44:**
141,n1,2; and shipbuilding issue, **44:**
51, 52, 70, 147-48,n1; invites U.S. to be
on inter-Allied councils, **44:** 195-96,
382, 385; W. Wiseman on, **44:** 230;
ideas of Americans aiding agriculture
and industry in, **44:** 337, 359, 461, 467

E. M. House sent as U.S. representative to Allied Council, **44:** 427, 433,
437-38; and F. C. Howe's memorandum
on an enduring peace, **44:** 475-77; and
formation of Supreme War Council, **45:**
47-48; and Inter-Allied Naval Council,
45: 190; war plans for 1918, **45:** 208-13;
use of U.S. troops, **45:** 248, 328, 372-73,
396, 397, 539-40, 571, 583; **46:** 9, 10, 43,
44, 211-12, 231-32, 337-38; French
need for gasoline and tankers, **45:** 302-
303, 492; G. Clemenceau on, **45:** 337;
J. J. Jusserand on success of House
mission, **45:** 365; and peace terms in Inquiry memorandum, **45:** 467, 467-68,
468, 473, 473-74; and Fourteen Points,
45: 476, 484, 513-14, 527, 537; and bicentennial of founding of New Orleans,
46: 100,n1; L. Colcord on German liberalism and, **46:** 113-14; and G. Creel
on U.S. Bureau of Information, **46:** 202-
203; WW on Allied councils not ex-
pressing political opinions, **46:** 360-
61,n1; and J. R. Mott's work with
French army, **46:** 496; and Inter-Allied
General Reserve, **46:** 558-60; and declaration on Poland, **46:** 587, 587-88;
G. Clemenceau and R. Poincaré to WW
on anniversary of U.S. entry into war,
47: 257-58, 277-78, 290, 291, 301; and
Liberia, **47:** 327, 353; joint Allied request for U.S. troops, **48:** 226-27; and
Blue Devils' visit to U.S., **48:** 307,n1;
T. H. Bliss on U.S. Army, **48:** 601-602;
WW on U.S. military commitment to,
48: 625, 641; and U.S. policy toward
Russia, **48:** 639-43; **51:** 17, 152-53, 209-
10; bridge in Lyon named for WW, **49:**
37,n1; military tonnage aid, **49:** 66, 67,
418-19; gift of Gobelin tapestry to
EBW, **49:** 156-57; T. H. Bliss on contin-
ued French artillery assistance, **49:**
279-80; suggestion to name bridge in
Washington after Marshal Joffre, **49:**
313-14, 314; and suggestion for High
Commissioner to Siberia, **49:** 323,n1;
military success in Lorraine, **49:** 547-
48; WW thanks Poincaré for message
on U.S. Army, **51:** 11; W. G. Sharp on,
51: 21-22,n1; H. F. Hollis on, **51:** 182-
83; W. G. McAdoo on financial situation and postwar reconstruction, **51:**
465-67; and intervention in Russia: *see*
Russia—Siberia, intervention in; Murmansk and Archangel, intervention in
*France et le Concours Américain, Fevrier
1917-Novembre 1918* (Kaspi), **44:** 52n1
Franchet d'Espérey, Louis Félix Marie
François, **51:** 199,n1, 200,n2, 581, 587
Francis, Alexander, **42:** 393,n1, 393-94,
395
Francis, David Rowland, **40:** 544n1; **41:**

408, 409, 415n1, 511, 544; **42:** 36, 37, 164-65,n2, 165, 258; **43:** 14, 150, 298-99; **44:** 270n1, 282, 532; **45:** 185, 220, 275, 427, 562; **46:** 22,n1, 46n3, 341-42, 358, 529-30, 550, 554, 586; **47:** 319-20,n3, 321, 397; **48:** 38, 103, 106, 262-63; **49:** 179, 312n1, 370-71, 517, 518n4; **51:** 31-32, 50; on demonstrations in Russia regarding Mooney case, **42:** 273; on Russian interpretation of WW's Peace without Victory speech, **42:** 318, 319, 320, 326; receives note on Russian Commission, **42:** 368-69,n1; on Russian situation and peace moves, **45:** 119-20, 411-14, 433-35; alleged scandal suggests recall of, **45:** 217-18,n5, 243, 543-45; and John Reed, **46:** 300,n7; and Diamandi incident, **46:** 300n8; and Sisson Documents, **46:** 372,n3; transfers staff from Petrograd to Vologda, **46:** 528,n1; on Bolsheviks and Russian situation, **48:** 112-14, 141-43, 264-65,n1, 276, 277-78; requests additional funds, **48:** 236; on need for supplies and food in Petrograd, **49:** 492, 493; on F. C. Poole and situation in Archangel, **49:** 495-96,n6, 508, 518-19; asks for reinforcements, **51:** 53, 54, 121-22; and American-Slavic legion, **51:** 178,n1

Francis H. Leggett and Company, **48:** 484n1

Francis Joseph I (of Austria), **45:** 463; death of, **40:** 34, 113-14

Francis W. Parker School, Chicago, **47:** 391,n1, 447-49, 477

Francke, Kuno, **43:** 410

Frank D. Beattys and Company, N.Y., **43:** 85n1

Frankfurt, S.M.S., **51:** 490

Frankfurter, Felix, **40:** 444; **42:** 462, 475, 486; **43:** 159,n1,2, 201, 206, 435, 460; **44:** 121, 149, 184, 217, 226, 298; **46:** 494; **47:** 425-26; **49:** 25, 26, 53,n1, 545; report on France, **43:** 442-48; and President's Mediation Commission, **44:** 104, 120, 161-64, 214, 520; **46:** 128-47; on meatpackers' labor settlement, **45:** 356; and Mooney case report, **46:** 68-74; on report on wage and hour stabilization, **51:** 363-67

Frankfurter Zeitung, **46:** 165, 267, 403

Franklin, Benjamin, **43:** 449; **45:** 130

Franklin, Philip Albright Small, **41:** 188,n1, 364, 369, 371; **47:** 66,n1

Franklin D. Roosevelt: The Apprenticeship (Freidel), **42:** 449n1; **44:** 303n1

Franklin K. Lane's Idea for Veterans' Colonization, 1918-1921 (Reid), **51:** 103n3

Franklin National Bank, Phila., **43:** 197

Franz Ferdinand, Archduke of Austria, **42:** 335

Frayne, Hugh, **43:** 25,n2, 26, 192, 341n1; **46:** 523; **47:** 495

Frazer, Lady, **42:** 394n4

Frazier, Arthur Hugh, **41:** 373, 376, 466,n2; **42:** 437-39; **43:** 275-76; **44:** 462; **46:** 233, 237, 388-89, 429; **47:** 86, 86-87, 108, 122; **49:** 404, 423; instruction for reporting Supreme War Council's activities, **46:** 254-56; and Supreme War Council meetings, **47:** 18, 59-60, 73-74, 74-76, 102, 505

Frazier, John Brown, **46:** 260,n2

Frazier, Lynn Joseph, **40:** 549,n1; **47:** 438,n1

Frear, Aaron H., **42:** 422,n1

Frederick the Great (Frederick II of Prussia), **42:** 335, 336; **51:** 331

Frederick VIII, S.S., **41:** 195n1

Free Federation of Workingmen of Puerto Rico, **40:** 146n1, 146-53, 213-14; **47:** 543,n1, 577; **48:** 35; **49:** 26, 297

freedom of speech, **42:** 118-19, 153; **43:** 421; **44:** 192; M. Eastman on, **44:** 170-72; G. Macfarland on, **44:** 366; W. Lippmann on, **44:** 393; WW on, **44:** 397; U. Sinclair on, **44:** 468; and *Masses* case, **48:** 59,n1,2: see also censorship

freedom of the press, **42:** 106-108; **44:** 266; M. Eastman on, **44:** 170-72; O. G. Villard on, **44:** 271-73

freedom of the seas, **51:** 47, 326, 349-50, 495-96, 511-12, 513, 515, 533, 569, 575, 581, 592, 594, 605, 613-14, 615, 633-34

Freeman, Henry R., **48:** 136,n1, 177n1

Freidel, Frank, **42:** 449n1; **44:** 303n1

Frelinghuysen, Joseph Sherman, **40:** 196,n3; **46:** 36

French, Francis Henry, **45:** 111,n14

French, John Denton Pinkstone, 1st Earl of Ypres and High Lake, **42:** 372,n2; **48:** 67,n2,3, 68; **49:** 545,n1

French, Thomas A., **43:** 231, 373, 393,n1, 419

French and American Independence (Jusserand), **48:** 491,n1

French Revolution, **41:** 302-303; **51:** 323

French Union for Woman Suffrage, **48:** 303

Frenzied Finance (Lawson), **40:** 349n11

Fresca, Carlo. **45:** 383,n2

Fresh Courage for Fearful Saints (Ogden), **51:** 296-97,n1

Fribourg, Switzerland, **49:** 193

Fribourg *La Liberté,* **49:** 188

Frick, Henry Clay, **44:** 290,n2

Fried, Alfred Herman, **47:** 65,n5

Friedberg, Robert, **45:** 34,n11

Friedensaktion der Meinlgruppe, 1917-18 (Benedikt), **46:** 198n1,2

Friedensappell Papst Benedikts XV. vom 1. August 1917 und die Mittelmächte (Steglich, ed.), **44:** 44n6, 351n2

Friedenspolitik der Mittelmächte 1917/18 (Steglich), **47:** 64n2

Friedjung, Heinrich, **41:** 56n2

Friedman, Isaiah, **45:** 149n2

Friedreich, August, **47:** 274-75

Friedrich Der Grosse, S.M.S., **51:** 490

Friedrich Wilhelm Viktor August Ernst, Crown Prince of Prussia, **49:** 399, **51:** 239,n7
Friend, Arthur S., **48:** 313n2
Friendly Sons of St. Patrick, **48:** 466n1
Friends, Society of: *see* Quakers
Friends Intelligencer, **41:** 304n
Friends of German Democracy: *see* Society of Friends of German Democracy
Friends of Irish Freedom, **43:** 217, 509-10; **48:** 118n1
Friends of Reconstruction Unit, **43:** 492,n1; **44:** 74, 75; **47:** 524
Friendship Under Stress (Meier), **44:** 484n1, 486n3, 489n5
Fries, Henry Elias, **49:** 450,n1
Frissell, Hollis Burke, **40:** 221-22, 293
Friuli, Italy, **44:** 549
Froelicher, Betty, **47:** 455
Froelicher, Frances Mitchell (Mrs. Hans), **47:** 454-55,n1
Froelicher, Hans, **47:** 453,n1,4, 454, 454-55,n1, 537n1
Froelicher, Hans III, **47:** 455
From Equal Suffrage to Equal Rights: The National Woman's Party, 1913-1923 (Lunardini), **44:** 561n8
From the Dreadnought to Scapa Flow: The Royal Navy in the Fisher Era 1904-1919 (Marder), **49:** 411n1; **51:** 124n2
Frontiers of Freedom (N. D. Baker), **48:** 30,n1
Frost, Richard H., **42:** 270n2; **44:** 274n1
Frost, Wesley, **40:** 38
Frothingham, Thomas Goddard, **43:** 79n1
Fryatt, Charles, **40:** 440; **51:** 326
Frye, William Pierce, **40:** 182,n1
Frye case, **41:** 284,n2
Fuel Administration, **45:** 61, 64, 66, 269, 343; **46:** 214; **47:** 405-11, 601; **48:** 24, 137; **49:** 53, 54, 367; **51:** 261; conservation order brings protest, **46:** 12,n1, 16, 18, 19, 23-24; WW on proclamation of, **46:** 25, 36; and N.Y. theaters, **46:** 28,n1, 41; and War Industries Board, **46:** 477, 521, 522,n1; and Colorado coal prices, **46:** 600, 610,n2; and railroad fuel question, **48:** 22-24, 81-93; and prohibition of use of fuel oil at country clubs, **48:** 643,n1; relationship with coal operators, **51:** 111-12,n3, 113-15, 116n1, 138; *see also* coal industry
Full Crew law, Pa., **43:** 21
Fuller, Melville Weston, **44:** 85
Fulton, John Farquhar, **41:** 482n3
Fund for the French Wounded, **43:** 415
Fundamental Social and Political Problems of Porto Rico (Yager), **48:** 36n1
Funk, Antoinette, **48:** 342-45,n1, 361
Funston, Eda Blankart (Mrs. Frederick), **41:** 259
Funston, Frederick, **40:** 100-101, 109, 123, 202-203, 476: **41:** 237; **42:** 139; death of, **41:** 259,n1
Furlong, Wesley J., **42:** 116

Furness, Marmaduke, 2nd Baron Furness of Grantley, **41:** 346,n1
Fürstenberg, Prince Karl Emilzu, **46:** 397,n2, 411-12, 418, 473,n1, 551-53; **47:** 124
Furuseth, Andrew, **51:** 587, 593, 610

Gadsden, Philip Henry, **48:** 598n1
Gaillard, David Dubose, **43:** 199,n2
Gaillard Cut, **43:** 199n1
Gajda (Gaida), Rudolf, **49:** 479,n1, 529n1, 543,n1,2, 544; **51:** 95, 99, 100-101, 609; photograph, *illustration section,* 49
Galicia, **41:** 220n4; **42:** 335; **43:** 523; **44:** 6, 21; **45:** 412, 459; **48:** 553; **51:** 501, 580
Gallagher, Thomas, **48:** 312,n1, 551n2
Gallatin, Albert (Abraham Alfonse), **42:** 28
Gallauner, Edmund, **51:** 175,n1
Gallego, Mex., **40:** 100
Gallenga-Stuart, Count Romeo Adriano, **49:** 64,n3
Gallinger, Jacob Henry, **41:** 11n1; **46:** 606n1; **51:** 155n1, 305n1, 537n2
Gallipoli, **43:** 115; **44:** 239n1; **45:** 72, 459
Galloo Island, Lake Ontario, **42:** 491,n1
Galloway, Charles Mills, **41:** 546,n1, 547-48; **45:** 336, 337
Gallup, New Mex., **43:** 340, 352, 353
Galt, Sterling, **47:** 217-18,n1
Galveston, Tex., **42:** 566; **48:** 238, 247-48, 280
Gama, Domicio da, **42:** 14,n1, 15, 81, 99-100, 105, 314, 314-15, 548-49; **43:** 11-12,n1
Game of Life and Death: Stories of the Sea (Colcord), **40:** 380,n2
Gamp-Massaunen, Baron Karl von, **46:** 191,n2
Gankin, Olga Hess, **46:** 457n3
Gannon, James Alonzo, **44:** 561,n7
García, Jesus y, **47:** 578-79
Gard, Warren, **42:** 245n2
Gard amendment, **42:** 343, 370n1
Gardener, Helen Hamilton (Mrs. Selden Allen Day), **42:** 237,n2, 269-70, 293, 474-75; **43:** 214-15,n1, 284-85; **44:** 523; **45:** 121, 277, 278, 306-307, 565; **46:** 608; **47:** 547; **49:** 264, 268-69, 304-305; **51:** 288, 294; and woman suffrage, **48:** 271, 303n1, 340-41, 347, 400-401, 404
Gardener, William Gwynn, **44:** 559-61,n1, 562; **45:** 39
Gardiner, Alfred George, **40:** 35,n3, 192
Gardner, Augustus Peabody, **40:** 494
Gardner, Frederick Dozier, **43:** 437,n1; **49:** 444-45,n1
Gardner, Gilson, **43:** 201-202
Gardner, Matilda Campbell Hall (Mrs. Gilson), **43:** 201n1
Garfield, Belle Hartford Mason (Mrs. Harry Augustus), **40:** 238; **44:** 65
Garfield, Harry Augustus, **40:** 238, 314, 334, 560; **41:** 344, 423-24, 468-69; **42:** 35, 214, 222, 495, 522-23; **43:** 25; **44:** 33,

36, 65, 89n1, 107, 144, 444, 474, 478, 498; **45:** 148n1, 173, 570; **46:** 3, 151n2, 219n5, 317, 444n2, 522,n1; **47:** 7, 43, 558-59,n1; **48:** 247, 612-13, 638; **49:** 3, 53, 144-45, 147, 173, 181, 225, 230, 424-25,n1, 461, 550; **51:** 116,n1, 302, 407, 411, 416; on keeping out of war, **41:** 101-102, 487-88; on coal prices, **44:** 450-52, 453; **45:** 176,n1; **46:** 599-601, 610,n2; **47:** 89-90; **48:** 148,n1; and Lansdowne letter, **45:** 173; and Alabama coal situation, **45:** 269, 276, 568,n1; on WW's State of the Union address of 1917, **45:** 215, 221; on draft exemptions, **45:** 547n1, 583, 585, 594; comments on coal conservation order of, **46:** 12,n1, 16, 18, 19, 23-24, 25, 28, 30, 33, 36, 41; and Hitchcock resolution to delay coal order, **46:** 31,n2; defends coal order, **46:** 31-33; death of mother, **47:** 8,n1, 35; and railroad fuel price question, **47:** 172, 241, 405-11, 419; **48:** 22-24, 31, 95; on oil prices, **47:** 404, 413; insists Allied representatives meet in Washington, **48:** 296-97; on intervention in Russia, **48:** 297-98; and prohibition of use of fuel oil at country clubs, **48:** 643,n1; on coal production, **48:** 646-47; urges WW to make western trip, **49:** 452; on anthracite coal strike and wage issue, **51:** 19, 545; and relationship between coal operators and Fuel Administration, **51:** 111-12,n3, 113-15, 138; photograph, *illustration section,* 44
Garfield, James Abram, **42:** 89; **46:** 314; **49:** 246
Garfield, James Rudolph, **48:** 279n5; **49:** 230,n1
Garfield, Lucretia Rudolph (Mrs. James Abram), **47:** 8,n1, 35
Garlington, Ernest Albert, **45:** 11,n1
garment industry: prices and, **49:** 375-77, 389-90
Garner, H. C., **51:** 193
Garner, John Nance, **41:** 84, 85; **42:** 21n1, 260-61; **48:** 119n2
Garnsey, Cyrus, Jr., **47:** 89
Garrecht, Francis Arthur, **44:** 345,n7
Garrett, Alonzo G., **41:** 236n1
Garrett, Daniel Edward: and woman suffrage, **45:** 307,n1; and water-power legislation, **45:** 301, 433,n1
Garrett, John Work, **40:** 113; **45:** 327
Garrett, Thomas Harrison, **42:** 168,n2
Garrigue, Charlotte: *see* Masaryk, Charlotte Garrigue
Garrison, Lindley Miller, **41:** 197; **48:** 52
Garrison, William Lloyd, **44:** 168
Garrod, William Heathcote, **42:** 266,n1
Garstin, Dennis, **47:** 319,n7
Gary, Elbert Henry, **42:** 534; **45:** 342-43; **51:** 150-51, 172
Gasparri, Pietro Cardinal, **40:** 556-57; **44:** 347,n2; **45:** 330,n1; **51:** 296
Gaston, Roy James, **47:** 260,n1

Gaunt, Guy (Reginald Archer), **40:** 60; **41:** 196, 214, 215; **42:** 142n1, 143; **46:** 438
Gavit, John Palmer, **40:** 29, 36, 40-42, 86, 91, 110-11, 124, 125-27, 164, 236; **41:** 32-33, 55, 467-68; **43:** 175; **49:** 128-29, 184; birthday wishes to WW, **45:** 395-96, 423; concern over health in training camps, **45:** 421-22,n1, 452, 453, 491-92; on censorship, **51:** 483, 521
Gavronsky, Jacob O., **48:** 376,n3
Gay, Edwin Francis, **46:** 309,n1; **48:** 484,n1
Gaylord, Winfield Romeo, **42:** 198,n7, 199, 253-54
Geddes, Sir Eric Campbell, **44:** 86-97,n3; **45:** 19-20,n1, 127; **47:** 73-74,n1, 172; **48:** 385,n4, 536-37, 565, 599; suggestions for U.S. shipbuilding, **49:** 410-13,n1; criticizes U.S. for not giving enough naval support, **51:** 124,n2, 179, 279-80; and peace terms, **51:** 313, 315,n3, 315-16, 325-26, 326, 327, 517, 594, 633-34
Geddes Deplores Peace Discussion (*New York Times*), **51:** 315n3
Geiger, Louis George, **48:** 115n2
Gelfand, Lawrence Emerson, **44:** 275n1; **45:** 459n1
Geliebler, Tucket [Tucker?], P., **44:** 79
General Assembly of the Presbyterian Church in the United States [Southern], **45:** 282,n1,2
General Board of the Navy, **40:** 506-507; **41:** 362, 428, 430, 432,n1; **43:** 345; **44:** 177, 465, 477; **51:** 344,n1
general deficiency appropriations bill, **41:** 319, 329
General Education Board, **47:** 289n2
General Electric Company, **41:** 113n1; **47:** 272n1; **48:** 375; **49:** 133, 290n3
General Federation of Trade Unions (Great Britain), **46:** 21,n2, 37, 356n6
general leasing bill, **40:** 544, 545, 560n1; **41:** 19, 64-65, 278, 290; **42:** 561; **43:** 36, 75,n1; **45:** 171, 172, 374-78, 402, 420-21, 453-54, 559; **48:** 170-71, 177; **49:** 481-85, 511; and Swanson amendment, **47:** 402, 415; S. Ferris on, **47:** 402-404; E. T. Thomas on, **47:** 451-52
General Munitions Board, **42:** 48, 138, 412, 498; **43:** 25,n1, 148n1
general staff bill, **41:** 481; **42:** 19, 76
General Supply Commission, **42:** 412
General Theological Seminary, **47:** 289n2
General Wood's Case (*Springfield*, Mass., *Republican*), **48:** 242,n1
Geneva, Switzerland: mentioned as possible site for peace conference, **51:** 516
Geneva, University of, **44:** 484n1; **48:** 210
Geneva *Nouvelliste*, **43:** 435n1
Gentry, Curt, **42:** 270n2
Geological Survey, (U.S.), **48:** 85
George III (of Great Britain), **40:** 64, 66
George V (of Great Britain), **40:** 319; **41:**

George V (of Great Britain) (*cont.*)
348n3; **42:** 82-83, 127, 355, 391n1; **43:**
482; **44:** 202, 411, 439; **45:** 4; **47:** 388n1;
48: 365-66, 366; **49:** 69, 70, 137, 302,
336; **51:** 39, 288-90, 422; message to
WW on anniversary of U.S. entry into
war, **47:** 265-66, 271, 309; on good Anglo-American relations, **47:** 596-97
George, James Zachariah, **43:** 369,n2
*George D. Herron and the European Set-
tlement* (Briggs), **40:** 540n1; **48:** 555n6
George Washington (Wilson), **47:** 421,n1
*George Washington, Fondateur des États-
Unis (1732-1799)* (Roth, trans.), **47:**
421,n1
Georgetown University School of Law,
44: 559n3
Georgia, **41:** 217; **44:** 107; **45:** 236; and
judgeship appointment in, **43:**
162,n2,3; senatorial contest in, **46:** 330;
47: 192, 312,n2, 325,n1, 382,n1; **49:** 80-
82, 114-16, 143, 205-206, 237,n1,
369,n1, 528,n1; politics in, **51:** 57, 632
Georgia, University of, **48:** 455n1
Georgia, Florida, and Alabama Railroad,
43: 530-32; **44:** 22-23, 82,n1, 90,n1, 106,
145, 198, 431
Gerard, James Watson, **40:** 21, 411, 429,
446; **41:** 70-71, 72, 127, 164, 183, 298;
42: 520-22; **43:** 404; **44:** 44; **48:** 311,n1;
news leaks and, **40:** 123, 130; W. J.
Bryan's peace plans and, **40:** 131-32,
137; departs for Germany, **40:** 132, 172;
J. H. Bernstorff on, **40:** 133; and German reply to WW's note, **40:** 331; meets
with Bethmann Hollweg on Allied reply, **40:** 383-84; gives indiscreet speech
on German-American relations, **40:**
461, 463,n1; on all-out submarine warfare, **40:** 552-53; **41:** 4, 78-80; on situation in Germany, **40:** 554-55; recall of,
41: 99, 111, 116, 124; meets with Bethmann Hollweg and Zimmermann on
German peace terms, **41:** 137-38; tem-
porary detention of by Germany, **41:**
195,n1, 240,n2, 502n1; on WW's war
message, **41:** 558; applies for ambassadorship, **49:** 423, 424
Gerard, Mary Daly (Mrs. James Watson),
40: 84; **48:** 63
Gercke (servant), **47:** 316,n2
Gerlach, Rudolph, **41:** 435,n5
German-American newspapers, **43:** 243,
247,n2; **44:** 236, 265, 318n1, 452
German Americans, **40:** 389; **41:** 208n1,
526, 556; **42:** 34,n1, 83-84; **43:** 86n2,3,
117, 134, 410; **44:** 39, 154-55, 190, 236;
45: 270, 455; **46:** 612-13; **47:** 19,n1, 141-
42, 274-75,n2, 275-76,n2,4, 324, 337,
360-61, 391-92, 394, 453n4, 518-20,
559,n2; fear confiscation of savings, **41:**
132; WW reassures, **41:** 157-58; attacks
against, **43:** 323-24,n1, 336; and P. M.
Warburg, **48:** 171-73
German Club of Cleveland, **42:** 34n1

German Consul-General at San Fran-
cisco sentenced for neutrality violation
(*Commercial and Financial Chronicle*),
41: 107
German East Africa, **51:** 514, 515
German intrigue in the United States,
43: 5, 103-104, 133-34,n1,2, 158, 168,
215-18,n5, 256, 395
German language, **44:** 364-65; **49:** 360n2;
controversy over teaching of, **46:**
459,n1, 491; **47:** 311,n1, 337; **48:** 192;
51: 259, 295
German Methodists in U.S., **46:** 612-13
German Naval Mutinies of World War I
(Horn), **45:** 33n8; **51:** 541n1
German Plot (*Springfield*, Mass., *Repub-
lican*), **41:** 451n2
German propaganda in the U.S., **41:** 347,
348; **45:** 137-38; **47:** 141-42, 238,
276,n2,3; in Switzerland, **47:** 219-
20,n1; in Mexico, **47:** 345,n3
*German Propaganda in the United
States, 1914-1917* (Hirst), **43:** 134n2
German Publishing Company, **44:** 493
*German Rulers Will Make a Stupid and
Disastrous Mistake if they Refuse to
Recognize the President's Reasonable
and Generous Terms of Peace* (*New
York American*), **44:** 307n1
Germany, **40:** 30n1, 404, 515, 527, 528;
45: 255, 461; **46:** 574; **47:** 590-91; **48:**
228,n1, 284; food situation in, **40:** 142-
44, 435, 485, 488, 555; **41:** 190, 227; **47:**
524; submarine warfare, **40:** 75, 144-
45, 478,n1, 506; Zeppelin warfare, **40:**
145-46; dispatch to Austria-Hungary,
July 1914, **40:** 204; J. H. Bernstorff on
England and, **40:** 213; British reaction
to December 1916 peace proposals of,
40: 229,n1, 247-48, 249, 342,n4; E. N.
Hurley on cost accounting and, **40:** 251;
J. Bryce on, **40:** 468-69; trench warfare,
40: 484-85; A. J. Balfour on, **40:** 501-
502; **42:** 329, 337-38, 340-41; and Costa
Rica, **41:** 142, 144; **46:** 450; and China,
41: 182-83, 185-87, 229-30,n1; **42:** 61;
and Mexico, **41:** 365, 459, 545-46; **42:**
92-93, 116, 225; **47:** 163-66, 165,n2,
474-75,n2, 552-53; **48:** 135, 238,n1,
278; **49:** 26-27, 30, 138, 153, 280,n2,
300; and Russia, **42:** 11-12, 36-37, 463-
65; **43:** 28n1, 471; **45:** 73, 282, 288-92,
316, 373, 393, 436, 442-47, 465; **48:** 61,
102-104,n1, 179-81, 184-85, 239-40,
299-300, 398-99,n1, 406-10, 498; **49:**
94-95, 197; **51:** 543, 602; Reichstag
"peace resolution," **43:** 185,n1,2; G. Michaelis succeeds Bethmann Hollweg as
Chancellor, **43:** 185,n1; and Cuba, **43:**
207; British War Cabinet memoran-
dum on submarine campaign of, **43:**
375-78; and N. Angell on calling Allied
conference to plan postwar association,
43: 401-409; and Poland, **44:** 4-6; **46:**
48-49; **49:** 382-83

R. Lansing on not trusting, **44:** 20-21; and G. Michaelis' speech in Reichstag, **44:** 43-44,n6; and Pope's peace appeal, **44:** 43-44,n6; and Argentina, **44:** 131, 140,n3, 164,n1, 181; and Sweden, **44:** 131, 140,n3, 164,n1, 412,n3; and Japan, **44:** 252; **45:** 393-94; **47:** 429, 430, 459; peace terms of, **44:** 318-20, 325; **45:** 384n2, 412, 415-17,n5, 433-35; **47:** 24-26; reply to Pope's appeal, **44:** 348-51; and official mail for neutrals, **44:** 412,n3; military advance into Italy, **44:** 506-509; **45:** 37-38; appoints new chancellor, **44:** 548,n2; J. C. Grew on political situation in, **45:** 30-37; and Norway, **45:** 81-82, 114; **49:** 333-34; and Turkey, **45:** 123-24; Lansdowne on, **45:** 173n1; railroads in, **45:** 310; and fear of postwar commercial economic isolation, **45:** 354-55, 462; and Brest-Litovsk peace talks and treaty, **45:** 384,n2, 411-12, 595,n2,3; **46:** 471,n3, 567; Austria will not abandon, **45:** 430-31; L. Colcord on liberalism in, **46:** 113-14; and propaganda in Italy, **46:** 157, 159-60, 376-77; general strikes in, **46:** 172, 184, 185-86, 225, 266-68, 310-13; and Austria-Hungary, **46:** 172-73, 271, 322, 473, 589-90; and comparison of G. Hertling's and O. Czernin's addresses, **46:** 183-93, 222-29; political situation in, **46:** 183-93, 557, 567-69; Von Muehlon on, **46:** 253-54; W. E. Walling on revolutions and, **46:** 310-13; and Sisson Documents, **46:** 341,n1; and armored aircraft, **46:** 434; Netherlands and, **46:** 615-17; **47:** 564-65; **49:** 548n1; military tactics and strategy of, **47:** 204, 243, 338-41, 366, 617-18; WW on decision making in, **47:** 268-70; and proposed suffrage reform in Prussia, **47:** 524,n1; and reconstruction plans, **47:** 530-31; WW on peace moves of, **48:** 54; and involvement in Ireland, **48:** 63-65, 65-66, 67-69, 192; G. D. Herron on possible peace moves by, **48:** 214-16; and woman suffrage, **48:** 304, 340; recalls some troops from Russia, **48:** 415; military strength on western front, **48:** 483, 568n1; R. L. Owen on commercial boycott of, **48:** 506,n1; and De Fiori-Herron peace talks, **48:** 552-55,n1,6,7; **49:** 228,n1, 229-30, 231, 436n1; R. von Kühlmann's attempt at peace negotiations with British, **48:** 555,n7; Catholics in, **49:** 190, 193; Bavaria's peace moves and, **49:** 228, 229-30; J. J. Pershing on certain defeat of, **49:** 404; and Bulgaria, **49:** 436n1; T. H. Bliss on possible peace proposals by, **51:** 46-47; training additional troops, **51:** 87; and Supreme War Council's note on Allied military policy, **51:** 195-203; R. De Fiori on military offensive of, **51:** 234, 235; resignation of Hertling and formation of coalition government, **51:** 253n1; inaugural speech of Prince Max von Baden, **51:** 269,n1; and Allied opinion on armistice terms, **51:** 272-75; W. Solf's attempt to oppose evacuation terms, **51:** 345-46, 348; WW on German colonies, **51:** 350; and evacuation of Belgium, **51:** 370-71,n2, 371-72,n1; press statement on hopeless military situation, **51:** 384-85; Pershing on armistice terms, **51:** 454-55; naval terms of armistice, **51:** 488-92; proposed final naval attack, **51:** 541n1; mutinies and peace riots in, **51:** 607; W. C. Bullitt on Bolshevik movement in, **51:** 622; *see also* Belgian deportations; Germany and the United States; World War

Germany and Belgium (Muehlon), **48:** 213n8

Germany and the Next War (Bernhardi), **40:** 487,n6,7

Germany and the Revolution in Russia, 1915-1918; Documents from the Archives of the German Foreign Ministry (Zeman, ed.), **48:** 398n1

Germany and the United States, **41:** 431; **43:** 26; **45:** 101n1, 358; **50:** 249, 391; and comments on peace prospects, **40:** 5-6,n2, 10-20, 21n1, 94, 134; and *Marina* and *Arabia* incidents, **40:** 38, 190-91, 191-92; and request for U.S. loan, **40:** 60, 62; possibility of severing relations, **40:** 65-66, 190-91, 378, 390; **41:** 3; German criticism of J. W. Gerard, **40:** 133; J. C. Grew reports conditions in, **40:** 141-46, 428-36; German peace offer, **40:** 231-32, 234-36; **45:** 415-17,n5; U.S. reply to German offer, **40:** 242-43, 250; WW's peace note of Dec. 18, 1916, **40:** 273-76; Lansing on submarine warfare, **40:** 313-14; and U.S. travel on seas, **40:** 316; reply to U.S. note, **40:** 331; reactions to German reply, **40:** 337, 353; and WW's secret negotiations with, **40:** 362-65, 477-78, 493, 504n1, 505-506, 507-508, 516-17, 524, 525-26, 528-29; Bethmann Hollweg on Allied reply to German offer, **40:** 383-84,n1; *U-53* affair and U-boat activities, **40:** 388-89, 405; N. Buxton on, **40:** 416-17; German decision for unrestricted submarine warfare, **40:** 448-52, 528-29,n1, 552-53; **41:** 59-63, 74-76, 76-78, 79-80, 80-82, 95-96; and Gerard's indiscreet speech, **40:** 461, 463,n1, 506; U.S. seeks statement of terms, **41:** 17, 18, 24-26, 51-52; Bernstorff on submarine warfare, **41:** 25; German refusal to state peace terms publicly, **41:** 59-63; Lansing on armed merchant ship question, **41:** 71-73, decision to send Bernstorff home, **41:** 87-88,n1; Lansing advocates break between, **41:** 96-99, 99-100; J. S. Williams on, **41:** 107-108; break in diplomatic relations, **41:** 111; Lansing in-

Germany and the United States (*cont.*)
forms neutrals of break, **41:** 116; reactions to break, **41:** 118-25, 126-27, 128, 216, 235, 376; alleged plot to assassinate WW, **41:** 127,n1; Gerard meets with Bethmann Hollweg and Zimmermann on peace terms, **41:** 137-38; G. Barthelme interprets U.S. sentiment for Germany, **41:** 149-51; and detention of Gerard and search of wives of American officials, **41:** 195-96, 240,n2, 282; efforts to restore relations between, **41:** 201-203, 203-204, 204-205, 242-46, 273, 273-77; and German intrigue in U.S. and abroad, **41:** 201,n1, 390, 502,n1, 523, 524-25; and Zimmermann telegram, **41:** 280-82, 322-27; and arming of U.S. merchantmen, **41:** 341-44, 360-61, 368-69, 369-72, 395-98, 534-35; German attacks on U.S. ships, **41:** 425,n1, 429, 431, 436; Lansing urges WW to enter war, **41:** 425-27; cabinet unanimously advocates war declaration, **41:** 436-44; and German submarines in American waters, **41:** 466n1, 473, 541, 556; and German threat to treat crews of armed ships as pirates, **41:** 496,n2; D. Lawrence on, **41:** 513-14

WW's war message to Congress, **41:** 519-27; and performance of German opera in the U.S., **42:** 7-8, 8-9; and seizure of German ships in U.S. ports, **42:** 9-10, 13, 27-28,n1, 29, 59, 98, 113,n1, 116-17, 133-34; **43:** 89,n1; and Prussian-American treaties, **42:** 10; A. J. Balfour and WW discuss, **42:** 140-41; and American Socialist party, **42:** 197-99; WW clarifies statement on Germany in Red Cross speech, **42:** 323-24, 326; E. M. House on Germany not stating peace terms, **42:** 425; and R. L. Owen's proposed peace-terms resolution, **42:** 444,n1; WW on how U.S. was forced into war, **42:** 499-504; W. H. Page on submarine warfare, **42:** 546-47; and idea of editorial forum in New York *World* and *Berliner Tageblatt*, **43:** 184, 219-20, 238, 285, 411-12; and transfer of Germans interned at Ellis Island, **43:** 239-40,n1; Lansing on Pope's appeal and, **43:** 523-24; alleged German plot to make war on the U.S., **44:** 74, 118; V. Ridder suggests sending German-American delegates to Germany, **44:** 154-55, 190; WW on not discussing peace now, **44:** 309; F. C. Howe on planning for an enduring peace, **44:** 475-77; WW on German objectives, **45:** 12-14; American press on peace proposals at Brest-Litovsk, **45:** 436; and Inquiry memorandum, **45:** 460-61, 467; WW on answering peace suggestions, **45:** 486; and Fourteen Points, **45:** 515-16, 530, 538-39; rumor of plan to destroy American shipping by explosives, **46:** 4, 50-51; Chamber of Commerce proposes postwar economic boycott, **46:** 6-7,n2, 7-8; R. Lansing on Germany not stating war aims, **46:** 110; G. Hertling answers WW's Fourteen Points, **46:** 110,n1, 162-67; WW on reply to Hertling, **46:** 167-68, 496-98; R. Ogden on use of economic boycott, **46:** 417-18; and teaching of German language, **46:** 459,n1, 491; and playing of German music, **46:** 459,n1, 491; German submarine warfare in American waters, **49:** 167,n1; WW on threat of economic boycott, **49:** 300-301, **51:** 8; and U.S. declaration recognizing Czechs, **49:** 405, 416; and WW's speech in Metropolitan Opera House, **51:** 127-33; and De Fiori-Herron meetings, **51:** 231-46; Germany's peace note of Oct. 6, 1918, **51:** 253; drafts and reply, **51:** 255-57, 263-64, 264-65, 268-69,n1; J. P. Tumulty's suggestions for WW's reply, **51:** 265-68, 329-32; Germany's reply to WW's note, **51:** 316,n6; U.S. note to Germany of Oct. 14, 1918, **51:** 333-34; WW and Wiseman discuss peace note, **51:** 347-48; Germany's reply of Oct. 20, 1918, **51:** 400n1, 403; drafts and comments on U.S. reply to note of Oct. 20, 1918, **51:** 399-400, 400-402, 408-409, 409-10, 412, 413, 413-15, 417-19; WW's note to Allies on German peace correspondence, **51:** 416-17; German memorandum on amendments passed by Reichstag, **51:** 518-20; *see also* Belgian deportations; Germany; World War

Germany *versus* the World (Harrison), **42:** 381,n5

Germany's Peace Proposal (*Springfield, Mass., Republican*), **51:** 266-67,n1

Germer, Adolph, **49:** 208,n2, 306

Gerry, Peter Goelet, **46:** 60, 61, 204; **51:** 301; and woman suffrage, **45:** 278, 279n1, 338, 339

Gersdorff, Carl August, **49:** 361n1

Geschichte der Republik Österreich (Goldinger), **51:** 564n3

Geter, John, **49:** 399-400

Gettysburg Address, **40:** 121; **41:** 8, 380n2, 558; T. Masaryk on, **49:** 485

Gettysburg Cemetery, **49:** 485

Gevork V: *see* Kevork V

Ghent, William James, **42:** 199,n9, 240

Gherardi, Walter Rockwell, **41:** 428; **42:** 365

Ghislain, Ludovic Alfred Joseph: *see* Moncheur, Baron

Giardino, Gaetano Ettore, **44:** 508,n3; **46:** 559,n4; **47:** 487,n1

Gibbons, James Cardinal, **41:** 45; **42:** 145; **44:** 320-21, 326, 343; **45:** 330, 334, 455; **46:** 438; **51:** 309, 374, 410, 600

Gibraltar, **42:** 264n3; **43:** 159n1, 172

Gibson, Braxton Davenport, **42:** 221,n1

Gibson, Charles Dana, **45:** 325n1; **48:** 63

Gibson, Irene Langhorne (Mrs. Charles Dana), **45:** 325,n1; **48:** 63
Gibson, Mrs. Mary E., **42:** 116
Gifford, Walter Sherman, **43:** 59, 60-61,n1, 90,n1, 102, 113; **44:** 502,n1; **46:** 444,n1; **47:** 528; **49:** 279,n1
Gilbert, Charles, **43:** 350n2
Gilbert, Joseph, **47:** 216, 226
Gilbert and Ela (attorneys, Madison, Wisc.), **46:** 119n1
Gilderhus, Mark Theodore, **49:** 230n1
Giles, W. N., **44:** 259
Gillet, Mr., **44:** 156-57,n1
Gillett, Frederick Huntington, **41:** 309n1
Gillmor, Reginald Everett, **44:** 175,n1
Gimeno y Cabañas, Amalio, **41:** 35,n1
Giolitti, Giovanni, **45:** 313,n2; **46:** 156,n2
Giovanniti, Arturo, **45:** 383,n2
Girard Trust Company, Phila., **43:** 197
Girl Behind the Gun (Bolton and Wodehouse), **51:** 314n1
Girsa, Vaclav, **49:** 44,n2, 219, 249-50, 262n1, 544,n3; **51:** 95
Gish, Dorothy, **48:** 313n1
Gish, Lillian, **48:** 313n1
Glad Adventure (Sayre), **43:** 53n1
Gladden, George, **48:** 491,n2
Gladden, Washington, **42:** 35; **47:** 19-20; death of, **48:** 491,n2
Gladstone, William Ewart, **41:** 530
Glasgow, William Anderson, Jr., **45:** 399,n4; **49:** 129-30,n1
Glass, Carter, **40:** 97, 138; **41:** 555-56; **42:** 21, 302, 303,n2, 474, 475; **45:** 307; **47:** 17
Glass, Carter, Jr., **41:** 555,n1
Glass, Franklin Potts, **41:** 328,n2, 329; **42:** 495, 496, 522; **43:** 433-34, 437, 506; **49:** 138, 224, 245; on investigation of Committee on Public Information and G. Creel, **48:** 148-49, 177-78
Glass, Powell, **41:** 555,n1
Gleaners, The, **49:** 291
Gleaves, Albert, **43:** 79n1
Glenn, John Mark, **41:** 527,n1
Glenn, Robert Broadnax, **41:** 63,n2
Glens Falls, N.Y., **51:** 535,n2
Globe, Ariz., **43:** 127; **44:** 135, 424; **46:** 131
Globe Theatre, N.Y., **48:** 52,n3
Glynn, Martin Henry, **40:** 185, 237; **43:** 514; **45:** 163n1
Gobelin tapestries, **49:** 156-57
Goddard, Robert Hutchings, **45:** 281,n1, 357
Godfrey, Hollis, **51:** 146,n1
Godham, Marguerite, **43:** 341,n1
Godnev, Ivan Vasil'evich, **41:** 416,n13; **42:** 419,n3
Godson, William Frederick Holford, **47:** 220n1
Goeben, S.M.S., **42:** 316; **49:** 411,n1
Goethals, George Washington, **44:** 71; **45:** 390n1; **46:** 105,n2; **47:** 145,n1; **48:** 266, 267; **49:** 281; on shipbuilding program and controversy with W. Denman, **42:** 32, 102-103, 145, 233-34, 235, 236, 248-49,n1, 399, 475-80, 523-25, 553-54,n1, 554-55, 555-56,n3, 567-68,n1; **43:** 50, 51, 72-73, 84-85,n1,2, 105, 106, 145, 198-99, 204-205,n1, 205,n1, 211, 211-12, 249-50, 257,n1, 285-86; resignation of, **43:** 233-34, 257, 259-60, 270, 272; replacement for, **43:** 271
Goethals Commission, **42:** 218n1
Goethals: Genius of the Panama Canal (Bishop and Bishop), **42:** 554n1
Goethals Wins Fight (Washington *Post*), **42:** 567n1
gold, **40:** 78; **43:** 227; and Mexico, **51:** 12,n2, 65-66
Gold Exports Committee, **51:** 12,n2
Golden, Peter, **47:** 520
Goldinger, Walter, **51:** 564n3
Goldman, Emma, **43:** 165n2; **44:** 290n1
Goldmark, Josephine, **40:** 8
Goldsborough, Philips Lee, **47:** 267n1
Golitsyn, Nikolai Dimitrievich, **41:** 416,n3
Goltra, Edward Field, **47:** 138, 167, 168
Gómez, José Miguel, **41:** 268n1, 384
Gompers, Samuel, **40:** 188n1, 266; **41:** 329, 407-408; **42:** 242, 271, 296,n1, 297, 471, 472; **43:** 267, 433, 511n1; **44:** 162, 172, 214, 302, 421, 482, 483, 498n1, 499; **45:** 8, 11,n1, 15, 167,n1, 269-70, 276, 348-49, 349, 383, 448; **46:** 269, 334, 364, 379, 578; **47:** 76, 105, 105n1, 114, 207, 272, 372, 462; **48:** 275, 309, 377, 404-405, 546,n1; **49:** 23-25, 34-35, 71, 73, 78, 159, 181, 185, 212, 394; **51:** 55n1, 407, 621; on Mexican commission, **40:** 114-15; and labor situation in Porto Rico, **40:** 146, 213-14; **47:** 543-44, 577; **48:** 637n6; **49:** 135-36, 158, 246, 296-98, 334; clemency appeal for incarcerated union members, **40:** 174-75, 177; **43:** 513n1; and railroad crisis, **41:** 430n2, 432; and Russian Commission, **42:** 30, 36, 43, 45,n3, 95, 111, 165; and article "Program for Labor," **42:** 134-35, 135-38; on British labor commission, **42:** 265-66; suggests WW address Congress on food legislation, **42:** 488-89, 497; on keeping Clayton Antitrust Act intact, **43:** 20-23; and war-risk insurance, **43:** 94; on East St. Louis assault on Negroes, **43:** 175,n2; on labor problems in western states, **43:** 230-31, 238-39, 352-54, 393, 416-19; on West Virginia district attorneyship, **43:** 278-80; and WW's interview with E. Martinez, **43:** 381, 383, 449, 449-50, 505; H. Todd and, **43:** 536-38; and American Alliance for Labor and Democracy, **44:** 47-48, 60, 95-100, 101-102; and Shipbuilding Labor Adjustment Board controversy, **44:** 219, 220, 226, 227, 233-34, 234-36, 242; and housing for workers on war contracts, **44:** 448,n1,2; **45:** 141; invites WW to address A.F. of L. convention, **44:** 556; urges publicity of President's Mediation Commission's

Gompers, Samuel (*cont.*)
report, **45:** 94; on proposed prohibition amendment, **45:** 295-98; and A.F. of L. resolution supporting WW, **45:** 298; against international labor conference, **46:** 21,n2, 37: and meat-packing industry, **46:** 25, 26; on Russian situation, **46:** 39, 53, 310-12; and criticism of labor movement, **47:** 126-28; on Mexican-U.S. relations, **47:** 351, 420,n1, 545-46; and A. Yager and labor situation in Porto Rico, **48:** 3, 4, 15, 17-18, 35, 37, 74-75, 130; on government takeover of telegraph companies, **48:** 313, 349-50; on investigation of detective agencies, **48:** 438-39; on Borland amendment to legislative, executive, and judicial appropriation bill, **48:** 444-45,n1; drops charges against Yager, **48:** 637-38; on labor commission to Mexico, **49:** 25-26; and proposed labor newspaper for Mexico, **49:** 89-90, 137; on draft legislation, **49:** 255-56, 328; on taking action against Bolshevik terrorism, **51:** 643-44; photograph, *illustration section,* 43
Gondrecourt, France, **43:** 443
Gonzáles, Francisco, **40:** 109,n2, 110
Gonzáles, Pablo, **44:** 331n3; **47:** 351n1; **49:** 29, 32, 33
Gonzales, William Elliott, **41:** 131,n2, 132n3, 268n1, 384; **42:** 51; **43:** 207; and sugar prices, **45:** 163,n2, 178
Gonzáles Flores, Alfredo, **41:** 140-44,n1, 248n1, 257,n1,2; **44:** 232n1; **45:** 388-89, 405, 406; **46:** 450; **49:** 6,n2, 431,n4
Good Government Club of Butte, Mont., **43:** 341n1
Good Gracious Annabelle (Kummer), **44:** 427n1
Good Time To Start (*Saturday Evening Post*), **46:** 575,n2
Goodnow, Frank Johnson, **40:** 444; **42:** 448
Goodwin, Elliot Hersey, **46:** 5-6,n1, 7-8; **49:** 314n1; **51:** 207-208
Goodwin, George E., **42:** 347,n2
Goodwin, William Shields, **45:** 169,n1
Gordon, Charles Blair, **43:** 365,n1
Gordon, Charles George (Chinese Gordon, Gordon Pasha), **48:** 588
Gordon, William, **47:** 381n2
Gore, Thomas Pryor, **42:** 343n1, 529, 532n1; **44:** 121-22,n1; **46:** 345; **47:** 16; **48:** 42n2; **49:** 310n1, 442; on controller of supplies, **42:** 314, 382-84; and Lever bill, **43:** 48n1, 160-61,n1, 162n1, 208, 393n1; and woman suffrage, **45:** 278, 338; and wheat prices, **47:** 139
Gorgas, William Crawford, **42:** 311; **45:** 390,n3, 452, 491; **46:** 210,n6
Gork'ii, Maksim (Aleksei Maksimovich Peshkov), **42:** 508,n1
Gorman, Patrick Emmet, **51:** 120,n1, 122, 149-50, 214-15
Gotō, Shimpei, **46:** 571,n2; **47:** 426,n1, 426-27,n3, 427-29, 472-73; **48:** 461-62, 505; **49:** 107,n2

Goucher, John Franklin, **47:** 453n2
Goucher College: *see* Woman's College of Baltimore
Gough, Hubert de la Poer, **47:** 443,n1
Gould, Alice, **47:** 139,n1
Gould, Elgin Ralston Lovell, **40:** 117,n1, 165
Gould, John H., **49:** 399-400
Government Hospital for the Insane, Washington, D.C.: *see* St. Elizabeth's Hospital
Government Takes Over the Nation's Colleges (*Current History*), **49:** 242n1
Government Under the Constitution (Wilson), **49:** 129, 184
Grabski, Wladyslaw, **42:** 544,n2
Grace Episcopal Church, N.Y., **40:** 89n1
Graham, Edward Kidder, **51:** 486,n1
Graham, Mary Owen, **51:** 486,n1
Graham, Samuel Jordan, **40:** 244-46
Grain Corporation: *see* United States Grain Corporation
Grand Junction, Colo., **43:** 73, 74
Grand Rapids, Mich., **43:** 423; **44:** 193
Grand Rapids *Herald,* **45:** 188n1
Granite Cutters International Association, **42:** 165n1
Grannon, Ryley, **43:** 154
Grant, Albert Weston, **43:** 191,n1
Grant, Ulysses Simpson, **42:** 89, 170; **45:** 264, 332n1; **48:** 461
Grant, Ulysses Simpson, III, **51:** 429,n5
Grant-Smith, Ulysses, **46:** 45,n2, 48, 49; **48:** 98n3; **51:** 623
Grasset, R. A., **47:** 121,n1
Grass-Roots Socialism: Radical Movements in the Southwest, 1895-1943 (Green), **43:** 434n2
Grasty, Charles Henry, **40:** 187,n2; **45:** 164n1
Graves, Henry Solon, **40:** 287,n1
Graves, John Temple, **43:** 175
Graves, William Sidney, **49:** 543-44,n1; **51:** 8,n2, 86n1, 99, 100, 101, 121, 122, 140, 152, 480; N. D. Baker wishes to replace, **51:** 356-57; on Japanese troops in Siberia, **51:** 384, 448-51; on Siberian situation, **51:** 608-609; photograph, *illustration section,* 49
Gray, George, **41:** 55,n1; **43:** 11; and Joint High Commission, **40:** 54, 55, 115, 300, 390-92, 397-401, 478-79, 479-81
Gray, L. S.: photograph, *illustration section,* 49
Gray, Natalie Hoyt, **44:** 110,n2
Grayson, Alice Gertrude Gordon (Mrs. Cary Travers, Altrude), **41:** 358; **44:** 173-75; **48:** 564
Grayson, Cary Travers, **40:** 402, 445, 572-73, 574; **41:** 359, 364, 424, 425, 431, 448, 473, 496, 498, 530, 531, 550; **42:** 13, 323; **44:** 151; **45:** 317; **46:** 485; **47:** 215, 310, 391, 605; **48:** 52, 62, 70, 71, 95, 168, 404; **49:** 267, 275, 276, 286, 298n1, 397, 398; **51:** 144, 277, 316, 342; and controversy over promotion to rear admiral, **40:** 443,n1, 463, 523, 562,n3;

and WW's views on need to combat submarine situation, **44:** 173-75; files insurance report on WW's burned hand, **48:** 201, 280

Grayson, James Gordon, **48:** 564,n1

Graz, Charles Louis Des, **47:** 36,n1

grazing homestead bill, **40:** 192-93,n1, 214, 263, 287-89, 526, 548; **51:** 287-88; passage of, **40:** 290,n1

Great Britain, **40:** 234, 239, 294, 435, 540; **41:** 162; **43:** 365; **45:** 549; and external debts, **40:** 75-76; cabinet change in, **40:** 172, 186, 187, 201; Bernstorff on relations with Germany, **40:** 213; British reaction to German peace proposals, **40:** 229,n1, 231, 233-34, 247-48, 249; and Germany's decision for unrestricted submarine warfare, **40:** 448-52; **41:** 75-76, 77, 85-86; will not talk peace with Austria-Hungary, **41:** 211-14; and requisitioning of Danish ships, **41:** 338; and Mexico, **41:** 366, 459; **42:** 37-38, 38, 96; public opinion in, **42:** 66, 67; conscientious objectors in, **42:** 69; and food crisis, **42:** 109; and Russia, **42:** 165, 381, 435, **43:** 369-72; **45:** 188-89,n1, 444, 445-46, 548; **46:** 419-21; and Japan, **42:** 354, 450; **44:** 251; need for oil tankers, **42:** 400; and training of army, **42:** 408; Kitchener's letter to his troops, **42:** 558; tonnage loss and need of replacements, **43:** 9-11, 18-19, 45-46, 140-42; W. H. Page compares financial and submarine crises, **43:** 47; and Turkey, **43:** 159n1; and Russian Jews, **43:** 159n2; Lloyd George on British war aims, **43:** 291,n1; and Poles and Poland, **43:** 301-302; **44:** 187-89, 189, 316-17; **46:** 120, 121; **51:** 447; and Asia Minor, **43:** 355; and China, **43:** 364n1; and Ireland, **43:** 451-52, 45: 560-61; and submarine warfare, **44:** 16,n1, 16-17; and reply to Pope's appeal, **44:** 23-24, 30; W. H. Page on finances of, **44:** 133; and woman suffrage, **44:** 167; **48:** 24n1, 25-26, 272; and German peace offer through Spain, **44:** 311, 318-20, 325, 342; on Ishii Mission to U.S., **44:** 314-16; and Zionist movement and Balfour Declaration, **44:** 323-24, 391, 546-47; **45:** 149,n2, 286n1; **46:** 333, 493, 516; **49:** 364, 403; W. H. Page on peace terms of, **44:** 329-31; and note from Vatican on German and Austrian reply to Pope's appeal, **44:** 347-51; and Sweden, **44:** 412,n3; and war labor problems, **44:** 501,n2, 569; **45:** 167; and Norway, **45:** 78-79; and Lansdowne letter, **45:** 173,n1, 174-75, 193, 548

and Inter-Allied Naval Council, **45:** 190; holds secret negotiations with Austria-Hungary, **45:** 430-31, 436; and Italy, **46:** 180; **47:** 468; **51:** 135; proposes Russian policy for Allies, **46:** 154-55; Gen. Robertson's resignation, **46:**

351n3; and Rumania, **46:** 373-74; and Labour party program, **46:** 435-36,n3; G. Hertling on, **46:** 496n1; and negotiations with Austria-Hungary, **46:** 577; **47:** 11, 122-23; and requisitioning Dutch ships, **47:** 27-28; on Vatican proposal for Easter armistice, **47:** 63,n1; conscription in, **47:** 130, 182, 204; and Irish conscription issue, **47:** 182, 204, 266-67,n1, 401n2, 412, 432,n1, 432-33, 442, 457-58, 466, 469-71, 520, 582, 620; and military losses, **47:** 204, 48: 246; and Vladivostok, **47:** 242-43, 244-45, 263n1; effect of war on colleges and universities in, **47:** 264; and Irish Home Rule issue, **47:** 266-67,n1, 401, 411-12, 442, 465-66, 469-71, 575-76, 582-84, 620; **48:** 68; and price fixing, **47:** 495; and organization for postwar reconstruction, **47:** 529-30, 531; and the Netherlands, **47:** 564, 565; and proposed U.S. war declaration against Turkey and Bulgaria, **47:** 568-69, 570-71; taxation in, **48:** 19, 21, 124; comments on troops of, **48:** 207, 243-45, 246, 332, 568n1; G. D. Herron on Labour party and league of nations, **48:** 212; and draft of memorandum on non-military activities of Allies, **48:** 324-29; and military strength on western front, **48:** 483, 568n1; and Phillimore Report, **48:** 501-502,n1, 550, 647,n1; **49:** 549; **51:** 327,n1; and Supreme War Council and Balkan situation, **48:** 545; industrial and economic problems in, **49:** 217-18; instructions to Gen. F. C. Poole, **49:** 285-86; recognition of Czechs as sovereign nation, **49:** 287,n1; and Germany and peace terms, **51:** 47-48, 511-13; and Murmansk Region Council, **51:** 79,n1; Lloyd George on Germany's peace note, **51:** 313; and Japan and Russian railroads, **51:** 481; S. L. Whipple on war aims of, **51:** 484; and declaration on near eastern liberated territories, **51:** 539-40,n2, 574-75; W. C. Bullitt on absence of revolutions in, **51:** 567-68; *see also* Russia—Siberia, intervention in; Russia—Murmansk and Archangel, intervention in; World War

Great Britain and the Creation of the League of Nations: Strategy, Politics, and International Organization, 1914-1919 (Egerton), **45:** 487n2; **47:** 104n1; **49:** 226n2; **51:** 327n1

Great Britain and the United States, **40:** 212, 464-65, 494; **41:** 346, 347-48, 388, 390, 463, 481; **42:** 33,n1, 194, 551-52; **43:** 4, 136, 452,n1, 453, 458; **44:** 56-57, 130-34, 230,n1, 411, 546; **45:** 272-73, 311-13, 322-23, 332; **46:** 3, 235n1; **49:** 125, 399; **51:** 187; comments on peace terms and, **40:** 4-6,n1,2, 133, 134-35, 178-80, 294,n2; and Federal Reserve Board warning against purchase of Allied short term notes, **40:** 19-20,n1, 77-

Great Britain and the United States
(*cont.*)
80, 87-88, 112, 136-37,n2, 137,n3;
WW's peace note of Dec. 18, 1916, and
Anglo-French reply, **40:** 222-25, 273-
76, 439-41,n1; and R. Lansing's reas-
surances on peace note, **40:** 307n1; and
Anglo-French conference of Dec. 26,
1916, **40:** 439n1; British views on
WW's note and peace terms, **40:** 316-
18, 319-20, 332-33, 355-58, 361-62,
366-68, 446n2,3, 465n2, 468-69, 469-
70; A. J. Balfour's addendum, **40:** 500-
503; W. H. Page on arming of merchant
vessels, **40:** 509-11; and American loan
to China, **40:** 515; **45:** 97-98; **48:** 519-20,
521; and Page's fear of peace without
victory phrase, **40:** 531-32; and arming
of merchantmen, **41:** 3, 4, 66, 71;
W. Wiseman and E. M. House discuss
early peace movement, **41:** 26,n1; reaction to WW's peace note, **41:** 36;
W. H. Page on C. A. Spring Rice as ambassador, **41:** 115; WW asks C. H.
Dodge to consider ambassadorship, **41:**
133; and British public opinion, **41:**
136-37, 372-73, 374-75; and Federal
Reserve Board reversal of policy on
loans, **41:** 256-57, 349,n2; and Austrian
peace proposal, **41:** 260, 270-73; and
Zimmermann telegram, **41:** 280-82,
297; and India, **41:** 301,n1; and bunkering agreements, **41:** 418-19,n1; T. B.
Hohler meets with House, **41:** 460; U.S.
will provide aid in war, **41:** 532-36; and
Balfour mission to U.S., **41:** 544-45,
553, 553-54; **42:** 14, 18,n1, 18-19, 20,
120, 121, 123, 125-26, 127, 140-41, 142-
43, 396-401; and Ireland and Home
Rule issue, **42:** 24-25, 41-42, 93, 111-12,
219-20, 222, 223,n1; **44:** 133-34,n2,
210; question of recruitment of British
subjects in U.S., **42:** 193; Poet Laureate
composes poem to U.S., **42:** 209-10; and
export restrictions, **42:** 224; A. J. Balfour addresses joint session of Congress, **42:** 232-33; British labor commission sent to U.S., **42:** 265-66; and
U.S. shipbuilding program, **42:** 296,
564; **43:** 124, 125, 172-73, 209-10,n1,
293-96; A. J. Balfour sends WW texts of
some secret agreements with Allies,
42: 327,n1; and plans for anti-subma-
rine barrier in North Sea, **42:** 348,n2;
fear of Japan's reaction to an Anglo-
American defensive alliance, **42:** 354;
plans for Polish Army, **42:** 355-56, 431-
32; and effect of German sea warfare on
British economy, **42:** 379-81; J. J. Jusserand on British mission, **42:** 402-403;
and need for U.S. army troops, **42:** 408-
10; **45:** 328; comments on Northcliffe as
special representative in U.S., **42:**
428,n2, 429, 432, 445-46, 461, 487-88;
43: 194-95, 451; Cecil on naval cooperation, **42:** 450-51; and counter-propaganda campaign in Russia, **42:** 463-65,
527, 529-30,n2; and British financial
crisis, **41:** 336-37; **43:** 34, 38-39, 44, 46-
47, 66, 67, 67-69, 97-98, 114, 139-40,n2,
147, 173-74, 194, 195, 223, 223-30; 326-
33, 335-36, 347, 356,n1; **44:** 280-81; and
German submarine warfare, **43:** 46-48,
65-66; WW on ineffectiveness of British navy, **43:** 79-80; and convoys, **43:**
80, 87, 88-89, 112; and Spring Rice and
Northcliffe, **43:** 97, 451, 452, 453; **44:**
56, 203; and Balfour's proposed treaty,
43: 113-14
WW's concern over reinstatement of
Hearst correspondents in, **43:** 132-33;
British desire for closer naval cooperation, **43:** 171,n1; Admiral Sims' naval
strategy recommendations, **43:** 179-82;
U.S. participants in secured British
loans, **43:** 194, 195, 196-97; financial
assistance given to Allies, **43:** 225; J. A.
Salter and T. Royden interview with
WW on shipping, **43:** 285-87, 287-90;
and War Cabinet memorandum on
submarine situation, **43:** 375-78;
J. Bryce wishes U.S. regiments to
march through London, **43:** 499; and
WW's reply to Pope's appeal, **44:** 40-41,
57-59, 130-31; shipping and shipbuilding issues, **44:** 70-72, 178, 362-64, 501-
502; and issue of U.S. representation
on inter-Allied councils, **43:** 94-95, 150,
302, 302-305, 463,n1; **44:** 80, 128-30,
195, 369-70, 373-75, 382, 385; H. T.
Mayo's visit to London, **44:** 86-88;
Lloyd George on war plans, **44:** 125-30;
Wiseman and house confer on various
issues, **44:** 200-203; Reading on meeting with WW, **44:** 237-38; and British
request for loans, **44:** 280-81; and British embargo of neutrals, **44:** 298, 298-
99, 388-89, 392, 396,n1; public reaction
to large numbers of British in Washington, **44:** 424; E. M. House to be representative to Allied council, **44:** 427,
438-39; and plan to mine North Sea,
44: 464-66; F. C. Howe on planning for
an enduring peace, **44:** 475-77; and
G. G. Barnard statue of Lincoln, **44:**
536n1; Milner on, **44:** 546-49; and
House mission, **45:** 3-4, 70-71;
W. Churchill (American) on naval relations and future war strategy, **45:** 19-
24; and formation of Supreme War
Council, **45:** 47-48, 93,n1,2; and war
plans and supplies for 1918, **45:** 208-13;
and U.S. and funds for Russia, **45:** 275,
322; cable censorship between, **45:** 321;
and Russian situation, **45:** 369-70, 417-
19; Lloyd George's New Year greetings, **45:** 405; WW's goodwill message,
45: 421; Reading appointed new ambassador to U.S., **45:** 454,n1; and Inquiry memorandum, **45:** 467-68; WW
informs Britain he must soon answer
German peace proposals, **45:** 486; and

Lloyd George's war aims statement, **45:** 487,n2, 488-89, 518; and WW's Fourteen Points, **45:** 577-78,n1, 578; and British request for U.S. troops, **46:** 8-11,n1, 11-12, 42, 43-44, 44-45, 162, 196-98, 211-12, 220, 231-32, 236-37, 337-38; and labor, **46:** 21,n1,2; and food crisis, **46:** 75, 76-78, 125-26, 461; Wiseman on interview with WW, **46:** 85-88; and Polish National Committee, **46:** 121, 149; Admiral Sims offered appointment to British Admiralty Board, **46:** 194,n1, 203; and subject of Bolshevik recognition, **46:** 333-34, 389, 419-21; Reading meets with WW on various issues, **46:** 353-57; and controversy over political declaration by two Allied councils, **46:** 359-61,n1, 390, 419, 465-67; and International News Service, **46:** 380, 393, 408, 413; and Charles I's message to WW: **46:** 418, 432, 435, 464; and Palestine, **46:** 493-95; Britain informed of WW's reply to Charles I, **46:** 507-508; and Inter-Allied General Reserve, **46:** 558-59; Britain proposes a league of nations committee, **46:** 574-75; WW declines membership in Britain's Institute of Naval Architects, **47:** 67; comments on and plans to alleviate critical need for U.S. troops and the Abbeville agreement, **47:** 130-31, 213-14, 256, 302-303, 305-306, 307, 313-15, 338-41, 372-76, 386-87, 393-94, 433-34, 436, 455-58, 497-98, 517, 535, 567, 595, 611-12, 615, 616-20; *see also* United States Army
Wiseman on WW's attitude toward crisis, **47:** 184-85; and statement acknowledging U.S. support, **47:** 206, 214,n1; WW and House discuss attitude of Britain, **47:** 215; George V and WW exchange messages on anniversary of U.S. entry into war, **47:** 265-66, 271; and Liberia, **47:** 327; Wiseman as important link between WW and British government, **47:** 444; **48:** 203-206; and Ireland, **47:** 444, 575-76; and proposed visit of Lord Mayor of Dublin to U.S., **47:** 432,n1, 506, 516; Balfour's concern over Mexican situation, **47:** 552-53; George V and WW exchange messages on friendship and cooperation, **47:** 596-97; **48:** 365-66; and Belgian relief, **48:** 46-48, 80; and German plot in Ireland, **48:** 63-64,n1,2 65-66, 67-69, 71,n1, 79, 195-97, 206; and Reading's frequent requests for interviews with WW, **48:** 381; WW refuses to make public comment on Ireland, **48:** 471-72; Wiseman on importance of Reading as ambassador, **48:** 524-25; tonnage shortages and transport of U.S. troops, **48:** 418-19, 544, 546; **49:** 66-67, 82-83, 217, 224, 279, 293, 354, **51:** 34-35, 94-95; public opinion on delay of Siberian decision, **48:** 566-67;

and WW's aide-mémoire on policy toward Russia, **48:** 639-43; clarification of British position on Russia, **49:** 58-60, 67-69; George V on naval cooperation between, **49:** 69, 70; and league of nations, **49:** 83, 225-28, 273; and China, **49:** 102-103; Page asks to be relieved of ambassadorship, **49:** 155; Remembrance Day, **49:** 168, 173,n1; and Irish conscription, **49:** 178; and the Vatican, **49:** 189,n4; and Czech Legion and Siberian issue, **49:** 248-50, 261-62, 302-303, 345, 366-67, 373; and British appointment of High Commissioner to Siberia, **49:** 250n1, 323; WW against publication of Phillimore Report, **49:** 265, 266, 273-74, 549; **51:** 327,n1; and German propaganda in Mexico, **49:** 280; and WW's policy toward Mexico, **49:** 299-300; and postwar economic boycott of Germany, **49:** 300-301; relations between, **49:** 303, 453-54,n1; and question of U.S. war declaration against Bulgaria and Turkey, **49:** 365,n1,2; and prices charged by Britain for supplies, **49:** 373-74, 435; and proposed visit by Australian Prime Minister, **49:** 409, 466; Geddes on U.S. shipbuilding and naval efforts, **49:** 410-13; **51:** 124,n2, 279-80, 633-34; and trade issues, **49:** 453-54,n1; E. N. Hurley on shipbuilding plans and, **49:** 473-74,n1, 491; R. Lansing on F. C. Poole's behavior in Archangel, **49:** 516-17; and Sisson Documents, **51:** 4, 246-47, 252, 352; and needed supplies and troops for Archangel, **51:** 31-32, 33, 75; H. F. Hollis on, **51:** 182-83; WW on, **51:** 222-23; and German peace note and terms, **51:** 324-25, 335-36, 411-12, 514-17; and Turkey, **51:** 389; W. G. McAdoo on postwar reconstruction and Britain's financial obligations, **51:** 465-67; *see also* Great Britain; Russia—Siberia, Murmansk and Archangel, intervention in; World War

Great Britain and the War of 1914-1918 (Woodward), **44:** 501n2
Great Decision (*New Republic*), **41:** 537-38,n1
Great Divide (Moody), **41:** 454,n1
Great Falls, Mont., **46:** 432n2
Great News (Ferguson), **40:** 542n4
Greatest Crime of History: Iron Hun Rule Has Made Russia a Hell Beyond Self-Redemption (Bernstein), **48:** 410,n2
Greathouse, Charles Ashford, **46:** 285-86,n1
Greble, Edwin St. John, **45:** 390,n2,4
Greece, **40:** 13, 15, 185, 219, 234, 235, 453-55, 486; **41:** 34-35, 78; **42:** 330-31, 339; **43:** 10, 268; **44:** 282; **45:** 123, 190; **46:** 581,n1; **47:** 513, 569; **48:** 79n1, 617; **49:** 538; **51:** 45, 156n2, 163, 169, 187, 501, 607; on anniversary of U.S. entry

Greece (cont.)
into war, **47:** 263-64, 271, 308-309; in Asia Minor, **51:** 180-81,n1
Greek Currant Company, **51:** 180n1
Greek Line, **51:** 180n1
Greeley, Horace, **44:** 168
Green, Charles Ewing, **45:** 231,n2
Green, James R., **43:** 434n2
Green, Jerome, **40:** 418
Green, Mary Livingston Potter (Mrs. Charles Ewing), **45:** 231,n3
Green, Paul, **47:** 482-83,n2
Green, William, **40:** 217; **43:** 340, 352, 353, 368; **46:** 297n1; **51:** 545-47
Green Corn Rebellion, **43:** 434,n2
Green Corn Rebellion (Bush), **43:** 434n2
Greene, Elbridge Gerry, **48:** 417,n1,2
Greene, Henry Alexander, **45:** 111,n8
Greene, William Conyngham, **44:** 314-16; **46:** 46,n1, 571
Greenough, William, **48:** 482,n2
Greenport Company, **41:** 377
Greenslet, Ferris, **46:** 605,n1; **51:** 621
Greenville, Tex., Banner, **47:** 521n1
Gregg, James Edgar, **51:** 176,n1
Gregory XVI (Pope), **49:** 190n5
Gregory, Francis Robert, **46:** 496,n1
Gregory, Jeremiah P., **45:** 547,n2
Gregory, John Duncan, **42:** 545,n6
Gregory, Julia Nalle (Mrs. Thomas Watt), **45:** 398
Gregory, Mary Cornelia Watt (Mrs. Francis Robert), **46:** 316,n1, 496
Gregory, Thomas Montgomery, **42:** 321-22,n1
Gregory, Thomas Watt, **40:** 240, 466, 467, 547; **41:** 88, 340, 403, 454, 484, 498, 518; **42:** 77n1, 113, 134, 158, 244,n2, 546; **43:** 5, 86, 116, 117, 146-47, 154-55, 160, 161, 187, 191, 336, 503; **44:** 8,n1, 31, 60, 107, 119-20, 151, 152, 157, 246, 247, 265, 290, 323, 347, 380, 397n1, 405, 415, 463, 480, 492-93, 514-15; **45:** 39, 92, 95, 148n1, 223, 268-69, 271, 398, 557, 562; **46:** 4n2, 63, 104, 206,n1, 213, 438, 469, 553; **47:** 136, 215, 363-65, 414, 616; **48:** 192, 193, 209, 220, 241, 290-91, 405, 612; **49:** 69, 247, 357; **51:** 105, 109, 144, 257, 270-71, 341, 618, 646

and on Trade Commission appointments, **40:** 413, 417; and naval oil reserves, **40:** 545, 560, 561n2; **41:** 247-48, 288; **42:** 533n1, 561; **45:** 374-78, 448, 454,n1, 559; advocates war entry, **41:** 442; and controversy with W. G. McAdoo over American Protective League, **42:** 440, 441-43, 446, 508-18; and Patria, **42:** 489, 490; and coal price fixing, **43:** 33, 41n1, 54, 61-64; and East St. Louis assault on blacks, **43:** 116, 247, 297-98; and woman suffrage, **43:** 201n1; and Yorke affair in San Francisco, **43:** 215-18; on German-
American newspapers and censorship, **43:** 243; on Henry Rule's arrest, **43:** 253-54; on Trading With the Enemy Act, **43:** 315-17; and railroads, **44:** 90, 422-23; **45:** 311; on Section 3 of Lever Act, **44:** 238n1; on illegal price fixing by corporations, **44:** 313; and Pacific Telephone and Telegraph Company, **44:** 497, 552-54; on New York mayoralty, **44:** 504, 512; on investigation of W. B. Hale, **45:** 28-29, 101-102,n1; on Frachtenburg investigation, **45:** 154; on German plot to destroy U.S. shipping, **46:** 50-51; on F. C. Miller case, **46:** 97-98, 119; on bill establishing war zone around shipbuilding plants, **46:** 283-85; on deferring Supreme Court decisions in antitrust suits, **46:** 297,n2; death of mother, **46:** 316,n1, 496; and Hog Island, **46:** 361n1; **51:** 13-14; on Swedish Americans who failed to register, **46:** 560-61; **47:** 135-36, 169; on dynamite conspiracy case and F. Ryan, **47:** 179, 219,n1, 232,n1; and I.W.W., **47:** 232-33, 479n4, 587; and court-martial bill, **47:** 381n2; and Mooney case, **47:** 467n1; and aircraft investigation, **47:** 584, 588, 603; on Walsh bill, **47:** 604; on sedition bill, **48:** 12-14; on antiprofiteering rent bill, **48:** 222, 238, 269; on Max Eastman, **48:** 251,n2; on breakup and investigation of Washington State Grange meeting, **48:** 322; **49:** 79-80; on Mrs. Stokes and Kansas City Star case, **48:** 422-24; defends Espionage Act, **49:** 306-308; on slacker raids, **49:** 451-52, 499-503, 513; K. Pittman on general leasing bill and, **49:** 484-85; on Vernon case, **51:** 68-70; and J. W. Davis, **51:** 107; and Pollak case, **51:** 125,n1, 171-72, 211, 281, 376-80; and Bouch case, **51:** 310-12; and Busch case, **51:** 395, 446
Grenard, Joseph-Fernand, **48:** 239,n1
Greve, Tim, **42:** 110n3
Grew, Joseph Clark, **40:** 21,n1, 83, 94, 106-107, 178, 191; **41:** 268,n2, 298; **45:** 30-38; **46:** 412, **47:** 358n1; **51:** 316, 638; reports on German situation, **40:** 141-46, 160-61, 184-85, 231, 428-36, 442; on news leaks in German Foreign Office, **40:** 216-17
Grey, Albert L., **48:** 356n1
Grey, Sir Edward (Viscount Grey of Fallodon), **40:** 5n1, 24n1, 60-61, 62, 201, 204, 212, 358; **41:** 17, 211, 272, 373, 535; **42:** 169, 327n1, 331, 520; **44:** 202, 251; **45:** 175; **48:** 523n1, 592-93,n1; **49:** 9, 269; **51:** 298
Gridiron Club: WW talks to, **40:** 193-97,n1; **41:** 240, 259; **45:** 238-40
Grieg, Edvard, **40:** 570
Griff nach der Weltmacht: Die Kriegszielpolitik des kaiserlichen Deutschland, 1914/18 (Fischer), **48:** 114n2
Griffin, Franklin A., **42:** 272,n6; **46:** 72,n4; **49:** 51n1

Griffin, Solomon Bulkley, **40:** 167n1; **47:** 499-500; **51:** 376
Griffin, Thomas F. A., **44:** 308,n1
Griffith, Arthur, **48:** 67n3
Griffith, David Wark, **48:** 313-14,n1, 356,n1
Griffith, Kathryn, **43:** 165n2
Griffith, Pearl Merril, **41:** 269,n2, 278-79
Griggs, John William, **40:** 466,n1
Grimes, W. W., **45:** 154,n2,4
Grimké, Archibald Henry, **41:** 218,n2
Grimm, Robert, **43:** 28n1
Grinberg, Suzanne, **48:** 26
Grinnell College, **40:** 540n1
Griscom, Lloyd Carpenter, **43:** 11; **49:** 78,n1; **51:** 373,n1, 385,n1
Grodno, Lithuania, **48:** 98
Groh, Theodore, **44:** 481,n2, 527-30; **45:** 28-29
Gronna, Asle Jorgenson, **41:** 318n1, 328; **44:** 36
Grosscup, Edward E., **47:** 82n1
Grosse Politik der Europäischen Kabinette, 1871-1914, **44:** 296n1
Grosser Kurfürst, S.M.S., **51:** 490
Grotius, Hugo, **43:** 462,n2
Grove Park Inn, Asheville, N.C., **49:** 427n1
Groves, J. Philip, **48:** 142,n5
Grovno, *see* Grodno, Lithuania
Grow, Malcolm Cummings, **42:** 287,n2, 292; **43:** 455n2
Grozier, Edward Atkins, **51:** 552,n2
Gršković, Don Niko, **40:** 104-105,n1, 165
Grubb, William Irwin, **43:** 70n1
Grubbs, Frank L., Jr., **44:** 47n1, 166n3
Grunewald, Jacques, **40:** 504n1; **41:** 49n1
Grunniije, Mr., **51:** 153,n3
Guanica Centrale, **47:** 543n1
Guantánamo, Cuba, **41:** 298n1
Guaranty Trust Company, N.Y., **40:** 89n1; **43:** 196; **45:** 332; **48:** 372, 519,n1; **49:** 233
Guatemala, **41:** 143,n17, 145,n1, 546; **42:** 46-47, 54, 359; **44:** 331,n1, 358, 388,n1; **47:** 553
Guchkov, Aleksandr Ivanovich, **41:** 416,n7; **42:** 218n2, 320,n1,2
Guelph, John Edward, **46:** 50-51
Guerlac, Othon Goepp, **43:** 135,n1
Guffey, Joseph Finch, **44:** 278
Guggenheim Brothers, **47:** 396n1
Guiffrey, Jean, **49:** 156,n2
Guillaumat, Louis, **47:** 513,n2
Guion, Walter, **48:** 233,n1, 237n2
Gulf Oil Refining Company, **49:** 230n1
Gulliver, John P., **46:** 460
Gumberg, Alexander, **46:** 300n7; **48:** 142,n4
Gumpertz, I. (or J.), **41:** 127n1
Gunsaulus, Frank Wakely, **45:** 143,n4
Gunter, Julius C., **47:** 194
Gustafson, Mr. (of National Wheat Growers' Association), **49:** 427,n2
Gustavus V (of Sweden), **45:** 114,n2
Guth, William Westley, **47:** 453,n3, 454, 536, 537,n1

Guthrie, George Wilkins, **40:** 216: **41:** 181-82, 186, 295; **43:** 83n3; death of, **41:** 374,n1 382, 403
Gutterson, Herbert Lindsley, **51:** 228,n2, 271-72
Guy, Jean Arthur, **40:** 542,n3
Guyot, Arnold Henry, **40:** 46

H. M. Byllesby and Co., Chicago, **41:** 514n1
Haakon VII (of Norway), **42:** 110n2,3: **45:** 114,n2
Haas, Jacob de, **45:** 572n1; **46:** 494, 516-17
Haas, Leon Samuel, **48:** 237,n1,2, 352
Haase, Hugo, **45:** 32; **46:** 183,n1, 190, 228, 312,n2
Habarovsk, Russia: *see* Khabarovsk
Habsburg Empire in World War I (Kann et al.), **45:** 57n4
Hadji-Mischef, Pantcho, **51:** 134,n1, 141, 155
Hadley, Arthur Twining, **40:** 90, 444: **42:** 495
Hagan, J. N., **51:** 212,n2
Hagedorn, Hermann, **44:** 367n2; **48:** 173n1
Hague, The, Netherlands, **41:** 40
Hague Conference (1899), **51:** 535n1
Hague Conference (1907), **51:** 331, 535n1
Hague Conventions, **40:** 172; **42:** 9-10; **49:** 201, 271
Haig, Sir Douglas, **44:** 319, 332; **45:** 112, 151, 571, 583; **46:** 211, 240,n1, 351n3, 558, 559; **47:** 161, 166, 201, 209, 238, 309, 434, 455, 456, 457, 465, 487, 501, 505, 517; **48:** 5, 33-34, 232, 387, 389; **51:** 373, 385, 414, 455, 462,n2, 473, 511n1, 544n1; WW's message of praise to, **47:** 131, 134, 160
Haight, Thomas Griffith, **49:** 210,n2, 212,n1
Hailar, Manchuria, **49:** 284; **51:** 479,n1
Haines, Robert B., Jr., **43:** 244n1
Haiti, **42:** 359
Haldeman, William Birch, **49:** 268n1
Hale, Edward Joseph, **41:** 140,n3,6, 145
Hale, George Ellery, **47:** 353n2
Hale, Matthew, **40:** 166-67; **41:** 490-93; **42:** 118-19,n1, 237,n3; **44:** 165-66, 205,n3, 221-22, 292, 292-93; **47:** 467, 537-38, 540, 557; **48:** 43,n1; and "Liberty Guard" proposal, **45:** 103,n1, 152, 160; on standardizing labor policies and appointing Director General of Labor, **47:** 376-79, 391; W. B. Wilson refutes ideas of, **47:** 461, 465
Hale, Olga Unger (Mrs. William Bayard), **44:** 481-82,n1, 527-30
Hale, William Bayard, **40:** 21,n1, 39, 160, 429; **44:** 528n2; **45:** 270,n3; **47:** 275-76,n4, 362-63; protests investigation, **44:** 480, 481-82, 514-15, 527-30; **45:** 28-29, 74, 101-102,n1
Halévy, Daniel, **43:** 135n2
Halévy, Elie, **43:** 135,n2
Halévy, Ludovic, **43:** 135

Halifax, Nova Scotia: and munitions explosion in harbor, **45:** 230,n1, 253
Hall, Benjamin Franklin, **42:** 86,n1
Hall, Charles Lacey, **40:** 551,n3
Hall, Henry Clay, **42:** 213,n1; **43:** 296-97, 300; **47:** 166-67
Hall, Henry Noble, **40:** 406n1; **43:** 476-77; **44:** 12; **48:** 66-69; on Ireland, **47:** 581, 582-84, 586
Hall, José, **41:** 269
Hall, Mrs. Mary C., **42:** 116
Hall, Ruth Preble, **40:** 551-52; **41:** 15
Hall, Willard Merrill, **40:** 551,n4; **41:** 15-16
Hall, William Reginald, **44:** 140,n3, 181-82, 245; **45:** 445; **46:** 397; **47:** 176; **48:** 65; **51:** 345, 528
Haller, Joseph, **51:** 447, 448
Hallett, George Hervey, **47:** 155,n3
Halperin, Yehiel, **45:** 572,n2
Halpern, Mr., **46:** 341,n3
Halsey, Abram Woodruff, **45:** 575
Ham, France, **47:** 129, 130; **51:** 421
Hamburg, Germany, **46:** 266; **51:** 607
Hamburg-America Line, **43:** 133n1
Hamilton, Alexander, **41:** 302; **47:** 201
Hamilton, George Ernest, **44:** 559,n3, 561
Hamilton, John William, **45:** 455,n2; **46:** 612-13,n1
Hamilton, Mary Agnes, **49:** 11n4
Hamilton, Peter Joseph, **41:** 180,n2; **48:** 17-18, 48-49
Hamilton College, **42:** 267
Hamlin, Charles Sumner, **40:** 76-77, 87, 112; **41:** 231-32, 233; **44:** 423-24; **48:** 569n1; and plans for Seattle hydroelectric plant, **49:** 118-19, 119-21, 143, 148, 295-96,n1
Hammer v. Dagenhart, **49:** 23n1
Hammerstein, Oscar, **45:** 239,n3
Hammerstein, Oscar II, **45:** 239n3
Hammond, John Hays, **40:** 35; **47:** 215
Hamon, Jacob (Jake) L., **47:** 10,n1
Hampton, George P., **49:** 304, 355, 357, 427,n2, 452; **51:** 212, 249, 250, 257, 310, 520; on water-power legislation, **49:** 289-92,n1, 499, 515; on governmental development of natural resources, **49:** 289-92,n1; suggests Federal Trade Commission appointments, **49:** 430-31
Hampton, Vernon Boyce, **44:** 199n
Hampton, William Judson, **44:** 199,n1
Hampton Institute, **40:** 221, 222; **42:** 321, 322; **51:** 176,n1,2
Hampton Roads, Va., **43:** 112; labor problems at, **47:** 379
Hanburg-Williams, Sir John, **49:** 9,n3
Hancock, Attilia Aldridge Anderson (Mrs. Lewis), **45:** 399,n3
Hancock, Dorothy, **45:** 399,n3
Hancock, Margery, **45:** 399,n3
Hancock, Winfield Scott, **42:** 217n1
Hand, Learned, **43:** 165n2; **44:** 171
Handel, Georg Friedrich, **46:** 604n1
Handelskrieg mit U-Booten (Spindler), **40:** 389n1

Hands Across the Sea: An Open Letter to Americans (Trevelyan), **40:** 124n3
Hanger, Glossbrenner Wallace William, **44:** 431,n1, 458-59; **46:** 448
Hankey, Maurice Pascal Alers, **42:** 327n2; **47:** 59: **51:** 34,n2
Hankey: Man of Secrets (Roskill), **42:** 327n2
Hankow, China, **49:** 213
Hanna, Paul, **43:** 383,n1, 394
Hannis Taylor, Legal Authority, Says Supreme Court Will Forbid Sending Militia or Conscripts Abroad (*New York American*), **44:** 60n1
Hanover National Bank, N.Y., **43:** 196
Hanson, Gladys, **41:** 454n1
Hanson, Ole, **40:** 167n1; **42:** 347; **46:** 566; and Seattle hydroelectric plant, **49:** 118-19, 120-21, 122, 170, 296n2
Hanson, Victor Henry, **49:** 245,n1
Haparanda, Sweden, **47:** 11
Hapgood, Norman, **40:** 10n1, 173, 173-74, 240, 493, 496-97; **41:** 56, 501; **43:** 364: **44:** 72; **48:** 144
Hapsburgs, **46:** 315
Hapsburg Monarchy, 1867-1914 (May), **41:** 56n2
Harbin, China, **46:** 118, 344,n1, 387, 391, 392, 511, 512, 540, 541, 555; **47:** 22, 71, 397-98; **48:** 38, 105; **49:** 283, 494; **51:** 121, 140, 384, 479, 480, 481n1, 549, 609
Harbison, Ralph Warner, **48:** 78,n2
Hard, William, **40:** 315,n1; **44:** 472,n6; **47:** 16,n3; **51:** 111,n1,2, 113
Harden, Maximilian, **40:** 66, 375-78; **42:** 256; **43:** 246,n1; **44:** 105, 154
Harding, Alfred, **48:** 466,n1
Harding, Arthur, **47:** 137-38, 138
Harding, Chester, **48:** 417n4
Harding, Warren Gamaliel, **42:** 245n2
Harding, William Procter Gould, **40:** 77, 77-78, 87-88, 112, 136,n2; **43:** 224, 425; **45:** 266; **48:** 611, 612,n1; **49:** 4, 6, 120-21, 472; **51:** 12,n2; on federal control of public utilities, **48:** 597-99; on cotton prices, **48:** 646; **49:** 47-50, 73-74; on interest rates, **49:** 503-504, 511
Hardinge, Arthur Henry, **44:** 311,n1
Hardinge, Charles, 1st Baron Hardinge of Penshurst, **41:** 458-59,n1; **43:** 24; **44:** 318; **45:** 430n1; **47:** 59
Hardwick, Thomas William, **42:** 302, 303,n2, 505; **43:** 162, 481n5; **45:** 237; **46:** 330; **47:** 16; **51:** 616; and woman suffrage, **45:** 278, 339; and senatorial race in Georgia, **47:** 192, 325n1, 382n1; **49:** 80-82,n2, 114, 137, 143, 206, 237n1, 245, 528n1
Hardy, D. Heywood, **48:** 142,n4
Hardy, Fred, **47:** 574
Hardy, Guy Urban, **51:** 645n1
Harlan, James Shanklin, **47:** 408,n1
Harlan, John Marshall, **47:** 274,n1
Harm From Censorship Greater Than Benefit (Price), **42:** 246,n4
Harmon, Judson, **40:** 466,n1

Harmsworth, Alfred Charles William: *see* Northcliffe, 1st Viscount
Harnedy, D. J., **43:** 217n5
Harper, Belle Dunton Westcott (Mrs. George McLean), **45:** 335,n3
Harper, George McLean, **43:** 540; **45:** 334-35,n2
Harper, Paul V., **41:** 415n1, 417n14; **43:** 150n2
Harper, Robert Newton, **40:** 163,n2
Harper, Samuel Northrup, **41:** 415,n1, 415-16; **42:** 44, 45, 417
Harper, William Rainey, **41:** 415n1; **43:** 150n2
Harper and Brothers, **46:** 259-60, 285, 448-49,n1, 506; **47:** 41; **48:** 120, 143, 479, 482-83; **49:** 129; **51:** 15, 172n1
Harper's Weekly, N.Y., **40:** 421n1
Harriman, Job, **42:** 199
Harriman, Joseph Wright, **44:** 212, 231, 360
Harrington, Emerson Columbus, **42:** 138,n3, 139; **48:** 248-49,n1, 270
Harris, Ernest Lloyd, **48:** 113,n4; **49:** 448,n1; **51:** 101-102, 481n2; photograph, *illustration section*, 49
Harris, Frederick Leverton, **40:** 367-68,n2
Harris, Gertrude Richardson (Mrs. Frederick Leverton), **40:** 367,n3
Harris, Joel Chandler, **40:** 169
Harris, Peter Charles, **51:** 139,n1, 448-51
Harris, William Julius, **41:** 45-46, 146-48,n1, 205-206, 288, 309; **46:** 38; **47:** 153, 221, 222,n2, 558-59,n1; **49:** 456, 461; resigns from Federal Trade Commission, **46:** 330, 335; and Georgia senatorial campaign, **47:** 192, 312,n2, 383n1; **49:** 80-82,n1, 114-16, 143, 206, 237,n1, 369-70, 528,n1
Harrisburg (Pa.) *Patriot and Union,* **41:** 380n2
Harrison, Austin, **42:** 381,n5
Harrison, Benjamin, **46:** 41n1, **51:** 573
Harrison, Carter Henry, **44:** 107, 146
Harrison, Fairfax, **42:** 540n2
Harrison, Floyd Reed, **44:** 82,n2
Harrison, Francis Burton, **40:** 112; **41:** 63, 152, 153, 345, 418; **42:** 541, 542; **44:** 8-9, 446-47; **45:** 49, 75; **49:** 407, 408
Harrison, Frederic, **42:** 381,n6
Harrison, George Paul, **42:** 451n1
Harrison, Leland, **40:** 388; **41:** 474n2; **51:** 345,n1
Harrison, Byron Patton (Pat), **42:** 21n1; **47:** 209
Harrison, Russell Benjamin, **49:** 185,n1, 238, 247-48
Harrison, Thomas Walker, **45:** 307,n1
Harrison, William, **51:** 168n1, 191-93
Hart, Hugh D., **44:** 142n1
Hart, William O., **44:** 79
Harte, Archibald Clinton, **48:** 412,n1
Hartman, Edward T., **44:** 79
Harvard Church, Brookline, Mass., **51:** 69
Harvard Divinity School, **46:** 22n3

Harvard Law School, **46:** 169n3
Harvard Medical School, **41:** 481; **46:** 22
Harvard University, **40:** 444; **42:** 284, 322n1; **44:** 105n2, 484n1, 540n2; **45:** 271n4; **46:** 309n1; **47:** 155n3, 198; **48:** 484n1; **49:** 12; **51:** 422
Harvey, George Brinton McClellan, **42:** 371,n1,2; **45:** 193-94, 326, 332; **47:** 15,n1, 16, 583n1; **51:** 483n1, 521
Harvey Cushing: A Biography (Fulton), **41:** 482n3
Haskell, Lewis Wardlaw, **45:** 415,n2; **47:** 133,n2
Haskell, William Nafew, **43:** 492,n1, 514
Haskell and Barker Car Co., Inc., Michigan City, Ind., **44:** 227n2
Haskins, Charles Homer, **46:** 169,n1
Hatzfeldt-Trachenberg, Hermann, Prince von, **41:** 274,n1
Hauber, C. A., **43:** 200,n3
Haugen, Gilbert Nelson, **45:** 300,n3, 335, 379
Haussmann, Konrad, **45:** 415,n1; **46:** 428; **47:** 24; **48:** 214; **51:** 242
Havana *Heraldo de Cuba,* **41:** 384n1
Havenith, Emmanuel, **40:** 26, 83-84, 170-71, 220, 316
Haverford College, **43:** 492n1; **44:** 29n1; **47:** 155
Haviland airplanes: *see* DeHaviland
Hawaii, **43:** 505, 506
Hawes, Thomas Samuel, **44:** 82,n1, 106, 145, 328
Hawkins, John Russell, **46:** 614,n1; **51:** 193,n1
Hawkins, Pompey Long, **45:** 547,n2, 579-80
Hawkins, William Walter, **51:** 538,n1
Hawley, Alan Ramsey, **47:** 293n1
Hawley, James Henry, **40:** 175,n2
Hay, John, **43:** 250n1
Hay, Mary Garrett, **44:** 532-33, 537
Hay-Bunau-Varilla Treaty, **48:** 417n4
Hay-Pauncefote Treaty, **40:** 550
Hayashi, Gonsuke, **40:** 514,n1, 515; **49:** 213,n2
Hayden, Carl, **51:** 404,n2
Hayes, Carlton Joseph Huntley, **41:** 164,n1,2, 165-67, 167n1,2, 168, 185
Hayes, Frank J., **43:** 368; **44:** 540; **46:** 297n1, 578,n1; **47:** 233,n2, 248, 252, 283; **49:** 216; **51:** 19, 545-47
Hayes, Rutherford Birchard, **49:** 246
Haynes, Robert Vaughn, **44:** 41n1; **45:** 546n1; **46:** 16n1
Hays, William Harrison, **46:** 566,n2; **47:** 389, 532; **48:** 347, 348
Hays, Kaufman and Lindheim, N.Y., **43:** 134,n2
Haywood, William Dudley, **43:** 325-26,n1, 336; **45:** 383, 384; **47:** 587n1, 604; **51:** 377, 378; on Walsh bill, **47:** 573-74
Hazelton, George Cochrane, **48:** 356n2
Hazen, Azel Washburn, **44:** 154
Hazen, Mary Butler Thompson (Mrs. Azel Washburn), **44:** 154

Hazleton, Richard, **44:** 133n2; **48:** 195,n1, 195-97

He Belongs to the Ages: The Statues of Abraham Lincoln (Durman), **44:** 536n1

Health Conservation Board, **42:** 138

Healy, Charles B., **48:** 168,n1

Heard, Dwight B., **46:** 386n1, 409,n1, 503, 547

Hearley, John, **51:** 282,n1, 294

Hearst, William Randolph, **41:** 483n1; **42:** 447, 488; **43:** 318n1, 379, 381, 450; **44:** 275, 301-302,n1, 333n1, 334, 528n2, 536,n1; **45:** 270, 320n1, 321; **46:** 63, 393, 437; **49:** 157n1

Hearst newspapers, **40:** 506; **43:** 132, 132-33,n1,2, 258, 259; **48:** 220,n1

Hearts of the World (film, Griffith), **48:** 313-14,n1, 356,n1

Hebrew language, **51:** 626

Hebrew University, Jerusalem, **49:** 364, 403

Heflin, James Thomas, **42:** 21n1, 323-24, 326, 370-71, 382, 474, 475, 497; **43:** 36, 71

Heflin, Robert Stell, **45:** 307

Hegge, Fred, **47:** 574

Helena, Mont., Commercial Club, **43:** 75n2

Helfferich, Karl Theodor, **40:** 463n1; **41:** 32-33; **46:** 254,n5; **48:** 213n8

Helgeson, Henry Thomas, **44:** 153n1

Helgoland, **43:** 180; **45:** 24; **51:** 275, 373, 464

Helgoland, S.M.S., **51:** 492

Hellier, Frank Oscar, **40:** 516,n1; **41:** 408

Hellingrath, Philipp von, **48:** 552,n2

Help to Russia Waits (*Washington Post*), **48:** 465,n1

Helsingfors University, **49:** 321

Helvering, Guy Tresillian, **42:** 96-97,n1, 97-98

Hemphill, Alexander Julian, **40:** 89,n1

Henderson, Arthur, **41:** 214,n1; **43:** 454; **45:** 167,n1; **46:** 21, 312, 435n3, 582; **47:** 86, 86-87, 102, 105, 122, 442-43; **49:** 11,n4, 225,n1; **51:** 566

Henderson, Charles Belknap, **51:** 453,n3, 612

Henderson, Robert Randolph, **41:** 354,n3; **45:** 411n2

Hendrick, Burton Jesse, **49:** 346n

Heney, Francis Joseph, **40:** 166, 370-71; **41:** 462,n3; **48:** 511; **49:** 215

Hengtowhotze, Manchuria, **51:** 479,n1

Henke, Charles W., **47:** 236,n6

Henkes, David A., **47:** 485-86,n5

Hennessy, Charles O'Connor, **51:** 283,n1,2, 403, 452

Henri, Florette, **48:** 157n4, 160n6

Henry (Prince of Prussia), **43:** 405,n2

Henry VII (of Great Britain), **49:** 227

Henry, Vida, **44:** 42n2

Henry Cabot Lodge and the Search for an American Foreign Policy (Widenor), **41:** 11n1

Henry IV (Shakespeare), **45:** 130

Henry Ford Hospital, **51:** 280,n1

Henry Holt and Company, **41:** 83n1

Hensley Resolution, **41:** 150,n3, 246,n1

Hepburn, Alonzo Barton, **40:** 93; **48:** 582,n1

Herald Publishing Company, Grand Rapids, Mich., **45:** 188n1

Herbert, Hilary Abner, **42:** 451n1

Herink, Albert, **47:** 300,n1

Hermanas, New Mex., **43:** 158n1, 170; **44:** 518

Herrick, Myron Timothy, **42:** 169

Herrick, Robert Frederick, **49:** 443,n1

Herriot, Éduard, **49:** 37n1

Herron, Carrie Rand, **40:** 540n1

Herron, George Davis, **40:** 540,n1, 541-42,n1,2; **44:** 287,n2; **45:** 256,n1; **46:** 198, 199, 235,n1, 241, 242-47, 253-54, 261, 353, 357, 388, 428, 473, 483, 510, 580, 580n1, 589, 615, 616; **47:** 24-26, 64-65,n1,2,4, 128; **48:** 549-50, 609, 621, 639; **51:** 9-10, 387, 388, 565; on a league of nations, **48:** 210-17, 473-74, 538-40, 592; meetings with R. de Fiori, **48:** 552-55,n6; **49:** 228-29, 229-30, 231-32; **51:** 229, 230-41, 241-46; on papal politics and the league of nations, **49:** 187-93; on Bulgaria, **49:** 436,n1, 447; on Austria-Hungary proposing peace terms, **51:** 240; compares German mind to Anglo-Saxon mind, **51:** 242-43

Herron, Mary Everhard (Mrs. George Davis), **40:** 540n1

Herron, William Collins, **43:** 276,n1

Hertling, Georg Friedrich, Count von, **44:** 548,n2; **45:** 34-37, 415, 595; **46:** 557; **47:** 25, 64n2,3,4, 269, 524,n1; **48:** 552,n1; **49:** 193; **51:** 233, 234, 236,n6, 239; speech on WW's Fourteen Points, **46:** 110,n1; comments on speech and comparison made to Czernin's address, **46:** 113,n2, 162-67, 172, 173, 186-87, 198, 207, 222-29, 273, 277-78, 567-69, 581, 592, 593; mentioned in Four Points address, **46:** 274-79, 291-97, 318-24; and peace terms, **46:** 428; WW's draft of answer to, **46:** 496-98; and Dutch reaction to speech of, **46:** 615, 616, 617; resignation of, **51:** 253n2; photograph, *illustration section,* **46**

Hertz, Friedrich Otto, **51:** 232,n2, 233

Hervé, Gustave, **41:** 466,n3

Hervey, William Addison, **45:** 154n3

Herzegovina, **41:** 212; **42:** 156, 333, 334; **45:** 412; **46:** 244

Herzl, Theodore, **49:** 363n2

Heuermann, Minnie, **40:** 212n1

Heyen, Carl, **43:** 133-34,n1

Heyworth, J. O., **46:** 363n4

Hibben, John Grier, **40:** 567; **42:** 458; **45:** 568; **47:** 380; **51:** 147n1

Hickling, Daniel Percy, **44:** 561,n8

Hicks, Amy Mali, **44:** 79

Hicks, John D., **49:** 441n7

Hieber, A. J., **42:** 34n1
Higginson, Francis Lee, Jr., **49:** 281,n1
Higginson, Henry Lee, **43:** 85-86, 282, 338; **44:** 425-26, 444: **45:** 44-45, 53-54; on prohibition, **43:** 52-53; on price fixing, **43:** 251-53; on Liberty Bonds and the economy, **43:** 337
Higginson, Hetty Appleton Sargent (Mrs. Francis Lee, Jr.), **48:** 391,n1; **49:** 281,n1
High-Brow Hearstism. The Peace Agitation of the New Republic (Walling), **45:** 153n1
Highways Transport Committee (Council of National Defense), **47:** 9
Hildebrand, Jesse Richardson, **47:** 388,n1
Hilfe (Berlin), **42:** 389n1
Hilfsverein, **48:** 98-99
Hill, Benjamin H., **44:** 331n3
Hill, David Jayne, **51:** 147n1
Hill, Ebenezer J., **42:** 324,n1
Hill, Johnson W., **42:** 116
Hill, Lucius D., **42:** 260n2
Hilles, Florence Bayard (Mrs. William Samuel), **43:** 201n1
Hillis, Newell Dwight, **45:** 142,n3
Hillman, Sidney, **44:** 164
Hillquit, Morris, **42:** 197,n1, 198, 199, 217, 253; **44:** 79; **45:** 318, 319; on international socialist conference, **42:** 268, 268-69, 350; and New York mayoralty, **44:** 272,n2, 333n1, 334, 393, 408, 463,n1, 504, 512, 556n2
Hillstrom, Joseph (Joe Hill), **51:** 377,n1, 378,n3
Hindenburg, Paul von, **40:** 144, 146, 378, 463n1, 555; **41:** 24, 26n1, 518; **42:** 160-61; **43:** 185,n2; **44:** 45,n7; **45:** 385, 595n3; **46:** 162, 163, 173, 190, 267; **51:** 253n2
Hindenburg, S.M.S., **51:** 490
Hindenburg Line, **51:** 384
Hine, Charles De Lano, **43:** 514,n3; **44:** 12
Hines, Walker Downer, **47:** 408,n2; **49:** 186,n1,2, 206; **51:** 408
Hinshaw, Virgil Goodman, **42:** 237n4
Hintze, Paul von, **40:** 515,n2; **41:** 182,n1; **44:** 296n1; **49:** 382,n2; **51:** 253n2
Hipper, Franz von, **51:** 541n1
Hirst, David Wayne, **43:** 134n2
Hirst, Francis Wrigley, **40:** 126-27, 494
Hirth, William, **47:** 90-91
His Initial Effort (Herron), **40:** 542n2
His Own Interpretation (London *Westminster Gazette*), **41:** 251n3
Hiss, Philip, **45:** 349,n2; **46:** 98-99,n1
Hiss and Weeks (architectural firm, N.Y.), **46:** 98n1
Historian, **45:** 487n2
Historische Zeitschrift, **48:** 63n1
History of the American People (Wilson), **40:** 560; **43:** 540; **46:** 570; **47:** 302, 336; **48:** 120; WW receives a special edition, **48:** 479, 482-83; WW against making film of, **51:** 14-15,n1, 172-73

History of the Great War (proposed text, Howland), **40:** 455-56,n1,3
History of the Labour Party from 1914 (Coles), **46:** 435n3
History of the Peace Movement in the Netherlands (Jong van Beek en Donk), **46:** 198n3
History of the Roumanians from Roman Times to the Completion of Unity (Seton-Watson), **47:** 240n1
History of the Shipbuilding Labor Adjustment Board, 1917 to 1919 (Hotchkiss and Seager), **44:** 220n1; **49:** 229n1
Hitchcock, Gilbert Monell, **40:** 103, 458n2; **41:** 121-22, 365; **44:** 81, 392; **45:** 566; **47:** 16, 234, 490; **48:** 51, 591; **49:** 508; **51:** 277n7, 392,n3, 405, 423-24; and armed-ship bill, **41:** 318n1, 323-24, 328; advocates testing armed neutrality, **41:** 498-500, 510; and woman suffrage, **45:** 278, 339; **46:** 61; and resolution on fuel proclamation, **46:** 31n1; and Chamberlain bills, **46:** 101n1, 204-205, 257n2
Hitchcock, James Ripley Wellman, **46:** 449,n1, 570-72; **47:** 302, 336
Hitchcock, Jessie Crounse (Mrs. Gilbert Monell), **49:** 508
Hitchman Coal and Coke Company *v.* Mitchell, Individually, *et al.*, **46:** 297n1
Hizen (Japanese ship), **49:** 150
Hoan, Daniel Webster, **44:** 339-40,n1, 344; **47:** 439
Hobby, William Pettus, **45:** 76-77, 161, 253; **47:** 144n2
Hoboken, N.J., **49:** 503
Hoboken *Observer*, **51:** 650,n2
Hobson, John Atkinson, **42:** 422,n2; **48:** 212,n5
Hochbaum, Hays L., **49:** 543,n1
Hodge, Frederick Webb, **45:** 154n2,4
Hodgson, Robert MacLeod, **47:** 72n3; **48:** 39,n1; **49:** 44,n1
Hoffman, Aaron, **46:** 520
Hoffmann, Arthur, **40:** 320-24, 348-54, 457-62; **41:** 102-107, 193-94; **43:** 28n1; **45:** 594
Hoffmann, Max, **45:** 384n2, 411n1, 595n3; **46:** 163, 471n3
Hoffstot, Frank Norton, **42:** 539, 540-41,n1
Hog Island, Pa., **46:** 124,n2, 361,n1; **51:** 13-14; launching of *Quistconck*, **49:** 164n1; photograph, *illustration section, 49*
Hoge, Peyton Harrison, **42:** 86,n1
Hogue, Richard W., **44:** 79
Hohenlohe, Prince Alexander von, **45:** 416n5; **47:** 65; **51:** 623
Hohenzollern (yacht), **42:** 521
Hohenzollerns, **46:** 315
Hohler, Thomas Beaumont, **41:** 366,n3, 458-60; **43:** 496; **49:** 550,n1
Holden, Hale, **45:** 373-74,n1, 403
Holder, Frans van, **40:** 530,n1

Holding Fast the Inner Lines: Democracy, Nationalism and the Committee on Public Information (Vaughn), **42:** 55n1; **43:** 3n1, 168n2; **44:** 248n1, 505n2

Holland: *see* Netherlands, The

Holland House, Washington, D.C., **40:** 85n1

Hollis, Christopher, **40:** 488n9

Hollis, Henry French, **42:** 149, 495, 532n1; **43:** 207-208,n1, 530; **44:** 23; **48:** 363; **49:** 264; **51:** 182-84,n1, 255, 510, 593-94; and railroad crisis, **41:** 241, 251-52, 262; and woman suffrage, **45:** 278, 338; **47:** 34, 399, 414; effect of son's suicide, **51:** 185,n2, 425; on peace conference, **51:** 298-99; on peace notes, **51:** 319, 421-22; on destruction in France and Belgium, **51:** 421-22

Hollis, Henry French, Jr., **51:** 185,n1, 425

Hollister, William R., **47:** 129,n1

Holloman, James Arthur, **47:** 382,n1

Hollond Memorial Presbyterian Church, Phila., **48:** 531n1

Holman, Charles William, **49:** 440,n1, 441

Holman, William Arthur, **44:** 213,n1

Holme, W. E., **43:** 230

Holmes, George Frederick, **44:** 260,n2

Holmes, John Haynes, **44:** 266-67; **51:** 12n2

Holmes, Lydia Wickliffe, **48:** 352,n1; **51:** 537

Holmes, Oliver Wendell (1841-1935), **46:** 297n1; **47:** 425

Holstein, Germany, **51:** 607

Holt, Hamilton, **46:** 14,n1, 460, 469; **48:** 627-28; **49:** 277, 347

Holtzendorff, Henning von, **40:** 463n1

Holy Roman Empire, **46:** 246, 261; **47:** 240

Holyrood Palace, Edinburgh, **42:** 89n2

homestead bill: *see* grazing homestead bill

Hommerich, August, **46:** 163,n2

Honduras, **41:** 143,n18, 144, 145,n1; **42:** 359

Honnold, Fred C., **47:** 409,n4, 410

Honnold, William Lincoln, **40:** 418,n1; **41:** 113,n3

Honolulu, **42:** 133

Honolulu Consolidated Oil Co., **40:** 561n2; **41:** 69n1

Hoo Wei Teh, **43:** 58

Hood, Edwin Milton, **41:** 324,n1

Hooker, Edith Houghton, **42:** 138-39,n1

Hooker, Richard, **41:** 295; **48:** 242

Hooker Electrochemical Company of Niagara Falls, **42:** 347n3

Hoover, Herbert Clark, **40:** 388, 484, 540, 554, 558; **41:** 3, 7, 113,n3, 214,n1, 239, 330; **42:** 48, 220, 323, 411n1 419, 420, 494-95; **43:** 35, 192, 319n1, 437n3, 493,n1; **44:** 32,n1, 38, 53, 107, 146, 160,n1, 247n1, 268, 343n1, 411, 501, 515; **45:** 74, 86, 148n1, 167n1, 238n1, 246, 570; **46:** 3, 30, 151n2, 265n1, 386, 387, 444n2, 489, 547, 614; **47:** 43, 137, 153, 178, 246, 558-59; **48:** 75, 169, 191, 247, 390, 392, 606; **49:** 304, 341, 368, 423, 424-25, 440; **51:** 26, 70, 109, 272, 372, 407, 416, 615, 638; W. H. Page on, **40:** 369; on Belgian deportations, **40:** 409, 409-11; on steps to be taken if U.S. enters war, **41:** 226, 227-29; on control of American food consumption, **41:** 228; **44:** 443-44,n1; on WW's war message, **41:** 543; on food crisis, **42:** 108-109; accepts position as Food Administrator, **42:** 345; on Lever bill, **42:** 430-31,n1, 532-33; **43:** 48-49,n1,6, 56, 57, 160-61, 207-208, 210, 339; and organization of Food Administration, **42:** 437, 480-85, 485-86, 522-23; meets with E. M. House, **43:** 99-100; urges embargo due to grain crisis, **43:** 117-18; concern over misrepresentation of Food Administration, **44:** 36; on draft exemptions, **44:** 72-73, 123; **49:** 509-10,n1; on wheat supply and prices, **44:** 88, 89n1,2, 215; **45:** 58-60, 178; **46:** 214, 304-309, 345-47, 368, 461, 565, 572-73; **47:** 120-21; **48:** 580; **49:** 352-53, 354, 356, 391-93

WW on making statement on farm prices, **44:** 191-92; and transportation of food, **44:** 544n1; **46:** 126-27,n1, 394, 424-26; on grain restrictions in brewing industry, **45:** 83-85, 91, 113, 228; **48:** 166-67, 209,n1; on resignations in Food Administration, **45:** 85; on unjust profits in food industries, **45:** 124-25, 128, 178-79,n2; on sugar prices, **45:** 115-16, 163,n1, 178; **49:** 419n; on legislation to be considered in Congress, **45:** 179-81; on conservation, **45:** 181; **46:** 19-21, 109,n1; corrections made in Food Administration poster, **45:** 256-57; sugar investigation and, **45:** 344-45,n1, 347-48, 352-54; E. M. House on, **45:** 399; **46:** 317; on beef surplus, **46:** 77, 125-26, 565,n1; requests grain investigation, **46:** 401, 407; on meat-packing industry, **46:** 409-10; **47:** 4, 47, 48, 49, 50, 90; **49:** 129-30, 460, 461, 464, 498, 504, 509, 522-28; C. Spreckels and sugar, **46:** 501-502, 546; D. F. Houston on livestock prices and, **46:** 504, 505,n2; and War Industries Board, **46:** 522,n1; proposes meat industry commission, **47:** 149-53, 192, 221; and western grain exchanges, **47:** 158-59,n1; F. W. Taussig and, **47:** 224, 225, 255; on Belgian relief, **47:** 293-94; **48:** 46-48, 80; on meat-packing investigation and Trade Commission's report, **48:** 7-9, 44, 107-10, 178, 562,n1; **51:** 18, 80; suggested as head of proposed Russian relief commission, **48:** 305-306, 306, 310, 315-16, 611; **49:** 408; plans European trip to visit his counterparts, **48:** 308-309, 310-11, 466-68; on monthly Food Administration reports,

48: 313; memorandum on coordination of Allied nonmilitary activities, **48:** 324-29; on reduction of activities of nonwar industries, **48:** 484-85; on coordination of inter-Allied agencies, **49:** 258-59, 337, 362-63; on brewing industry proclamation, **49:** 550; on food export program, **51:** 88-89; and Fuel Administration problems, **51:** 113, 114, 116; on hog prices, **51:** 126-27; on the draft, **51:** 228,n2; on price indices and Food Administration, **51:** 357-61; on postwar food management and Belgian Relief Commission, **51:** 397-99, 437-38, 457-59, 461, 605, 618-20, 634-36; praises WW's negotiations for peace, **51:** 554-55, 578; on German plan to destroy Belgian coal mines, **51:** 576, 577

Hoover, Irwin Hood (Ike), **40:** 380-81; **41:** 364, 383, 424, 506, 515, 557; **42:** 31, 426; **44:** 430; **47:** 309; **48:** 22, 148,n2; **51:** 475

Hoover-Wilson Wartime Correspondence, September 24, 1914 to November 11, 1918 (O'Brien, ed.), **44:** 160n1

Hopkins, Alison Low Turnbull (Mrs. John Appleton Haven), **43:** 201n1, 235,n1, 436

Hopkins, Charles Howard, **44:** 270n1

Hopkins, Charlotte Everett Wise (Mrs. Archibald), **46:** 37n1, 195,n1, 206-207; **47:** 53

Hopkins, Ernest Jerome, **42:** 270n4

Hopkins, John Appleton Haven, **40:** 166; **42:** 237n4; **47:** 254n1; and woman suffrage, **43:** 213,n2, 235, 250, 436-37

Hopkins, Mark, **41:** 423

Hopkins, Prince (Prynce or Pryns) Charles, **49:** 208,n2, 306

Hopper, John J., **46:** 15n1

Hopwood, Francis John Stephens, **43:** 360,n1

Horace S. Ely and Company, N.Y., **51:** 644n2

Horn, Daniel, **45:** 33n8, **51:** 541n1

Horn, Henry John, **47:** 428,n3

Hornblower, George S., **49:** 62n3

Hornbrook, James Joseph, **46:** 598

Hornsby, John Allen, **46:** 209,n3

Horodyski, Jean Marie de, **42:** 352, 355-56, 454-55, 520, 543-45; **43:** 37-38, 256, 426; **44:** 316; **48:** 335

Horthy de Nagybánya, Miklós, **51:** 562n1

Horvat (Horvath), Dmitrii Leonidovich, **47:** 99,n6, 397, 398; **48:** 72,n2; **49:** 221, 494; **51:** 480, 481n1, 608

Horvat (Horvath) movement, **47:** 397, 398, 592, 594

Hot Springs, N.C., **51:** 69, 70

Hotchkiss, Willard Eugene, **44:** 220n1; **49:** 299n1

Hôtel de Ville, Paris, **46:** 100n1

Hough, Charles Merrill, **40:** 551,n2; **43:** 165n2; **44:** 171

Houghton Mifflin and Company, **46:** 449, 605,n1; **47:** 41

Housatonic, S.S., **41:** 284

House, Edward Mandell, **40:** 20-21, 30-33, 60-61, 62-63, 96-97, 118, 132, 133, 160, 178, 189, 192, 237, 237-41, 243n2, 326, 339-42, 343, 345-46, 359-60, 379, 402-405, 406, 407, 407-409, 418-19, 429, 462-63, 468-69, 469,n1,2, 474, 493-94, 494-95, 495; **41:** 3-4, 69, 115, 122, 127,n1, 134, 137, 149, 164-65, 185, 190, 196-97, 200, 201, 214, 215-16, 217, 226, 227-29, 235, 250, 292-93, 304n3, 317-18, 322, 331-32, 340-41, 346, 349,n1, 373-74, 374-75, 376, 388, 411, 429-30, 454-55, 466, 468, 473, 496-98, 501, 511, 528-30, 531, 543-44, 554-55; **42:** 22, 24, 29-30, 45, 64, 89-91, 141, 145, 160, 220, 248, 267, 372, 378, 437-39, 520, 527, 529; **43:** 24, 38, 66, 167, 172, 183-84, 185-86, 194-96, 197-98, 242-43, 313-14, 356-57, 364-65, 365-66, 409-10, 425-26, 457, 485-87, 497; **44:** 16, 30, 31, 56-57, 69-70, 80, 105, 120-21, 141, 149-50, 164-65, 175-79, 203, 213, 242, 244, 278, 284-85, 310, 323-24, 328, 342, 353-54, 362-64, 371, 378-82, 385, 388, 390, 392-93, 426-27, 454-55, 541, 545, 546; **45:** 3-4, 69, 82, 86, 151-52, 174-75, 186, 187, 221, 245, 311-13, 316-17, 317-18, 322-23, 323-27, 332-33, 370, 384, 397-400, 423, 430-31, 438, 445, 458-59, 486; **46:** 36n1, 114-17, 167-68, 169, 172, 178, 181-83, 213, 220-21, 221, 255, 266, 266-68, 271-72, 279n, 316-18, 327-28, 350-51, 382-83, 429-30, 432-33, 435-38, 444-45, 445, 448-49, 460, 473, 483, 485, 487-89, 507, 516, 530-31, 532, 555-56, 567, 570-71, 597, 601n1; **47:** 12, 59, 85-86, 102-103, 103-104, 105-106, 185-86, 307-10, 313, 334, 391, 468, 477, 503, 505, 523-25, 605; **48:** 50-53, 62-63, 69-71, 94-95, 143-44, 144-45, 152, 153, 283-84, 288-90, 331, 366, 374, 382, 391-92, 454, 523, 549-50; **49:** 83, 90, 140, 202, 269-72, 273, 280, 286-87, 302, 303, 303-304, 366, 404, 454, 455, 499, 548; **51:** 6-7, 10, 64, 102-10, 116-17, 142-44, 145-46, 164, 188, 226, 275-80, 291, 314-17, 325, 326, 328, 348, 352, 372, 471, 495, 504-505, 511, 533, 544, 562, 575, 583, 616-17, 634, 635

on peace moves, **40:** 4-6, 29-30, 39, 74-75, 84-85, 110-11, 131-32; and W. J. Bryan, **40:** 85-86,n1, 137-38, 173; resists WW desire to send him abroad, **40:** 85, 96, 118, 134-35; on politics in England, **40:** 172-73, 185-86, 187, 201, 212, 294; on reply to German peace proposal, **40:** 233-34; advice and comment on WW's peace note, **40:** 238, 276, 293, 304-305, 345, 359; meets with W. Wiseman, **40:** 262, 464-65; **41:** 26, 39-40; **44:** 200-203; efforts to reassure Britain after WW's note, **40:** 307n1; meetings with J. H. Bernstorff, **40:** 337, 364-65, 477-78, 505, 507, 508, 516-17, 524, 525,

House, Edward Mandell (*cont.*)
526-29; **41:** 17-18, 18-19, 24-26, 26, 51,
69, 80-82, 95-96, 117, 117-18; and L. R.
Colcord, **40:** 371-72,n2, 374-75, 380; appointment suggestions, **40:** 408, 413;
46: 518; advice and comments on Peace
without Victory speech, **40:** 445-46,n1,
462-63, 491, 539, 558; meets with
H. Hoover, **40:** 540; and J. H. Whitehouse, **41:** 85-86; meets with WW and
R. Lansing on break with Germany,
41: 86-89; and alleged German plot to
assassinate WW, **41:** 127n1, 201n1; desires to be on WW's staff, **41:** 134, 149;
and Zimmermann telegram, **41:** 288,
296-97, 308,n1; and H. Bergson, **41:**
315n2; **48:** 317,n2; not at inauguration,
41: 328; suggested as replacement for
W. H. Page, **41:** 341; suggests V. C.
McCormick as ambassador for Japan,
41: 374; on W. Denman and Shipping
Board, **41:** 418; advocates recognition
of Russian government, **41:** 422-23; on
Allied need of war supplies, **41:** 428-29;
T. B. Hohler meets with, **41:** 458, 459-
60; and WW's war message, **41:** 482-84,
497, 528-29,n1; J. A. Baker on interviews with, **41:** 532-36; and Balfour
mission to U.S., **41:** 544-45, 553; **42:** 18-
19, 20, 120, 142n1, 142-43, 155-57, 168-
73, 288-89; suggestions for Russian
commission, **42:** 30, 43, 58, 111, 194-95;
on Pan-American Pact, **42:** 80; on Norway and war, **42:** 110,n1,3; on J. Joffre,
42: 170; and shipbuilding program, **42:**
233-34, 235-36, 553-54, 554-55, 555; on
Japanese alien rights, **42:** 275, 276,
277, 278

on peace terms, **42:** 288-89, 354-55,
425, 433, 523; suggests Anglo-American defensive alliance, **42:** 296; on R. E.
Swing, **42:** 388; **43:** 29; on Northcliffe,
42: 428,n2, 432, 445-46, 461, 487-88,
542; on WW's Flag Day address, **42:**
456, 520, 523; on winning the war with
air power, **42:** 530-31; on British financial crisis, **43:** 44, 147, 223, 425; on
Central Purchasing Commission, **43:**
76; on H. Hoover, **43:** 99-100; on Balfour's proposed Allied treaty, **43:** 123-
24; on Morgenthau mission, **43:** 183-
84; on exchange of war views by New
York *World* and *Berliner Tageblatt*, **43:**
184, 198, 219-20, 220-21, 237-38, 274-
75, 285, 366-67, 411; and W. Wiseman
and shipbuilding program, **43:** 209-
10,n1; on Russia, **43:** 248-49, 522-23;
45: 73, 166n1, 184-85, 188-89; on Denman-Goethals controversy, **43:** 265; on
D. F. Malone, **43:** 283, 290-91, 424-25;
on W. G. McAdoo, **43:** 390-91; on N. Angell memorandum on Allied diplomatic
strategy, **43:** 400, 401; on Spring Rice
and Northcliffe, **43:** 451; on Pope Bene-

dict's appeal and WW's reply, **43:** 471-
72, 488-89, 508-509, 521,n1; **44:** 33, 40-
41, 49-50, 83-84, 157; on WW, **43:** 486;
has more complete picture of war than
WW, **43:** 486-87; on possible resignation of R. Lansing, **44:** 176, 184; on bat-
tleships, **44:** 178; WW meets with, **44:**
184-86; **49:** 275-76, 281-82, 293-94; and
preparatory work for peace conference,
44: 184, 216-17, 226, 229, 246-47, 275-
76,n2, 279, 298, 299,n1,2, 380-81, 454-
55; as representative to inter-Allied
council, **44:** 200-201, 203, 297, 373-75,
378-79, 381, 382, 385, 392, 427, 433,
437-39, 445-46, 448, 455, 461; on Massachusetts politics, **44:** 221-22; on Mooney case, **44:** 246; warns McCormick
about embargo of neutrals, **44:** 396,n1;
newspaper reveals mission of, **44:** 459-
60,n2; on Pershing-Pétain conflict, **44:**
462, 463
House Mission (1917): **44:** 532, 537,
545, 546, 547-49; **45:** 3-4, 14, 47-48, 54,
68, 70-71, 73-74, 93, 112-13, 122, 151,
151-52, 156-57, 166,n1, 177, 184-85,
188-89, 309, 313; report of, **45:** 166n1,
327, 368-69,n1, 398, 401; W. Wiseman
on, **45:** 311; J. J. Jusserand on, **45:** 365;
and Paris inter-Allied conference, **45:**
3, 112-13, 122, 151, 156, 166, 176, 323-
24; on formation of Supreme War
Council, **45:** 47-48, 69, 93,n1,2, 112-13,
151; and league of nations, **45:** 68; **46:**
574-75; **47:** 323-24; **48:** 289-90, 424-26,
561, 592-93, 608, 630-37, 647,n1; **49:**
12, 13 14, 225, 265-68, 428-29, 466,
468n1, 508; and Great Britain, **45:** 70-
71; on political conditions in Europe,
45: 73; approves constitution of Inter-
Allied Naval Council, **45:** 189-91; on
WW's State of the Union message of
1917, **45:** 232; returns from European
mission, **45:** 309, 313

urges W. Wiseman to return to U.S.,
45: 332; on possible Anglo-French
peace proposal discussion, **45:** 421; on
Fourteen Points, **45:** 476n1, 493n1,
506n1, 550-59, 564; and proposal for
postwar economic boycott of Germany,
46: 6, 8; reaction to coal proclamation,
46: 23-24; WW on, **46:** 88; **51:** 351-52;
on peace delegates, **46:** 115-16; on Italy, **46:** 207; on proposed Japanese intervention in Siberia, **46:** 214-15, 518-
19, 519, 549, 553, 561-62, 571-72, 576-
77, 590-91; **47:** 156-57, 170-71, 412,
417-18; on Supreme War Council's declaration, **46:** 250-51; on E. R. Stettinius
and War Industries Board, **46:** 259; on
WW's Four Points Address, **46:** 290-91,
313-14, 317,n2, 318, 327; on Hog Island
investigation, **46:** 361; and F. I. Cobb's
and S. G. Blythe's news plan, **46:** 367;
and Charles I message to WW, **46:** 464,

467-68; and WW not recognizing Bolsheviks, **46:** 485; and Austria-Hungary and peace moves, **47:** 11, 122; **51:** 23-24; and League to Enforce Peace, **47:** 101-102; on WW's sending message of admiration to British troops, **47:** 131; and British request for U.S. troops, **47:** 157, 158, 170, 227, 302-303, 433, 436, 444, 471, 585; discusses speech WW to deliver in Baltimore, **47:** 186, 308; and Britain's acknowledgement of U.S. help, **47:** 206, 256, 308; on anxiety during German offensive, **47:** 215; D. Lloyd George on, **47:** 229, 338; and Irish conscription issue, **47:** 238, 266n1, 441-42; and Wisconsin campaign, **47:** 388-90; on Gen. R. Hutchinson, **47:** 465; and H. Plunkett on Irish situation, **47:** 469-71; on W. G. McAdoo and railroad fuel issue, **47:** 498-99; on Italy wanting to celebrate first anniversary of entrance into war, **47:** 525-26; on J. D. Ryan, **47:** 526; annoyed at publicity given him, **47:** 534,n1; on aircraft investigation, **47:** 546, 584; George V on, **47:** 596-97; on J. J. Pershing, **47:** 616; request for his presence at Supreme War Council meeting, **48:** 61-62, 79, 135; on Reading, **48:** 95; and Gen. L. Wood, **48:** 173n1; on plan for military reorganization in France, **48:** 231-33, 261, 265-68; on plan for a Russian relief commission, **48:** 240, 306-307, 310; as possible representative in Paris, **48:** 266-67; **49:** 267; on Reading's frequent requests for meetings with WW and WW's refusals, **48:** 381; on WW making statement on food situation, **48:** 390-91; suggests WW address Congress and Allies on number of U.S. troops in France, **48:** 400; and intervention in Siberia, **48:** 430-31; **49:** 96; on meeting with K. Ishii, **48:** 540-41, 577-78; on son-in-law's draft rejection, **48:** 541,n1; on third term for WW, **49:** 275; on crank letters, **49:** 303; suggests J. W. Davis for British ambassadorship, **49:** 348, 350; Wiseman on staying in Magnolia, Mass., with, **49:** 397; and W. Lippmann, **49:** 402,n3, 429; **51:** 9; on Allies being committed to U.S. program, **49:** 428-29; on Spain, **49:** 453; meets with W. G. McAdoo, **49:** 488-89; and Bulgaria, **51:** 145; on German-U.S. peace notes, **51:** 254, 276-77, 278-79, 316, 340-42; suggestions for peace conference and commissioners, **51:** 314, 315, 316-17, 406-408, 473, 606-607; participation in peace negotiations, **51:** 462, 473, 511-13, 513, 514-17, 531-32, 534, 541, 542, 562-63, 568-69, 580-82, 594-95, 596, 606-607; on Pershing's peace terms letter to Supreme War Council, **51:** 523-25, 596-98, 617; on need for unbiased information, **51:** 637

38; on establishing international relief organization, **51:** 638-39; *see also* House Mission

House, Loulie Hunter (Mrs. Edward Mandell), **40:** 132; **41:** 297, 317, 340; **43:** 186; **44:** 175-76; **45:** 4, 397-98; **46:** 23; **47:** 86; **48:** 50, 63, 391; **49:** 265, 294, 488; **51:** 142, 316, 483

House of Representatives: *see* United States Congress, House of Representatives

House Journal, **45:** 448n1

House to go to Paris War Conference (Philadelphia *Public Ledger*), **44:** 459n2

housing: for government workers in Washington, D.C., **46:** 37,n1, 67, 195, 206-207; **47:** 38,n1,2, 53, 58, 66; and shipyard workers, **46:** 98-99, 124, 150, 171; WW signs bill to alleviate problems, **46:** 443,n1; and alley legislation, **47:** 192-93,n2, 255,n1; Negroes and, **48:** 159-60; and antiprofiteering rent bill, **48:** 190,n1, 192-93, 222; and women, **48:** 199; W. B. Wilson on establishing a housing corporation, **48:** 594; program, **49:** 72

Housing Administration, **48:** 150

Houska, Vaclav, **49:** 219,n1

Houston, David Franklin, **40:** 9,n1, 28, 37, 173, 193, 207, 347, 348; **41:** 55n1, 88, 94n1, 282, 340; **42:** 220, 301,n2; **43:** 11, 35, 177, 183, 433, 486; **44:** 82-83, 160, 207,n2, 263, 392, 454; **45:** 76, 148n1, 555; **46:** 116, 117, 174n1, 196, 212, 306, 335-36, 347, 409, 493, 547, 582, 614; **47:** 47, 48, 153, 221, 353; **48:** 52, 69; 107, 219-20,n1, 298, 432, 434, 444; **49:** 78, 90, 104, 451; **51:** 412, 414, 415, 604, 616; and Washington University, **40:** 215-16,n1, 303; and grazing homestead bill, **40:** 214, 287, 288, 290; and meat-packing investigation, **41:** 32, 112, 208; **48:** 7; advocates break with Germany, **41:** 123; on entering war, **41:** 439, 444, 503; E. M. House on, **44:** 176; and commercial policy of U.S., **44:** 456-57; on Texas drought and cattle crisis, **45:** 105-107, 161; on water-power legislation, **45:** 168-69, 301; **49:** 316, 329-32, 344, 356, 357; and draft exemptions, **45:** 583, 585, 594; on B. M. Baruch, **46:** 91, 215, 218; on cattle and meat-packing industry, **46:** 503-505; **49:** 439-40; WW on War Industries Board and, **46:** 522; WW advised to dismiss, **46:** 602; and Baer bill, **47:** 20,n1, 178,n2; and price fixing, **47:** 117, 138, 445; and Nonpartisan League, **47:** 177-79, 188; on potatoes, **47:** 449; on national forests, **47:** 589; on A. F. Lever, **48:** 259; on aid to drought-stricken farmers, **49:** 99-100, 101; suggested for Russian commission, **49:** 407, 408; on Federal Board of Farm Organizations,

Houston, David Franklin (*cont.*)
  49: 440-42; W. G. McAdoo on, 49: 489;
  photograph, *illustration section,* 47
Houston, Helen Beall (Mrs. David
  Franklin), 41: 505,n1
Houston, Herbert Sherman, 48: 29n1
Houston, William Cannon, 40: 292n1,
  305, 315
Houston, Tex.; racial clash in and subsequent courts-martial, 44: 41-42,n1,2,
  49, 63-64, 77-78; 45: 546-47,n1, 577,
  579; courts-martial and clemency appeal for condemned men, 46: 13, 16,n1,
  339, 383-84,n1, 385,n1; sentencing of
  rioters, 49: 324-28, 399-402
Hovelaque, Émile Lucien, 42: 169-70,n3,
  210n1; 46: 100,n1,2
Hovey, Carl, 48: 147,n5
How Allied Capitals View Wilson's Ad-
  dress (New York *Evening Post*), 40:
  588n1
How the Kaiser, Weeks Ahead, Fixed the
  Date for War to Begin, Now Revealed
  by Morgenthau (New York *World*), 45:
  123n1
How the War Came to America (Bullard
  and Poole), 43: 168n2; 47: 522,n4
*How We Advertised America: The First
  Telling of the Amazing Story of the
  Committee on Public Information that
  Carried the Gospel of Americanism to
  Every Corner of the Globe* (Creel), 43:
  168n2; 45: 241n1
How We Found a Cure for Strikes
  (Disque), 46: 218n2
Howard, Daniel Edward, 47: 315,n1
Howard, Roy Wilson, 40: 133, 134-35,
  307n1, 345-46, 374, 381-82, 412, 413;
  41: 308,n1; 45: 596, 597-98; 46: 610n2;
  51: 621n1; on press censorship and
  peace negotiations, 51: 538-39
Howard, William Schley, 47: 325,n1,2,
  382,n1; and Georgia senatorial campaign, 49: 80-82,n1, 114, 115, 143, 205-
  206, 237, 369, 528n1
Howard University, 42: 321, 322,n1
*Howard University: The First Hundred
  Years, 1867-1967* (Logan), 42: 322n1
Howe, Annie Josephine Wilson (Mrs.
  George, Jr.) sister of WW, 40: 93, 108,
  128, 574; 41: 259, 458; 43: 241
Howe, Frederic Clemson, 42: 215; 43:
  175; 44: 290n1, 478, 498; 48: 93,
  241,n1; memorandum on issues to be
  settled for an enduring peace, 44: 474-
  77; on governmental ownership of railroads, 45: 283-85, 309-11, 334
Howe, George III, nephew of WW, 41:
  172, 210, 259-60, 457, 458; 43: 236
Howe, James Wilson, nephew of WW, 41:
  457, 458; 43: 236, 242,n2; 51: 27
Howell, Clark; and Georgia senatorial
  campaign, 49: 80-82, 114, 115, 116,
  205, 237, 528
Howells, William Dean: WW's birthday
  greetings to, 41: 311,n1

Howland, Harold Jacobs, 40: 455n2
Howland, William Bailey, 40: 455-
  56,n1,2,3, 464
Hoyt, Mary Eloise, cousin of EAW, 47:
  139-40
Hoyt, Sadie (Saidie) Cooper (Mrs.
  Thomas Alexander), 40: 568,n1
Hoyt, Thomas Alexander, uncle of EAW,
  42: 88
Hsü Shih-ch'ang, 51: 292-93, 318-19,
  457n2, 550,n5
Huber, Ernst Rudolf, 51: 253n2
Hübscher, Carl P., 40: 44n2
Huddleston, George, 49: 138n1, 224,
  236,n1, 245,n2
Hudson, James Alexander, 47: 90-91
Hudson, Manley Ottmer, 47: 155,n3
Hudson Guild, 44: 267n3
Hudspeth, Robert Stephen, 47: 82n1; 49:
  210
Hughes, Charles Evans, 40: 40, 41, 60n1,
  61, 90, 117, 359, 370, 414n3; 41: 341,
  400, 498; 44: 167, 333n1; 46: 238,n2,
  566; 47: 542, 616; 49: 402n1; 51:
  618,n1; A. G. Gardiner on, 40: 35n3;
  congratulatory message to WW, 40: 38,
  46: 238,n2, 566; and 1916 election, 47:
  437, 438, 453n4; and Italy's anniversary of entry into war, 47: 525, 553,
  554; and aircraft investigation, 47:
  584, 603; 48: 3, 15, 45-46, 50, 305
Hughes, Margaret Hughes (Mrs. William), 46: 169
Hughes, William, 46: 61,n1; 49: 139n1;
  51: 283,n1; and woman suffrage, 45:
  278, 338; and water-power legislation,
  45: 301; death of, 46: 169,n1, 288,
  332n1, 349
Hughes, William Morris, 48: 228,n1; 49:
  408-409,n1, 409, 466
*Hugo Grotius, the Father of the Modern
  Science of International Law* (Vree-
  land), 43: 462,n2
Hukuang Railway, 49: 407
Hulbert, Allen Schoolcraft, 43: 502; 44:
  82-83, 207,n1,2
Hulbert, Mary Allen, 43: 502; *see also*
  Peck, Mary Allen Hulbert
Hulen, John A., 44: 42,n4
Hull, Cordell, 45: 307; on taxation, 48:
  19-21, 27
Hull, William Isaac, 41: 302,n2, 303,
  304,n3
Hull-House, Chicago, 41: 303; 51: 181n1
Hulun, Manchuria: *see* Hailar
Humboldt, Ariz., 43: 157
Humphreys, Benjamin Grubb, 41: 198,n2
Hungarian Americans, 45: 138-39,
  241n1; 48: 435
Hungary and Hungarians, 40: 234; 41:
  211, 212, 260, 267; 42: 156, 334, 501;
  45: 57,n4; 46: 244; 48: 435, 436; 51: 502,
  541; and woman suffrage, 48: 340
Hunt, George Wylie Paul, 43: 53, 72, 87,
  98, 104,n1, 104-105, 109, 113, 127, 128,
  131, 171; 44: 172; 45: 403,n1, 46:

573,n1, 584, 598-99; **47:** 194; **49:** 28; report on Arizona copper strike settlement, **44:** 134-39; on H. C. Wheeler's army commission, **47:** 115-16, 187, 347
Hunt, Henry Thomas, **42:** 272,n2
Huntington, Elizabeth Wainwright Dodge (Mrs. George Herbert), **44:** 93,n3; **45:** 185,n2
Huntington, George Herbert, **45:** 185,n2
Hurban, Vladimir S., **49:** 194-200,n1, 221
Hurd, Richard Melanchthon, **47:** 141-42,n1; **51:** 147,n2
Hurley, Edward Nash, **42:** 252,n2; **44:** 13, 148n1, 211, 242, 243, 289, 394-95, 411, 437, 449, 482, 495, 501, 515, 544,n1; **45:** 46, 246, 272; **46:** 4n2, 30, 101, 107, 151n2, 171, 329, 338-39, 444n2, 546, 582; **47:** 5-6, 43, 73, 241, 294, 385,n6, 558-59,n1; **48:** 46, 140,n1; **49:** 71n1, 84, 85, 105,n1, 147, 164, 181, 210, 424-25,n1, 456, 490-91, 529; on cost accounting, **40:** 58-60, 250-55, 268-69, 278; resigns from Federal Trade Commission, **40:** 419-20, 427-28, 490; **41:** 46; meat-packing investigation, **40:** 519-21; **41:** 31,n1, 32, 37; on Webb bill, **41:** 84, 93; appointed chairman of Shipping Board, **43:** 260, 270-71, 286, 291; on shipbuilding, **44:** 209,n2; **45:** 314; **47:** 233-34,n1; **49:** 374, 473-74,n1; and Shipbuilding Labor Adjustment Board controversy, **44:** 219-21, 224, 226, 227, 228,n4,5, 233, 234-36; on coordinating needs of various departments for shipping, **45:** 42-44; and national employment service, **45:** 130,n1; and draft exemptions, **45:** 583, 585; and housing of shipyard workers, **46:** 123-24, 150, 151, 171; and carpenters' strike, **46:** 356,n5, 362-63, 378-79; and Hog Island, **46:** 361,n1; on electrical welding of ships, **46:** 503, 513; on reorganization of War Industries Board, **46:** 610; on profiteering in shipbuilding industry, **46:** 610-11; on restricting industrial development in eastern U.S., **47:** 336; and launching of *Tuckahoe,* **47:** 500,n1; and Georgia senatorial campaign, **49:** 144-45; on Public Service Railway Co., **49:** 474-75; photograph, *illustration section,* 44
Hurrah and Hallelujah: The Spirit of New Germanism, a Documentation (Bing), **42:** 394n5
Hurst, Cecil James Barrington, **48:** 501n1
Hurst, John, **41:** 218,n1
Husarek, K., **49:** 543,n1, 544
Husbands, Julia M., **49:** 264,n1
Husted, James William, **42:** 277n1
Husting, Paul Oscar, **40:** 523; **41:** 498; **42:** 146-50, 200-201; **43:** 117, 319; **45:** 376-77; **46:** 61,n2, 566n5; **47:** 40n1; on Socialist for Russian commission, **42:** 253-55, 259; death of, **44:** 421,n1, 429
Hustings, Jean Pierre, **44:** 421

Hustings, Mary Magdelena Juneau (Mrs. Jean Pierre), **44:** 421
Hutcheson, William Levi, **46:** 356n5, 364-65, 366, 367, 379, 578,n1; **47:** 223,n2, 248, 252, 283
Hutchins, Robert Grosvenor, Jr., **44:** 424,n1, 435
Hutchinson, William Thomas, **43:** 512n1
Hutchison, Robert, **47:** 230,n1, 305, 306, 369, 374, 386, 465
Hutten-Czapski, Bogdan Graf von, **41:** 139n2
Huysmans, Camille, **47:** 76,n5
Hyde, Mr. (of National Wheat Growers Association), **49:** 427,n2
Hyde, Clayton H., **51:** 212,n2
Hyde, Frank M., **46:** 383n1
Hyde, James Hazen, **49:** 169,n4, 173
Hyde, William DeWitt, **42:** 570,n1
Hylan, John Francis, **44:** 333n1, 458, 556n2; **45:** 157; **48:** 16; **51:** 20
Hyman, Mark, **46:** 361n1
Hymans, Paul, **42:** 338,n3; **51:** 569,n1, 570

Iakovlev, Nikolai Nikolaevich, **47:** 100,n2
Iceland, **40:** 248
Ickes, Harold LeClair, **44:** 165,n2
Idaho, **41:** 107; **44:** 14, 18; **45:** 234; **46:** 478; **47:** 194; labor problems in, **49:** 200, 222n1, 281; politics in, 145-46, 147; **51:** 180,n1, 589, 632
If I Were Wilson (Harden), **40:** 375,n2
Ifft, George Nicholas II, **49:** 487,n2
Iglesias Pantín, Santiago, **40:** 146-53,n1, 213; **41:** 407,n1; **47:** 543,n1, 577; **48:** 15-16, 35-37,n2, 75, 130, 637,n2; **49:** 26-36, 71, 135, 246
Ihlen, Nils Claus, **45:** 74,n3, 83, 114; **49:** 333,n1; **51:** 186
Iliodor (Monk Iliodor; Sergei Mikhailovich Trufanov), **42:** 465,n1
Illinois, **41:** 215; **42:** 83, 122; **43:** 512,n1; **44:** 165; **47:** 135-36, 410; **48:** 603-604; the draft and Swedes in, **46:** 458-59, 560; **51:** 552,n5,6, 589, 632
Illinois, S.S., **41:** 425,n1, 431, 436
Illinois, University of, **46:** 174n1
Illinois Central Railroad, **44:** 458; **46:** 426n6
Illinois Coal Operators Association, **47:** 409n4
Illinois Federation of Labor, **44:** 104n1
Illinois Manufacturers' Casualty Company, **46:** 124n1
Illinois National Guard, **44:** 42,n2, 63, 78
Illinois State Federation of Labor, **46:** 578n1
Illinois Trust and Savings Bank, **43:** 196
illiteracy, **47:** 30-32, 610,n1; **48:** 11
Im Weltkriege (Czernin), **46:** 115n1
Imienpo, Manchuria, **51:** 479,n1
Immigration, Committee on (Senate), **49:** 310n1
Immigration and Naturalization, Committee on (House of Reps.), **43:** 191n2

immigration legislation: Wilson's veto of second Burnett bill, **41,** 52-53

Imo, S.S., **45:** 230n1

Imperial University, Tokyo, **48:** 569n1, 582n1

Imperial War Cabinet, **42:** 327,n2, 339n4, 346, 531n1

Imperial War Conference, **42:** 327n2

Imperiali, Marquis Guglielmo (dei Principi di Francavilla), **44:** 318,n1; **45:** 351,n1

Improper Activities of German Officials in the United States (Lansing), **41:** 502n1

Improved Mailing Case Co. of New York, **40:** 215n1

In Defense of Yesterday: James M. Beck and the Politics of Conservatism, 1861-1936 (Keller), **45:** 596n1

In the Footsteps of Joseph Hampton and the Pennsylvania Quakers (Hampton), **44:** 199n

In the Fourth Year: Anticipations of a World Peace (Wells), **51:** 298,n2

In the Front Line Trenches (Harbison), **48:** 78n2

In Time of War I Sing (Crafton), **47:** 540,n1

income tax, **43:** 350n2; **44:** 182; **51:** 108n9, 205, 206, 219-20; and war costs, **41:** 448n2, 518; **46:** 15n1; WW deducts from his salary, **41:** 449; C. Hull on, **48:** 20-21; W. G. McAdoo on, **48:** 122-23, 127; W. B. Wilson on, **48:** 223;

Independent, The, **40:** 240, 455n2; **42:** 216; **46:** 14n1, 460; **47:** 276n3; **48:** 144n1; **49:** 277,n1, 347

Independent Labour party, Great Britain, **41:** 36,n1; **42:** 435n1

Independent Oil Producers' Agency of California, **45:** 350n1

India, **41:** 191, 301,n1; **42:** 340, 500; **45:** 412, 428-29, 573; **46:** 591; **47:** 245, 334, 356, 366, 422; **49:** 463,n2

Indian Council, **47:** 10, 20

Indiana, **40:** 230, 243; **42:** 83, 85, 122; **44:** 231; **46:** 285-86,n1; and F. C. Miller case, **46:** 97-98, 119; Democratic convention and platform for, **48:** 318-20,n1; **49:** 265,n2,3, 308, 309, 315; politics in, **51:** 632

Indianapolis, Ind., **43:** 421

Indianapolis dynamite case: *see* dynamite conspiracy case

Indianapolis *Freeman,* **43:** 119n1

Indianapolis News, **48:** 319n1

Indians, American: *see* American Indians

Indochina, **45:** 412

Industrial Arbitration Commision: *see* United States Industrial Arbitration Commission (proposed)

Industrial Bank of Japan, **42:** 63n5

Industrial Peace League of Jerome, Ariz., **44:** 86n1

Industrial Relations Commission: *see*

United States Commission on Industrial Relations

Industrial Service and Equipment Company, **47:** 385n1

Industrial Violence in Bayonne (Reed), **48:** 147,n4

Industrial Workers of the World (I.W.W.), **42:** 271,n1, 563, 564; **43:** 17,n4, 156-59, 191, 200,n1,2,3, 202, 203, 222n1, 231, 237, 267, 280-81, 325n1, 336, 341, 352, 417, 418, 419, 470n3, 494, 495, 510; **44:** 17-18, 27, 86n1, 107, 262; **45:** 261, 383,n3, 384; **46:** 139, 144n1, 145, 196, 348, 481-82, 508-509; **47:** 224; **49:** 538-39; arrest and indictment of leaders of, **44:** 17-18,n2, 158n1; F. Frankfurter on, **44:** 161-64; activities in Spokane, **44:** 50,n1, 345; and President's Mediation Commission, **44:** 103-104, 120; and Arizona, **44:** 136-37, 479; and Mesaba strike, **44:** 163n1; and Swedish Americans and draft evasion in Illinois, **47:** 135-36; activities in western states, **47:** 194-98, 232-33, 479; and Mooney case, **47:** 396; on Walsh bill, **47:** 573-74,n2,3,6,7, 604; and Pollak case, **51:** 125n1, 376-80

inflation: S. J. Graham on, **40:** 244-46

Information, Bureau of, **43:** 458; **47:** 217

Ingersoll, Raymond Vail, **46:** 89,n1

Ingersoll-Sergeant Drill Company, **49:** 455n1

Ingraham, William Moulton, **44:** 446-47

Inn, S.M.S., **51:** 493

Inouye, Kazutsugu, **51:** 549,n3

Inquiry: American Preparations for Peace, 1917-1919 (Gelfand), **44:** 275n1; **45:** 459n1

Inquiry memorandum, **45:** 17-19, 324, 459-74

Insincerity Already Exposed (New York *Evening Post*), **51:** 265,n1, 296-97,n1

Institute for Government Research, **40:** 443-44, 497-99

Institute of Economics, **40:** 443n1

Institution of Naval Architects of Great Britain, **47:** 67

Insular Affairs, Bureau of (War Dept.), **40:** 402; **49:** 252

Insular Affairs, Committee on (Senate), **40:** 295

Inter-Allied Board to Siberia (proposed), **49:** 323,n1, 323,n2

Inter-Allied conference, Paris: *see* Paris inter-Allied conference

Inter-Allied Conference on Propaganda, London, **49:** 434n1

Inter-Allied Council on War Purchases and Finance (Inter-Allied Purchasing Council; Supply Council), **45:** 351,n2, 362, 424; **46:** 75, 79, 324, 498; **47:** 173-74,n1; **48:** 467; **49:** 361n1; **51:** 182n1; W. G. McAdoo on need for creation of, **43:** 136,n2, 356n1; **44:** 195, 284, 355; **45:** 54-55; background and formation

of, **44:** 195-98, 284, 310, 312, 324, 353-54, 355, 369, 373-75; **45:** 245-46; controversy over political advice by, **46:** 359-60, 360-61,n1, 379-80, 393, 409, 415, 419, 465-67
Inter-Allied Embargo Council (Blockade Council, Joint Embargo Council); background of, **44:** 355-56, 369-70, 373-75, 380
Inter-Allied Food Council, **51:** 437, 634, 635, 636
Inter-Allied General Reserve, **46:** 241, 558-59
Inter-Allied Labor and Socialist Conference at London (Feb. 23, 1918), **47:** 74,n1, 75; **49:** 536
Inter-Allied Maritime Transport Council, **45:** 208-209, 213; **48:** 467; **51:** 634, 635, 636
Inter-Allied Naval Conference, **51:** 512-13
Inter-Allied Naval Council, **45:** 127, 190-91, 215,n1; **47:** 27, 332-33; **48:** 219, 285n3, 356, 385-86; background of, **44:** 86-87; and naval terms for armistice, **51:** 487, 488-95
Inter-Allied Purchasing Commission (in U.S.): W. G. McAdoo proposes creation of, **43:** 136-38,n1, 189, 319-20
Inter-Allied Shipping Board, **46:** 217, 324; recommendations for formation of, **45:** 351, 424-25
Inter-Allied Transportation Council, **48:** 200n2, 219
Interborough Rapid Transit Company, N.Y., **40:** 35n3
Interior, Department of the, **40:** 382, 402, 521; **41:** 290; **45:** 168,n1; **46:** 104,n1; **47:** 402, 403; **48:** 85, 219-20,n1; **51:** 103,n3
Internal Revenue, Bureau of, **48:** 89, 93
International Association for Woman Suffrage, **48:** 340
International Association of Bridge and Structural Iron Workers, **40:** 176,n1, 188n1, 207-208; **47:** 179n3
International Association of Industrial Accident Boards and Commissions, **44:** 314
International Association of Machinists, **47:** 223n2, 272, 359n1; **49:** 104,n2; strike in Bridgeport, Conn., **49:** 465,n1, 519-20, 537, 539-40, 547
International Brotherhood of Electrical Workers, **44:** 307-308; **45:** 96; **46:** 136
International Boundary Commission, **42:** 260,n2
International Chinese Public Loan Consortium, **49:** 311
International Committee of the Red Cross, **46:** 395,n2, 395-97, 406,n1
International Committee of Women for Permanent Peace, **45:** 586
international court (proposed), **48:** 631, 633-34
International Film Company, **41:** 483n1

International Film Service, Inc., **42:** 467n1, 489; **43:** 501
International Harvester Co., **42:** 167; **48:** 145n3; **49:** 55; **51:** 443
International Institute of Agriculture, Rome, Italy, **46:** 377,n2
International Maritime Council: see Inter-Allied Maritime Council
International Mercantile Marine Company, **41:**188
International News Service, **43:** 132, 133; **46:** 380,n1, 393, 408, 413, 437, 443, 601n1, 602; **47:** 267, 442
International Nickel Company, **43:** 177, 193
International Peace: Speech of Hon. Robert L. Owen ... in the Senate of the United States, **42:** 444n1
International Seamen's Union of America, **46:** 578n1
International Socialism and the World War (Fainsod), **42:** 199n10
International Socialist Bureau, **42:** 268
international socialist conference, Stockholm, **42:** 199,n10, 265, 268, 268-69, 274, 438; **43:** 522, 524; U.S. denies passports for, **42:** 350; postponement of, **42:** 364
International Socialist Review, **42:** 254n2; **43:** 165; **44:** 39n1
International Sugar Company, **45:** 344n1
International Woman Suffrage Alliance, **42:** 215
International Workers Defense League of San Francisco, **44:** 274n1; **47:** 359n1
Interstate and Foreign Commerce, Committee on (House of Reps.), **41:** 156, 157, 160; **42:** 34n1, 299; **43:** 21, 22, 39, 111n4; **44:** 116; **45:** 266,n2, 300, 301, 302, 335,n1, 379, 406; **48:** 457n1, 532n1; **49:** 329-30, 330, 371, 381; **51:** 90
interstate commerce, **40:** 264-65; and right to strike issue, **41:** 238n1
Interstate Commerce, Committee on (Senate), **40:** 246,n1, 278; **41:** 14,n2, 20, 156, 157; **42:** 299; **45:** 319; **46:** 361n1, 443n1; **51:** 166; and coal transportation, **42:** 206, 207, 208, 212, 213n1; and railroads, **42:** 218,n1, 505n2; and wire-control bill, **48:** 534n1, 535,n1, 556,n2
Interstate Commerce Commission, **40:** 155, 156, 156-57, 266; **41:** 207, 208, 254, 319; **43:** 7n1, 37, 252, 296, 367, 425, 504; **44:** 520; **45:** 266,n1,3, 401n1; **46:** 109, 238n2; **47:** 166-67, 408, 446; **51:** 192; W. M. Daniels nominated to, **40:** 255, 279; and railroads, **44:** 336, 400-405, 406-407, 413, 422-23,n1, 425, 428, 429-30, 444; **45:** 225n1, 287, 360; and public utilities, **49:** 253, 389, 405-406, 421; and transit companies, **51:** 247,n3, 258; and meat-packing legislation, **51:** 442
interurban railroads: see railroads

Intervention and Dollar Diplomacy in the Caribbean, 1900-21 (Munro), **40:** 82n1; **41:** 141n2

Intervention and the War (Ullman), **47:** 319n6, 355n1, 367n4

Investigation, Bureau of (Justice Department), **44:** 17n1, 514-15; **48:** 322; and W. B. Hale, **45:** 28-29; and Frachtenberg case, **45:** 92n2, 154; and W. J. Flynn, **45:** 101n1

Ioffe, Adolf Abrahamovich: *see* Joffe, Adolf Abrahamovich

Iowa, **41:** 215, 216; **42:** 83, 122; **47:** 428; politics in, **51:** 632

Iowa College, **40:** 540n1

Ireland, John, Archbishop, **51:** 191,n2

Ireland, Merritte Weber, **49:** 235n1

Ireland, **41:** 347, 536; **42:** 112, 113, 193; **43:** 215-18, 360-61, 451, 451-52, 509n2; **45:** 412, 428-29; **46:** 244, 249; **47:** 204, 552, 580; **51:** 26, 74; and Home Rule, **42:** 24-25, 41-42, 93, 111-12, 115, 219-20, 222, 223,n1, 543,n1; **44:** 133-34,n2, 210; **47:** 228n1, 266-67,n1, 401, 411-21, 442, 466, 620; **48:** 68, 206, 300,n2; National Gallery asks WW to sit for portrait, **42:** 390-91, 403-404, 545; and Friends of Irish Freedom, **43:** 217, 509-10,n2; and Irish Convention, **43:** 360,n1, 361, 365, 451-52; and Phelan-Wilson exchange, **45:** 560-61, 573; and conscription, **47:** 182, 227-28,n1, 266, 412, 432,n1, 432-33, 442, 457-58, 466, 620; **48:** 178; **49:** 67, 71, 206, 300,n2,3; and proposed U.S. visit of Lord Mayor of Dublin, **47:** 432,n1, 432-33, 506, 516; WW's position regarding, **47:** 441-42; **48:** 192; W. Wiseman on, **47:** 443-44, 465-66; H. Plunkett requests WW send representative to Great Britain on, **47:** 575-76; H. N. Hall on, **47:** 582-84, 586; and Easter Rebellion, **48:** 63, 65; German involvement in, **48:** 63-65, 67-69, 195-97; American public opinion toward, **48:** 67; Wiseman and WW discuss, **48:** 206; J. D. Phelan on, **48:** 466, 471-72; C. McCarthy on, **49:** 545-47

Irías, Julían, **41:** 143,n15; **45:** 388

Irish Americans, **41:** 347; **42:** 24, 41, 223n1, 353; **43:** 215-18, 509-10; **44:** 262; **45:** 455, 560, 560-61; **46:** 4; **47:** 228n2, 238, 401n2, 470; **48:** 64, 67, 118,n1; **49:** 275, 399, 545, 546; and New York's 69th National Guard regiment, **43:** 492, 514; rally against Britain's conscription efforts, **47:** 520

Irish Convention, **43:** 360,n1, 361, 365, 451-52; **47:** 228,n1, 266-67,n2, 442,n2, 469, 575-76, 580, 582; **48:** 300,n1,2

Irish Convention, 1917-18 (McDowell), **42:** 543n1; **47:** 228n1, 267n2

Irish Nationalist party, **48:** 195

Irish Progressive League, **47:** 520

Irkutsk, Russia, **46:** 34,n2, 35, 387, 540, 541; **47:** 15, 22, 57, 70, 97, 100, 131, 132, 242, 245, 281, 318, 460, 473, 488,

490; **48:** 105, 131, 186, 460, 480, 497, 505, 542; **49:** 97, 151, 152, 198, 220, 262n1, 283, 494; **51:** 85, 101, 384, 549

Iron Mountain Railroad, **41:** 402, 412

Irvine, Camille Hart (Mrs. William Mann), **44:** 513,n1,2; **47:** 450,n2

Irvine, W. I., **43:** 383,n1, 394

Irvine, William Mann, **44:** 513; **47:** 450,n1

Irving National Bank, N.Y., **41:** 142; **43:** 196

Is a Peace Conference Now Possible? (Eliot), **44:** 185n4

Isaacs, Alice Edith Cohn: *see* Reading, Lady

Isaacs, Gerald Rufus: *see* Erleigh, Viscount

Isaacs, Rufus Daniel: *see* Reading, 1st Marquess of

Isabella Thoburn College, Lucknow, India, **45:** 158,n1

Iseghem, Belgium, **51:** 421

Iselin, Adrian, **48:** 63,n2

Iselin, Sara Grace King Bronson (Mrs. Adrian), **48:** 63,n2

Ishii, Kikujiro, **43:** 57-58,n1; **45:** 128, 392; **46:** 250, 591; **48:** 288, 448-49, 544, 639; **49:** 39, 92, 95, 110, 178, 282; **51:** 457,n1,2; mission to U.S., **44:** 249-55, 264,n1,2, 314, 340-42, 356-57, 367-69, 376-78, 412-15, 418-20, 453-54,n1, 531; meetings on Russian intervention, **47:** 440, 441, 459-61,n1, 472-73, 488-90, 496, 586, 622; **48:** 540-41, 559-60, 577-78, 621-22; visit to Fairhaven, Mass., **48:** 569,n1, 569-70; and chief commander of joint forces, **48:** 579-80, 622; on Japan's proposal for intervention in Russia, **49:** 107-109,n1, 175-76,n1; on Soviet forces in China, **49:** 284; meets with WW on Russian and Chinese situations, **51:** 548-51, 592; photograph, *illustration section,* 45

Isthmian Canal Commission, Second, **40:** 35n3; **43:** 199n1

Istria, **51:** 262

Italia Irredenta, **40:** 501; **42:** 333, 389n4; **46:** 180, 244, 262; **51:** 156n2, 388

Italian-American Union, **48:** 120

Italian Americans, **47:** 525-26, 553, 554

Italy, **40:** 13, 15, 16, 204, 231, 250, 307n1, 357, 361, 496, 501; **41:** 61, 77, 211, 212, 223, 300, 338; **42:** 109, 173, 327n1, 330, 331, 436; **43:** 9, 65, 98, 124, 126, 136, 238, 269, 296, 304, 355, 356, 464, 471; **44:** 20, 37, 361n1, 547; **45:** 47, 73, 151, 164n1, 222n1, 248, 313, 592,n13, 595; **46:** 120, 154n1, 244, 249, 311-12, 471, 483-84; **47:** 63-64, 74, 205, 269; **48:** 96-97, 218; **49:** 111, 404; **51:** 44, 46, 47, 175n1, 187, 567; and Germany's arming of merchant ships, **40:** 449, 452, 453; and Russia, **42:** 110, 165; and peace terms, **42:** 156, 157, 333, 456; **48:** 553; **51:** 233, 262, 273, 274 500-501; and mission to U.S., **42:** 177; **43:** 12, 27-

28, 28; and financial assistance from U.S. and Britain, **43:** 225, 227; and Pope's peace appeal, **44:** 26, 34, 57; D. Lloyd George on war plans and, **44:** 126; German advance into and military situation in, **44:** 480, 506-509, 513-14; 549, 557; **45:** 37-38; and Switzerland, **44:** 489; and Bersaglieri, **44:** 507,n2; and formation of Supreme War Council, **45:** 47-48; and Inter-Allied Naval Council, **45:** 190; shipping and food crisis in, **45:** 351, 425; effect of Russia's separate peace on, **45:** 413, 414; and British war aims statement, **45:** 487n2; German propaganda in, **46:** 157-60; and territorial claims under Treaty of London, **46:** 180, 473; and Austria-Hungary, **46:** 199-200, 262, 272; **47:** 122, 125-26, 239, 240, 589-90,n1; **51:** 119, 532; and comparison of Hertling's and Czernin's views on, **46:** 224, 228, 275, 292; and Rumania, **46:** 373-74; Charles I on, **46:** 442; troops of join Foch's command, **48:** 468, 513,n6; and Corfu, **47:** 514; and proposed U.S. war declaration against Bulgaria and Turkey, **47:** 568, 570-71; and woman suffrage, **48:** 24n1, 25-26; G. D. Herron on desire for league of nations by, **48:** 212; and memorandum on coordination of nonmilitary activities of Allies, **48:** 324-29; naval action by, **48:** 385-86; and Supreme War Council and Balkan situation, **48:** 545; and Serbians, **48:** 545; combat strength on French front, **48:** 568n1; N. Angell on, **48:** 616-17; and recognition of Czechs as sovereign nation, **49:** 287,n1; and Yugoslavs, **49:** 288; and France, **51:** 41, 43, 386-87, 387-88; will not send High Commissioner to Siberia, **51:** 135; E. M. House suggests military offensive by, **51:** 146; Supreme War Council's note on military policy and, **51:** 195, 196, 198; question of sending troops to, **51:** 386-87, 388; and Turkey, **51:** 389, 456; and Polish Army, **51:** 447; and danger of separate peace with Germany and Austria-Hungary, **51:** 529-30; W. C. Bullitt on Bolshevism in, **51:** 565; armistice signed with Austria-Hungary, **51:** 576,n1; T. N. Page on, **51:** 600-603; and Austria-Hungary's troops in Ukraine, **51:** 616-17, 618; and intervention in Russia: *see* Russia—intervention in; Vatican

Italy and the United States, **44:** 69, 123-24, 411, 495; **45:** 95; **46:** 86-87, 360-61,n1; **49:** 398, 418-19; J. R. Mott recommends financial assistance to Italian army, **44:** 94; and loans, **44:** 281, 494; T. N. Page on, **44:** 295-96; **46:** 155-60, 178, 207; **49:** 63-65; and House mission, **44:** 427, 438-39; and shipping crisis, **44:** 437, 449, 501-502; and F. C. Howe's memorandum on an enduring peace, **44:** 475-77; WW exchanges notes with new premier of, **44:** 510, 511; and U.S. war declaration against Austria-Hungary, **45:** 262-63, 267-68; Lansing on sending U.S. hospital units to Italy, **45:** 364-65; and Inquiry memorandum, **45:** 459, 466, 469, 473; and Fourteen Points, **45:** 478, 484, 514, 527, 537; **46:** 78, 96, 96-97, 149; WW on, **46:** 178, 486, 487, 552; uneasiness between, **46:** 199-200; Page on Sonnino and peace moves, **46:** 365-66; and U.S. military mission to, **46:** 365, 376-78, 414, 456-57,n2; food and fuel crisis in, **46:** 454-56; and Inter-Allied General Reserve, **46:** 558-60; Victor Emmanuel (Vittorio Emanuele) on anniversary of U.S. entry into war, **47:** 278, 280; and U.S. troops, **47:** 486-87, 501, 566, 567; **48:** 601, 625, 641; **49:** 136-37, 369,n1, 533-35; U.S. on anniversary of Italy's entry into war, **47:** 525-26, 553, 554, 600; and WW's aide-mémoire on Russia, **48:** 639-43; T. H. Bliss clarifies term "Supreme Command," **49:** 126-27; and shipbuilding plans, **49:** 312-13; and intervention in Russia: *see* Russia—intervention in

Italy America Society, **47:** 525, 553, 554

Ivanov-Rinov, Pavel Pavlovich, **51:** 450,n5

Ives, Eugene Semmes, **43:** 53,n1

I.W.W.: *see* Industrial Workers of the World

Ixtapalapa, Mex., **47:** 475n2

Izegem, Belgium: *see* Iseghem

J. and W. Seligman and Co., N.Y., **40:** 444n3; **48:** 518n3

J. D. Spreckles and Brothers Co., **42:** 272n5

J. H. Williams and Co., **47:** 321-22

J. P. Morgan and Co., N.Y., **40:** 19,n1, 136n2; **41:** 257,n1, 550; **42:** 162, 372n3, 530; **43:** 20, 37, 44, 140n3, 147, 194, 195, 224; **44:** 528n2, 556; **45:** 407; **46:** 111, 112, 259, 269; **47:** 372, 519,n1, 521-23; **49:** 233; **51:** 221,n4, 223n6

Jack O'Lantern (Caldwell and Burnside), **48:** 52,n3

Jackson, Andrew, **42:** 139; **45:** 332n1

Jackson, Charles Samuel, **43:** 266

Jackson, Frank Watterson, **51:** 180-81,n1

Jackson, Frederick Mitchell, **49:** 245n2

Jackson, Jesse B., **44:** 337,n1, 359

Jackson, Richard Harrison, **43:** 503,n1; **51:** 429,n6

Jackson, Robert R., **43:** 392,n1

Jackson, Wilson, **42:** 31-32

Jackson, Miss., *Daily Clarion-Ledger,* **49:** 180n,n1

Jackson, Miss., *Daily News,* **46:** 104n1

Jackson County, Minn., **47:** 216,n2, 235n3

Jacksonville, Fla., **45:** 150n1

Jacob Jones, U.S.S., **45:** 238n2

Jacobus, Melancthon Williams, **41:** 320-21, 548-49; **42:** 6
Jacoway, Henderson Madison, **45:** 169,n1
Jaffé, Edgar, **48:** 213,n7; **51:** 243,n11
Jagow, Gottlieb von, **40:** 161,n1; **41:** 298
Jakaitis, J. J., **47:** 492n1
James, Edmund Janes, **46:** 174n1
James, Elizabeth (Mrs. L. H.), **44:** 365n1
James, Ollie Murray, **41:** 359,n3; **44:** 117,n1, 151, 154; **47:** 571; **48:** 404; **51:** 208; death of mother, **44:** 365,n1; and woman suffrage, **45:** 278, 338, 339; **46:** 60, 61; and water-power legislation, **45:** 301, 302; and Chamberlain bills, **46:** 82-83, 101,n1, 147n2, 204, 368-69,n1; death of, **49:** 368,n1; successor chosen, **49:** 381, 384, 388, 480, 481
James, Rorer Abraham, **47:** 17,n10
James, Ruth Thomas (Mrs. Ollie Murray), **49:** 368; **51:** 208
James, William, **44:** 225,n1; **48:** 620,n3
Jameson, John Butler, **51:** 537,n2
Janeway, Frank Latimer, **46:** 260-61,n1, 286, 330
Janik, Frantisek, **49:** 45,n3
Janin, Pierre Thiébaut Charles Maurice (Maurice Janin), **51:** 84n1, 85, 95,n2, 96
Janvier, Caesar Augustus Rodney, **48:** 531-32,n1
Janvier, Ernest Paxton, **48:** 532,n4
Japan, **40:** 15, 231, 239, 250, 294n2, 416, 557; **41:** 518; **42:** 173, 196, 296, 330, 331-32, 354; **43:** 174, 229, 256, 365, 464-65; **44:** 131, 239n1; **48:** 433n1; and China, **41:** 178, 181-82, 186, 187, 382, 394; **43:** 268, 362, 364n1; **46:** 331n2, 500, 501; **47:** 61, 441, 442, 462; and Zimmermann telegram, **41:** 281, 282, 405, 430, 546; J. W. Jenks on China and, **42:** 61-63; and Great Britain, **42:** 327n1, 450; **46:** 77; **47:** 428-29, 429-30; **51:** 614; size of mercantile marine, **43:** 10; and Chengchiatun affair, **43:** 83,n3; and Russia, **44:** 494, 496; **45:** 336, 347, 393, 420; **46:** 407n1, 539,n1; and Inter-Allied Naval Council, **45:** 190; A. Satō on fears of German or Russian expansion, **45:** 393-95; and Germany, **46:** 389; political changes in, **47:** 426-27; the Genrō in, **48:** 461,n2; Russia's attitude and treatment of, **48:** 478, 541, 577-78; and Czechs, **49:** 248-49, 417; and troops in Russia, **51:** 25, 98, 384, 396, 449-51, 608, 609; suggests joint action with U.S. in China, **51:** 457,n1,2; and railway control in Russia, **51:** 478, 479-81,n1; *see also* Russia—Siberia, intervention in
Japan and the United States, **43:** 98; **45:** 73, 392-95; **48:** 495-96, 540-41, 583-85; and China, **41:** 38-39, 176; **43:** 55-56, 80-83; **49:** 102-103; and anti-Japanese land laws, **41:** 107; condolences on G. W. Guthrie's death, **41:** 382, 403; new ambassador to Japan, **41:** 374, 510; **42:** 244-45, 347,n1; **43:** 333-34, 347,n1; and Vatican, **41:** 433, 435; and film *Patria,* **41:** 483,n1; **42:** 447, 467,n1, 489-90, 527; **43:** 432; **44:** 13; C. R. Crane on, **41:** 493-94; and U.S. loan to China, **42:** 53, 54; **45:** 97, 98; and Grand Canal project, **42:** 63n5; need for better U.S. news service in Japan, **42:** 275; A. Satō and E. M. House discuss Japanese aliens' rights, **42:** 275, 276-78; Belgium's suggestion for checking ambitions of Japan, **43:** 7-8; Ishii and mission to U.S., **43:** 57-58,n1; **44:** 249-55, 255-56, 264,n2, 314-16, 340-42, 356-57, 367-68, 376-78, 413-15, 417-20, 453-54,n1, 510, 530-31; Lansing on sending mission to Japan, **43:** 106; and Balfour's proposed Allied treaty, **43:** 113-14, 124, 125-26; House on, **44:** 213; and Megata financial mission, **44:** 315-16,n2; and navy patrol, **44:** 413; Gotō discusses war and peace with R. S. Morris, **47:** 427-30; F. N. Doubleday meets with Gotō, **48:** 461-62; and chief command of forces in Russia, **48:** 513, 579-80; and aid to Czech troops, **48:** 542-43, 559-60; Reading on WW's views on, **48:** 565-66; Ishii visits Fairhaven, Mass., **48:** 569,n1, 569-70; and WW's aide-mémoire on policy toward Russia, **48:** 639-43; H. Bergson on Russian situation and, **49:** 94-96; and Trans-Siberian Railway, **49:** 396,n1; *see also* Russia—Siberia, intervention in
Japan, Germany, Russia and the Allies (Mason), **48:** 585,n3
Japanese Expansion and American Policies (Abbott), **48:** 451,n3
Japanese Thrust into Siberia 1918 (Morley), **46:** 620n1; **47:** 99n5, 426n1; **48:** 72n2, 448n1; **49:** 5n1
Jarrett, J. L., **43:** 130
Jassy, Rumania, **43:** 95,n1; **49:** 142
Jay, John, **41:** 302
Jay, Peter Augustus, **44:** 26,n1
Jay's Treaty, **41:** 302
Jefferson, Thomas, **42:** 28, 29n1; **43:** 160n1; **44:** 114-15, 176,n1, 186; **47:** 38
Jeffreys, George, 1st Baron Jeffreys of Wem, **49:** 258,n1
Jellicoe, Florence Gwendoline, Countess Jellicoe, **41:** 270
Jellicoe, John Rushworth, 1st Earl Jellicoe, **40:** 452; **41:** 136,n2, 270, 271; **43:** 19, 171; **44:** 87,n1,2; **45:** 19, 23; **48:** 385
Jenkins, Charles Francis, **44:** 239n1, 241n2, 269-70,n1
Jenkins, Douglas, **49:** 519,n8
Jenks, Jeremiah Whipple, **42:** 60-64,n1; **45:** 97
Jensen, Joan Maria, **42:** 441n2
Jernagin, William H., **51:** 168n1, 193
Jerome, Ariz., **42:** 473; **43:** 157; **44:** 86; **46:** 144,n1
Jersey City, N.J., **49:** 503

Jewish Americans, **42:** 58, 164, 204, 234-35, 506-507; **44:** 391, 503-504, 512; **45:** 286, 316, 572; and Balfour Declaration, **45:** 149,n2; at Camp Upton, **45:** 157, 160

Jewish Relief Committee, **45:** 86

Jewish Welfare Board, **45:** 100; **49:** 425-26; **51:** 636

Jews, **44:** 39, 298; **49:** 78; **51:** 504, 604; in Germany, **40:** 146, relief for, **40:** 346, **45:** 100, 471; **47:** 555-56, 608; and Palestine and Zionism, **43:** 159n2,3; **44:** 324; **45:** 149,n2; **46:** 333; **49:** 363-64, 403; WW and House on numbers of, **46:** 489-90; and draft, **46:** 525n1; in Poland, **51:** 625

Jiménez Oreamuno, Ricardo, **41:** 142,n13

Joe Boyle: King of the Klondike (Rodney), **48:** 100n2

Joe Tumulty and the Wilson Era (Blum), **45:** 18n2, 93n3; **46:** 332n1, 406n1

Joffe (Ioffe), Adolf Abrahamovich, **45:** 384n2, 595n3; **51:** 622

Joffe document, **46:** 372,n3

Joffre, Joseph-Jacques Césaire, **42:** 264n2; **44:** 462; **47:** 4; **48:** 332-33; **49:** 314; and French mission, **42:** 20,n2, 69, 133, 176; E. M. House on, **42:** 160, 169, 169-70, 172; and U.S. expeditionary force, **42:** 175; conversation with WW, **42:** 186-91, 202, 230

Joffre et son destin (Fabry), **42:** 191n1

John Adams (Morse), **42:** 246n4

John Ericsson League of Patriotic Service, **46:** 458n1

John Lambert, S.S., **40:** 191

John Purroy Mitchel: The Boy Mayor of New York (Lewinson), **44:** 333n1

John R. Mott, 1865-1955 (Hopkins), **44:** 270n1

Johns, George Sibley, **42:** 130

Johns Hopkins Medical School, **45:** 108n3

Johns Hopkins University, **40:** 165, 444; **42:** 448; **47:** 394

Johns Hopkins University Hospital, **48:** 404n1

Johnson, Allen, **45:** 352

Johnson, Ben, **47:** 192-93,n1, 255,n1; **48:** 190,n1; on anti-Catholic weekly, **49:** 169, 174,n1

Johnson, Donald, **43:** 175n1; **44:** 266n2

Johnson, Edwin Stockton, **45:** 338

Johnson, Francis, **41:** 36,n1

Johnson, Hiram Warren, **40:** 86; **42:** 107; **45:** 301,n5; **46:** 116, 316; **51:** 83, 377, 455n1

Johnson, J. L., **45:** 28

Johnson, James A. Courvoisier, **49:** 210,n1

Johnson, James P., **46:** 12n1

Johnson, James Weldon, **46:** 383n1, 384n, 385n1

Johnson, O. E., **51:** 91n1

Johnson, Robert Underwood, **40:** 237

Johnson, Royal Cleaves, **45:** 278

Johnson, Stewart, **43:** 160n1

Johnson, Walter, **40:** 21n1

Johnson, William Hannibal, **40:** 330,n1

Johnson, William Hugh, **47:** 272,n2, 283

Johnston, Albert Sidney, **44:** 156

Joint Anglo-French Financial Committee, **40:** 19n1

Joint Distribution Committee: *see* American-Jewish Joint Distribution Committee

Joint Embargo Council: *see* Inter-Allied Embargo Council

Joint High Commission: *see* Mexico and the United States

Joint State and Navy Neutrality Board, **41:** 71,n1, 73n4

Jones, Captain, **49:** 448,n4

Jones, Andrieus Aristieus, **42:** 343n1; **43:** 213n1; **46:** 204; **49:** 264,n2; and woman suffrage, **45:** 278, 388; **51:** 189n1

Jones, Claude Motley (Mrs. William Atkinson), **47:** 372,n1

Jones, David Benton, **45:** 230

Jones, E. M., **49:** 327-28

Jones, (Ernest) Lester, **42:** 348,n1,2

Jones, Jenkin Floyd, **44:** 79

Jones, Jesse Holman, **47:** 604-605,n1; **51:** 144; and Red Cross, **48:** 6, 16, 59, 116; B. M. Baruch mentions for Price-Fixing Committee, **48:** 607, 611

Jones, John Paul, **41:** 455

Jones, Mary Harris (Mrs. George E.), Mother Jones, **40:** 154,n1, 207-208

Jones, Paul, **44:** 79

Jones, Richard Lloyd, **45:** 221n1; **46:** 119n1; **51:** 148

Jones, Rufus Matthew, **43:** 492n1; **44:** 74, 75; **47:** 155

Jones, Thomas Davies, **40:** 238, 241; **41:** 208; **43:** 291, 325, 347; **45:** 78-80, 80-81, 82-83, 230; **46:** 230,n4; and Tariff Commission, **41:** 24: 58-59, 93; and food and neutrals, **45:** 116-17; resigns from War Trade Board, **45:** 350, 367

Jones, Thomas Jesse, **47:** 289,n3

Jones, Wesley Livsey, **41:** 198-99; **43:** 200n1; **46:** 106,n1, 107-108, 218; **48:** 428n1; **49:** 296n2; and sugar investigation, **45:** 344, 348

Jones, Wiley Emmet, **43:** 113,n1

Jones, William Atkinson, death of, **47:** 372,n1

Jones, Willie, **41:** 455

Jones Act (Puerto Rico), **41:** 180, 278, 312, 407n1, 515-16; A. Yager on, **40:** 57-58; WW on, **40:** 90-91, 159; S. Iglesias Pantín on, **40:** 147-53; W. B. Wilson on, **40:** 295-97,n1,2

Jones and Laughlin Steel Co., **44:** 242, 277

Jones bill (Philippine Islands), **40:** 57

Jong van Beek en Donk, Benjamin (Baron Jong), **46:** 198-99,n3, 388,n1, 580-81,n1, 589-90, 615; **47:** 24,n1, 64-65,n1,4, 128,n1, 133, 142

Jordan, Doctor, **45:** 77

Jordan, David Starr, **41**: 515; **42**: 382; **46**: 326
Jordan, Sir John Newell, **49**: 213,n2
Joseph Fels Commission, **46**: 494n2
Joseph W. Folk of Missouri (Geiger), **48**: 115n2
Jouhaux, Léon, **47**: 75,n3
Journal of Interamerican Studies and World Affairs, **47**: 357n1
Journal of Modern History, **46**: 341n1
Journal of Southern History, **47**: 144n2
Journal of the American Bankers' Association, **49**: 430, 471n1, 472
Journal of the Senate, **42**: 302n1; **43**: 207n1
Jowett, Frederick William, **42**: 422,n2
Jowett, John Henry, **47**: 420-21,n1
Juárez, Mex.: *see* Ciudad Juárez
Judge Learned Hand and the Role of the Federal Judiciary (Griffith), **43**: 165n2
Judiciary Committee (House of Reps.), **41**: 197n1; **42**: 113, 269; **43**: 213n1, 222n2; **44**: 314; **47**: 573n1; **49**: 62,n2; and woman suffrage, **45**: 242, 277
Judiciary Committee (Senate), **40**: 386n1, 471; **41**: 197; **42**: 106n2, 113, 289, 299; **43**: 222n2; **47**: 94,n1, 109, 381n2, 573,n1
Judson, Frederick Newton, **46**: 238,n3
Judson, William Voorhees, **45**: 104-105,n1, 216, 217,n4, 220; **46**: 22n1, 179n1, 408-409, 414, 554; **47**: 304; on Russian situation and proposed intervention in Siberia, **46**: 532, 533-40
Jugo-Slavs: *see* Yugoslavs
Jusserand, Elise Richards (Mme. Jean Jules), **42**: 169; **48**: 352
Jusserand, Jean Jules, **40**: 119n1, 132, 139, 504, 519; **41**: 4n1, 354-57, 359; **42**: 18,n2, 69-71, 168, 175, 210-12, 229n2, 299-301, 375; **43**: 24, 99, 255, 273, 274, 525; **44**: 24, 120, 371, 380, 433,n1, 439; **45**: 323, 396, 432, 438, 550, 557; **46**: 34n1, 350, 361n1, 390, 464, 488, 585; **47**: 497n1, 563; **48**: 202, 294-95, 295, 352, 353, 391, 415, 454, 469, 473, 503,n2, 561, 574, 575, 576; **49**: 67, 94, 110, 111-12, 113, 149, 156-57, 282; **51**: 84-85, 173, 389; on WW's peace note, **40**: 307n1; on American unpreparedness, **40**: 408; meets with E. M. House, **41**: 149,n1; and H. Bergson, **41**: 315-17,n2; **48**: 317; and proposed French mission to U.S., **41**: 554; and British mission, **42**: 127-29, 402-403; House on, **42**: 161; on WW's absence from French mission reception, **42**: 233; meets with WW on food situation, **43**: 142-44; on France's hope for league of nations, **43**: 359-60; and Pope's peace appeal and WW's reply, **44**: 153, 157, 185; urges U.S. to send representative to inter-Allied conference, **44**: 297, 385; on WW's State of the Union message, **45**: 219-21; on success of House mission, **45**: 365; and Fourteen Points Address, **46**: 78, 83; on wheat crisis, **46**: 213-14; and Supreme War Council's Versailles Declaration, **46**: 415, 429, 444-45; and intervention in Russia, **46**: 474-75, 476, 482, 547, 548, 555; **47**: 14-15, 20-23, 55, 56-57, 317, 318-21, 430-31, 432, 585-86, 621; **48**: 239-40, 273-74, 355-56, 416, 421n1, 446-47, 621; **49**: 36, 91-93, 123-24, 127-28, 211,n1; and France and Polish declaration, **46**: 585, 587-88; and France's telegram on anniversary of U.S. entry into war, **47**: 257, 290; on Abbeville resolution, **47**: 585, 595, 615; and Allied request for U.S. troops, **48**: 243, 244-45, 252-55; presents inscribed book to WW, **48**: 491,n1; on coal crisis, **49**: 239-40; on inter-Allied Civilian Board, **49**: 323,n1, 332,n2; on German atrocities, **49**: 497-98; on I.W.W., **49**: 538-39; indignant over WW's Russian policy, **51**: 152-53, 209-10; on aviators captured by Austria-Hungary, **51**: 174-75; on peace terms and Bulgaria, **51**: 169; on WW's reaction to Allied note, **51**: 307-309, 313; and Turkey, **51**: 456; and Anglo-French declaration on liberated territories, **51**: 540, 574-75
Just Government League of Maryland, **42**: 124,n1, 138n1
Justice, Department of, **41**: 48, 290; **42**: 16, 17, 77n1, 225, 308, 437n1; **43**: 17, 297, 315; **44**: 17n1, 158,n1, 192-94, 290-91, 313, 522; **46**: 104n1, 383; and cost of living inquiry, **40**: 244n1, 264, 519-20; Easby-Smith on illegal invasion of privacy by, **40**: 466-69; and War Trade Committee, **42**: 29n1, 49, 117-18; and censorship, **42**: 163, 387; and American Protective League, **47**: 441-43, 510, 517; and Frachtenberg case, **45**: 141,n2, 154,n1,4; and general leasing bill, **47**: 402, 403; and aircraft investigation, **47**: 542, 545, 603; **48**: 3; and antiprofiteering rent bill, **48**: 193, 222, 238, 269; and lynchings, **48**: 476; and slacker raids, **49**: 463 499-503; and Pollak case, **51**: 376-80
Justicia, S.S., **49**: 217
Jutland, Battle of, **43**: 463

Kahn, Julius, **42**: 94, 144n1; **43**: 272, 299; **46**: 49n1
Kahn, Otto Herman, **42**: 7-8,n1, 8-9; **43**: 12; **44**: 511,n1
Kaiser, S.M.S., **51**: 490, 607
Kaiser as I Know Him (Davis), **47**: 499n1
Kaiser Karl VI, S.M.S., **51**: 492
Kaiserin, S.M.S., **51**: 490
Kaiser's Dynasty Shaken by Defeat (*New York Times*), **51**: 331,n4
Kaledin, Aleksei Maksimovich, **45**: 217n4, 229,n2, 251, 263-64, 274-75, 444; **46**: 421n3; **47**: 104
Kalmykov, Ivan Pavlovich, **51**: 450,n6
Kalmyks, **48**: 105n1

Kamchatka, Russia, **48:** 186
Kampf um die preussische Wahlreform im Ersten Weltkrieg (Patemann), **45:** 34n13; **47:** 524n1
Kandalaksha, Russia, **47:** 431
Kane, Mr. **48:** 356n1
Kaneko, Hisakazu, **48:** 569n1
Kann, Robert Adolph, **45:** 57n4
Kansas, **41:** 63n1; **42:** 83, 122; **44:** 293-94; **47:** 438; **48:** 486-87; **49:** 99; and farm labor problem and draft, **44:** 53, 432; politics in, **49:** 308-309, 315-16; **51:** 375, 589, 623-24, 632
Kansas, University of, **44:** 105n2
Kansas City, Mo., **42:** 85
Kansas City (Mo.) *Star,* **44:** 394n1; **46:** 63n2; **48:** 235n1; **49:** 442; and Rose Pastor Stokes case, **48:** 405, 422-24,n1
Kansas City *Tribune,* **41:** 63n1
Kansas Farmers' Union, **49:** 427n1
Kaplan, Fania Efimovna Roidman, **51:** 4n2
Kapp, Wolfgang, **46:** 163n1
Karakhan, Lev Mikhailovich, **48:** 40,n1
Karch, Otto Herman, **43:** 297,n1, 300
Karelia, **48:** 285n3
Kargé, Joseph, **43:** 115,n2
Karl I (of Austria-Hungary): *see* Charles I
Karl, Barry Dean, **40:** 489n2
Karl Helfferich, 1872-1924: Economist, Financier, Politician (Williamson), **45:** 32n4
Karnebeek, A. C. van, **46:** 615n4
Károlyi, Count Mihály, **51:** 565,n6
Karymskaya, Russia, **47:** 71, 99, 592; **48:** 105; **49:** 493,n1, 494
Kaspi, André, **42:** 229n2; **44:** 52n1, 156n1
Katsura, Taro, **47:** 427,n3
Katz, Friedrich, **41:** 327n5; **46:** 354n3; **47:** 165n2, 345n2, 475n2; **49:** 280n1,2
Kaufman, William, **51:** 311-12, 394
Kautsky, Karl, **42:** 197,n3
Kazan, Russia, **51:** 556; fall of, **51:** 50,n1, 51n2
Kean, Jefferson Randolph, **43:** 86n2
Keasbey, Lindley M., **44:** 79
Keating, Edward, **43:** 22; **48:** 395, 444, 474,n1; and child labor legislation, **51:** 165, 181; and congressional election, **51:** 312, 460-61,n1, 482, 645,n1
Keating-Owen Child Labor Act of 1916, **40:** 7, 37, 42, 91-92; **49:** 23,n1
Kedleston, 1st Marquess of, *see* Curzon, George Nathaniel
Kedrov, Mikhail Sergeevich, **49:** 495,n1
Keeley, James, **49:** 434,n1
Keen, William Williams, **48:** 220n1, 324
Keene (Keene Valley), N.Y., **44:** 124n3
Keeping the Negro at Home (Atlanta Constitution), **40:** 153,n1
Kegley, Carey B., **51:** 249,n1
Keith, Minor Cooper, **41:** 143,n14; **46:** 450,n1
Keith's Theater, Washington, D.C., **42:** 13, 447, 490

Keller, Morton, **45:** 596n1
Kelley, Florence, **42:** 208, 214
Kelley, Francis Clement, **46:** 406,n1
Kellogg, Charles Flint, **48:** 159n5
Kellogg, Frank Billings, **42:** 505,n1; **44:** 89n1; **46:** 348n1; **49:** 476n3; **51:** 414; on proposed Federal License Act, **51:** 70-73, 80
Kellogg, Paul Underwood, **41:** 8, 164, 168, 305n1; **42:** 118-19,n1
Kellogg, Emery, and Cuthell, N.Y., **41:** 365
Kelly, Peter, **43:** 299
Kem, Russia, **47:** 431
Kemp, Thomas Webster, **47:** 606,n2; **49:** 530,n1, 531; **51:** 52
Kendall, Calvin Noyes, **42:** 458
Kendall, Mrs. Frederick W., **44:** 453,n1
Kendrick, John Benjamin, **40:** 263,n1, 278; **42:** 343n1; and woman suffrage, **45:** 278, 338
Kenly, John Reese, **45:** 118,n1, 125-26, 129-30, 155, 162
Kenly, William Lacy, **47:** 509n2, 545; **48:** 73-74,n3, 628; **51:** 15n1
Kennamer, J. R., **44:** 144,n1
Kennan, George (1845-1924), **42:** 217,n2; **49:** 346-47; advocates Siberian intervention, **48:** 183,n1, 183-87; suggestions for Russian commission, **49:** 320-23
Kennan, George Frost, **44:** 367n2, 483n1; **45:** 217n5, 252, 411n1; **46:** 22n1, 46n3, 300n7,8, 341n1,4, 372n3; **47:** 68n2, 79n2, 281n1, 319n6, 440n1; **48:** 96n2, 113n3, 142n6,8, 335n1, 489n1; **51:** 4n2
Kennedy, Alfred Ravenscroft, **48:** 501n1
Kennerly, Mitchell, **44:** 287,n1
Kennerly, Taylor, **46:** 63
Kennicott mine, Ala., **43:** 37
Kent, Charles William, **44:** 474,n1
Kent, Eleanor Smith (Mrs. Charles William), **44:** 474
Kent, Elizabeth Thacher (Mrs. William), **40:** 426,n3; **47:** 547,n1, 572
Kent, Fred I., **51:** 12,n1
Kent, Stephenson Hamilton, **44:** 562-70,n1, 571; **45:** 25
Kent, William, **41:** 23; **43:** 400, 432-33, 495-97, 536; **46:** 547, 614; **47:** 389; **48:** 141n3; **51:** 147-48, 161, 175; on grazing homestead bill, **40:** 192-93, 214, 287-89, 290,n1, 526, 548; **51:** 287-88; and Tariff Commission, **40:** 173, 173-74; **41:** 379, 380; and cost of living inquiry, **40:** 519; on WW's Peace without Victory speech, **40:** 561; and meatpackers investigation, **41:** 31-32, 37, 84-85, 112, 207-208, 208; **46:** 195-96,n1,2; **47:** 45-51; on V. Berger and Socialists, **43:** 190, 193; on water-power legislation, **45:** 299-301, 302, 335, 379-80; **49:** 505-506; **51:** 20-21; on Federal Trade Commission appointments, **46:** 492-93, 493; on Nonpartisan League, **47:** 399-400, 475; on M. Eastman, **48:** 93, 116, 235, 241,

Kent, William (*cont.*)
251; on Russian situation, **49:** 54-55; on G. Norris reelection, **49:** 384; on Pollak case, **51:** 125,n1, 171-72, 203-204, 281, 376-80; on Washington State Grange and Bouck case, **51:** 249-50, 257, 310, 393-94, 520

Kent School, **45:** 231n5

Kentucky: and coal, **47:** 410; and woman suffrage, **49:** 268,n1, 381,n1, 388, 529; **51:** 30-31, 49; A. Krock on Democratic politics in, **49:** 480; **51:** 76, 81, 120, 149-50, 214-15, 395, 589, 632; and teaching of German language, **51:** 259, 295

Kenyon, William Squire, **41:** 199; **42:** 301n2, 532n1; **44:** 49: **45:** 344; **46:** 588; **47:** 19; **48:** 347,n1; **49:** 384, 477

Keppel, Frederick Paul, **49:** 385

Kerenskii, Aleksandr Fedorovich, **41:** 416,n12; **42:** 198, 320n2, 418n1,2, 419n3; **43:** 371,n2; **44:** 38,n1, 39, 91-92; **45:** 73, 105, 192, 216, 251, 407, 444; **46:** 372; **47:** 504, 549n2; **48:** 374, 504, 616; photograph, *illustration section*, **42**

Kern, Albert E., **44:** 405,n1, 415, 492

Kern, Araminta Cooper (Mrs. John Worth), **43:** 512

Kern, John Worth, **40:** 354; death of, **43:** 512,n1

Kernan, Francis Joseph, **48:** 265n1, 267

Kernek, Sterling J., **45:** 430n3, 487n2; **46:** 577n3; **47:** 11n1

Kerney, James, **49:** 169,n3, 173

Kerr, Philip, **46:** 577,n3; **47:** 11,n1, 122,n2, 123

Kerth, Monroe Crawford, **45:** 217n4

Kerwin, Hugh Leo, **42:** 471,n2; **44:** 80,n1, 81, 183; **45:** 60, 260, 262; **51:** 181

Ketcham, John Clark, **44:** 258-59,n2

Kevork V, **40:** 105-106,n1, 311

Khabarovsk (Habarovsk), Russia, **48:** 459,n2, 528; **49:** 152, 262n1, 479; **51:** 449,n2, 450,n6, 609

Kharkov, Russia, **46:** 341n4

Kholm: *see* Chelm

Kiaochow, China, **49:** 213

Kibbey, Joseph Henry, **46:** 598,n2

Kiefer, Daniel, **44:** 79

Kiel, Germany, **46:** 266; mutiny at, **51:** 541n1, 607

Kiel Canal, **44:** 477

Kiev, Russia, **46:** 310, 341n4; **48:** 102n1, 103; **49:** 195

Kikuchi, Giro, **48:** 39n1

Killen, Linda, **51:** 104n4

Kimball, A. D., **43:** 253

King, Caroline Blanche, **45:** 423n1

King, Charles Dunbar Burgess, **47:** 317,n1

King, Edward John, **43:** 347,n1

King, Ernest Joseph, **43:** 182,n2

King, F. Lacy, **45:** 184,n3

King, Stanley, **45:** 426,n1, 427; **46:** 171,n1

King, William Henry, **40:** 89,n1; **43:** 455,n1; **46:** 204; **47:** 416n2, 490; **48:** 433,n1; and woman suffrage, **45:** 278, 338, 339; **46:** 60, 61

Kingman, Ariz., **43:** 157

King's College, Cambridge, **47:** 401n1

Kinmonth, J. Lisle, **51:** 552,n8

Kipling, Rudyard, **43:** 314

Kirby, William Fosgate, **40:** 523,n1; **47:** 321n1; and woman suffrage, **45:** 278, 338

Kirchwey, George Washington, **41:** 242-46, 274, 275

Kirk, Alexander Comstock, **40:** 555,n3

Kirk, Clara Comstock (Mrs. James A.), **40:** 555,n3

Kirov, Russia: *see* Viatka

Kirstein, Louis, **47:** 557,n4

Kitchener, Herbert Horatio, 1st Earl Kitchener of Khartoum, **40:** 32, 294n2; **41:** 541; **49:** 9; letter to his troops, **42:** 557, 558

Kitchin, Claude, **41:** 530,n4, 531, 550; **42:** 25, 27, 269, 270, 302-303,n1,2; **44:** 92; **46:** 15, 37; **47:** 562; **48:** 119,n2, 154, 173, 393, 405; **51:** 90, 108n9, 219; and Alaska fisheries bill, **40:** 293, 305, 318-19; and woman suffrage, **45:** 242, 243, 277; and civil service retirement bill, **48:** 474n1; and wire control bill, **48:** 535n1; and revenue legislation, **49:** 86, 87, 105, 124-25, 162,n1, 163, 163-64; WW on, **49:** 258

Kitchin, Samuel, **42:** 27,n1

Kittrell College, N.C., **51:** 193n1

Klotz, Louis Lucien, **45:** 245,n1; **46:** 359, 360, 465

Klück, Carl, **49:** 357n1; **51:** 68-70

Knapp, Harry Shepard, **40:** 82

Knecht, Marcel, **42:** 30,n3

Knickerbocker Hotel, N.Y., **45:** 41n1

Knight, Austin Melvin, **42:** 59,n2; **46:** 33, 46, 47, 338, 555, 620; **47:** 68, 206; **49:** 142, 149, 177, 278, 282, 543-44; **51:** 100; on Japanese intervention in Siberia, **47:** 69-72, 623,n1; on helping Siberia set up government, **47:** 92,n1,2; and munitions protection in Russia, **47:** 162,n2; on Czech troops in Russia and need to keep Vladivostok open, **48:** 458, 459-60, 480-81, 527-528, 543, 544; **49:** 150-53, 262-63, 479

Knight, John George David, **49:** 215,n1

Knight, Samuel Howell, **45:** 459,n1

Knights of Columbus, **44:** 551-52; **48:** 221: **49:** 385

Knox, Alfred William Fortescue, **45:** 444,n1; **48:** 602,n1, 603; **49:** 9; **51:** 8,n3, 100

Knox, Dudley Wright, **43:** 182,n2

Knox, Edmund Francis Vesey, **49:** 9,n2

Knox, Philander Chase, **40:** 466,n1; **41:** 456; **42:** 67

Knoxville Journal and Tribune, **46:** 381

Knudsen, Gunnar, **51:** 186,n1

Koch, Metod, **51:** 562,n1

Koch, Robert, **40:** 145n3

Kodama, Gentaro, **47:** 427,n2

Kohlsaat, Herman Henry, **48**: 62,n1
Kohns, Lee, **51**: 644,n2
Kola, Russia, **48**: 626, 642
Kola Peninsula, **48**: 285n3
Kolchak, Aleksandr Vasil'evich, **51**: 102n1
Kollontai, Aleksandra Mikhailovna, **46**: 341,n2
Köln, S.M.S., **51**: 490
Kölnische Zeitung, **41**: 149,n1,2; 242; **51**: 255n1
Konenkamp, S. J., **48**: 281,n4, 282-83,n1, 329, 546
König, S.M.S., **51**: 490
König Albert, S.M.S., **51**: 490
Königsberg, **42**: 336
Konovalov, Aleksandr Ivanovich, **42**: 419,n3; **44**: 179-80,n1; **48**: 374,n1, 382, 406-10, 415, 454,n1, 570; **49**: 321,n1, 322
Konow, Henri, **41**: 362,n1
Konta, Alexander, **45**: 135, 135-40, 161, 241,n1
Koo, Vi Kyuin Wellington (Ku Wei-chün), **42**: 126,n2; **45**: 336,n1; **48**: 561
Koons, John Cornelius, **44**: 289,n2
Kopelin, Louis, **45**: 203
Korea, **44**: 255; **47**: 98
Korff, Sergei Aleksandrovich, **49**: 321-22,n4
Kornilov, Lavr Georgievich, **44**: 216,n1; **45**: 264, 274, 444; **46**: 341; **47**: 549,n2; **48**: 104
Kortrijk, Belgium: *see* Courtrai
Kosciusko, Thaddeus (Kosciuseko, Tadeusz Andrzej Bonawentura), **44**: 305, 317
Kostowski, Mr., **46**: 48
Kotlas, Russia, **49**: 518,n3
Kovno, Lithuania, **48**: 98
Kozlowski, Joseph, **46**: 404
Kraft, Barbara S., **41**: 90n2
Kraft, Frederick, **49**: 208,n2, 306
Kram, Matilda von: *see* Cram, Matilda von
Kramář, Karel, **51**: 565,n5
Krasnoyarsk, Russia, **47**: 100, 245; **49**: 198
Krause, Paul von, **45**: 32n3
Kreher, Hulda, **46**: 604,n3
Kreher, Paul, **46**: 604
Kress von Kressenstein, Friedrich Sigmund Georg, Baron, **51**: 345,n1
Krivoshein, Aleksandr Vasil'evich, **48**: 239,n2
Krock, Arthur Bernard, on Democratic politics in Kentucky, **49**: 480,n1
Kronprinz Wilhelm, S.M.S., **51**: 490
Kronprinzessin Cecile, **47**: 371
Kropotkin, Pëtr Alekseevich, **44**: 67,n1
Kroupensky, B. N. de, **40**: 514,n1
Krueger Auditorium, Newark, **47**: 82n1
Krupenskii, Vasilii Nikolaevich, **46**: 46,n1; **47**: 15,n1
Krupp von Bohlen und Halbach, Gustav, **46**: 253n2

Krupp Company, **46**: 253,n2
Kruse, Charles, **44**: 79
Krylenko, Nikolai Vasil'evich, **45**: 120,n4, 217n4
Ku Klux Klan, **43**: 540,n1
Ku Wei-chün: *see* Koo, Vi Kyuin Wellington
Kuantung, China, **49**: 213
Kucharzewski, Jan, **46**: 403n1
Kudashev, Nikolai Aleksandrovich, **41**: 178,n1
Kudriasheff (German agent), **47**: 69,n1
Kuehl, Warren Frederick, **40**: 386n1
Kühlmann, Richard von, **43**: 186n5, 410; **44**: 37, 329; **45**: 32, 33, 36, 289, 384n2, 415, 416n5, 595,n2,3; **46**: 187-88, 188, 190-91; **48**: 398n1, 555,n7; **49**: 382n2; **51**: 239
Kuhn, Joseph Ernst, **40**: 161,n2, 455; **42**: 33n1, 550,n1
Kuhn, Loeb and Co., N.Y., **40**: 60, 62; **42**: 7n1, 163; **47**: 555; **48**: 372, 519,n1
Kuibyshev, Russia: *see* Samara
Kulakowski, Bronislaw D., **44**: 6-7; **46**: 402-405
Kummer, Clare Rodman Beecher (Mrs. Frederic Arnold), **44**: 427n1
Kurdistan and Kurds, **41**: 220n4
Kurland: *see* Courland
Kuroki, Shinkei, **47**: 593,n2
Kuroki, Tamemoto, **42**: 285,n1
Kwanchengtze, Manchuria, **51**: 479,n1

L 24 (airship), **40**: 145n3
L 31 (airship), **40**: 145n2
L. Straus and Sons, N.Y., **51**: 644n2
La Crosse, Wash., **43**: 200
La Fayette, Ben, **51**: 444,n1
La Follette, Belle Case, **46**: 348n1
La Follette, Fola, **44**: 79; **46**: 348n1
La Follette, Robert Marion, **41**: 359; **43**: 319, 455,n1; **44**: 365,n1; **45**: 221n1, 238n1; **47**: 40, 390n1; **48**: 343, 345; and armed-ship bill, **41**: 318n1, 328, 350; and WW's Peace without Victory speech, **41**: 11n1; and WW's war message, **41**: 531; and war declaration against Austria-Hungary, **45**: 224n1; and WW's State of the Union Message of 1917, **45**: 237; brings libel suit against *Wisconsin State Journal*, **46**: 119,n1; Nonpartisan League speech and senatorial investigation of, **46**: 348,n1; and woman suffrage, **51**: 83
La Follette, William Leary, **43**: 200,n1; **45**: 300,n4
La Monte, George Mason, **49**: 212n1; and Pollak case, **51**: 204, 210-11, 378, 380, 451, 606, 640; and N.J. politics, **51**: 283,n1,2, 403-404, 640
La Pallice, France, **42**: 189
La Rochelle, France, **42**: 189
LaBarre, George B.: on G. Creel, **48**: 11-12,n1,2
labor and labor unions, **43**: 6, 16-18; **44**: 60, 81,n1, 232, 282-83, 320n1, 418,

labor and labor unions (*cont.*)
511n1; **44:** 161-64, 244, 302-303, 430-
31, 500, 564-65, 565-66; **46:** 21,n1, 87,
176, 343; **48:** 137, 138; **49:** 104; National Consumers' League resolutions
on, **40:** 7-9; W. B. Wilson on establishing a Railway Labor Commission, **40:**
97-100; Porto Rico and, **40:** 146-52,
213-14; **47:** 543-44, 577; **48:** 3-4, 15-16,
17-18, 35-37, 48-49, 637-38,n6; **49:** 135-
36, 158, 236,n1, 246, 252, 296-98, 334,
394; appeals for pardon for union members convicted in Dynamite Conspiracy
Trial, **40:** 154,n1, 174-77,n1, 207-208;
WW commutes sentences of some
United Mine Workers, **40:** 217,n1; and
bill to create an Industrial Arbitration
Commission, **41:** 253-55, 258, 262; and
Russian Commission, **42:** 165; and coal
industry, **42:** 205-206, 460-61, 473-74;
and selective service bill, **42:** 209, 214;
and Council of National Defense, **42:**
135-38, 266, 296-98, 459-60,n1, 471-73;
railroad unions delay shipments, **42:**
242-43, 304,n1; British labor commission sent to U.S., **42:** 265-66; and
Mooney case, **42:** 270,n1, 271-72,n1,
273; **44:** 246, 267; **47:** 467; and Pennsylvania, **42:** 434, 446; comments on union
organization, **42:** 460-61, 473-74, 496,
504-505; WW meets with leaders of
railroad brotherhoods, **42:** 495; L. D.
Brandeis and, **42:** 533,n1; W. B. Wilson
on, **42:** 563-64; problems in Montana,
43: 16-18, 299, 341, 345,n1; S. Gompers
on keeping Clayton Antitrust Act intact, **43:** 20-23; problems in Arizona
copper mines, **43:** 53, 72, 98, 104-105,
157, 157-58, 158-59, 170, 171, 230-31,
237n2, 238-39, 325, 336, 339-40, 373,
393, 416-17; **44:** 134-39, 172, 516-20,
521-22; and strike at International
Nickel Company, **43:** 177; problems in
California, **43:** 248,n1; and Washington State, **43:** 266-67; **44:** 50,n1, 86n1,
276-77, 344-45; Bell memorandum for
western governors on I.W.W. and, **43:**
280-81; W. Green and miners' eviction
in New Mexico, **43:** 340, 352, 353, and
Covington mission, **43:** 361-62,n2, 386,
494, 495; and Alabama situation, **43:**
368, 433-34, 437, 506; **44:** 144n1; **45:**
568n1; and Mare Island explosion and
investigation, **43:** 470,n2,3; WW commutes sentence of F. Ryan, **43:**
513,n1,2; W. L. Chambers on railroad
situation in Georgia, **43:** 530-32; and
American Alliance for Labor and Democracy, **44:** 47-48,n1, 95-100, 101-
102; and Georgia, Florida and Alabama Railroad, **44:** 106, 198; and
F. Frankfurter on dealing with troubles of **44:** 161-64; and national Nonpartisan League convention, **44:** 182-
83; and Boston and Maine Railroad, **44:**
183; and Shipbuilding Labor Adjust-

ment Board, **44:** 219-21,n1, 226-29,
233-34, 234-36, 242-44, 256-57,n1, 268;
and shipbuilding strike in Oregon, **44:**
247; and copper situation in Montana,
44: 259-63; **45:** 321-22; and steel strike
in Pittsburgh, **44:** 277-78; and workmen's compensation law and shipping
industry, **44:** 313-14; N. D. Baker on
WW not making statement on eight-
hour day, **44:** 421-22; housing problems, **44:** 448, 482; **45:** 141; **46:** 98-99,
124; W. L. Chambers on railroad arbitration, **44:** 458-59; A. S. Burleson on,
44: 470n3
A.F. of L. and Russia, **44:** 483-84;
F. K. Lane on Council of National Defense and strike mediation, **44:** 498-
501; S. H. Kent's report on, **44:** 562-70;
45: 25; Wehle memorandum on war
production and labor disputes, **45:** 7-
11; WW's address to A.F. of L. convention, **45:** 11-17; **48:** 275, 309; and railroads, **45:** 25-26, 49; and shipbuilding
projects, **45:** 41,n2; H. L. Higginson on
National Industrial Conference Board
proposal and, **45:** 44-45; settlement of
Pacific Telephone and Telegraph Co.
strike, **45:** 95-96; and Atlantic Coast
Line strike, **45:** 117-18; and need for
national employment service, **45:** 130-
32, 162; need for studies on, **45:** 132-
33,n2; W. C. Redfield on, **45:** 246-47;
and Twin City Rapid Transit Co.
strike, **45:** 331; **47:** 189-91, 272-73; **49:**
181; offers support for WW and war ef-
fort, **45:** 350; oil strikes canceled, **45:**
350; and meatpackers' labor settle-
ment, **45:** 355, 356; L. Steffens on class
war, **45:** 382-83; S. Gompers against international conference on, **46:** 21,n2;
urges WW to take over meat-packing
plants, **46:** 25-27; report of President's
Mediation Commission, **46:** 127-47;
Texas and Louisiana oil disputes settled, **46:** 170; and Hitchman case, **46:**
297n1; and carpenters' strike, **46:**
356,n5, 362-65, 366-67, 379; W. B.
Swope urges WW to address, **46:** 416-
17; R. N. Baldwin on I.W.W. trial, **46:**
481-82; and vocational rehabilitation,
47: 29, 153; Texas Federation affirms
support for war effort in face of labor
critics, **47:** 104-105, 126-28, 144; and
the I.W.W., **47:** 194-98, 232-33, 573-74;
proposal assuring day and piece
workers steady employment, **47:** 210-
12, 291, 291-92; R. W. Woolley and
M. Hale coordinating federal labor pol-
cies, **47:** 376-79; suggestions for a Director General of, **47:** 377, 391, 425-26;
and cost of living, **47:** 384; seniority
controversy on N.Y. Central Railroad,
47: 446-47; W. B. Wilson on Woolley's
and Hale's criticism, **47:** 461-65, 537-
38; and Mexican-U.S. conference on,
47: 545-46; **49:** 73; protest against

Wheeler's army commission, **47**: 597-98; WW on appropriations and, **47**: 601; W. G. McAdoo on coal workers, **48**: 87-88; and Maryland's compulsory work law, **48**: 248-49,n1, 270,n1; strikes and the war effort, **48**: 261-62,n1; WW on American Alliance for Labor and Democracy, **48**: 275-76; threatened telegraphers' strike, **48**: 281,n1, 282-83,n1, 298, 329, 337-40, 349-50, 374-75, 393-94; and Democratic platform of Indiana, **48**: 319; WW and U.S. Employment Service, **48**: 320-21, 333-34; A. J. Sabath on effect of prohibition on, **48**: 376-77; and detective agencies, **48**: 438-39; and Borland amendment to legislative, executive, and judicial appropriation bill, **48**: 444-45,n1; WW's veto of bill to increase working hours for government employees, **48**: 471; report of labor commission to Mexico, **49**: 26-36; plan for international conference, **49**: 35-36; McAdoo compares wages in railroad and shipbuilding industry, **49**: 84-85; and proposed U.S. newspaper in Mexico on, **49**: 89-90, 137; and steel industry, **49**: 145; issue of discrepancies in wage rates, **49**: 147, 181, 186,n2, 206-207, 211n1, 251, 367; and the draft, **49**: 255-56, 294-95, 328, 386; **51**: 212, 250-51; and Shipbuilding Labor Adjustment Board, **49**: 298-99,n1, 367; WW's Labor Day message of, 1918, **49**: 414-15, 429; machinists' strike and settlement in Bridgeport, **49**: 465,n2,3, 519-20, 539-40, 547; **51**: 49-50; C. Merz on London inter-Allied Labor Conference, **49**: 536-37; anthracite coal strike, **51**: 19, 545-47; and wages in shipbuilding industry, **51**: 32, 59-60, 83-84, 396-97; and P. Gorman's withdrawal from Kentucky's congressional race, **51**: 149-50; and coordination of wages and rates by government agencies, **51**: 260-61, 280, 363-67; and overtime wages, **51**: 366-67; WW on proposed all-American war labor board, **51**: 368-70,n1,2; F. P. Walsh suggests women be appointed to National War Labor Board, **51**: 522-23; *see also* strikes; President's Mediation Commission; War Labor Conference Board; National War Labor Board; War Labor Policies Board; Shipbuilding Labor Adjustment Board
Labor, Committee on (House of Reps.), **51**: 166, 214
Labor, Department of, **41**: 151-52; **42**: 437n1, 504-505, 567; **43**: 93, 292; **44**: 104; **45**: 8, 182; **46**: 127, 171, 481; **47**: 29, 58, 464; **48**: 219-20, 336; **49**: 53n1, 386, 405, 424; **51**: 69-70, 181-82, 357; and national employment service, **45**: 131-32, 162, 182-83,n1; **48**: 334; and Twin City Rapid Transit Co. strike, **45**: 258-62; and educational program for

workers regarding war and labor, **48**: 222-25; and Speakers' Bureau, **48**: 225
Labor Adjustment Board: *see* National War Labor Board
labor commission: *see* President's Mediation Commission
Labor Statistics, Bureau of, **45**: 132-33,n2, 150
Labour and the New Social Order (Webb), **46**: 435n3
Labour party (Great Britain), **41**: 5n2; and development of natural resources, **49**: 291
LaBudde, Otto A., **41**: 360,n4
Lacaze, Marie Jean Lucien, **40**: 449,n1
Lackawana Bridge Co., Buffalo, N.Y., **42**: 477,n2
Laconia, S.S., **41**: 373,n1
Lademacher, Horst, **46**: 457n3
Ladies Home Journal, **41**: 22n1; **42**: 182n1; **48**: 362,n1, 382-83
Lafayette, Marquis de (Marie Joseph Paul Yves Roch Gilbert du Motier) **42**: 23,n3; **47**: 401n2; birthday celebration in U.S., **49**: 313-14
Lafayette Hotel, Washington, D.C., **40**: 129n2
Lafoon (Laffoon), Polk, **51**: 259,n1, 295
LaGuardia, Fiorello Henry, **46**: 456n2
Lahovary, N. H., **47**: 450,n1,3
Laibach, Slovenia, **47**: 125,n2
Lakefield, Minn., **47**: 194n1, 216-17,n1,2
Lamar, Joseph Rucker, **47**: 425
Lamar, William Harmong, **43**: 165,n1,2, 394-96; **44**: 171; **47**: 471-72; **49**: 174n1; **51**: 55n1, 57,n2
Lamb, Charles, **45**: 15-16
Lamb, William E., **47**: 348
Lamennais, Hugh Félicité Robert de, **49**: 190,n5
Lammasch, Heinrich, **46**: 198,n1, 199, 200, 241-47, 253, 261-63, 315-16, 353, 388, 412, 483-84, 510n1, 580,n1, 581, 589; **48**: 553
Lamont, Thomas William, **45**: 407, 444-45,n2, 446, 547-48, 569-70; **46**: 160-61, 179-80, 585-86n2; **51**: 220-26, 296-97, 372, 530-31, 576
Lancashire, England, **42**: 379; **49**: 217
Lancken-Wakenitz, Baron von der (Oscar Hans Emil Fritz), **51**: 370,n1, 371n2
land-grant colleges, **46**: 175
Landis, Kenesaw Mountain, **46**: 458n2; **47**: 135,n2, 136
Landon, Archer A., **47**: 322,n4, 557,n4
Landon, Francis Griswold, **40**: 165,n1
Landry, Marguerite Pichon, **48**: 26
Landsberg, Otto, **45**: 32,n7
Lane, Anne Wintermute (Mrs. Franklin Knight), **41**: 185n, 196n, 240n, 260n, 283n, 350n, 518n, n1; **43**: 521; **46**: 429, 515n; **51**: 415n, 548n, 605n, 616n
Lane, Arthur Bliss, **41**: 435,n4
Lane, Frances (Mrs. George W.), **41**: 196,n3

Lane, Franklin Knight, **40:** 161-62, 173, 214, 218, 278, 279, 383, 412, 498; **41:** 88, 135, 331, 350, 445, 556; **42:** 58, 142, 153-54,n1,3, 167, 168n1, 471, 533; **43:** 61, 84, 177, 183, 385, 486; **44:** 293-94, 301, 495, 498-501, 512, 556; **45:** 148n1, 168, 176, 271, 329, 332, 342, 448; **46:** 101, 215, 429, 439, 581; **47:** 206, 233, 557; **48:** 11, 69-70, 85, 219-20,n1; **49:** 241,n1; **51:** 21, 55n1, 56, 125, 213, 412, 604-605; on Carranza's rejection of protocol and termination of Joint High Commission, **40:** 33-34, 48-56, 114-15, 297-98, 298-301, 390-92, 397-401, 478-79; death of brother, **40:** 162,n1, 193; on Germany's dispatch to Austria-Hungary on July 29, 1914, **40:** 204; on naval oil reserves, **40:** 205-206, 382, 383, 420, 560-61,n1,2; **41:** 19, 69n1, 248, 288, 289,n2, 289-90, 290-91; on water-power legislation, **40:** 206-207, 287, 424; **45:** 171-72, 300, 301, 406, 433n1; **49:** 316, 329-32, 344, 356, 357, 505, 506; **51:** 206; on grazing homestead bill, **40:** 263, 287, 288, 289, 290; **51:** 103,n3; and H. Bergson, **41:** 315n2, 316-17; on cabinet meetings, **41:** 183-84, 195-96, 239-40, 260-61, 282-83, 517-19; **51:** 413-15, 548; and railroad crisis, **41:** 425, 430n2, 437; advocates war entry, **41:** 443, 444, 506; on railroad rate increase, **42:** 218, 221; WW supports an appointment in Montana, **42:** 346-47; on Bering River coal field, **43:** 36-37, 43; and coal price fixing, **43:** 41n1, 62, 63; on opening coal mines in Colorado and Wyoming, **43:** 73-74; on governmental purchase of coal fields, **43:** 367, 399; and Russian Commission, **43:** 424; **49:** 321; on Pope Benedict's peace appeal, **43:** 521,n1; on legislation Congress should consider, **45:** 171-72; on British politics and Lansdowne letter, **45:** 193-94; and general leasing bill, **45:** 374, 375, 402,n1, 453-54; WW on, **45:** 555-56; on cabinet discussion of proposed Japanese intervention in Siberia, **46:** 515; on vocational rehabilitation, **46:** 608-609; on leasing oil lands, **47:** 10, 20; on adult illiteracy bill, **47:** 30-32, 610,n1; on Mooney case, **47:** 148; on elections, **51:** 616

Lane, Franklin Knight, Jr. (Ned), **41:** 196,n2, 518

Lane, Frederick T., **40:** 162,n1, 193

Lane, George Whitfield, **41:** 183-84,n1, 195-96, 239-40, 260-61, 282-83, 350, 517-19

Lane, Harry; and Alaska general fisheries bill, **40:** 291, 292, 366, 387n1, 417; **41:** 179, 207, 230

Lane, Hugh, **42:** 390-91,n2, 404

Lane, Jack C., **48:** 173n1

Lane-Mondell bill, **51:** 103n3

Lang, Cosmo Gordon, Archbishop of York, **47:** 84,n1, 102, 103, 117, 137, 138, 323

Lansdowne, Henry Charles Keith Petty-Fitzmaurice, 5th Marquess of, **45:** 518, 545, 546; **48:** 214

Lansdowne letter, **45:** 166n1, 173,n1, 174-75, 193, 215, 312, 548

Lansing, Eleanor Foster (Mrs. Robert), **41:** 318, 429; **42:** 127; **45:** 67; **46:** 551; requests and receives WW's Red Cross contribution, **48:** 45, 78, 94

Lansing, Robert, **40:** 48, 88, 118, 129, 163, 173, 189, 229, 240, 247-48, 279, 298, 304, 305, 306, 319-20, 326, 331, 359, 385, 388, 405, 425, 442, 442-43, 444, 445, 453, 503, 546n2, 547-48, 549-50, 554, 556, 562-63; **41:** 4, 18-19, 33, 34-35, 35, 36, 44-45, 68, 79-80, 138-39, 172-73, 179, 183, 187, 193-94, 195-96, 210, 218, 224-25, 282, 340, 349n2, 367,n4, 381, 386, 393-94, 403, 433-35, 466, 484, 496, 502, 549, 556; **42:** 18,n1, 59,n2, 77n1, 79, 90, 104, 108, 161, 165, 170, 176, 176-78, 222, 258, 264, 274, 281, 314, 358, 376, 385-86, 392-93, 396, 410, 417, 439-40, 453-55, 498n1, 530, 548, 552-53, 566; **43:** 13, 29-32, 34, 38, 39, 40, 67-69, 71, 80, 94-95, 111, 124, 133, 134, 140, 144, 183, 201, 267-70, 355-56, 413, 457-58, 459-60, 482; **44:** 3, 16, 22, 23-24, 24-26, 27, 38n1, 65-66, 66, 74, 90, 143, 179, 180-81, 187, 207, 211, 222, 347-48, 358, 385, 398, 411, 433, 483, 495, 496, 510, 513-14, 532; **45:** 30, 55, 115, 119-20, 147, 148,n1, 151-52, 166, 216-18, 243, 271, 274, 307, 323, 332, 342, 349-50, 384, 388, 398, 415, 417, 433, 474, 492, 533, 601, 603n1; **46:** 46, 51-52, 64-65, 88-89, 168, 172-73, 194,n1, 198-200, 203, 212, 232, 235,n1, 241, 253-54,n4, 261-63, 265, 334, 341-42, 352, 357, 358, 358-59, 360-61, 375, 388, 412, 418, 428, 429, 444, 465-66, 467, 488, 499, 550-51, 580-81, 589-90, 606, 620

47: 64, 85, 128, 140, 163, 173-74, 206, 219-20, 225, 226, 241, 323, 332, 344, 430, 432, 512-14, 526, 544, 555; **48:** 27, 72, 73, 96, 112, 131-32, 141, 141n3, 183, 194, 200-201, 206-207, 303, 312, 335, 358, 359, 364, 382, 391, 406, 428-29, 434, 444, 448, 453, 454, 456-57, 461, 469n1, 473, 488, 542, 544, 551, 552, 591; **49:** 178, 230, 248, 250, 267, 305, 310, 320, 346-47, 373, 373-74, 382, 403, 404, 409, 416, 417, 423, 436, 448, 529, 536-37, 540, 543; **51:** 17, 23, 24, 25, 50, 61-62, 76-77, 86, 91, 93-94,n1, 95, 121-22, 153, 161, 169, 171, 173, 178, 186, 258, 276, 277, 290, 291, 307, 328, 334-35, 341, 345, 403, 416, 505, 506, 518, 526, 527-28, 542, 576, 592, 592-93, 603-604, 605,n1, 615, 616, 618, 622, 634 on Belgian deportations, **40:** 24-27, 94-95, 106-107, 112-13, 170-71, 180, 220, 409, 411-12, 518; on *Marina* incident, **40:** 38; and proposed conference of neutrals, **40:** 46, 80-81,n1; on Dominican Republic, **40:** 82; E. M. House meets with, **40:** 96; on appointment of minister to Netherlands, **40:** 113; on leaks, **40:** 122-23, 130, 216, 419, 462; on Chinese loan, **40:** 140-41, 160, 512-13, 514-15, 563-64; **42:** 53-54; **45:** 96-97; **48:** 371-74, 382, 517, 518-23; **49:** 348; and J. C. Grew's reports, **40:** 141, 184, 428; on taking action on German submarine warfare, **40:** 190-91, 313-14, 478,n1; and WW's peace note of Dec. 18, 1916, **40:** 197, 209-11, 238, 243,n1, 256-59, 259-62, 276,n1, 273n1,2, 324-25; on German peace proposal, **40:** 230-31, 234-36, 241; on *Americanism*, **40:** 276-77,n1, 557-58,n1; "verge of war" statement and subsequent remarks and comments on, **40:** 306,n1, 307n1, 323-24, 406n1, 407; and possible forced resignation of, **40:** 307n1, 406-407, 445; **44:** 176, 184; meetings with P. Ritter, **40:** 323-24, 352; meets with Spanish ambassador, **40:** 378-79; opinion of Count Bernstorff, **40:** 445; and WW's Peace without Victory speech, **40:** 447, 478, 491, 524; on armed-ship question, **40:** 447-48, 509; **41:** 71-73,n1, 232, 233, 263-66, 341-44, 360-61, 368-69, 387, 387-88; on French banking interests in Mexico, **40:** 519; on unrestricted German submarine warfare, **40:** 552; on Colombian treaty, **41:** 27-28, 420n1, 456,n1; meets with Japanese ambassador, **41:** 37-38; **47:** 440, 441, 459-61, 472-73, 488-89; on W. H. Page and British ambassadorship, **41:** 70, 128-29, 137; and break with Germany, **41:** 87, 88, 96-99, 99-100, 110, 111, 116, 118-25, 126-27, 131; and Austria-Hungary, **41:** 95, 129-30, 158-59, 185, 267-68, 297-98, 299-300, 312, 313, 421-22, 476, 477, 477-78; on bases of peace, **41:** 132n1, 160-64; and Costa Rica, **41:** 139, 145, 146,n1, 248, 257; **45:** 405-406, 417; **46:** 450-51; **47:** 231; and China, **41:** 175, 181-82, 182-83, 185-86, 186, 195, 383-84, 394, 401-402; on Swiss efforts to restore German-American relations, **41:** 201-203, 203-204, 204-205, 273-75; and Saulsbury resolution, **41:** 225, 232, 235; and G. W. Kirchwey, **41:** 242-45, 247; and Mexico's peace proposal, **41:** 249, 258, 352; and Logan Act, **41:** 277; and Cuba, **41:** 278-79; **42:** 51; on Zimmermann telegram, **41:** 297, 321-27; E. M. House on, **41:** 318; **46:** 313; **51:** 104-105, 109, 110, 116; and Mexico, **41:** 350, 391, 404-406; **42:** 92-93, 95-96; **43:** 384,n1; **47:** 357; advocates war entry, **41:** 385, 425-27, 429-30, 436-37, 439-41; on new Russian government, **41:** 408, 415, 544, 552; **43:** 473, 475-76; and W. Denman and bunkering agreements, **41:** 418, 418-19; and Danish West Indies, **41:** 427-28, 475-76; on cabinet discussion of war resolution, **41:** 436-44; proposed statement to press on war power of Congress, **41:** 471-72, 475; on Cuba and Panama if U.S. enters war, **41:** 472-73, 476; WW on, **41:** 497; aids WW in war message, **41:** 516; and requests by French and British for missions to U.S., **41:** 553-54; on German ships in U.S. ports, **42:** 9-10, 13, 28-29; and Pan-American Pact, **42:** 14-15, 44, 54, 55, 81-82, 94, 99, 105; on coordinating secret service, **42:** 16-17; on Irish situation and Home Rule, **42:** 24-25

suggestions for Russian Commission, **42:** 36-37, 43-44, 45, 95, 164, 196, 203-204, 204, 216, 238, 239, 240, 262, 368-69; concern over possible Mexican oil embargo, **42:** 37, 38; and Panama, **42:** 51; and Committee on Public Information, **42:** 59, 71; on list of contraband, **42:** 101-102, 106; on WW's message to provisional Russian government, **42:** 109-10, 318, 326, 360, 365-67, 434, 466-67; on question of U.S. attendance at V. Carranza's inauguration, **42:** 116, 130-31, 154-55; on interdepartmental committee, **42:** 117-18; meets with WW and A. J. Balfour, **42:** 140, 141, 142; on censorship, **42:** 163, 195, 245n1, 387; on representative to British War Trade Intelligence Department, **42:** 224, 236; on Stevens' Commission to Russia, **42:** 238, 239; **43:** 439; on U.S. publicity office in Russia, **42:** 252, 284, 289, 377, 507; and International Boundary Commission appointment, **42:** 260-61,n2; and Mooney case, **42:** 271-72, 273n; on Morgenthau mission, **42:** 315-17; on refusing passports for international socialist conference, **42:** 350; on R. L. Owen's resolution on peace terms, **42:** 444,n1; on counter-propaganda campaign in Russia, **42:** 463; on arousing patriotism, **42:** 469, 490-91; on Belgium's idea of consortium of Allies, **43:** 7-8; and Japan and China, **43:** 55, 83n3; on reply to Cardinal Mercier, **43:** 74-75; W. G. McAdoo and, **43:** 204; on Pope Benedict's appeal and WW's reply, **43:** 438, 520, 523-24, 525; **44:** 18-22, 56; on F. Frankfurter report on France, **43:** 442; and B. Whitlock articles on Belgium, **43:** 477-78, 493; **44:** 84-85; E. M. House and F. L. Polk on, **43:** 485-86; and Poland, **44:** 188-89, 318; **46:** 47, 120-22, 149; and Shipping Board, **44:** 209; and House's preparatory work for peace conference, **44:** 217-19, 226, 229, 380-81; and Ishii mission, **44:** 249-55,

Lansing, Robert (*cont.*)
264,n2, 340-42, 356-57, 367-69, 376-78,
413-15, 417-20, 453-54,n1, 530-31; and
proposed inter-Allied conference, **44:**
297-98; on Guatemala, **44:** 331; on
House mission, **44:** 445-46; **45:** 368-69;
and *Public Ledger* disclosure of House
mission, **44:** 459, 460,n2, 524; on death
of father-in-law, **45:** 67,n1; on legislation Congress should consider, **45:** 177-
78; on Russian recognition and policy
toward, **45:** 205-207, 263-65, 283,n1,
369, 427-30, 562-64; on Palestine, **45:**
286; E. M. House on WW's attitude toward, **45:** 327; and Japan and Russia,
45: 336, 347, 370; on Germany's fear of
postwar trade and commercial isola-
tion, **45:** 354-55; and railroads, **45:** 361;
on sending hospital units to Italy, **45:**
364-65; and WW's Fourteen Points, **45:**
506n1, 555; and Chamber of Commerce's proposal for postwar economic
boycott of Germany, **46:** 6, 7-8, 14-15

proposed Japanese intervention in Siberia, **46:** 34,n2, 219-20, 236, 301-302,
339-41, 474-76, 482; **47:** 55-57, 67-68,
91-92, 96, 106, 131-32, 299, 317, 441,
496; on Bolsheviks, **46:** 45-46,n3, 299-
300; on Italy's frontiers and Adriatic
question, **46:** 96-97; on Germany not
stating war aims, **46:** 110; discussed as
peace commissioner, **46:** 115-16; on
H. A. Smith's relief plan, **46:** 298-99;
sends additional consular officers to
Russia, **46:** 301; and Four Points address, **46:** 313; on H. Lammasch, **46:**
315-16; on Rumania, **46:** 326, 373-75;
47: 450-51, 474,n1; suggests Admiral
Knight visit Vladivostok, **46:** 338; on
Russian Railway Service Corps, **46:**
344, 357, 358, 387; on W. E. Walling
memorandum on revolution, **46:** 349-
50; on proposed Socialist meeting, **46:**
350; **47:** 108-109, 210,n1; on possible
postwar financial aid to Austria-Hungary, **46:** 353; on Sisson Documents, **46:**
372,n3; **51:** 3-4, 18, 246; and Red Cross
appeal for halt to poisonous gas warfare, **46:** 395; and International News
Service, **46:** 393, 408; on Versailles
Declaration of Supreme War Council,
46: 415; on Austria-Hungary's peace
moves and proposals, **46:** 424; **51:** 10-
11,n2,3, 526, 527; on Zionist Committee, **46:** 493-94; on setting limits on relief, **47:** 44-45; on French telegram on
anniversary of U.S. entry into war, **47:**
257, 258; and Liberia, **47:** 315, 327,
353, 358; on relief for enemy aliens in
U.S., **47:** 360-61, 380-81; on movements for autonomy in Siberia, **47:**
397-99, 591-92; and proposed U.S. war
declaration against Bulgaria and Turkey, **47:** 416, 490-91,n1, 568-70; **48:** 79-

80; on political changes in Japan, **47:**
426; on defining U.S. policy toward
Austria-Hungary, **47:** 589-91; on intervention in Russia, **47:** 605, 621-22; **48:**
37, 99, 104, 236; on German plot in Ireland, **48:** 63-65, 71, 195; on Italy and
the Yugoslavs, **48:** 96-97; on relief
problem, **48:** 97-99, 136-37; on D. R.
Francis' request for funds, **48:** 236, 247;
on sending Marines to Galveston, **48:**
238, 247-48; on creation of Russian relief commission, **48:** 305-306, 465;
Reading on, **48:** 381; on Czech troops in
Russia, **48:** 398, 458; **49:** 282-84, 383,
417, 434-35, 446, 491-93; **51:** 86-87, 97-
98; on Panama's election, **48:** 417; on
dismemberment of Austria-Hungary
and issue of oppressed minorities in,
48: 435-37, 437-38, 447-48, 464, 485;
and R. Robins, **48:** 489,n1; memorandum of conference at White House on
Siberian situation, **48:** 542-43; on Bavarian peace program, **48:** 555n8; on
negotiations with Japan on Siberian
intervention, **48:** 559-60, 560-61, 574-
75, 579-80; and recognition of Czechs
as sovereign nation, **49:** 287-89, 313,
404-405, 415-16; and Tereshchenko,
49: 312,n1; and inter-Allied civilian
board, **49:** 323, 332; on Norway, **49:**
333, 346; on Italy's desire for U.S.
troops, **49:** 369; **51:** 386-87; on Chinese
Eastern Railway, **49:** 396,n1; and
W. Lippmann, **49:** 433; on prices British charge Allies for supplies, **49:** 435;
and A. Smith, **49:** 465; McAdoo on, **49:**
489; on Russian policy, **49:** 506-507; on
Gen. Poole's behavior, **49:** 515-17; on
keeping Col. Stewart in Archangel informed of policy, **49:** 517-18; and Samperio case, **49:** 542,n1; on McCarthy
memorandum on Ireland, **49:** 544-45;
on supplies for Russia, **51:** 31-32, 75,
139-41; and the Red Terror, **51:** 78, 642-
43; and Murmansk Region Council resolution, **51:** 79; on currency for Siberia,
51: 87-88; on Bulgaria, **51:** 133-34, 143,
154, 162-63, 163-64, 187; on atrocities
by retreating Germans, **51:** 135; WW
and House on, **51:** 144; on WW's speech
at Metropolitan Opera House, **51:** 147;
on aviators captured by Austria-Hungary, **51:** 174-75; on destruction of St.
Quentin, **51:** 215; and Herron report,
51: 229; and German-U.S. peace notes,
51: 268-69, 279,n8, 400-402, 417-18; on
Prince Max's inaugural speech, **51:**
269-70; and peace conference talk, **51:**
315, 316, 346; and peace notes to Austria-Hungary, **51:** 383n1; and note to
Allies on negotiations with Germany,
51: 416-17; on joint action with Japan
on China's internal differences, **51:**
457,n1,2; on Polish army, **51:** 446; on
Turkey, **51:** 456; and Russian railroad

situation, **51**: 478, 481,n1,2; on Italy's request for joint peace negotiations with Austria-Hungary and Germany, **51**: 528-30; on aid and support for Siberia, **51**: 598; photograph, *illustration section*, **42; 45**
Lansing-Ishii Agreement, **49**: 109
Lansing Papers, **48**: 489n1
Lara, Carlos, **41**: 143
Laredo, Tex., **49**: 35
Larned, Kan., *The Tiller and the Toiler*, **51**: 375
Larsen, William Washington, **45**: 307,n1
Larso, Bruce L., **49**: 536n1
Larson, Cedric, **43**: 168n2
Lasater, Edward Cunningham, **45**: 85,n1; **51**: 212,n2
Lascelles, Frank Cavendish, **45**: 255,n2
Lasch, Christopher, **40**: 371n2
Lassiter, William, **43**: 92,n2; **44**: 196,n1, 197
Last of the Radicals: Josiah Wedgwood (C. Wedgwood), **40**: 361n1
Latané, John Holladay, **46**: 549n1; **47**: 202n5, 507n1
Lathrop, Julia, **48**: 463-64,n1
Latin America, **40**: 164, 550; **41**: 8-9, 140-44, 258; **42**: 356-58; **45**: 388, 597; **48**: 257-58; **49**: 26, 34, 299-300
Latin American Affairs, Division of, **44**: 331,n1
Latta, Maurice C., **41**: 557,n1
Latvia and Letts, **45**: 289n1; **46**: 471n3; **49**: 197; **51**: 498
Lauck, William Jett, **45**: 183; **49**: 521,n1
Laughlin, Irwin Boyle, **40**: 369-70; **48**: 249n1; **49**: 155; **51**: 346, 528
Lausanne, Switzerland; mentioned as possible peace conference site, **51**: 473, 517, 551
Lauzanne, Stéphane Joseph Vincent, **42**: 30,n3; **48**: 288,n1, 289
Lavit, Samuel, **49**: 465,n1,2; **51**: 24
Law, Herbert Edward, **41**: 309n1
Lawrence, David, **40**: 550; **41**: 27-28, 40-44, 69, 512-14; **42**: 108, 386-87, 395-96; **44**: 226, 275, 299-300,n2, 309, 321-22; **46**: 152-53,n1; **47**: 4-5, 39-40; **48**: 361, 362; on G. Lorimer, **47**: 295, 301; disclosures on G. Borglum, **47**: 587,n1, 587-88; on public reaction to German note of Oct. 12, 1918, **51**: 320-24
Lawrence, Frederick William Pethick, **42**: 422n2
Lawrence College, Wisc., **42**: 557
Lawrenceville School, **40**: 169n1; **43**: 540,n3
Lawson, Thomas William, **40**: 349n11
Lawson, Victor Fremont, **48**: 62,n1; **49**: 203-204,n1
Lawyers Mortgage Company of New York, **47**: 141n1
Lazo, Sergei Georgievich, **47**: 100,n4, 101
Le Havre, France, **42**: 228
Le Verrier, Marie Louise, **48**: 26

Leacock, Stephen, **45**: 558
League for National Unity, **44**: 320n1, 325-27, 343
League for Political Education, **40**: 117
league of nations, **40**: 21n1, 60n1, 61, 348n5, 371, 405, 423, 439, 470, 477, 516; **41**: 36, 64, 90, 154, 173, 235, 250-51, 375, 390, 466n3, 493, 498; **42**: 89-90, 212, 436n5; **43**: 114, 273, 274, 359-60, 401, 403, 446, 447, 468, 513, 533, 534; **43**: 488, 488-89; **45**: 68; **46**: 149, 244, 496n1, 549n1, 556, 572; **47**: 24; **49**: 14-16, 16-20; **51**: 104, 107, 422; mentioned in WW's peace note, **40**: 72-74, 199, 200, 224, 228, 257, 274; R. Lansing on, **40**: 96, 276,n1, 558,n1; **41**: 440; O. G. Villard on, **40**: 236-37; J. Bryce on, **40**: 317-18, 446n2, 469; **47**: 507-508,n1, 535; N. Buxton on, **40**: 496; WW on, **40**: 534-35; **47**: 85-86, 105, 258-59, 535; **49**: 83; **51**: 129-30, 223-24, 351, 352, 513, 573, 574; H. D. Croly suggests WW make speaking tour on, **40**: 559; M. Poindexter on, **41**: 11n1; and H. C. Lodge, **41**: 11n1; WW on idea of speaking tour, **41**: 13; T. von Bethmann Hollweg on, **41**: 62; W. Lippmann on, **41**: 83,n1, 389; L. D. Wald on, **41**: 168; M. Eastman on, **41**: 305-308; J. J. Jusserand on, **41**: 356-57; H. G. Wells on, **45**: 340n1; and Inquiry memorandum, **45**: 463, 465, 467, 472; and Fourteen Points, **45**: 483; A. J. Balfour on, **45**: 577n1; comparison of G. Hertling's and O. Czernin's views on, **46**: 225, 275, 293, 320; Britain wants committee to formulate plans for, **46**: 574-75,n2; St. Loe Strachey on, **46**: 618-19; W. H. Taft's and A. L. Lowell's study group on, **47**: 102-103, 199-202, 202n5, 323-24; T. Marburg on, **47**: 507n1; **49**: 201-203; and League to Enforce Peace's plan for, **48**: 29-30,n1; G. D. Herron on, **48**: 210-17, 473-74, 538-40; **49**: 191-93; E. M. House on, **48**: 289-90, 424-26, 592-93; **49**: 225, 429, 508-509; report of Phillimore Committee, **48**: 501-502,n1, 550; WW asks House to rewrite Phillimore Committee's report on, **48**: 549; A. L. Lowell on, **48**: 561-62, 586, 590-91; House's draft for, **48**: 608, 630-37; and N. Angell, **48**: 613-14, 617-18; H. Holt on, **48**: 627-28; W. Wiseman on, **49**: 11-14; R. Cecil on, **49**: 225-28, 549; French proposal for société des nations, **49**: 226,n2; and Bavaria's peace terms, **49**: 229, 230; WW against publicity on, **49**: 265, 266, 273-74; House and WW discuss plans for, **49**: 265-68; first Paris draft, **49**: 266n4; and E. Root, **49**: 269-72, 286; Wilson's first draft of Covenant of, **49**: 266, 467-71; and the Netherlands, **49**: 508-509; comments, opinions and suggestions, **51**: 21n1, 23, 119, 182n2, 182, 183, 188, 223-24, 226,n1,

league of nations (*cont.*)
237, 244, 245, 255, 269n1, 298-99, 323, 327,n1, 430-31, 432-33, 444,n1, 496, 504, 535n1, 557-58, 594, 599, 615; freedom of the seas and, **51**: 326, 349, 496; *see also* postwar organization and security; Phillimore Report
League of Nations (Brailsford), **41**: 375,n6
League of Nations (Grey), **48**: 592-93,n1
League to Enforce Peace, **41**: 91; **42**: 221; **43**: 513; **44**: 12; **46**: 549n1; **47**: 85, 101, 103, 147-48, 208,n2; **48**: 29-30,n1, 561-62, 586, 590-91; **49**: 241; and forthcoming meeting of, **47**: 42,n2, 119,n1, 123, 198; and W. H. Taft's meeting with B. Colby and WW, **47**: 198-202
'Leak' Investigation of 1917 (Blum), **40**: 349n11
Leap into the Dark: The Issue of Suffrage in Hungary during World War I (Vermes), **45**: 57n4
Leary, John Joseph, Jr., **42**: 29n1
leasing bill: *see* general leasing bill
leather industry, **47**: 383-84, 395, 495
Leatherbee, Frances Anita Crane (Mrs. Robert William), **48**: 273,n1
Leavell, William Hayne, **42**: 46-47
Leavenworth Prison, **49**: 209
Ledebour, Georg, **40**: 433,n8; **42**: 197,n3
Lednicki, Aleksander, **42**: 544,n2
Ledoyen, Olon, **47**: 484-86, 516
Ledvinko, Frank, **40**: 217,n1
Lee, Algernon, **44**: 79
Lee, Clayton, **47**: 522,n6
Lee, Elisha, **41**: 54, 415, 420
Lee, Fitzhugh, **42**: 139
Lee, Gordon, **45**: 307,n1; **49**: 369,n1
Lee, Henry (Light-Horse Harry), **42**: 29n1
Lee, Joseph, **43**: 479
Lee, O. C., **47**: 235,n3
Lee, Robert Edward, **44**: 156
Lee, William Brewster, **41**: 354,n2; **45**: 411n2
Lee, William Granville, **40**: 246n2; **41**: 29, 54, 251,n1, 353, 420,n1
Lee, William J., **43**: 109,n1
Lee, Higginson and Company, **43**: 76,n1; **48**: 372, 519,n1; **49**: 281n1
Leffingwell, Russell Cornell, **48**: 518,n4, 593,n1; **49**: 87, 162, 218,n1; **51**: 407
Legalistas (Mexico), **40**: 110,n4
Legge, Alexander, **48**: 145,n3
legislative, executive, and judicial appropriations bill, **48**: 444,n1
Lehigh and Wilkes-Barre Coal Co., **40**: 102
Lehigh Valley Railroad Co., **40**: 103
Leinster, S.S., **51**: 362,n2
Leipnik, Ferdinand, **40**: 507-508,n2
Leipziger Neueste Nachrichten, **49**: 548n1
Leissler, Annie B. (Mrs. George A.), **51**: 172,n1, 270-71
Leissler, George A., **51**: 172,n1, 271

Leland, Henry Martyn, **44**: 540,n3
Lema, Marquis de, **44**: 319,n2
Lenin, V. I. (Vladimir Il'ich Ul'ianov), **42**: 273,n2; **43**: 474n1; **45**: 120, 147, 205, 251, 252, 253, 274, 430, 443, 444; **46**: 300, 310,n1, 341n5, 408, 457n3, 471n3, 542; **47**: 69, 79, 245, 440, 441, 606; **48**: 41, 101-102, 113, 142n6, 144, 410n2; **49**: 55, 197, 199; **51**: 4, 246; and Sisson Documents, **46**: 341,n1; R.H.B. Lockhart on, **48**: 39-40; G. Kennan on, **48**: 186, 187; and R. Robins, **48**: 489n1; L. Colcord, **48**: 548, 549; assassination attempt on, **51**: 4n2, 61n1; photograph, *illustration section*, **45**
Lennon, John B., **47**: 558,n5
Lenroot, Irvine Luther, **40**: 424; **41**: 23; **42**: 91; **46**: 566,n5; **49**: 505, 506; **51**: 21, 206, 616; and water-power legislation, **45**: 172, 300, 301, 335, 379, 380, 406; and naval oil bill, **45**: 454; and Wisconsin election, **47**: 40,n1, 326,n1, 390n2
Lens, France, **51**: 216
Leo XII, **41**: 434n2
Leonard Wood: A Biography (Hagedorn), **48**: 173n1
Leopard, H.M.S., **42**: 29n1
Leslie, Shane (John Randolph), **47**: 401,n1,2, 411-12, 552; **48**: 300
Leslie Woman Suffrage Bureau, **48**: 303n1
Leslie's Illustrated Weekly Newspaper, **47**: 352n1
Lesson for the Attorney General (New York *World*), **42**: 245n3
LeSueur, Arthur, **44**: 79; **47**: 235,n2
Letters and Journal of Brand Whitlock (Nevins, ed.), **44**: 450n1
Letters and Papers of Chaim Weizmann, **43**: 159n1; **45**: 149n2
Letters of an American Friend (Bullard), **47**: 522n3
Letters of Franklin K. Lane, Personal and Political (Lane and Wall, eds.), **41**: 185n, 196n, 240n, 260n, 283n, 350n, 518n; **46**: 515n; **51**: 415n, 548n, 605n, 616n
Letters of Theodore Roosevelt (Morison *et al.*, eds.), **41**: 469n1; **42**: 29n1; **51**: 455n1
Lever, Asbury Francis, **42**: 294n1,2, 301,n2, 323; **43**: 242, 245; **44**: 10; **46**: 368; **47**: 117, 138, 445; **49**: 73-74; on water-power legislation, **45**: 300, 335, 379, 433,n1; abandons senatorial quest on WW's request, **48**: 259-60, 268, 272
Lever, Samuel Hardman, **41**: 257,n1; **43**: 44, 46, 67, 147, 183; **46**: 489
Lever bill, **42**: 294n2; **43**: 76, 118, 210, 221, 272, 393n1, 437n3; **44**: 89, 155-56, 238n1; WW's statement on, **42**: 344-46; H. Hoover on, **42**: 430-31,n1, 532-33; **43**: 48-49,n1,6, 56, 160-61, 207-208; revision of, **42**: 529,n1; and Section 25 and coal provisions, **43**: 7n1, 397,n1, 400; S. Gompers on Clayton Act and,

43: 22, 23; and amendments, **43:** 42,n2, 84n1, 107-108, 120, 131, 148, 163-64, 207-208, 234-35, 242,n1, 245,n1, 246, 339, 347, 348-50, 357-58; and prohibition, **43:** 42,n2, 48n1, 52, 64, 84n1; and Gore substitute for, **43:** 160-61,n1, 162-63,n1; and cotton, **43:** 190-91, 210,n1; passage of, **43:** 415,n1; Lever Food and Fuel Control Act, 1917, **45:** 83, 124, 168-69, 410; **48:** 161n2, 168
Levetzow, Magnus von, **51:** 541n1
Levine, Evelyn L., **48:** 311,n1
Lewin-Epstein, Eliahu Ze'ev Halevi: *see* Epstein, Lewis
Lewinson, Edwin Ross, **44:** 333n1
Lewis, Mr., **46:** 564,n3
Lewis, Charles Lee, **46:** 459n1
Lewis, David John, **40:** 438, 492; **41:** 379, and telegraph legislation, **48:** 556,n1, 623, 628-29
Lewis, Ernest William, **44:** 478,n1, 483; **47:** 558
Lewis, Fred W., **48:** 294
Lewis, James Hamilton, **40:** 240; **41:** 88n1; **42:** 467-68; **45:** 318; **46:** 48,n1, 49; **48:** 307, 435n1; **49:** 74,n1, 264; **51:** 552,n5,6; on railroad bill, **41:** 33, 37; and Chicago postmastership, **41:** 67, 208n1; on armed-ship bill, **41:** 393-94; and woman suffrage, **45:** 278, 338; on inviting E. Debs to White House, **45:** 319; on governmental ownership of railroads, **45:** 319; and peace terms resolution, **45:** 601,n1; WW urges to seek reelection in 1920, **48:** 603-604
Lewis, John Llewellyn, **46:** 297n1; **51:** 545-47
Lewis, William Henry, **46:** 480,n2; **47:** 289
Lexington, Battle of, **41:** 555n1; **46:** 177
Leygues, Georges, **45:** 190,n1
Li, Tien-yi, **41:** 394n1
Li Yüan-Hung, **40:** 437,n1, 512, 562-64; **41:** 175,n2; **42:** 61,n4, 466n1; **43:** 363,n3
Liang Ch'i-ch'ao, **42:** 61,n3; **43:** 363,n4,5
Libby, Henry W., **47:** 236,n5
Libby, McNeill and Libby, **40:** 291n2
Liberator, The (N.Y.), **48:** 93,n1
Liberia, **46:** 480; **47:** 315-17, 327, 353; U.S. sends vessel to, **47:** 358n1; loan to, **49:** 522
Liberty airplane engine, **44:** 538-41; **45:** 155; **47:** 321n1, 322, 518,n1; **49:** 69
Liberty Bonds; Liberty Loans, **46:** 442n1; **49:** 80, 233, 234; and Bouck statement on, **51:** 311; WW on, **51:** 80-81, 180n1 *first*: **42:** 294-95, 401,n1, 455, 470, 526; **43:** 68, 114, 140n3, 186, 253, 337; **45:** 409-10; **48:** 123, 125-26; **51:** 466; WW purchases, **46:** 168 *second*; **44:** 257n1, 270n1, 278, 294, 336, 346, 351-53, 383, 395, 400-405, 406, 423, 424, 426, 452, 463n1, 503, 512; **45:** 146, 410 *third*, **47:** 186, 236, 237, 274-75, 289-90, 383n1, 388, 401n2, 520-21,n1, 562; **48:**

126, 307n1; and WW's address in Baltimore, **47:** 267-68,n1, 295-96, 335, 343; and Hollywood stars, **47:** 302n2; *Chicago Tribune* wishes to know WW's subscription to, **47:** 436-37,n1 *fourth*: **51:** 285; W. G. McAdoo on, **49:** 85-86; WW on, **49:** 99,n1; **51:** 75,n1, 103, 127, 146-47; WW considers tour on behalf of, **49:** 361-62, 445-46, 490; and E. Caruso, **51:** 251-52,n2; WW participates in campaign, **51:** 314n1; photograph, *illustration section*, **51**
Liberty Guard, **45:** 152, 160
Liberty Loan Committee, **44:** 352
Liberty National Bank of New York, **43:** 196
License Act (proposed), **51:** 70-73, 80
Lichnowsky, Karl Max, Prince Lichnowsky, **40:** 527
Lie, Mikael, **41:** 90n3
Liebenfels, S.S., **41:** 106, 484n1
Liébert, Gaston Ernest, **41:** 502,n2
Liebknecht, Karl, **42:** 197,n4; **46:** 312,n2; **51:** 565, 622n1
Liège, Belgium, **40:** 484
Lieghley, Per Lee, **41:** 55-56,n3
Life and Letters of Walter H. Page (Hendrick), **49:** 346n
Life Extension Institute, **42:** 323n2
Liggett, Hunter, **45:** 111,n6
Lighthouse Service; and pensions, **40:** 95,n1, 218
Lika, S.M.S., **51:** 492
Likhoidov, K. T., **47:** 594,n2
Liliuokalani, Queen of the Hawaiian Islands, **43:** 505, 506
Lille, France, **40:** 25; **44:** 332; **51:** 275, 385, 421
Limberg Railway: *see* Limburg Railway (Netherlands)
Limbourg, Belgium, **40:** 84
Limburg Railway (Netherlands), **47:** 564, 565
Lincoln, Abraham, **40:** 121, 220, 342n4, 494; **41:** 8, 181, 302, 303, 321, 345, 380n2, 466n3, 530, 558; **42:** 29n1, 89, 107-108, 171, 210n1, 371n1; **43:** 245, 246, 350, 364; **44:** 29n1, 114, 115-16, 156, 178-79, 417; **45:** 223, 255, 270n2, 371n1, 382; **46:** 41n1, 42, 335, 368n1, 460, 469; **47:** 296, 298, 349n1, 483, 529; **49:** 485; **51:** 343, 355, 392; G. G. Barnard's statue, **44:** 536,n1
Lincoln, Robert Todd, **44:** 536n1
Lincoln in Marble and Bronze (Bullard), **44:** 536n1
Lincoln University, **42:** 321-22,n1
Lind, John, **46:** 459; **47:** 53, 55, 376, 377, 557; **51:** 390; and Twin City Rapid Transit Co. strike, **45:** 261, 262, 279
Linda Vista, Ca., **44:** 522
Lindbergh, Charles Augustus, **49:** 536,n1; **51:** 64-65,n2; on woman suffrage demonstration and riots, **44:** 108-16

Lindbergh of Minnesota: A Political Biography (Larson), **49:** 536n1
Lindley, Curtis Holbrook, **43:** 49,n2, 56, 160; **45:** 348,n1
Lindley, Oswald, **49:** 518,n1
Lindquist, A. E., **47:** 235,n3
Lindsay, Samuel McCune: on child labor legislation, **51:** 165-67,n1, 214
Lindsey, Benjamin Barr, **42:** 118-19,n1; **49:** 208; **51:** 645,n2
Lindsey, Washington Ellsworth, **43:** 170,n1
Line of advance through Russia (Lochridge), **44:** 361n1
Lines of advance against the Central Powers (Lochridge), **44:** 361n1
Link, Arthur Stanley, **40:** 19n1, 76n1, 82n1, 137n3, 349n11, 383n1, 529n1; **41:** 11n1, 59n1, 88n1, 94n1, 149n2, 280n1, 318n1, 349n2, 352n1, 393n1, 418n1, 425n1, 430n2; **42:** 526n1
Link Belt Co., Chicago, 46, 124n1
Linsingen, Alexander von, **49:** 195,n1
Lippincott, Horace Mather, **47:** 415-16,n1
Lippmann, Walter, **40:** 237, 360, 406, 423, 539; **41:** 83,n1, 113, 146, 388-89, 537-38; **42:** 4, 65, 120, 525, 528; **43:** 410, 454,n1; **44:** 27, 244, 459n2; **45:** 153, 162; **51:** 9; on the draft, **41:** 134-35, 538; on censorship, **41:** 135; **44:** 392-93; on WW's war message, **41:** 537; on N. Angell's memorandum, **43:** 400, 401; on reply to Pope Benedict's proposal, **43:** 532-34; on labor disputes in private shipyards, **44:** 219-21; E. M. House on, **44:** 226; on New York City's mayoralty, **44:** 333-34; and Inquiry memorandum, **45:** 459-74, 476n1; and military intelligence work abroad, **49:** 402,n3, 423, 429, 433-34, 447, 487-88; Cobb-Lippmann report on Fourteen Points, **51:** 495-504
liquor: *see* prohibition
Lister, Ernest, **43:** 200,n2,5, 494; **44:** 13, 14, 15, 345; **47:** 194; **48:** 293,n4
literacy test: WW on, **41:** 52-53
Literary Digest, **51:** 649
Lithuania and Lithuanians, **40:** 446n4, 477; **44:** 5; **45:** 289, 412, 433; **46:** 162, 533, 568; **47:** 492-94, 549, 555-56; **48:** 97-98, 630,n1; **51:** 269n1, 498
Lithuanian Americans, **47:** 492-94
Lithuanian National Council, **47:** 492,n1, 492-94, 534; **48:** 630n1
Littell, Eliakim, **40:** 336n1
Littell, Robert Smith, **40:** 336n1
Littell's Living Age, **40:** 336n1, 347; **41:** 133,n1; **45:** 346
Little, Arthur W., **43:** 413,n1
Little, Arthur W., Jr., **43:** 413,n1
Little, Frank, **43:** 341, 354, 510; **46:** 144,n1
Little, Winslow, **43:** 413,n1
Littmann, Richard Ludwig Enno, **47:** 623-24

Litvinov, Maksim Maksimovich, **47:** 245,n3; **48:** 265, 276; **51:** 351n2
Livermore, Seward, **43:** 48n1, 245n1; **46:** 40n1, 49n1; **47:** 388n1; **48:** 50n1, 260n2; **51:** 604n1
Liverpool, England, **43:** 308
livestock industry: *see* cattle industry; meat-packing industry
Living Age: see Littell's Living Age
Livingston, Deborah Knox (Mrs. B. F.), **44:** 144-45,n1
Livonia, **45:** 289,n1; **46:** 568
Ljubljana, Slovenia: *see* Laibach
Lloyd George, David, **40:** 133, 172, 187, 189, 201, 233, 403, 439n1, 477, 488, 497, 517, 524; **41:** 136, 211, 214, 262, 270-73, 501, 535; **42:** 140-41, 265, 320, 414, 436, 437, 461; **43:** 44, 66-67, 115, 140n3, 355, 465; **44:** 16,n1, 70, 86-87, 200, 222, 379, 381, 386, 427, 441, 494, 545; **45:** 3, 156, 166n1, 173, 175, 318, 322, 323, 421, 430n2, 432n1, 436,n2, 444, 445, 458, 574, 578; **46:** 76, 161, 162, 197, 211, 240, 259, 406,n1; **47:** 428, 433, 471; **48:** 33, 47, 153, 245, 381, 395, 546, 586, 602-603, 615; **49:** 52, 110-11, 273, 303, 354, 428, 466; **51:** 23, 34, 39, 41, 182, 183, 235n4, 298, 325, 396, 422

accepts premiership, **40:** 185, 185-86,n1; on Germany's peace offer, **40:** 306,n1, 342,n4; R. W. Howard on interview with, **40:** 345-46; W. H. Page on, **40:** 355, 366; **41:** 270-71, 272; speech on war loan campaign, **40:** 486,n4; on need of U.S. entry into war and WW's presence at peace conference, **41:** 213-14; and Irish Home Rule, **42:** 24-25, 93, 111, 223n1, 543n1; **47:** 412, 582; and Balfour statement on foreign policy, **42:** 328, 334, 339, 341, 342; on British war aims, **43:** 291,n1; **45:** 487,n2, 488-89, 509, 518, 521, 535, 556-57, 577,n1, 594; **46:** 4, 86, 87, 110, 274, 318; talk of visiting U.S., **43:** 451, 453; war plans of, **44:** 125-30, 213,n1; on shipping issues, **44:** 362-64; **45:** 317; **49:** 217-18, 293; on Italian situation, **44:** 480; on Russian army, **44:** 496-97; E. M. House on, **45:** 70-71; and Supreme War Council, **45:** 93,n1, 112-13, 151; **46:** 233-35, 250-51, 268n3, 415; and labor, **45:** 167; New Year greeting of, **45:** 405; and British peace terms, **45:** 436,n2; and Russia, **45:** 446, 548; House compares to WW, **45:** 558; and wheat crisis, **46:** 213, 214; and Gen. Robertson's resignation, **46:** 351,n3; Reading on, **46:** 438; T. H. Bliss on, **47:** 13-14; and Supreme War Council's discussion of Japanese intervention in Siberia, **47:** 59, 60, 61; on proposed international socialist conference, **47:** 74, 75-76, 76; Reading informed of U.S. troop disposition plans, **47:** 86, 202, 213-14, 256, 280-81, 369-71, 386-88, 512, 517; critical need for

U.S. forces leads to Abbeville resolution, **47:** 181-83, 185,n1, 203-205, 221-22, 229-30, 262, 303-304, 305-306, 307, 338-41, 373-76, 393-94, 566, 567, 568, 618; telegram to American people read publicly by Reading, **47:** 185,n1, 206; on F. Foch, **47:** 209, 238, 349; on U.S. surprising Germans, **47:** 284n1, 286; talk of having to leave office, **47:** 442, 465; on postwar reconstruction, **47:** 531; on German plot in Ireland, **48:** 65, 68; wishes to have E. M. House at Supreme War Council meeting, **48:** 79, 94-95; and Belgian relief, **48:** 80; and joint Allied request for more U.S. troops, **48:** 226-27, 243, 246, 252; and intervention in Russia, **48:** 448,n1, 587-88; **49:** 9-11; on postwar economic problems and Germany, **49:** 300,n1; and peace negotiations, **51:** 261, 272n1, 272-73, 290, 291-92, 313, 427, 428, 429, 511,n1, 511-12, 513, 514-17, 532, 562, 568, 569, 571, 580, 582; on freedom of the seas, **51:** 313, 569, 570, 594, 614; on Pershing's peace terms, **51:** 523; photograph, *illustration section*, **43**

Lloyds of London, **44:** 394

Lobdel, Charles Elmer, **49:** 91,n1

Lochner, Louis Paul, **40:** 507,n1; **41:** 89-92, 515; **43:** 481-82; **44:** 78-79

Lochridge, P. D., **44:** 361n1; **51:** 429,n5

Lockhart, Frank Pruit, **47:** 427,n4

Lockhart, Robert Hamilton Bruce, **46:** 419,n1; **47:** 60, 171, 239, 319n7, 367n4, 440, 466, 621; **48:** 99, 100, 101, 102-104, 274, 378, 431; on Russian situation and views of intervention, **47:** 245-46, 606-607; **48:** 448,n1, 587-88; imprisonment of, **51:** 4n2, 18n2, 351,n2

Lockwood, Alfred Collins, **46:** 599,n3

Lodge, Henry Cabot, **40:** 406, 492n1, 494; **41:** 498; **42:** 29; **45:** 270; **46:** 60, 63n1, 116, 602; **49:** 266, 273, 310n1; **51:** 23, 303, 304, 305,n1, 341, 439, 455n1, 572, 573; WW refuses to speak at same function with, **40:** 345, 412; and WW's Peace without Victory speech, **41:** 11n1; and Zimmermann telegram, **41:** 324; and filibuster in Senate, **41:** 350; and Colombian treaty, **41:** 411, 456; meets WW after war message, **41:** 532; and sugar investigation, **45:** 344,n1; opposes WW's peace terms, **51:** 156,n2, 277n7, 297n1; and Fuel Administration, **51:** 111, 112, 113

Logan, James Addison, **42:** 437,n1

Logan, Rayford Whittingham, **42:** 322n1

Logan, Thomas Francis, **41:** 240n1, 259; **51:** 640; on G. Creel, **47:** 342,n1, 343

Logan Act, **41:** 277; **42:** 350n1

London, Meyer, **42:** 154,n1, 179, 198; **43:** 481,n5; **45:** 224n1

London, England, **40:** 144; **43:** 308; Zeppelin raids on, **40:** 142, 145; proposed Allied shipping conference in, **43:** 302, 304; proposed naval conference in, **44:** 87, 132; as site for some inter-Allied councils, **45:** 190, 245

London, Treaty of, 1915, **46:** 181-82, 472; and Article 15, **46:** 157,n3, 365,n1

London *Daily Chronicle*, **40:** 320, 465,n1, 494; **45:** 436; **49:** 202

London *Daily Express*, **43:** 405n2; **45:** 436

London *Daily Mail*, **40:** 319; **42:** 379, 428n2; **45:** 93n3, 387n1; **47:** 12n1; **51:** 298

London *Daily News*, **40:** 35,n3, 229,n1; **46:** 250; **47:** 297-99; **51:** 277,n6

London *Daily Review of the Foreign Press*, **45:** 384n2

London *Daily Telegraph*, **45:** 166n1, 173n1, 436

London Declaration of 1909: *see* Declaration of London

London *Justice*, **45:** 430n3

London *Morning Post*, **40:** 494, 511

London *Nation*, **40:** 126, 180, 204, 218; **41:** 250; **42:** 435,n4

London *National Review*, **40:** 495

London *New Europe*, **46:** 156,n1

London *Nineteenth Century*, **40:** 495

London *Sketch*, **40:** 555,n4

London *Spectator*, **51:** 444n1

London *Star*, **42:** 379n1

London *Times*, **40:** 60n1, 319, 406n1, 413, 414n3, 488n9, 497; **41:** 250; **42:** 164n1, 209, 264n3, 393n3, 428n2, 435, 436; **43:** 291n1, 299; **44:** 43n3; **45:** 149n2, 436n2, 577n1; **46:** 110n1, 113n2, 191n11; **47:** 214n1, 581; **48:** 66, 67,n1,3, 187; **49:** 189n4, 300n1; **51:** 235n4, 326n2

London *Westminster Gazette*, **40:** 204, 319, 333, 495; **41:** 215,n3; **45:** 175

Long, Boaz Walton, **41:** 143,n19

Long, Breckinridge, **41:** 70; **42:** 123, 155, 236-37, 351; **43:** 12, 124; **47:** 18; **49:** 479; appointment as Third Assistant Secretary of State, **40:** 305, 425,n1, 548; on newspapers, **45:** 87-88, 152-53, 329,n2; on proposed Japanese intervention in Siberia, **46:** 301, 302-303, 303-304, 513-15, 527-30, 584; and Chinese loan, **48:** 517, 518-19, 519-20

Long, J. Weller, **51:** 212,n1

Long, John Wendell, **49:** 516n1

Long, Richard Henry, **51:** 624,n1

Long, Samuel Wesley, **45:** 53,n1

Long, Walter Hume, **41:** 374,n3; **48:** 228,n1

Long Live the Constitution of the United States (pamphlet), **43:** 421

Longuet, Jean, **51:** 565,n7

Longworth, Alice Roosevelt (Mrs. Nicholas), **46:** 63n1

Longworth, Nicholas, **46:** 63n1; **51:** 60,n3

Lord, Chester Sanders, **43:** 333,n2

Lord, James, **42:** 471, 472; **49:** 26-36, 136

Lord, James Revell, **51:** 165-67,n1, 214

Lord's Day Alliance of the United States, **47:** 311n1

Loreburn, Earl: *see* Reid, Robert Threshie

Loree, Leonor Fresnel, **46:** 578,n2; **47:** 223,n2, 248, 283

Lorimer, George Horace, **46:** 575,n3; **47:** 295, 301, 348

Lorraine: *see* Alsace-Lorraine

Los Angeles Times, **43:** 379n1; **47:** 127

Los Angeles Times Building, **40:** 176n1

Los 8 Años (Cañas), **45:** 388n2

Lothian Road United Free Church (Edinburgh), **49:** 295n1

Lotos Club of New York, **47:** 185n1, 214

Loucheur, Louis, **45:** 209,n2

Loudon, John, **46:** 615-16,n3, 617; **47:** 87, 133-34, 142-43

Louisiana: oil strike in, **45:** 44, 60, 350; **46:** 170, 179; and bicentennial of founding of New Orleans, **46:** 100,n1; and woman suffrage, **48:** 237,n2, 352; politics in, **51:** 632

Louisiana Historical Quarterly, **46:** 100n1

Louisville, Ky.; politics in, **51:** 81, 120

Louisville *Courier-Journal*, **49:** 268,n1, 480,n1; **51:** 31

Louisville Presbyterian Theological Seminary, **49:** 122n1

Louisville Times, **49:** 268n1, 480,n1

Lovcen, S.M.S., **51:** 492

Lovejoy, Owen Reed, **40:** 42; **41:** 8; **42:** 118-19,n1; **51:** 182,n2,4

Lovett, Robert Scott, **42:** 448; **43:** 192,n1, 341, 504, 515; **44:** 208, 212, 222, 223-24, 233; **45:** 311,n1, 314; **46:** 23, 85, 336; **47:** 117; resigns from War Industries Board, **46:** 39,n1, 52, 439, 476, 477, 491, 524; on copper prices, **46:** 58-59, 68

Lowden, Frank Orren, **43:** 512n1; **46:** 560,n1; **47:** 136,n4

Lowden of Illinois: The Life of Frank O. Lowden (Hutchinson), **43:** 512n1

Lowell, Abbott Lawrence, **40:** 444; **43:** 52, 513; **44:** 12; **46:** 116, 574-75; **47:** 101, 102, 105, 123, 137, 147-48, 198, 323; **48:** 152, 153,n1; **49:** 12; on a league of nations, **47:** 102-103, 200-201; **48:** 561-62, 586, 590-91; and Red Cross, **48:** 250-51,n2

Lowell, James Russell, **40:** 475

Lowenthal, Max, **43:** 159n2, 442; **46:** 74, 147

Lowrie, Mr. (of National Wheat Growers Assoc.), **49:** 427,n2

Lowrie, Barbara Armour (Mrs. Walter), **46:** 105,n1

Lowrie, Walter, **44:** 123-24, 249; marriage of, **46:** 105,n1

Lowry, Edward George, **40:** 414,n3; **42:** 486-87, 497

Lowry, Horace, **47:** 189

Lowther, James William, **47:** 442,n1

Loyal Legion of Loggers and Lumbermen, **46:** 218n2

Lubin, David, **46:** 337,n2

Lubin, Simon Julius, **47:** 194-98,n1, 233,n1, 325-26, 479

Lucas, Benjamin H., **43:** 392,n1

Lucke, Max, **44:** 493

Ludendorff, Erich Friedrich Wilhelm, **40:** 378, 384, 463n1, 555; **41:** 24, 26n1; **42:** 160; **43:** 185n1,2; **45:** 415, 417, 595,n3; **46:** 162, 163, 173, 190; **48:** 552, 554-55,n6; **51:** 76n1, 253n2, 384

Ludwig III (of Bavaria), **48:** 553,n3; **49:** 228, 229

Ludwigshafen, Germany, **46:** 266

lumber industry, **44:** 13, 14, 15, 248, 255, 277; **45:** 233-34, 234, 295; and eighthour day, **46:** 106,n1, 106-108, 218, 508-509, 509-10; President's Mediation Commission report on, **46:** 138-41

Lunardini, Christine, **44:** 561n9

Lundeen, Ernest, **45:** 224n1

Lundquist, Charles P., **44:** 463,n1, 504

Lundy, Theodore, **44:** 323,n1

Luneville, France, **47:** 612

Lungkiang, Manchuria: *see* Tsitsihar

Lunn, George Richard, **42:** 195,n1

Lupin, Manchuria: *see* Manchuli

Lusitania, S.S., **40:** 317; **42:** 390n2, 464, 522; **46:** 348n1

Lusitania case, **51:** 331

Luxburg, Karl-Ludwig von, **44:** 140n3

Luxembourg, **40:** 440; **43:** 466; **45:** 468, 476; **46:** 568; and peace terms, **51:** 262, 273, 463, 470, 472, 500

Luxemburg, Rosa, **42:** 197,n4; **51:** 622n1

L'vov, Georgii Evgen'evich, **41:** 416,n6; **42:** 109,n1, 419,n3; **43:** 455n3; **44:** 179; **47:** 57; **51:** 481n1

Lyell, Charles Henry, **51:** 10,n8

Lyman, Charles Adelbert, **49:** 441,n6

Lyman M. Law, S.S., **41:** 284

Lynch, Frederick Henry, **41:** 302n2; **51:** 644n2

Lynch, James Kennedy, **49:** 120,n8

lynching, **40:** 153,n1; **41:** 217; **43:** 130, 343, 412n2; **46:** 380-81,n1, 385n1, 550; **48:** 160-61, 463,n3; **49:** 113-14, 166; **51:** 137-38, 191-92; L. A. Walton on, **48:** 302; R. R. Moton on, **48:** 323-24, 416; and WW statement against, **48:** 323-24, 476; **49:** 88-89, 97-98; N. D. Baker on, **48:** 476; L. C. Dyer on, **49:** 61-62,n2,3

Lynn, Mass., **49:** 133

Lyon, Ernest, **47:** 289

Lyon, Peter, **43:** 134n2

Lyon, France, **49:** 37,n1

Lyttelton, Edward, **40:** 488,n8,9

McAdoo, Eleanor Randolph Wilson (Mrs. William Gibbs), daughter of WW and EAW, **40:** 336, 551, 570,n6, 575; **41:** 328, 531; **42:** 560; **43:** 248; **44:** 55, 65, 278, 347; **45:** 277,n1, 558; **46,** 167, 314, 371, 485; **47:** 310, 506, 533; **48:** 70, 313n1; **49:** 219, 319; **51:** 110, 315; and WW's last will and testament, **42:** 426;

persuades husband not to resign, **47:** 498

McAdoo, Malcolm Ross, **47:** 136n1, 172

McAdoo, William Gibbs, **40:** 136, 173, 181, 241, 265, 313, 347-48, 422, 498; **41:** 69, 88, 123, 132, 252, 261, 279, 280n1, 282, 299, 323, 328, 332, 340, 349,n2, 418, 424, 445, 448n1, 466, 473, 484, 506, 506-507, 514, 528, 541, 556; **42:** 16, 58, 134, 158, 185, 256, 260, 274-75, 278, 496, 560; **43:** 44, 66, 147, 155, 173, 194, 249, 314, 337, 347, 356n1, 425, 470, 486; **44:** 80, 171, 230, 246, 373, 379, 380, 556; **45:** 143, 148n1, 237, 283, 362, 407, 602; **46:** 30, 37, 150, 151, 438, 444n2, 446, 448, 467, 468, 476, 479n1, 485, 488, 489, 518, 554, 582, 620; **47:** 6-7, 9, 43, 82, 171, 172-73, 173, 310, 533; **48:** 219-20,n1, 313n1, 570, 593-94; **49:** 120, 147, 181, 246, 295n1, 319, 375, 389, 462, 472; **51:** 105, 109-10, 194n1, 217, 228, 300, 344, 605,n1

and alleged peace note leak to Wall Street, **40:** 349n11, 353; and B. N. Baker resignation from Shipping Board, **41:** 16,n1; EBW on, **41:** 318; recommendations for Tariff Commission, **41:** 379-80; advocates war entry, **41:** 438-39; WW on, **41:** 474-75; on purchase of Danish West Indies, **41:** 485, 485-86, 500; on WW's war message, **41:** 541; on War Loan bill and Liberty Loan, **42:** 25-27, 27, 126, 294-95, 455, 526; **44:** 401; suggestions for Russian Commission, **42:** 80-81; on need for WW to consult him on Shipping Board expenditures, **42:** 285-87; on amendment to Federal Reserve Act, **42:** 302-303; and price fixing, **42:** 411,n1, 419; **44:** 29; and controversy with T. W. Gregory over American Protective League, **42:** 440-43, 510-18, 518n5; on war-risk insurance, **42:** 455, 527,n1, 565; **43:** 6, 93-94, 385,n1, 478,n1; **44:** 92,n1,2; and British financial crisis, **43:** 46, 68, 69, 97, 98, 139-40, 223, 224, 226, 228, 326, 335, 452n1; on arrest of C. Heynen, **43:** 133-34; proposes inter-Allied purchasing commission in U.S. and coordination of Allied purchases, **43:** 136,n2, 356n1; **44:** 195-98, 284, 355; **45:** 54-55, 245-46, 424, 532-33, 546; **46:** 324; **43:** 136-38, 189, 319-20; desires State Department information for decisions on loans, **43:** 203-204; and Trading With the Enemy Act, **43:** 281, 311, 312, 314, 315, 316, 320-23; taxation views of, **43:** 350n2; E. M. House on, **43:** 390-91; **45:** 398-99; **49:** 286, 287; talk of presidential candidacy of, **43:** 391; **45:** 558; **46:** 116, 318; **47:** 506; **48:** 70; on B. Newton as New York Port Collector, **44:** 208-209; mentioned as U.S. representative on Supreme War Council, **44:**

246; on war revenue bill and postal rate increase, **44:** 257,n1; on foreign loan requests, **44:** 280-84; on concern over health conditions in war industries, **45:** 26-28, 51, 91-92, 92; urges creation of Inter-Allied Shipping Board, **45:** 351, 424-25; on war expenditures and U.S. treasury, **45:** 424-25, 532, 533, 546, 588-92; and W. B. Hale investigation, **45:** 74, 101-102,n1; J. P. Tumulty on, **45:** 232-33; and War Emergency Finance Corp., **45:** 266,n1; and Russia, **45:** 274, 275; on governmental control of railroads, **45:** 225-28, 287, 304-306, 313, 324, 358-61, 362, 374, 401; fears railroad crisis may bring panic to Wall Street, **45:** 287

becomes Director General of railroads, **45:** 360-61, 451; sends WW birthday greetings, **45:** 380; sends message without WW's approval, **45:** 546, 588-92; on embarkation regulations under Espionage Act, **45:** 561-62,n1, 587-88; and the draft, **45:** 583, 585, 594; **48:** 12, 151-52,n1; **49:** 377-78, 379-81, 514, 541; and precautions taken regarding explosives threat aboard ships, **46:** 3-4, 17-18; appointment suggestions for War Industries Board, **46:** 17, 111-12, 259; on Russia's respecting treasury obligations as condition of recognition, **46:** 65-66; on Britain's food crisis and U.S. Treasury, **46:** 75, 76-78, 79, 126, 356; and H. C. Hoover and problem of food transport, **46:** 126n1, 394, 424-26, 469, 478; on J. T. Robinson, **46:** 252-53; Hoover on, **46:** 317; and controversy over political advice by Inter-Allied Council on War Purchases and Finance, **46:** 359, 379-80, 393, 409; and International News Service, **46:** 413, 437, 443; rejects proposal to tighten financial blockade of Central Powers, **46:** 423n1; on War Finance Corporation board, **46:** 442-43; on priorities committee of War Industries Board, **46:** 477-78, 490-91, 506, 522,n1, 524; on diverting industry from eastern U.S., **47:** 159,n1, 180; and railroads, **47:** 488, 498-99; **48:** 31, 51-52, 62, 80-93, 148,n1; **49:** 84-85, 393-94; contemplates resigning, **47:** 498, 499; **48:** 52, 69, 70, 95; **49:** 287, 489; on need for revenue legislation, **47:** 561-62; **48:** 119n2, 121-27, 128; House and WW discuss, **48:** 70-71; with H. A. Garfield issues joint statement on fuel issue, **48:** 148,n1; on revolving fund for federal operation of coal mines, **48:** 168; and Chinese loan, **48:** 371; on passage of revenue bill, **49:** 85-87, 103, 124-25, 134, 162,n1, 163-64; **51:** 204-206; on P. M. Warburg's appointment, **49:** 218-19, 222; supports P. Cravath on Inter-Allied Council

McAdoo, William Gibbs (*cont.*)
on War Purchases and Finance, **49:** 361,n1; on WW's support for Liberty Loan, **49:** 361-62; **51:** 285; on his health, **49:** 218-19, 362; on order forbidding railroad employees to engage in political activities, **49:** 372,n1; on public utilities, **49:** 405-406; discusses WW and cabinet with House, **49:** 488-89; and Mexico, **51:** 65-68, 446; and tax on WW's and federal judges' salaries, **51:** 109; wishes to be peace commissioner, **51:** 314-15; on German-U.S. peace notes, **51:** 412, 414, 416; and financing postwar reconstruction in Belgium, **51:** 461-62; on financial situation in France, **51:** 465-67; on financial questions to be considered at peace conference, **51:** 468-70
McAllister, James Gray, **49:** 122,n1
McAlpin, Charles Williston, **40:** 219,n1
MacArthur, Douglas, **41:** 474n2
Macauley, Charles Raymond, **44:** 494, 512-13; **48:** 29-30
McAuliffe, Maurice, **49:** 427,n1
McBride, John, **43:** 17,n6, 18, 104-105, 109, 171; **44:** 135
McCain, Henry Pinckney, **40:** 522; **44:** 345,n6; **45:** 208-13, 439; **46:** 45, 162, 196-98, 220, 240-41, 391, 584,n1, 619; **47:** 261, 616; **48:** 219, 331, 386, 418, 481, 577; **49:** 57, 67, 137, 262; **51:** 139n1
McCain, William J., **40:** 175,n1, 176-77
McCall, Samuel Walker, **43:** 469,n4; **44:** 204,n1, 292; **51:** 314, 316-17, 342
McCandless, Byron, **41:** 557
McCann agency, **51:** 114
McCarter, Thomas Nesbitt, **42:** 458; **49:** 405,n2
McCarthy, Charles, **49:** 440,n1, 441, 544-47; **51:** 26
McCarthy, John, **43:** 299
McCarthy, Thomas, **41:** 359; **43:** 239n1; **48:** 146,n2
McCauley, Alice Bournonville, **51:** 547,n3
MacCauley, Harvey, **51:** 547,n1, 578
MacCauley, Nell Carolyn Deatrick (Mrs. Harvey), **51:** 547,n2
Macchi di Cellere, Count Vincenzo: *see* Cellere, Count Vincenzo Macchi di
McChord, Charles Caldwell, **45:** 255n1; **47:** 557; **51:** 247,n1, 248
McClintock-Bunbury, Thomas Kane: *see* Rathdonnell, 2d Baron
McClure, Samuel Sidney, **43:** 134n2
McClurg and Company, **41:** 309
McCombs, William Frank, **42:** 244n2; **45:** 326; **46:** 445,n3; **47:** 546
McCormack, George Bryan, **45:** 269,n1, 270
McCormick, Andrew Phelps, **40:** 190,n1
McCormick, Anne (Mrs. Vance Criswell), **40:** 164,n3; **49:** 350,n1
McCormick, Annie Criswell (Mrs. Henry), **40:** 164,n3; **49:** 350,n1

McCormick, Cyrus (Princeton, 1912), **42:** 167,n1
McCormick, Cyrus Hall, Jr., **41:** 48; **42:** 167-68, 208; **44:** 66, 94n1, 142n1; **46:** 23; and Russian Commission, **42:** 45,n3, 81, 95, 143-44, 166-67, 178, 194, 262
McCormick, Harriet Bradley Hammond (Mrs. Cyrus Hall, Jr.), **42:** 166,n1
McCormick, Harold Fowler, **45:** 416n5
McCormick, Joseph Medill, **46:** 63n1; **51:** 298, 552,n5
McCormick, Vance Criswell, **40:** 162n1, 163-64, 305, 408; **41:** 374, 497, 510; **42:** 347; **43:** 34-35, 71, 76, 535,n1; **44:** 11, 28, 284, 326, 390, 392, 396n1,2, 411, 434, 437; **45:** 69, 235, 323, 327, 349; **46:** 91, 380, 444n2, 488, 546,n1, 611; **47:** 43, 53, 120, 172, 558-59,n1; **49:** 157, 350, 435n1, 493, 529, 550; **51:** 87, 104n4, 146, 300, 353, 407, 416, 537, 598, 638; and Norway, **45:** 74, 78, 79-80, 82-83; on tonnage, **45:** 339; on commandeering of Dutch ships in U.S. ports, **45:** 366; on army absentee voting, **51:** 287,n1; and WW's appeal to voters, **51:** 389-90, 392-93
McCosh, Isabella Guthrie (Mrs. James), **42:** 168
McCosh, James, **42:** 168, 343; **48:** 532,n5
McCoy, Edwin T., **47:** 597-98,n1
McCoy, Frank Ross, **42:** 324
MacCracken, Henry Noble, **44:** 554-55,n1
McCulloch, James Edward, **47:** 326-27,n1
McCumber, Porter James, **44:** 89n1; **46:** 345; **51:** 277n7
McDonald, Charles F., **47:** 82n1; **51:** 552,n9
McDonald, Duncan, **44:** 79
McDonald, James, **44:** 522
MacDonald, James Ramsey, **40:** 446n4; **42:** 418n2, 420-22, 435
McDonald, Rhoda Isabel (Mrs. William Jesse), **46:** 5
McDonald, Thomas, **49:** 327-28, 400
McDonald, William Jesse (Bill), **40:** 133,n2; **41:** 340; death of, **46:** 5,n1,2
Macdonogh, George Mark Watson, **42:** 355,n1; **45:** 313,n1
MacDougall, William Dugald, **41:** 496,n1; **42:** 380,n4
McDowell, Robert Brendan, **42:** 543n1; **47:** 228n1, 267n2
Macedonia, **40:** 234, 454; **42:** 156, 334; **44:** 218, 361n1; **45:** 470; **48:** 481,n1; **51:** 45-46, 143, 155, 187, 199-200, 502; front in, **51:** 64
McElroy, Isaac Stuart, **49:** 292n3
McElroy, Isaac Stuart, Jr., **49:** 292n3
McElroy, Robert, **40:** 566,n1
McElwain, James Franklin, **47:** 557,n4
McEwan, William Leonard, **42:** 313,n1
McFarland, Bates H., **51:** 226,n1
Macfarland, Charles Stedman, **41:** 93
Macfarland, Grenville Stanley, **42:** 489-90,n1, 527; **43:** 431; **44:** 536n1; **45:** 270-

71; **46:** 601-602,n1; **48:** 449-50, 474; **51:** 19-20, 76, 193,n2; and *Patria*, **44:** 231,n1, 287,n1, 307,n1; takes charge of editorial policy of *New York American*, **44:** 275,n1, 286; on censorship and A. S. Burleson, **44:** 366,n1, 371-72, 389, 397, 416-17

MacFarland, Superintendent (of Railway Mail Service), **43:** 374

McGarrity, Joseph, **48:** 63n1

Macgowan, David Bell, **48:** 429,n1

McGranahan, James, **51:** 74,n1

McGrath, Captain, **49:** 495,n5

McGraw, James Joseph, **51:** 444n1

McGraw, John Thomas, **51:** 437,n2, 538, 540

Machado da Franca, José Francisco de Horta: *see* Alte, Viscount of

McIlhenny, John Avery, **41:** 546, 547-48; **42:** 3; **45:** 336, 337

McIlherron, Jim, **46:** 380,n2

McIlvaine, James Hall, **40:** 571,n2

McIlwaine, Charles Howard, **42:** 570,n2,3

McIntyre, Frank, **40:** 57, 97, 112, 149; **48:** 35, 35-37, 75, 130, 637,n3; **49:** 135, 394

Mack, Julian William, **43:** 94,n1, 385n1; **47:** 557,n2; **49:** 56,n2

Mackay, Clarence Hungerford, **48:** 281,n5, 282-83, 298, 301

Mackaye, Percy W., **44:** 266,n1

McKellar, Kenneth Douglas, **42:** 260n2, 343n1; **43:** 107-108, 120-22, 131, 148-49, 163-64, 234-35; **48:** 395, 444; **51:** 312; and woman suffrage, **45:** 278, 338

McKelway, Alexander Jeffrey, **40:** 42; **45:** 331, 333-34, 346; **47:** 15-17; death of, **47:** 359,n1

McKelway, Alexander Jeffrey III, **47:** 16,n5

McKelway, Benjamin Mosby, **47:** 16,n5

McKelway, Catherine Scott Comfort (Mrs. John Ryan), **47:** 16,n4

McKelway, Ruth Smith (Mrs. Alexander Jeffrey), **47:** 359

McKenna, Reginald, **40:** 493, 494,n1, 497; **45:** 175

Mackensen, S.M.S., **51:** 490

McKeown, Thomas Deitz, **43:** 434-35,n1; **45:** 307,n1

Mackenzie, William Douglas, **42:** 392-95, 395

McKibben, Ross, **46:** 435n3

McKinley, William, **46:** 41n1; **51:** 573

McLachlan, James Douglas, **44:** 312,n1; **47:** 386; **51:** 208-209,n1

Maclay, Joseph Paton, **40:** 452,n2; **43:** 179,n1, 303,n2; **45:** 379; **46:** 211; **49:** 217

McLean, Edward Beale, **43:** 154, 182-83; **46:** 525-26, 527; **47:** 256, 292-93, 310; **51:** 452, 464, 485

McLean, John, **51:** 560,n2

Mclennen, Edward Francis, **41:** 49,n4

McManus, Robert C., **46:** 492,n2

McMillan, Duncan James, **46:** 41n1

Macmillan and Company, **41:** 502n3, 555; **42:** 21, 254

Macmillen, Francis, **44:** 266,n1

McMillin, Benton, **40:** 164

MacMurray, John, **48:** 155-61

MacMurray, John Van Antwerp, **46:** 539n1; **48:** 609n1; **49:** 212, 449

McNab, Gavin, **42:** 525-26, 547; **43:** 265; **44:** 243, 243-44; **49:** 489,n1; and aircraft investigation, **47:** 41n1, 328-32, 508, 545n1; on abolishing Aircraft Board, **47:** 332; on WW's participation in Wisconsin senatorial race, **47:** 388-90; *see also* Marshall-Wells-McNab Committee

McNally, James Clifford, **46:** 428,n1

McNamara, James B., **40:** 176n1; **51:** 377,n1

McNamara, John J., **40:** 176n1; **51:** 377,n1

McNamara dynamiting case: *see* dynamite conspiracy case

McNamee, Luke, **43:** 182,n2

MacNaughton, Edgar, **46:** 479,n3

McNeil, Myron S., **49:** 180,n1

McNulty, Frank Joseph, **45:** 9,n7

McRoberts, Samuel, **46:** 111,n4; **47:** 437,n1

McSparran, John Aldus, **44:** 258,n1; **46:** 602

McWade, Robert Malachi, **45:** 184,n2

Macy, Valentine Everit, **44:** 219, 220,n2, 226-29, 233, 234, 242, 256-57,n1, 268, 277; **45:** 132n1; **46:** 362,n1, 364; **47:** 557; **49:** 298-99; **51:** 32, 59-60, 83-84; and wages in shipbuilding industry, **51:** 194, 396-97, 406, 422-23

Mad Monk of Russia, Iliodor, **42:** 465n1

Madagascar, **45:** 412

Madden, Martin Barnaby, **51:** 92n1

Madero, Francisco Indalecio, **49:** 280n1

Madeyski, Jerzy Wiktor, **46:** 403,n2

Madison *Wisconsin Botschafter*, **44:** 318n1

Madison *Wisconsin State Journal*, **45:** 142,n1,2, 221n1; **46:** 119n1

magazines: and war effort, **47:** 295; *see also* under names of specific periodicals, such as *Saturday Evening Post*

Magennis, Peter Elias, **48:** 118n1

Maggie (servant at Sayre household), **49:** 388

Magie, William Francis, **45:** 92,n1, 154

Maginnis, Marguerite, **48:** 118n1, 118,n1

Maglione, Luigi, **49:** 188,n2

Magnate: William Boyce Thompson and His Time, 1869-1930 (Hagedorn), **44:** 367n2

Magnes, Judah Leon, **44:** 79; **48:** 98,n6

Magnolia, Mass.: W. Wiseman on week spent with E. M. House and WW in, **49:** 397

Magyars, **46:** 244-45; **49:** 45, 198, 199, 220, 221, 448; **51:** 502

Mahany, Rowland Blennerhassett, **44:** 183,n1; **47:** 557; **48:** 43

Mahdesian, Arshag, **49:** 20n2
mail censorship: *see* Post Office Department
Maine, **44:** 144,n1; **46:** 478; politics in, **51:** 632
Mainz, Germany, **51:** 463
Maitland, Mary Jones (Mrs. Alexander), **40:** 570,n2
Making Democracy Efficient (*American Review of Reviews*), **47:** 385,n4
Making Democracy Efficient: The Overman Bill as an Opportunity (Cleveland), **47:** 385,n2
Making of a State: Memories and Observations, 1914-1918 (Masaryk), **47:** 552n6; **48:** 358n1; **49:** 287n1
Maklakov, Vasilii Alekseevich, **45:** 166n1, 185,n2; **46:** 302,n5; **47:** 398
Malaby, Zachary Taylor, **51:** 477,n1
Malcolm, James, **49:** 157n1
Mali, Pierre, **40:** 89,n1
Malines, Archbishop of: *see* Mercier, Désiré Félicien François Joseph, Cardinal Mercier
Malinov, Aleksandŭr, **51:** 134,n2, 141, 154, 154-55
Mallet, Claude Coventry, **45:** 388,n3
Malone, Dudley Field, **41:** 530, 543-44; **43:** 175, 187, 283,n1, 298, 425, 514; **49:** 275; resigns as Collector of Port of New York, **43:** 290-91,n1; **44:** 169, 190, 200; WW on, **43:** 313-14; and woman suffrage, **44:** 167-69, 185; and WW's reply to Pope's appeal, **44:** 184,n3
Maltbie, Milo Roy, **51:** 20,n1
Malvy, Louis Jean, **43:** 444,n3
Mamatey, Victor Samuel, **48:** 358n1; **51:** 562n1
Man, The (Morley), **42:** 182n1, 202
Man and the President (Herron), **40:** 542n1
Man Who Heads the 'Spruce Drive' (Clay), **46:** 218n2
Manchester, England, **41:** 5n2; **44:** 536n1
Manchester Guardian, **40:** 558,n1; **41:** 250; **44:** 386,n1; **46:** 511-12; **51:** 277,n6
Manchuli, **49:** 282-83, 494; **51:** 479,n1
Manchuria, **41:** 38, 39; **43:** 82; **44:** 255; **46:** 475n4, 514; **47:** 98, 131; **49:** 107, 213, 262
Manchuria, S.S., **41:** 364
Manchuria Station, **46:** 387
Manchurian Railway, **46:** 220n2
Mandel, Bernard, **44:** 47n1
Mangan, John J., **45:** 18,n1
Mangum, Franc, **46:** 38,n1
Manikovskii, Aleksei Alekseevich, **45:** 217n4
Manila, P. I., **41:** 152
Manila Bay: and Adm. Dewey, **44:** 296n1, 387
Manjiro, the Man Who Discovered America (Kaneko), **48:** 569n1
Mann, James Robert, **42:** 91; **47:** 584,n2
Mann, Louis, **46:** 519-20

Mann, William Abram, **45:** 111,n2
Mann Act, **41:** 246-47, 261
Manners, John Hartley, **47:** 476,n2
Mannheim, Germany, **46:** 266
Mannheimer Volksstimme, **46:** 164, 227
Manning, Natalie, **46:** 520
Manning, Richard Irvine, **51:** 110, 294, 337, 375
Manning, Vannoy Hartrog, **42:** 561,n1
Manning, William Thomas, **40:** 89,n1
manpower bill, **49:** 347
Mansfield, Frederick William, **44:** 205,n2, 293n1
Mantle of Elijah, A Novel (Zangwill), **45:** 369n1
Manufactures, Committee on (Senate), **46:** 31n1; and sugar investigation, **45:** 344n1, 348, 353
Manufacturers Record (Baltimore), **47:** 540,n2,3
Manuilov, Aleksandr Apollonovich, **41:** 416,n8; **42:** 419,n3
Mapa, Victorino, **44:** 9
Marburg, Theodore, **41:** 250n3; **46:** 549,n1, 572; **47:** 86, 200, 202n5, 535; **49:** 214-15; on league of nations, **47:** 507, 507-508,n1; **49:** 201-203
Marbury, William Luke, **51:** 28,n1
March, Peyton Conway, **45:** 110,n7; **46:** 560,n1, 562,n1; **47:** 26, 129, 237-38, 262, 271, 509, 545, 616; **48:** 73, 74, 243, 353, 357, 401-403, 418, 484,n1, 503, 542, 544, 577, 599; **49:** 117, 126-27, 258-61, 276, 279-80, 285-86, 293, 373,n1, 487, 517, 529-30; **51:** 26, 51-55, 139, 146, 261, 337-38, 403, 416, 425-26, 472, 545; on U.S. troop commitment, **47:** 145-47, 260-61, 279; appointed Chief of Staff, **48:** 181,n6; on intervention in Russia, **48:** 182, 418-21, 479-80; **49:** 57; on importance of all-American divisions, **48:** 244; J. J. Jusserand meets with, **48:** 253-54; on sending 80 divisions to France, **49:** 66-67, 262; clarifies U.S. position regarding troops and Italian front, **49:** 136-37; and Supreme War Council's note on military policy, **51:** 195, 211; on WW's reply to German note of Oct. 6, 1918, **51:** 272; on J. J. Pershing's interference in Armistice terms, **51:** 525
Marchand, C. Roland, **43:** 175n3, 512n1
Marchant, H. P., **46:** 615n4
Marchienne, Baron de Cartier de, **43:** 8,n2
Marder, Arthur Jacob, **49:** 411n1; **51:** 124n2
Mare Island Navy Yard, **43:** 470n2
Margerie, Pierre de, **44:** 43,n1
Marghiloman, Alexandru, **47:** 240,n1, 451,n2
Margulies, Herbert F., **47:** 388n1
Maria Theresa, **42:** 335
Marie (of Rumania), **43:** 95, 460n1
Marie Therese, S.S., **40:** 449

Marina incident, **40:** 5, 38, 75, 95, 107, 190, 191, 212, 272, 307n1, 389,n1, 430, 432

Marine Corps: *see* United States Marine Corps

Maritime Transportation, Committee on: *see* Inter-Allied Maritime Transport Council

Market Bureau (Department of Agriculture), **41:** 32, 207

Markgraf, S.M.S., **51:** 490

Markham, Charles Henry, **46:** 426,n6

Markovic, Ivan, **49:** 45,n3

Marling, Alfred Erskine, **51:** 644,n2

Marmande, R. de, **42:** 435,n3, 436

Marmon, Howard C., **44:** 540,n4

Marquand, G. H., Jr., **43:** 336n1, 373

Marsh, Arthur Richmond, **44:** 105,n2, 105-106

Marsh, Benjamin Clarke, **44:** 206; **49:** 335,n1

Marsh, Ernest P., **43:** 267,n6; **44:** 104,n1, 214, 520; **46:** 74, 147

Marshall, Hudson Snowden, **42:** 443; **47:** 41n2, 313,n1, 328-32, 335, 336, 508, 545n1; *see also* Marshall-Wells-McNab Committee

Marshall, Josephine Banks (Mrs. Charles Henry), **48:** 63,n2

Marshall, Leon Carroll, **47:** 558,n6

Marshall, Lois I. Kimsey (Mrs. Thomas Riley), **40:** 230, 243; **41:** 358; **47:** 548

Marshall, Louis, **46:** 525n1; **51:** 644; on relief for Jews, **47:** 555-56, 608; on Polish Jews, **51:** 625-27

Marshall, Thomas Riley, **40:** 230, 243-44; **41:** 358; **46:** 31, 57, 194, 208; WW's birthday greetings to, **47:** 40, 57-58; asked to campaign in Wisconsin, **47:** 40-41; on child welfare, **47:** 547-48, 560, 596

Marshall, Sir William Raine, **51:** 201,n4

Marshall-Wells-McNab Committee, **47:** 512; establishment of, **47:** 41n1, 193, 259; report of, **47:** 328-32, 335,n1, 509-10,n1, 545,n1, 554, 587, 587-88, 588

Martel, Damien Joseph Alfred Charles, Viscount de, **40:** 514,n1, 515

Marti y Zayas Bazan, José, **42:** 295

Martin, Chalmers, **41:** 321,n1

Martin, Charles Douglas, **43:** 412,n2

Martin, Daniel Hoffman, **47:** 360,n1

Martin, Edward Sandford, **46:** 328; **48:** 152n1

Martin, Franklin Henry, **41:** 170n3; **42:** 138,n1; **43:** 148n1, 222n1

Martin, George Brown, **49:** 480, 481, 486, 529; **51:** 294-95; and woman suffrage, **51:** 30, 31, 49, 58, 133, 288

Martin, Gertrude S., **48:** 345n1

Martin, Henderson S., **40:** 37,n2; **41:** 63,n1

Martin, Hugh Street, **47:** 140,n1, 141; **48:** 142n8, 288,n1

Martin, Joseph, **41:** 360

Martin, Julia Whitney (Mrs. Edward Sandford), **46:** 328,n1

Martin, Luther (1749?-1846), **46:** 33

Martin, Thomas Staples, **40:** 291; **41:** 309n1, 393; **42:** 343, 532n1; **44:** 117, 150-51, 154, 199, 273-74, 279-80; **46:** 37, 60, 204, 368,n1; **47:** 94-95; **48:** 10, 14, 51, 119,n2, 129, 154, 405, 592; and Lever bill, **43:** 42,n2, 162-63; and woman suffrage, **45:** 278, 338, 339; **47:** 572; and Overman bill, **47:** 94n1; and wire-control bill, **48:** 526, 534, 535,n1

Martin County, Minn., **47:** 216n2

Martine, James Edgar, **40:** 523

Martinez, Edmundo E., **43:** 378,n1, 378-79, 381, 383, 449-50, 505

Marushevski, V. V., **45:** 217n4

Marx, Karl, **51:** 565n7

Maryland, **47:** 217n1, 411; and woman suffrage, **42:** 124,n1, 138-39; and labor laws, **43:** 418,n1; **48:** 248-49,n1, 270; politics in, **51:** 632

Maryland League for National Defense; WW's remarks to, **41:** 10,n1

Maryland Shipbuilding Company, **42:** 477

Masaryk, Charlotte Garrigue (Mrs. Thomas), **41:** 56n1

Masaryk, Thomas (Tomáš) Garrigue, **41:** 56,n1,2; **43:** 150, 299; **47:** 548, 549-52,n6, 561, 610-11; **48:** 106, 202,n1, 273, 274, 335n1, 353, 353-54, 354, 355, 398; **49:** 41, 44, 53, 154, 194, 203, 219, 287n1, 288, 345, 373, 434, 435, 446, 511-12; **51:** 8, 26, 51, 95,n2, 349, 395; WW meets with, **48:** 283, 358,n1; and U.S. recognition of Czechs as sovereign nation, **49:** 185, 485-86; concern over Anglo-American relations, **49:** 550-51; on situation in Russia, **51:** 86-87, 96-97,n1,2, 210,n3; on Austria-Hungary's peace note, **51:** 506-507; on peace terms, **51:** 507-508

Masaryk (Newman), **41:** 56n1

Masaryk: A Biography (Selver), **41:** 56n1

Masaryk in England (Seton-Watson), **41:** 56n1

Mason, Gregory, **48:** 585,n3

Mason, James Murray, **41:** 303

Mason City, Ia., **47:** 236

Massachusetts, **47:** 472; politics in, **44:** 204-205, 221, 292,n2, 292-93,n1; **51:** 28, 552,n1, 590, 624, 632; and transit companies, **49:** 422, 459

Massachusetts Institute of Technology, **49:** 242n1

Massachusetts State Board of Arbitration and Conciliation, **49:** 133

Masses, The (N.Y.), **43:** 164, 165,n2, 188, 481,n5; **44:** 171-72,n2, 394, 469, 470n3, 471; **49:** 208n2; **51:** 57, 521; comments on trial of editors, **48:** 59n1,2, 93n1, 146,n1, 197-98, 208-209, 220, 251n2

Masses Publishing Company, **43:** 165n2

Massey, William Ferguson, **42:** 341,n7

Massingham, Henry William, **40:** 126, 140, 180
Mather, Samuel, **41:** 55n1
Mathy, Heinrich, **40:** 145-46,n2
Matsui, Keishiro, **43:** 256,n1
Matthews, Mark Allison, **51:** 16,n1,2
Matthias Erzberger and the Dilemma of German Democracy (Epstein), **43:** 185n1; **45:** 32n3
Maugham (William) Somerset, **43:** 278,n2
Maura y Montaner, Antonio, **42:** 264,n3
Maurer, James H., **44:** 79
Mauretania, S.S., **44:** 375, 381
Maury, Annie Lee Bolling (Mrs. Matthew H.), **41:** 288,n1, 297
Maury, Henry Lowndes, **44:** 259-63,n1
Maxa, Prokop, **49:** 45,n3
Maxim, Hudson, **40:** 35,n3
Maximalists: *see* Bolsheviks
Maximilian Harden: Censor Germaniae: The Critic in Opposition from Bismarck to the Rise of Nazism (Young), **43:** 246n1
Maximilian Harden und die "Zukunft" (Weller), **43:** 246n1
Maximilian von Baden (Prince Max of Baden), **51:** 235,n4, 268, 269, 316n6, 331n5, 607; assumes chancellorship, **51:** 253,n2; and peace correspondence with U.S., **51:** 255-57, 263-65, 266-67,n3, 276-79; inaugural speech of, **51:** 269,n1, 277n6
May, Arthur James, **41:** 56n2; **46:** 403n1; **47:** 589n1; **48:** 114n2
May, Paul, **43:** 7, 8
Mayer, Arno Joseph, **45:** 487n2; **47:** 74n1
Mayflower, U.S.S., **40:** 119n1, 189; **42:** 123, 160; **43:** 238, 240, 317, 318; **44:** 175, 182n2; **48:** 440: **49:** 167, 240
Mayflower Company, **51:** 173
Mayo, Dermot Robert Wyndham Bourke, 7th Earl of, **42:** 403,n2
Mayo, Henry Thomas, **41:** 298n1, 381; **43:** 178, 179, 427, 463,n1, 503; **44:** 86-87, 131-32, 174-75, 411, 464; **46:** 213n2; **47:** 348; background of Inter-Allied Naval Conference and, **44:** 87-88
Mays, John, **41:** 474,n3
Mazzini, Giuseppe, **41:** 530
M'Donnell, Randel Mark Kerr: *see* Dunluce, Viscount
meat-packing industry, **45:** 178-79,n2, 331; **46:** 76, 386; **47:** 8-9, 19; **48:** 308, 487n1; settlement reached, **45:** 355-56; WW urged to take over, **46:** 25-27, 588; report of President's Mediation Commission on, **46:** 128, 141-43; WW on labor situation in, **46:** 149-50,n1,2; FTC investigation of and recommendations, **41:** 31-32, 112, 146-48, 205-206, 207, 208, 309, 309-10,n1; **46:** 195-96,n1,2, 462-63,n3, 492, 493; **48:** 7-9, 44, 75-77, 107-10, 179,n1, 507-11, 564n1; **49:** 130-32, 164,n1, 372,n1, 460-61, 522-28; **51:** 18, 80, 90,n1; H. Hoover on, **46:** 409-10;

47: 149-53, 192, 221, 222, 255; W. Kent on, **47:** 47, 49-50; D. F. Houston on, **49:** 439-40; and complaints of no profits, **49:** 498,n1; J. Daniels on navy and, **49:** 509n1; and export program, **51:** 89; W. B. Colver on, **51:** 441-43
Mechanics and Metals National Bank, N.Y., **43:** 197
Mecklenburg, Duke of, **46:** 163n1
Meda, Filippo, **46:** 454,n1
Medal of Honor, **45:** 173
Mediation and Conciliation Act, **40:** 246n4
Mediation Board: *see* United States Board of Mediation and Conciliation
Medvedev, A. S., **51:** 450,n7
Meeker, Arthur, **49:** 498,n1
Meeker, Jacob Edwin, **49:** 235,n1
Meeker, Royal, **49:** 433,n1; on need for labor and cost surveys, **45:** 132-33,n2, 149-50, 150, 183; on vocational rehabilitation, **47:** 28-30, 95, 123-24, 153; suggests a textile and clothing administration, **49:** 375-77, 389-90; fears for WW's safety if he makes a tour, **49:** 445-46
Megata, Tanetaro, **44:** 315-16,n2, 3
Mehring, Franz, **51:** 565, 622n1
Meier, Heinz Karl, **44:** 484n1, 486n3, 489n5
Meiklejohn, Alexander, **44:** 146
Meinl, Julius, **45:** 415,n1, 415-17,n5; **46:** 198,n1, 199, 388, 580-81, 589; **47:** 24,n2
Meléndez, Carlos, **41:** 143,n20; **49:** 118,n1
Melendy, H. Brett, **51:** 213n1
Meletii, Metropolitan of Moscow, **49:** 63,n3
Mellon National Bank, Pittsburgh, **43:** 197
Melton, Alger, **44:** 121n1
Memoirs of My Life (Giolitti; Storer, ed.), **46:** 156n2
Memoirs of Prince Max of Baden (Calder and Sutton, trans.), **51:** 235n4
Memoranda and Letters of Dr. Muehlon (Smith, trans.), **48:** 213n8
Memorandum as to Price Fixing Through Establishment of Maximum Price to Consumers as Compared with the Fixing of a Uniform Average Price by Means of a Government Pool (Colver), **43:** 6,n1
Memorandum: Desirable Federal Activities in the Field of Hygiene and Sanitation of Industries during War (Blue), **45:** 27,n1
Memorandum for the Adjustment During the War of Wages, Hours and Conditions of Labor in Production of Munitions and Supplies, **45:** 7-8,n4, 9,n6
Memorandum for the Adjustment of Wages, Hours and Conditions of Labor in Shipbuilding Plants, **45:** 7,n3
Memorandum for the Secretary of the Treasury (Strauss), **46:** 423n1
Memorandum of Conference with Presi-

dent Wilson, March 28, 1918 (Lowell), 47: 202n6
Memorandum of Conversation with Swedish Minister (Lansing), 40: 81n1
Memorandum of the cost of production of copper in 1917 (Federal Trade Commission), 44: 64,n1
Memorandum of War Aims (Inter-Allied Labor and Socialist Conference—London, Feb. 23, 1918), 47: 74n1
Memorandum on a strategic comparison of the Western Front with the Eastern Mediterranean (Lochridge), 44: 361n1
Memorandum on Power of President to raise Street Railway Rates, 48: 526,n1
Memorandum on Russia (Strunsky), 46: 422n1
Memorandum on the General Strategy of the Present War Between the Allies and the Central Powers (Sargent), 44: 239n1; 45: 4-6,n1
Memorandum on the Status of Armed Merchant Vessels . . . March 25, 1916, 41: 72,n3
Memorandum to the Representatives of the Mine Workers of Alabama (W. B. Wilson), 44: 144n1
Memorial Day: WW's address on, 42: 422-23
Memphis, Tenn., 42: 137; 46: 384
Men and Power (Beaverbrook), 46: 351n3
Menace, The (Aurora, Mo.), 49: 169,n1, 174,n1
Menace of Peace (Herron), 49: 188n3
Méndez, Joaquín, 44: 331,n1,2
Mendieta, Carlos, 41: 339,n2
Menocal, Mario García, 41: 268n1, 339, 384, 385,n2; 42: 295,n1; 43: 207; 45: 116, 178
Men's League for Woman Suffrage, 43: 462n1
Mensdorff-Pouilly-Dietrichstein, Albert von, 45: 430n3; 46: 577
Mercantile Bank of America, 45: 388
Mercersburg Academy, 44: 513,n1,2; 47: 450n1
merchant marine: *see* United States Merchant Marine
Merchant Marine and Fisheries, Committee on (House of Reps.), 40: 291, 417-18; 41: 209n1; 46: 151, 283
Merchant's Association of N.Y., 47: 218,n1; 48: 472n1
Merchants National Bank of New York, 48: 644n1
Mercier, Désiré Félicien François Joseph, Cardinal Mercier, 43: 40-41,n1, 74, 75, 101-102; 51: 370-71
Mere Literature and Other Essays (Wilson), 46: 449, 605; 47: 41
Meredith, Edwin Thomas, 44: 289,n1, 291
Meredith, Ellis (Mrs. Henry H. Clement), 51: 304,n2
Merrheim, Charles, 51: 560,n3

Merriam, Charles Edward, 40: 489,n1,2, 492; 51: 118,n1
Merrill, James M., 49: 167n1
Merrill, Oscar Charles, 45: 300,n1; 49: 330,n3, 331, 351; 51: 21,n2
Merrill water-power bill, 45: 168-69,n1, 300,n1
Merton College, 42: 266n1
Merz, Charles, 40: 421-23,n1; 49: 487,n1, 536
Mes Missions, 1917-1918 (Bergson), 41: 315n2; 48: 441n1
Mesaba, Minn., 44: 163,n1
Meserve, Harry Fessenden, 46: 89,n1, 118
Mesopotamia, 40: 435; 41: 191; 42: 157; 43: 115, 291n1; 44: 361n1, 387; 45: 459, 460, 471, 487n2, 553; 47: 422; 49: 339, 404; 51: 48, 200-201, 503, 514, 539,n2
Message from the President of the United States . . ., 41: 53n
Message from the President of the United States Vetoing H.R. 9054, 48: 597n
Message from the President of the United States Vetoing H.R. 10358, 48: 471n
Message from the President of the United States Vetoing Senate Joint Resolution 159, 48: 590n
Message from the United States Government to the American People (Creel), 47: 276,n3
Message May Swing Russians Into Line (Colcord), 45: 222,n1
Message sent by the President to the Farmers Conference . . ., 46: 178n
Messiah (Handel), 46: 604n1
Meston, James Scorgie, 48: 531,n3
Metal Mine Workers Union, 44: 262; of Butte, Mont., 43: 299, 339-40
Metal Trades Council, 44: 244
Metcalf, William Penn, 51: 478,n1
Metcalf, Ariz., 44: 478, 483
Methodist Episcopal Church, 42: 259n1; 47: 337n1; and post office appropriations bill, 41: 311,n1, 312
Methodist Episcopal Church, South, 49: 317n1; and temperance, 48: 190-91
Methodist Episcopal Church of Bernardsville, N.J., 41; 257n1
Methodist Episcopal Church of Butler, N.J., 44: 199n1
Metropolitan, 44: 472,n6; 47: 16n3; 48: 147,n4,5
Metropolitan Opera Company, 42: 7-8,n1, 8-9,n1; 47: 584n1; 48: 16, 53n1, 63
Metropolitan Opera House: E. M. House and WW discuss proposed speech at, 51: 103, 104; WW's address at, 51: 127-33; House on setting and delivery of speech, 51: 144; comments on WW's speech at, 51: 124, 147, 148, 149, 150-51, 151, 156, 164, 172, 175, 176, 182-83,n2, 221-22, 224; benefit concert at, 51: 314n1, 316
Metropolitan Museum of Art: and J. S. Sargent portrait of WW, 46: 219n6

Metternich, Klemens Wenzel Nepomuk Lothar von, **51:** 567
Metz, Herman August, **41:** 327,n4
Metz, France (Germany), **47:** 240; **51:** 275, 415
Mexican-American Joint High Commission, **47:** 425n3
Mexican-American Labor Conference, **49:** 73
Mexican Constitution, **47:** 346n5
Mexican Federation of Labor, **49:** 29
Mexican Northern Railway, **40:** 282, 284, 302
Mexico, Balthasar Henry, **51:** 248,n5
Mexico, **42:** 359; **49:** 303; Legal Peace party formed, **40:** 110n4; French banking interests in, **40:** 519; and Germany, **42:** 82, 92-93, 225; **43:** 217,n5; **48:** 135, 238,n1, 278; German propaganda and intrigue in, **44:** 90,n1, 412,n3; **47:** 163-66, 474-75,n2; **49:** 26-27, 30, 137-38, 153, 280,n2; and Guatemala, **44:** 331,n2,3; and oil situation, **49:** 225, 230-31, 300
Mexico and the United States, **40:** 3, 123, 161-62, 162, 269, 270, 371, 421, 476; **41:** 4, 303, 348, 350-51,n3, 423,n1, 459, 545-46; **42:** 92, 95-96, 116; **43:** 39-40; **46:** 354-55,n2,3,4, 406n2; **47:** 246, 662; **48:** 134-35, 551, 612; **49:** 154, 462; **51:** 446; U.S. withdrawal and boundary control plans, **40:** 33-34, 48-56, 115-16; F. Funston's strategy for Villa's capture, **40:** 100-101; renewal of border attacks, **40:** 109-10, 130-31,n2, 202-203; **41:** 236-37,n1; F. K. Lane on hostile attitude of Mexican commissioners, **40:** 114-15; V. Carranza wishes changes in protocol, **40:** 279-87, 297-98; U.S. gives ultimatum, **40:** 298-301, 301-303; V. Carranza vetoes proposal, **40:** 390-92, 393-94; termination of Joint High Commission, **40:** 394-96, 397-401, 478-79; American commissioners urge U.S. troop withdrawal, **40:** 479-81; Pershing's troops begin withdrawal, **40:** 522, 546; and clergy imprisoned in Mexico, **41:** 34, 44-45; D. Lawrence on, **41:** 40-44, 512-13; and Switzerland, **41:** 106; and Carranza's peace proposal, **41:** 249-50,n2, 351, 392, 404-406; and Zimmermann telegram, **41:** 280-82, 392-93,n1; and American interests in Mexico, **41:** 365-67; C. P. Anderson on, **41:** 385-87; and the Vatican, **41:** 433, 435; and film *Patria*, **41:** 483,n1; and oil, **42:** 37-38, 38; **47:** 404, 475, 552; WW receives new ambassador, **42:** 79-80,n1; and Carranza inauguration, **42:** 130-32, 154-55; Pershing on border situation, **42:** 225-27; and E. Martinez interview with WW, **43:** 378-79, 381, 449, 449-50, 505; and loan, **43:** 384,n1; **49:** 141, 153, 166; and attitude toward the war, **47:** 163-66; WW on his past policy regarding, **47:** 288-89; and gold and sil-

ver, **47:** 345,n2, 357,n1; **51:** 12,n2; H. P. Fletcher on worsening relations between, **47:** 345-47; S. Gompers on, **47:** 351, 420; **49:** 24-25; WW on importance of passing passport bill, **47:** 474-75; WW answers Gompers on, **47:** 545-46; A. J. Balfour on, **47:** 552-53; proposed movement of Marines to Galveston, **48:** 238,n1, 247-48, 279-80; WW's remarks to Mexican editors, **48:** 255-59, 278; report of American Federation of Labor Commission to Mexico, **49:** 26-36; plan for international conference, **49:** 35-36; W. B. Wilson on creation of labor newspaper in Mexico, **49:** 89-90; F. L. Polk on L. Warfield's suggestions on, **49:** 140-41,n2,3; WW against Britain recognizing Domínguez, **49:** 299-300; WW intervenes on behalf of Mexican exchange tutor, **49:** 305
Mexico City *Boletín de la Guerra*, **49:** 26-27, 27
Mexico City *El Democrata*, **49:** 26, 27
Mexico City *Excelsior*, **49:** 27
Mexico City *El Pueblo*, **49:** 26, 28
Mexico City *El Universal*, **49:** 27
Mexico City *La Defensa*, **44:** 331,n3
Meyer, Eugene, Jr., **46:** 208,n1, 209, 229-30; **47:** 51, 579-80; and Russian Commission, **42:** 81,n1, 95, 143,n1, 165, 194-95, 204
Mezes, Annie O. Hunter (Mrs. Sidney Edward), **40:** 237; **48:** 63,n2
Mezes, Sidney Edward, **40:** 237; **41:** 544; **42:** 554, 555; **44:** 226, 244, 381, 426, 439, 454, 541, 549-51; **45:** 17-18, 324; **46:** 116; **47:** 12, 323, 534,n2,3; **48:** 63,n2; **51:** 314,n2, 408; and Inquiry Memorandum, **45:** 459-74, 476,n1
Mézières, France, **51:** 385-86
Miami Herald, **46:** 604n1
Miami Metropolis, **46:** 604,n2
Michael (Mikhail Aleksandrovich), Grand Duke of Russia, **44:** 180,n3
Michael, Charles Edwin, **46:** 578,n2; **47:** 223,n2, 248, 252, 283
Michaelis, Georg, **43:** 185,n2, 406,n3, 448, 498,n1; **44:** 25, 43-46,n6,7; **45:** 31-33
Michailovitch, Lioubomir (Ljubo Mihajlović), **47:** 416-17,n1; **48:** 437,n1,2
Michaud, Jennie W., (Mrs. Regis), **40:** 570,n3
Micheler, Joseph Alfred, **42:** 190,n2
Michigan, **42:** 83, 122; **43:** 325; senatorial campaign in, **48:** 347n1; **49:** 84,n1, 438-39,n3, 461, 498; politics in, **51:** 590, 632
Michigan, University of, **46:** 29n1, 404,n6
Michigan City, Ind., **46:** 97-98, 119
Michigan Socialist, **43:** 165
Michigan State Grange, **44:** 259
Midland National Bank of Minneapolis, **47:** 236n5
Midleton, St. John Brodrick, 9th Viscount, **47:** 267n2

Mihajlović, Ljubo: *see* Michailovitch, Lioubomir

Miles, Basil, **44:** 143,n1; **45:** 543-45, 562n1; **46:** 302, 303, 303-304, 451-52; **47:** 69, 226-27; **48:** 112, 145, 479-80; **49:** 517; **51:** 478; on movements for autonomy in Siberia, **47:** 397-99

Miles, Sherman, **46:** 533, 540-44, 554

Miley, E. L., **51:** 395,n1

Milhaud, Edgard, **48:** 210-11,n1

Military Academy, United States: *see* United States Military Academy

Military Affairs, **49:** 167n1

Military Affairs, Committee on (House of Reps.), **41:** 550; **42:** 91, 103,n1, 104n2; **45:** 585; **46:** 147, 153, 329; **48:** 457n1, 532n1

Military Affairs, Committee on (Senate), **40:** 267n1; **41:** 550; **42:** 274n1, 542; **43:** 16; **44:** 361n1; **45:** 390n1, 585; **46:** 103, 257; **47:** 381n2, 458-59; **48:** 73-74, 413; **49:** 255; **51:** 15,n1; and G. Borglum, **46:** 95, 106; Chamberlain bill controversy, **46:** 40n1, 54-55, 82, 147,n1,2, 204, 257n2; and aircraft matters, **47:** 207n1, 321,n1, 511, 542; and conduct of the war, **48:** 10,n1, 14, 50n1; photograph, *illustration section,* **49**

military appropriations bill: *see* Army Appropriations Act

Military Critic on Allied Attacks Along West Front . . . Imperative Need of Rebuilding Russian Front by Some Form of Intervention (*New York Times*), **49:** 93n1

Military missions of liaison with belligerent countries (Kuhn), **42:** 33n1

Military Policy of the United States (Upton), **47:** 483n3

Miliukov, Pavel Nikolaevich, **41:** 416,n10, 455, 466, 552; **42:** 218n2, 232, 265, 273, 319,n2, 320,n2, 436; **45:** 418, 444; **49:** 220

Miller, Adolph Caspar, **40:** 77; **41:** 316-17; **43:** 183

Miller, Charles Ransom, **51:** 106n7

Miller, David Hunter, **44:** 105,n1, 105-106, 426, 439; **46:** 490; **47:** 185; **48:** 63,n2; **49:** 226n2; **51:** 408; and Inquiry memorandum, **45:** 459-74, 476n1; on Alsace-Lorraine, **45:** 469, 473-74

Miller, Fred C., **46:** 97-98, 119

Miller, George Frazier, **46:** 383n1

Miller, Henry John, **41:** 454

Miller, Lucius Hopkins, **40:** 169-70; **46:** 260,n3

Miller, Mae Coffeen (Mrs. Lucius Hopkins), **40:** 170,n3

Miller, Ransford Stevens, **51:** 457,n2

Miller, Thomas A., **44:** 86n1

Miller and Auchincloss (N.Y. law firm), **44:** 105n1

Mills, Anson, **42:** 260n2

Mills, Charles B., **47:** 236,n5

Milne, George Francis, **51:** 141n3

Milner, Alfred, 1st Viscount Milner (1854-1925), **41:** 214; **42:** 435; **44:** 202, 386, 546, 546-49; **45:** 418; **46:** 211, 240; **47:** 433, 435, 455, 456, 457, 471, 512, 567, 595, 618; **48:** 33, 50, 218, 285, 353, 386, 388, 395, 418; **49:** 82-83; **51:** 55, 462,n2, 473,n1, 571; becomes Secretary of State for War, **47:** 436,n2; and agreement on U.S. troop transport, **48:** 227; and request for U.S. troops for Russia, **48:** 330, 536, 537; and plan for intervention in Russia, **48:** 330, 367, 368, 369, 396-97, 418; on peace terms, **51:** 373; N. D. Baker on, **51:** 385, 386; photograph, *illustration section,* **47**

Milton, Robert, **46:** 520

Milwaukee Journal, **43:** 194, 319,n1; **45:** 345,n2

Milwaukee Leader, **42:** 253,n1, 254; **43:** 190n1; **44:** 245; and censorship, **44:** 272, 338-40, 344,n1, 396-97,n2

Mineola, Tex., **47:** 260,n1, 521n1

Miners' Position: Organizer Harrison's Card (*Birmingham News*), **43:** 434n1

Miners' Reply to Recent Editorial in News Columns (*Birmingham News*), **43:** 434n1

mining industry: *see* coal industry

Minneapolis, Minn., **43:** 117, 512n1; **44:** 47,n1, 78; **51:** 91,n1; and Twin City Rapid Transit strike, **45:** 258-62, 279, 331; **47:** 189-91, 272-74, 292; **49:** 181

Minneapolis Chamber of Commerce, **40:** 102

Minnesota, **42:** 83, 122; **43:** 325, 512n1; **44:** 17, 78; transit strike in Minneapolis, **45:** 258-62, 279, 331; **47:** 189-91, 272-74, 292; Nonpartisan League in, **46:** 348,n1; **47:** 54, 87-88, 194n1, 216-17,n2, 226, 235-37, 400, 406; and potato crop transport problems, **46:** 463-64, 478; politics in, **47:** 53-55,n1; **51:** 301, 390,n1, 590, 632; and C. A. Lindbergh appointment, **49:** 536,n1

Minnesota, University of, **45:** 272n1

Minnesota Commission on Public Safety, **45:** 258n2; **46:** 348,n1, 369, 464; **47:** 189-91, 226, 236n5, 273, 400

Minor, Robert, **48:** 143,n9

Minsk, Russia, **46:** 48, 403

Minutes of a Meeting held at 10, Downing Street, S.W. on December 26, 1916, **40:** 439n1

Minutes of the General Assembly of the Presbyterian Church in the United States of America, **42:** 535n1

Minutes of the University Commission on Southern Race Questions, **48:** 462,n2

Mirbach-Harff, Count Wilhelm von, **48:** 41,n3, 239, 239-40, 398-99,n1; assassination of, **49:** 63,n1

Mireles, Gustavo Espinosa, **49:** 34,n3

Misme, Jane, **48:** 26

Mission Sir Roger Casements im Deutschen Reich, 1914-1916 (Doerries), **48:** 63n1

Missionary Review of the World, **48:** 78n2

Mississippi, **46:** 104,n1; **47:** 209; **48:** 400-401; senatorial campaign in, **49:** 180, 369,n2; politics in, **51:** 632

Mississippi, S.S., **40:** 450

Mississippi Valley Historical Review, **46:** 218n2

Missouri, **42:** 83, 122; **43:** 437; **47:** 90-91; **48:** 115,n1,2; politics in, **49:** 210, 224,n1,2,3,4, 235,n1, 239, 370-71, 444-45; **51:** 82,n2, 85, 138-39, 171, 589, 612, 632

Missouri, University of, **47:** 115n3

Missouri Democratic State Convention, **49:** 444-45

Missouri Farmer, 47: 91

Missouri Farmers' Association, **47:** 90-91

Missouri Peace Society, **47:** 155n3

Mr. Wilson's Opportunity (*Springfield, Mass. Republican*), **40:** 241,n1

Mr. Wilson's speech on Peace Conditions (New York *Commercial and Financial Chronicle*), **41:** 107

Mrs. Stokes for the Government and Anti-War at the Same Time (*Kansas City Star*), **48:** 422-23

Mitchel, John Purroy, **40:** 35n1, 119n1, 215n1; **41:** 555,n1; **43:** 175n2, 239; **45:** 157; and New York mayoralty, **44:** 333-34,n1, 458, 464, 556n2; and military service of, **45:** 399-400,n5; death of, **48:** 568,n2

Mitchel, Olive Child (Mrs. John Purroy), **48:** 568,n1

Mitchell, Charles Wellman: death of, **45:** 404,n1, 411, 423, 575

Mitchell, Ewing Young, **48:** 115n1

Mitchell, Florence Crowe (Mrs. Charles Wellman), **45:** 404

Mitchell, James H., **49:** 399-400

Mitchell, John, **42:** 448, 471; and Hitchman case, **46:** 297,n1

Mitchell, Max, **45:** 160,n1

Mitteleuropa (Naumann), **42:** 389n1

Mixed-flour Act (1898), **42:** 294n2

Mob Treatment of Disloyalists Worries Wilson: President Will Issue Statement Demanding Respect Be Shown to Law (St. Louis *Republic*), **49:** 61,n1

Mobile, Ala., WW's speech mentioned, **44:** 438,n1

Mock, James Robert, **43:** 168n2

Moderate Opinion in England (Whitehouse), **40:** 465n2

Moffett, Cleveland Langston, **43:** 499-500,n1, 504, 509, 510; **44:** 31

Mohilev, Russia, **46:** 403

Mohonk Conference, 1915, **48:** 36,n1

Moje Paměti: Československá Anabase (Gajda), **49:** 543n1

Moldavia, **43:** 371

Moltke, S.M.S., **51:** 490

Moncheur, Baron (Ludovic Alfred Joseph Ghislain), **43:** 8,n1, 465-69

Mondell, Frank Wheeler, **51:** 103,n3

Monell, Ambrose, **43:** 177,n1

Money, Hernando DeSoto, **43:** 369,n2

Monge, Ricardo, **45:** 388,n5

Mongolia and Mongols, **43:** 82, 83n3; **48:** 105n1

Monk Iliodor: *see* Iliodor

Monroe Doctrine, **40:** 65, 66, 348n5, 461, 539, 543; **41:** 9, 11n1, 166, 512; **42:** 6, 37, 38, 94, 96, 105, 314; **44:** 254; **45:** 394-95; **48:** 257-58; **49:** 270

Monrovia, Liberia, **47:** 315-17, 327, 353, 358

Mont Blanc, S.S., **45:** 230n1

Montagna, Giulio Cesare, **49:** 333,n2

Montague, Andrew Jackson, **41:** 55n1; **45:** 567,n1

Montague, Robert Latané, **45:** 567n3

Montana, **42:** 346-47,n3; **44:** 17, 107, 259-63; **45:** 234; **47:** 195, 411; **48:** 220n1; **49:** 99, 100, 449n1; labor problems in, **43:** 17, 18, 299, 339, 341, 345, 494; **45:** 321-22; coal prices in, **43:** 75-76; politics in, **51:** 213, 302, 589, 612, 632

Montana State Metal Trades Council, **43:** 354

Montauk Point, N.Y., **41:** 152

Montdidier, France, **48:** 387, 388n9; **51:** 421

Montealegre and Bonilla (coffee exporters), **41:** 141; **49:** 6

Montenegro, **40:** 16, 234, 441, 477; **42:** 425n1; **43:** 268, 448, 524; **44:** 19, 20; **45:** 412; **46:** 224, 228; **51:** 256, 262, 263, 264, 274, 502; and peace terms and Inquiry memorandum, **45:** 459, 470, 473; and Fourteen Points, **45:** 479, 484, 514, 528, 553; and British war aims statement, **45:** 487n2

Monteux, Pierre, **48:** 53,n1

Monteglas, Count Adolf von, **40:** 552,n1; **47:** 64,n2

Monteglas, Count Maximilian von (Maximilian Maria Karl Desiderius), **47:** 64,n2; **48:** 214

Montgomery, James, **47:** 414n1

Montgomery, W. A., **42:** 5,n3

Montgomery Ward and Company, **43:** 169

Monthly Review of the United States Bureau of Labor Statistics, **43:** 511n1; **48:** 338n2

Monticello, **41:** 179-80, 234, 310-11; **47:** 38

Moody, William Vaughn, **41:** 454n1

Moon, John Austin, **43:** 481n5

Mooney, Rena (Mrs. Thomas Joseph), **46:** 69, 71, 72

Mooney, Thomas Joseph (middle name incorrectly given in Vol. 42), **42:** 270,n2, 271-72, 273n1, 279; **44:** 246, 267, 274n1, 290,n1, 307, 307-308; **46:** 69, 74, 84; **47:** 467; **48:** 237, 247, 404; **49:** 24, 51,n1; **51:** 377,n1

Mooney-Billings Report: Suppressed by the Wickersham Commission, **42:** 270n2

Mooney case, **44:** 267, 290-91; **45:** 382; **46:** 170; **47:** 148, 160,n1, 210, 359, 396-97,

467; **48:** 237, 247, 404-405; **49:** 23, 24, 90, 244; President's Mediation Commission's report on, **46:** 68-74; WW asks for postponement of execution, **46:** 74; publicity of report on, **46:** 84

Mooney Case (Frost), **42:** 270n2; **44:** 274n1

Moore, Frank Gardner, **46**, 119-20,n1,2

Moore, George Gordon, **42:** 372,n2, 373-74, 377, 405, 408, 410

Moore, John Bassett, **43:** 11

Moore, John Denis Joseph, **43:** 509-10,n1,5

Moore, Joseph Hampton, **46:** 561, 562

Moore, Walter William, **42:** 87-89,n1

Moorland, Jesse Edward, **49:** 179,n1

Morales, Cristobel, **42:** 438-39

Moran, William Herman, **42:** 517,n4

Moravia, **45:** 553n2

Morawetz, Victor, **49:** 168-69,n2, 173

Morbid Neutrality (*Springfield*, Mass., *Republican*), **41:** 451n2

Morehead, John Henry, **51:** 477,n2

Morehouse College, **42:** 322n1

Morel, Edmund Dene, **42:** 422,n2

Morenci, Ariz., **43:** 157; **44:** 478, 483

Morgan, Edward M., **40:** 41,n1

Morgan, Edwin Vernon, **42:** 105,n1, 439,n1

Morgan, J. Edward, **44:** 274,n1

Morgan, Jane Norton Grew (Mrs. John Pierpont, Jr.), **46:** 23,n1

Morgan, John Pierpont, **44:** 470n3; **49:** 168n2

Morgan, John Pierpont, Jr., **40:** 19n1; **41:** 257, 466, 550; **42:** 6; **46:** 23,n1; **48:** 518; **49:** 233; **51:** 221,n4

Morgan, J. P. and Co.: *see* J. P. Morgan and Co.

Morgan, William Fellowes, **47:** 218,n1; **48:** 472,n1

Morgan State College, **42:** 322n1

Morgenthau, Henry, **42:** 58, 316-17, 462-63, 475; **43:** 134, 159,n1, 172, 201, 206; **44:** 299n2, 333n1, 461, 467; **45:** 122-24, 128,n1, 185; **49:** 537; E. M. House on, **43:** 183-84; on his book and movie rights, **48:** 284,n1, 311, 350

Morgenthau mission, **42:** 316-17,n3; **43:** 159n1,2,3, 172, 183-84, 206

Morison, Elting Elmore, **41:** 469n1; **42:** 29n1, 82n1, 83n1; **51:** 455n1

Morlan, Robert Loren, **44:** 153n1; **45:** 167n1; **47:** 194n1

Morley, Christopher Darlington, **42:** 182n1, 202

Morley, James William, **46:** 620n1; **47:** 99n5, 426n1; **48:** 72n2, 448n1; **49:** 5n1

Mormons, **44:** 294

Morocco, **42:** 264n3; **44:** 476

Morones, Luis N., **49:** 34

Morris, Edward, **45:** 179n2

Morris, Emery T., **42:** 115, 202; **46:** 550

Morris, Ira Nelson, **40:** 240,n2; **44:** 298; **48:** 93,n3, 194-95; **49:** 436,n1, 437-38

Morris, Robert Hugh, **49:** 420,n1

Morris, Roland Sletor, **41:** 510; **44:** 213; **46:** 34,n1, 118, 339, 344,n2, 545, 620; **47:** 77-78, 91-92, 427-30; **49:** 96,n1, 304, 408, 506-507; appointed ambassador to Japan, **42:** 347,n1; **43:** 333-34, 347,n1; on Czechs, **49:** 493-94; **51:** 98-101; travels to Vladivostok, **49:** 507n1; **51:** 86,n1; WW's instructions on U.S. position in Russia, **51:** 121; on Japanese control of Russian railways, **51:** 478, 479-81,n1

Morris and Company, **46:** 28, 462n3; **48:** 508

Morrison, Frank, **44:** 483,n1; **46:** 26; **49:** 25; **51:** 81, 120, 122, 150; death of, **46:** 28,n2

Morrison, John Frank, **45:** 109,n5

Morrow, Dwight Whitney, **51:** 226,n6

Morrow, Ian F. D., **43:** 185n1; **51:** 253n2

Morrow, Jay Johnson, **41:** 153,n1

Morrow, John DeLorma Adams, **47:** 409,n4; **51:** 111,n2,3, 113, 115

Morse, John Torrey, Jr., **42:** 246n4

Morse, Perley, **49:** 132

Moscow, **44:** 180; **46:** 411n1; **47:** 141, 355; **48:** 380; **49:** 196, 250; Red Terror in, **51:** 3, 4, 4,n2, 18,n2, 61, 78,n2

Moscow Cooperative Societies, **48:** 359n1

Moscow Is Become a City of Despair (Williams), **46:** 411n1

Moscow *Izvestia*, **45:** 597; **46:** 539n1

Moscow *Pravda*, **45:** 384n2

Moscow *Russko Slavo*, **42:** 320

Moser, Charles Kroth, **47:** 96,n2, 397n1, 594; **48:** 105,n2; **51:** 481n1

Most Critical Food Situation in the Country's History Will Come Within Next Sixty Days, Says Administrator Hoover (*Official Bulletin*), **46:** 424,n1

Mother Jones: *see* Jones, Mary Harris

Mother Nature's News, **48:** 491n1

motion pictures: and Sunday showings at training camps, **47:** 311,n1,2; H. Morgenthau on making his book into a movie, **48:** 284; WW on, **48:** 311; EBW's criticism of D. W. Griffith's *Hearts of the World*, **48:** 313-14,n1; WW meets with Griffith's representatives, **48:** 356,n1; *see also Patria* (film)

Moton, Robert Russa, **40:** 153-54, 218; **41:** 412, 414; **43:** 119,n1, 132, 208; **47:** 289; **48:** 475, 476, 530; **49:** 113-14, 166, 522, 541; on Liberia, **46:** 480,n3; on lynchings and request that WW make statement against, **48:** 323-24, 416; WW promises statement, **48:** 346

Motono, Ichiro, **44:** 314-16,n1; **46:** 35,n1, 118, 344n2, 474, 475, 476, 539n1, 571,n1, 620; **47:** 57; resignation of, **47:** 426n1, 440

Mott, John R., **40:** 54, 55, 56, 221, 281, 300, 390-92, 397-401, 478-79, 479-81; **41:** 113,n3, 505, 527; **42:** 160, 393n1, 395; **43:** 13-14, 149-50, 424; **44:** 27, 94,n1, 142n1, 434; **47:** 304-305; **48:** 142, 240, 303; **49:** 63, 154, 384-85; **51:** 636-

Mott, John R. (*cont.*)
37; and Russian Commission, **42:** 45,n3, 95, 262; **44:** 15-16, 66-69, 270,n1; on WW's reply to Pope's appeal, **44:** 94; and YMCA fund-raising campaign, **44:** 270n1, 551, 551-52; on need for funds for programs, **46:** 479, 495-96; on proposed Japanese intervention in Siberia, **46:** 604-605,n1; and proposed Russian relief commission, **48:** 306,n2, 315; **49:** 77-79, 123; and passport clearance for YMCA workers, **49:** 387, 390
Mott, Thomas Bentley, **51:** 53,n3
Motzkin, Leo, **45:** 572,n2
Moulliens-au-Bois, France, **51:** 39
Mount Carmel Baptist Church, Washington, D.C., **51:** 168n1
Mt. Moriah Baptist Church, Washington, D.C., **51:** 193n1
Mount Vernon, **42:** 160
Mount Vernon Address: *see* Fourth of July
Mount Vernon, July 4, 1918 (poem, Davis), **49:** 462,n1
Moudros, Greece, **49:** 411n1
Moves for a War Cabinet (*New York Times*), **46:** 40n1
Mozart, Wolfgang Amadeus, **49:** 360n2
Muehlon, Wilhelm von, **46:** 253-54,n2,6; **47:** 64n2; **48:** 213,n8, 554, 558n6
Mueller, Fred William, **46:** 613,n6; **47:** 337,n1
Mueller, Georg Alexander von, **40:** 463n1; **45:** 36n14
Mueller, Lauro Severiano, **42:** 14,n2, 15; resignation of, **42:** 265n4
Mueller-Meiningen, Ernst (Ernst Müller), **45:** 32,n3
Muenchner Neueste Nachrichten, **46:** 165, 227, 267
Muhlfeld, George Oscar, **51:** 14,n3
Muling, Manchuria, **51:** 479,n1
Muller, Julius W., **45:** 249n2, 257
Mullowny, Alexander R., **43:** 201n1
Munich, Germany, **51:** 607
Munich, University of, **46:** 198n2; **49:** 229
Municipal Auditorium (St. Paul), **44:** 182
Municipal Research, Bureau of, N.Y., **40:** 498n1
Munitions Ministry (proposed), **46:** 40n1, 41, 49n1, 54, 63n1, 82, 92, 101n1, 204, 217
Munitions of War Act (England), **44:** 569
Munitions Standards Board, **41:** 530n1
Munn, Charles Allen, **46:** 151-52,n1
Muñoz Rivera, Luis, **40:** 57
Munro, Dana Gardner, **40:** 82n1; **41:** 141n12
Munsey, Frank Andrew, **40:** 35,n3; **43:** 416n1; **46:** 574; **51:** 221
Munsey, J. E., **40:** 176,n1
Munsey's Magazine, 40: 35n3
Munson, William Benjamin, **47:** 354,n1, 395
Murdock, Victor, **48:** 44, 507-11; **49:** 130-32, 431

Murguia, Francisco, **40:** 109,n1, 130n2
Murmansk (Murman), Russia, **48:** 112, 113, 142: *see also* Russia—Murmansk and Archangel, intervention in
Murmansk Railway, **48:** 285n3
Murmansk Region Council, **51:** 79,n1, 161n1
Murphy, Charles Francis, **41:** 359-60; **49:** 157n1
Murphy, Grayson H. P., **42:** 252,n2
Murphy, Joseph E., **41:** 328, 331, 357, 531-32
Murray, Arthur, **44:** 344,n2
Murray, Arthur Cecil, **48:** 523-25,n1; **49:** 397-99; **51:** 6-10
Murray, George Gilbert Aimé, **45:** 215; **48:** 212,n4
Murray, John, **49:** 26-36
Murray, Katie, **40:** 568,n2
Murray, Robert H., **49:** 29, 30
Muscle Shoals dam, **47:** 191
Musings Without Method (*Blackwood's Magazine*), **42:** 381n7
Musser, George Washington, **45:** 44,n1, 60
Mutineries de 1917 (Pedroncini), **43:** 31n5
Mutsuhito, Emperor of Japan (1867-1912), **48:** 461,n1
My Experiences in the World War (Pershing), **42:** 391n1; **43:** 236n1; **45:** 107n1, 109n4; **47:** 209n, 219n
My Four Years in Germany (Gerard), **42:** 520n1; **43:** 404; **48:** 311,n2; film from, **48:** 311n2
My Life and Work (Ford), **51:** 280n1
My Memoir (E. B. Wilson), **49:** 156,n3, 292n3, 443n4
My War Memories (Beneš), **49:** 287n1
Myers, Gustavus, **42:** 148n1
Myers, Henry Lee, **40:** 424, 561n2; **41:** 278; **43:** 480; **47:** 321n1; and water-power legislation, **45:** 172, 301; and woman suffrage, **45:** 278, 338; and general leasing bill, **45:** 402n1, 453-54
Myers, Jerome A., **51:** 251-52,n1
Myers, Joseph S., **43:** 105,n1
Myers water-power bill, **40:** 207, 543

NAACP: A History of the National Association for the Advancement of Colored People (Kellogg), **48:** 159n5
Nabokov, Konstantin Dmitrievich, **42:** 381,n8; **44:** 318,n1
Naboth's Vineyard: The Dominican Republic, 1844-1924 (Welles), **40:** 82n1
Nagasaki, Japan, **46:** 344; **48:** 106
Nagel, Charles, **43:** 410
Nagle, Patrick, **44:** 79
Nail, John E., **46:** 339,n3
Nakahama, Manjiro, **48:** 569,n1, 569-70
Nakahama, Toichiro, **48:** 569n1
Namur, Belgium, **51:** 386
Nancy, France, **40:** 482
Nansen, Fridtjof, **45:** 74,n2, 79, 80, 81, 83, 114-15,n1

Nantucket Island, **42:** 158; **49:** 167
Naón, Rómolo Sebastian, **42:** 358, 359-60, 376
Napoleon I, **40:** 376; **41:** 309; **42:** 340; **51:** 331
Napoleon in His Own Words From the French of Jules Bertaut (Law and Rhodes, trans.), **41:** 309,n1
Napoleonic wars, **51:** 323
Naramore, Chester, **47:** 404,n2
Nash, Harry Fletcher, **47:** 90,n1
Nashville Globe, **43:** 119n1
Nasmyth, Florence (Mrs. George William), **47:** 155,n3
Nasmyth, George William, **47:** 155,n3
Nason, Charles Pinckney Holbrook, **49:** 257,n4
Nast, Albert Julius, **46:** 613,n5
Nast cartoons, **48:** 143
Nation, The (N.Y.), **51:** 55n1, 56-57,n2, 57,n1; and censorship, **51:** 55n1, 56-57,n2, 57,n1
'Nation' and the Post Office (New York *Nation*), **51:** 55n1
Nation at War (March), **46:** 560n1; **48:** 484n1
National Adjustment Commission, **47:** 378
National Advisory Board for Aeronautics, **45:** 155
National Agricultural Advisory Committee, **49:** 440n2, 442
National American Woman Suffrage Association, **41:** 400,n2, 401-402; **42:** 215, 237, 269; **45:** 121n1, 277; **47:** 547n1; **48:** 26, 111, 303n1, 303, 340, 363; **51:** 30, 82
National Association for the Advancement of Colored People, **41:** 217-18; **43:** 104,n1; **46:** 380-81,n1,5; **49:** 88n1; clemency appeal for Houston rioters, **46:** 339n1,2, 383-84,n1, 385n1
National Association of Colored Women of the United States, **43:** 284
National Association of Manufacturers, **46:** 18; **47:** 127
National Association of Railway and Utilities Commissioners, **48:** 624; **49:** 253
National Association of the Motion Picture Industry, **47:** 311n1
National Association Opposed to Woman Suffrage, **43:** 250n1; **45:** 345n1
National Bank of Commerce, N.Y., **43:** 197; **44:** 424,n2
National Bank of Mexico, **40:** 519
National Board of Farm Organizations, **49:** 441n6
National Cash Register Company, **46:** 94n1
National Catholic War Council, **49:** 425-26; **51:** 636
National Cattlemen's Association, **46:** 462n3
National Child Labor Committee, **45:** 331, 334,n1; **51:** 165,n1, 182n2
National City Bank of New York, **42:**

352; **43:** 197; **46:** 89n1, 111, 112, 118; **47:** 437n1; 613n1; **48:** 519,n1; **49:** 233
National Civic Federation, **44:** 220n2
National Civil Liberties Bureau, **43:** 175n1; **44:** 266n2; **46:** 196, 481-82
National Civil Service Reform League, **40:** 28
National Cloak and Suit Company, **45:** 157,n1
National Coal Association, **51:** 113, 115
National Committee on Prisons and Prison Labor, **48:** 248n1
National Conference Committee of Railways, **40:** 246n2; **41:** 352, 414-15, 415
National Conference of American Lecturers, **47:** 334n1
National Conference on Marketing and Farm Credits, **49:** 440,n2, 441
National Consumers' League, **40:** 7-9, 37, 91
National Council of Defense: *see* Council of National Defense
National Council of Farmers' Cooperative Associations, **49:** 441n1
National Dairy Union, **49:** 440
national defense: *see* preparedness
National Defense Act: *see* Army Reorganization Act of 1916
National Defense Committee (K.O.N.) of Poland, **42:** 11n1
National Defense Fund, **44:** 28
National Equal Rights League, **42:** 113-16; **46:** 550
National Erectors' Association, **47:** 127
National Farmers' Advisory Council, **49:** 104, 441
National Farmers' Union, **44:** 259; **49:** 440n2, 441n7
National Federation of Federal Employees, **48:** 395n1
National Foreign Trade Council, **41:** 84
National Gallery of Ireland, **42:** 390-91,n1, 403, 545; **43:** 191, 243; **44:** 360; **46:** 219n6
National Grange, **48:** 293, 343; **49:** 232,n2, 290-91, 291
National Guard, **41:** 151, 500n1, 540, 551; **42:** 52, 56, 75, 76, 98, 103, 200; **44:** 60n1; **45:** 408, 409; **46:** 43; and conscription, **40:** 327, 329-30; and New York's 69th regiment, **43:** 492, 514
National Hotel, Washington, D.C., **46:** 15n1
National Industrial Conference Board, **45:** 45, 53; **46:** 578; **47:** 272, 282; **51:** 522-23
National Labor Adjustment Agencies: conference of and recommendations by, **51:** 363-67, 423
National Livestock Growers Association, **40:** 263
National Museum, Washington, D.C., **45:** 559,n1
National Nonpartisan League: *see* Nonpartisan League
National Park Bank, N.Y., **43:** 197

National party (U.S.), **47:** 253,n1; **51:** 390n1
National Polish Committee: *see* Polish National Committee
National Press Club, **45:** 598n1; **46:** 63n1
National Public Utilities War Board (proposed), **49:** 389n1, 420-21
National Race Congress of the United States of America, **51:** 168n1, 191
National Research Council, **42:** 36; **47:** 114, 353,n2
National Review (London), **40:** 495
national security: *see* preparedness
National Security League, **42:** 83n1; **46:** 49n1, 459n1; **47:** 584n1; **51:** 175
National Service Commission of the Presbyterian Church, **42:** 535-37,n1
National Suffrage News, **42:** 237n1
National Theater, Washington, D.C., **46:** 314; **48:** 119n1, 356n2
National Union of Manufacturers (Great Britain), **49:** 300,n1
National War Fund Finance Committee, **48:** 16
National War Labor Board, **47:** 231, 376, 464; **49:** 28, 53n1, 186,n2, 240n1, 367; **51:** 24, 49n1, 247,n2, 258, 285n1, 363, 364; creation of, **46:** 578,n1, 578-80, 582; **47:** 247-53, 282-84; W. B. Wilson on members of, **47:** 272; union support of, **47:** 343n1; suggestions for umpires, **47:** 557-58; **48:** 43; and proposed telegraphers' strike, **48:** 281,n1, 282, 329, 337,n1, 339, 350, 374-75, 393-94; and interurban railways, **48:** 526-27,n1; and Porto Rico, **48:** 637n6; **49:** 135, 297-98; W. B. Wilson on strikes and, **49:** 133, 134; and Twin City Rapid Transit Co. strike, **49:** 181; and railroad wage discrepancies, **49:** 206, 211,n1, 251; and machinists' strike, **49:** 519, 520-22, 539-40; F. P. Walsh recommends appointment of women to, **51:** 522; photograph, *illustration section,* **47:** *see also* War Labor Conference Board
National War Labor Board: Stability, Social Justice, and the Voluntary State in World War I (Conner), **46:** 578n1; **49:** 53n1, 223n1, 540n1
National War Labor Conference Board: *see* War Labor Conference Board
National War Savings Committee, **49:** 216
National Wheat Growers' Association, **49:** 427n1,2; **51:** 212n2
National Woman's Liberty Loan Committee, **48:** 342n1
National Woman's Party, **40:** 379n1,4; **41:** 330; **42:** 237,n4, 560,n1; **45:** 243,n1; **47:** 547,n1; **48:** 111; **49:** 264; demonstrations at White House by, **43:** 201n1, 235n1, 476-77,n1; A. Wadsworth on, **43:** 250; and hunger strikes, **44:** 560
Nationalism (R. Tagore), **41:** 502,n3
Nationalism and War in the Near East (Young), **41:** 56n5

Natural Bridge National Forest, **47:** 589
naturalization law, **42:** 277
Nauen, Germany, **47:** 474, 475n2
Naumann, Friedrich, **42:** 389,n1; **46:** 184,n2, 189-90, 190, 191, 227
Naval Academy: *see* United States Naval Academy
Naval Affairs, Committee on (House of Reps.), **51:** 124,n1, 344n1
Naval Affairs, Committee on (Senate), **40:** 420; **45:** 448; **47:** 223n2
Naval Appropriations Act of 1916, **41:** 246, 331
Naval Consulting Board, **41:** 169n2; **42:** 457; **43:** 305n1
Naval Fuel Oil Board, **40:** 382
Naval History of the World War (Frothingham), **43:** 79n1
naval oil reserves, **40:** 205-206, 214, 382, 420, 560; **41:** 19, 64-65, 69,n1, 247-48, 278, 288-92; **42:** 525-26, 533, 547-48, 559, 561; **43:** 43, 75; **45:** 374-78, 402, 448, 556, 559; **49:** 291, 484; *see also* general leasing bill
Naval Oil Reserves and Pending Legislation (memorandum), **40:** 560,n1
Naval War College, **41:** 362; **42:** 82n1
Navigation, Bureau of, **42:** 257; **43:** 312
Navy, Department of the, **40:** 382, 402; **41:** 152, 290; **42:** 40, 49, 118, 134, 399, 412, 445, 559; **43:** 63, 89,n1, 490; **44:** 174, 283, 502; **45:** 10-11, 44, 63-64, 65, 424; **46:** 18, 40n1, 171, 217; **47:** 378-79, 402, 403, 562; **49:** 53n1, 312,n1, 410-13; and Lighthouse Service, **40:** 95n1; rear admiral nominations, **40:** 523,n2; and C. T. Grayson promotion, **40:** 562,n1,3; and wireless stations, **41:** 159, 484; and Danish West Indies, **41:** 361-62, 362-63, 427-28, 485; and steel prices, **41:** 407; and bond issue for preparedness, **41:** 448n1; notifies ships at sea of war declaration, **41:** 557-58; and Mare Island explosion, **43:** 470,n2,3; and War Industries Board priorities committee, **46:** 477, 602-603, 607
Navy League, **43:** 470,n2,3
Naylor, Wilson Samuel, **42:** 556-57,n1; **44:** 55
Neal, George Ira, **43:** 279-80,n1
Neale, James Brown, **48:** 647,n1; **49:** 53, 144-45, 148, 173
Nearing, Scott, **44:** 79; **47:** 472,n1; **49:** 208, 306; **51:** 57n2
Nebraska, **41:** 365; **42:** 83, 122; **44:** 18; **47:** 438; **49:** 99, 384; politics in, **51:** 477,n2, 590, 632
Need for a National Budget, **40:** 498n1
Needles, Ca., **43:** 157
Neely, Matthew Mansfield, **42:** 21n1
Nef, Walter T., **47:** 574,n7
Negotiations (Harvey), **51:** 521,n1
Negro Silent Protest Parade (*The Crisis*), **43:** 412n2
Negroes, **40:** 153-54,n1, 221, 293; **41:** 217-18, 412; **42:** 49-51, 98; **43:** 106-107, 208; **44:** 10, 564, 568; **46:** 480, 614,n3; **47:**

521; **49:** 139, 179-80,n2, 204; on ending discrimination, **42:** 112-16; **43:** 128-30; and U.S. Army training camps and service, **42:** 321-22,n1, 357-58; **43:** 392, 506-507; and Dockery-Young affair, **43:** 4, 16, 78, 79, 118, 119, 132; **48:** 156-58,n2,3,4; **49:** 179n2, 391; and silent protest parade, **43:** 342-43, 412n2; meeting with WW, **43:** 412,n1,2,3; race riot in Houston, **44:** 41-42,n1,2, 49, 63-64, 77-78; **45:** 546-47,n1,2, 577, 579-80; **49:** 324-28, 401-402; and antilynching campaign, **46:** 380-81, 385,n1, 550; clemency appeal for Houston rioters, **46:** 13, 16,n1, 339, 383-84,n1, 385,n1; and Liberia, **47:** 353; 49: 522; and *Birth of a Nation,* **47:** 388,n2; G. B. Clarkson on postwar reconstruction and, **47:** 533; memorandum on Negroes as voters, **48:** 155-61; Civil Service complaints by, **48:** 158-59,n5; and housing in Washington, D.C., **48:** 159-60; comments and requests that WW speak out against lynching, **48:** 302, 323-24, 416, 462-63,n3, 475-76, 476; G. Creel on unrest among, **48:** 341-42; conference of Negro editors, **48:** 342, 346, 528-30, 607; and lynching, **49:** 88-89; WW remarks, **49:** 97-98, 113-14; **51:** 168; problems in Newport News, **51:** 136-37, 162, 185; and charges of discrimination in Army, **51:** 170,n1, 191-93; *see also* East St. Louis assault; lynching

Neill Primary Act of 1917 (Georgia), **49:** 114n1, 115

Nekrasov, Nikolai Vissarionovich, **41:** 416,n11; **42:** 419,n3; **43:** 441,n1

Nelson, Herman, **48:** 294

Nelson, John Mandt, **41:** 327,n1

Nelson, Knute, **44:** 89n1; **47:** 54, 55n1; **48:** 136,n2; **51:** 301, 390; and senatorial campaign of, **48:** 347,n1

Nesbit case (Houston riot of 1917), **49:** 324-25, 326, 400-402

Netherlands, The, **40:** 15, 45, 248, 457n1; **41:** 40, 125-26, 130-31, 200; **42:** 339, 342, 464, 494; **43:** 10; **45:** 80, 114, 595; **46:** 329, 615-17; **48:** 200n2, 219, 426, 539, 613; **51:** 240-41; and proposed conference of neutrals, **40:** 46-48, 81n1; minister named, **40:** 113; and commandeering of Dutch ships in U.S. ports, **45:** 366; **47:** 26-28, 261; and peace moves, **47:** 64-65,n4, 128,n1, 133-34, 142-43; **49:** 548,n1; and shipping available to U.S., **47:** 205, 294; and relief for Polish Jews, **47:** 555; and German demands on, **47:** 564-65; and league of nations, **49:** 19, 467, 508-509

Neubriesach, Germany (now Neuf-Brisach, France), **51:** 275

Neukoelln (Berlin, Germany), **45:** 595,n4

Neutral Ally: Norway's Relations with Belligerent Powers in the First World War (Riste), **45:** 74n2

Neutral Conference for Continuous Mediation, **41:** 89-92,n2,3

neutrality: *see* World War

Neutrals and Armed Neutrality Leagues (*Springfield*, Mass., *Republican*), **41:** 295,n2

Nevada, **47:** 194; labor problems in, **43:** 222n1, 281; politics in, **51:** 453, 589, 612, 632

Neville, Keith, **48:** 191,n1,4

Nevins, Allan, **44:** 450n1

New Amsterdam Theatre, **51:** 314n1

New Armenia (N.Y.), **49:** 20n2

New Bedford Evening Standard, **48:** 569n1

New Bedford *Morning Mercury,* **49:** 569n1

New Catholic Encyclopedia, **41:** 434n2

New Europe (London), **45:** 430n3

New Freedom (Link): *see* Wilson: The New Freedom

New Freedom (Wilson), **49:** 233

New Freedom Society, **48:** 435,n1

New Guinea, **48:** 228

New Hampshire: politics in, **51:** 537,n2, 589, 633

New Haven Railroad, **42:** 45n1; **44:** 425,n1; **45:** 367n1

New Ideas in Business: An Account of their Practice and their Effects upon Men and Profits (Tarbell), **40:** 373,n1

New Jersey, **40:** 265; **45:** 325, 573-74; **48:** 567; and port facilities, **44:** 502; WW's letter to Democrats of, **47:** 82-84, 253-54; and transit companies, **49:** 72, 183,n1, 405, 424; 463-64, 474-75; machinists' strike in, **49:** 133; German submarine activities and, **49:** 167,n1; and woman suffrage, **49:** 182; **51:** 404, 452; senatorial campaign in, **49:** 210,n1,2, 211-12,n1; **51:** 283,n1,2, 403-404, 452, 590, 606n2; slacker raids in, **49:** 502-503; and congressional election, **51:** 179,n3, 632; politics in, **51:** 552,n8

New Jersey Central Railroad, **40:** 102

New Jersey Harbor Commission, **49:** 455n1

New Jersey Public Service Corporation: *see* Public Service Corporation of New Jersey

New Jersey Zinc Company, **41:** 58

New Machine (editorial, Philadelphia *Public Ledger*), **40:** 315n1

New Machine Fights High Costs (Philadelphia *Public Ledger*), **40:** 315n1

New Mexico, **44:** 17; **47:** 411; labor problems in, **43:** 170, 171, 239, 353; politics in, **51:** 478,n1, 579, 580, 590, 612, 632

New National Museum, Washington, D.C., **43:** 509n4

New National Theater, Washington, D.C., **46:** 519; **47:** 476,n1

New Orleans, La., **45:** 150n1; bicentennial of founding of, **46:** 100,n1; and street railways, **49:** 223, 240,n1; **51:** 247

New Orleans Railway and Light Company, **49:** 240n1

New Radicalism in America, 1889-1963: The Intellectual as a Social Type (Lasch), **40:** 371n2

New Republic, The, **40:** 359, 360, 374n1, 380, 381, 421n1; **41:** 13,n1, 83n1,2, 135, 448n2, 537-38,n1; **42:** 135, 254, 273n1, 361,n1, 362, 435; **44:** 410; **45:** 153,n1; **46:** 109; **47:** 253, 254n4; **48:** 241n1, 482n3; **49:** 402, 429, 487n1; **51:** 111

New Russia in the Balance: How Germany's Designs May be Defeated and Russian Democracy Preserved (Browne), **48:** 299n1

New Ulm, Minn., **43:** 319n1

New Willard Hotel, Washington, D.C., **40:** 193n1; **41:** 240n1, 358; **44:** 231n1, 529; **45:** 238n1

New World, **48:** 620n3

New York (Bynner), **45:** 258,n1

New York (state): and 69th National Guard unit, **43:** 492, 514; woman suffrage campaign and amendment passage in, **44:** 62, 79, 144n1, 372, 391, 440-41, 441-43, 523,n1, 533, 537, 556n2; **45:** 40n1; and H. A. Garfield's fuel order, **46:** 19, 24; petition for Houston rioters, **46:** 339,n1,2,3, 383-84; WW on not naming Democratic club after him, **49:** 103; Democratic politics and A. E. Smith, **49:** 105-106,n1, 157,n1, 465; slacker raids in, **49:** 451, 451-52, 463, 499-503, 513; **51:** 28, 535,n2,3, 632, 747

New York City, **43:** 112, 146-47, 421; **45:** 150n1; and postmastership, **40:** 74,n1, 272; **41:** 67; and harbor protection, **41:** 152; politics in, **41:** 359-60; and district attorneyship, **42:** 244,n2; mayoralty in, **44:** 272,n2, 333-34,n1, 428,n1, 458, 464, 504, 512, 556,n2; and coordination of port facilities, **44:** 502-503, 515; **45:** 573-74; fuel order affects theaters in, **46:** 28,n1, 41; and airmail service, **47:** 615n1; and public opinion on the war, **45:** 123, 128; WW's address in on behalf of Red Cross, **48:** 53-57; and street railways, **51:** 20

New York, U.S.S., **49:** 69, 70

New York Academy of ·Medicine, **46:** 404,n7

New York Age, **43:** 119n1; **48:** 302n1

New York American, **40:** 21,n1, 44n2, 429; **41:** 127; **44:** 60n1, 119, 275, 286, 307,n1; **45:** 270n2, 320n1; **48:** 220n1

New York Avenue Presbyterian Church, Washington, D.C., **42:** 535n2

New York Bar Association, **40:** 359

New York Book Buyer, **43:** 540

New York Call, **43:** 383n1; **44:** 393, 408, 428,n1, 446, 471,n4

New York Central Federated Union, **44:** 47

New York Central Railroad, **42:** 81; **46:** 426n5, 447n1; **47:** 446, 488

New York City Woman Suffrage Party, **44:** 532-33, 533

New York *Commercial and Financial Chronicle,* **41:** 107

New York Cotton Exchange, **44:** 105n2

New York Democratic County Committee, **42:** 327n1

New York Evening Journal, **42:** 106n1

New York Evening Mail, **42:** 22,n1,2, 237n4; **43:** 134,n2; **45:** 55

New York *Evening Post,* **40:** 86, 110, 414n3, 558n1; **41:** 308n2, 463, 463-64; **42:** 316n1; **43:** 175, 359,n1; **44:** 275, 299,n2, 322; **45:** 423n1, 436, 437; **46:** 422n1, 539n1; **47:** 534n1, 587n1; **48:** 143n9; 647,n2; **51:** 28, 221,n3,5, 265n1, 297,n1, 531, 534n1

New York *Evening Sun,* **44:** 445n1; **48:** 11, 541n1; **49:** 344,n1; on prohibition, **49:** 476-77

New York *Forum,* **49:** 165n1

New York *Gaelic-American,* **41:** 347n1

New York *Globe,* **42:** 197n1; **43:** 412n3; **45:** 153n1; **48:** 16n1

New York Herald, **40:** 136n2, 348n5, 459n4; **41:** 374,n2; **42:** 230, 363n3, 487,n1; **45:** 437; **46:** 525n2; **47:** 51n1; **48:** 11n2, 119n2, 410,n2; **49:** 5n1

New York *Il Prolitero,* **44:** 446

New York *Jewish Daily Forward,* **43:** 175, **44:** 393, 446, 452

New York *Journal of Commerce and Commercial Bulletin,* **42:** 245,n3; **43:** 108n1, 111; **48:** 644n2

New York, New Haven and Hartford Railroad, **41:** 402, 412; **44:** 423,n2, 458; **47:** 488

New York *Novy Mir,* **45:** 147,n1

New York Peace Society, **41:** 302n2

New York *Public,* **44:** 469-70,n3

New York Red Book, **49:** 157n1

New York Republican Club, **42:** 29,n2

New York *Russky Gollos,* **44:** 446

New York Sabbath Committee, **46:** 41n1

New York Shipbuilding Company, **42:** 477; **47:** 500,n1

New York Society for Ethical Culture, **44:** 267n3

New York State Bankers' Association, **41:** 67,n5

New York State Bar Association, **45:** 598,n2

New York State Federation of Labor, **42:** 136

New York State Food Commission, **45:** 163n1; **46:** 297n1

New York State Industrial Commission, **46:** 297n1

New York State Modern Language Association, **44:** 364

New York State Woman Suffrage Party, **43:** 462n1; **44:** 335, 384, 440,n1, 533, 537

New York Stock Exchange, **41:** 358; **45:** 287-88; alleged peace note leak and inquiry, **40:** 349n11, 353, 462, 506; **41:** 69,n1

New York *Sun,* **40:** 35n3, 349n8, 352; **41:**

374; **43:** 333, 359,n1; **45:** 437; **46:** 63, 574,n1; **47:** 562; **48:** 612n1

New York Times, **40:** 4, 24,n1, 30,n1, 60n1, 75n1, 83, 119n1, 124n1, 130n2, 176n1, 187,n2, 188n1, 212n1, 244n1, 246n2, 267n1, 306n1, 307n1, 346n2, 386n2, 421n2, 427n, 460n5, 463n1, 476n4, 486n4, 487n5, 491n, 544n1, 546n2, 547n3, 554n1, 561n2, 562n3, **41:** 5n2, 11n1, 14n2, 16n1, 64n3, 88n1, 96n1, 126n2, 229n1, 240n2, 243n1, 268n1, 280n1, 287n1, 294n1, 298n1, 318n1, 320n, 326n3, 349n2, 352n1, 367n,n1, 388n1, 448n1, 461n1, 462, 463, 474n2, 484n1, 551n; **42:** 9n1, 29n1,2, 38n2, 75n, 79n, 80n, 104n2, 118n1, 145n2, 153n1, 237n4, 245n1,2,3, 266n1, 326n, 361n2, 363n1, 370n1, 386n1, 389n4, 425n1, 439n, 459n1, 468n1, 498n1, 540,n2, 554n1, 556,n3, 560n1, 567n1; **43:** 11n1, 28n1, 48n1, 57n1, 61n2, 70n1, 133n1, 148n1, 158n1, 160n1, 165n2, 175n2, 185n1, 201n1, 217n4, 246n1, 263n1, 283n1, 291n1, 319n1, 333n1, 336n2, 351,n1,2, 405n2, 412n2, 415n2, 437n, 470n2,3, 481n5, 498n1, 501,n2, 509n2, 512n2

44: 50n1, 89n1, 141n1, 142n1, 164n1, 176n2, 185n4, 236n4, 266n1, 290n1, 299n1, 315n2, 327n, 333n1, 366n1,2, 423n2, 428n1, 443n1, 504n1, 511n1, 523n1, 532n1; **45:** 11n1, 18n2, 41n1, 101n1, 114n2, 164,n2, 215n1, 225n1, 230n1, 238n2, 329n2, 340,n1, 344n1, 354n, 368n1, 390n1,4, 405n, 422n2, 545n,n1, 565n3, 577n1, 596n1, 598n1,2; **46:** 6, 8, 12n1, 31n1, 40n1, 49n1, 54, 63n1, 84n1, 109n2, 110n1, 113n2, 115n1, 124n1, 150n1, 213n2, 219,n5, 254n6, 263n1, 281n2, 287n1, 297n1,2, 318n1, 329,n1, 332n1, 356n5, 361n1, 372n1, 380n2, 403, 411,n1, 420n2, 433n2, 437,n4, 453, 458n3, 496n1, 505n2, 520n, 539n1, 565, 567n1, 620n2; **47:** 41n2, 51n1, 72n1, 82n1, 94n1, 178n2, 185n1, 186n, 207n1, 221n1, 254n1, 276n2, 281n1, 284n1, 310, 321n1, 324n1, 334n1, 381n2, 383n1, 385n6, 412, 413, 420n1, 453n4, 476n2, 478n2, 511, 524n1, 573n2, 584n1, 589n1, 615n1; **48:** 10n, 45n1, 52n3, 53n1, 118n1, 119n2, 146n1, 161n2, 162n1, 173n1, 191n3, 196, 202n1, 213n8, 235n1, 251n2, 274,n1, 281n1, 300n3, 307n1, 313n1, 347n1, 417n5, 433, 434n, 469n1, 487n1, 555n7, 582n1; **49:** 4n2, 5n1, 37n1, 56n2, 157n1, 292n3, 315n2, 439n3, 443n4, 546n2, 778n13, 786n2, 788n5

51: 5n1, 10n1, 24n2, 55n1, 57n2,3, 57n1, 84, 108n9, 117n1, 156n2, 189n1, 253n1, 259n1, 277n5,6, 279n8, 314n1, 315n3, 326n2, 330n2,3, 331n4,5, 395n1, 446n2, 551,n1, 554n1, 555n;

and article advocating WW replace cabinet members, **41:** 446n1, 450; articles favoring intervention in Russia, **49:** 93,n1, 94; editorials on Austria-Hungary's peace proposals, **51:** 106,n7

New York Times Index, **44:** 528n2

New York Times Magazine, **44:** 133n2; **45:** 123n1

New York Tribune, **40:** 335n1; **43:** 395n1; **44:** 301n1; **45:** 241n1, 341n1, 559: **46:** 36n1; **47:** 35n2, 114, 154n1, 390n2; **48:** 11n2, 147n4; **49:** 5n1

New York Trust Company, **43:** 197

New York University, **42:** 60n1

New York University Law School, **44:** 39n1

New York *World,* **40:** 4, 119n1, 122, 133, 229n1, 294, 338, 349n10, 352, 375, 406,n1; **41:** 23n1, 40, 127, 408,n2, 463; **42:** 161, 223n1, 245,n2,3, 446n2; **43:** 167, 175, 235n1, 239n1, 334n1, 404, 412n2; **44:** 334, 390; **45:** 123n1, 153, 421n1, 432,n1; **46:** 22n1, 49,n1, 53, 205n, 230, 264,n1; **47:** 51n1, 52n3, 253, 254,n4, 296, 310, 335,n1; **48:** 11n2, 53n1, 119n2, 196, 259n; **49:** 5n1, 162,n2; **51:** 28, 189n; and Statue of Liberty, **40:** 35n2; and idea of editorial forum on war in *Berliner Tageblatt* and, **43:** 184, 198, 219, 220, 237-38, 274, 285, 366, 411-12; on prohibition, **49:** 477; supports Democratic candidates for Congress, **51:** 293,n1,2

New-Yorker Staats-Zeitung, **40:** 323, 324, 348n7, 353; **43:** 410n1; **44:** 154-55, 236

New Zealand, **49:** 217

Newark, N.J., **45:** 150n1; **49:** 502, 503

Newark Evening News, **45:** 437; **47:** 253, 254n4; **51:** 283n1

Newark Museum, **51:** 211n2

Newark Public Library, **51:** 211n2

Newberry, Barnes, **49:** 438n2

Newberry, Phelps, **49:** 438,n2

Newberry, Truman Handy, **49:** 438,n2

Newchwang, China, **49:** 213

Newdick, Edwin W., **48:** 393,n2, 488

Newlands, Francis Griffith, **40:** 246,n3,4, 265, 278; **49:** 456; and railway mediation legislation, **41:** 14, 20,n1, 21, 156-57, 160, 197, 238,n1, 241, 258, 262; on flood-control legislation, **41:** 197-99; and railroad priorities bill, **42:** 290,n2, 299, 462, 505-506, 529; and woman suffrage, **45:** 278, 338; death of, **51:** 453n1

Newlands railroad bill, **40:** 421n2; **44:** 328, 431, 449

Newman, Edward Polson, **41:** 56n1

Newman, Oliver Peck, **40:** 167

Newspaper Publishers Association, **48:** 177-78

newspapers, **42:** 382, 396; **43:** 185, 431; **44:** 44-46, 143, 295, 306, 309, 450, 452, 535; 47: 342; and leak on Belgian deportation protest, **40:** 122-23, 130; proposed European news bureau, **40:** 243,n2, 337-38, 371, 371-72,n1,2, 374,n1,2, 380-81; WW's press confer-

newspapers (*cont.*)
ences, **40:** 264-72, 421-23, 470-77, 543-
47; **41:** 63-68; R. W. Howard suggests
WW give interview on peace note to,
40: 345-46; H. D. Croly, **40:** 360; WW
on, **40:** 422-23, 474-75; **42:** 68, 243; **45:**
88-90, 329; and break with Germany,
41: 124; and K. von Wiegand's complaint, **41:** 134; and Zimmermann telegram, **41:** 308,n1; given armed-ship
statement, **41:** 381-82; eager for news
on war situation, **41:** 445, 449; and censorship, **41:** 474,n2, 530, 555, 556; **42:**
245-46,n1,2,3, 369-70,n1, 371,n1, 386-
87, 433n1; **43:** 175, 239, 246,n1, 276-77,
333n1, 383; **44:** 272, 338-40, 361n1,
393-94, 405,n1, 408, 415, 416-17,
428,n1, 452, 468, 472-73, 491; **46:** 382-
83, and Committee on Public Information's guidelines on: **42:** 40, 41, 304-13;
H. L. Stimson on lack of reporting in
western states, **42:** 84; A. Brisbane on
freedom of the press, **42:** 107-108, E. M.
House on, **42:** 445-46; and Scripps
chain on patriotic duty of American editors, **42:** 446n1; F.I. Cobb on, **43:** 167;
and idea of editorial forum on war in
New York *World* and *Berliner Tageblatt,* **43:** 184, 198, 219-20, 220-21, 237-
38, 274-75, 285, 366, 411-12; comments
on German-American press, **43:** 243,
319,n2; G. S. Macfarland takes charge
of *New York American's* editorial policy, **44:** 275, 286; House mission revealed by Philadelphia *Public Ledger,*
44: 459-60,n1; rumors and false statements in, **45:** 18,n1, 53,n1, 95; B. Long
on, **45:** 87-88, 329n2; A. Konta on Hungarian, **45:** 139-40; G. Creel on, **45:** 152-
53; editorials on Brest-Litovsk peace
proposal, **45:** 436-37; and fuel order, **46:**
12n1, 23, 40; plans for a purchase by
B. M. Baruch, **46:** 36n1, 113n1; libel
suit against *Wisconsin State Journal,*
46: 119n1; F. Cobb's and S. Blythe's
plan for, **46:** 367; R. N. Baldwin on censorship and, **46:** 382-83; House and
WW discuss, **46:** 437n4; S. Gompers on
criticism of labor movement by, **47:**
127; W. S. Rogers on foreign correspondents, **47:** 276-77; WW's remarks
to foreign correspondents, **47:** 284-89; a
foreign correspondent's impression of
WW, **47:** 297-99; comments on news
conferences, **47:** 355, 359; and Borglum
affair, **47:** 509; proposed labor newspaper in Mexico, **49:** 89-90, 137-38; and
peace notes and negotiations, **51:**
279n8, 415, 538-39; F. Dixon on trip
abroad for *Christian Science Monitor,*
51: 579-80; *see also* under names of individual newspapers
Newton, Byron Rufus, **43:** 310,n2; **44:**
208-209,n1
Newton, U.S.S., **47:** 66
Newton D. Baker and the American War

Effort, 1917-1919 (Beaver), **43:** 25n1;
44: 158n1; **45:** 390n1; **46:** 444n2; **48:**
32n4, 173n1; **49:** 335n1
Nicander, Edwin, **44:** 427n1
Nicaragua, **41:** 143,n16, 144, 145,n1; **42:**
359; **45:** 388-89
Nicholas I (of Russia), **42:** 329
Nicholas II (of Russia), **40:** 205, 388n1,
441; **41:** 408n2, 409, 416; **42:** 337, 435,
456; **44:** 180n3, 557, 558; **47:** 549n2; **48:**
184n3; **51:** 567
Nicholls, E. H., **47:** 194n1
Nicholls, Samuel Jones, **45:** 307,n1
Nichols, Jesse Brooks, **49:** 519,n7
Nicolaevsk, Russia, **47:** 98
Nieman, Lucius William, **43:** 117, 194,
243, 318, 319,n1; **44:** 236, 429
Niemojowski, Bonawentura, **41:** 139n2
Niemojowski, Waclaw Jósef, **41:** 139,n2
Niessel, Henri Albert, **48:** 38n1, 131
Nieto, Rafael, **49:** 27
Nieuport, Belgium, **51:** 184
*Night of Violence: The Houston Riot of
1917* (Haynes), **44:** 41n1; **45:** 546n1; **46:**
16n1
Nikolayevsk-on-Amur,   Russia,   **49:**
150n3
Nikolsk, Russia, **48:** 459; **49:** 152
nitrate plant provision: *see* Army Reor-
ganization Act of 1916
Nitti, Francesco Saverio, **51:** 386,n1
Nivelle, Robert Georges, **42:** 264,n2; **43:**
31n5, 262; **44:** 52,n1
Nivelle offensive, **43:** 444,n1
Nixon, Lewis, **43:** 11
Nizhneudinsk, Russia, **48:** 459,n1
No Divided Counsels at Washington (*The
Independent*), **49:** 277,n1, 347
No Divided Government (New York
World), **51:** 293,n1
No Negotiated Peace (*New York Times*),
51: 106n7
No Peace with the Hohenzollerns!
(Borah), **51:** 330n2, 331
Nobel Institute, **41:** 90n3
Nobel Peace Prize: of 1909, **42:** 255n1; of
1911, **47:** 65n5
Noble, Herbert, **41:** 142
Nock, Albert Jay, **51:** 55n1
Nockels, Edward M., **40:** 175,n1, 176-77;
43: 513,n1; **46:** 26
Noel, Edmund Favor, **49:** 369n2
Noel-Buxton, Noel Edward: *see* Buxton,
Noel
Nolan, E. D., **46:** 71
Nollen, John Scholte, **46:** 479,n4
Nonpartisan Leader (Minneapolis), **47:**
178,n2, 521n1
Nonpartisan League, **44:** 153n1, 182,n1,
206; **45:** 167n1; **46:** 160, 270,n1, 347-49,
369, 386-87; **47:** 193-94,n1; **48:** 290,
322, 343, 345; **49:** 80, 172; **51:** 65, 645;
and House resolution on attack on
woman suffrage demonstrations, **44:**
112-14; in Minnesota, **47:** 53, 87-88,
194n1, 216-17, 235-37, 399-400; D. F.

Houston on, **47:** 177-79, 188; G. Creel on, **47:** 226; in Texas, **47:** 260, 521,n1; question of WW's endorsement of, **47:** 260, 352,n2,3; W. Kent on, **47:** 399-400; WW on Kent's concerns about, **47:** 414,n1 475; A. W. Ricker on, **47:** 438, 439; C. R. Crane on and WW's answer to, **47:** 466, 478; and Washington State Grange and Bouck case, **51:** 249, 310, 311, 312

Norfolk, Va., **45:** 117-18

Norfolk Navy Yard, **46:** 546,n1,2,3

Norman, Erik-Wilhelm, **42:** 110,n1,3

Norman Foster Company, **47:** 479,n1; **48:** 201, 280; **51:** 120

Norman Institutions (Haskins), **46:** 169,n1

Norman Thomas, A Biography: 1884-1968 (Fleishman), **51:** 12n3

Norman Thomas: The Last Idealist (Swanberg), **51:** 12n3

Norris, George William, **49:** 384; **51:** 477n2; and armed-ship bill, **41:** 318n1, 328

Norris, Lydia Hutton Shortlidge (Mrs. Augustus C.), **40:** 169,n3

Norris, Percival Chandler, **40:** 169,n1

Norris, R. V., **47:** 89

Norristown, Pa., **49:** 165

North, Frank Mason, **44:** 326

North American Review, **42:** 371n1; **47:** 15,n1

North American Review's War Weekly, **51:** 483n1, 520-21,n1

North Carolina, **43:** 115; **46:** 90; and woman suffrage, **48:** 110, 233; politics in, **51:** 207, 482, 632

North Carolina, University of, **43:** 174n1; **51:** 486,n1

North Dakota, **43:** 512n1; **46:** 347, 348, 386; **47:** 178, 438, 466; **48:** 628,n1; grants woman suffrage, **40:** 549; **41:** 13; and wheat prices, **44:** 36, 88n1, 191; politics in, **51:** 632

North Sea, **49:** 312n1; mining of, **42:** 220, 348,n2, 358, 449n1, 457; **43:** 180; **44:** 465-66, 477-78; **45:** 22

Northcliffe, 1st Viscount (Alfred Charles William Harmsworth), **40:** 5, 133, 187, 233, 307n1, 319, 413-14, 488, 497; **41:** 196; **42:** 111; **43:** 24: 44, 184, 194-95,n2, 238, 268,n1, 278, 332-33, 356,n1, 357n4, 365, 409, 425; **44:** 16, 56, 70, 80, 203; **45:** 70, 71, 194, 313, 321; **47:** 582; in U.S. as British special envoy, **42:** 428,n1; 429, 432, 461, 487-88, 521, 542; WW on, **42:** 432, 446-47,n2; and C. A. Spring Rice, **43:** 24, 97,n2, 451, 452, 453; and British financial crisis, **43:** 66-67, 229; E. M. House on, **43:** 219, 220; on U.S. sending representative to inter-Allied conference, **44:** 195

Northcliffe Glad 'Old Gang' is Out; Scorns Hollweg (New York *World*), **40:** 229n1

Northern Pacific, U.S.S., **51:** 406

Northern Pacific Railway Company; **45:** 367n1

Northern Railroad Company of Costa Rica, **46:** 450

Northwestern Miller (Minneapolis), **42:** 481n1

Northwestern Oklahoma Wheat Growers' Association, **51:** 212n2

Norton, Charles Dyer, **42:** 252,n2

Norton, Patrick Daniel, **42:** 245n2; **46:** 345,n1

Norway, **40:** 46-48, 81n1, 358-59, 552; **41:** 40, 249n1; **42:** 110-11, 339, 342; **43:** 299; **44:** 284, 299, 396n1; **45:** 74,n2, 272, 366; **48:** 539; **49:** 312,n1, 333-34, 346; **51:** 623; and exports, **45:** 78-83, 114-15,n1; and United States, **51:** 186

Not Accepted (*New York Times*), **51:** 106n7

Notes on Sovereignty in a State (Lansing), **45:** 603n1

Nothing but the Truth (Montgomery), **47:** 414,n1

Nottingham, England, **46:** 435n3

Noulens, Joseph, **44:** 43,n2; **47:** 319-20,n5, 430,n1, 430-32, **48:** 100,n3, 239; **49:** 495,n2

Novara, S.M.S., **51:** 492

Novo-Cherkassk, Russia, **46:** 421n3

Novosseloff (Novoselov), S.S., **49:** 321,n2,3

Noyes, Frank Brett, **41:** 308,n2; **43:** 333,n2; **47:** 380

Noyes, Pierpont Burt, **48:** 484n1; **51:** 115,n4

Noyon, France, **48:** 387, 388n9; **51:** 421

Nowaka, A. H., **44:** 344, 345

Nuevo Leon, state, Mex., **40:** 203

Nugent, James Richard, **47:** 82n1

Nugent, John Frost, **49:** 145-46,n2, 147; **51:** 180,n1, 612

Nunn, P. N., **48:** 222n1, 225

Nuremberg, Germany, **46:** 266; **51:** 607

Nürnberg, S.M.S., **51:** 490

Nye, Joseph M., **42:** 23,n2; **46:** 290

Nye, William, **45:** 317

Oates, James, **40:** 217,n1

Obregón, Álvaro, **41:** 545-46; **44:** 331n3; **49:** 28

O'Brian, John Lord, **47:** 363-65,n1; **49:** 463

O'Brien, Dermond, **42:** 403,n4

O'Brien, Francis William, **44:** 160n1

O'Brien, John, **43:** 299

O'Brien, William, **43:** 452,n1

Occoquan, Va., **44:** 453,n1

Oceanic Steamship Company, **42:** 272n5

Ochoa, Manuel, **41:** 351,n1

Ochs, Adolph Simon, **40:** 4; **51:** 106n7

O'Connell, John, **44:** 243, 244n1

O'Conner, Andrew, Jr., **45:** 560,n4

O'Connor, Joseph, **49:** 546

O'Connor, Thomas Power ("Tay Pay"), **44:** 133,n2; **48:** 195-97

October and Other Poems (Bridges), **49:** 463n2

Odegard, Peter Holtan, **43:** 42n2

Odell, George Talbot, **42:** 22,n1; **45:** 55, 55-57

Odell, Joseph Henry, **46:** 194,n1

Odessa, Russia, **46:** 310; **47:** 431; **48:** 299

Odum, Howard Washington, **48:** 455n1

Oederlin, Friedrich, **51:** 252,n1, 268, 518

Official Bulletin, **42:** 258n, 346n, 391n1; **43:** 3,n1, 15n, 145n1, 154n, 380n1; **44:** 89n, 92n1, 148n1, 323n1, 444n2, 555n1; **45:** 128n1, 176n1, 268n1, 599; **46:** 12n1, 21n2, 25n1, 33n1, 41n1, 56n, 68n1, 84n1, 109n1,2, 174n1, 424n1, 425n,n1, 459n1, 505n2; **47:** 28n3, 41n2, 72n1, 192n2, 207n1, 353n2, 484n4, 488n1; **48:** 43n2, 64,n2, 73n1, 117n1, 148n3, 281,n2, 334n, 337n1, 392n1, 464n2, 482n1, 487n1; **49:** 56n2, 98n, 170n1, 173n1, 359n1, 372n1, 393n2, 400n1, 403n1, 415n1, 416n2, 432n1, 439n1, 440n2, 474n1, 476n2, 503n1, 541n1; **51:** 75n2, 78n2, 91n1, 126n1, 127n2, 147n1, 618n1

Official German Documents relating to the World War, Translated under the supervision of the Carnegie Endowment for International Peace, Division of International Law, **40:** 504n1

Official Proceedings of the Central States Conference on Rail and Water Transportation Held Under the Auspices of the Evansville Chamber of Commerce, **40:** 246n2

Official Statements of War Aims and Peace Proposals, December 1916 to November 1918 (Carnegie Endowment for International Peace, Scott, ed.), **46:** 110n1

Offley, William M., **42:** 513

Ogarev, Mr., **51:** 450,n7

Ogden, Rollo, **44:** 322; **46:** 417-18; **51:** 223, 296-97,n1, 531

Ogle, Alfred McCartney, Jr., **51:** 115,n5

O'Gorman, James Aloysius, **43:** 147

O'Gorman, Thomas, **51:** 191,n1

O'Hern, John K., **46:** 28

Ohio, **47:** 410, 608-609; and judgeship appointment, **41:** 55-56; and farmers and wool prices, **49:** 278; J. P. Tumulty on prohibition and, **49:** 478; politics in, **49:** 510,n2; **51:** 28, 632; woman suffrage, **51:** 177

Ohio State Bankers' Association, **49:** 511

Ohl, Josiah Kingsley, **41:** 374,n2; **42:** 487,n1

oil: and prices, **42:** 534; strikes in Texas and Louisiana, **45:** 44, 46, 60; **46:** 170, 179; California strike averted, **45:** 121, 122, 126, 129; President's Mediation Commission report on California's, **46:** 134-35; F. K. Lane on leasing lands, **47:** 10, 20; H. A. Garfield on prices, **47:** 404; Standard Oil of Indiana's finances, **47:** 413; and Mexico, **47:** 475, 552; **48:** 180, 204, 398

oil leasing bill: *see* general leasing bill

oil reserves: *see* naval oil reserves

Oil Producers Association, **49:** 230n1

Okeh, W. W. (Lawrence), **47:** 40n2

Oklahoma, **44:** 3,n1, 121-22,n1, 191, 293-94; **49:** 99; and woman suffrage, **51:** 444,n1,2; politics in, **51:** 633

Oklahoma Farmers' Union, **51:** 212n2

Olander, Victor A., **46:** 578,n1; **47:** 223,n2, 248, 252, 283

O'Laughlin, John Callan, **40:** 114; **42:** 29n1

Old Hundred (hymn), **45:** 565n3

Old Master and Other Political Essays (Wilson), **46:** 259,n1, 285, 449; **49:** 128, 184

Older, Fremont, **45:** 382,n1

Olds, Frank Perry, **43:** 247,n2

O'Leary, B. A., **44:** 308

O'Leary, Jeremiah A., **41:** 347,n1; **45:** 238n1

O'Leary, Michael A., **51:** 552,n3

Oliver, Frederick Scott, **42:** 161,n5

Oliver, James Harrison, **40:** 405n1; **41:** 73n4, 430,n1

Oliver, William Bacon, **47:** 223,n1

Olmsted, Frederick Law, Jr., **49:** 513-14

Olney, Agnes Thomas (Mrs. Richard), **42:** 22

Olney, Richard (1835-1917), **40:** 9, 466,n1, 559-60; **41:** 23,n1; **44:** 205n3; death of, **42:** 22,n1

Olney, Richard (1871-1939), **44:** 205,n3

Olson, Harry, **46:** 459,n4

Olson, Keith Waldemar, **43:** 385n1; **51:** 103n3

Olympia, U.S.S., **44:** 375, 381; **47:** 290n1; **51:** 79,n1

Omaha Bee, **44:** 50n2

Omsk, Russia, **46:** 471, 548; **47:** 355, 424; **48:** 180, 204, 398; **49:** 198, 312n1; **51:** 102n1, 121, 140, 450, 481n1

On the Firing Line: Extracts from the Report of the General Executive Board to the Seventh Annual Convention of the Industrial Workers of the World, **47:** 573,n3

One Hundred Red Days: A Personal Chronicle of the Bolshevik Revolution (Sisson), **46:** 341n1

One Thing Needful (New York *Nation*), **51:** 55n1, 57n2

One Thing Needful: Central Powers Must Be Democratic, If Peace Is to Endure (Bohn), **51:** 330n3

Oneal, James, **44:** 79

Oneida Community, Ltd., **48:** 484n1

O'Neill, Lawrence, **42:** 403,n1; **47:** 432,n1, 432-33, 506, 516, 582

Onon River, Mongolia and Russia, **49:** 494

Onou, Constantin, **42:** 177,n2, 417; **43:** 473,n1

open-door policy, **40:** 13; **43:** 82; **44:** 249, 251-52, 253-56, 264,n2, 315, 340-42, 342, 415, 420, 531; **48:** 520

open-shop policy, **44:** 244

Oppenheim, Maurice L., **43:** 254,n5
Opponents of War, 1917-1918 (Peterson and Fite), **43:** 434n2, 512n1; **44:** 17n1; **47:** 276n2
Ordeal by Battle (Oliver), **42:** 161,n5
Order of Railway Conductors, **45:** 26
Ordnance, Bureau of, **43:** 71n1
ordnance program, **47:** 358,n1
Oregon, **41:** 107; **45:** 234; **46:** 478; **47:** 194; labor problems in, **43:** 222n1, 281; **44:** 14, 18, 191n1, 242, 243, 244, 247, 268; politics in, **51:** 633
Oren, Nissan, **51:** 563n1
Orenburg, Russia, **46:** 310
Organic Act (Porto Rico), **40:** 147, 149, 159, 295
Oriente Province, Cuba, **42:** 295,n1; **43:** 207
Origins and Intent of David Lloyd George's January 5 War Aims Speech (Woodward), **45:** 487n2
Origins of American Intervention in North Russia (1918) (Strakhovsky), **51:** 79n1
Origins of Teapot Dome: Progressives, Parties, and Petroleum, 1909-1921 (Bates), **40:** 561n2
Orjen, S.M.S., **51:** 492
Orlando, Vittorio Emanuele, **44:** 510,n1, 511; **45:** 156, 166n1; **46:** 86, 149, 156, 213, 233-35, 268n3, 454, 457; **47:** 11,n2, 59, 60, 75, 76, 513, 517, 566, 567, 568; **48:** 386, 545; **51:** 41; and joint Allied request for more U.S. troops, **48:** 226-27, 243, 246, 252; and Japan and intervention in Siberia, **48:** 448,n1; strife with S. Sonnino, **51:** 175n1, 386, 387-88; and peace negotiations, **51:** 261, 272n1, 272-73, 290, 291-92, 427, 428, 429, 517, 532, 562, 568, 569, 580, 582
Orsza, Russia, **46:** 403
Osage Indians, **47:** 10; reservation of, **40:** 382
Osborn, Henry Fairfield, **43:** 247n1
Osborn, Lucretia Thatcher (Mrs. Henry Fairfield), **43:** 247,n1
Osborn, William Church, **49:** 157,n1
Osborne, Benjamin, **40:** 175,n1
Osborne, John Eugene, **40:** 240
Osborne, Loyall Allen, **46:** 578n2; **47:** 223,n2, 248, 252, 283; **48:** 394
Osborne, Thomas Mott, **49:** 208
Oscawana Building Company of New York, **48:** 129
Osgood, Charles Grosvenor, Jr., **49:** 257,n3
O'Shaughnessy, George Francis, **45:** 518,n1; **51:** 537,n1
Osler, Sir William, **49:** 155
Oslo, Norway: *see* Christiania
Ostend, Belgium, **44:** 332, 333
Osuna, Gregorio, **40:** 109,n3
Otani, Kikuzo, **49:** 345,n1
Otis, Harrison Gray, **43:** 379,n1, 450
Ottoman Empire, **46:** 292, 487; **51:** 503: *see also* Turkey
Oulahan, Richard Victor, **41:** 64,n3

Our Times: The United States, 1900-1925 (Sullivan), **51:** 621n1
Out There (Manners), **47:** 476,n2
Outdoor Advertising Company, **42:** 511n1
Outlook, The, **42:** 216, 570; **46:** 194,n1, 218,n1, 239; **48:** 183,n1,2, 585n3; **51:** 15,n1
Over the Top (Empey), **48:** 356n1
Overman, Lee Slater, **41:** 197,n1, 234, 357; **42:** 245n2; **46:** 61; **47:** 94, 109, 109-10, 350, 381, 394, 395, 446,n1; and woman suffrage, **45:** 278, 339; **48:** 110, 233; **51:** 133; on postwar reconstruction, **51:** 216,n2, 227, 270, 280
Overman presidential war-powers Act, **47:** 94,n1, 109, 109-10, 255, 349n1, 350, 381, 385,n2, 385,n4, 395, 446, 447, 526; **48:** 489n1; **49:** 268; passage of, **47:** 573n1
Owen, H. N., **51:** 212,n2
Owen, Robert Latham, **40:** 42, 269; **41:** 359n3; **42:** 303, 444,n1; **43:** 11, 455; **45:** 582; **46:** 88, 89-90, 204, 206; **49:** 384, 515; **51:** 276; and woman suffrage, **45:** 278, 338; **51:** 76, 83; and Fourteen Points Address, **45:** 541; and Lever bill, **43:** 246, 348-50, 357-58; on commercial boycott of Germany, **48:** 506,n1; on oppressed nationalities in Austria-Hungary, **48:** 530-31; on credit curtailment for nonwar industries, **49:** 6-8, 61; on interest rates, **49:** 471,n1; on WW's speech at Metropolitan Opera House, **51:** 148; and postwar reconstruction plans, **51:** 217,n1, 217-18, 270; on WW's reply to German note, **51:** 439
Oxford University, **48:** 212n4; **51:** 594
Oxman, Frank C., **42:** 271,n2,7, 273n1; **46:** 71-72,n3
Oxman, Stephen A., **40:** 307n1

Pacelli, Eugenio (Archbishop, later Pius XII), **46:** 488,n2
Pacheco, Leonidas, **41:** 141,n10
Pachitch, Nikola P.: *see* Pašić, Nikola P.
Pacific Gas and Electric Company, **46:** 69
Pacific Historical Review, **51:** 103n3, 213n1
Pacific Northwest Quarterly, **46:** 144n1
Pacific Telephone and Telegraph Company, **44:** 497, 552-54; **45:** 39; strike settlement, **45:** 95-96; President's Mediation Commission report on, **46:** 135-38
Pack Up Your Troubles (Hazelton), **48:** 356,n1,2
Packard Corporation, **44:** 540
packing industries, **47:** 8-9; **48:** 107-10; *see also* meat-packing industry
Paderewska, Helena de Rosen (Mrs. Ignace Jan Paderewski), **47:** 576-77,n1,2
Paderewski, Ignace Jan, **41:** 388,n1, 511, 544; **42:** 372, 431, 454; **43:** 344, 426; **44:** 187, 211, 278, 303-305, 316, 318; **45:** 569; **46:** 120, 122-23, 404; **51:** 446
Padgett, Lemuel Phillips, **51:** 124,n1
Padua, Italy, **44:** 506

Page, Alice Wilson (Mrs. Walter Hines), **40:** 367; **41:** 117, 271; **51:** 388
Page, Arthur Wilson, **40:** 65, 388; **41:** 171; **43:** 465, 493
Page, Charles R., **51:** 587, 593, 610
Page, Florence Lathrop Field (Mrs. Thomas Nelson), **49:** 65
Page, Frank Copeland, **51:** 356,n1
Page, Thomas Nelson, **40:** 556-57; **41:** 218-20, 221-24: 433-35; **42:** 109-10; **43:** 27-29; **44:** 124, 392, 411, 427, 437, 439, 510; **45:** 95; **46:** 207; **47:** 261; **48:** 96; **49:** 63-65, 533; **51:** 175, 600-603; on Peace Without Victory speech, **41:** 224; on Italian situation, **44:** 295-96, 506-509; **46:** 155-60, 178, 365-66, 454-58; on sending military mission to Italy, **46:** 376-78, 457-58; on food and coal crisis in Italy, **46:** 454-56
Page, Thomas Walker, **51:** 610,n1
Page, Walter Hines, **40:** 63, 63-67, 118, 140, 178, 234, 250, 256, 260, 439n1, 442-43, 444, 445; **41:** 201,n1, 496, 553; **42:** 14, 20, 24: 25, 90, 109, 121-22, 265, 289, 531; **43:** 66, 150; **44:** 23-24, 30, 57, 70-72, 130-34, 140, 181-82, 245, 318-20, 342, 375, 388-89, 412, 427, 439, 456; **45:** 272, 273, 445; **46:** 46, 203, 339-41, 360, 411-12, 418, 467n1; **47:** 27, 85, 444, 491n2, 506; **48:** 249n1, 266, 335; **49:** 275, 536-37; **51:** 17, 107
C. N. Carver on, **40:** 5; wishes U.S. to take up Allied cause, **40:** 65-66; question of replacing or resignation of, **40:** 85, 240-41, 360, 365, 403, 463; **41:** 70,n1, 128-29, 137, 171, 341, 497; **44:** 177; on British reaction to German peace proposal, **40:** 247-48; on reaction to WW's peace note of Dec. 18, 1916, **40:** 319-20, 332-33, 355-58, 366-68; on his term of service, **40:** 367; on H. Hoover, **40:** 369; on I.B. Laughlin, **40:** 369-70; E. M. House and WW on dispatches from, **40:** 403; on British views of arming merchant ships, **40:** 509-11; on Peace Without Victory speech, **40:** 531-32; on C. A. Spring Rice, **41:** 115; on break with Germany, **41:** 116-17, 136-37; on Austria-Hungary's peace moves, **41:** 158-59, 211-14, 260, 262-63, 270-73; **46:** 397-400, 473-74: on D. Lloyd George, **41:** 270-71, 272; and Zimmermann telegram, **41:** 280-82, 297, 322, 324; on Anglo-French financial crisis, **41:** 336-37; on British requisitioning of Danish ships, **41:** 337-38; on British public opinion on American inaction, **41:** 372-73; on Lady Paget, **41:** 494; on WW's war message, **41:** 538; on meeting with George V, **42:** 82-83; on Home Rule for Ireland, **42:** 93; **44:** 133-34,n2; and Northcliffe, **42:** 401; on naval situation and submarine crisis, **42:** 546-47; **43:** 18-19, 26, 47-48, 114-15, 171, 463-65; on British financial crisis, **43:** 34, 38-39, 46-47, 114, 114,n3, 223-24, 374; on A. J. Balfour's proposed U.S. treaty

with Allies, **43:** 113-14; on Great Britain and Hearst newspapers, **43:** 132-33; recommends sending J. J. Pershing and W. S. Sims to Allied war conference in Paris, **43:** 208-209, 236-37; on sending H. T. Mayo to naval conference in London, **43:** 463,n1; Pope Benedict's appeal and WW's reply, **43:** 482; **44:** 130-31, 390-91; on German peace proposal and Allied peace terms, **44:** 329-31; and embargo issue, **44:** 396; on separate peace with Turkey, **45:** 148-49; and Charles I's peace moves and WW's response, **47:** 176-77; on proposed visit to U.S. of Dublin's Lord Mayor, **47:** 432-33; and German involvement in Ireland, **48:** 63-64, 65-66, 71,n1; and war declaration against Turkey and Bulgaria, **48:** 79n1; poor health of, **49:** 155, 346, 348; **51:** 356, 375, 388
Paget, Mary Fiske Stevens (Mrs. Arthur Henry Fitzroy), Lady Paget, **40:** 133, 135, 138, 178; **41:** 494, 494-95
Paine, Ralph Delahaye, **48:** 604,n2
Painlevé, Paul, **40:** 496,n1; **44:** 141n1, 462; **45:** 54n1, 93n1, 108,n2
Palavicini, Félix Fulgencio, **49:** 27,n1
Paléologue, Maurice, **42:** 327n1
Palestine, **42:** 235, 316,n1; **43:** 159n3, 184, 206; **44:** 324, 546-47; **45:** 53, 460, 471, 572; **46:** 333, 493-95, 516, 49: 339, 363, 364, 403, 549; **51:** 47, 48, 151, 156n2, 200, 503, 514; and Balfour Declaration, **45:** 149,n2; R. Lansing on, **45:** 286,n1
Palermo, S.S., **40:** 191
Pálffy von Erdöd, Moritz, Count, **46:** 199,n5
Palmer, Alexander Mitchell, **41:** 510; **45:** 101n1; **46:** 611; **47:** 275,n1; **48:** 49; **49:** 432; **51:** 408; on Allied property seizures, **48:** 228-29,n1; and Busch case, **51:** 395, 445-46,n2
Palmer, Bradley Webster, **46:** 450,n2; **51:** 408,n3
Palmer, Edgar, **44:** 238,n1
Palmer, Frederick, **40:** 39; **41:** 555; **42:** 43, 372
Palmer, John McAuley, **46:** 456n2
Palmer, Leigh Carlyle, **41:** 364,n1, 370-71
Pan American Building, Washington, D.C., **42:** 126
Pan-American Federation of Labor, **47:** 351
Pan-American Pact, **48:** 257-58,n1; Brazil and, **42:** 14, 15, 45, 80, 99-101; WW on, **42:** 44, 45, 54, 94, 105; R. Lansing on, **42:** 81-82
Pan American Union, **42:** 281n1
Pan Americanism, **41:** 9, 513
Panama, **41:** 131,n1, 152, 153, 293,n1, 456n1, 472-73, 476, 496; **42:** 51; **45:** 388-89, 405; **48:** 417,n2,3,5
Panama and the United States (Buell), **48:** 417n3,5

Panama Canal, **40:** 402, 550; **41:** 292, 456n1; **43:** 199; bonds for, **40:** 271-72
Panama Canal tolls controversy, **46:** 80
Panama City, Panama, **48:** 417,n3,5
Panama Railroad, **42:** 343
Panaretov, Stephan, **45:** 186,n4; **47:** 569,n1; **51:** 134,n3, 141, 154, 162-63
Pangerman Plot Unmasked: Berlin's Formidable Peace Trap of "The Drawn War" (Chéradame), **42:** 394n4
Panhuys, F. G. van, **46:** 615,n2
Pani, Alberto J., **40:** 51, 52, 54, 55, 56, 269, 280, 281, 285-87, 297, 393-94, 394-97; **42:** 38n2; **49:** 33
Panken, Jacob, **44:** 79
Pantín, Santiago Iglesias: *see* Iglesias Pantín, Santiago
Papen, Franz von, **41:** 506
Paraguay, **42:** 359
parcel post, **40:** 28
Pardo y Barreda, Josè, **40:** 164
Parecchia letter, **46:** 156,n2
Paris, Robert C., **51:** 100,n3, 608-609
Paris, France, **44:** 179; **48:** 288, 332, 333, 387, 389; and New Orleans bicentennial, **46:** 100,n1; inter-Allied war conference in, July 25, 1917, **43:** 208-209, 236-37,n1, 255, 269; attack on Corpus Christi Day, **49:** 189, 190; mentioned as site for peace conference, **51:** 473
Paris, University of, **48:** 210; and WW's honorary degree from, **48:** 575, 579
Paris Declaration of 1856: *see* Declaration of Paris
Paris Economic Conference and Treaty, 1916, **41:** 162-63; **42:** 65; **43:** 403, 404; **49:** 300n1
Paris inter-Allied conference, Nov. 1917, **45:** 3, 112-13, 122, 151, 156, 166, 208, 213, 245, 323-24; **46:** 115, 304-305, 556, 574, 590
Paris *Journal des Débats,* **44:** 46
Paris *La Liberté,* **44:** 44
Paris *La Victoire,* **41:** 466n3
Paris *Le Figaro,* **44:** 45
Paris *Le Gaulois,* **44:** 45-46
Paris, *L'Heure,* **51:** 255
Paris *L'Humanité,* **48:** 213n8; **51:** 565n8
Paris *L'Information,* **51:** 255n1
Paris *L'Intransigeant,* **51:** 255n1
Paris *Le Journal,* **44:** 44-45
Paris *Le Matin,* **40:** 462; **42:** 30n3; **44:** 45
Paris *Les Nations,* **42:** 435,n2
Paris *Le Populaire,* **42:** 364-65,n1
Paris *Le Temps,* **42:** 229n1,2; **44:** 44
Park, Frank, **43:** 539,n1
Park, Maud May Wood (Mrs. Charles Edward), **45:** 121,n1, 129, 169, 306-307; **48:** 271, 303n1; **49:** 264; **51:** 444n1
Parker, Alton Brooks, **51:** 644,n1
Parker, Charles Bailey, **41:** 351,n2
Parker, Edwin Brewington, **46:** 491,n2; **47:** 117,n1; **48:** 484,n1
Parker, James, **43:** 156,n1; **44:** 42,n6; **45:** 111,n4; **49:** 324,n3
Parker, James Southworth, **51:** 535,n2
Parker, John Milliken, **40:** 89, 92

'Parliament of Man': Mr. Henderson on the Task of a League of Nations (newspaper article), **49:** 225n1
Parliamentary Debates, **40:** 342n4, 414n1, 494n1; **42:** 389n4; **44:** 16n1; **46:** 419n
Parmoor, 1st Baron: *see* Cripps, Charles Alfred
Parrish, Mrs. L. C., **42:** 116
Parrish, Michael E., **49:** 53n1
Parry, William H., **41:** 46
Parsons, Elsie Clews, **44:** 79
Pasha, Rifaat, **44:** 43,n5
Pašić, Nikola (Nicola), **43:** 269,n6; **44:** 75-76,n1; **47:** 36-37
Passaic, N.J., **49:** 503
Passchendaele, Belgium, **44:** 333n1, 480; **45:** 175
Passing of the Hapsburg Monarchy, 1914-1918 (May), **46:** 403n1; **47:** 589n1; **48:** 114n2
Passion for Anonymity: The Autobiography of Louis Brownlow, Second Half, **43:** 201n1
passport bill, **47:** 364,n5, 474, 501
Patchin, Philip Halsey, **42:** 284-85,n1, 377, 378, **43:** 458; **44:** 459-60, 524; **51:** 134, 144
Patemann, Reinhard, **45:** 34n13; **47:** 524n1
Paterson, N.J., **49:** 503
Pathé Exchange, Inc., **42:** 447,n1
Patria (film), **41:** 483,n1; **42:** 447, 467,n1, 489-90, 527; **43:** 431-32, 501-502; **44:** 13, 231-32,n1, 287n1, 307
patriotism: WW on, **43:** 151
patronage: C. H. Dodge on, **41:** 171-72
Patten, Thomas Gedney, **43:** 165n2
Patterson, David Calvin, Jr., **47:** 70,n2
Patterson, Robert Urie, **46:** 456n2
Paul (Pavel Aleksandrovich), Grand Duke of Russia, **44:** 180,n3
Paul, Alice, **40:** 379, 420, 423; **45:** 40n1, 243n1, 345; **51:** 304; hunger strike of, **44:** 559,n4
Paul S. Reinsch: Open Door Diplomat in Action (Pugach), **41:** 394n1; **42:** 63n5
Paulucci di Calboli, Marquis Raniero, **48:** 212,n6; **51:** 233,n3
Pavlu, Bohdan, **51:** 50n1
Payer, Friedrich von, **45:** 34,n10; **46:** 567,n1, 569, 581; **48:** 213n8
Payne, Christopher Russell, **47:** 72,n3
Payne, John Barton, **44:** 289,n1
Peabody, Francis Greenwood, **46:** 22,n3
Peabody, Francis Stuyvesant, **42:** 471,n1, 472-73, 561; **43:** 62; **51:** 552,n4
Peabody, Francis Weld, **46:** 22,n2
Peabody, George Foster, **40:** 221; **41:** 115, 296, 532; **44:** 77, 83; **45:** 203-204, 225, 570; **46:** 40, 52, 53; **48:** 475; **49:** 125, 179-80, 204; **51:** 57-58; on R. N. Baldwin, **51:** 534-35
Peabody Coal Company, **42:** 471n1
Peace and Bread in Time of War (Addams), **41:** 304n3

peace commission: *see* World War—peace moves

Peace Conference: *see* World War—Peace Conference

Peace Inquiry Bureau, **45:** 458

Peace Ship: Henry Ford's Pacifist Adventure in the First World War (Kraft), **41:** 90n2

Peace With Victory (*The Independent*), **46:** 14n1

Peace Without Victory (*The New Republic*), **41:** 13,n2

Peale, Rembrandt, **45:** 568n1; **46:** 103n2

Peale, Peacock and Kerr, **46:** 103n2

Peano, Camillo, **46:** 156n2

Pears, Sir Edwin, **41:** 375,n7

Pearse, Padraic (Patrick) Henry, **43:** 509,n3

Pearson, Weetman Dickinson: *see* Cowdray, 1st Baron

Pearson's Magazine, **43:** 381,n1, 382, 396, 413, 480; **44:** 471,n5; 47: 477

Peçanha, Nilo, **42:** 265,n4, 314,n2, 315

Peck, Mary Allen Hulbert (Mrs. Thomas Dowse), **40:** 571,n1; **43:** 502

Pedroncini, Guy, **43:** 31n5

Peek, George Nelson, **46:** 229,n3, 603,n1, 607

Peffer, E. Louise, **40:** 192n1

Peláez, Manuel, **41:** 386,n1; **42:** 38,n1; **46:** 354,n2

Pelham Bay Naval Training School, **48:** 69, 94

Penfield, Frederic Courtland, **40:** 23-24; **41:** 477; and peace moves with Austria-Hungary, **41:** 129-30, 164, 267, 297-98, 299, 312, 313, 398-99; on desperate situation in Austria-Hungary, **41:** 300-301; possible recall of, **41:** 478

Penfield, Walter, **41:** 140

Pennsylvania, **42:** 434; **46:** 611,n1; **47:** 410, 411; steel strike in, **44:** 277-78; and farmers in, **46:** 602,n1; politics in, **51:** 633; and woman suffrage, **51:** 82

Pennsylvania, University of, **42:** 569n1; **47:** 155n3, 415n1; **48:** 306n1, 532; **51:** 649n3

Pennsylvania, U.S.S., **42:** 274, 278, 303; **43:** 427n1

Pennsylvania State Grange, **44:** 258; **49:** 232,n2, 440n2

Penrose, Boies, **41:** 350; **45:** 340; **46:** 60, 63n2, **47:** 584; **48:** 347, 348, 349; **51:** 572, 573

Penwell, Lewis, **49:** 277,n2

Penza, Russia, **49:** 285

People's College, Fort Scott, Kan., **47:** 235n2

People's Council of America for Democracy and Peace, **43:** 175n3, 382, 383, 394-96, 396-97, 415,n2, 437, 480-81, 512,n1; **44:** 47,n1, 78-79, 107,n4, 366n2, 470; **47:** 472n1

People's Counselor, **44:** 323,n1

People's National Bank, Philadelphia, **43:** 197

People's Relief Committee, **47:** 555

Percy, Lord Eustace Sutherland Campbell, **42:** 224,n1; **48:** 114; **49:** 402

Pereira Gomez, Wenceslao Braz: *see* Braz Pereira Gomez, Wenceslao

Pereverzev, Pavel Nikolaevich, **42:** 418n1, 419,n3

Perham, Henry B., **44:** 483,n1; **49:** 136,n2

Perkins, Cleveland, **41:** 430,n2

Perkins, George Walbridge, **40:** 185; **48:** 612-13,n1, 638; **49:** 384, 385

Perkins, James Handasyd, **47:** 613,n1

Perkins, Thomas Nelson, **45:** 209,n2, 213; **46:** 23,n3; **47:** 215

Perkins Urged for Fuel Administrator (New York *Sun*), **48:** 612n1

Perley Morse and Company, **49:** 132

Perlowski, Jan, **49:** 382

Perm, Russia, **49:** 285, 448

Permanent Court of Arbitration, The Hague, **49:** 540,n1, 540-41

Péronne, France, **47:** 130

Perry, F. J., **43:** 230

Perry, Matthew Calbraith, **48:** 569n1

Pershing, John Joseph, **40:** 100, 109, 130, 131, 522; **41:** 486, 545-46; **42:** 95, 242, 437; **43:** 389, 435,n1; **44:** 51-52, 69, 461, 467; **45:** 113, 208, 209, 322, 323, 332,n1, 373, 396, 397, 409, 438, 439-40; **46:** 452; **47:** 131, 279, 280, 443, 480, 487, 498, 501, 505, 614, 616, 617; **48:** 79, 218, 301, 331, 386, 451-52; **49:** 52, 74, 127, 235,n1, 246, 281, 293, 336-37, 517, 532, 533, 535, 543n1, 547; **51:** 17, 39, 53, 287n1, 373-74, 384-85, 407, 414, 562

on F. Villa's successes, **40:** 202-203; and troop withdrawal from Mexico, **40:** 546; **41:** 40,n1, 42-43; on universal selective service, **42:** 225; on Mexican border situation, **42:** 225-27; and expeditionary force to be sent to France, **42:** 249, 250, 264, 391-92,n1, 404-405; reception on arrival in Paris, **43:** 32n6, 275; and Paris conference, July 25, 1917, **43:** 209, 236,n1, 304n5; promoted to general, **44:** 328-29,n1; and H. Pétain, **44:** 462, 463; on military situation and recommendation concerning, **45:** 107-11,n1; evaluation of army officers, **45:** 111-12; E. M. House on, **45:** 332n1; **48:** 231-33; exchange of holiday greetings between WW and, **45:** 363, 364, 366, 424, 426; agreement reached with France regarding use of U.S. troops, **45:** 438, 439-40, 571, 583; on European situation, **45:** 594-95; and Britain's request for U.S. troops and subsequent proposals, **46:** 8-11,n1, 11-12, 43, 44, 45, 162, 196-98, 211, 231-32,n1, 236, 237-38, 248, 272, 337-38, 354, 439; L. Wood and, **46:** 259, 297,n3; **48:** 173n1, 192, 242,n1; on N. D. Baker making inspection tour, **46:** 400; **47:** 160, 166, 170, 174, 176, 183, 205, 261n2, 262; WW gives military decision-making authority to, **47:** 158, 183, 284-85; WW's message to on anniversary of U.S. entry into war, **47:** 172,n1; and F. Foch's title, **47:** 209,n, 238, 348; and transport and brigading of U.S. troops, **47:** 302-303, 305-306, 314-15,n2, 369, 370, 374, 375, 386, 393, 435, 455, 456-58; **48:** 227; on Italian troops joining Foch's command, **47:** 468; and Abbeville resolution, **47:** 512-13, 517-18, 535, 563, 566-68, 595, 615-16, 618; **48:** 32-34; on disposition of U.S. forces in France, **47:** 611-13; and work overload, **47:** 616, 619; and powers enforcing death penalty, **48:** 5-6; on German and American aircraft, **48:** 49,n1; W. Wiseman and WW discuss, **48:** 205, 206; on separate American army divisions, **48:** 243-44; on troop crisis in France, **48:** 245-46; and plans for reorganization of military in France, **48:** 265-68; on Supreme War Council's resolution on Russian intervention, **48:** 504; on combat strength on French front, **48:** 568,n1; and troop request for Russia, **48:** 537; W. S. Sims on, **48:** 605; and Murmansk expedition, **49:** 43, 44; on Britain's tonnage reduction, **49:** 217-18; on united Allied effort to end war, **49:** 404, 416-17; and issue of propaganda, **49:** 487, 488; WW's congratulations to, **51:** 3, 61; Baker on strategy of, **51:** 385-86; receives Distinguished Service Award, **51:** 400, 583; and peace negotiations, **51:** 454-55, 470-72, 473,n1, 595-96; G. Clemenceau's criticism of, **51:** 462,n2; and impact of letter to Supreme War Council on peace terms, **51:** 523, 524-25, 544,n1, 544-45, 596-98, 617; photograph, *illustration section,* **42; 46**

Persia, **42:** 501; **44:** 476, 477; **45:** 417, 419; **47:** 244, 334, 356, 366, 368, 422, 423, 424; **51:** 47, 200-201

Perth Amboy (tug boat), **49:** 167n1

Peru, **40:** 164; **41:** 9; **42:** 359

Peshekhonov, Aleksei Vasil'evich, **42:** 418n1, 419,n3

Peshkov, Aleksei Maksimovich: *see* Gor'kii, Maksim

Pétain, Henri-Philippe Benoni Omer Joseph, **42:** 264,n1,2, 438; **43:** 31,n5, 262-65,n1, 444; **44:** 462, 463; **45:** 108, 122, 151, 332n1, 399, 438, 571, 583; **46:** 10, 439, 496, 558,n2, 559; **47:** 166, 209, 238, 434, 487, 501, 505; **48:** 5, 232; **51:** 455, 473,n1

Peter Ibbetson (Du Maurier), **46:** 264,n1

Peter Ibbetson (play), **46:** 264,n1

Peters, Andrew James, **43:** 266, 267; **51:** 624

Peterson, Horace Cornelius, **43:** 434n2, 512n1; **44:** 17n1; **47:** 276n2

Peterson, O. G., **47:** 235,n3

Petigru, James Louis, **40:** 194

Petrograd, Russia, **44:** 180; **47:** 355; **48:** 179, 380; demonstrations in, **42:** 218,n2, 271, 272, 273,n1; **43:** 474,n1; U.S. staff transferred from, **46:** 528n1; Red Terror in, **51:** 3, 4, 61, 78,n2

Petrograd Telegraph Agency, **45:** 194,n1

Petroleum War Industries Board, **51:** 114

Petroleum War Service Board, **51:** 114

Pettit, Walter W., **48:** 142n6

Petty, Calvin H., **46:** 449n1

Petty, May Randolph (Mrs. Calvin H.), **46:** 449,n1

Pew, J(ohn) Howard, **41:** 232n1

Pewee Valley, Ky., Presbyterian Church, **42:** 86n1

Phelan, James Duval, **40:** 205, 420, 560n1, 561n2; **41:** 278, 454; **42:** 343n1; **43:** 11, 216, 218, 372, 473, 509n4; **44:** 133n2; **46:** 204; **47:** 396-97; and woman suffrage, **45:** 278, 279, 338; on R. Emmet, **45:** 559-60; and exchange with WW on Ireland, **45:** 559-60, 573; and Irish situation, **48:** 195, 466, 471-72

Phelps, Wilbur Franklin, **49:** 169,n1

Phelps Brothers, **46:** 412

Phelps Dodge Corporation, **42:** 563; **43:** 3, 127, 373; **44:** 518

Phelps Stokes Fund, **47:** 289

Philadelphia, Pa., **43:** 421; **45:** 132, 150n1; **47:** 401,n2, 615n1; **49:** 165; and German-American support in, **47:** 559,n2

Philadelphia, S.S., **41:** 187

Philadelphia and Reading Coal Co., **40:** 102

Philadelphia and Reading Railroad, **40:** 102

Philadelphia *Evening Bulletin,* **47:** 19n1

Philadelphia Evening Ledger, **46:** 352,n1, 353

Philadelphia *Farm Journal,* **44:** 269n1

Philadelphia Inquirer, **41:** 240n1; **46:** 611,n1; **47:** 342n1

Philadelphia National Bank, **43:** 197

Philadelphia North American, **42:** 569n1

Philadelphia Orchestra, **49:** 360,n1

Philadelphia *People's Press,* **43:** 165

Philadelphia *Public Ledger,* **40:** 112, 243n1, 316, 371,n1, 380; **41:** 191,n2; **45:** 222,n1; **47:** 278-79; **48:** 143, 598n2; reveals E. M. House's confidential work and mission, **44:** 275-76,n1,2, 298, 459-60,n2,3, 478-79, 524-25

Philadelphia Record, **40:** 35n1, 167n1; **42:** 245,n3; **45:** 437; **48:** 597n1

Philadelphia Trust Company, **43:** 197

Philander Priestly Claxton: Crusader for Public Education (Lewis), **46:** 459n1

Philip Dru: Administrator: A Story of Tomorrow, 1920-1935 (House), **42:** 161,n3

Philippine bill: *see* Jones bill

Philippine Islands, **40:** 112; **42:** 161,n2,3, 541-42; **43:** 16, 174; appointment of vice governor, **40:** 37: **41:** 63,n1,2, 417-18, 505; N. D. Baker on German ships in harbors of, **41:** 152-53; sends inaugural congratulations to WW, **41:** 345

Philippines and the United States, **44:** 8,n1, 8-9, 296n1, 387, 446-47, 449; **47:** 578-79, 579; **48:** 483-84; shipbuilding offer made by Philippines, **45:** 49-50, 75

Philips, August, **47:** 24,n1, 87,n1,2, 133-34, 142-43

Phillimore, Sir Walter George Frank, **47:** 104,n2; **48:** 501n1, 502, 647; **49:** 168

Phillimore Committee, **48:** 425n1, 501n1, 549n1

Phillimore Report, **48:** 647,n1; **49:** 12, 13, 14,n4, 16,n1, 19, 83, 168, 226, 228; **51:** 327,n1; WW does not wish publication of, **49:** 265, 266, 273, 274; Britain agrees not to publish, **49:** 549

Phillips, Charles Francis, **46:** 458n3

Phillips, Wendell, **40:** 237; **44:** 168

Phillips, William, **40:** 7, 96, 240, 339, 408, 492,n1, 508; **41:** 17, 18, 70n1, 124, 126, 185, 248, 321, 340, 542; **42:** 127, 217, 232-33, 360, 378-79, 417, 434, 453; **43:** 12, 86n3, 171n1, 302, 486; **44:** 38n1, 80, 139, 147-48, 156-57, 380, 513; **45:** 221-22, 349, 398; **46:** 395, 488; **47:** 474n2, 506, 516; **48:** 239, 249, 250-51, 575-76, 579; **51:** 24: 276; promoted to Assistant Secretary of State, **40:** 425, 457; on WW's war message, **41:** 539; on Central Polish Agency, **42:** 454; on replacing minister to Switzerland, **42:** 454-55; on Liberia, **47:** 353; on intervention in Russia, **49:** 51, 97, 178-79, 261-62; on Bulgarian peace moves, **51:** 141-42, 154; on German atrocities in France, **51:** 216

Philosophy of Politics (projected, Wilson), **46:** 285,n1

Phipps, Lawrence Cowle, **51:** 645,n1

Phoenix, Ariz., **43:** 158n1

P.I.C.: see Committee on Public Information

Piave River, Italy, **44:** 480

Picardy, France, **47:** 612; **48:** 33

Pichon, Jean, **47:** 96-97,n4, 101, 320

Pichon, Stéphen Jean Marie, **45:** 166n1, 418, 550; **46:** 429,n1; **47:** 59, 60, 318,n4; **48:** 202, 252, 273-74, 421n1, 443,n1, 446-47; **49:** 111, 124, 149, 156-57, 239-40, 538; **51:** 21n1, 33, 187, 209-10, 512, 616-17; on Japanese intervention in Siberia, **48:** 384,n3

Pickford, Mary, **47:** 301-302,n1,2

Pickford, Thomas H., **40:** 128,n1

Picot, Georges, **42:** 327n1

Pierce, Franklin, **43:** 160n1

Pierce, Palmer Eddy, **43:** 341n1; **46:** 523,n1

Piez, Charles, **46:** 124,n1, 171, 379; **47:** 233n1

Pig Iron Up to $55 in Rush for Steel (*New York Times*), **42:** 540n2

Pigott, W., **46:** 363n4

Piłsudski, Jósef Klemens, **42:** 11n1; **46:** 48, 404-405, 405

Piltz, Erasme (Erazm), **42:** 355,n2; **44:** 187,n1

Pinchot, Amos Richards Eno, **41:** 8, 305n1; **44:** 266-67; on postal censorship, **43:** 164, 165, 175-76, 176, 187, 193, 276-77; on widespread opposition to the war, **43:** 277-78; on *Masses* trial, **48:** 146-47, 220, 251

Pinchot, Gertrude Minturn (Mrs. Amos Richards Eno), **40:** 418; **44:** 559n1

Pinchot, Gifford, **40:** 116-17; **45:** 85; **49:** 440, 441-42,n8; **51:** 6; WW on, **45:** 91

Pindell, Henry Means, **46:** 331

Pine, Max, **44:** 79

Pineton, Charles Louis Antoine Pierre Gilbert: see Chambrun, Marquis de

Pininski, Count Leon, **42:** 544,n5

Pinkham, Lucius Eugene, **43:** 505

Pipes, Richard Edgar, **46:** 341n4; **48:** 102n1

Pitchfork Ben Tillman, South Carolinian (Simkins), **48:** 260n2

Pitkin, Wolcott Homer, Jr., **49:** 394,n2

Pitney, Mahlon, **46:** 297,n1

Pittman, Key, **40:** 561n2; **41:** 478-79, 485; **42:** 562; **43:** 5; **51:** 301, 303, 620; on Diggs-Caminetti decision, **41:** 246-47, 261; and woman suffrage, **45:** 279, 338; **49:** 264; **51:** 30-31, 59; and water-power legislation, **45:** 301; and general leasing bill, **45:** 375, 376, 377, 378, 402n1, 454; **49:** 481-85, 511; on congressional election results, **51:** 611-13

Pittsburgh, Pa., **42:** 313,n2; steel strike in, **44:** 242, 277

Pittsburgh Dispatch, **40:** 193n1

Pittsfield, Mass., **49:** 133

Pius IX, **41:** 434n2

Pius X, **41:** 434n2

Pius XII, **46:** 488,n2

Plancarte, Francisco, **46:** 406n2

Plans for American Cooperation to Preserve and Strengthen the Morale of the Civil Population and the Army of Russia, **43:** 526,n1

Planta, Alfred von, **43:** 28n2

Platt Amendment, **41:** 268n1, 298n1

Playground and Recreation Association of America, **43:** 478-80

Pleasant, Ruffin Golson, **51:** 537,n1

Plehve, Viacheslav Konstantinovich, **49:** 495n3

Pleshkov, Mikhail Mikhailovich, **47:** 398,n2; **48:** 105,n3

Pless, Germany: Imperial Conference at, January 29, 1917, **41:** 59n1

Plumb, Glenn Edward, **45:** 401,n1

Plummer, Edward Hinkley, **45:** 111,n9

Plunkett, George Noble, **44:** 133,n3

Plunkett, Sir Horace, **40:** 29, 30-33, 212, 294,n2, 305, 307n1, 339-42; **42:** 162, 542-43,n1; **43:** 356, 360-61, 365, 451; **44:** 210; **48:** 300; **49:** 546; and Irish Convention report and Home Rule and conscription issues, **47:** 228n1, 442,n2,

443, 444, 465-66, 469-71, 575-76, 580, 620
Plymouth Congregational Church, Brooklyn, N.Y., **45:** 142n3
Pocahontas, **42:** 58n1
Pocatello, Idaho, **46:** 432n2
Podolsky, Michael M., **42:** 218-19,n1
Pogranichnaya, Russia (now Suifenhe, Manchuria), **51:** 449,n3, 479,n1
Pohick, Va., **43:** 142
Poincaré, Raymond, **41:** 219, 314; **44:** 439; **45:** 54n1, 327; **46:** 213; **47:** 309,n6, 589n1; **48:** 301, 582-83; **49:** 547-48; **51:** 11, 21n1; on U.S. troops joining French, **45:** 372-73, 396, 397, 539-40; on anniversary of U.S. entry into war, **47:** 257, 258
Poindexter, Miles, **41:** 11n1, 37; **42:** 347; **43:** 200,n1, 202-203, 248; **44:** 276, 277; **47:** 396; **48:** 274,n1, 433; **51:** 277n7, 331,n5, 341, 455n1
Pokotu, Manchuria: see Bukhedu
Pola, Yugoslavia, **51:** 562,n1, 563
Poland, William Babcock, **48:** 46,n1; **51:** 586,n4
Poland and Poles, **40:** 13, 16, 65, 161, 186n1, 234, 240, 307n1, 318, 357, 404, 435, 441, 446n4, 477, 537; **41:** 25, 26n1, 56, 62, 80, 220n4, 225, 388; **42:** 68-69, 104,n1, 425, 433, 493-94, 502; **43:** 38, 246n1, 439, 485, 487, 523, 524; **44:** 6-7, 150, 317, 330; **45:** 86, 220, 412, 416, 418; **46:** 47, 48-49, 191,n11, 198n2, 244, 312, 487, 533, 552, 568; **47:** 44-45, 493, 555; **48:** 436, 437n2,3, 485, 530-31; **49:** 229, 382-83; **51:** 438, 567; thanks WW for his declaration on Polish rights, **41:** 139; and Polish Army, **42:** 12, 352-353, 355-56, 357, 385-86, 431-32, 454, 543; **44:** 304, 305, 316; **46:** 121, 123; **47:** 576n2; **51:** 446, 447-48; and peace terms, **42:** 104n1, 155, 156, 157, 334, 335-36, 354, 385, 389n4, 441n1; **45:** 461, 463, 470-71, 473; **48:** 553-54; **51:** 43, 44, 47, 156n2, 265n1, 269n1, 331, 335, 411, 420, 498, 503, 557, 558; and Jews, **42:** 234, 235; A. J. Balfour on, **42:** 335-38; and Central Polish Agency, **42:** 454; and Poles in Russian army, **42:** 493; plan for formation of provisional Polish government, **42:** 520, 544-45, 552-53; Britain's proposal for, **43:** 300-302, 344; F. L. Polk on sending relief to, **43:** 345,n1, 346; G. J. Sosnowski on, **44:** 4-6; Pope's peace appeal and, **44:** 19, 21, 34, 57; and Polish National Committee, **44:** 187-89, 211, 278, 304-305, 316-17, 318; **46:** 120-23; I. J. Paderewski on, **44:** 303-305; and U.S. financial aid, **45:** 349; and Fourteen Points, **45:** 480-81, 485, 515, 529, 538, 553,n2, 569; and British war aims statement, **45:** 487n2; comparison of G. Hertling's and O. Czernin's views on, **46:** 162, 164, 186, 187, 222, 224, 226, 275, 277, 292,

295, 322; W. R. Wilder on, **46:** 401-402; and Polish National Defense Committee, **46:** 402-405; and France, **46:** 585, 587; and Supreme War Council declaration on, **46:** 587-88,n1, 597; relief and, **48:** 97-99, 136-37; and T. Gallagher's resolution, **48:** 312, 551; WW on G. M. Hitchcock's bill on independence for, **48:** 591; in Moscow, **49:** 250; L. Marshall on rights of Jews in, **51:** 625-27; Benedict XV on, **51:** 641
Polis Theater, Washington, D.C., **48:** 313n1
Polish Alma Mater, **44:** 303
Polish Americans, **41:** 68, 507-508, 508-509, 511-12; **42:** 60, 68-69, 104, 352-53; **43:** 38, 256-57, 346, 426; **44:** 188, 211, 303-304; **47:** 576
Polish Army: see Poland and Poles
Polish Brotherhood of St. Joseph, **44:** 303
Polish Central Relief Committee, **41:** 508,n1, 512; **47:** 44, 556
Polish Falcons Alliance College, **41:** 508
Polish Falcons Alliance of America, **41:** 508, 511-12; **42:** 12, 44, 60; **44:** 303
Polish National Committee (National Polish Committee, Paris), **42:** 355n2, 356n1; **44:** 187-88, 278, 304-305, 316-17, 318; financial needs of, **46:** 120-22, 122-23, 149; desires U.S. recognition of Polish Army, **51:** 446, 447-48; and Jews, **51:** 625-27
Polish National Council, **41:** 508, 512; **44:** 303
Polish National Defense Committee, **41:** 68n1; **44:** 5,n1, 6-7; proposes conference in Washington, **46:** 402, 402-405
Polish National Department of Chicago, **44:** 303
Polish Roman Catholic Union of America, **41:** 508, 512; **44:** 303
Polish Uniformed Society, **44:** 303
Polish Union of Buffalo, **44:** 303
Polish Union of Wilkes-Barre, **44:** 303
Polish Women's Alliance, **44:** 303
Political Conditions of Allied Success: A Plea for the Protective Union of the Democracies (Angell), **48:** 614n, 616n2
Political History of Poland (Corwin), **46:** 404n7
Political Origins of the New Diplomacy, 1917-1918 (Mayer), **45:** 487n2; **47:** 74n1
Political Prairie Fire: The Nonpartisan League, 1915-1922 (Morlan), **44:** 153n1; **45:** 167n1; **47:** 194n1
Politics Is Adjourned: Woodrow Wilson and the War Congress, 1917-1918 (Livermore), **43:** 48n1, 245n1; **46:** 40n1, 49n1; **47:** 388n1; **48:** 50n1, 260n2; **51:** 604n1
Polk, Frank Lyon, **40:** 82, 83, 84, 96, 97, 122, 136, 241, 326, 353, 358, 367; **41:** 120, 122, 124, 201, 274, 340, 367,n1, 418, 474n2, 482, 528, 530, 549; **42:** 90,

Polk, Frank Lyon (*cont.*)
131, 160, 169, 199, 239, 240, 320, 446, 463, 527, 529, 530; **43:** 83n4, 86n3, 124, 134, 150, 155, 159,n2,3, 183, 236, 257,n2, 273, 286, 293, 302, 335, 345-46, 346, 378, 381, 386-87, 388n1, 416, 442, 458; **44:** 176, 177, 184, 380, 450n1; **45:** 40, 52, 78, 317, 323, 398, 562; **46:** 64-65, 78, 83, 153, 327, 408, 409, 438, 488, 510, 567, 580, 592, 615, 621; **47:** 5, 18, 24, 36, 64n1, 226, 234, 280, 313; **48:** 264, 609, 621, 621-22, 637, 639; **49:** 4, 5, 41, 42, 44, 51, 53, 96, 118, 126, 150, 168, 174, 175, 187, 212, 219, 225, 230; **51:** 175, 252, 291, 315, 316, 529
on Swiss efforts to restore German-American relations, **41:** 203-204; and Zimmermann telegram, **41:** 322, 323, 324; and Mexico, **41:** 365, 386-87; **48:** 279; **49:** 140-41, 153, 166; and China, **41:** 382-83; **43:** 362; on Cuba, **41:** 384; **43:** 206-207; and Colombia, **41:** 420; on Pan-American Pact, **42:** 14, 15; meets with D. da Gama, **42:** 314-15; and *Patria,* **42:** 467,n1, 489-90, 527; and Hearst newspaper correspondents, **43:** 132, 133; on Morgenthau mission, **43:** 206; and Great Britain's proposal for independent Poland, **43:** 300-301, 344; on WW's views of French idea of society of nations, **43:** 359-60; discusses WW and cabinet with E. M. House, **43:** 485-86; on proposed Japanese intervention in Siberia, **46:** 33, 34, 35, 41, 117-18, 547, 548, 550-51, 553, 554-55, 574, 584-85, 585-86, 594-95; **47:** 20-21; on procedure for reporting Supreme War Council's activities, **46:** 254-56; and Costa Rica, **46:** 450-51,n5; **49:** 5-6; on WW's message to Fourth All-Russia Congress of Soviets, **46:** 597; and requisitioning Dutch ships, **47:** 26-27; and Russian policy, **48:** 262-63, 276, 276-77,n1; WW's condolences to, **48:** 441; on former Austrian soldiers and Italy, **49:** 21; on proposals and counterproposals leading to American-Japanese intervention in Russia, **49:** 37-39, 75, 97, 107, 107-109, 175-76, 178-79; on American Group, **49:** 77, 101-103; on Russian legation in Rumania and Spain, **49:** 142; on Czech troops' need of clothing, **49:** 176-77; on internationalization of Chinese concessions, **49:** 213-14; on Herron-De Fiori talks, **49:** 228, 231-32; immigration resolution of, **49:** 310,n1; and Al Smith, **49:** 465
Polk, William Mecklenburg, **48:** 441,n1
Pollak, Theodora, **51:** 125,n1, 171-72, 203-204, 210-11, 211, 281, 376-80, 451, 520
Pollard, Albert Frederick, **48:** 501n1
Pollen, Arthur Joseph Hungerford, **42:** 379,n1; **43:** 71,n1; **44:** 177
Pollock, William Pegues: and woman suffrage, **51:** 294,n1, 337, 375

Pollyanna (Porter), **46:** 314n2
Pollyanna: The Glad Girl (play, Cushing), **46:** 314n2
Polo de Bernabé, Luis, **40:** 231,n1, 233; **51:** 528,n1
Pomerene, Atlee, **40:** 523; **41:** 55-56, 88n1; **42:** 561; **43:** 234; **46:** 61; **51:** 21, 176-77, 227, 280; and woman suffrage, **45:** 279, 339; **47:** 608-609; on wheat prices and Gore amendment, **47:** 95-96, 139; and telegraph legislation, **48:** 534, 535, 556,n3, 592
Pond, Allen Bartlit, **43:** 168-70,n1, 193-94; **44:** 236, 265
Ponsonby, Arthur Augustus William Harry, **41:** 374-75,n2; **42:** 422,n2
Poole, DeWitt Clinton, Jr., **42:** 507, 508,n1; **48:** 96n2, 113, 359-60,n1; and Red Terror, **51:** 4,n2, 18n1, 61,n1
Poole, Ernest Cooke, **42:** 254,n3,6, 268, 269; **47:** 522n4
Poole, Frederick Cuthbert, **48:** 285,n2, 286, 330, 380, 536, 537, 599, 600-601; **49:** 43; **51:** 8-9, 37, 52-53, 153, 209; British instructions to, **49:** 285-86; interferes in Archangel affairs, **49:** 448, 496, 508, 516-17, 518, 530-31
Poor's Manual of Railroads, **44:** 423n2
Pope, Alexander, **40:** 208
Pope, Joseph, **42:** 360
Popham, John Nichols, **46:** 450,n4
Popov, Christo I., **45:** 384n2
Popov, Mikhail Konstantinovich, **47:** 96,n2, 99,n5
Popović, Evgenije, **43:** 268,n2
Populist party, **47:** 438
pork industry, **48:** 308
Porras, Belisario, **48:** 417n2,5
Port and Harbor Development Commission (N.Y.-N.J.), **45:** 573-74
Porter, Edward Jr., **49:** 399-400
Porter, Eleanor Emily Hodgman (Mrs. John Lyman), **46:** 314n2
Porter Military Academy (Charleston, S.C.), **48:** 203
Portland, Ore., *American,* **44:** 493
Portland, Ore., *Argus,* **42:** 161
Portland, Ore., *Deutsche Zeitung,* **44:** 493; **47:** 524
Portland, Ore., *Nachrichten aus dem Nordwesten und Freie Presse,* **44:** 405n1, 415, 492-93
Portland *Oregon Voter,* **47:** 352,n2
Porto Rico, **40:** 57-58, 90, 146-53, 213-14, 402; **41:** 407-408,n1, 485, 515-16; A. Yager and labor situation in, **47:** 543-44, 577; **49:** 71, 236,n1, 252; S. Gompers charges against Yager, **48:** 3-4, 15-16, 17-18, 35-37, 48-49, 74-75, 130; and commission to investigate labor in, **48:** 637-38,n5,6; **49:** 135-36, 158, 246, 296-98, 334, 394; *see also* Jones Act
Porto Rico bill: *see* Jones Act
Portugal, **40:** 231; and woman suffrage, **48:** 24n1, 25-26

Posen (Poznán), **42**: 336; **44**: 317; **48**: 553-54; **51**: 504

Post, Louis Freeland, **40**: 3; **43**: 104-105, 108-109, 175n3; **44**: 205; **45**: 8, 60; **48**: 235; **51**: 204; on Atlantic Coast Line strike and settlement, **45**: 117-18, 125-26, 184; on need for national employment service, **45**: 130-32, 162, 182-83; and Twin City Rapid Transit Co. strike, **45**: 258-62, 279; on pardon for early draft resisters, **46**: 289, 324-25

Post Bellum (proposed journal), **41**: 90,n2

Post Office, Committee on the (House of Reps.), **43**: 481n5

Post Office appropriations bill, **41**: 311-12,n2

Post Office Department, **40**: 28, 41, 89, 89-90, 97, 438; **44**: 143n1; **45**: 382; **47**: 211, 372; **48**: 12-14; and Secret Service, **42**: 16; and censorship, **42**: 163, 195-96; **43**: 164, 164-65,n1,2, 175-76, 176, 187-88, 382, 383, 396, 413, 423-24, 480-82; **44**: 49, 147,n1, 171, 193, 266n1, 338-40, 344,n1, 358,n1, 371-72, 389-90, 393-94, 396n1, 408, 428n1, 467-72, 491; **46**: 382-83; **51**: 12,n1,2,3, 15-16, 55,n1, 56-57, 77; and Revenue Act of 1917, **43**: 350n2; postal rates and revenue bill, **44**: 257n1, 289, 291; and airmail service, **47**: 615,n1; and *The Menace* case, **49**: 174,n1

Post Telegraph-Cable Company, **48**: 281,n1, 282,n5, 298, 313, 375

postwar organization and security, **40**: 21,n1, 403-404; **41**: 334, 551; **42**: 89-90, 151, 367, 535n1; **43**: 273, 274, 360, 401-402, 407, 467, 468, 513; **44**: 76, 177, 226, 299-300,n1,2, 349-51, 374, 379-80, 474-77, 488, 549-51; **45**: 17-18, 68, 198; **47**: 101, 102-103, 103-104, 201; **48**: 501-502,n1; N. Angell on, **40**: 10-19; **48**: 614-21; A. G. Gardiner on, **40**: 35n3; and conference of neutrals, **40**: 47; E. Grey on, **40**: 60n1; WW on, **40**: 67-70; **48**: 516-17; **49**: 225-26; J. Bryce on, **40**: 317-18, 469; J. H. Bernstorff on WW's desire for, **40**: 364-65; N. Buxton on, **40**: 414n1; L. P. Lochner and WW discuss, **41**: 90-92,n1,2; R. Lansing on, **41**: 123; W. H. Taft on, **41**: 154; D. Lloyd George on, **41**: 213-14; **45**: 489; and Fourteen Points, **45**: 515, 529, 538; and Indiana Democratic platform, **48**: 318; E. M. House on, **48**: 424-26; R. L. Owen on economic preparedness and, **49**: 8; N. D. Baker on military service and, **49**: 117-18; E. Root on, **49**: 269-72; WW and House discuss, **49**: 281; WW on Great Britain's proposed economic boycott of Germany, **49**: 300-301; E. A. Filene on a reconstruction commission, **49**: 444, 472; idea of economic boycott of Germany, **51**: 8; W. G. Sharp on France and, **51**: 21n1; Lippmann-Cobb memorandum on Fourteen Points, **51**: 495-

504; *see also* league of nations; World War—Peace Moves

Posyet Bay, Russia, **51**: 450,n4

potatoes, **46**: 307, 478; **47**: 449

Potomac Park airfield, **47**: 615n1

Potsdam, Germany, **42**: 521

Potter, Elizabeth Herndon (Mrs. J. Edwin), **46**: 573,n1; **47**: 42,n1, 104

Potter, William Chapman, **47**: 396,n1; **49**: 349,n1

Pou, Edward William, **47**: 474-75, 501; **48**: 45n1, 592; on selective service bill, **42**: 42-43, 52; and woman suffrage, **42**: 269, 270, 293, 320-21; on WW's speech being misinterpreted, **42**: 349, 357; and water-power legislation, **45**: 301, 406, 433,n1; **49**: 316, 317, 329, 330, 406, 425; **51**: 21; on Democratic majority in Congress, **51**: 299-300

Powell, Adam Clayton, **43**: 412n2

Powell, D. F., **48**: 292,n2

Powers, E. W., **44**: 522

Powhatan Hotel, Washington, D.C., **46**: 610n2

Powles, Allen H., **40**: 487n6

Prager, Robert Paul, **47**: 276n2; **49**: 61n1

Pratt, Edward Ewing, **43**: 12, 117

Pratt, William Veazie, **43**: 182,n2; **45**: 72-73,n1; **51**: 486,n1, 487-88

Pratt Consolidated Coal Company, **45**: 269n1

Precautions Advisable in Export Contracts (*Commerce Reports*), **43**: 110,n3

Preece, Ambrose, **41**: 451,n1

Preliminary Note on the Organization of the Food Administration (Hoover), **42**: 437,n1

Preliminary Report on Aeronautic Conditions (Borglum), **46**: 94,n1

Preliminary Statement to the Press of the United States, **42**: 313n5

Prentis, Percy L., **43**: 267,n2

preparedness, **40**: 270, 348n5; **42**: 3, 4, 55; E. M. House and J. Daniels discuss, **40**: 238-39; and Chamberlain bill, **40**: 267,n1, 475; and draft provisions of National Defense Act, **40**: 327-30; House and WW discuss, **40**: 408-409; WW answers memorial for compulsory universal military training, **41**: 10,n1; and national relief fund, **41**: 113n3; N. D. Baker on delaying mobilization, **41**: 114; WW on, **41**: 239, 287; and vocational education bill, **41**: 295,n2; and Danish West Indies, **41**: 362-63; and finances for, **41**: 448n1; and L. Wood, **41**: 461,n1; J. P. Tumulty on, **41**: 462-63; K. Pittman on, **41**: 479; M. Hale on, **41**: 492-93; G. Creel statement on, **47**: 334n1; *see also* World War—U.S. preparations for entry into

Presbyterian, The (Phila.), **42**: 537n5

Presbyterian Church in the United States (southern), **45**: 282n2, 286

Presbyterian Church in the United States of America, **42**: 535-37,n1; **45**:

Presbyterian Church in the U.S.A. (*cont.*)
282,n1,2, 286, 315, 330; and prohibi-
tion, **41:** 311
President, The (Child), **47:** 15,n2
President Grant, S.S., **42:** 274, 278, 303
President and his Day's Work (Law-
rence), **47:** 4n1
President and the Kaiser (*Springfield,
Mass., Republican*), **51:** 330n1
President Lincoln, S.S., **42:** 274, 278, 303
President of the United States (Wilson),
42: 69,n2
President Supports Harris for the Senate
(*Atlanta Constitution*), **49:** 237,n1
President to Speak (Fox), **46:** 525,n3
Président Wilson (Halévy), **43:** 135,n2
President Wilson on principles which
would serve to enlist United States in
Peace Federation (New York *Commer-
cial and Financial Chronicle*), **41:** 107
President Wilson's Appeal (Eliot), **51:**
551,n1
President Wilson's Epoch Making Mes-
sage Comes as a Reply to Lord Lans-
downe's Demand to Restate War Aims
(Macfarland), **45:** 270,n2
President Wilson's Peace League com-
pared with the Holy Alliance (New
York *Commercial and Financial
Chronicle*), **41:** 107
*President Wilson's State Papers and Ad-
dresses* (Shaw, ed.), **44:** 273,n2
President Woodrow Wilson (*Semaine Lit-
téraire*), **40:** 542n1
President Woodrow Wilson Urges Voters
of State to Support Harris Against
Hardwick for the Senate (*Atlanta Con-
stitution*), **49:** 237n1
*Presidential Messages and State Papers:
Being the Epoch-Marking National
Documents of All the Presidents from
George Washington to Woodrow Wilson, Collected and Arranged with Brief
Biographical Sketches* (Muller, ed.), **45:**
249-50,n2, 257
President's Cabinet (*New York Times*),
41: 446,n1
President's Demands (Ogden), **51:** 296-
97,n1
President's Mediation Commission (Labor Commission), **44:** 103-104, 120,
161-64, 191, 213-14, 214, 223, 241,n1,
257,n1, 478, 479; **45:** 121,n1, 127, 331;
46: 26, 27, 482; **47:** 574; and Mooney
case, **44:** 267; **46:** 68-74, 74, 84; on Bisbee deportations, **44:** 515, 516-20, 521-
22; **45:** 94, 95, 95-96, 134-35; **47:** 115,
167, 597-98; and Pacific Telephone and
Telegraph settlement, **45:** 95-96, 103-
104; and northwestern lumber industry, **45:** 234, 244, 295; **46:** 107; and
meatpackers' labor settlement, **45:**
356; report and recommendations of,
46: 127-47, 149-50; and settlement of
oil disputes in Texas and Louisiana,
46: 170; and rapid transit strike in
Minneapolis, **47:** 189-91, 273

press: *see* newspapers
Press Censorship Substitute (Washing-
ton *Evening Star*), **42:** 245n3
Pressed Steel Car Company, **42:** 540n1
*Pressure Politics: The Story of the Anti-
Saloon League* (Odegard), **43:** 42n2
Preston, John White (*not* John William)
43: 86,n2, 215-18,n2, 254; **47:** 479,n2,3;
51: 125,n1, 211, 376-80
Preston, William, Jr., **44:** 17n1
Preussische Jahrbücher, **42:** 389n2
Price, Joseph Morris, **40:** 215,n1
Price, Lucien, **42:** 264,n4
Price, Theodore Hazeltine, **42:** 255-56,
259
Price, William Jennings, **42:** 51,n1; **45:**
388-89,n6
price-fixing bill, **47:** 117
Price-Fixing Committee (War Industries
Board), **48:** 474, 487-88, 607; **51:** 218-
20, 285,n1; and F. W. Taussig, **47:** 208,
224, 225, 255
Price of Vigilance (Jensen), **42:** 441n2
prices and price fixing, **44:** 182-83, 409;
45: 244, 344, 571; **49:** 145; and coal industry, **43:** 6,n1, 7,n1, 33,n1; **44:** 3,n1,
29, 144n1, 450-51, 453,n1; **45:** 176n1;
46: 599-601, 610,n2; **47:** 7, 33, 89-90;
WW on, **43:** 151-54; War Industries
Board and, **43:** 489-91; **46:** 521, 602-
603, 603, 607; and copper, **44:** 64,n1,
223-24; **46:** 58-59, 68; **48:** 487-88, 489;
and grains, **44:** 88,n1, 89, 191-92,
215,n2; **45:** 59-60; **46:** 306-307, 345-47,
368, 430-32, 505; **47:** 88, 90-91, 95-96,
139; **49:** 104, 352-53, 354, 354,n1, 356,
391-93, 427,n1, 433; T. W. Gregory on
enforcing law on, **44:** 313; and Chamber of Commerce's proposal, **45:** 62-63;
and Cuba and sugar, **45:** 115-16,
163,n1, 353; R. Meeker on, **45:** 132n1;
J.   Daniels   on,   **45:**   171;
H. Hoover on, **45:** 179-80; and meat-
packing industry, **45:** 179,n2; **47:** 49;
48: 8-9, 76-77, 109-10, 562,n1; WW's
recommendations to Congress on, **45:**
201; lumber industry and, **45:** 233-34;
W. C. Redfield on, **45:** 246-47; and steel
industry, **45:** 342-43, 344; **47:** 118-
19,n1, 138, 167-68; **51:** 90-91, 285-86,n1;
W. G. McAdoo on, **46:** 75; and cotton,
46: 83-84, 84; **47:** 138, 168-69, 173; **48:**
646; **49:** 47-50, 461; **51:** 5,1n, 372,
610,n1, 611; and cattle, **46:** 125-26,
409-10,n2, 588; WW on agriculture
and, **46:** 177; farmers on, **46:** 280-81,
602n1; and potatoes, **46:** 307; and zinc,
46: 336; A. C. Townley on, **47:** 88; Hoover commission for meat industry approved by WW, **47:** 149-53, 192; and
railroads and fuel issue, **47:** 241, 405-
11, 418-19; **48:** 24: 81-93; and leather
and wool, **47:** 383-84, 395, 444-45; H. A.
Garfield and fuel, **47:** 404; **48:** 148n1;
and Standard Oil of Indiana finances,
47: 413; and plan for "Liberty garments," **47:** 494-96, 502; and wheat, **48:**

42,n1, 74, 488, 580, 593-94, 628n1; W. B. Wilson on, **48:** 223; R. S. Brookings and, **48:** 392-93; **51:** 218-20; A. Capper on profiteering and, **48:** 486-87; and WW's veto on wheat prices, **48:** 595-97; and public utility rates, **49:** 159-62; Ohio farmers and wool prices, **49:** 277-78; suggestion for textile and clothing administrator to control, **49:** 375-77, 389-90; and sugar, **49:** 419n1; and Federal Board of Farm Organizations, **49:** 441,n9; and agriculture, **51:** 118n1; H. Hoover on hog prices, **51:** 126-27,n1,2; H. Hoover on indices and, **51:** 357-61; and anthracite versus bituminous coal, **51:** 545-47; *see also* World War—economic impact

Priest, George Madison, **45:** 92,n1, 154

Priest, Joseph, **49:** 257,n2

Prime Minister's Secretariat, 1916-1920 (Davies), **42:** 266n1

Princeton, N.J., **42:** 31n1; **51:** 110

Princeton Alumni Weekly, 45: 334-35,n2, 568n2; **48:** 78n2

Princeton Bank, **41:** 260, 457-58

Princeton Packet, **46:** 105n1

Princeton Theological Seminary, **45:** 570n1; **49:** 420n1

Princeton University, **40:** 35n1, 108n1, 165n1, 169, 169n1, 255n1, 443n1, 551n1, 566n1; **41:** 321n1; **42:** 67-68, 439n1, 570,n2,3; **43:** 136, 462n1; **44:** 237, 239n1; **45:** 41n1,92n1,256n3, 325, 411n2, 558, 570n1; **46:** 28n2, 260n1, 286, 508n1, 553,n1; **47:** 264, 311n1, 540n1; **48:** 310; **49:** 235, 257, 398, 420,n1, 435n1, 480n1, 487n2; **51:** 12, 115n5, 547n1, 649; club-quad controversy of 1907, **40:** 567-69, 570; military training at, **42:** 458; **47:** 380; trustees support WW's Fourteen Points, **45:** 568,n2; and Liberty Loan, **47:** 274

Principle of Censorship (*The New Republic*), **42:** 245n3

Prinz Eugen, S.M.S., **51:** 492

Prinzregent Luitpold, S.M.S., **45:** 33,n8, **51:** 490

Pritchett, Henry Smith, **41:** 250,n4

Proceedings of the Brest-Litovsk Peace Conference: The Peace Negotiations between Russia and the Central Powers, 21 November, 1917–3 March, 1918 (U.S. Department of State), **45:** 384n2

Proctor, Frederick Cocke, **49:** 230,n1

Program for Labor (*The New Republic*), **42:** 135-38

Programme Wilson d'inspiration allemande (Paris *L'Intransigeant*), **51:** 255n1

Progressive Era in Minnesota, 1899-1918 (Chrislock), **45:** 258n2; **46:** 348n1

Progressive party, **41:** 490,n1; **42:** 237n1, 284; and National party, **47:** 254n1; in Illinois, **44:** 165,n2; in Colorado, **48:** 197n1

prohibition, **45:** 40n1, 83-85, 275, 542; **46:** 553-54, 620-21,n2; **47:** 88, 106-107; **49:**
476,n1; **51:** 28-30, 103, 105; J. P. Gavit on, **40:** 41-42; E. M. House on, **40:** 86, 173; in Porto Rico, **41:** 278n1; Post Office appropriations bill and, **41:** 311-12,n1; and Washington, D.C., **41:** 329, 432; and navy, **42:** 123, 526,n3; J. Fisher on, **42:** 323,n2; and Presbyterian Church, **42:** 535n1; Lever bill and, **43:** 42,n2, 48n1, 64, 84n1, 160n1; H. L. Higginson on, **43:** 52-53; A. Capper on, **43:** 112; and army camps, **43:** 115-16; B. Swope on, **43:** 334-35; S. Gompers on proposed amendment on, **45:** 295-98; and White House, **45:** 541; and Randall amendment, **48:** 161,n2, 247; H. Hoover on, **48:** 166-67, 209,n1; WW on, **48:** 175; J. Cannon, Jr., on, **48:** 190-91; J. H. Small on Anti-Saloon League, **48:** 350-51; A. J. Sabath on, **48:** 376-77; and Jones amendment, **48:** 428,n1; J. Daniels on, **48:** 432; and Kansas, **49:** 309; J. P. Tumulty on, **49:** 476-78; Eighteenth Amendment, **49:** 477n5; proclamation on brewing industry, **49:** 550,n1

Prohibition National Committee, **45:** 541

Prohibition party, **51:** 390n1

Pro-Hyphen German Socialist (Walling), **42:** 197n1

Prologue: Journal of the National Archives, **46:** 12n1

Proper Perspective of American History (Wilson), **49:** 165,n1

Proposal for the Organization of a *National Reconstruction Plan Commission* for the United States, **51:** 146n1

Proposed Additions to Selective Service Regulations of November 8, 1917 (H. A. Garfield), **45:** 547n1

Protopopov, Aleksandr Dmitrievich, **41:** 416,n2; **48:** 184,n3

Prouty, Charles Azvo, **45:** 266,n3

Providence Journal, **44:** 83

Prudential Insurance Company, **42:** 527n1, 565

Prussia, **42:** 425, 444n1, 493; **43:** 185; **46:** 245; **47:** 64n2, 244

The Public: An International Journal of Fundamental Democracy (N.Y.), **43:** 175,n3

public buildings appropriations bill, **40:** 422, 476

Public Buildings and Grounds, Committee on (House of Reps.), **41:** 179; **46:** 443n1

public health: and war industries, **45:** 91-92, 92; and army training camps, **45:** 390n4, 421n1, 423, 452-53, 491-92

Public Health Service, **45:** 27, 51; W. G. McAdoo on, **49:** 379-81

Public Information, Committee on: *see* Committee on Public Information

Public Lands, Committee on (House of Reps.), **40:** 192, 206, 289; **45:** 300, 301, 335n1, 375, 377, 378, 406, 454; **47:** 402, 403,n1, 452; **49:** 291, 482; **51:** 206

Public Lands, Committee on (Senate), **40:**

Public Land, Committee on (*cont.*) 206; **42:** 561; **45:** 375n1, 377, 378, 453, 454

public opinion: in the United States, **44:** 165-66, 305-306, 408-10, 424; and Inquiry memorandum, **45:** 468; on the war, **45:** 236, 315; on U.S. troops joining British, **46:** 248; on proposed Japanese intervention in Siberia, **46:** 530, 531; U.S. Army and death penalty, **48:** 5-6; concern in England over delay in Siberian intervention, **48:** 566-67; E. Root on, **49:** 270-71; on German note, **51:** 320-24

Public Service Corporation of New Jersey, **49:** 183, 405, 424, 463-64, 474-75

Public Service Reserve, Labor Dept., **45:** 131

Public Service Trolley Lines, N.J., **49:** 183, 474-75

public utilities, **48:** 597-99, 611, 612,n1; **51:** 76, 92,n1, 193, 247-48; S. R. Bertron on, **49:** 54; in New Jersey, **49:** 72, 405, 463-64; WW on, **49:** 72, 159, 204, 205, 232, 389,n1; W. C. Redfield on, **49:** 156-62; W. M. Daniels on, **49:** 183-84, 252-55, 420-22; W. G. McAdoo on, **49:** 389,n1, 405-406; proclamation on, **49:** 457, 458-59, 460,n1; K. Pittman on, **49:** 482; *see also* transit companies

Public Utilities Commission of New Jersey, **49:** 72, 405, 424: 463-64, 474-75

Public Utilities War Board (proposed): *see* National Public Utilities War Board

Pudd'nhead Wilson (Twain), **44:** 124n2

Puerto Rico: *see* Porto Rico

Puerto Rico and the United States, 1917-1933 (Clark), **48:** 18n1

Pugach, Noel H., **41:** 394n1; **42:** 63n5

Pujo, Arsène Paulin, **49:** 233

Pulitzer, Ralph, **40:** 3-4, 119,n1, 337; **46:** 351-52, 370; **51:** 293,n1

Pulj, Yugoslavia: *see* Pola

purchasing: B. M. Baruch on, **46:** 251, 288-89

Purchasing Council: *see* Inter-Allied Council on War Purchases and Finance

Pure Food and Drug Act, 1906, **42:** 294n2

Put Patriotism in Education (Madison *Wisconsin State Journal*), **45:** 142,n2

Pye, William Satterlee, **43:** 182,n2

Pyne, Moses Taylor, **40:** 568,n5, 569

Quadruple Alliance, **45:** 384n2

Quakers, **40:** 122, 125; **42:** 159; **43:** 492n1; **44:** 29,n1, 74, 75, 267n3, 288; **47:** 415-16

Quantico, Va., **47:** 539

Quai d'Orsay, France, **51:** 512

Queenstown, Ireland, **44:** 346n1

Quesada, Manuel Castro: *see* Castro Quesada, Manuel

Question of Palestine, 1914-1918: British-Jewish-Arab Relations (Friedman), **45:** 149n2

Quezon, Manuel Luis, **40:** 112

Quick, John Herbert, **49:** 512,n1, 514

Quincy, Josiah, **46:** 617,n1

Quinn, Arthur Hobson, **51:** 649,n3

Quinn, John, **41:** 347,n2

Quistconck, S.S.: launching of, **49:** 164n1, 443,n4; photograph, *illustration section, 49*

R. N. Baldwin, Draft Violator, Sentenced (New York *Evening Post*), **51:** 534,n1

Race Riot at East St. Louis, July 2, 1917 (Rudwick), **43:** 103n1

Radcliffe, Wallace, **42:** 535,n2

Radek, Karl, **48:** 40,n2; **49:** 495,n5

Radetzky, S.M.S., **51:** 492

Radoslavov, Vasil', **48:** 457n1; **51:** 563,n2

Raemaekers, Louis, **43:** 416,n2

Railroad Administration, **45:** 101n1, 451; **46:** 432, 491; **47:** 408n3, 488; **48:** 590; **49:** 53n1, 253; **51:** 261, 363, 442; W. G. McAdoo and, **46:** 112, 443; **49:** 287, 393-94, 489; priorities committee of War Industries Board and, **46:** 477-78, 506, 521, 522,n1, 524; and fuel question, **47:** 405-11, 418-19; **48:** 81-93; and meat-packing industry, **48:** 508-509; **49:** 460, 461, 504, 525; *see also*, railroads

Railroad brotherhoods, **42:** 495; **43:** 21; and 1917 strike crisis, **41:** 20, 21, 29-30, 54, 66, 238, 241, 251-52,n1, 262, 352,n1, 402, 409, 412-13, 424, 425, 430n2, 432

Railroad Wage Commission, **47:** 211; **48:** 81; **49:** 84, 206, 367; **51:** 260

railroads, **40:** 421-22,n2,3, 476; **42:** 3, 74; **44:** 309, 352; **45:** 401,n1, 403; **46:** 108-109, 506; **49:** 256; crisis of 1916, **40:** 155, 155-56, 246,n2,3,4, 265-67, 278, 303; **41:** 13-14,n1,2, 29-31, 53-54, 64, 66, 238,n1, 241, 409-11, 412-13, 414, 414-15, 420, 424-25, 519; and mediation, **41:** 13-14,n1,2, 32, 37, 156-57, 160, 197, 253-55, 258; **44:** 430-31, 448-49, 458-59; **45:** 25-26, 49; and preparedness, **41:** 151; crisis of 1917; **42:** 153-54,n1,3; and U.S. aid to France for, **42:** 192-93, 201-202; and coal, **42:** 206; **49:** 290; and rate increases, **42:** 218,n1, 221; **44:** 402-405, 406-407, 425-26, 428, 429-30, 444; and Russia, **42:** 222, 238,n2,3; **43:** 387; **46:** 344,n1, 357, 358; **51:** 478-81,n1; and unions delaying needed shipments, **42:** 242-43; priorities bill for, **42:** 289-90, 298-99, 299, 462,n1, 505-506,n2; **43:** 504; H. C. Hall on building cars and locomotives for, **43:** 296-97; and Georgia, Florida and Alabama Railroad controversy, **43:** 530-32; **44:** 22-23, 82,n1, 90,n1, 106; and Boston and Maine strike, **44:** 152,n1, 183; labor and draft law and, **44:** 565; Atlantic Coast Line strike and settlement, **45:** 117-18, 129-30, 155, 162, 184; comments on governmental ownership of, **45:** 170-71, 225-28, 271,

304-306, 309-11, 313, 319, 324, 334, 383-85; J. P. Tumulty on W. G. Mc-Adoo's ability to manage, **45**: 232-33; G. W. Anderson on, **45**: 265-66; Mc-Adoo on Wall Street and, **45**: 287-88; WW on, **45**: 318, 401,n1, 403; and governmental takeover of, **45**: 358-61, 367, 373, 373-74, 389, 391, 398, 448-51; **46**: 620,n1; and draft exemptions, **45**: 584; **48**: 12, 115; **49**: 377-78, 514; and food crisis, **46**: 126n1, 214, 306-309, 394, 424-26, 463-64, 469, 478; W. L. Chambers on Mediation Board and, **46**: 446-48; and plan for restricting northeastern industrial development, **47**: 159,n1, 336; and fuel price controversy, **47**: 172, 241, 405-11, 418-19, 498-99; **48**: 22-24, 31, 80-93, 148,n1; McAdoo and House discuss, **47**: 498-99; and Negroes, **48**: 160; **51**: 192; and Indiana Democratic platform, **48**: 319; and interurban railways, **48**: 526-27,n1, 567-68, 589-91, 623-24; and wage issue, **49**: 84-85; **51**: 194,n1, 260, 261; order forbidding political activity by employees of, **49**: 372,n1; meat-packing industry and, **49**: 523; *see also* Russian Railroad Commission; under name of specific railroad

Railroads' War Board, **42**: 540n2; **47**: 418

Railway Labor Adjustment Board, **47**: 378

Railway labor commission (proposed), **41**: 14,n1; W. B. Wilson on establishing, **40**: 97-100

Railway Mediation Act of 1913, **41**: 20n1, 238n1

Railway Service Corps in Russia: *see* Russian Railway Service Corps

Rainey, Henry Thomas, **41**: 23; **42**: 21n1; **48**: 119

Raker, John Edward, **45**: 300,n4

Raleigh, U.S.S., **47**: 358n1

Raleigh Hotel, Washington, D.C., **41**: 359; **44**: 529

Raleigh *News and Observer,* **40**: 443n3

Ralston, Oliver Cromwell, **42**: 347,n3

Rand, Carrie: *see* Herron, Carrie Rand

Rand, Mrs. E. D., **40**: 540n1

Rand School of Social Science, **47**: 472n1

Randall, Charles Hiram, **48**: 161,n2; **51**: 477,n3

Randall prohibition amendment, **48**: 161,n2, 247; **51**: 28,n2

Randolph, James Harvey, **51**: 193,n1

Rankin, Jeanette, **42**: 126,n3; **43**: 299, 339-40, 345,n1; **45**: 238n1, 321-22, 363

Ransdell, Joseph Eugene, **41**: 198; **43**: 311, 312-13; **46**: 450; **47**: 34; and woman suffrage, **45**: 279,n1, 338; **48**: 237n2, 352

Rapallo, Italy, **45**: 47; **46**: 234

Raphael, John N., **46**: 264n1

Rapid Fire Gun of Rot (San Juan *Times*), **48**: 36,n2

Rapley, William Harryman, **47**: 476,n1

Rappard, Willem Louis Frederik Chris-

tiaan van, **41**: 22, 125-26, 130-31, 190,n1, 200; **51**: 422

Rappard, William Emmanuel, **44**: 484-90,n1

Rasputin, Grigorii Efimovich, **41**: 416,n1; **42**: 465,n1

Rathbun, Don S., **42**: 272n10; **47**: 196,n4

Rathdonnell, 2d Baron (Thomas Kane McClintock-Bunbury), **42**: 403,n2

Ratibor und Corvey, Maximilian Klaus Wilhelm von, **51**: 345n1

Ratner, Sidney, **43**: 350n2

Rawlinson, Henry Seymour, **46**: 453,n3, 558; **47**: 107,n1, 443,n2

Rawll, Herbert Frederic, **44**: 494n1

Ray, George Washington, **44**: 193,n3

Ray, Ariz., **43**: 157

Rayzacher, Stanislaus, **46**: 403

Rea, Cleveland Dodge, **44**: 93,n1

Rea, George Bronson, **42**: 487,n2

Rea, Grace Dodge, **44**: 93,n1

Rea, Julia Parish Dodge (Mrs. James Child), **44**: 93,n1

Rea, Ruth, **44**: 93,n1

Rea, William Holdship, **44**: 93,n1

Read, Caroline Seaman (Mrs. William Augustus), **48**: 28-29,n1, 46, 111

Read, Harlan Eugene, **49**: 235

Read, Isaac, **47**: 16

Reading, Alice Edith Cohen Isaacs, Lady, **46**: 438,n1; **47**: 116, 137; **48**: 354,n6, 391

Reading, 1st Marquess of (Rufus Daniel Isaacs), **40**: 137, 186n1, 201; **43**: 453; **44**: 56, 125,n1, 132-33, 200, 201, 202, 203, 230, 284, 299, 351, 380, 381, 480, 494-95, 496-97; **45**: 40, 69, 70-71, 166n1, 245, 313, 323, 445, **46**: 86, 161, 180, 248, 250, 259, 297, 317, 328, 333-34, 438, 439, 461, 467, 488, 489, 565,n1; **47**: 18, 63, 64, 92, 96-99, 120, 130, 221-22, 305-306, 307, 307-308, 334-35, 338, 343, 355-57, 412, 585; **48**: 33, 61-62, 66, 94, 114, 132-35, 228, 253, 274, 310, 352-54, 365-66, 367, 378, 383, 390, 418, 463, 561, 574-75, 593-94, 595, 622; **49**: 9, 57, 70, 94, 125, 177, 273-74, 300-301, 345, 354, 417, 452-55, 549; **51**: 7, 94, 145, 188, 208, 290-91, 291, 295, 328, 511, 539-40

delivers Lloyd George's letter to WW, **44**: 222,n2, 237-38; and inter-Allied councils, **44**: 238, 369-70, 373-75, 385; **46**: 361n1, 415, 465-67; ambassadorship of, **45**: 454,n1, 457, 594; **48**: 95, 524-25; meetings with WW, **46**: 353-57; **47**: 116-17, 137, 138; **48**: 381, 391, 429-31, 453-54, 469; on WW's reaction to Supreme War Council's declaration, **46**: 390, 415, 419; on intervention in Russia, **46**: 470, 474, 475, 482, 506-507, 555, 561-62, 576, 605-606,n1; **47**: 78-82, 82, 170-71, 281-82, 299, 366-69, 417,n1, 436,n1, 440-41, 488-90, 496, 544, 605, 620-22; **48**: 37-38, 39, 40-41, 99-102, 112, 133-34, 202, 236, 285-86,n1, 333, 395, 429-31, 453-54, 470,

Reading, 1st Marquess of (*cont.*)
493-501, 511-14, 543-44, 565-66, 586-87, 587-88, 602-603; **49:** 36-37, 52, 67-69, 110-11, 302-303, 366-67; and critical need for U.S. troops in Europe, **47:** 181-83, 203-205, 213-14, 229-30, 256, 271, 280-81, 313, 314-15, 369-71, 373-76, 615; publicly reads Lloyd George's cable and angers WW, **47:** 185-86,n1, 206, 214; and British cable acknowledging U.S. help, **47:** 206, 214,n1; E. M. House on nervousness of, **47:** 215; and King George's message on anniversary of U.S. entry into war, **47:** 265; and G. Auchincloss, **47:** 308, 310, 313; and N. D. Baker on troop disposition, **47:** 386-88, 393-94, 455, 618; and Irish issue, **47:** 411-12, 575-76, 580, 582; on confusion between J. J. Pershing and F. Foch, **47:** 595; and Mexican situation, **47:** 552-53; **48:** 134-35; on request that House attend Supreme War Council meeting, **48:** 79, 135; on WW not sending agent to Vatican, **48:** 132-33; on Phillimore Report and league of nations, **48:** 501-502, 550; **49:** 14, 83, 265; on U.S. need for assistance with troop transport, **49:** 82-83; on U.S. change of attitude toward Britain, **49:** 453n1; W. Wiseman advises trip to London for, **49:** 455; on W. M. Hughes, **49:** 466; and postwar shipping plans, **49:** 473, 491; meets with T. H. Bliss in Paris, **49:** 535; and peace terms, **51:** 313-14, 324, 571, 594; on WW and Phillimore Report, **51:** 327n1; photograph, *illustration section,* **46**

Reading Holding Co., **40:** 102, 103
Real Colonel House (Smith), **47:** 310,n7, 534n1
Realpolitik in Russia (Howe), **48:** 241,n1
Reames, Clarence L., **44:** 405n1, 415, 492, 493; **51:** 249,n3, 311, 393
Rebel, The (Halletsville, Tex.), **43:** 165
Rebel at Large (Creel), **44:** 367n2
Rebels of the Woods: The I.W.W. in the Pacific Northwest (Tyler), **44:** 50n1; **46:** 144n1, 218n2
reconstruction, **51:** 146,n1; various plans, **51:** 207-208, 216,n1,2, 217n1, 217-18, 226,n2, 227, 229, 270; H. Hoover on Belgium and, **51:** 457-59; W. G. McAdoo on financial obligations and France, **51:** 465-67; to be considered at peace conference, **51:** 469; House on establishing international relief organization, **51:** 638-39; *see also,* postwar organization and security
Record of the Actual Accomplishments of the United States During Our First Year of War (*Scientific American*), **46:** 151n2
Record Publishing Co., Phila., **40:** 35n1
recruiting: *see* selective service
Red Cross: *see* American National Red Cross; American Red Cross Mission to Russia; International Committee of the Red Cross
Red Cross Magazine: The Official Publication of the American Red Cross, **43:** 455n3; **45:** 187,n1
Red Cross Society: and Sargent portrait of WW, **42:** 403-404
Red Terror, **51:** 4n2, 18n2, 61,n1, 62-63, 72n2; R. Lansing on, **51:** 642-43; petition urging WW to make statement against, **51:** 643-44
Redfield, Elise Mercein Fuller (Mrs. William Cox), **45:** 247
Redfield, William Cox, **40:** 188n1, 498; **41:** 282, 461, 506, 556; **42:** 134, 449; **43:** 35, 144, 177, 291; **44:** 10, 263; **45:** 148n1, 177, 272; **46:** 91, 117, 554, 581; **47:** 557; **48:** 303, 434, 444, 465; **49:** 71n1, 267, 394; **51:** 104, 217-18, 227, 270, 280, 412; and exchange with W. C. Adamson about pensions for Lighthouse Service, **40:** 95,n1, 163,n1, 182, 183, 218; on Alaska fisheries bill, **40:** 290-92,n1, 305-306, 366, 387,n1; on railway strike crisis, **41:** 409-11; advocates war entry, **41:** 439, 444; and antisubmarine barrier in North Sea, **42:** 220, 348, 358; on combined purchasing by U.S. and Allies, **42:** 256-57, 260; on shipbuilding program, **42:** 257; and war-risk insurance, **43:** 94; alleged statements on requisitioned ships by, **43:** 108,n1, 109-11, 116-17; and Trading With the Enemy Act, **43:** 281, 310, 311-12, 312-13, 316, 321-23; and Exports Council, **43:** 512,n2, 518, 519; **44:** 11, 11-12, 27-28; on using more women in labor force, **44:** 337-38, 359; on New York City's mayoralty, **44:** 458, 464; on prices and wages, **45:** 246-47, 256; sends WW birthday greetings, **45:** 380-81; on restricting exports and imports, **46:** 309; on truck transportation, **47:** 9; on aircraft production and Liberty Engine, **47:** 321-22; on U.S. commercial influence, **48:** 269; on public utilities, **49:** 159-62, 183, 184, 205, 218
Redmond, John Edward, **47:** 266-67,n2, 401n1
Reed, James Alexander, **41:** 24,n1, 359,n3; **42:** 505; **43:** 437,n3; **44:** 36, 37, 38; **45:** 16; **48:** 51, 115,n2; **49:** 224; **51:** 82,n2, 277n7; and prohibition, **41:** 311,n2; and woman suffrage, **45:** 279, 339; and sugar investigation, **45:** 344,n1, 352-53
Reed, John (Silas), **43:** 164, 165, 175, 187; **46:** 300,n7; **51:** 57n2; and *Masses* trial, **48:** 144,n1, 146-47,n1,4, 197-98, 208, 220, 251,n2
Reed Verner Zevola, **44:** 104,n1, 214, 497, 552; **45:** 121,n1, 122, 126, 127, 129, 350; **46:** 74, 134, 147
Regan, James B., **45:** 41,n1
Register of the Commissioned and Warrant Officers of the United States Navy

and Marine Corps, January 1, 1917,
    43: 182n2
Registration Day, **42:** 452-53, 514
Regnault, Eugène Louis Georges, **46:**
    46,n1, 474,n2, 476; **47:** 56,n1; **48:** 283n1
'Regularization' of Shops By a Business
    Individual (Hard), **40:** 315n1
Reid, Bill G., **51:** 103n3
Reid, Doris Fielding, **46:** 596,n2
Reid, Edith Gittings (Mrs. Harry Field-
    ing), **42:** 36; **46:** 596
Reid, Harry Fielding, **42:** 36; **46:** 596
Reid, Ogden Mills, **47:** 16,n3
Reid, Robert Threshie, Earl Loreburn,
    40: 139
Reinsch, Paul Samuel, **40:** 140, 160, 335,
    548; **41:** 38-39; **42:** 53, 468n1, 487n2;
    43: 55, 83n4, 457; **44:** 510, 530, 531,n2;
    45: 307, 308; **47:** 592-93; **48:** 72,n2, 335-
    36, 609; **49:** 294, 304; and Chinese fi-
    nances, **40:** 128, 436-38, 512, 514-15,
    563-64; **49:** 310, 311, 348; on China and
    European war, **41:** 175-79, 182-83, 185,
    186, 195, 229-30, 352, 382, 394, 401-
    402; **43:** 362-63; on deteriorating situ-
    ation in China, **46:** 331,n2; on Ameri-
    can role in Russia, **46:** 407,n1; **49:** 407-
    408; on international commission to
    China, **46:** 499, 595
Relief Committee for Greeks, **51:** 180-
    81,n1
Remington Arms Company, **47:** 378; **51:**
    24
Renaudel, Pierre, **51:** 565-66,n8, 566
Renner, Karl, **51:** 564n3
rent-profiteering resolution: *see* antiprof-
    iteering rent bill
Report of Committee on Aircraft Investi-
    gation Appointed March 15, 1918, **47:**
    509n1
*Report of the Proceedings of the Irish Con-
    vention,* **47:** 228n1
*Report of the 33rd Annual Lake Mohonk
    Conference on the Indian and Other De-
    pendent Peoples,* **48:** 36n1
Republican Club of New York, **42:** 29,n2
Republican National Committee, **40:**
    359n1; **41:** 165; **46:** 60, 566n2; **47:** 389,
    390,n2, 532; and woman suffrage, **45:**
    242-43
Republican party and Republicans, **40:**
    559; **42:** 29n2, 81; **43:** 35, 349-50; **44:**
    147, 153n1; **46:** 63n1, 518, 565-66,n2,
    602; **51:** 92n1, 117, 614; and Senate re-
    action to WW's Peace without Victory
    speech, **41:** 11n1, 12; and general leas-
    ing bill, **41:** 19; and Colombian treaty,
    41: 28; and plans for extra session of
    Congress, **41:** 282-83, 287,n1; and
    armed-ship bill, **41:** 327-28,n1, 350;
    and woman suffrage, **45:** 277-78, 338,
    542, 545; **46:** 60, 61, 608n1; **47:** 34, 572;
    48: 363; **51:** 117, 158, 189n1; and water-
    power legislation, **45:** 301; F. I. Cobb
    urges WW to work with sympathizers
    in, **45:** 340-41; and W. J. Stone's attack

on, **46:** 63n2; W. G. McAdoo on appoint-
    ments and, **46:** 111; and peace dele-
    gates, conference, and terms, **46:** 115;
    49: 267; **51:** 156n2, 277n7, 405, 423-24;
    and Chamberlain bills, **46:** 204-205;
    WW on, **46:** 264; **51:** 60; and Wisconsin
    senatorial race in 1918, **47:** 389-90,n2;
    A. W. Ricker on, **47:** 437-39; on postwar
    reconstruction, **47:** 532; E. Root and
    J. R. Mann on national loyalty above
    partisanship, **47:** 584n1,2; E. M. House
    on, **47:** 584; and revenue legislation,
    48: 128, 153; Negroes and, **48:** 155-56;
    and Nonpartisan League, **48:** 290; J. P.
    Tumulty on congressional campaign
    tactics of, **48:** 347-49; election to Con-
    gress of (1918), **51:** 293,n1, 305-306,
    590, 604n1, 612, 627-33; R. Ogden on,
    51: 297n1; WW's drafts and final ap-
    peal to voters, **51:** 317-18, 343, 353-54,
    381-82; G. B. Clarkson on, **51:** 459-60;
    C. W. Eliot on, **51:** 551,n1, 599-600;
    news advertisement urging defeat of,
    51: 572-74
Republican party in California, **51:**
    213n1
Republican party in Idaho, **49:** 145-46,
    147
Republican party in Kansas, **49:** 309,n3;
    51: 623-24
Republican party in Massachusetts, **44:**
    204-205
Republican party in Michigan, **49:**
    438,n2
Republican party in Minnesota, **47:** 54-
    55,n1
Republican party in Missouri, **49:** 235,
    444; **51:** 139
Republican party in Nebraska, **49:** 384
Republican party in New Mexico, **51:** 478
Republican party in Ohio, **49:** 510n2
Republican party in Oklahoma, **51:**
    444,n1
Republican party in Pennsylvania, **46:**
    611
Republican party in Tennessee, **51:** 482-
    83,n3
Republican Publicity Association, **51:**
    92n1
Republican Stones Thrown from Glass
    House (Hearst), **45:** 320,n1
Republicans Plan on Early Campaign
    (Penrose), **45:** 340,n1
Requa, Mark Lawrence, **47:** 404,n2; **49:**
    230; **51:** 114-15
Reshetar, John Stephen, **48:** 102n1
Resignation of Ex-President Taft as
    Head of Worlds Court (New York *Com-
    mercial and Financial Chronicle*), **41:**
    107
Resisting the Draft (Bryan), **44:** 54n1
*Resolution Relating to Certain Measures
    now Pending in Congress,* **47:** 399n1
Resolutions adopted at the Twenty-first
    Annual Convention of the American
    National Livestock Association at Salt

Resolutions adopted (*cont.*)
Lake City, Utah, January 14, 15, and 16, 1918, **46:** 386,n1
Restoration of Trade Union Conditions (Webb), **47:** 159,n1
Reuters Agency, **41:** 276; **44:** 457
Revel, Paolo Thaon di, **48:** 356, 385,n4
Revenue Act of 1916, **43:** 350n2
Revenue Act of 1917: **42:** 27; **44:** 121,n1, 280, 289, 291, 351; **48:** 122-23; **51:** 205; history and provisions of, **43:** 314-17, 350n2
Revenue Act of 1918, **51:** 108n9, 204-206; W. G. McAdoo on, **48:** 119,n2, 121-27, 128; **49:** 85-87; F. M. Simmons on, **48:** 153-54, 168-69,n1; WW's address to Congress on, **48:** 162-65, 167; support for, **49:** 103, 124-25, 134-35; J. P. Tumulty on, **49:** 162; R. C. Leffingwell and, **49:** 162-63,n1; WW on war-profits tax and, **49:** 163-64; A. Capper on farmers' views on, **49:** 232-34
Review of Reviews: see American Review of Reviews
Revised Memorandum on Cost of Producing Gasoline and Fuel Oil for Certain Companies Supplying the Navy, June—1917 (Federal Trade Commission), **44:** 444,n1
Revolution Administered: Agrarianism and Communism in Bulgaria (Oren), **51:** 563n1
Revolution in Russia (*Springfield*, Mass., *Republican*), **41:** 451n2
Revues Hommes et Mondes (Paris), **41:** 315n2; **48:** 441n1
Reynolds, George McClelland, **40:** 93
Reynolds, Lynn, **44:** 539
Rheem, L. M., **43:** 75n2
Rheims, France, **40:** 482
Rhett, Robert Goodwyn, **40:** 194,n2; **44:** 148-49,n1; **45:** 61-67, 265, 276, 299; **46:** 93
Rhine River, **51:** 262, 273, 455, 463, 470, 472
Rhoads, Charles J., **42:** 118-19,n1
Rhoades, Nelson Osgood, **48:** 279n5
Rhode Island: and woman suffrage, **47:** 399,n1, 414; politics in, **51:** 28, 537,n1, 590, 633
Rhodes, Charles Lincoln, **41:** 309n1
Rhondda, 1st Baron, David Alfred Thomas, **46:** 76n1, 77
Riaño y Gayangos, Don Juan, **40:** 323, 339n1, 353, 378-79; **41:** 219,n3, **46:** 467,n1; **47:** 177,n1
Ribot, Alexandre, **42:** 229n2, 320, 374-76, 425,n1, 433; **43:** 255, 273, 274; **44:** 24, 25, 548; **47:** 200
Ricardo, David, **44:** 262
Rice, Edwin Wilbur, Jr., **49:** 290,n3
Rice, Melvin Augustus, **40:** 174, 177; **42:** 458
Rice, William North, **43:** 85,n1,2
Richards, Charles Russell, **44:** 458,n1
Richardson, Mrs. Dee, **43:** 272-73,n1
Richardson, James Daniel, **45:** 250,n3

Richmond *Virginian,* **43:** 65n1
Rickard, Edgar, **48:** 629,n1,2,3; **49:** 104
Ricker, Allen [not Arthur] W., **43:** 381,n1, 382, 386, 396, 413, 480; **44:** 79; **47:** 471-72, 477,n1,2, 516; **48:** 16-17; on 1916 election and Nonpartisan League and Republican party, **47:** 437-39
Rickert, Thomas A., **47:** 223,n2, 252, 283
Ridder, Bernard Herman, **43:** 409, 410,n1, 411
Ridder, Herman, **43:** 410n1
Ridder, Victor, **44:** 154, 190
Riga, Russia (now Soviet Latvia), **44:** 180
Rigall, F. Edward, **42:** 273n1
Riggs, Elisha Francis, **51:** 53-54,n4, 55
Rihani, Ameen Fares, **45:** 4-5,n2
Rinehart, Mary Roberts (Mrs. Stanley Marshall), **44:** 232,n1
Riste, Olav, **45:** 74n2
Ritter, Gerhard, **48:** 555n7
Ritter, Paul, **40:** 7,n1, 42-46, 320-24, 348-54, 457-62; **41:** 102-107, 126, 172-73,n1; efforts to restore German-American relations, **41:** 201-203, 203-204, 204, 244, 245, 273-77
Riva-Agüero, Enrique de la, **40:** 164
Rivera, Luis Muños: *see* Muñoz Rivera, Luis
rivers and harbors bill, **40:** 422, 476; **41:** 198
Road to Peace (Bryan), **40:** 131,n1
Road to Safety: A Study in Anglo-American Relations (Willert), **40:** 262n1; **47:** 401n1
Roads Want Federal Aid (*New York Times*), **42:** 540n2
Robbins, Thomas, **42:** 457
Robert Brookings Graduate School of Economics and Government, **40:** 443n1
Robert College, Istanbul, **45:** 185n1, 207
Robert M. La Follette, June 14, 1855-June 18, 1925 (La Follette and La Follette), **46:** 348n1
Roberts, Albert S., **40:** 237,n1
Roberts, William Henry, **45:** 282,n1, 286
Robertson, Absolam Willis, **47:** 16,n7
Robertson, David Stephen, **47:** 592,n1
Robertson, Malcolm Arnold, **44:** 513,n1
Robertson, William Robert, **41:** 136,n1; **45:** 3,n1, 112, 151, 208; **46:** 8-9, 11, 43, 44, 162, 197, 211, 237, 240,n1, 353; **47:** 434, 465; resignation of, **46:** 351n3, 439; **47:** 12,n1, 13-14
Robilant, Mario Nicolis di, **47:** 571n1; **49:** 534; **51:** 203, 580
Robins, Raymond, **46:** 232,n1, 232-33, 300, 341, 408-409, 414; **47:** 239; **48:** 112-13, 141-42, 234, 353,n4, 489,n1; **49:** 54-55; **51:** 509, 558; WW on, **48:** 355-56; on proposed Russian relief commission and intervention, **48:** 489-90,n1
Robinson, Douglas Hill, **40:** 145n2
Robinson, Flora Lois, **45:** 158-59,n1, 214
Robinson, James, **49:** 327-28, 400
Robinson, Joseph C., **47:** 478,n2
Robinson, Joseph Taylor, **40:** 246, 278;

41: 156; **42:** 505; **43:** 84n1; **44:** 142n1; **46:** 204; **47:** 602-603; **48:** 9; and woman suffrage, **45:** 279, 338; and senatorial campaign of, **46:** 252-53, 258, 583
Robinson, Leonidas Dunlap, **45:** 307,n1
Robinson, Samuel Shelburne, **51:** 315,n5
Robles Domínguez, Alfredo: *see* Domínguez, Alfredo Robles
Robson, Herbert Thomas, **46:** 461,n1
Rochester, Edward Sudler, **43:** 3n1
Rochester, N.Y., **44:** 567
Rockefeller, John Davison, Jr., **47:** 539
Rockefeller Foundation, **41:** 113n3; **45:** 272n1
Rockford, Ill., **46:** 458, 560; **47:** 135
Rodgers, James Linn, **41:** 459
Rodman, Hugh, **49:** 69,n1, 137,n1
Rodney, William, **48:** 100n2
Rodzianko, Mikhail Vladimirovich, **41:** 409,n1; **45:** 229,n3; **49:** 220
Roe, Gilbert Ernstein, **43:** 165n2
Rogers, Elizabeth S. White (Mrs. John), **43:** 201n1
Rogers, Gustavus Adolphus, **51:** 535,n2
Rogers, Henry Huttleston, **43:** 367,n1
Rogers, James Edwin Thorold, **44:** 260,n3
Rogers, Ralph M., **42:** 426,n1
Rogers, W. H., **43:** 17-18,n7
Rogers, Walter Stowell, **42:** 275,n2; **43:** 456-59,n2; **47:** 276-77,n1; **51:** 409,n5
Rohaczev, Russia, **46:** 403
Rolfe, John, **42:** 58n1
Rolph, George Morrison, **45:** 344n1, 354
Roman Catholic Church, **40:** 407,n2; **41:** 434n2; **42:** 145; **43:** 40n1, 147, 216, 452; **44:** 19, 25, 37, 43, 302, 320, 330; **48:** 300,n3; **51:** 191, 548; WW on appointments and, **44:** 177; J. P. Tumulty and, **45:** 326; and Mexico, **46:** 406n2; and Irish issue, **47:** 228,n1,2, 238, 267, 444, 466, 469, 470; and *The Menace*, **49:** 169,n1, 174,n1; G. D. Herron on papal politics and league of nations, **49:** 187-93
Roman Holiday in Texas (*Nonpartisan Leader*), **47:** 521n1
Romantic Revolutionary: A Biography of John Reed (Rosenstone), **48:** 251n2
Romberg, Baron Gilbert von, **51:** 76n1, 91
Rome *Avanti*, **49:** 64
Romjue, Milton Andrew, **46:** 100,n1, 102-103
Roosevelt, Edith Kermit Carow (Mrs. Theodore), **46:** 287
Roosevelt, Franklin Delano, **41:** 215, 340; **42:** 449,n1, 457; **44:** 226, 227, 233, 302-303, 310; **45:** 8, 9, 10, 11; **46:** 171; **47:** 234, 297, 358n1; **49:** 106, 410-13; on arming mechant ships, **41:** 189, 189-90, 403; on mining North Sea, **44:** 464-67, 473; on carpenters' strike, **46:** 363-64; and gubernatorial candidacy, **48:** 356, 563-64; and naval terms, **51:** 486-87
Roosevelt, Quentin, **49:** death of, 37,n1, 50
Roosevelt, Theodore, **40:** 29, 31-32, 86, 117, 180, 185, 420, 468, 493, 541,

562n3, 565; **41:** 9, 63n1, 197, 293n1, 328, 423, 461n2; **42:** 56-57, 139, 230; **43:** 175n2, 372, 510; **44:** 85, 333n1, 394,n1, 410, 536n1; **45:** 71, 173, 186, 250, 320, 320-21, 325, 332n1, 341; **46:** 49n1, 54, 63n1, 68, 102,n1, 480, 566; **47:** 212, 303, 308, 471, 584, 616; **48:** 153, 630; **49:** 267, 442, 445; **51:** 147-48,n1, 225, 250, 297n1, 341, 521, 551n1, 572-73; desires to raise volunteer division, **41:** 469,n1, 469-70, 478, 501-502; **42:** 324, 325, 346, 356, 470; meetings with WW, **42:** 29,n1, 31-32n1; and Russian Commission, **42:** 287, 292; and woman suffrage, **46:** 60; W. J. Stone's attack on, **46:** 63,n2; A. C. Townley on, **46:** 160n2; hospitalized, **46:** 287,n1; death of Quentin, **49:** 37,n1, 50; on unconditional surrender, **51:** 331,n5, 455,n1
Roosevelt Hospital, N.Y., **46:** 287n1
Root, Elihu, **40:** 89; **41:** 250,n3, 251, 498; **42:** 6, 29,n2, 267, 289, 530, 551; **43:** 15,n2, 414, 416n1, 439, 459, 510; **44:** 15-16, 27, 66, 68, 69, 94n1, 142n1, 177, 281, 299n2; **45:** 191, 341; **46:** 49n1, 116, 518, 519, 530, 574, 575; **47:** 102, 105, 137, 323, 584,n1; **48:** 561; **49:** 12; **51:** 109; and appointment to Russian Commission, **42:** 45n3, 80, 95, 124-25, 126, 152, 154, 177, 194, 216, 216-17, 238,n2,3, 239, 240, 262, 560n1; suggested as special envoy to Japan, **42:** 244; and peace commission, **49:** 267, 286; on league of nations and postwar security, **49:** 269-72; G. Kennan on, **49:** 320-21; and Permanent Court of Arbitration appointment, **49:** 540-51,n1; photograph, *illustration section,* **46**
Root, Robert Kilburn, **42:** 291
Root and Van Dervoort Engineering Company of East Moline, Ill., **46:** 578n2
Root Mission: *see* Russian Commission
Root-Takahira Agreement, **42:** 245; **43:** 81,n1, 82; **44:** 377, 413-14, 418
Roper, Daniel Calhoun, **41:** 379; **42:** 448; **49:** 438-39, 461, 498
Rosales, Maximo, **41:** 143
Rose, Hans, **40:** 388-89
Rose, John Holland, **48:** 501n1
Rosen, Roman Romanovich, **41:** 416,n3; **42:** 381n9
Rosenbaum, Herman S., **45:** 157n1
Rosenbaum, Sol G., **45:** 157,n1
Rosenbaum, William, **45:** 157n1
Rosenberg, Arthur, **51:** 253n2
Rosenberg, Emily S., **47:** 357n1
Rosenburg, A. H., **42:** 557
Rosenstone, Robert Allan, **48:** 251n2
Rosenwald, Julius, **42:** 449; **43:** 148n1, 177, **46:** 563; **47:** 539; **49:** 78
Roskill, Stephen, **42:** 327n2
Rosner, Ignace, **46:** 403
Rosov, Israel Benjamin, **45:** 572,n2
Ross, Edward Alsworth, **47:** 427,n2; **48:** 450-51,n1, 457, 485, 590; **49:** 78; on

Ross, Edward Alsworth (*cont.*)
methods of helping Russia, **48:** 570-73,n1
Ross, Isaac Nelson, **51:** 168n1, 193
Rostankowski, Peter, **41:** 508
Rostov, Russia, **46:** 421n3
Roth, Georges, **47:** 421,n1
Rothschild, 2nd Baron Rothschild, Lionel Walter, **45:** 149,n2
Rouaix, Pastor, **49:** 140,n3
Roumania: *see* Rumania
Rouse, Arthur Blythe, **51:** 301,n1, 302
Roussos, George, **43:** 269,n4; **51:** 180n1, 268
Rowan, James, **43:** 494; **44:** 50,n1
Rowe, Leo Stanton, **43:** 12; **48:** 209,n1, 278
Royden, Thomas, **43:** 10,n3, 46, 105, 141, 285-87, 287-90
Roye, France, **51:** 421
Rubel, Lawrence, **47:** 207n1
Rubin, William Benjamin, **48:** 438n1, 439
Rublee, George, **40:** 417; **41:** 45-49; **43:** 49,n5, 425; **51:** 223,n6, 422
Rublee, Juliet Barrett (Mrs. George), **51:** 184,n5
Rucker, William Waller, **41:** 357,n1; **46:** 614,n2; **47:** 3n1
Ruckstall, G. E., **43:** 502,n1
Ruddock, Albert Billings, **40:** 555,n2
Ruddock, Margaret Kirk (Mrs. Albert Billings), **40:** 555,n2
Rudin, Harry Rudolph, **51:** 621n1
Rudwick, Elliott M., **43:** 103n1
Ruggles, James A., **47:** 140-41,n1; **48:** 96,n3, 263,n1; **51:** 53,n5
Ruiz, Leopoldo, **46:** 406n2
Rule, Henry, **43:** 254,n3
Rules and Regulations Governing Licenses for the Importation, Manufacture and Refining of Sugar, Sugar Syrups and Molasses (Hoover), **44:** 247n1
Rules Committee (House of Reps.), **40:** 349n11, 419; **41:** 358; **42:** 43; **43:** 71n1, 222n2; **45:** 300, 301, 335n1, 406; **47:** 72, 474n1; **48:** 45n1; and woman suffrage, **42:** 269, 270, 320-21,n1, 474, 475; and water-power bill, **49:** 316, 329
Rules Committee (Senate), **45:** 379; **46:** 606,n1
Rumania, **40:** 21, 69, 144, 185, 204, 231, 234, 239, 317, 361, 435, 441, 484, 496, 540, 555; **41:** 61, 89, 138, 211, 212, 221, 300; **42:** 156, 327n1, 333, 334, 425n1, 444n1, 501; **43:** 268, 371, 414,n1, 460n1, 524; **44:** 4, 20, 196-97, 476; **45:** 73, 312, 412, 418, 419; **46:** 187, 198n2, 388, 533, 568, 576, 590, 605-606; **47:** 122, 240,n1, 450-51,n1, 474,n2, 590; **48:** 27, 100n2, 436; **49:** 142, 436n1; **51:** 587; C. Vopicka incident, **40:** 554n1; Queen Marie's plea for U.S. aid, **43:** 95; and loans, **44:** 282; and peace terms, **45:** 459, 470, 473; **51:** 47, 163, 256, 262, 263, 264, 274, 420, 502; and Fourteen

Points, **45:** 479, 484, 514, 528, 538, 553-54; and British war aims statement, **45:** 487n2; comparison of G. Hertling's and O. Czernin's views on, **46:** 224, 228; King Ferdinand's financial problems, **46:** 235,n1, 326; and Diamandi incident, **46:** 300,n8; R. Lansing on, **46:** 373-75; and Russia, **46:** 420,n2; and Jews, **51:** 625-26
Rumbold, Sir Horace George Montagu, **42:** 455,n1, 544,n3; **44:** 514,n1; **45:** 255,n1; **46:** 577,n2
Rumeley, Edward Aloysius, **42:** 22,n2, 237n4; **43:** 134n2
Runciman, Sir Walter (1847-1937), **42:** 379n3
Runciman, Walter (1870-1949), **42:** 379,n3, 380, 381; **45:** 175
Rupprecht, Crown Prince of Bavaria (Maria Luitpold Ferdinand von Wittelsbach), **48:** 387-88,n1, 553,n4; **49:** 229
Russel, Nicholas, **49:** 322,n5
Russell, Charles Edward, **42:** 289; **43:** 424, 456, 530, 537, 538; **44:** 557-58, 558; **45:** 167n1, 191, 371; **48:** 375-76,n1, 492; and St. Louis Resolution, **42:** 148n1, 198; and appointment to Russian Commission, **42:** 204, 240, 252, 259, 262, 267, 280; and international socialist conference, **42:** 268, 269, 350-51
Russell, Isaac K., **51:** 49-50,n1
Russell, Winter, **44:** 79
Russell Sage Foundation, **41:** 505, 527
Russia, **40:** 5n2, 15, 16, 35n3, 39, 160, 161, 204, 231, 234, 239, 250, 307n1, 357, 361, 388, 404, 416, 435, 441, 446, 452, 453, 494, 495, 496, 503-504, 527, 528, 540; **41:** 26n1, 62, 80, 162, 184, 219, 220, 221, 347, 408n2, 409, 426, 440, 464, 518, 527, 553; **42:** 104, 157, 173, 275, 381, 435, 436; **43:** 57, 95, 255, 269, 394, 395, 402, 409, 413, 464 471, 487; **44:** 34, 125, 132, 167, 179-80, 201, 271, 282, 297, 350, 361n1, 367,n2, 379, 389, 547; **45:** 184-85, 190, 372; **46:** 257n1; **51:** 47, 256

treatment of German prisoners in, **40:** 212n1, 213; Uniates in, **40:** 407,n2; and American loan to China, **40:** 514, 515; S. N. Harper on, **41:** 415-17; and U.S. recognition of Provisional Government, **41:** 422-23, 457,n1, 461, 544; C. R. Crane on, **41:** 493,n1; **42:** 232; **43:** 13-14; **49:** 154; and Trans-Siberian Railway, **41:** 511; WW on new democracy in, **41:** 552; Germany and, **42:** 11-12, 36-37, 389n4, 502, 503; **47:** 524; **49:** 197; **51:** 602; Jews in, **42:** 113, 115, 164-65,n2, 463-64; **45:** 572; antiwar demonstrations in, **42:** 218-19,n2, 232; agreements with Allies, **42:** 327n1; A. J. Balfour on, **42:** 328-29, 335, 337-38; and Poland and Polish Army, **42:** 352, 432, 491-94; **43:** 37-38; **44:** 4-6 **46:**

48-49, 121, 123; and separate peace with Germany, **43:** 28n1; **45:** 73, 147, 151, 166n1, 188-89,n1, 193, 196, 216, n1, 312, 384,n2, 411-14, 418, 432n1, 433-35, 446-47, 572; **46:** 471n3, 585-86,n2; and Asia Minor, **43:** 355; transportation problems in, **43:** 369-72; H. L. Scott on, **43:** 414,n1; "July Days," **43:** 474,n1; D. Lloyd George on war plans and, **44:** 126; L. G. Kornilov's attempted coup, **44:** 216,n1; R. Lansing and J. J. Jusserand discuss situation in, **44:** 297-98; comments on crisis and civil strife, **44:** 387, 532; **45:** 104-105, 191-93, 228-29, 250-53, 263-65, 271, 274-75, 282-83, 288-95, 442-47, 574-75, 575-76; and Japan, **44:** 494-95; **45:** 336, 347, 370, 393; **46:** 539,n1; **48:** 360, 478, 541; C. E. Russell on, **44:** 557-58; and inter-Allied conference, **45:** 166n1; and Great Britain, **45:** 188-89, 312-13, 418, 420, 487n2, 548, 549; **49:** 250n1; Trotsky-Judson exchange on separate peace, **45:** 216-18,n4; Trotsky's declaration on Brest-Litovsk negotiations, **45:** 411-14; and Allied policy agreed to at Paris conference, **45:** 417-19; W. J. Bryan on, **45:** 599; Constituent Assembly dissolved by Bolsheviks, **46:** 46n3, 53, 232; P. Scheidemann on, **46:** 113, n2, 188; as inspiration for strikes in Germany and Austria-Hungary, **46:** 184-85; O. Czernin and G. Hertling on, **46:** 193, 222-28, 274-77; Semenov expedition, **46:** 220-21,n2; and Diamandi incident, **46:** 300,n8; W. E. Walling on, **46:** 310-12; Sisson Documents, **46:** 341, n1, 372,n1,3; and resolution of Inter-Allied Council on War Purchases and Finance, **46:** 359-60; and Rumania, **46:** 420,n2; movements for autonomy in Siberia, **47:** 92,n1,2, 357, 397-99, 591-94; and Czech troops, **47:** 513-14,n7, 551-52, 565; and woman suffrage, **48:** 27 *intervention in*: comments on intervention, **48:** 37-40, 40-41, 61, 96n3, 99-102, 102-104, 112-14, 194-95, 202,n1, 203-204, 283-84, 288, 297-98, 364-65, 375-76, 414-15, 415, 449-50, 489-90,n1, 505, 511-14, 523, 625-27

M. Summers on divergent trends in, **48:** 96,n1; D. R. Francis on, **48:** 141-43; W. C. Bullitt on, **48:** 144-45; Red Cross in, **48:** 234; cooperative societies in, **48:** 359-60,n1; L. Colcord on Brest-Litovsk treaty, **48:** 576-77; France will not abandon, **49:** 123-24; Soviet forces enter China, **49:** 284; and Supreme War Council's note on military policy and, **51:** 201-202; and peace terms and Fourteen Points, **51:** 262, 263, 264, 274, 350-51, 498, 499, 508-10; T. H. Bliss on U.S. policy and, **51:** 426-27; Bolshevik and German terrorism, **51:** 542-43; Austria-Hungary wishes to keep troops in Ukraine, **51:** 616-17, 617

Murmansk and Archangel, intervention in: **46:** 451-52, 555; **48:** 384n1, 481n1; **49:** 495,n6, 518,n5; Great Britain urges U.S. to support, **47:** 62, 356, 367-68, 503-505, 606-608; **48:** 37-38, 206-208, 388; British troops land at Murmansk, **47:** 140-41; and sending of U.S. vessel to, **47:** 226-27, 246, 263, 290,n1; T. H. Bliss on Supreme War Council's views on, **47:** 333, 513-14,n7; **49:** 530-32; J. Noulens urges Allied intervention, **47:** 431-32; Bolsheviks may ask British troops to leave, **47:** 544; R. Lansing on, **47:** 605, 621-22; distinction between Siberian intervention and, **48:** 37-38, 73, 134; R. H. B. Lockhart on, **48:** 101, 103, 380; T. H. Bliss on, **48:** 181, 401-403, 577, 599-602; **51:** 52-53, 337, 426-27; WW on, **48:** 182, 204, 626, 641-42; **51:** 50-51, 75, 85, 121-22, 139, 140-41; U.S. willing to send troops to, if Foch approves, **48:** 236, 285,n1, 286, 330-31; French views on, **48:** 239; Supreme War Council on, **48:** 285-86,n3, 330-31; G. T. M. Bridges on WW and, **48:** 353; Foch's recommendations regarding, **48:** 396-97; P. C. March on, **48:** 419, 420; people of Archangel resent English there, **48:** 478; A. J. Balfour on Supreme War Council's resolution supporting, **48:** 496, 498, 501; Gen. Poole at, **48:** 536-37; **49:** 285-86, 448, 508, 516, 518-19; Reading on WW's views on, **48:** 565; N. D. Baker and WW on sending troops, **49:** 43-44, 52, 57; and U.S. purpose and policy, **49:** 171, 506-507; Lansing on, **49:** 492-93; Lansing on keeping Col. Stewart informed of policy on, **49:** 517-18; W. Wiseman on Gen. Poole and, **51:** 8-9; request for more U.S. troops, **51:** 17, 33, 52-55, 85; and resolution of Murmansk Region Council, **51:** 79,n1; T. G. Masaryk and Gen. Janin and, **51:** 95n2, 96-97,n2; G. V. Chicherin on, **51:** 556 *Siberia, intervention in*: **46:** 451-52, 530-31; **47:** 82, 206, 224,n1,2, 513,n7; **48:** 37-38, 73, 419,n1, 479-80, 481n1, 609n1; **49:** 42-43; **51:** 95n2; Japanese policy toward, **46:** 35, 41, 46-47, 118, 221, 407n1, 571-72, 574, 584-85, 604-605; **47:** 77-78; **48:** 495-96, 499, 639; **49:** 75, 75-76, 96, 107-109, 110, 149, 175-76,n1, 178-79; British policy toward, **46:** 154-55, 182, 270-71, 302-303, 340, 470-71, 472, 547-48, 576-77, 605-606, 620; **48:** 333, 378-79; **49:** 58-60; E. M. House on, **46:** 214, 445, 518-19, 519, 530, 532, 597; U.S. policy on, **46:** 219-20, 236, 248, 250, 301-302, 302-303, 303-304, 339-41, 498-99, 506-507, 508, 531, 544,n1; **47:** 91-92, 106, 131-32, 605, 620-22; **48:** 542-43, 559-60, 574-75, 578, 586-87, 621-22; **49:** 278, 332,n2, 345, 448, 506-507; **51:** 598, 618; France on, **46:** 339-40, 388-89, 451-52, 471; **47:** 14-15, 20-23, 55-57, 282, 318-

Russia (*cont.*)
21, 430-32, 472-73, 585-86; **48:** 131-32,
179-80, 202, 254, 273-74, 288, 317,n2,
352-53,n1, 355, 441-43,n1, 621-22; and
Russian Railway Service Corps, **46:**
344n2; Reading on WW on, **46:** 355,
482; **47:** 440-41; Supreme War Council
on, **46:** 391; **47:** 59-61, 333, 422-24, 491-
92; **48:** 496-501, 503-506; **51:** 202; T. H.
Bliss on, **46:** 391-92; R. Lansing on, **46:**
474-76; **48:** 104; **49:** 323,n1; W. C. Bullitt memorandum on, **46:** 510-13; Russian embassy protests, **46:** 513-15; cabinet discusses issue of, **46:** 515;
B. Long's memorandum on, **46:** 527-30;
W. V. Judson memorandum on, **46:**
533-37, 537-40; S. Miles memorandum
on, **46:** 540-44; WW on, **46:** 545, 547,
550-51, 551, 553, 594-95; **48:** 133-34,
182, 285,n1, 421,n1, 432-34, 470, 542-
43, 544; **51:** 25-26, 50-51, 85, 121-22,
139, 140-41, 152-53, 188, 209-10;
House and Reading meet on, **46:** 561-
62; Japan on, **46:** 571-72, 584-85; **47:**
77-78; **48:** 495-96, 499, 639; **49:** 75, 75-
76, 96, 107-109, 110, 149, 175-76,n1,
178-79; Wiseman on WW's and House's
attitudes toward, **46:** 248, 530-31, 590-
91; **47:** 35-36; 503-504; **51:** 8; Britain
presses U.S. to support, **47:** 61-63, 78-
82, 156-57, 170-71, 239, 243-44, 299,
355-57, 366-69, 412, 417n1, 436,n1,
472-73, 606-608; U.S. public opinion
on, **47:** 67-69; A. M. Knight on, **47:** 69-
71, 92,n1,2, 162,n2

on Germany and, **47:** 97-99, 100-101,
131-32, 171, 398-99, 459, 590-91; and
protection of British and Japanese munitions and supplies, **47:** 162,n2, 242-
43; Trotsky's willingness to accept Allied forces encourages Britain, **47:** 245-
46, 412, 436,n1; Japan and Britain
land forces, **47:** 263,n1, 281-82,n1, 299;
Ishii's meetings with Lansing, WW
and Reading on, **47:** 459-61, 472-73,
488-90, 496; Wiseman on four courses
for Allied action, **47:** 503-505; P. S.
Reinsch on, **47:** 592-93; G. Kennan advocates Japan and U.S. cooperate in,
48: 185-87; comments on WW's attitude toward and opposition to, **48:** 202,
254, 273-74, 315, 316, 421n1;
L. Browne against, **48:** 299; proposed
Russian relief commission and, **48:**
305-306, 429-31, 432-34; proposed Allied plans for Japan's involvement in,
48: 383-84,n3; A. I. Konovalov on, **48:**
406-10; W. T. Ellis on, **48:** 412; and
weather, **48:** 416, 446, 589; P. C. March
opposed to Japanese, **48:** 419-21; Foch
recommends immediate action, **48:**
445-46; Allies on effect of Japan's involvement on U.S. commitment, **48:**
430-31, 448-49,n1; S. Gotō on Japan
and, **48:** 461-62; M. Bochkareva's views

on, **48:** 469,n1, 473; C. T. Williams on
need for joint action, **48:** 478-79; Czechs
take Vladivostok, **48:** 544; British concern over public opinion, **48:** 566-67;
E. A. Ross on, **48:** 572-73; J. F. Abbott
on Japanese, **48:** 581-85; D. Lloyd
George on, **48:** 587-89; **49:** 9-11; Gen.
A. Knox and, **48:** 602-603; Italy and,
48: 637; **49:** 4, 21; WW's aide-mémoire
on U.S. policy, **48:** 624-27, 641-42; news
reports that Japan accepted U.S. proposal on, **49:** 5,n1; comments on U.S.
decision, **49:** 36-37, 52, 57-58, 67-69,
91-93, 97; U.S. press statement, **49:** 37-
39, 39-40, 51, 53, 170-72, 179, 211,n1,
278; W. Kent discourages idea of, **49:**
55; J. J. Jusserand on, **49:** 91-93, 124,
127-28; H. Bergson meets with WW on,
49: 94-96, 112-13; comments on need
for more troops, **49:** 261-62, 282-84,
345, 373, 532; effect on Anglo-American relations, **49:** 302-303, 366-67, 550-
51; WW meets with Ishii on, **51:** 548-
51; G. V. Chicherin on, **51:** 556; W. S.
Graves on, **51:** 608-609: *see also* Russian Revolution; Bolsheviks; Russia
and the United States; Czech troops in
Russia; Vladivostok

Russia (Wallace), **42:** 393n3
Russia and Peace (*Springfield*, Mass., *Republican*), **41:** 451n2
Russia and the United States, **43:** 37n1,
98, 124, 126, 136, 149-50, 248-49, 386-
87, 389, 522; **44:** 556, 558; **45:** 119, 151-
52, 165, 176, 235, 316, 339, 368, 369-70;
46: 301; and Polish Falcons, **42:** 11-12,
60; on separate peace efforts, **42:** 36-37,
141, 268, 318, 360-64, 418-19, 434, 463;
46: 585-86,n2; WW and J. H. Whitehouse discuss, **42:** 67; and WW's message to Provisional Government, **42:**
109-10,n2, 319, 320, 326, 365-67,
385,n1, 458-59,n1,2, 466-67, 487; Russia's sense of exclusion from conferences, **42:** 165, 176-78; R. Lansing's
comments on, **42:** 176-77; **45:** 205-207,
263-65, 427-30, 562-64; **51:** 642-43;
WW declines to meet former Russian
ambassador, **42:** 236-37; and U.S. effort
to set up publicity agency in Russia, **42:**
252-53,n1,2,3, 258, 267, 284-85, 289,
377, 378, 508-509; **43:** 15n2, 460n1; **44:**
67-68, 90n1, 270,n1, 424,n1, 434, 435,
435-36; **45:** 194, 367-68, 387, 474, 543-
44; **46:** 407,n1, 479; **47:** 522; **48:** 449-50;
and Mooney case, **42:** 271-72, 273,n1;
44: 246n1, 267, 290n1; Russia's an-
nouncement of war aims and peace
terms, **42:** 420-22; and Great Britain,
42: 463-65, 527, 529-30,n2, 551-52; **43:**
20, 159n2; militant suffragists greet
Russian commission, **42:** 560,n1; and
financial situation, **43:** 66, 67, 68,
140n2, 225; **44:** 281; WW's greetings to
new ambassador, **43:** 100-101; and proposed Allied conferences on war objec-

tives, **43:** 255, 388, 407; and Russian railways, **43:** 370-72; **46:** 344,n1, 357, 358, 387; C. E. Russell on, **43:** 456-57; Russia's assurances to Allies, **43:** 473-74, 474-75; and Pope's peace appeal and WW's reply, **44:** 22, 41, 181; WW's message to President of National Council Assembly and acknowledgement, **44:** 38, 91-92; and labor, **44:** 483-84; suggestion of sending U.S. troops to, **44:** 494-95, 496-97; L. R. Colcord on, **45:** 222n1; **48:** 546-49; and U.S. aid, **45:** 322; and passport issue, **45:** 342,n3; and Inquiry memorandum, **45:** 465, 467; and Fourteen Points, **45:** 483, 506-10, 512-13, 519, 520, 522, 526, 534-35, 535-36, 537, 553, 596-97; B. Miles on, **45:** 543-45; and issue of recognition, **46:** 22,n1, 45-46,n3, 65-66, 233, 299-300, 485; S. Gompers on, **46:** 39; WW will not meet with W. B. Thompson, **46:** 160-61, 179-80, 193,n1; and replacement for W. V. Judson, **46:** 179,n1; and R. Robins, **46:** 232,n1, 232-33, 408-409, 414; J. S. Williams advocates "watchful waiting," **46:** 287; W. E. Walling on, **46:** 311; and Sisson Documents, **46:** 341-42n1; **51:** 3-4; S. Strunsky on, **46:** 422n1; WW's message to Fourth All-Russia Congress of Soviets **46:** 598; **47:** 79,n2; comments on WW's message of support to Russians, **46:** 611, 619; **47:** 12; WW on B. Long's memorandum on, **47:** 18; and YMCA, **47:** 304-305; WW intends to stand by Russia, **48:** 54, 134, 256-57; and Bolshevik request for recall of U.S. consul, **47:** 544; and U.S. preemptive purchase of supplies needed by Germany, **48:** 236, 247, 262-63; Bolsheviks' plan to send representative to Washington, **48:** 264-65, 276; W. C. Redfield on U.S. commercial influence, **48:** 269; U.S. policy on recognition in event of Bolshevik collapse, **48:** 276-77,n1, 277-78; memorial urging U.S. to intervene in Russia, **48:** 375-76,n2; E. M. House on, **48:** 390; WW on W. F. Morgan's plan for Russian exiles, **48:** 472; and M. Tereshchenko, **49:** 175,n1, 312,n1; F. L. Polk on Russian diplomatic missions in Rumania and Spain, **49:** 142; question of Russia as neutral or belligerent, **49:** 185n1, 238-39, 247-48; U.S. opposition to Red Terror, **51:** 62-63, 78,n2, 643-44; and Russian Bureau, Inc., **51:** 104n4; WW on U.S. military policy, **51:** 121-22, 139; D. R. Francis' plan for Slavic American legion, **51:** 178,n1,2; G. V. Chicherin on, **51:** 508-10, 555-61; *see also* Russian Commission; Russian Railroad Commission; Czech troops in Russia

Russia Expiring under Reds' Rule (Williams), **46:** 411n1

Russia from the American Embassy,

April, 1916-November, 1918 (Francis), **49:** 495n6

Russia I Believe In: The Memoirs of Samuel N. Harper, 1902-1941 (P. Harper, ed.), **41:** 415n1, 417n14; **43:** 150n2

Russia in Upheaval (Ross), **48:** 570,n1

Russia Leaves the War (Kennan), **44:** 367n2; **45:** 217n5, 411n1; **46:** 22n1, 46n3, 300n7,8, 341n1,4, 372n3, **47:** 79n2, 440n1

Russian-American Relations, March, 1917-March, 1920: Documents and Papers (Cumming and Pettit, eds.), **48:** 142n6

Russian Americans, **44:** 39; **47:** 68

Russian Bureau: A Case Study in Wilsonian Diplomacy (Killen), **51:** 104n4

Russian Bureau, Inc., **51:** 104n4

Russian Commission (Root Commission), **42:** 141, 350, 351; **43:** 424, 460n1, 526-30; **44:** 15-16, 27, 39, 66-67, 94, 142n1, 143; **45:** 191, 283, 288; **49:** 320-21; appointment suggestions for, **42:** 30, 36-37, 43-44, 45,n1,2,3, 58, 80-81, 95, 111, 124-25, 143-44,n1, 152, 154, 164-65, 166-67, 194-95, 197, 204, 215-16, 216-17, 222, 239, 240, 252, 253-55,n2,3, 259, 262, 263, 287-88, 378; WW informs Russia of, **42:** 177-78, 365, 366-69; prepares to leave, **42:** 178, 179, 262, 281; relationship to Stevens Commission, **42:** 238,n2,3, 239; and work in Russia, **43:** 13-14, 15,n1,2, 101, 106, 165n2; meets with WW, **43:** 416n1

Russian Empire, 1801-1917 (Seton-Watson), **43:** 455n3

Russian Far Eastern Committee, **47:** 594

Russian Information Bureau, New York, **44:** 483,n1

Russian Orthodox Church, **40:** 407n2

Russian Provisional Government, 1917: Documents (Browder and Kerensky, eds.), **42:** 418n2

Russian Railroad Commission (Stevens Commission), **42:** 222, 238,n2,3, 239; **43:** 387, 424; **49:** 396n1; report of, **43:** 439, 440-43, 459-60

Russian Railway Service Corps, **46:** 344,n1, 357, 358, 387, 393; **47:** 106,n4; **51:** 549, 598

Russian Relief Commission: *see* Commission on relief in Russia

Russian Revolution, **41:** 409, 415-17, 425, 429, 438, 440, 441, 445, 451n2, 461, 466, 481, 513, 524; **42:** 44, 141, 232, 263, 435; **43:** 275, 278, 454n1, 455,n2, 474; **44:** 557, 558; **45:** 414, 464, 543, 544; **46:** 541, 545; G. Kennan on, **48:** 183-87; and Czech legion, **48:** 335-36,n1; W. Ellis on, **48:** 411; E. A. Ross on meaning of, **48:** 570-71; *see also* Bolsheviks

Russian Revolution (Slobodin), **44:** 39n1

Russian Revolution, 1917-1921 (Chamberlin), **42:** 218n2, 418n1; **43:** 474n1; **44:** 180n3, 216n1; **46:** 421n3; **49:** 349;

Russian Revolution, 1917-1921 (cont.)
  51: 4n2, 100n2, 102n1
Russian Union, **48:** 472n1
Russia's Agony (Wilton), **48:** 187n5
Russia's Dual Government (Kennan), **48:** 183n2
Russo-Japanese War, **42:** 329; **43:** 455n3; **48:** 478
Ruthenians, **44:** 5; **45:** 471
Ryan, Frank M., **40:** 176,n1, 177,n1; **43:** 513n1,2; **47:** 179n3, 212, 219; sentence commuted, **47:** 232,n1,2
Ryan, John Dennis, **46:** 91-92, 111,n2; **47:** 509, 526, 545, 558-59,n1; **48:** 74; **49:** 349; **51:** 408; appointed chairman of Aircraft Board, **47:** 436, 437, 494, 501
Ryan, Thomas Fortune, **40:** 89
Rye, Thomas Clark, **46:** 381,n4; **47:** 6n2
Ryerson, Martin Antoine, **40:** 444,n2

Saavedra, Rodrigo de: *see* Villalobar, Marquis de
Sabath, Adolph Joseph: on prohibition, **48:** 376-77
Sabine, Wallace Clement Ware, **44:** 540,n2
Sabotage Act, **47:** 364,n2, 381
Sack, Arkady Jack, **43:** 455n3; **44:** 483,n1; **48:** 183n2
Sackville-West, Charles John, **47:** 565-66,n1, 568, 571; **51:** 203
Sacramento, Ca., **47:** 196,n4,5, 479
Sacramento Bee, **47:** 196,n5
Sadeleer, Etienne de, **47:** 324n1
Sadeleer, Louis de, **47:** 324
Sadoul, Jacques, **47:** 319n6; **48:** 113,n2; **51:** 509
Sagamore, S.S., **44:** 159
Saida, S.M.S., **51:** 492
St. Clair, Labert, **49:** 99n1
St. Clair, Leonard Pressley, **45:** 350n1
St. Elizabeth's Hospital, Washington, D.C., **44:** 559n5; **48:** 78, 129
Saint-Gaudens, Augustus, **44:** 536n1
St. James, Minn., **47:** 235
St. John, Irwin, **44:** 79
St. John's Protestant Episcopal Church, Washington, D.C., **40:** 354n1, 383
St. Louis, Mo., **42:** 85; **43:** 323
St. Louis, S.S., **41:** 184, 188,189, 377
St. Louis *Globe-Democrat*, **43:** 323-24,n2
St. Louis Labor, **43:** 165
St. Louis Platform: *see* Democratic Platform, 1916
St. Louis Post-Dispatch, **42:** 245,n3; on prohibition, **49:** 476
St. Louis Proclamation (or Resolutions), **42:** 148n1, 197n1, 199, 253, 274
St. Louis *Republic*, **49:** 61,n1, 370-71
St. Louis Union Bank, **43:** 197
St. Louis Women's Club, **41:** 458
St. Mary's School, Raleigh, N.C., **40:** 570n6
St. Mihiel, France, **51:** 3n1, 385
St. Nazaire, France, **43:** 79n1, **45:** 108
St. Omer, France, **48:** 389

St. Patrick's Church, Washington, D.C., **40:** 113
St. Paul, Minn., **47:** 178; **49:** 181; and Twin City Rapid Transit Co. strike, **45:** 258-62, 279, 331; **47:** 189-91, 272-74
St. Paul's American Church, Rome, Italy, **46:** 105n1
St. Paul's Cathedral, London, **42:** 112
St. Paul's Cathedral of Fond du Lac, Wisc., **44:** 302n1
St. Peter's Church, San Francisco, **43:** 216n1
St. Quentin, France, **51:** 215, 421
St. Thomas, V.I., **41:** 362
Salem Methodist Episcopal Church of New York, **43:** 412n2; **46:** 339n1
sales tax, **41:** 448n2
Salis, John Francis Charles, Count de, **44:** 23,n2, 347-48,n3
Salisbury, 3d Marquess of: *see* Cecil, Robert Arthur Talbot Gascoyne-
Salisbury, 4th Marquess of: *see* Cecil, James Edward Hubert Gascoyne-
Salonika, **40:** 454; **43:** 269; **45:** 6,n5, 459-60; **47:** 513; **49:** 404; **51:** 45, 162
Saloutos, Theodore, **49:** 441n7
Salt Lake City, Utah, **44:** 294; **46:** 432n2
Salter, James Arthur, **43:** 11,n4, 46, 141, 285-87, 287-90
Saltillo, Mex., **49:** 34
Saltonstall, John Lee, **46:** 429,n2
Salvation Army, **49:** 425-26; **51:** 636
Samalayuca, Mex., **40:** 101
Samara, Russia, **47:** 304n1, 424; **48:** 180; **51:** 50n1, 84, 95n2, 556
Samperio, Telesforo, **49:** 542,n1
Samson and Good Samaritan: Address . . . To be Delivered December 11, 1916 (J. S. Williams), **40:** 202,n2
Samuel Gompers: A Biography (Mandel), **44:** 47n1
San Antonio *Light*, **49:** 73n1
San Francisco, **43:** 216, 253-54; and Mooney case, **42:** 270n2, 271, 273n1; **44:** 290,n1, 307; **46:** 68-74
San Francisco *Blast*, **44:** 290n1
San Francisco *Bulletin*, **42:** 272n10; **45:** 382n1; **46:** 519n1
San Francisco Examiner, **43:** 215, 216,n2
San Francisco *Leader*, **43:** 216, 217,n5
San Jose, Ca., **43:** 248n1
San Juan, P.R., **41:** 312
San Juan *La Justicia*, **48:** 35, 37
San Juan *Times*, **48:** 36,n2
San Salvador, **42:** 359; **46:** 621
San Stefano, Treaty of, **45:** 470
San Ysidro, Mex., **40:** 203
Sanborn, Joseph Brown, **51:** 39-40,n1
Sanger, Joseph P., **47:** 483n3
Santa Fe Railroad, **41:** 412
Santiago de Cuba, **41:** 268n1
Saratoga, S.S., **44:** 413
Sargent, Herbert Howland, **44:** 239,n1; **45:** 4-6,n1
Sargent, John Singer, **42:** 390-91, 403, 545; **43:** 191, 203, 243; **44:** 360, 372,

383, 439; **49:** 66, 101; on G. G. Barnard's statue of Lincoln, **44:** 536,n1; and WW's portrait by, **45:** 400; **46:** 219,n6, 239
Sargent, Marion Cooldige (Mrs. Lucius Manlius), **49:** 286,n1
Sargent, Nathan, **44:** 296n1
Sarrail, Maurice Paul Emmanuel, **45:** 6,n5
Sartwell, Edward R., **51:** 115,n3
Sassman, Otto, **43:** 323,n1, 336n1, 373-74
Satō, Aimaro, **41:** 37,n1, 38-39, 359; **42:** 275,n1, 276, 276-77, 278; **43:** 55-56, 57n1; **45:** 370,n1, 392,n1, 393-95; photograph, *illustration section,* 45
Satō, Naotake, **47:** 99,n7
Saturday Evening Post (Phila.), **42:** 126, 486; **44:** 142n1; **45:** 385n3; **46:** 575,n2,3; **47:** 40n2, 301, 348
Saulsbury, Willard, **41:** 20, 225, 225-26, 226, 234-35,n1; **42:** 567-68; **43:** 4; **46:** 60, 61; **49:** 450; **51:** 589; and woman suffrage, **45:** 279, 339; and antiprofiteering rent bill, **48:** 190n1, 192-93, 193, 222, 238, 269
Saulsbury resolution, **41:** 225, 225-26, 226, 232, 234-35
Saunders, Charles B., Jr., **40:** 443n1
Saunders, William Lawrence, **49:** 455-57,n1, 541
Sauz, Mex., **40:** 109, 110
Savage, George, **43:** 397
Savage, Thomas J., **47:** 223,n2, 248, 252, 272
Savinkov, Boris Viktorovich, **49:** 495,n3
Savoy Hotel, London, **40:** 186,n1
Saxony, **40:** 144; **42:** 425
Saye, Albert Berry, **49:** 114n1
Sayles, William R., **51:** 621n1
Sayre, Eleanor Axson, granddaughter of WW, **40:** 108, 576; **42:** 152, 158, 556, 557, 560; **47:** 154, 392, 454, 455, 536; **49:** 388
Sayre, Francis Bowes, **40:** 108, 336, 574, 575; **41:** 474, 549; **42:** 5, 158-59, 215, 551, 556-57, 560; **43:** 53,n1; **44:** 55, 56, 64, 65; **45:** 158; **46:** 169n3; **47:** 154, 392, 502; **49:** 167, 292, 319; **51:** 316; and letter of introduction from WW, **42:** 557, 559-60,n1; rumor of shooting of, **45:** 53n1
Sayre, Francis Bowes, Jr. (Francis Woodrow Wilson Sayre until Feb. 1919), grandson of WW, **40:** 108, 574, 575; **42:** 152, 158, 556, 557, 560; **47:** 154, 392, 454, 455, 536; **49:** 167, 388
Sayre, Jessie Woodrow Wilson (Mrs. Francis Bowes), daughter of WW and EAW, **40:** 108, 336; **41:** 328, 549; **42:** 5, 151-52, 158, 215, 551, 556, 557, 560; **43:** 240-42; **44:** 55-56, 64-65; **45:** 158,n1, 214; **47:** 154, 392-93, 502-503; **48:** 6; **49:** 167, 292, 318-19, 388; **51:** 316; letters from EAW (1906-1914), **40:** 566-72; letters from H. W. Bones, **40:** 572-76; and WW's last will and testament, **42:** 426;

and H. Froelicher, **47:** 453n1, 454, 454-55, 536, 537; and YWCA war effort, **47:** 502,n1, 613, 614; informs WW he is to become grandfather again, **49:** 292
Sayre, John Nevin, **42:** 158, 159-60, 179,n2, 557,n3; **49:** 292, 319; **51:** 12,n3, 77
Sayre, Martha Finley Nevin (Mrs. Robert Heysham), **42:** 557,n4, 559; death of, **49:** 292.n2
Says Immediate Aid Will Save Russia (*New York Times*), **49:** 93n1
Sazonov, Sergei Dmitrievich, **42:** 327n1; **46:** 539n1
Scalapino, Robert Anthony, **47:** 427n3; **48:** 462,n2
Scales, Dabney M., **42:** 5,n2
Scandinavia, **40:** 15, 248; **41:** 91; **42:** 464; **44:** 284, 388; **45:** 114,n2; **48:** 613
Schack, Eckhard von, **43:** 217,n4,5
Schauffler, Grace Jarvis (Mrs. Henry Park), **49:** 388,n1
Schauffler, Henry Park, **49:** 388,n1
Schauffler, William Gray, **49:** 388,n2
Scheer, Reinhard Karl Friedrich Heinrich, **51:** 541n1
Scheiber, Harry N., **48:** 146n3
Scheidemann, Philipp, **42:** 197,n2, 388, 389; **43:** 406, 410; **44:** 154; **45:** 31, 37; **46:** 113,n2, 163, 164, 183, 188; **51:** 232, 565, 566
Schelde (Scheldt) River (Escaut River), **43:** 466,n2
Schelking, Eugene de, **49:** 93n1
Schenectady, N.Y., **49:** 133
Schérer, André, **40:** 504n1; 41n1
Schermerhorn, Sheppard Gandy, **46:** 450,n3
Schick, Joseph, **49:** 165-66
Schiff, Jacob Henry, **40:** 62; **43:** 410; **45:** 100
Schiff, Mortimer Leo, **49:** 384
Schlesinger, Benjamin, **44:** 79
Schleswig-Holstein, **44:** 218; **51:** 244, 607
Schlossberg, Joseph, **44:** 79
Schlumberger, Marguerite de Witt (Mme. Paul de), **48:** 26,n3
Schmedeman, Albert George, **45:** 78,n1; **51:** 186, 623
Schmidlapp, Jacob Godfrey, **41:** 250,n5; **43:** 410
Schneiderman, Rose, **44:** 79
Schoenfeld, Hans Frederick Arthur, **49:** 333,n1, 333-34
Schuette, Oswald Francis, **41:** 79,n2
Schulthess, Edmund, **40:** 459,n4, 462; **46:** 594,n2; **51:** 240,n10
Schulthess, Louis, **46:** 556
Schulthess' Europäischer Geschichtskalender, **44:** 44n6, 45n7, **46:** 110n1, 113n2, 163n1, 496n1, 567n1; **47:** 75,n2; **48:** 555n7; **51:** 235n4, 236n6, 239n7,8, 269n1
Schultz, Mr., **41:** 201,n1, 215
Schultz, Max, **41:** 127n1, 201n1
Schulze-Gaevernitz, Gerhart, **45:** 57,n5

Schurman, Jacob Gould, **48:** 230,n1
Schwab, Charles Michael, **47:** 385,n6, 436, 437; **48:** 488,n1; **49:** 443n4, 475
Schwabe, Klaus, **48:** 555n6; **51:** 253n2
Schwarz, Jordan A., **46:** 36n1
Scialoja, Vittorio, **41:** 408,n1,2
Scientific American, **46:** 151n1,2
Scilly Islands, **43:** 308
Scotland, **47:** 227
Scott, Charles Prestwich, **44:** 386,n1
Scott, Emmett Jay, **46:** 480,n1; **47:** 289-90; **48:** 323, 528, 529-30, 607; **49:** 139; **51:** 185
Scott, Frank Augustus, **41:** 530,n1; **42:** 449; **43:** 25, 192, 341n1, 515; **44:** 212, 232; resignation of, **44:** 450, 464
Scott, Frank Hamline, **41:** 49,n3
Scott, Helen Evans (Mrs. Townsend), **40:** 426,n2
Scott, Hugh Lenox, **40:** 123; **41:** 239, 481n2; **42:** 33n1, 133, 191, 225-27, 295; **43:** 414,n1; **44:** 196-97, 282; **45:** 111; **46:** 449n1; retirement of, **44:** 164, 232n1; photograph, *illustration section,* 46
Scott, James Brown, **40:** 547,n3; **46:** 110n1
Scott, Leroy, **42:** 254,n3,7
Scott, Mary Merrill (Mrs. Hugh Lenox), **42:** 281n1
Scribner, Arthur Hawley, **48:** 112
Scribner, Charles, **46:** 259-60, 285, 449; **48:** 111-12
Scribner's Magazine, **46:** 371n1
Scribner's Sons: *see* Charles Scribner's Sons
Scripps, Edward Wyllis, **40:** 37n1; **51:** 60n1
Scripps, James George, **51:** 60,n1
Scripps-McRea newspapers, **40:** 37n1, 374,n2; **42:** 446,n1; **43:** 201; **51:** 60n1
Scruples of Mr. Wilson (Hervé), **41:** 466n3
Scudder, Wallace McIlvaine, **42:** 458
Scully, Thomas Joseph, **51:** 552,n7
Sdobnikov, Yuri, **46:** 310n1
Sea Power (Wash.), **40:** 267
Seabury, Samuel, **41:** 12
Seager, Henry Rogers, **44:** 220n1; **45:** 132, 150, 183; **49:** 299n1
Seamen's Act, **42:** 566-67; **45:** 177
Search—A Parable (Holmes), **51:** 12n2
Searing, Annie Eliza Pidgeon (Mrs. John W.), **48:** 208n1, 209
Sears, William Joseph, **47:** 30,n1, 610
Sears, Roebuck and Company, **43:** 169
Seattle, Wash., **43:** 266; **45:** 562; hydroelectric plant construction in, **49:** 119,n2, 119-21, 121-22, 143, 148, 170, 295-96,n2
Seattle Post-Intelligencer, **43:** 267n4,5
Sebastian, Forest D., **47:** 481-84,n4, 516
Sechzig Jahre Politik und Gesellschaft (Hutten-Czapski), **41:** 139n2
Secret Service, Treasury Dept., **42:** 16, 308, 441, 516-18,n1; **43:** 133, 154-55; **46:** 18; and investigation of W. B. Hale,

44: 481-82, 514, 527-30; **45:** 28-29, 74, 101,n1; and WW's security, **45:** 237
Secret Service Division, American Protective League, **42:** 440-43, 446, 515-16
Secret Treaty Between Japan and Russia for Joint Armed Demonstration Against America and Great Britain in the Far East (*Izvestia*), **46:** 539n1
Secret War in Mexico: Europe, the United States and the Mexican Revolution (Katz), **41:** 327n5; **46:** 354n3; **47:** 165n2, 345n2, 475n2; **49:** 280n1,2
Secretary M'Adoo Withdraws Request for Editor's Help (R. Smith) 44: 257n1
Secretary Redfield Warns Shipowners (New York *Journal of Commerce*), **43:** 108n1
Sedgwick, Ellery, **44:** 178,n5; **49:** 350; **51:** 221,n5
Sedgwick, Mabel Cabot (Mrs. Ellery), **49:** 350,n2
Sedition Act, **47:** 364,n4; **48:** 146,n3; T. W. Gregory on, **48:** 12-14,n1; WW signs, **48:** 14n2
Seeking World Order: The United States and International Organization to 1920 (Kuehl), **40:** 386n1
Seeley, Fred Loring, **49:** 427-28,n1
Seested, August Frederick, **48:** 424,n2
Seibold, Louis, **42:** 245n2; **43:** 19-20, 23, 95-96, 102; on Nonpartisan League, **46:** 347-49, 369,n1, 386
Seidler, Ernst von, **46:** 589,n1
Seitz, Don Carlos, **42:** 161,n4; **43:** 175
Selective Draft and Adjustment of Industrial Man Power (Crowder), **47:** 264-65,n1
Selective Service: *bill,* **40:** 327-28, 329-30; **41:** 500n1, 551; **42:** 91, 93-94; **43:** 393n1; W. H. Taft on, **41:** 154; N. D. Baker on, **41:** 155-56; **42:** 75, 91-92; and J. P. Mitchel, **41:** 555,n1; C. Glass on, **41:** 555-56; WW on, **42:** 4, 52, 97-98, 130, 144, 179,n2, 179-80, 200-201, 214, 274, 324-26; various comments on, **42:** 19, 31, 42-43, 76, 85, 93-94, 96-97, 103-104, 122, 139-40, 146-50; and St. Louis (Socialist) resolutions on, **42:** 148,n1, 253; and J. N. Sayre on religious exemptions, **42:** 159-60, 179,n2; N. D. Baker and WW and Proclamation on, **42:** 179-82, 201, 342; women fear effect on labor standards, **42:** 208-209, 214; G. E. Chamberlain and passage of, **42:** 285; American Protective League and registration, **42:** 514
Act: **42:** 455; **43:** 318; **44:** 470, 554, **45:** 171, 177n1, 408; **46:** 280, 285, 289, 324-25, 329, 458n3; **47:** 135; **49:** 221,n1, 500; **51:** 534n1; WW on, **42:** 452-53; and aliens, **43:** 191, 461; **45:** 177n1; various exemptions to and requests for, **43:** 273,n2, 515-17, 534, 535; **44:** 565; **45:** 230, 231, 232, 254-55, 547n1, 583-86, 594; German-American resistance to, **43:** 319,n1,2; and T. E. Watson, **43:**

389n; question of farmers' exemptions, **43:** 539; **44:** 53, 61, 72-73, 150, 239-40, 258, 269-70, 343n1; **46:** 176, 428n1, 431, 446, **51:** 212, 250-51; Quakers and, **44:** 29,n1; and noncombatant service, **44:** 74, 75; **47:** 72-73,n1, 154, 155-56; and A. S. Hulbert, **44:** 82-83; T. P. Gore on, **44:** 121n1, N. D. Baker on special exemptions, **44:** 123: M. Eastman and The Masses and, **44:** 171; and display of registration card, **44:** 193-94; and lumber industry, **44:** 225; and teachers, **44:** 231; 513,n2; and drafting married men, **44:** 432; support from Jews of New York City, **44:** 503-504; and Bisbee deportations, **44:** 518, 520, 521-22; new regulations issued for, **44:** 522, 533-35; WW on success of, **45:** 408; request for pardon for early resisters, **46:** 289, 324-25; and J. I. France's bill to expand, **46:** 325-26,n1, 343; and Swedish-Americans, **46:** 458-59, 560; **47:** 135-36; and prejudiced statement on Jews in medical manual, **46:** 525n1; and illiteracy problem, **47:** 30-32, 610n1; and rejection despite correctable defects, **47:** 180; and Crowder bill on industrial mobilization, **47:** 264-65,n1, 296,n1, 299-300; and Herink case, **47:** 300,n1,2,3; railroad workers and, **48:** 12, 115, 151-52,n1; **49:** 377-78, 514, 541,n1; W. B. Wilson on labor and, **48:** 225; and rejection of G. Auchincloss, **48:** 541,n1; and extending draft age, **49:** 66, 67, 68; and G. E. Chamberlain on universal military training, **49:** 129; and coal industry, **49:** 144; and effect on Russian citizens in U.S. if Russia classified belligerent, **49:** 185n1, 238-39; and volunteers, **49:** 221,n1; R. C. Maclaurin on Student Army Training Corps, **49:** 242,n1; H. B. Fine on student exemptions, **49:** 242-44; and labor's concern over amendment to, **49:** 255-56, 294-95, 328-29; WW declines to make exception for son of friend, **49:** 305-306; WW opposes "Work or Fight" amendment, **49:** 347; WW and proclamation for new, **49:** 349-50, 358-59; and public health personnel, **49:** 379-81; and question of exemption by class of labor, **49:** 386-87; and clergy, **49:** 419-20; H. Hoover on Food Administration personnel, **49:** 509-10,n1; WW on priority classifications, **49:** 515; and selection of candidates for commissions, **51:** 228,n2, 271-72; F. Dixon on exemption of newspapermen, **51:** 579-80
Seligman, Edwin Robert Anderson, **45:** 244
Seligman, J. and W. Company, **48:** 519n3
Selph, Colin M., **43:** 324n2
Selver, Paul, **41:** 56n1,2; **49:** 287n1
Semaine Littéraire (Geneva), **40:** 541, 542n1
Semenov, Grigorii Mikhailovich, **46:** 220-
21,n2, 472; **47:** 69, 70, 99, 100n4, 101, 244, 318, 397, 398, 549, 592, 593; **48:** 72, 73, 104-106, 106,n4, 133-34, 142, 185, 239, 420, 480; **49:** 151, 221, 284; **51:** 608,n1; photograph, *illustration section,* **49**
Semple, Lorenzo, **41:** 418,n1
Senate (U.S.),: *see* United States Congress
Senate Journal, **40:** 458n2
Senate Report No. 48, **42:** 462n1
Senator Lenroot of Wisconsin: A Political Biography, 1900-1929 (Margulies), **47:** 390n1
Senator Poindexter Urges Action in Russia. Wants Military Expedition Chiefly Japanese Troops—U.S. Government, He Says, Has Misconceived the Bolsheviki (*New York Times*) **48:** 274,n1
Serbia (Servia) and Serbs, **40:** 13, 16, 28, 65, 69, 104-105, 204, 226-29, 231, 234, 239, 240, 307n1, 318, 340, 341, 404, 440, 441, 446n4, 477-78, 484, 554n1; **41:** 56-57,n2, 138, 211, 212; **42:** 155, 156, 333, 333-34, 425n1, 501; **43:** 225, 268, 268-69, 345,n1, 346, 355-56, 524; **44:** 19, 20, 21, 75-76, 330, 547; **45:** 255, 330, 412; **46:** 224, 228, 399, 404, 442, 483, 568; **47:** 36-37, 121, 125, 416-17, 569; **48:** 27, 79n1, 96-97, 213n8, 285n3, 464, 485, 545, 553, 617; **49:** 126,n1, 229, 288, 436n1, 538; **51:** 142, 143, 163, 169, 187, 256, 262, 263, 264, 274, 420, 502, 557, 558, 607; King Alexander's gratitude to U.S., **44:** 436-37; and peace terms and Inquiry memorandum, **45:** 459, 466, 470, 473; and Fourteen Points, **45:** 479, 484, 514, 528, 538, 553-54, 573; and British war aims statement, **45:** 487n2; and immigration resolution, **49:** 310,n1
Serbian Americans, **42:** 353; **43:** 346
Sergius Aleksandrovich, Grand Duke, **49:** 495n3
Seton-Watson, Hugh, **43:** 455n3
Seton-Watson, Robert William, **41:** 56n1,2,4; **47:** 240n1
Sevasly, Miran, **49:** 20,n1,2
Seventy Years of It: An Autobiography (Ross), **47:** 427n2
Seventy Years of Life and Labor: An Autobiography (Gompers), **44:** 47n1
Sever, George Francis, **49:** 119,n2, 120, 121
Seward, Anne Leddell, **40:** 565-66,n1
Seward, William Henry, **40:** 565
Seyda, Marjan, **42:** 356,n2, 544; **44:** 187
Seyda, Wladislaus Kasimir, **46:** 191,n11
Seydlitz, S.M.S., **51:** 490
Shackleford, Dorsey William, **49:** 224,n2
Shadow Lawn, Long Branch, N.J., **40:** 219,n2
Shafroth, John Franklin, **40:** 147, 386,n1, 471, 523; **41:** 403, 417,n1; **49:** 484; **51:** 590, 612, 645n1; and woman suffrage, **45:** 279, 338; **48:** 400; on L. Wood, **48:**

Shafroth, John Franklin (*cont.*) 189, 193-94

Shafter, William Rufus, **49:** 323,n7

Shaine, Isaac M., **51:** 424,n1

Shakespeare, William, **41:** 544; **45:** 130; **51:** 108

Shakespeare on the Stage (Winter), **40:** 335n2

Shall We Have a Coalition Cabinet (Bridges), **46:** 218n1

Shanghai, China, **49:** 213

Shanks, Hershel, **43:** 165n2

Shannon, David Allen, **42:** 148n1

Shantung Province, China, **41:** 39; **43:** 82

Shapiro, Nathan D., **44:** 10,n1

Sharp, Mr. (of Secret Service), **51:** 275,n2

Sharp, William Graves, **40:** 140, 439-41, 446, 481-89, 532-33 544n1; **41:** 3; **42:** 14, 227-31; **43:** 201, 364n1, 379, 387-89,n1; **44:** 75-76, 216, 427, 439; **45:** 327, 332n1, 387n1; **46:** 235, 238, 256, 302, 395, 406,n1, 601n1; **47:** 24-26, 73-74, 74-76, 108, 186,n2,3, 231, 570-71; **48:** 27,n1, 38,n1, 266; **49:** 543; **51:** 21-22,n1, 229-30, 230-31, 241; refutes R. E. Swing's estimate of French situation, **43:** 29-33; on Baron Ishii and Japanese mission, **43:** 57-58; on Allied conference in Paris, July 25, 1917, **43:** 255-56, 267-70; J. J. Pershing on, **43:** 264; and Asia Minor, **43:** 335, 355-56; on French attitude toward Pope's appeal and WW's reply, **44:** 24-26, 43-46, 103; on gasoline and tanker needs in France, **45:** 302-303, 492; on Japanese intervention in Siberia, **46:** 388-89; **48:** 131-32; on French reaction to WW's objection to Supreme War council's declaration, **46:** 429; on J. Joffre's military observations, **48:** 332-33

Sharpe, Henry Granville, **44:** 164,n2; **45:** 390,n1

Sharpless, Isaac, **44:** 29,n1

Shaw, Albert, **40:** 117-18, 165; **41:** 135; **42:** 150-51, 153; **44:** 273; **45:** 247-50, 257; **46:** 611; **47:** 5, 73, 394, 395, 446; on Overman bill, **47:** 385-86,n1,2

Shaw, Anna Howard, **40:** 548; **41:** 399-401; **42:** 237, 269, 270; **44:** 551; **48:** 28, 303n1; **51:** 189; on mourning badges, **48:** 111, 117; and Woman's Committee resolution on WW and EBW, **48:** 169-70, 174-75; on more responsible government positions for women, **48:** 198-99, 221, 250; on religious discrimination by YWCA, **48:** 208n1, 209, 221-22,n1

Shaw, Emmet R., **49:** 528n1

Shaw, George Bernard, **44:** 536n1; **45:** 175

Shaw, Leslie Mortier, **51:** 424,n1

Shaw, Matthew A. Neil, **42:** 115

Shcherbachev, D. G., **45:** 217n4

Shea, Timothy, **43:** 530; **44:** 23

Sheehan, Joseph, **41:** 557

Sheldon, Edward Wright, **41:** 380, 452; **44:** 395, 406, 447; **48:** 66, 120

Sheldon, Ernest Alfred, **40:** 451

Sheldon, Louis Pendleton, **46:** 380,n2

Shelly, Rebecca, **40:** 124n1

Shenandoah National Forest; **47:** 589

Shepherd, A. S., **51:** 396n1

Shepherd, Clifford John, **49:** 120,n4

Sheppard, Lucius Elmer, **41:** 14,n1, 29, 251,n1, 352-53, 420,n1; **43:** 530; **44:** 23

Sheppard, Morris, **46:** 573; **47:** 39, 321n1; **48:** 413, 440; **49:** 476, and woman suffrage, **45:** 279, 338; on prohibition, **45:** 295n1; **47:** 88, 106-107; **48:** 161, 175

Sherley, Joseph Swagar, **41:** 23, 82, 309n1; **42:** 427; **47:** 38, 53, 58, 600-602; **48:** 119n2, 137-39, 139, 140, 335,n1, 405; **49:** 233; **51:** 138; and water-power legislation, **45:** 301, 379; and congressional candidacy, **51:** 81, 120, 122, 149, 150, 215; and hospital construction, **51:** 281-82

Sherman, Lawrence Yates, **41:** 11n1; **47:** 584

Sherman, William Tecumseh, **45:** 544

Sherman Antitrust Act, **40:** 102n1; **43:** 21, 33n1; **51:** 71

Sherwood, Isaac Ruth, **49:** 510,n2

Shidehara, Kijuro, **43:** 82,n2

Shidlovsky, Dr. C., **44:** 39,n2

Shields, John Knight, **40:** 215, 287, 424,n1, 523; **41:** 23; **42:** 260n2; **49:** 139,n1, 264, 505; **51:** 483; and water-power legislation, **40:** 116-17,n1, 207, 215, 424, 522-23, 543; **41:** 19, 82-83; **45:** 301, 302, 335, 379, 406; **49:** 316, 355; and woman suffrage, **45:** 279, 339; **48:** 370, 371, 427, 440; **51:** 30, 133; senatorial campaign of, **47:** 6,n2, 6-7, 34, 37

Shillady, John R., **46:** 380-81,n1; **49:** 88-89,n1

Shiloh Baptist Church, Washington, D.C., **42:** 49n1, 50

Shiloh National Park, Tenn., **42:** 243,n3

Shine, F. E., **43:** 104n1

Shingarev, Andrei Ivanovich, **41:** 416,n9; **42:** 419,n3

Ship Control Committee, **47:** 66, 146

shipbuilding industry: and wages, **49:** 84-85, 105; **51:** 194,n1,2, 364-65, 396-97, 406, 422-23; Italy unable to build transports in U.S., **49:** 312-13; WW on not publicizing postwar plans on, **49:** 374; E. Geddes on, **49:** 410-13; E. N. Hurley on, **49:** 473-74,n1

Shipbuilding Labor Adjustment Board, **44:** 220,n1, 226-29, 233-34, 234-36, 242-43,244, 256-57,n1, 268, 277, 289; **45:** 7n1,132, 150, 183; **47:** 378; **49:** 298-99,n1,367; **51:** 32, 59-60, 83-84, 194,n2, 260, 396n1; and carpenters' union, **46:** 356n5, 362-63, 364, 366, 367

shipbuilding program, **43:** 51, 205n1, 212, 288; **46:** 86; **47:** 145; WW on, **42:** 32, 235-36, 564; G. W. Goethals and,

42: 102-103, 233-34, 248-49,n1, 475-80, 523-25; 567-68,n1; **43:** 72-73; and Denman-Goethals controversy, **42:** 248-49, 398-99, 553-54,n1, 555-56; **43:** 198-99, 204-205,n1, 205n1, 211, 211-12, 233-34, 249-50, 257,n1, 257-60, 265, 271, 285-87; W. C. Redfield on, **42:** 257; W. Saulsbury on, **42:** 567-68; Executive Order on requisitioning ships and, **43:** 144-45, 206, 293-96; WW discusses, **43:** 172-73, 287-90; J. Daniels on, **43:** 178, 305-10; W. S. Sims on, **43:** 181, 302-305; issue of foreign ships built in U.S. yards, **44:** 70-72, 209,n2,3, 211; and France, **44:** 156-57; strike in Oregon, **44:** 247; Japan and, **44:** 250; wage rates agreed upon, **44:** 302-303; E. N. Hurley on, **44:** 394-95; **45:** 42-44, 314; **47:** 233-34,n1; D. Lloyd George on, **44:** 362-64; and labor, **45:** 7, 131; **46:** 356,n5, 362-63, 363-64, 364-65, 366, 378-79; **47:** 291, 291-92, 463; and Philippines, **45:** 49-50; T. H. Bliss' war plans for 1918 and, **45:** 208-209; and British, **45:** 317, 322, 332; **46:** 8n1; V. C. McCormick on, **45:** 339; G. Creel on, **45:** 408; W. G. McAdoo on, **45:** 424-25; and Council of National Defense report on Allied needs, **45:** 489-91; and draft exemptions, **45:** 585-86, 594; and electrical welding, **46:** 101, 503, 510; and lumber industry, **46:** 107, 138; and housing crisis, **46:** 123-24, 171; and Hog Island facility, **46:** 124,n2; and copper industry, **46:** 128; and bill establishing "war zones" around shipyards, **46:** 283-85, 329; and reorganization of War Industries Board, **46:** 610; and elimination of profiteering in, **46:** 610-11; and *Tuckahoe,* **47:** 500,n1

Shipkoff, Theodore K., **46:** 235n1

Shipley, Arthur Everett, **47:** 264,n1, 396; **48:** 249,n1, 250

Shipman, Samuel, **46:** 520

shipping, **44:** 544n1; **47:** 73-74, 145-47; priority shipments, **42:** 289-90, 298-99; rumor of German plot to destroy, **46:** 3-4, 17-18, 50-51; and troop transport, **46:** 42, 43, 44-45; **47:** 204-205, 230, 260-61; W. C. Redfield on restricting imports and exports, **46:** 309

Shipping Act of 1916, **42:** 3, 32, 286

Shipping Board: *see* United States Shipping Board

Shipping Board Operations. Testimony of William Denman, Esq., First Chairman of the United States Shipping Board, relating to the policies and activities of his administration and reviewing shipping conditions in general . . . December 13,14, and 15, 1920, **42:** 272,n4

Ships Sunk with Loss of American Life (Lansing), **41:** 502n1

Shipyard Employment Managers, **45:** 130n1

shoe industry, **47:** 495

Shonts, Theodore Perry, **40:** 35,n3

Shope, Bella Wilson (Mrs. William Krebs), **40:** 170,n1

Shoreham Hotel, Washington, D. C., **41:** 543; **46:** 40

Short, William Harrison, **47:** 119,n2,3, 147, 199

Short Ballot Association, **46:** 109

Shortridge, Samuel Morgan, **42:** 272,n4

Shouse, Jouett, **41:** 296; **51:** 375, 623-24; and farmers, **44:** 53-54, 61, 150, 153, 343,n1,2; **48:** 629,n2; on woman suffrage, **48:** 263-64, 279; on Kansas Democratic politics, **49:** 308-309, 315-16

Shwangliao: *see* Chengchiatun

Siasconset, Nantucket Island, **42:** 158, 551, 557

Siberia, **42:** 144; **43:** 387; **45:** 294, 347, 370, 393, 418, 420; **48:** 72,n2, 73, 104-106, 528, 577-78; and Semenov expedition, **46:** 200-21,n2; and Russian Railway Service Corps, **46:** 344,n1,2, 357, 358, 387; China and, **46:** 501; movements for autonomy in, **47:** 92,n1,2, 357, 397-99, 591-94; reports on conditions in, **47:** 96-99, 100-101, 131; protection of Japanese and British munitions in, **47:** 162,n2; Czech troops in, **47:** 513-14,n7, 551-52, 565; T. G. Masaryk on, **47:** 550; cooperative societies in, **48:** 359-60,n1; politics in, **49:** 220-21; Great Britain appoints High Commissioner to, **49:** 250n1; currency plan for, **51:** 67, 87-88,n1; Italy will not send High Commissioner to, **51:** 135; Supreme War Council's military policy and, **51:** 202; intervention in: *see* Russia—Siberia, intervention in

Siberian Intervention (White), **51:** 100n2

Siberian Provincial Conference, **47:** 71

Siberian Provisional Government, **51:** 100,n2, 102n1

Siberian Railway: *see* Trans-Siberian Railway

Sibert, William Luther, **43:** 199,n1; **45:** 111,n7

Siems-Carey Company, **48:** 372-73

Signal Corps, U.S. Army, **47:** 321n1, 329, 332, 396n1; **48:** 73-74

Silberer, Geza: *see* Sil-Vara, G. A.

Silesia, **42:** 335; **45:** 553n2; **51:** 504

Sil-Vara, G. A., **45:** 55-57,n1

Silver, Horace Percy, **42:** 281n1

silver: and Mexico, **51:** 12,n1,2

Simbirsk, Russia, **51:** 50n1, 51n2, 556

Simkhovitch, Vladimir Grigorievitch, **42:** 111,n4; **43:** 219

Simkins, Francis Butler, **48:** 260n2

Simmons, Furnifold McLendel, **40:** 270; **43:** 162; **44:** 117,n1; **46:** 83-84; **47:** 561; **49:** 450; **51:** 204-206, 475, 476-77; and woman suffrage, **45:** 278, 279, 339; and

Simmons, Furnifold McLendel (*cont.*)
　revenue legislation, **48:** 119,n2, 129,
　153-54, 167, 168-69,n1, 173, 175-76;
　49: 86, 105,n2, 134-35; and wire-con-
　trol bill, **48:** 535n1
Simmons Hardware Company, St. Louis,
　43: 76
Simon, John Allsebrook, **40:** 342,n3,4
Simons, Algie Martin, **42:** 198,n6, 199,
　240, 253-54,n2, 259
Simons, Kate Drayton Mayrant (Mrs.
　S. Lewis), **49:** 305-306,n1
Simons, Mayrant, **49:** 305-306
Simpson, Alexander, **51:** 283,n1,2
Simpson, Mrs. Cravath, **42:** 115
Simpson, John A., **51:** 212,n2
Simpson, S. D., **40:** 175,n1
Simpson, W. G., **40:** 175,n1
Sims, Thetus Willrette, **41:** 23; **43:** 7,n1;
　45: 265-66,n2, 403; **48:** 452; **51:** 86, 90,
　206; and water-power legislation, **45:**
　300, 335, 379, 380,n2, 433,n1; **49:** 289,
　316, 317, 329-32, 351, 406; on railroad
　proclamation, **45:** 391,n1; and wire-
　control bill, **48:** 457, 458,n1, 532-33,n1,
　533; and public-health legislation, **49:**
　381
Sims, William Sowden, **42:** 82,n1, 121,
　121-22; **43:** 26, 47, 79-80, 88, 112, 173,
　178, 179,n1, 191, 463; **44:** 173-75, 465;
　45: 19, 20, 21, 23; **47:** 27, 161-62, 204,
　327, 348; **48:** 356, 604-606; **49:** 137, 158,
　413; **51:** 20, 79,n1, 528; reports on Al-
　lied naval situation, **43:** 114-15, 179-
　82, 302-304; on convoy system, **43:** 181;
　and Allied conference in Paris, July 24-
　27, 1917, **43:** 209, 236,n1, 304,n5; and
　proposed honorary appointment in
　British Admiralty, **46:** 194,n1, 203; on
　naval peace terms, **51:** 474-75,n1,2;
　photograph, *illustration section,* **42**
Sinclair, Upton Beall, **42:** 148n1, 198; **44:**
　467-72, 491; **47:** 254n1; **48:** 118n1; on
　Masses case, **48:** 59,n1,2; on conscien-
　tious objectors, **48:** 610-11; **49:** 56, 207-
　209, 247, 306
Sinn Fein movement, **43:** 17,n3, 361, 451-
　52; **44:** 133,n2,3, 210; **47:** 267, 432, 442,
　469, 552; **48:** 118n1; **49:** 545; and
　charges of conspiracy with Germany,
　48: 63-65, 65-66,n1, 67-68, 71, 195-97,
　206; and conscription issue, **48:** 330n3
Sisca, Michael, **51:** 251n2
Sisson, Edgar Grant, **44:** 434,n2, 435-36;
　45: 194, 216,n2, 367-68, 441, 444-45,
　543-44, 596-97; **46:** 233, 300n7, 358,
　479; **47:** 522; **49:** 24, 25, 26, 434; **51:**
　18,n1; and Sisson Documents, **46:**
　341,n1; **47:** 440,n1; and question of
　publication, **51:** 3, 4,n1, 18n1, 104,n5,
　246-47, 252, 352
Sisson Documents (Kennan), **46:** 341n1
*Six Centuries of Work and Wages: The
　History of English Labour* (Rogers), **44:**
　260n3
Six Power Consortium: *see* American

Group of the Six-Power Consortium
Sixtus of Bourbon-Parma, Prince, **47:**
　589,n1
Sixtus letter, **47:** 589,n1; **48:** 114n2,
　205,n2, 435
*64th Congress, 1st, 2nd and 3rd Sessions,
　1915-1917 . . . ,* **42:** 277n1
Skagerrak, **42:** 348n2
Skagit hydroelectric power project, **49:**
　119,n2, 296n2
Skeffington, Henry J., **51:** 69,n2
Skinner, Robert Peet, **48:** 233,n1
Skobelev, Mikhail Ivanovich, **42:** 418n1,
　419,n3
Skoropadski, Pavlo Petrovich, **48:** 102n1
slacker raids, **49:** 451, 499-503, 513
Slagle, Robert Lincoln, **46:** 459n1
Slama, Charles H., **48:** 191,n2
Slater, George H., **47:** 104-105, 126, 144
Slattery, Charles Lewis, **40:** 89,n1
Slavic National Congress, Second, **40:**
　104, 165
Slavonia, **46:** 244
Slavs, **40:** 104-105, 165; **41:** 211, 212; **48:**
　485-86, 591
Slayden, Ellen Maury (Mrs. James Lu-
　ther), **49:** 73n3
Slayden, James Luther, **49:** 73,n3,
　137,n3, 138; **51:** 616
Sleicher, John Albert, **47:** 352,n1
Slidell, John, **41:** 303
Slivinski, Anton, **49:** 357n1; **51:** 68-70
Slobodin, Henry (Harry) Leon, **44:** 39,n1,
　65-66
Slocum, Grant, **51:** 212,n2
Slocum, Herbert Jermain, **41:** 41
Slocum, Stephen L'Hommedieu, **44:** 332-
　33,n2; **51:** 384
Sloss Sheffield Steel and Iron Company,
　43: 511; **46:** 29-30
Slovaks, **45:** 224
Slovenes, **40:** 104-105; **49:** 126n1
Sly, Henry Edward, **47:** 96,n1
Small, John Humphrey, **42:** 98; **46:** 90;
　48: 350-51; on water-power legislation,
　49: 344, 356-57
Small Bore Editor Gloats Over Atrocity
　(*Nonpartisan Leader*), **47:** 521n1
Smileage Book campaign, **47:** 220n1
Smith, Alfred Emanuel (Al Smith), **49:**
　105-106,n1, 157,n1, 465; **51:** 535,n3
Smith, Alfred Holland, **42:** 81,n2; **46:**
　426,n5; **51:** 408,n4
Smith, Arthur Douglas Howden, **47:**
　310,n7, 534n1, 546
Smith, Charles Hadden, **48:** 72,n1
Smith, Charles Stephenson, **48:** 142,n5
Smith, Earl Baldwin, **40:** 551,n1
Smith, Edward North, **42:** 469,n1, 469-
　71, 490-91
Smith, Edward Parson, **51:** 477,n1
Smith, Ellison DuRant, **40:** 272; **41:** 20;
　46: 204; **48:** 535, 556n2; **51:** 5; and
　woman suffrage, **45:** 279, 339; **51:** 30,
　58
Smith, Felix Willoughby, **49:** 519,n8

Smith, George McLeod, **44:** 445,n1
Smith, Henry Clark, **44:** 86n1
Smith, Hoke, **41:** 359n3; **42:** 427, 505; **43:** 162, 515; **47:** 30, 610; **48:** 51; **49:** 115; and woman suffrage, **45:** 279, 338, 339; and vocational rehabilitation bill, **47:** 29n1
Smith, Howard Alexander: on relief work, **46:** 265,n1, 298-99
Smith, Jane Norman (Mrs. Clarence Meserole), **40:** 379,n3
Smith, John Watson, **47:** 596; and woman suffrage, **45:** 279, 338, 339
Smith, Joseph, **49:** 327-28, 400
Smith, Kirby, **42:** 457,n2
Smith, Lucy Marshall, **40:** 336, 347, 568,n1, 569; **45:** 581-82; **46:** 371
Smith, Marcus Aurelius, **40:** 523: **43:** 127, 128; **46:** 598; **47:** 116; **51:** 277n7; and woman suffrage, **45:** 279, 338
Smith, Mary Randolph, **40:** 336, 347, 568,n1, 569; **45:** 581, 582; **46:** 371
Smith, Munroe, **48:** 213n8
Smith, Ralph, **44:** 257n1
Smith, Robert, **49:** 399-400
Smith, Robert A. C., **44:** 502,n1
Smith, Robert Freeman, **46:** 354n2; **48:** 279n5
Smith, Roland Cotton, **40:** 354,n1, 383, 412
Smith, William Russell, **40:** 466,n3
Smith and Wesson Company, Springfield, Mass.: strike at, **49:** 133-34, 519, 520, 521, 539-40
Smith-Hughes vocational education bill, **40:** 159,n1,2
Smith-Lever Act, **46:** 175
Smithe, Douglas, **46:** 433,n1
Smithsonian Institution: and Frachtenberg case, **45:** 92n2, 141,n2, 154; request for WW's typewriter, **46:** 461-62,n1, 468-69, 502-503
Smokeless Coal Operators' Association, **43:** 70n1
Smolensk, Russia, **46:** 403
Smolny Institute, Petrograd, **46:** 403
Smoot, Reed, **41:** 11n1; **45:** 338, 340; **46:** 602; **49:** 310n1
Smoot resolution, **43:** 237n1
Smulski, John F., **41:** 508
Smuts, Jan Christiaan, **42:** 531,n1; **45:** 430n2,3; **46:** 473, 577; **47:** 11; **48:** 271, 555n7
Smyrna, Turkey, **45:** 52, 53
Snell, Bertrand Hollis, **47:** 72,n1, 85
Snook, John Stout, **45:** 307,n1
Snow, Kneeland S., **44:** 41,n1
Snowden, Philip, **41:** 375,n4; **42:** 422
Snyder, Carl, **47:** 40n3
Snyder, Edgar Callender, **44:** 50,n2
Snyder, Homer Peter, **40:** 289n2; **48:** 475,n1
Sobánski, Wladyslaw, **42:** 544,n2; **44:** 187
Social and Economic Background of Woodrow Wilson (Dodd), **46:** 518n1

Social Insurance Conference: WW's remarks to, **40:** 188-89
Social Revolution (St. Louis), **43:** 165
Socialist and Sinclair (*Pearson's Magazine*), **44:** 471-72,n5
Socialist Conference, Stockholm: see international socialist conference
Socialist party and socialists, **40:** 540n1; **43:** 190, 193, 422; **44:** 39n1; **45:** 203, 318, 319; **47:** 178, 438, 439, 471-72; **48:** 16-17,n1, 147, 235,n1; peace policy and efforts by, **42:** 36-37, 268-69, 318, 360-63, 364, 364-65, 463-64; and Russian Commission appointment, **42:** 154,n1, 166, 197-99,n1-10, 203-204, 216-17, 240, 253-54,n2,3; and G. R. Lunn, **42:** 195n1; in France, **42:** 364; William II on Reichstag members of, **42:** 521; raids on headquarters of, **44:** 158n1; comments on censorship of, **44:** 158, 172, 272, 339, 366n1, 392, 393-94, 408-409, 467-72; and labor, **44:** 483-84; proposed international conference of, **47:** 74-76, 105-106, 108-109, 210,n1; and National party, **47:** 254n1; *see also* international socialist conference; St. Louis Proclamation
Socialist Party of America: A History (Shannon), **42:** 148n1
Socialists and the War: A Documentary Statement of the Position of the Socialists of All Countries (Walling), **42:** 203-204,n1
Société des Nations (Milhaud), **48:** 210-11,n1
Society for the Propagation of the Faith, **44:** 184n3
Society of Equity: *see* American Society of Equity
Society of Friends: *see* Quakers
Society of Friends of German Democracy, **47:** 19,n1, 324,n1, 559n2
Solf, Wilhelm, **40:** 463n1; **51:** 235,n4, 239, 316n6, 345-46, 348, 400n1
Solovetski Island, Russia, **49:** 518n4
Soma scandal, **47:** 426,n1
Some Particular Advices for Friends and a Statement of Loyalty for Others, **47:** 415
Somme, Battle of the, **42:** 373
Sonnenburg, Alphons Falkner von, **49:** 228,n5, 229
Sonnino, Sidney, **41:** 223,n1, 224; **42:** 110,n1; **43:** 355,n1; **44:** 26, 348, 350; **45:** 166n1, 189n1; **46:** 157, 158, 159, 178, 207, 365, 415, 454, 456; **48:** 212, 504, 545; **49:** 65, 428; **51:** 230, 233; and peace terms, **51:** 118-19, 512, 513, 515, 516, 529-30; tension with V. Orlando, **51:** 175n1, 386, 387-88
Sons of Confederate Veterans, **42:** 451n1
Sons of Liberty, **42:** 440, 443
Sookine, George Jan, **46:** 513-15; **48:** 383-84,n2
Sophie (of Greece), **40:** 486,n3
Sosnowski, George Jan, **42:** 11-12,n1,

Sosnowski, George Jan (*cont.*)
44,n1, 60, 140,n1, 134, 491-94; **44:** 4-6;
45: 575, 575-76; **46:** 404
South Africa, **41:** 213
South America, **40:** 14, **41:** 9; **42:** 309,
356-58; **45:** 597; **46:** 153; **48:** 257-58; **49:**
431
South Carolina, **41:** 217; **44:** 10; **47:** 597;
49: 246-47,n4; politics in, **48:** 259-
60,n2, 268; **51:** 633
South Dakota, **47:** 466; politics in, **51:**
590, 633
South Dakota, University of, **46:** 459n1
South Manchurian Railway, **47:** 71; **49:**
396n1
Southampton, England, **46:** 8n1, 10, 12
Southern Commercial Congress, **40:**
202,n2, 214
Southern Pacific Railroad Co., **40:** 206;
46: 491
Southern Railway System, **42:** 540n2; **47:**
408n3
*Southern Slav Question and the Habs-
burg Monarchy* (Seton-Watson), **41:**
56n2
Southern Sociological Congress, **47:** 326-
27,n1
Southern Sociological Congress: Ration-
ale of Uplift (Chatfield), **47:** 326n1
Southwick, Henry Lawrence, **49:** 351n1
Southwick, Jessie Eldridge (Mrs. Henry
Lawerence), **49:** 351,n1,2
Soviet Documents on Foreign Policy (De-
gras, ed.), **45:** 119n1; **46:** 341n5; **51:**
509n1
Soviet-Polish   Relations,   1917-1921
(Wandycz), **46:** 403n3
Spa, Belgium, **48:** 555n7; **51:** 253n2
Spacek, V., **49:** 44,n2, 219
Spaeth, John Duncan, **40:** 571,n5
Spahn, Peter, **45:** 32,n3
Spain, **40:** 45, 231, 234, 304, 378-79, 405,
461, 552, 556; **41:** 35, 40, 116, 219,
249n1; **42:** 264,n3, 438-39; **43:** 10, 144;
46: 621; **47:** 139-40,n1, 454; **48:** 539,
613; **49:** 404, 453; **51:** 184, 567; and conference of neutrals, **40:** 46-48, 81n1;
ambassador gets early information on
WW's peace note, **40:** 323; reaction to
Pope's peace appeal, **44:** 84,n1; role in
peace moves, **44:** 311, 318-20, 325; **46:**
397-400, 412, 418, 424: 432, 435, 442;
recall of U.S. naval attaché in, **46:** 49-
50,n1, 59, 67, 79; Russian legation in,
49: 142; and military service of Spanish citizens in U.S., **49:** 542,n1
Spangler, Jackson Levi, **44:** 104,n1, 214,
520; **46:** 74, 147
Spanish American War, **41:** 154, 155-56,
512; **46:** 54
Spargo, John, **42:** 148n1, 198, 237n4, 240;
44: 490, 491-92; **45:** 50, 68, 542; **47:**
254n1
Spartacus   League   (Spartacists),   **42:**
197n4; **51:** 622,n1
Spartanburg (S.C.), *Herald,* **49:** 246n1

Spaulding, Claude M., **48:** 578-79,n1
Special Privilege Mobilizes (New York
World), **47:** 254
Spector, Ronald, **44:** 296n1
*Speculator: Bernard M. Baruch in Wash-
ington, 1917-1965* (Schwarz), **46:** 36n1
Spencer, Henry Benning, **47:** 408,n3
Spencer, Willing, **47:** 68n2
Spiers, Edward Louis, **46:** 388,n1; **47:** 59
Spindler, Arno, **40:** 389n1
Spingarn, Joel Elias, **41:** 218; **49:** 62n3
Spiritual, Moral and Intellectual Society
of the First Emanuel Church, N.Y., **43:**
106n1
Spokane, Wash., **44:** 344-45; **46:** 432n2
Sport, Mrs. Emeline, **42:** 116
Sprague, Frank Julian, **43:** 305,n1, 306,
307, 309
Sprague, Oliver Mitchell Wentworth, **41:**
448,n2
Spreckels, Claus August, **45:** 344n1, 353;
46: 501-502, 546
Spreckels, John Diedrich, Jr., **42:** 272,n5
Spreckels, Rudolph, **40:** 312, 313,n1
Spreckels Sugar Company, **42:** 272n5
Spring Rice, Sir Cecil Arthur, **40:** 406-
407, 493, 499-500; **41:** 38, 40, 126-27,
256-57, 381, 411, 431-33; **42:** 18, 120,
354, 355, 372, 428,n1, 445, 450-51, 520,
530, 564; **43:** 44, 65-66, 124, 438; **44:** 56,
83-84, 153, 203, 317, 385, 388, 494-95;
45: 255, 267, 316, 322, 399, 431-32, 518,
566, 572, 577-78, 578; on U.S. policy toward purchase of Allied notes, **40:** 136-
37; **41:** 349; on German peace offer, **40:**
249; on WW's peace note and Allied reply, **40:** 307n1, 316, 469-70; W. H. Page
on, **41:** 115; E. M. House on, **41:** 196; **42:**
142n1, 143, 161, 169; sends WW words
from Isaiah LXI, **42:** 112-13; and British mission, **42:** 125, 126, 140-41, 232,
296; Northcliffe and, **43:** 24, 97, 195,
451, 452, 453; on Poles and Poland, **43:**
37-38, 256-57, 301-302; **44:** 187-88,
316-17; and British financial crisis, **43:**
38, 97-98, 224, 228, 230, 326-33, 335-
36, 347; on war losses by gross tons, **43:**
140-42; on settlement of controversy on
U.S. Shipping Board, **43:** 285-87; on
resolution to requisition vessels, **43:**
293-96; and submarine crisis, **43:** 374-
78, talk of recalling, **44:** 202; on Japan
and the Russian situation, **45:** 336,
347, 369-70, 392, 393-95; on WW's
thoughts on the war, **45:** 454-57, 459;
death of, **46:** 343,n2
Spring Rice, Florence Lascelles, Lady
Spring Rice, **45:** 399; **46:** 343
Springfield, Mass.: strike in, **49:** 133-34,
519, 520, 539-40
Springdale Golf Club, Princeton, N.J.,
40: 347n2
Springfield Arsenal, **42:** 165
Springfield (Mass.) *Republican,* **40:**
167n1, 241,n1; **41:** 295n2, 450-51,n1,2,
462; **42:** 556,n3; **44:** 204, 292n2, 293n1;

47: 509; **51:** 28, 330,n1; on postal censorship, **44:** 358,n1; on German peace proposal, **45:** 436-37; on L. Wood, **48:** 242,n1; on prohibition, **49:** 476; on German peace note, **51:** 266-68

Sprout, Harold, **51:** 344n1

Sprout, Margaret, **51:** 344n1

Sprunt, Alexander, **42:** 88

Sprunt, James, **42:** 86, 99, 203n1

Sprunt, John Dalziel, **42:** 203,n1,2

Spry, William, **51:** 377

Spurgeon, John J., **44:** 459-60,n3, 478-79, 524-25; **47:** 278-79,n1

Square Deal, **47:** 127

Squier, George Owen, **42:** 192,n1, 530, 549, 550; **44:** 538,n1; **45:** 155, 426, 427; **46:** 94n1, 95, 230; **47:** 509, 541, 545

S. S. McClure Newspaper Corporation, **43:** 134n2

Staal, Aleksei Fedorovich, **47:** 397,n2

Staatskunst und Kriegshandwerk (Ritter), **48:** 555n7

Stabler, Jordan Herbert, **40:** 82,n1; **41:** 139, 140-44; **49:** 5-6,n1

Stack, E. J., **44:** 243

Stafford, William Henry, **41:** 327n1

Stakes of Diplomacy (Lippmann), **41:** 83,n1, 113

Stambuliiski, Aleksandŭr, **51:** 563,n1

Stämpfli, Wilhelm, **44:** 484n1

Standard Oil Co., **40:** 205; **43:** 367n1; **44:** 260

Standard Oil Company of Indiana, **47:** 412-13, 413

Standard Oil Trust, **46:** 111

Standards, Bureau of, **45:** 492; **49:** 162

Staněk, František, **51:** 506,n1

Stanford University, **40:** 369; **44:** 146n1

Stanislaus, Ignatius Valerius Stanley, **41:** 68,n1; **46:** 404

Stanley, Albert Henry, **40:** 452,n4

Stanley, Augustus Owsley, **49:** 381,n1, 388, 480, 481, 486, 529; and woman suffrage, **51:** 31,n1, 49, 288, 294; WW supports, **51:** 76, 395; and teaching of German language, **51:** 259, 295

Stanley, Edward George Villiers, Earl of Derby; *see* Derby, 17th Earl of (Edward George Villiers Stanley)

Stanny Zjiednoczone a odrodzenie Polski [The United States and the Rebirth of Poland] (Wedrowski), **42:** 355n2

Stanton, Elizabeth Cady, **40:** 426

Starling, Edmund William, **41:** 557,n2

Starr, Western, **44:** 79

Stars and Stripes (newspaper), **47:** 172n1

Starzynski, Teofil A., **41:** 388n1, 507-508, 508-509, 511-12

State, Department of, **2:** 16-17, 29n1, 40, 49, 117, 118, 163, 437n1, 559, 567; **43:** 204, 315, 458-59; **44:** 287,n1, 459; **45:** 177,n1; **47:** 44, 600; **48:** 240, 305; **51:** 87

State, The (Wilson), **40:** 567; **44:** 487-88; **51:** 535-36,n1,2

States Revisited (Lowry), **40:** 414n3

Statler Hotel, Buffalo, **44:** 556

Statue of Liberty: WW's remarks at first illumination of, **40:** 35,n1,2, 119, 119-21; **41:** 5

Statutes at Large, **41:** 278n1, 310n2, 311n2; **42:** 179n2; **43:** 7n1, 397n1, 415n1, 519; **44:** 257n1, 266n1, 323n1; **47:** 193n2, 364n2,3,4,5, 589n1,2, **48:** 150n1, 228n1; **49:** 185n1, 550n1; **51:** 108n9

Stavka (at Mogilev, Russia), **45:** 217n4

Stead, Alfred, **51:** 45,n11, 46

Steamboat Inspection Service, **43:** 312

Stedman, Charles Manly, **45:** 307

Steed, Henry Wickham, **47:** 552n6

Steel, Richard Alexander, **48:** 537,n4

Steel, Ronald, **45:** 459n1; **49:** 402n3, 434n2

Steel and Iron Institute, **43:** 373

steel industry, **42:** 242-43, 248-49, 279, 401, 539, 540-41,n2; **44:** 250, 421; **47:** 118-19,n1, 138, 167-68, 255; **48:** 392; **49:** 70, 145; **51:** 220; and prices, **43:** 105-106, 122, 155-56, 221, 366, 373, 380; **45:** 342-43, 344; **51:** 90-91, 285-86,n1; strikes, **44:** 242, 244, 272-78

Steffens, Lincoln, **40:** 371, 374; **45:** 593; **51:** 645; on class war, **45:** 381-84

Steglich, Wolfgang, **44:** 44n6, 351n2; **47:** 64n2

Stein, Hermann Christlieb Matthäus von, **45:** 32,n2

Stein, Leonard, **45:** 149n2

Steiner, York, **46:** 412

Stelzle, Charles, **42:** 323n2

Stenberg (or Strenberg), Mr. (Soviet military commander), **47:** 100,n3

Stephen S. Wise: Servant of the People (Voss, ed.), **41:** 181n

Stephens, Dan Voorhees, **42:** 21n1

Stephens, Frank, **44:** 79

Stephens, Hiram, **40:** 217n1

Stephens, Julius, **43:** 130

Stephens, Richard, **44:** 172-73, 223

Stephens, William Dennison, **42:** 270,n1, 271, 272, 279; **43:** 386; **44:** 81,n1, 290,n3; **46:** 73, 74, 170; **47:** 194; **51:** 213n1, 377; and Mooney case, **47:** 148, 160, 210, 359, 397, 467; **48:** 237,n1, 247, 405

Sterling, Mr., **41:** 182,n3,4

Sterling, Bruce Foster, **45:** 307,n1

Sterling, Frederick Augustine, **43:** 171n1

Sterling, Thomas, **44:** 89n1; **51:** 83

Stetson, Francis Lynde, **40:** 89; **49:** 168n2

Stettinius, Edward Reilly, **42:** 372,n3; **46:** 111,n1, 112, 269,n1; **47:** 321, 325, 436, 437; **48:** 232-33, 266, 267, 331, 381; **49:** 279, 281, 286, 349, 350-51; **51:** 35, 337

Steuben, S.S., **42:** 236

Stevens, Edwin Augustus: death of, **46:** 583,n2

Stevens, Emily Contee Lewis (Mrs. Edwin Augustus), **46:** 583

Stevens, George Walter, **43:** 242,n1

Stevens, John Frank, **43:** 249, 424, 439, 459; **44:** 281; **46:** 89-90, 344,n1, 345,

Stevens, John Frank (*cont.*)
387, 472, 474; **48:** 72n1; **49:** 63, 77-78, 396n1; **51:** 86n1, 478, 480, 481n1, 598; and Russian Railroad Commission, **42:** 95,n1, 222, 238,n2,3, 239; **43:** 440-42; photograph, *illustration section,* 49
Stevens, Raymond Bartlett, **41:** 49; **43:** 50-51,n1; **44:** 313-14; **45:** 8-9,n5; **46:** 324,n2, 327; **47:** 172,n2; **48:** 233,n1, 331
Stevens Commission: *see* Russian Railroad Commission
Stewart, George E., **49:** 516,n1, 517-18,n1, 518-19; **51:** 102n1
Stewart, Joseph, **44:** 289,n2
Stewart, Samuel Vernon, **43:** 494; **44:** 107,n2; **49:** 449,n1; **51:** 213,n1
Stillman, James, **49:** 233
Stimson, Frederic Jesup, **40:** 463n2
Stimson, Henry Lewis, **40:** 89; **42:** 83-86, 122; **43:** 92,n1, 102, 201n1
Stirling, Yates, Jr., **43:** 182,n2
Stock Market inquiry: *see* New York Stock Exchange
Stockbridge, Horace Edward, **44:** 257n1
Stockholm, Sweden, **40:** 48; **41:** 40
Stockholm Conference: *see* international socialist conference
Stockholm Dream (Harden), **43:** 246n1
Stoddard, Richard C., **49:** 56,n2
Stokes, Edward Casper, **42:** 458
Stokes, Helen Louisa Phelps (Mrs. Anson Phelps), **47:** 350,n1
Stokes, James Graham Phelps, **42:** 198,n8, 199
Stokes, Rose Harriet Pastor (Mrs. James Graham Phelps), **48:** 235,n1, 405, 422-23; **49:** 208, 306
Stokowski, Leopold Anthony: on playing German music, **49:** 360,n1,2
Stone, Fred Andrew, **48:** 52,n3
Stone, Harlan Fiske, **49:** 56,n2
Stone, Melville Elijah, **41:** 308,n2; **46:** 437
Stone, Sarah Louis Winston (Mrs. William Joel), **47:** 350
Stone, Warren Sanford, **41:** 14,n1, 29, 54, 251,n1, 353, 420,n1; **43:** 530; **44:** 22
Stone, William Joel, **40:** 213, 249, 405, 447; **41:** 121, 124, 280n1, 324, 358-59, 419, 430; **45:** 582; **46:** 63,n1,2, 116; **48:** 115n1; and Danish West Indies, **40:** 385, 385-86, 424-25; and WW's Peace without Victory speech, **40:** 445, 478, 491, 524; on water-power legislation, **41:** 19-20, 23; and Colombian treaty, **41:** 28, 240-41, 261-62; and decision for break with Germany, **41:** 88,n1; on Saulsbury resolution, **41:** 225-26, 232; and armed-ship bill, **41:** 294n1, 318n1, 328, 534-35; greets WW after war message, **41:** 532; on woman suffrage, **45:** 279, 338; death of, **47:** 350,n1
Stone and Webster Corporation, Boston, **43:** 266, 267,n3; **49:** 120, 122, 143
Storer, Edward, **46:** 156n2
Storey, Moorfield, **41:** 217-18

Story, Daisy Allen, **41:** 310-11
Story of the Nonpartisan League: A Chapter in American Evolution (Russell), **45:** 167n1
Stout, Ralph Emerson, **48:** 405,n1, 422-24
Stovall, Pleasant Alexander, **40:** 22-23, 277, 323; **41:** 127,n1, 193-94, 214, 275-77; **42:** 454; **46:** 580-81, 589-90, 594, 615-17; **47:** 64-65,n1,4, 128, 525; **48:** 228n1, 457n1, 473, 540, 552n1, 555, 609, 621; **49:** 228,n3, 231, 436,n1, 447; **51:** 76,n1, 154-55, 603, 623; on U.S. recognition of Swiss neutrality, **45:** 235-36; talk of recalling, **45:** 332; on Poland, **49:** 382-83
Strachey, John St. Loe, **46:** 617-19; **47:** 258-59; **51:** 444,n1, 444-45
Strachey, William, **46:** 618
Straight, Dorothy Payne Whitney (Mrs. Willard Dickerman), **42:** 118,n1
Straight, Willard Dickerman, **41:** 39; **42:** 30, 43, 45, 63n5
Straits of Gibraltar, **44:** 477
Strakhovsky, Leonid Ivan, **51:** 79n1
Strange, James F., **46:** 621,n3
Strange News from Russia (*The New Republic*), **42:** 273n1
Stránský, Adolf, **51:** 506,n1
Strassburg, Germany (now Strasbourg, France), **51:** 275, 415, 463
Strategy of the present war (Lochridge), **44:** 361n1
Stratton, Samuel Wesley, **45:** 492n1; **47:** 322
Straus, Oscar Solomon, **41:** 55n1, 250; **42:** 30, 43, 45, 58, 276; **44:** 299n2, 333n1; **51:** 644
Strauss, Albert, **46:** 423n1; **48:** 518,n3; **51:** 407
Strauss, Frederick, **40:** 444,n3
Strauss, Joseph, **49:** 137,n1
Strawn, Tex., **46:** 433n1
Strayer, Louis William, **40:** 193n1
Street, Mrs. J. G., **42:** 116
street railways: *see* transit companies
Strenberg, Mr.: *see* Stenberg, Mr.
Stresemann, Gustav, **45:** 31,n2; **46:** 190,n8
Strickland, Mr., **44:** 328
strikes (labor), **42:** 137; **47:** 574; W. B. Wilson on, **40:** 97-100; **47:** 461-62; **49:** 132; WW on, **40:** 156, 157-58, 476, 543-44; **48:** 275-76; antistrike legislation and railroads, **41:** 14n1,2, 26,n1,2, 29-31, 33, 37, 54, 238n1, 253-55, 409-11; mining industries and, **43:** 16-18, 53, 325, 336, 340, 433-34, 494; **44:** 15, 134-39, 163n1, 172, 424-25, 478, 516-20, 521-22; **45:** 269-70, 321-22; **51:** 19, 545; and lumber industry, **44:** 14, 225; and railroads, **44:** 152,n1, 183, 198; and steel industry, **44:** 242, 244, 277-78; in Oregon shipyards, **44:** 247; Council of National Defense on, **44:** 498-501; in oil industry, **45:** 44, 60, 121, 122, 129, 350;

46: 179; statistics on, **45:** 45; settlement of Pacific Telephone and Telegraph Co., **45:** 95-96; Atlantic Coast Line, **45:** 117-18, 125-26, 129-30, 155, 162, 184; Twin City Rapid Transit Co., **45:** 258-62, 279, 331; **47:** 189-91, 272-74; and President's Mediation Commission report, **46:** 128-47; and carpenters' union, **46:** 356,n5, 362-63, 363-64, 364-65, 366, 367, 378-79; R. W. Woolley and M. Hale on, **47:** 376, 379; and T. J. Mooney, **47:** 467; W. G. McAdoo on coal workers and, **48:** 87-88; J. P. Tumulty on, **48:** 261-62,n1; and telegraph workers, **48:** 281,n1, 282-83, 329, 337-40, 374-75, 393-94; machinists in Bridgeport, **49:** 265,n3, 519-20, 537, 547; **51:** 24,n1,2, 49-50; *see also* railroad crisis of 1917; labor; under the names of individual states

Stroehlin, Henry, **47:** 231,n2

Stromquist, Carl Eben, **47:** 311,n1

Strong, Benjamin, **40:** 137; **44:** 346, 351-53, 383; **51:** 103, 144,n3, 407

Strong, Frederick Smith, **45:** 111,n5

Strong, John Franklin Alexander, **43:** 385,n1

Strong, Sidney, **44:** 79

Structural Iron Workers Organization, **47:** 212

Struggle for Labor Loyalty: Gompers, the A.F. of L., and the Pacifists, 1917-1920 (Grubbs), **44:** 47n1, 166n3

Struggle Is Unto Death (*Manufacturers' Record*), **47:** 540,n2

Strunsky, Simeon, **46:** 422,n1

Stuart, Henry Carter, **40:** 222,n1; **48:** 562,n3; **51:** 127n2

Studd, Herbert William, **47:** 505,n1

Students' Army Training Corps, **49:** 242,n1; **51:** 168-69

Stumm, Wilhelm August von, **40:** 552,n2; **41:** 49n1

Stürmer, Boris Vladimirovich, **40:** 388,n1; **46:** 372n3; **48:** 184,n3

Stuttgart, Germany, **51:** 607

Stuttgart Congress (A. M. Simons), **42:** 254n2

Stuttgart *Schwäbische Tagwacht*, **46:** 164

Submarine Boat Corporation, **47:** 223n2

Submarine Scare, 1918 (Merrill), **49:**167n1

submarine warfare: *see* World War—strategic plans

Success Story: The Life and Times of S. S. McClure (Lyon), **43:** 134n2

Suez Canal, **44:** 477

Suffolk, H.M.S., **47:** 72n3, 243; **48:** 493,n1, 494

suffrage: *see* woman suffrage

Suffrage Committee (House of Reps.), **45:** 545n1

sugar, **46:** 431, 501-502, 546; **47:** 543n1; **51:** 89; and prices, **45:** 115-16, 163,n1, 353; **49:** 419n1; and Senate investiga-tion, **45:** 344-45,n1, 347-48, 352-54

Sugar Equalization Board, **49:** 419n1

Suggested Amendment to the Draft Act of May 18, 1917 (Woolsey), **45:** 177n1

Suhr, Herman D., **51:** 377,n1

Suifenho, Manchuria: *see* Pogranichnaya

Sukhomlinov, Vladimir Aleksandrovich, **48:** 184,n3

Sullens, Fanny, **40:** 217,n1

Sullens, Frederick, **46:** 104n1,2

Sullivan, (James) Mark, **43:** 197-98; **47:** 40n3; **51:** 621n1

Sulzer, Madame, **48:** 283, 289

Sulzer, Hans Adolf, **44:** 484n1; **45:** 80,n1, **48:** 283-84, 289; **49:** 437,n1; **51:** 76-77,n1, 91, 422

Summers, Leland Laflin, **51:** 407,n2

Summers, Maddin, **45:** 228-29,n1, 474; **48:** 96,n1,2, 141; death of, **48:** 96,n2, 113

Summit, N.J., **51:** 211n2

Sumner, Samuel Storrow, **41:** 470,n2

Sun Company of Philadelphia, **41:** 232,n1

Sun Yat-sen, **42:** 466,n1, 468,n1

sundry civil appropriations bills, **41:** 310n2, 329; **51:** 138

Supply Council: *see* Inter-Allied Council on War Purchases and Finance

Supreme Command, 1914-1918 (Hankey), **42:** 327n1

Supreme War Council, **46:** 352; **47:** 13,n2, 158, 294, 443n2, 487n1, 505,n1, 566n1, 571n1, 617; **48:** 32, 205, 232, 367n1, 463, 481n1, 493, 545, 566; **49:** 43-44, 201, 277, 279, 293, 336-37, 338, 341-42, 343, 530; **51:** 315; background and formation of, **44:** 80, 128-30, 179-80, 201, 203, 211, 246, 297, 353, 355, 369; **45:** 47-48, 54, 69, 93,n1,2, 112-13, 122, 151, 156, 317-18, 332n1, 546; E. M. House to attend, **44:** 380, 381-82, 427, 433; **48:** 61-62, 79, 94; and T. H. Bliss, **45:** 364, 532, 533, 539; **46:** 212, 240-41; **47:** 458-59, 512-14,n7; **48:** 200; **51:** 34, 39, 42, 43, 44, 45, 46, 47, 49, 337-38, 434-36,n1, 571; on need of U.S. battalions, **46:** 162, 211-12, 220, 221; Versailles Declaration and reactions to, **46:** 233-35, 249-50, 250-51, 268,n3, 390, 393, 415, 419, 429, 465; and Inter-Allied General Reserve, **46:** 241, 558-59; U.S. procedures and instructions for reporting on activities of, **46:** 254-56; suggestions for appointment to, **46:** 324, 327; U.S. on political opinions not being expressed by, **46:** 360-61,n1, 409; and intervention in Russia, **46:** 391-92; **47:** 59-61, 333, 491-92, 514,n7; **48:** 285-86,n3, 330-31, 367-70, 383-84,n3, 395-97, 416, 448,n1, 496-501, 503-506, 511-14, 588-89; resolution on joint notes, **46:** 453-54; and declaration on Poland, **46:** 587-88,n1 and requisitioning of Dutch ships, **47:** 26-27; and A. H. Frazier as observer, **47:** 102; on Italian participation in war, **47:** 130; **48:** 385; and

Supreme War Council (*cont.*)
Versailles resolution of March 27, 1918 on U.S. troops, **47:** 174, 175, 186-87, 205; and U.S. troop commitment, **47:** 260-61, 262-63,n2, 271, 315n2, 369, 369-70, 373, 374, 387, 455, 512,n1; and Abbeville agreement, **47:** 471, 497-98, 517-18, 535, 563-64, 567-68, 585, 595, 615, 618; and proposed U.S. war declaration against Bulgaria and Turkey, **47:** 491,n2, 568-70; **48:** 79-80; and Dutch situation regarding Germany, **47:** 564-65; J. J. Pershing on depression at, **48:** 245-46; N. D. Baker on U.S. permanent representative to, **48:** 266, 267; WW insists recommendations for troop use must come from, **48:** 418, 431; and resolution on minorities in Austria-Hungary, **48:** 437,n2; duties of military representatives to, **48:** 537,n5; on Balkan situation, **48:** 545; and Russia, **51:** 50, 52, 53, 337; joint note on Allied military policy for 1918 and 1919, **51:** 195-203, 211; E. M. House on progress of peace negotiations, **51:** 401, 462,n2, 517, 532, 568, 581-82, 592, 595, 605, 638; and Pershing's letter on peace terms, **51:** 523-25, 544,n1, 545, 596-98; agrees to armistice terms for Austria-Hungary, **51:** 544; resolution on food supplies, **51:** 595
Supreme War Council: Mr. Lloyd George's Statement (London *Daily Mail*), **47:** 12,n1
Surgeon Grow: An American in the Russian Fighting (Grow), **42:** 287n2; **43:** 455n2
Surgeon's Life: The Autobiography of J. M. T. Finney, **49:** 235n1
Survey, The (N.Y.), **40:** 124n3; **41:** 164,n2, 167n1
Sussex incident, **40:** 190-91; **41:** 96, 109-10, 120, 122
Sutphen, Henry Randolph, **42:** 477n1
Sutton, Mr., **46:** 212,n1
Sutton, C. W. H., **51:** 235n4
Sutton, George M., **43:** 480-82,n1
Sutton, William Seneca, **48:** 463n3
Suzzallo, Henry, **46:** 509,n1; **47:** 557
Swan Island, Caribbean, **47:** 353,n1
Swanberg, W. A., **51:** 12n3
Swanson, Claude Augustus, **41:** 234, 247, 288-92, 324, 359n3, 456; **46:** 41, 450; **51:** 83; and woman suffrage, **45:** 278, 279, 338; and general leasing bill and oil reserves, **45:** 374-75, 377, 402, 420, 448, 454,n1, 559
Swanson, Martin, **46:** 70,n2
Swanwick, Helena Maria Sickert (Mrs. F. T.), **42:** 422n2
Swarthmore College, **41:** 302n2; **44:** 36n1
Sweden, **41:** 40, 90, 249n1; **42:** 11, 339; **43:** 10; **44:** 389, 495; **45:** 80, 82, 114,n1; **47:** 361, 380-81, 430; **48:** 539; **49:** 312n1, 437-38; **51:** 18,n1,2, 102; and Germany, **44:** 131, 140,n3, 164,n1, 181, 412,n3;

and conference of neutrals, **40:** 23, 46-48, 81n1; and embargo, **44:** 284, 298, 298-99, 396,n1; and Russian mission to, **46:** 341,n2; and Austria-Hungary's peace negotiations, **51:** 258-59, 505-506, 526, 527
Swedish Americans, **44:** 236; **46:** 458-59, 469, 560; and draft evasion in Illinois, **47:** 134-36, 169
Sweet, Edwin Forrest, **43:** 385,n1
Sweet, Richard C., **40:** 442, 447, 491; **41:** 120, 124
Swem, Charles Lee, **40:** 159n2; **41:** 113n1; **43:** 159n2, 240, 368, 454; **44:** 215n2, 338, 397n1, 446n1; **45:** 125, 130, 179n3, 184, 262; **46:** 193n1, 313, 317n2, 318, 460; **48:** 32, 303n1, 319n1, 428, 463-64,n1, 564-65, 628; **49:** 4n2
Swift, A. V., **44:** 259
Swift, Eben, **45:** 111,n13; **46:** 456,n2
Swift, Louis Franklin, **45:** 179n2; **46:** 27, 462, 463
Swift, Gustavus, **46:** 27
Swift and Company, **46:** 27, 28, 195n1, 462,n3, 492; **47:** 50; **48:** 508
Swift and Company *v.* United States, **41:** 84
Swing, Raymond Edwards, **42:** 388, 388-90; **43:** 29-32,n1,2, 58; **46:** 36n1, 114, 181
Swinton, Ernest Dunlop, **51:** 7,n1
Switchmen's Union of North America, **47:** 447
Switzerland, **40:** 7, 15, 22, 42n1, 42-46, 231, 234, 457n1; **41:** 91, 102-107, 435; **43:** 144, 233; **44:** 484-90,n1,3,5, 514; **45:** 310, 332, 549, 595; **46:** 556, 592-94, 621; **47:** 64; **48:** 251,n2, 426, 457n1, 608; **51:** 184, 617; and conference of neutrals, **40:** 46-48, 81n1; **41:** 91-92, 131, 172-73,n1; and WW's peace note and Swiss reply, **40:** 320-24, 325-26, 348-54, 457-62; neutrality of, **41:** 193-94; **45:** 235-36; efforts to restore German-American relations, **41:** 203-204, 204-205, 244, 273-77; mobilizes troops, **41:** 222; C. W. Eliot on army and military training system of, **41:** 480-82, 540; **42:** 4, 19-20, 35-36, 76; and Morgenthau mission, **42:** 317; suggestion of new minister to, **42:** 454-55; and expulsion of Swiss minister to Russia, **43:** 28-29,n1; German activities in, **47:** 219-20,n1, **49:** 193, 436n1; and relief to enemy aliens in U.S., **47:** 361, 380-81; and league of nations, **49:** 19, 467; and Sulzer's alleged mission from WW, **51:** 76-77,n1, 91; R. de Fiori on German peace terms and, **51:** 240, 241; transmits peace message from Germany, **51:** 252,n1; Bolshevik movement in, **51:** 622-23
Swope, Herbert Bayard, **40:** 375n1; **43:** 404; **45:** 581; **46:** 22n1, 75, 416-17, 423; **47:** 93, 159; **48:** 302, 317, 486, 492; **51:** 284-85; on prohibition, **43:** 334-35,n1;

on aircraft program, **47**: 51-52; and Japanese intervention in Siberia, **47**: 224,n1,2; on investigation of ordnance program, **47**: 358,n1
Sykes, Mark, **42**: 327n1
Sylph, S.S., **44**: 81,n1
Sylvan Theater, Washington, D.C., **42**: 498n1
Symington, Powers, **42**: 379,n2
Syracuse, N.Y., **43**: 423; **44**: 193
Syria and Syrians, **40**: 318, 440, 501; **42**: 316, 332; **43**: 346, 355; **44**: 93; **45**: 330, 471, 553; **47**: 44; **51**: 503, 539,n2
Syria-Mt. Lebanon League of Liberation, **45**: 4n2
Syrovy, Jan, **51**: 51n2
System, the Magazine of Business, **46**: 218n2
Syz, John, **44**: 484n1
Syzran, Russia, **51**: 556
Szebeko, Ignacy, **42**: 544,n2
Szeklers, **51**: 502,n5
Szeptycki, Stanislaw, **46**: 403n2
Szold, Robert, **49**: 394,n1

Tacoma, Wash., **43**: 37, 266
Taft, Annie Sinton (Mrs. Charles Phelps), **44**: 536n1
Taft, Charles Phelps, **44**: 536n1
Taft, Robert Alphonso, **48**: 313,n1, 526n1
Taft, William Howard, **40**: 31, 420, 498n1, 565; **41**: 153, 154, 155-56, 197, 250n3, 251; **42**: 158, 448, 43: 11, **44**: 299n2, 536n1; **45**: 250, 272-73, 325, 374; **46**: 116, 480, 574, 578; **47**: 85-86, 102, 105, 137, 147-48, 276, 323, 584, 605; **48**: 561; **49**: 12, 186,n2, 211, 223n1, 251, 267; **51**: 363, 551n1, 630; and Red Cross, **42**: 261,n1, 281n1, 295-96; WW's get-well message to, **43**: 393, 399; confers with WW about proposed League to Enforce Peace convention, **47**: 42,n1, 119,n1,3, 123, 198-99; 199-202; and National War Labor Board, **47**: 248, 252, 272, 283, 302, 464; **49**: 520-22; F. P. Walsh on, **47**: 252-53; and interurban railways, **48**: 432, 526n1, 567-68, 598,n2, 623; **51**: 247-48, 258; on labor questions, **48**: 337, 338, 375, 394; **51**: 367-68; suggested as peace commissioner, **51**: 109; photograph, *illustration section*, **44**
Tagliamento River, Italy, **44**: 480, 507, 508
Tagore, Debendranath, **41**: 502n3
Tagore, Rabindranath, **41**: 502,n3, 554-55; **42**: 21
Talat Pasha, Mehmet, **42**: 316,n2, 317
Talcott, Charles Andrew, **40**: 289,n1,2; **41**: 354,n1; **45**: 411n2
Talk About Peace (*New York Times*), **40**: 30,n1
Talk with Abraham Lincoln (Gulliver), **46**: 460
Talk with Mr. Burleson (G. P. West), **44**: 470n3

Talks with T. R. (Leary), **42**: 29n1
Tallman, Clay, **40**: 560-61,n2; **41**: 69n1, 291-92
Tammany Hall, **41**: 359; **44**: 458; **49**: 106, 157n1, 465
Tammany Society, **42**: 327,n1
Tampa Morning Tribune, **46**: 604n3
Tampico, Tamaulipas, Mex., **42**: 37, 38,n2, 92, 96; **47**: 475; **48**: 238n1, 279; and Mooney case, **42**: 271,n1
Tanaka, Tokichi, **46**: 574,n1, 584,n1
Tangier, **42**: 264n3
Tansill, Charles Callan, **48**: 118n1
Tarbell, Ida Minerva, **41**: 191, 215-16; **42**: 210n1; **47**: 476; **48**: 57-58, 120; and Tariff Commission, **40**: 305, 343, 372-74, 384
Tardieu, André Pierre Gabriel Amédée, **42**: 229,n1, 374-76, 445, 488; **43**: 219, 220, 238, 286, 356n1, 358, 385, 426; **44**: 51, 52, 70, 147-48, 156-57,n1,2, 195-96, 462; **45**: 312, 322, 337, 399; **46**: 390, 490, 565n1; **48**: 236, 525; **51**: 34, 465, 577
Tariff Commission: *see* United States Tariff Commisson
tariff system: D. F. Houston on, **44**: 456-57; F. W. Taussig on, **44**: 541-44; WW on, **51**: 476-77
Tarnowski von Tarnow, Count Adam, **40**: 123,n2, 132, 139,n1; **41**: 88-89, 95, 106, 129,n2, 130, 149, 185, 473, 476, 477, 477-78, 525-26; **42**: 141, 493
Tatra, S.M.S., **51**: 492
Taube, Aleksandr Aleksandrovich, **49**: 152,n1
Taussig, Frank William, **41**: 379; **44**: 454, 455, 541-44, 545; **46**: 401, 407; **47**: 153, 221, 222,n2; **48**: 7; appointed to Tariff Commission, **40**: 347-48, 422; differs with a WW statement in address to American Federation of Labor, **45**: 101, 104, 127; on German peace proposal and U.S. response, **45**: 440-41; decision to remain on both committees of War Industries Board and Food Administration, **47**: 208, 224-25, 225, 233, 255
Taussig, Joseph Knefler, **44**: 346n1
taxation, **40**: 474; **42**: 25; **43**: 78, 91-92, 152, 350,n2, 491; **44**: 336; and war, **41**: 448n2, 522; **49**: 162-63,n1, 163-64; C. Hull on, **48**: 19-21, 27; W. G. McAdoo on need for increases, **48**: 122-27; WW's address to joint session of Congress on, **48**: 162-65; A. Capper on farmers and, **49**: 232-34, 241; A. S. Burleson on, **51**: 29-30; and President's and judges' salaries, **51**: 108-109,n9; R. S. Brookings on price fixing and, **51**: 219-20: *see also* revenue legislation; and under the name of specific tax, such as excess-profits tax
Taylor, Mr., **49**: 119
Taylor, A. Elizabeth, **47**: 144n2
Taylor, Abraham Merritt, **49**: 474,n1
Taylor, Alonzo Englebert, **42**: 323,n2; **48**:

Taylor, Alonzo Englebert (*cont.*)
306,n1; represents Food Administration on House mission, **45:** 69,n1, 78, 80, 86
Taylor, Charles Henry, Jr., **48:** 149,n2
Taylor, David Watson, **41:** 377,n1, 377-79, 381; **42:** 549; **43:** 470,n1; **49:** 313,n1
Taylor, Edward Thomas, **45:** 300,n4, 402n1; **46:** 79, 80-81; **47:** 451-52,n3
Taylor, Hannis, **42:** 526,n1; **44:** 60,n1, 119-20
Taylor, James Henry, **45:** 46; **46:** 582-83
Taylor, Thomas, Jr., **43:** 338,n2
Tchita, Russia: *see* Chita
Teapot Dome oil reserve, **40:** 206,n4
Tedcastle, Agnes Vaughn (Mrs. Arthur W.), **42:** 151
Tegetthof, S.M.S., **51:** 492
Tehuantepec Railway, Mex., **42:** 92, 96
Telefunken company, **46:** 621
telegraph system: and proposed strike, **48:** 281,n1, 282-83, 298, 301, 329, 337-40, 349-50, 374-75, 393-94, 546,n1; recommendations for legislation for governmental takeover of, **48:** 313, 440, 457,n1, 458,n1, 488, 526, 532-33,n1, 533, 534, 535,n1; and Aswell resolution on, **48:** 457,n1, 458,n1; and passage of wire-control bill, **48:** 556,n1,2, 591-92, 623,n1, 628-29
Temes, S.M.S., **51:** 493
temperance: *see* prohibition
Temperance, Prohibition and Public Morals, Board of (Methodist Episcopal Church), **41:** 311n1
Tempest, The (Shakespeare), 45:130
Temps des Américains: Le Concours Américain à la France en 1917-1918 (Kaspi), **42:** 229n2
Tennessee, **42:** 138,n2; and woman suffrage, **41:** 299, 48: 427; lynching in, **46:** 380-81, 384; politics in, **47:** 6,n2, 6-7, 34, 37; **51:** 482-83,n3, 633
Tennessee Historical Quarterly, **47:** 326n1
Terauchi, Masatake, **46:** 513, n2, 571,n2; **47:** 426n1, 427, 428; **48:** 582, 585; **49:** 107,n1, 322,n6
Tereshchenko, Mikhail Ivanovich, **41:** 416,n13; **42:** 320n2, 419,n3; **43:** 371,n1, 407n4; **44:** 43, 179, 180; **49:** 175,n1, 312,n1
Tergnier, France, **51:** 421
Territories, Committee on (House of Reps.), **40:** 292n1
Terry, Edward B., **45:** 547,n2
Testimony of Kolchak and Other Siberian Materials (Varneck and Fischer, eds.), **51:** 100n2, 102n1
Teusler, Rudolf Bolling, **49:** 529n1
Texas, **41:** 535; **46:** 478; **49:** 99; racial clash in Houston, **44:** 41-42,n1,2, 49, 62-64, 77-78; **46:** 383-84,n1, 385,n1; oil strike in, **45:** 44, 46, 60, 350; **46:** 170, 179; drought and livestock crisis in, **45:** 76-77, 105-106, 161, 253; and woman suffrage, **46:** 573,n1; **47:** 42, 104, 144n2; and Nonpartisan League, **47:** 260, 521,n1; politics in, **49:** 73,n3, 137n3; **51:** 616, 633
Texas, S.S., **46:** 213n2
Texas Company, **43:** 99n1
Texas Equal Suffrage Association, **46:** 573n1; **47:** 42, 144n1
Texas National Guard, **44:** 42n2
Texas State Federation of Labor, **47:** 104-105, 126, 127, 144
textile industry: and prices, **49:** 375-76, 389-90
Thacher, Thomas Day, **45:** 543,n4; **46:** 233,n2; **48:** 141,n3, 142; **49:** 55,n1
Thanksgiving Proclamation, **44:** 525-26; **45:** 147
Thayer, Henry Bates: resignation from Aircraft Board, **47:** 400,n1, 414, 415
Their Only Hope (cartoon), **51:** 483,n1
Thelen, Max, **49:** 253,n1
Thilly, Frank, **43:** 135, 136
Thionville (Diedenhofen), Germany (now France), **51:** 275
Third Presbyterian Church of Pittsburgh, **42:** 313n1
Thomas, Mr., **49:** 319,n1
Thomas, Albert, **42:** 319,n1, 320; **48:** 211; **51:** 21n1, 566
Thomas, C. W., **44:** 345,n5
Thomas, Charles Spalding, **40:** 523, 561n2; **42:** 245n2, 343n1; **46:** 204, 563; and woman suffrage, **45:** 279, 338; and Colorado coal prices, **46:** 599, 600-601; **47:** 7, 33, 37, 89-90; and Borglum affair, **47:** 511-12, 535-36; and labor, **49:** 104, 132, 133, 166; and immigration resolution, **49:** 310n1
Thomas, David Alfred: *see* Rhondda, 1st Baron
Thomas, Harriet Park (Mrs. William Isaac), **44:** 79
Thomas, Irving, **40:** 187
Thomas, James Henry, **42:** 266,n1
Thomas, Martha Carey, **48:** 345n1
Thomas, Norman Mattoon, **44:** 266-67; **51:** 12,n1,2,3
Thomas, William E., **43:** 162,n2,3
Thomas A. Edison, Inc., **41:** 126n1,2
Thomas P. Gore: The Blind Senator from Oklahoma (Billington), **43:** 48n1, 393n1
Thompson, Alexander Marshall, **47:** 540,n1
Thompson, Caroline Cordes (Mrs. Samuel Huston, Jr.), **45:** 256,n2
Thompson, Charles Thaddeus, **40:** 29,n1, 36
Thompson, Henry Dallas, **42:** 458
Thompson, John, **47:** 235
Thompson, Robert Means, **43:** 470n3
Thompson, Samuel Huston, Jr., **43:** 33-34; **45:** 163, 255-56; **47:** 539-40, 559; on Federal Trade Commission, **40:** 490, 493
Thompson, Vance, **48:** 472n1

Thompson, William Boyce, **44:** 367,n2, 424, 434, 435; **45:** 407, 441-42, 474, 548, 570; **46:** 160-61, 179-80, 193,n1, 232,n1; **47:** 141, 142; on Russian situation, **45:** 442-47

Thompson, William Hale, **43:** 512n1; **44:** 236n4

Thompson, William Howard, **42:** 343n1; **47:** 8-9; and woman suffrage, **45:** 279, 338

Thompson, William McIlwain, **45:** 256n3

Thompson, William Ormonde, **47:** 557,n4

Thomson, Graeme, **43:** 303,n4; **47:** 230, 394

Thornton, Montrose, W., **42:** 116

Thrace, **51:** 47, 502

Threatened Miners' Strike: Is There Any Justification? (*Birmingham News*), **43:** 434n1

Three Centuries of Treaties of Peace and Their Teaching (Phillimore), **47:** 104,n2

3 Noted Germans Interned for War in Hunt for Spies (*New York Times*), **43:** 133n1

Through Darkness to Dawn (Rice), **43:** 85n1,3

Throw I.W.W. in River, Says Labor Committee (*Sacramento Bee*), **47:** 196,n5

Thurman, Albert Lee, **43:** 310n1, 519; **44:** 11

Thurman, Allen Granberry, **51:** 177,n2

Ticino, Switzerland, **48:** 553

Tidewater Coal Bureau, **43:** 242

Tientsin, China, **49:** 213, 214

Tikhon, Patriarch (Vasili Ivanovich Belyavin), **43:** 149,n1; **49:** 63,n2

Tillman, Benjamin Ryan, **40:** 420; **43:** 198-99; **48:** 203, 428,n1,2; and woman suffrage, **45:** 279, 339; **47:** 597; senatorial campaign of, **48:** 260n2; death of, **48:** 268n1, 492,n1

Tillman, John Newton, **49:** 63,n1

Tillman, Robert, **49:** 399-400

Tillman, Sallie Starke (Mrs. Benjamin Ryan), **48:** 492

Tillman case (Houston riot of 1917), **49:** 326, 327, 328, 400-402

Tin Plate Mills, Wheeling, W. Va., **42:** 473

Tinkham, George Holden, **42:** 202,n1

Tinoco Granadas, Federico, **41:** 140-44,n1, 145, 146,n1, 248, 386; **43:** 160n1; **44:** 232n1; **45:** 388, 405-406; **46:** 450; **49:** 5-6, 21-22, 431,n2

Tinoco Granadas, Joaquin, **41:** 143; **47:** 231n1

Tippy, Worth Marion, **41:** 353,n1, 353-54

Tirpitz, Alfred Peter Friedrich von, **40:** 141, 555; **42:** 160; **46:** 113n2, 163n1, 189,n7

Tisza, Count István (Stephen), **45:** 57,n4, 138

Title Guarantee and Trust Company, N.Y., **43:** 197

To All Those Engaged in Coal Mining (WW), **49:** 144-45; 173,n1

To End Water Power Graft (New York *Evening Sun*), **49:** 344,n1

To Raise Every Boy to Be a Soldier (*New York Times*), **40:** 267n1

To the United States of America (Bridges), **42:** 392

Todd, George Carroll, **40:** 102-104n1; **44:** 151,n2; **46:** 361n1; **48:** 612n1; **49:** 463

Todd, Helen, **43:** 432,n1, 433,n2 495, 497, 536,n1, 536-38

Todd, Robert Henry, **41:** 312,n1

Todorov, General (Bulgarian), **51:** 141n2

Tokoi, Antti Oskari, **48:** 100,n1, 101

Toledo, Ohio, *Blade*, **49:** 510

Toledo Herrarte, Luis, **42:** 46,n1

Tolstoi, Leo (Lev) L'vovich (1869-1945), **42:** 216

Tom Watson: Agrarian Rebel (Woodward), **43:** 389n1

Tomasi, Pietro Paolo, **47:** 319,n5

Tomsk, Russia, **47:** 22, 100; **48:** 398; movement for autonomy, **47:** 71, 92n1, 397,n1, 398, 592; **49:** 42

Tooele, Utah, **42:** 564; **43:** 17-18

Topeka, Kan., **42:** 83, 84

Topeka Plaindealer, **45:** 577; **51:** 170n1

Topics of the Day: The League of Nations (Strachey), **51:** 444,n1

Torrance, Jared Sidney, **41:** 423,n1,2, 468

Torres, Rodolfo, **49:** 305

Torretta, Marchese della, **47:** 319-20,n5

Totten, James, **41:** 430,n2

Toul, France, **47:** 612

Tours, France, **48:** 265, 389

Toward a New Order of Sea Power: American Naval Policy and the World Scene, 1918-1922, (Sprout and Sprout), **51:** 344n1

Toward the Truth (Muehlon), **48:** 213n8

Towner, Horace Mann, **44:** 54,n1

Townley, Arthur Charles, **44:** 182-83,n1; **45:** 167,n1; **46:** 160,n1,2, 270, 348, 387; **47:** 87-88, 177-78, 193-94,n1, 215-16, 216, 226

Townley, F. S., **44:** 193,n2

Townley, Walter Beaupré, **47:** 27,n2

T. P. Talks of Obstacles in Home Rule Fight: Nationalist Party, Seeking Autonomy, Is Trying to Keep Ireland from Committing Suicide—Futility of Sinn Fein's Hopes (*New York Times Magazine*), **44:** 133n2

trade: *see* commerce

Trade Commission: *see* Federal Trade Commission

trade unions: *see* labor unions

Trades Union Congress (London), **45:** 487n2; **47:** 74n1; **49:** 545

Tradesmen's National Bank, Phila., **43:** 197

trading with the enemy: *bill*, **43:** 111,n4, 281, 311, 312, 314, 315, 320-23, 518; **44:** 11, 208, 318; **47:** 275n1; and Section 19 (foreign-language publications), **44:**

Trading with the enemy (*cont.*)
266,n1, 318,n2; and censorship, **44:**
271-73, 366n1, 389, 409, 416, 470n3;
Act **51:** 395n1
Train, Charles Russell, **41:** 435,n3
Training for War and for Work (*Springfield*, Mass., *Republican*), **41:** 295n2
Trammell, Park, **42:** 343n1; **46:** 61, 608;
49: 268; and woman suffrage, **45:** 278,
279, 338; **47:** 34-35,n2; **48:** 43-44, 233;
51: 123, 165
Trans-Baikal Railroad, **47:** 70
Transbaikalia, Russia, **47:** 100n4
transit companies, **51:** 61, 76, 247, 258; issues of wage discrepancies and rate increases, **49:** 183, 186,n2, 206-207,
211,n1, 223, 251, 421-22, 474-75; G. S.
Macfarland on, **51:** 19-20, 193n2; *see
also* Twin City Rapid Transit Company
Trans-Siberian Railway, **41:** 511; **42:** 11-
12, 222; **43:** 424; **45:** 229; **47:** 15, 22, 80,
131, 132, 141, 592; **48:** 105, 131, 202,
204, 419, 441n1, 459, 460, 560; **49:** 10,
40n1, 45, 76, 285, 396n1; **51:** 99, 100,
394, 427, 481n1,2; and proposed Japanese occupation of, **46:** 89-90, 154-55,
181-82, 219-20, 220,n2, 220-21, 271,
302-303, 303-304, 340, 344,n1,2, 355,
387, 388, 391-92, 470-71, 515, 528-30,
535, 548, 590; *see also*—Russia Siberia,
intervention in
Transylvania, **40:** 361; **42:** 334; **45:** 412,
418; **46:** 244; **51:** 502
Trask, David F., **43:** 236n1; **51:** 474n1
Traum von Stockholm (Harden), **43:**
246n1
Traveller in War-time (Churchill), **43:**
354,n2
Travieso, Martin, Jr., **40:** 97
Treadway, Allen Towner, **46:** 256n1; **48:**
45n1
Treasury, Department of the, **42:** 412; **43:**
94, 204, 389; **44:** 198, 323n1, 502; **45:**
28-29, 561n1, 591; **46:** 75, 122, 408,
413; **48:** 162-65, 140,n1, 168, 219-
20,n1; **51:** 87, 205; and Secret Service,
42: 16, 17, 441; and War Trade Committee, **42:** 49, 118; and Shipping
Board, **42:** 286; and trading with the
enemy bill and control of clearances,
43: 281, 313, 314, 315, 316, 321-22; and
railroads, **45:** 225-26, 233; and Russian
obligations to, **46:** 65, 66; McAdoo on
Allied demands on, **45:** 424-25, 589-91;
and on Fourth Liberty Loan drive, **49:**
85-87; and aid to drought-stricken
farmers, **49:** 100-101; war savings and
thrift stamps deposits, **49:** 235,n2;
McAdoo considers resigning from, **49:**
287, 489; and public health responsibilities, **49:** 379
Treat, Charles Gould, **45:** 107,n1
*Treaties and Agreements with and con-
cerning China, 1894-1919* (Mac-
Murray, ed.), **46:** 539n1
*Treaties and Other International Agree-

ments of the United States of America,
1776-1949* (Bevans, comp.), **51:** 576n1
*Treatise on the Laws of Private Corpora-
tions Other than Charitable* (Stetson),
49: 168n2
Treaty of Berlin, 1878, **42:** 333
Treaty of London, 1915, **48:** 114n1
Tredwell, Roger Culver, **45:** 216-28,n1
Trego, Frank H., **44:** 541,n6
Trent, Austria (now Trento, Italy), **51:**
500-501
Trentino, **40:** 307n1; **41:** 217; **42:** 456; **44:**
21, 508; **45:** 418, 441; **47:** 240; **51:** 48,
262
Trešić-Pavičić, Ante, **51:** 562,n1
Treub, M. W. F., **46:** 615n4
Trevelyan, Charles Philips, **40:** 124,n3,
140, 164, 178, 178-80, 189; **41:** 374-
75,n2; **42:** 422, 435
Trevelyan, George Otto, **40:** 124n3, 180
Treviño, Jacinto B., **40:** 109
Treviso, Italy, **44:** 506
Trieste, Austria (now Italy), **42:** 156; **45:**
38, 469; **46:** 244, 262; **47:** 63-64, 125,n3,
240; **48:** 553; **51:** 156n2, 501, 564
Triglav, S.M.S., **51:** 492
Trinidad, **47:** 89
Trinity College, Dublin, **42:** 543n1
Trinity Episcopal Church, N.Y., **40:** 89n1
Tripoli, Lebanon, **44:** 476
Triumphant Success of the New Liberty
Loan is Necessary for Victory in The
Terrible War (Macfarland), **44:** 307,n1
Troelstra, Pieter Jelles, **51:** 232,n1, 233
Trotha, Adolf von, **51:** 541n1
Trotsky, Leon (Leib or Lev Davydovich
Bronstein), **43:** 474n1; **45:** 119,n1, 120,
147,n1, 176, 192, 205, 222n1, 251, 252,
253, 274, 341, 430, 443, 444, 543,n2,
573, 595n3; **46:** 22n1, 191, 299, 300,n7,
342, 408, 420,n2, 421, 471,n3, 542; **47:**
69, 79, 440, 441, 466, 504, 522, 551,
607, 621; **48:** 38, 41, 99-100, 101, 144,
204-205, 410n2, 428; **49:** 45,n3, 197,
199; **51:** 4, 246; on separate peace, **45:**
216-17,n4, 411-14; and passport issue,
45: 342,n2,3; and Sisson Documents,
46: 341,n1; "no war—no peace," **46:**
341n5; on intervention in Russia, **47:**
60, 141, 227, 245-46, 281, 319n6, 320,
356, 367,n3, 412, 436n1, 489, 496, 544,
605; WW on, **48:** 133; G. Kennan on, **48:**
186, 187; L. Colcord on, **48:** 548, 549;
photograph, *illustration section,* **45**
Trotter, William Monroe, **42:** 115; **46:** 550
Trowbridge, Daniel W., **46:** 433n2
Trubetskoi, Prince Grigorii Nikolaevich,
45: 229,n4; **48:** 239,n2
True Story of the Horror (*Nonpartisan
Leader*), **47:** 521n1
Truer Germany (Colcord), **40:** 374n1
Trufanov, Sergei Mikhailovich: *see* Ilio-
dor (Monk Iliodor)
Trumbull, Frank, **41:** 54; **43:** 242
Truth About New Russia (Gavronsky),
48: 376n3

Tschlenow, Jehiel, **45:** 572,n2
Tseretelli, Irakli Georgievich, **42:** 418n1, 419,n3; **45:** 216,n3
Tsinan, China, **49:** 213
Tsingtau, China, **49:** 213
Tsitsihar, Manchuria, **51:** 479,n1
Tsurumi, Yūsuke, **47:** 427,n1, 428; **48:** 585,n4
Tuan Ch'i-jui, **41:** 175,n4; **42:** 61,n2; **43:** 363,n1, 363,n5; **45:** 308,n1
Tuckahoe, U.S.S., **47:** 500,n1
Tucker, Henry St. George, **49:** 529n1
Tucker, Mona House (Mrs. Randolph Foster), **44:** 184,n1, 185; **49:** 275,n1, 276, 499
Tucker, Randolph Foster, **44:** 184,n1, 185; **49:** 275,n1, 276
Tumulty, Joseph Patrick, **40:** 7, 24, 35, 44n2, 96, 111, 154, 236-37, 255, 306, 324, 339, 352, 374, 423, 457n1, 465, 562-63; **41:** 31, 33, 37, 44-45,n1, 68, 70, 84, 113n3, 124, 134, 167, 168, 251-52, 255, 257-58, 329, 332, 359, 402, 412-13, 445, 496, 531, 557; **42:** 6-7, 8-9, 29n, 31, 42-43, 104, 123, 129n1, 138, 139, 153n1, 153-54, 219, 237, 287, 427, 437, 495, 505, 506, 532, 548; **43:** 13, 42-43, 71, 86,n3, 103, 106-107, 128, 135, 136, 145, 146, 149, 156-57, 175-76, 208, 221n1, 222,n1, 239-40, 266-67, 270, 272n1, 284, 318, 319, 345, 351-52, 386, 391, 393, 412,n3, 420, 501n2; **44:** 10n1, 17, 22-23, 40, 77,n1, 80, 84, 173n1, 183, 191-92,n2, 203, 206, 207, 208, 215, 223, 231-32, 239n1, 242, 268, 271, 273, 276-77, 277-78, 279, 287, 289, 302, 307, 308,n1, 346, 351-52, 364, 365, 383-84, 384, 398, 445, 448, 453, 467, 482, 490-91, 504, 524, 536,n1, 556, 559; **45:** 39, 40, 41n1, 46, 53, 68, 69-70, 93,n3 117-18, 125-26, 155-56, 214, 221, 250, 262, 275, 288, 306, 314, 318, 320, 344, 371, 397, 425, 426, 435, 541, 555, 577, 600; **46:** 30, 41, 41n, 57, 63, 79, 82, 83-84, 84, 109, 119,n1, 150, 152n1, 181, 193n1, 194, 256-57,n1, 264, 318, 339, 347-49, 380-81, 411, 422, 601-602, 604n3, 619; **47:** 82n1, 126, 129, 147, 200, 224n2, 260, 275n2, 311, 362-63, 420, 437, 449, 479n4, 552, 576n2, 578, 600, 604, 615; **48:** 32, 51, 62, 115, 118, 119, 166, 169n2, 230-31,n1, 237, 241, 300, 302, 311, 335,n1, 345n1, 345-46, 356, 364, 392, 428n1, 444, 488, 564-65, 578-79, 597, 627, 628, 643, 644-45; **49:** 20, 51, 90, 126, 164, 172, 211-12, 219, 222, 240, 246, 314-15, 360, 371n3, 419-20, 438, 449-50, 455, 541; **51:**, 14-15, 15, 23, 49-50, 57,n1, 84, 117, 120, 133-34, 170, 172n2, 186, 191, 293n2, 316,n6, 353, 356n1, 392, 476,n1, 483, 485, 616

and stock exchange leak inquiry, **40:** 349n11, 462; talk of resignation, **40:** 463,n3; and inauguration ceremony, **41:** 328, 329; and WW and arming of merchant ships, **41:** 367, 381; on A. S. Burleson, **41:** 382; on labor issues, **41:** 414, 424, 432, 42: 459; **43:** 104; **48:** 261-62, 526-27; **49:** 223; on being masters of our own destiny in war, **41:** 462-64; on WW's reaction to applause after war message, **41:** 541n1; on Irish Home Rule, **42:** 111-12, 222, 223, **47:** 401,n2, 411-12, 575; on espionage bill and censorship, **42:** 106-107, 108, 245-46; on reception for British mission, **42:** 125; on sending ambassador to Japan, **42:** 244-45; on evils of a separate peace, **42:** 360-64; suggests B. Whitlock tell of German atrocities, **42:** 427-28; and training camp at Princeton, **42:** 458; on WW's note to provisional Russian government, **42:** 458-59; on L. Seibold, **43:** 19-20; on East St. Louis assault, **43:** 139, 342, 343, 359; and Morgenthau mission, **43:** 172; on Massachusetts elections, **44:** 204-205; and Shipbuilding Labour Adjustment Board controversy, **44:** 229n6; on woman suffrage, **44:** 460-61; **45:** 565; **46:** 608,n1; **47:** 34-35, 42, 547, 571-72, 572n2, **48:** 24, 217-18, 271-72, 303n1, 370; **49:** 264-65, 381; **51:** 49; rumor of imprisonment, **45:** 18,n2; on declaring war on Austria-Hungary, **45:** 163-64,n1; suggestions for WW's State of the Union address, **45:** 164-65; on W. G. McAdoo's ability to manage railroads, **45:** 232-33; WW and E. M. House discuss, **45:** 325-26; sends WW birthday greetings, **45:** 369,n1; on investigation of supplies in training camps, **45:** 390; on editorial opinions, **45:** 436-37; **47:** 253-54; and G. Borglum, **46:** 95n2, 332; **47:** 51, 235, 293, 396, 508-509, 511-12,n2, 587, 587-88, 588; appointment suggestions for War Industries Board, **46:** 259, 269; on Father Kelley, **46:** 406,n1; on New York politics, **46:** 565-66; and Nonpartisan League, **47:** 193-94,n1; and Philadelphia *Public Ledger*, **47:** 278-79; and Mooney case, **47:** 396-97, 467n1; on *Chicago Tribune's* request for amount of WW's personal donation to Liberty Loan, **47:** 436-37; and T. G. Masaryk, **47:** 561n1; on revenue legislation, **48:** 128-29; **49:** 162; suggests a minister to Denmark, **48:** 143-44; and Negroes as voters, **48:** 155; on congressional campaigns, **48:** 347-49; **49:** 369-70; **51:** 304-306, 572; on wire-control bill, **48:** 591-92; on Al Smith, **49:** 105-106; on New Jersey politics, **49:** 210; **51:** 283; WW on, **49:** 275; on WW not making western tour, **49:** 439; on slacker raid, **49:** 451; on public utilities, **49:** 457, 458, 460; on prohibition legislation, **49:** 476-78; **51:** 105; on E. Root and Permanent Court of Arbitration, **49:** 540-41; and censorship of *The Nation*, **51:** 55,n1; on question of WW endorsing candidates,

Tumulty, Joseph Patrick (*cont.*)
  51: 63, 537-38, 552; and Unconditional Surrender Club, **51:** 91,n1; on relationship between coal operators and Fuel Administration, **51:** 111-12, 113-16; on peace correspondence with Germany, **51:** 265-68, 278-79, 329-32, 338-39; on West Virginia's elections, **51:** 437; on E. Keating's reelection bid, **51:** 460-61
Tunis, **44:** 476
Tupper, C. T., **43:** 200,n2
Turbulent Era: A Diplomatic Record of Forty Years 1904-1945 (Grew), **40:** 21n1
Turkestan, **47:** 356, 366, 422, 423, 424; **51:** 201
Turkey, **40:** 25, 231, 250, 307n1, 317, 318, 357, 361, 362, 404, 414n1, 446n2, 500-501; **41:** 25, 26n1, 61, 75, 76, 81, 128, 464; **42:** 149n1, 198, 288, 315-17,n1,2,3, 329, 332, 340, 403, 425, 433, 456, 463, 500, 501, **43:** 159n1,3, 236, 345,n1, 346, 406, 469, 471; **44:** 21, 43, 93, 119, 126, 200, 201, 239n1, 295, 361n1, 379, 387, 476, 547, 548; **45:** 13, 72-73, 197, 200, 249, 286, 416, 460, 559; **46:** 167, 172, 173, 182, 224, 240, 275, 277, 292, 295, 320, 322, 493; **47:** 269, 422-23, 424; **48:** 20n2, 29, 179, 399, 404, 416; **51:** 47, 151, 152, 156n2, 163, 183, 266, 455n1, 456, 488, 499, 501, 503, 517, 563-64, 595; A. I. Elkus on, **44:** 37; **45:** 52-53; H. Morgenthau on Germany and, **45:** 123-24; question of separate peace with, **45:** 148-49; **51:** 292, 349, 389; issue of declaring war against, **45:** 185-86, 207, 215; **47:** 416-17,n2, 490-91,n2, 568-70, 570-71; **48:** 70, 79-80,n1; **49:** 365,n1,2, 537; and Brest-Litovsk peace conference, **45:** 384n2, 411-12; and Inquiry memorandum, **45:** 464, 467, 471-72; and Fourteen Points, **45:** 482, 485, 507, 514, 520, 528, 534, 538, 553; and British war aims statement, **45:** 487n2; relief to, **47:** 44; **48:** 97-99, 136; Charles I on peace terms and, **47:** 125; and Allied war plans for 1918-1919, **51:** 200-201
Turkish Americans, **43:** 86n2,3
Turmoil and Tradition: A Study of the Life and Times of Henry L. Stimson (Morison), **42:** 83n1
Turn to the Right (play), **47:** 220,n1, 222
Turner, Hezekiah C., **49:** 399-400
Turner, Sheadrick Bond, **43:** 392,n1
Tuscania, S.S., **46:** 433,n2
Tuskegee Institute, **41:** 421; **42:** 321, 322; **46:** 480n1; **47:** 289; **48:** 530
Twain, Mark, **44:** 124n2
Twin City Rapid Transit Company, **49:** 181; strike, **45:** 258-62,n2, 279, 331; **47:** 189-91, 272-74
Twining, Nathan Crook, **43:** 182,n2; **45:** 21
Tyler, Robert L., **44:** 50n1; **46:** 144n1, 218n2

Tynan, Thomas J., **51:** 645,n2
Typhoon (Conrad), **44:** 82,n1
Tyrol, **51:** 564
Tyrrell, Sir William George, **48:** 501n1, 555n7; **49:** 402, 423, 429

U-Boat Attacks (*Springfield*, Mass., *Republican*), **41:** 451n2
U-boat warfare, **40:** 452; *U-53*, **40:** 85, 144, 388-89; *U-55*, **40:** 389n1; *U-69*, **40:** 144; *U-151*, **49:** 167n1; *U-156*, **49:** 167n1
Udine, Italy, **44:** 506, 508
Ufa, Russia, **51:** 50n1, 102,n1; Directorate, **51:** 100n2, 102n1
Uhlig, Otto, **46:** 189n6
Ujina, Japan, **49:** 494,n2
Ukraine, **45:** 418, 419; **46:** 187, 191, 268, 402, 421, 471n3, 533, 537, 568; **48:** 106n4, 186, 299, 419, 490; **49:** 195; **51:** 498, 501-502, 638; and Central Rada, **46:** 341n4, 421n3; **48:** 102-103,n1
Ukrainian Revolution, 1917-1920: A Study in Nationalism (Reshetar), **48:** 102n1
Ulan Bator, Mongolia: *see* Urga
Ul'ianov, Vladimir Il'ich: *see* Lenin, V. I.
Uliassutai, Mongolia, **49:** 448,n2
Ullman, Richard Henry, **45:** 189n1, 544n6; **47:** 245n3, 319n6, 355n1, 367n4; **49:** 518n4; **51:** 4n2
Ulyanovosk, Russia: *see* Simbirsk
Uncle Dudley: *see* Price, Lucien
Unconditional Surrender Club of the United States of America, **51:** 91n1
Underwood, Emory Marvin, **42:** 244n2
Underwood, Oscar Wilder, **40:** 523; **41:** 160, 199, 238; **42:** 31; **43:** 11; **46:** 204; and woman suffrage, **45:** 279, 339
Union College, Schenectady, N.Y., **44:** 364n1
Union des Patriotes Russes, **48:** 472n2
Union Française pour le Suffrage des Femmes, **48:** 25-26,n3
Union Legaue Club of Chicago, **43:** 168-70, 193-94; **44:** 236
Union Methodist Episcopal Church, Washington, D.C., **48:** 155n1
Union of Democratic Control, England, **42:** 422,n2, 435n1
Union of Polish Socialists, **44:** 6n1
Union of Siberian Cooperative Societies, **48:** 359n1
Union Pacific Railroad, **42:** 488; **43:** 74; R. Lovett and, **46:** 39n1, 52, 476
Union Theological Seminary, Richmond, Va., **42:** 87, 89n3
Union Trust Company, N.Y., **43:** 197
Union Trust Company, Pittsburgh, **43:** 197
Unionist party, Porto Rico, **48:** 18,n1
Unite and Win (Creel), **47:** 276,n3
United Brotherhood of Carpenters and Joiners of America, **46:** 356n5, 362-63, 363-64, 364-65, 366, 367, 379; **47:** 343,n1

United Commercial Travelers of America, **46:** 256n1
United Confederate Veterans, **42:** 450-53,n1
United Free Church of Scotland, **49:** 295
United Fruit Company, **46:** 450, 621; **49:** 431; and Costa Rica, **41:** 140, 143,n14, 143-44
United Garment Workers of America, **47:** 223n2
United Kingdom: *see* Great Britain
United Mine Workers Journal, **44:** 144n1; **46:** 103n2; **49:** 216
United Mine Workers of America, **40:** 217,n1; **43:** 340, 352, 353, 368, 511; **44:** 144n1; **45:** 269, 540, 568n1; **46:** 297n1, 578n1; **51:** 545; and Council of National Defense, **42:** 458, 458-59,n1, 471-73; in Alabama, **42:** 460-61, 504-505
United Press, **40:** 133, 345, 346, 374; **44:** 164; **51** 538,n1, 621n1; and Zimmermann Telegram, **41:** 308,n1
United Shoe Machinery Company, **46:** 362n3
United Society of Christian Endeavor, **51:** 149n1
United States and East Central Europe, 1914-1918: A Study in Wilsonian Diplomacy and Propaganda (Mamatey), **48:** 358n1; **51:** 562n1
United States and Pangermania (Chéradame), **45:** 410,n1, 423; **47:** 112,n1
United States and Poland (Wandycz), **42:** 11n1; **44:** 6n1
United States and Revolutionary Nationalism in Mexico, 1916-1932 (Smith), **46:** 354n2; **48:** 279n5
United States and the Rebirth of Poland (Wedrowski), **42:** 355n2
United States Army, **41:** 151, 462, 522; **42:** 4, 91-92, 98, 103, 139-40, 200, 200-201, 227, 406; **44:** 68, 119, 209,n2; **47:** 295; **49:** 169; and Cuba, **41:** 268n1; and Danish West Indies, **41:** 363; and increase in military departments, **41:** 455,n1, 474; and T. Roosevelt request for volunteer division, **41:** 469,n1, 469-70, **42:** 56, 324-26, 346; and bill to increase, **41:** 500-501,n1; plans for leisure and recreational program for, **41:** 505-506, 509, 527; **43:** 478-79; **47:** 220,n1, 311,n1,2; and Polish Americans, **41:** 507-509; C. W. Eliot and, **41:** 540; **42:** 19-20, 35-36, 76, 91; WW on, **41:** 550-51; **46:** 103; **48:** 205; and Polish army, **42:** 12, 352-53, 356, 357, 385-86; **43:** 426; **44:** 188, 189, and volunteerism in Civil War, **42:** 58, 146-50; **44:** 337; Wilson and Joffre discuss sending of U.S. troops to France, **42:** 186-91; plans for expeditionary force, **42:** 194, 249-51, 325, 400-401; **49:** 66-67; Negroes and, **42:** 321, 321-22, 357-58; **43:** 130, 392, 506-507; **44:** 10, 63-64; **48:** 156-58,n2,3,4; **49:** 179,n2; **51:** 137, 170n1,

192; J. J. Pershing appointed commander A.E.F., **42:** 404-405; and cantonments for, **42:** 406-407; T. H. Bliss on, **42:** 408-10; and recommendation to disband four months after war ends, **42:** 427; and insurance, **42:** 527n1, 565; **43:** 6, 93-94; **44:** 92, 116-17, 323; Philippines offers divisions for, **42:** 541-42: **43:** 16; and Young-Dockery affair, **43:** 4, 16, 118, 119,n1, 132; and diet in, **43:** 324-25; **45:** 423n1; WW's messages to, **43:** 380; **44:** 91, 142; **47:** 172; L. D. Wald on violation of civil rights by, **43:** 422-23; and New York's regiment, **43:** 492,n1, 514; and draft exemptions, **43:** 535; **48:** 151-52,n1; and Houston riot, **44:** 41-42,n1,2, 63-64, 77-78; **45:** 579-80; **46:** 13, 16,n1, 383-84,n1, 385,n1; **49:** 399-404; need for U.S. troops and question of amalgamation with French troops, **44:** 51, 52, 237, **45:** 122, 208-209, 316-17, 328, 372-73, 396, 397, 405, 438, 439-40, 539-40, 571, 583; and distribution of Bibles to, **44:** 85, 118, 152; WW leads parade for contingent from Washington, D.C., **44:** 107n3; C. A. Lindbergh report on woman suffrage demonstration and, **44:** 108-16; E. M. House on replacements for retiring generals, **44:** 164-65; new regulations for selective service, **44:** 522, 533-35; and YM-YWCA programs, **44:** 551-52; **48:** 208n1, 221-22,n1; and health issues, **45:** 108-109, 390n4, 421n1, 423; **46:** 290-10; **47:** 478,n2; **51:** 281-82; J. J. Pershing's evaluations and recommendations of officers, **45:** 109-12; and Jews at Camp Upton, **45:** 157; and N. D. Baker on, **45:** 173; **46:** 248-49, 400-401, 414, 612; and holiday greetings from, **45:** 364, 366, 426
Senate investigation of lack of supplies in training camps, **45:** 390,n1; statistics on, **45:** 408-409; **48:** 307, 476-77, 482; **51:** 404-405, 405; shipping needs of, **45:** 489-91; WW on not creating a munitions ministry, **45:** 566; and British and French request for battalions from, **46:** 8-11,n1, 11-12, 42, 43-44, 44-45, 162, 196-98, 211-12, 220, 231-32, 236-37, 237-38, 240, 248, 272-73, 337-38, 354; **48:** 226, 246, 285-86; WW on Sabbath observance and, **46:** 41-42,n1; G. E. Chamberlain on inefficiency and WW's reply, **46:** 53-55, 55-56; and housing appropriation, **46:** 171; J. I. France's bill to mobilize forces, **46:** 325-26,n1, 343; and request for military mission to Italy, **46:** 376-78; and inter-Allied General Reserve, **46:** 241, 558-59; and Sheriff Wheeler's commission, **46:** 584, 598-99; **47:** 115-16, 347, 597-98; and rehabilitation of wounded men, **46:** 608-609; **47:** 28-30, 95, 123-24, 153; and illiteracy problem, **47:** 30-32; and noncombatant service, **47:** 72-73,n1,

United States Army (*cont.*)
154-55; critical need for U.S. troops leads to Versailles resolution and Abbeville agreement, **47:** 130-31, 145-47, 157, 158, 166,n1, 170, 174-76, 181-83, 204-205, 213-14, 221-22, 229-30, 230, 256, 260-61, 262-63, 271, 279, 280-81, 302-303, 305-306, 307, 314-15, 369-71, 372-76, 386-88, 393-94, 434-35, 436, 455-58, 497-98, 517-18, 556-68, 611-12, 615-16, 616-20; **48:** 32-34; Bliss on Foch as military coordinator, **47:** 237-38; and Sedition Act, **47:** 364n4; and Bliss' rank, **47:** 458-59; and truck gardens at training camps, **47:** 478,n1; and court-martial case, **47:** 480-86, 516; and issue of sending troops to Italy, **47:** 486-87, 501; and Pershing's authority regarding death penalty, **48:** 5-6; and aviation, **48:** 73-74; and Freeman case, **48:** 136,n1, 177,n1; L. Wood affair, **48:** 173,n1, 194; and Foch-Milner-Pershing agreement on troop transport, **48:** 218, 227; J. G. Schurman to address soldiers in Europe, **48:** 231,n1; discussions on troop need and importance of homogeneous and independent divisions, **48:** 243-45, 252; and Service of Supply, **48:** 265-66; House's plan for European reorganization of, **48:** 265-68; J. Joffre on, **48:** 332; and absentee voting, **48:** 558,n1,3; **51:** 287,n1; and WW's decision to send troops to Murmansk, **49:** 43-44, 52, 57; and universal military service, **49:** 117, 203,n2; and issue of French versus Italian fronts, **49:** 136-37; and poll on three cardinal sins, **49:** 156; and possible reduction of tonnage by Britain, **49:** 217; appointment of Assistant Surgeon-General, **49:** 235,n1; and R. C. Maclaurin's plan for Student Army Training Corps, **49:** 242,n1; and intelligence checks of YMCA workers sent abroad, **49:** 359-60; and Public Health Service, **49:** 380-81; and fund appeal by various agencies, **49:** 425-26; and aliens mistakenly drafted, **49:** 542,n1; St. Mihiel salient, **51:** 3n1; and Russian situation, **51:** 17, 33; and candidate selection for officers' training, **51:** 228,n2, 271-72; and enlisted congressmen and senators, **51:** 302-303; Pershing on, **51:** 454; *see also* selective service; conscientious objectors

United States Army in the World War, 1917-1919, **47:** 261n2

United States as a Sea Power (Colcord), **40:** 374n1, 380,n1

United States Board of Mediation and Conciliation, **40:** 303,n1, 421n2; **41:** 156-57, 238; **42:** 279n1; **44:** 82, 431, 448-49, 499; **45:** 26;; **46:** 106, 446-47; **47:** 447

United States Bureau of Corporations, **47:** 50n1

United States Chamber of Commerce: *see*

Chamber of Commerce of the United States

United States Coast and Geodetic Survey, **42:** 348, 457

United States Coast Guard, **40:** 95,n1, 182

United States Commission on Industrial Relations, **44:** 261-62,n5; **47:** 557n4; **48:** 438-39,n2; **49:** 440n1

United States Congress, **41:** 318-20, 382, 487; **42:** 149,n2, 195n1, 200, 201, 260, 526; **44:** 145, 279-80, 324, 386, 552, 553-54; **45:** 272; **46:** 108-109; and eight-hour law for women, **40:** 7-9; and Porto Rico bill, **40:** 57, 58, 147, 151

WW's addresses to and comments on, **40:** 155:59; **41:** 108-12, 124-25, 283-87, 292, 293, 296, 482-83, 497, 506-507, 512, 516; **45:** 164-65, 194-202, 203, 203-204, 207, 215, 219-20, 221-22, 222,n1, 232, 237, 240, 241, 247, 254, 270,n2, 312, 324; **48:** 162-65; war message, **41:** 519-27; **42:** 5, 20, 41, 42, 162, 182n1, 214; **44:** 438, 454; Fourteen Points Address, **45:** 534-39; Four Points Address, **46:** 273-74, 274-79, 290-91, 291-97, 318-24

and the deficit, **40:** 270-71; and R. Spreckels on proxy voting at stockholders' meetings, **40:** 313,n1; and National Defense Act, **40:** 327-28, 329-30; C. A. Spring Rice on war views of, **40:** 406; and Alaska fisheries bill, **40:** 417-18; **41:** 209,n1; and revenue legislation, **40:** 474; **47:** 561-62; **48:** 119,n2, 121-27, 128, 128-29; **51:** 206; and WW's tribute to Admiral Dewey, **40:** 506-507; and extra session, **40:** 545; **41:** 64; **41:** 282-83, 287,n1, 367,n1, 381-82, 429-30, 430, 431, 437, 438-43, 445, 446, 448, 454-55; and WW's visits to, **40:** 546; and preparedness, **41:** 10, 462; and meat-packing investigation, **41:** 85, 310n2; and purchase of Monticello, **41:** 179-80, 310-11; and railroads, **41:** 238n1, 430n2; **45:** 225, 305-306, 311n1, 324, 358-61, 400, 401, 448-51, 451; and Porto Rico Act (Jones Act), **41:** 312; and W. Denman, **41:** 419; and Colombian Treaty, **41:** 420-21,n1; and raising armies, **41:** 469n1; R. Lansing on war power of, **41:** 471-72; and universal military training, **41:** 481n2; and requisition of German ships, **42:** 13, 28-29; A. J. Balfour addresses, **42:** 232; and woman suffrage, **42:** 241; **44:** 168, 523n1; **45:** 121,n2, 169n1, 242-43, 338-39; **47:** 578; **49:** 264; and International Boundary Commission, **42:** 260n2; and resolution on aliens, **42:** 277,n1; and peace resolutions, **42:** 444,n1; **43:** 455n1; Gompers urges WW address on control of food supplies, **42:** 488-89; and aircraft program, **42:** 550; and ship-building program, **42:** 564; **43:** 172-73; and Lever bill, **43:** 84n1, 121, 348-49, 357-58; and Negroes, **43:** 128-30; **48:**

155-61; and price control and Central Purchasing Commission, **43:** 137, 138; C. S. Jackson on, **43:** 266; and British financial crisis, **43:** 335; and mail censorship, **43:** 481n5; and Selective Service Act, **43:** 516; C. A. Lindbergh on Constitution and, **44:** 114; WW on oversight committee, **44:** 117-18, 155-56, 159; WW anecdote on determining how to vote, **44:** 237; and adjournment, **44:** 273-74; WW praises 65th Congress, **44:** 317; resolutions on days of prayer, **44:** 398-400; **47:** 598-99; and war emergency employment service appropriation, **45:** 130, 162; cabinet suggestions for legislation to be considered, **45:** 148,n1, 170-71, 171-72, 172-73, 177-78, 179-81; and war declaration against Austria-Hungary, **45:** 224n1; and prohibition, **45:** 275n1, 296; **49:** 477n5; **51:** 29; H. J. Ford on, **46:** 62; and Eight-Hour Commission, **46:** 105,n2; WW on addressing, **46:** 168; and housing crisis, **46:** 207; first Nonpartisan League member of, **46:** 270n1; H. A Smith's relief plan and, **46:** 298-99; E. M. House on passing an embargo law and, **46:** 490; and Overman bill, **47:** 94n1; W. B. Wilson on need for funds for Labor Department, **47:** 464; and responsibility for war declaration, **47:** 490; E. Root and J. R. Mann urge patriotic end to partisanship **47:** 584n1,2; C. Hull on tax increases and, **48:** 19-21; G. Creel's controversial statement about, **48:** 45n1; candidate endorsement by WW, **48:** 229-30; **51:** 63 J. P. Tumulty on Republican tactics for upcoming election, **48:** 347-49,n1; and appropriation for Children's Bureau, **48:** 463,n1; and resolution on wartime profiteering, **48:** 487,n1; question of recess and passage of wire-control resolution, **48:** 535,n1; and water-power legislation, **49:** 289, 291; and immigration resolution, **49:** 310,n1; H. Hoover urges consideration of meat-packing transportation problems, **49:** 528; comments, on WW's appeal for a Democratic Congress, **51:** 105, 225, 293,n1, 297, 299-300, 304-306, 317-18, 343-44, 353-55, 380-81, 381-82, 459-60, 548, 551,n1, 588, 599, 629, 630, 647; and child labor bill, **51:** 166-67; and proposed postwar reconstruction committees, **51:** 216,n1,2, 217n1; peace terms and, **51:** 277n7, 455,n1; and hospital construction, **51:** 281-82; newspaper advertisement urging reelection of WW's supporters in, **51:** 572-74; 1918 election results, **51:** 604,n1, 611-13, 616, 627-33, 639, 640, 645-46, 646-48

House of Representatives, **41:** 319-20, 332; **45:** 201; **49:** 277; and Interstate Commerce Commission, **40:** 155, 157; and vocational education bill, **40:**

159,n1; and Burnett immigration bill, **40:** 267,n2,3; and grazing homestead bill, **40:** 289, 290n1; and peace note leak to Wall Street, **40:** 349n11; and railroads, **41:** 14n2, 20,n1, 21; **46:** 620,n1; and water-power legislation, **41:** 19-20, 82; **45:** 302, 406, 433,n1, 448,n1; **48:** 453; **49:** 316, 317; **51:** 6; and bills relating to conditions of war, **41:** 197,n1; and flood control bill, **41:** 198; and Alaska general fisheries bill, **41:** 207; passes Porto Rico bill **41:** 278n1; and armed-ship bill, **41:** 280n1, 294,n1, 318n1, 327,n1; and war resolution, **41:** 550, 557; and selective service, **42:** 42-43, 144n1, 285; and espionage bill and censorship, **42:** 106n2, 245n2, 370,n1; **43:** 481,n5; E. M. House and WW on necessity of cabinet members to sit in, **42:** 162; and woman suffrage, **42:** 269-70, 293, 320-21,n1, 474, 497; **43:** 36, 212, 213, 214; **44:** 112-14; **45:** 242-43, 277, 278, 306-307, 518, 545n1, 565n3; **46:** 61, 80-81; **48:** 263-64; and Federal Reserve Act, **42:** 302-303,n1,2; and war risk insurance bill, **42:** 455; **44:** 92, 199; S. Gompers on interstate and foreign commerce bill in, **43:** 21, 22; and Lever bill, **43:** 42n2, 48,n1, 52, 221, 347, 415n1; and revenue legislation **43:** 350n2; **49:** 85, 86, 87, 125; and workmen's compensation law, **44:** 314; and prohibition, **45:** 295n1; **49:** 476n1,3 477n5; J. J. Fitzgerald resigns from, **45:** 422,n2; and housing crisis and appropriation to Shipping Board, **46:** 151; and bill establishing war zone around shipbuilding plants, **46:** 283; and War Finance Corporation bill, **46:** 561; and New York elections, **46:** 565n1; and J. M. Baer bill, **47:** 178,n2; and W. C. Adamson's resignation, **47:** 191n1; and alley-house legislation, **47:** 255n1; and children, **47:** 560; **51:** 165-66; passes Overman bill, **47:** 573; and Walsh bill, **47:** 573n1; and agricultural appropriations bill and Gore amendment, **48:** 42,n1; and Hoover on food bill and closing breweries, **48:** 166, 175; and general leasing bill, **48:** 170-71; **49:** 481-85; and antiprofiteering rent bill, **48:** 190,n1; Lever to remain in, **48:** 268, 272; and resolution on Poland, **48:** 312; J. H. Small on prohibition and, **48:** 351; WW's veto of appropriations bill, **48:** 417; and wire-control resolution, **48:** 526, 532-33,n1, 533, 535n1; members enlist in the military, **51:** 302-303; elections, **51:** 588, 604n1; campaigns for seats in: *see* under names of specific state or candidate; *see also* under names of individual committees, such as Public Lands, Committee on

Senate, **41:** 319-20; **42:** 343; **46:** 52; and Porto Rico bill, **40:** 58, 147; **41:** 278n1; and Interstate Commerce Commission,

United States Congress (*cont.*)
40: 155, 157; and Burnett immigration bill, 40: 267,n3; and Alaska fisheries bill, 40: 291, 417-18; 41: 207, 230; and Shafroth resolution on world court, 40: 386,n1, 471; approves resolution endorsing WW's notes, 40: 458n2, 460-61; and cloture, 40: 471, 472; 41: 357, 358, 359; and W. Phillips' nomination as Assistant Secretary of State, 40: 492,n1; and WW's Peace without Victory speech, 40: 533-39, 404, 405, 445, 447; 41: 11n1; and Colombian treaty, 40: 550; 41: 9, 28, 393n1, 420-21,n1, 425, 456, 465; WW on, 41: 11, 318-20; and general leasing bill, 41: 19; 45: 172, 375, 454; 49: 481-85; and B. N. Baker's resignation from Shipping Board, 41: 21; WW meets with senators to discuss possible break with Germany, 41: 88,n1; and bills relating to conditions of war, 41: 197,n1; and flood control bill, 41: 198; and Zimmermann telegram, 41: 324,n2; and armed-ship bill, 41: 280n1, 317-18,n1, 327-28, 332, 350, 534-35; and espionage bill, 42: 106n2, 245n2, 370n1; and woman suffrage, 42: 269; 43: 213,n1, 214; 45: 121n1, 277-79; 46: 60, 61; 48: 233-34, 263-64, 304, 340, 341, 363-64, 404; 49: 268; 51: 30-31, 58, 83, 158-61, 189n1; and selective service bill, 42: 285; 43: 515-16, 517; and Federal Reserve Act, 42: 302-303,n1,2; and resolution creating a controller of supplies, 42: 382-84; and war-risk insurance bill, 42: 455; 44: 279-80; and Lever bill, 42: 529,n1, 532-33; 43: 48,n1, 52, 56, 120, 162, 163, 190, 210, 221, 245,n1, 339, 393,n1, 415n1; rejects W. E. Thomas for district judgeship in Ga., 43: 162n3; and shipbuilding program, 43: 233, 237,n1; and trading with the enemy bill, 43: 313; confirms ambassador to Japan, 43: 347,n1; and revenue legislation, 43: 350,n2: 49: 86; J. S. Williams on reason for not seeking reelection to: 43: 368-69; and mail censorship, 43: 481n5; confirms new Collector of Port of New York, 44: 208n1; and workmen's compensation law, 44: 313-14; F. W. Taussig on bargaining tariff and, 44: 544; and war emergency employment service appropriation, 45: 130; and vote to declare war on Austria-Hungary, 45: 224n1; and prohibition, 45: 295n1; 48: 161,n2; and water-power legislation, 45: 301, 406; 49: 505-506; and sugar investigation, 45: 344,n1, 347-48; and peace terms, 45: 601,n1; 51: 338-40; and Hitchcock resolution on coal order, 46: 31,n2; and controversy over Chamberlain bills, 46: 40,n1, 101n1, 204-205, 257n2, 288, 368-69,n1; W. J. Stone's attack on T. Roosevelt in, 46: 63,n2; reaction to WW's Fourteen Points address in 46: 87; and appropriation for housing crisis, 46: 151, 171; and J. T. Robinson's campaign plans, 46: 252-53, 258; and bill establishing war zone around shipbuilding plants, 46: 283-85; and investigation of R. M. La Follette, 46: 348,n1; and proposed Japanese intervention in Siberia, 46: 475, 506; election to replace P. O. Hustings, 46: 566n5; and rules concerning treaties 46: 606n1; J. E. Davies to run for, 46: 609; and railroad bills, 46: 620,n1; and passage of Overman bill, 47: 94, 109, 573n1; and agricultural appropriations bill and Gore amendment, 47: 95-96; 48: 42,n1; and J. M. Baer bill, 47: 178n2; WW on a league of nations and, 47: 200; and alley-house legislation, 47: 255n1; and Wisconsin's election results, 47: 326,n1; and Mooney case, 47: 396-97; and Borglum and aircraft program, 47: 508-10, 511; passes Walsh bill, 47: 573,n1; and oil-leasing bill, 48: 171; and antiprofiteering rent bill, 48: 190,n1; and contest in South Carolina, 48: 259-60,n2, 268n1; and civil service retirement bill, 48: 395n2; and resolution on Russian Commission, 48: 433,n1; and passage of wire-control bill, 48: 526-27,n1, 532, 533, 534,n1, 535,n1, 556,n2, 591-92, 623,n1; resolution on daily noontime prayer 48: 578-79,n1; and natural resources legislation, 49: 291; and agricultural bill with prohibition rider, 49: 476n1,3, 477n5; and child labor legislation, 51: 165-66; members enlisted in the military, 51: 303; debate over WW's reply to Germany, 51: 303; election (1918) results, 51: 588, 589-90, 604n1, 611-13; campaigns for seats in: *see* under names of specific state or candidate; *see also* under the names of individual committees, such as Woman Suffrage, Committee on

United States Constitution, 40: 196; 42: 28, 277n1, 296; 43: 129, 222n2, 247n2, 500, 510; 44: 79, 138, 438, 470; 46: 108; 47: 201, 364n4; 48: 156, 557; 49: 89, 477; 51: 299; and Shafroth resolution, 40: 386, 471; and proclamation on treasonable acts, 42: 77-79; C. A. Lindbergh on right to petition, 44: 110, 114; and woman suffrage, 44: 523n1; S. Gompers on prohibition amendment and, 45: 296-98; and taxation, 51: 108-109,n9

United States Customs Service, 44: 169

United States Employment Service, 45: 130n1, 131; 49: 520,n1, 540; 51: 165n1; WW's remarks to delegates from, 48: 320-21; WW's appeal to labor and industry to use, 48: 333-34

United States Food Administration: *see* Food Administration

United States Forest Service, 40: 287n1

United States Fuel Administration: *see* Fuel Administration

United States Gas Mask Plant, **47:** 136, 172-73, 364

United States Government as Union Organizer: The Loyal Legion of Loggers and Lumbermen (Tyler), **46:** 218n2

United States Grain Corporation, **48:** 629,n2,3

United States Housing Corporation, **49:** 405

United States Industrial Arbitration Commission (proposed), **41:** 253-55,n1, 258

United States Marine Corps, **42:** 250, 404; women enlisted in, **49:** 546n1

United States Military Academy, **40:** 551; **41:** 15-16, 319, 528; **42:** 281n1; **43:** 4n3, 16; **44:** 445n1; **47:** 329; **48:** 203; and cancellation of Army-Navy game, **44:** 535, 571; **45:** 29-30

United States Naval Academy, **41:** 496; **43:** 354n3; **44:** 445n1; **46:** 50n1, 620-21,n2; **47:** 380; **49:** 139n1; and cancellation of Army-Navy game, **44:** 535, 571; **45:** 29-30

United States Naval War Code, **41:** 338

United States Navy, **41:** 522, 530, 544; **42:** 28n1, 220; **43:** 6, 470, 503; **44:** 177; **45:** 405, 566; **47:** 233, 328-29, 378, 48: 604-606; **49:** 169; **51:** 279; D. W. Taylor on method of protecting merchant vessels from attack, **41:** 377-79; J. Daniels on, **41:** 395-98; **43:** 344-45; **45:** 170-71; increase in, **41:** 461, 474; **51:** 344,n1; and prohibition order, **42:** 123, 526,n3; and antisubmarine barrier in North Sea, **42:** 220, 449,n1, 457; R. Cecil compares it to Japanese, **42:** 450; and British cooperation with, **42:** 450-51; and insurance, **42:** 527n1, 565; and steel prices, **42:** 534-35; and British deserters, **42:** 567; and German vessels in U.S. ports, **43:** 89,n1; discrimination in, **43:** 130; **51:** 192; W. S. Sims on, **43:** 179-82; WW's address to officers of the Atlantic Fleet, **43:** 427-31; and coal costs, **43:** 520; and distribution of Bibles in, **44:** 85, 118, 152; purpose of Admiral Mayo's visit to London, **44:** 86-88; and war-risk insurance bill, **44:** 92, 116-17, 323; C. A. Lindbergh report on woman suffrage demonstrations and, **44:** 108-116; and YMCA campaign for servicemen in, **44:** 551-52; WW against admirals becoming honorary members of British Admiralty, **45:** 127-28; G. Creel on, **45:** 408, 409; shipping needs of, **45:** 489-91; and Sabbath observance, **46:** 41-42,n1; and housing appropriation, **46:** 171; and F. Janeway's chaplaincy request, **46:** 260, 286, 330; effect of carpenters' strike on, **46:** 363-64; and rehabilitation of wounded men, **46:** 608-609; **47:** 28-30, 95, 123-24, 153; Supreme War Council on tonnage

obligations of, **47:** 145-47; and Sedition Act, **47:** 364n4; and Public Health Service; **49:** 380; and draft exemptions, **49:** 386; women enlisted in, **49:** 546n1; and chaplains, **51:** 16,n1; and hospital construction, **41:** 281-82; *see also* arming of U.S. merchantmen; naval oil reserves; shipbuilding program

United States Navy in the Pacific, 1900-1922 (Braisted), **42:** 59n2

United States neutrality: *see* World War—neutrality

United States Policy and the Position of Turkey, 1914-1924 (Evans), **42:** 317n3

U.S. Position Is That Slav Race Should Be Entirely Free From Teutonic Rule (*Official Bulletin*), **48:** 464,n2

United States Public Health Service: *see* Public Health Service

United States Railroad Administration: *see* Railroad Administration

United States Railway Commission: *see* Russian Railway Commission

United States Rubber Company, **49:** 133

United States Shipping Board, **40:** 269; **41:** 66; **42:** 32, 102, 113n1, 133-34, 145, 168n1, 234, 235, 257, 260, 278, 399, 475, 534, 556n3, 567; **43:** 49n4, 89,n1, 357, 385, 490; **44:** 13, 70, 147-48, 157, 283, 314, 449, 501, 502; **45:** 42, 44, 64, 65, 424, 435n1, 489; **46:** 18, 217, 329n1, 502; **47:** 233,n1, 294, 463, 562; **48:** 80, 86, 233n1; **49:** 210, 405, 424,n1, 464; **51:** 104n4, 276, 368, 587, 593, 610; B. N. Baker resigns from, **41:** 16,n1, 21; and bunkering agreements, **41:** 418-19,n1; and Emergency Fleet Corporation, **42:** 234, 248, 523-25, 554n1, 555,n2, 567n1; W. G. McAdoo on closer relations with executive departments, **42:** 285-87; Central Purchasing Agency and, **42:** 424; and Denman-Goethals controversy and resignations, **43:** 50-51,n3, 204-205,n1, 233, 260, 261, 285-86; and order on shipbuilding and requisitioning ships, **43:** 144-45, 293-96; and Smoot resolution, **43:** 237,n1; B. Colby appointed to, **43:** 260, 271, 310; and foreign ships built in U.S. yards, **44:** 209,n3, 219-21; and housing appropriation, **46:** 151, 171; and issue of restricting exports and imports, **46:** 309,n1; and carpenters' strike, **46:** 362, 364, 364-65, 367; and War Industries Board reorganization, **46:** 477, 491, 521, 522, 610, and wage policy, **47:** 377-78; *see also* shipbuilding program; Shipbuilding Labor Adjustment Board; Emergency Fleet Corporation

United States Steel Corporation, **41:** 556n1; **42:** 134n1, 248,n2, 496, 534; **43:** 197, 266, 367n1; **47:** 127; **48:** 392; **49:** 168n2

United States Supreme Court, **40:** 92, 103, 205, 217n1, 246n2; **42:** 28, 29; **44:**

United States Supreme Court (*cont.*) 313, 347; **45:** 297; **46:** 380; **47:** 425, 449, 467; **49:** 23n1, 89; **51:** 108-109,n9, 165; and Diggs-Caminetti decision, **41:** 246-47; and Adamson Act and railroad crisis, **41:** 352n1, 430n2, 432, 519

United States Tariff Commission **40:** 41, 271; **41:** 65, 282, 448; **44:** 541, 544; **46:** 521; **47:** 152; **48:** 197n1; **51:** 610n1; and cost accounting, **40:** 59; 252, 253, 269; appointments to, **40:** 173-74, 305, 343, 347-48, 372-74, 384, 422, 476, 489,n2, 544; **41:** 24, 58, 93, 379-80

United States Treasury: *see* Treasury, Department of the

U.S. v. W. D. Haywood, et al., **44:** 17n2

United War Work Campaign, **51:** 636-37

Universal Film Company, **48:** 582

Universal Military Training, 65th Cong., 1st sess., Senate Doc. No. 10, **41:** 481n2

Universal Military Training League, **49:** 203n2

University Commission on the Southern Race Question, **48:** 462-63

University of the State of New York at Albany, **51:** 93, 94n1

Unknown Soldiers: Black American Troops in World War I (Barbeau and Henri), **48:** 157n4, 160n6

Unnecessary Risk (Ogden), **51:** 531

Unpatriotic Teaching in Public Schools (American Defense Society, Inc.), **51:** 147n1

Unterberger, Betty Miller, **48:** 335n1

Untermyer, Samuel, **41:** 69, 145; **47:** 10, 20; **49:** 60

Upper Silesia, **42:** 335

Upton, Emory, **47:** 483,n1

Urbana, Ill., **46:** 174

Urga, Mongolia, **49:** 448,n3

urgent deficiency appropriation bill: *see* deficiency appropriation bill

Urgent Military and Naval Deficiency Appropriations Act, **42:** 555,n1

Urges Socialist Party to Back President Wilson: A. W. Ricker Says Executive is Hope of Liberals—Wants St. Louis Platform, Condemning War, Amended (New York *Globe and Commercial Advertiser*), **48:** 16-17,n1

Uritski, Moisei Solomonovich: assassination of, **51:** 4n2, 61n1

Urofsky, Melvin Irving, **49:** 363n2

Urriola, Ciro Luis, **48:** 417,n2

Uruguay, **41:** 249; **42:** 359

Usher, Nathaniel Reilly, **41:** 369,n1

Uskoke, S.M.S. **51:** 492

Ussishkin, Abraham Menahem Mendel, **45:** 572,n2

Ussuri River (Ussuri front), Russia, **49:** 151, 152, 219, 262, 494,n3; **51:** 609

Ustrugov, Leonid Aleksandrovich, **47:** 397,n1; **48:** 72,n1

Utah, **43:** 17, 222n1; **44:** 17; **47:** 89-90, 194; politics in, **51:** 633

Utilization of Yugo-Slav Prisoners of Serbian Race in the Serbian Army (Supreme War Council), **48:** 545n2

Vail, Theodore Newton, **40:** 444; **47:** 400, 414, 415

Vain Endeavor: Robert Lansing's Attempts to End the American-Japanese Rivalry (Beers), **43:** 57n1; **44:** 454n1

Valdés, Ramón M., **42:** 51,n2; death of, **48:** 417n2

Valentini, Rudolf von, **45:** 36,n14

Valentino, Pietro Arone de, **44:** 347,n1, 348

Valera, Eamon de: *see* De Valera, Eamon

Valkenburg, Edwin Augustus van, **47:** 16,n3

Valona (Vlonë, Vlona), Albania, **47:** 513,n3; **51:** 45, 501

Van Anda, Carr Vattel, **51:** 106n7

Van Dervoort, William Humphrey, **46:** 578n2; **47:** 223,n2, 248, 252, 283

Van Dyke, Carl Chester, **45:** 259,n4; **47:** 191,n3, 273

Van Dyke, Ellen Reid (Mrs. Henry), **46:** 596n4

Van Dyke, Harry Weston, **41:** 141,n11

Van Dyke, Henry, **46:** 596n4; resigns as minister to The Netherlands, **40:** 133; and club-quad controversy of 1907, **40:** 567; naval chaplaincy of, **51:** 16,n2

Van Hise, Charles Richard, **49:** 241, 407; and patriotism controversy at University of Wisconsin, **45:** 142-47, 221n1; on Fourteen Points Address, **45:** 586-87, 593

Van Raalte, Albert **48:** 98,n5

Van Tassell, Wardell C., **47:** 478n2

Vance, Zebulon Baird, **44:** 556,n1

Vandal of Europe (Muehlon), **48:** 213n8

Vandenberg, Arthur Hendrick, **45:** 188,n1

Vanderbilt, Alice Claypoole Gwynn (Mrs. Cornelius II), **40:** 133,n1

Vanderbilt, Grace Graham Wilson (Mrs. Cornelius III), **40:** 133n1

Vanderlip, Frank Arthur, **41:** 539; **42:** 63n5; **45:** 238n1; **48:** 518; **49:** 407

Vanderveer, George Francis, **46:** 196,n1

Vandiver, Frank Everson, **43:** 32n6

Vardaman, James Kimble, **40:** 128, 129; **46:** 104n1; **49:** 137, 180,n1, 245, 369n2; **51:** 616; and woman suffrage, **45:** 279, 338; and sugar investigation, **45:** 344

Varenne, Alexandre Claude, **51:** 566,n9

Varieties of Religious Experience (James), **44:** 255,n1

Varneck, Elena, **51:** 100n2, 102n1

Vassar College, **44:** 554n1

Vatican, **41:** 39, 40, 44-45, 218-20, 433-35; **43:** 472-73; **44:** 26, 330, 348-51; **45:** 31, 35-36, 432n1, 464-65; **47:** 466, 524; **48:** 31n1, 132-33; suggests U.S. can stop war, **40:** 556-57; and "Law of Guarantee," **41:** 434-35,n2; and peace moves, **46:** 156, 365, 488, 580n1; **47:** 63,n1; **51:** 282-83, 294, 309; G. D. Her-

ron on papal politics and league of nations, **49:** 187-93
Vaughn, Stephen, **42:** 55n1; **43:** 3n1, 168n2; **44:** 248n1, 505n2
Vaux, Léon Freiherr de, **51:** 623,n3
Vauxaillon, France, **48:** 245
Veeder, Henry, **46:** 492,n3
Vehouni, Arsène E., **40:** 105-106,n1, 311
Venetia (Venezia), **44:** 549
Venezuela, **41:** 9
Vénisélos, Eleuthérios, **42:** 331; **43:** 268; **51:** 45; on first anniversary of U.S. entry into war, **47:** 263-64, 271
Ventures in Diplomacy (Phillips), **40:** 492n1
Verdun, France, **40:** 70, 485; **42:** 373; **47:** 303, 523, 612
Verheerung Europas: Aufzeichnungen aus den ersten Kriegsmonaten (Muehlon), **48:** 213n8
Verkhneudinsk, Russia, **51:** 384, 449,n1
Vermes, Gábor, **45:** 57,n4
Vermont: politics in, **51:** 633
Vernon, Ambrose White, **40:** 116-17, 215; **49:** 357,n1; **51:** 68-70
Vernon, Katherina Tappe (Mrs. Ambrose White), **49:** 357,n1; **51:** 68-69
Vernon, Mabel, **42:** 237n4
Versailles, France, **45:** 48, 151, 156; **46:** 272; as possible peace conference site, **51:** 516, 617; *see also* Supreme War Council
Vesnić (Vesnitch), Milenko R., **43:** 268-70,n5; **45:** 553-54
veterans: and homestead bill, **51:** 103,n3
Veyra, Jaime C. de, **41:** 345
Viatka, Russia, **49:** 285, 448,n5
Vicious and Unconstitutional (New York *World*), **46:** 264,n1
Victor American Coal Company, **43:** 340, 353
Vittorio Emanuele III (of Italy), **43:** 27-28; **44:** 439; **45:** 262-63, 267-68; **49:** 64; **51:** 576; on anniversary of U.S. entry into war, **47:** 278, 280
Victor Talking Machine Company, **51:** 92n1
Vienna, **51:** 564,n1, 565
Vienna *Arbeiterzeitung*, **40:** 23-24; **46:** 183, 185-86, 226, 227, 228
Vienna *Fremdenblatt*, **46:** 186-87
Vienna *Neue Freie Press*, **40:** 23; **41:** 56n2; **46:** 187; **48:** 522n1
Vienna *Neues Wiener Journal*, **51:** 239n7
Viennese Ultimatum to Serbia (Muehlon), **46:** 254,n6; **48:** 213n8
Vierteljahreshefte für Zeitgeschichte, **48:** 213n8
Vigilancia, S.S., **41:** 425,n1, 431, 436, 451n2
Vignal, Paul, **45:** 143,n5
Villa, Francisco (Pancho), **40:** 114, 397; **41:** 34, 43-44, 106; on rampage again, **40:** 100,n1, 109-10, 202-203
Villa Ahumada, Chihuahua, Mex., **40:** 100, 101

Villa Giusti, Italy, **51:** 576n1
Villalobar, Marquis de (Rodrigo de Saavedra), **40:** 248,n1, 554; **44:** 320
Villard, Oswald Garrison, **40:** 236-37; **41:** 8, 218; **43:** 5n1, 12, 239-40,n1; **44:** 273, 322; **47:** 155; on freedom of the press, **44:** 271-73; and censorship of *The Nation*, **51:** 55,n1, 56, 57, 84; sells New York *Evening Post*, **51:** 221,n3; on liberal support, **51:** 646
Villard Makes Protest (*New York Times*), **51:** 57,n3
Villers-Cotterêts, France, **48:** 332, 387
Villistas, **40:** 110,n4, 130,n2, 202
Vilna, Lithuania, **48:** 98
Vincent, George Edgar, **45:** 272,n1
Violations of American Rights by Germany since the Suspension of Diplomatic Relations (memorandum), **41:** 502n1
Virgin Islands: *see* Danish West Indies
Virginia, **47:** 16-17, 410; politics in, **51:** 633
Virginia, University of, **40:** 444; **41:** 517,n1; **42:** 221n1; **44:** 260, 474n1; **51:** 453n1, 610n1
Virginia Bill of Rights, **47:** 288, 583; **48:** 68
Virginia Bridge and Iron Company, **46:** 578n2
Virginia Farmers' Union, **44:** 259
Virginia Union University, **42:** 322,n1
Virginian Railway, **43:** 367,n1
Viribus Unitis, S.M.S., **51:** 492
Vision, The (B. Bolling), **46:** 371n1
Vision of War (Colcord), **40:** 380,n3
Viskniskki, Guy Thomas, **47:** 172n1
Viviani, René Raphaël **42:** 20,n1, 132-33, 169, 175-76, 230; **43:** 238; **44:** 441; description of, **42:** 175-76; on meeting with WW, **42:** 182-85, 210-12; on success of French mission, **42:** 299-301
Vladivostok, Russia, **43:** 248-49; **45:** 336, 347, 420, **47:** 22, 72n3, 92,n1, 98, 319, 356, 503, 514; **48:** 38, 131, 182, 204, 262, 285n1, 398, 479, 483-84, 542; **49:** 92, 109, 152, 248, 262, 448, 494-95, 507n1, 544; **51:** 25, 99; Japanese ships at and Japanese occupation of, **46:** 33-34, 34, 35, 41, 46-47, 118, 355, 391, 392, 452, 470; **47:** 263n1, 281n1, 319, 320, 426n1, 489; and issue of supplies at, **46:** 338; 511, 512, 535, 536, 540-41, 548, 554-55; **47:** 69, 242, 243, 245, 355, 367; A. M. Knight on, **47:** 71, 206; **48:** 528; American warship at, **47:** 281; British land at, **47:** 281n1; **48:** 662; U.S. consul recalled, **47:** 544,n2; reports of conspiracy by Allied consuls at, **48:** 106n4; and Czech troops in, **48:** 453, 454, 469, 480-81, 494, 544; **49:** 40n1, 45-46, 197, 198, 220; order to land marines at, **48:** 543; U.S. and Japan send troops to, **49:** 40, 75, 75-76, 94, 107, 171, 175, 176n1, 179, 278, 282-84, 285; *see also* Russia—Siberia, intervention in

vocational education, **40:** 159,n1; **47:** 95, 123-24, 153; **48:** 319; and military training, **41:** 295,n2

Vocational Education Board, **46:** 468; **47:** 29

Vogelsang, Alexander Theodore, **48:** 78,n1, 129-30

Vokes, May, **44:** 427n1

Volga River, **49:** 199, 262n1

Völkerrecht nach dem Kriege (Lammasch), **46:** 198n1

Volio, Alfredo, **45:** 388,n2, 389, 405

Vologda, Russia, **46:** 528n1; **47:** 319n5; **48:** 113-14, 505; **49:** 448, 495,n6; **51:** 95n2

Vologodskii, Petr Vasil'evich, **51:** 100n2, 102n1

Von der Tann, S.M.S., **51:** 490

Vopicka, Charles Joseph, **40:** 544,n1; **41:** 473,n1; **46:** 235n1; **47:** 450

Voska, Emanuel Victor, **49:** 41,n1, 41-42

Voss, Carl Hermann, **41:** 181n

Voyager to Destiny: The Amazing Adventures of Manjiro, the Man Who Changed Worlds Twice (Warriner), **48:** 569n1

Voznesenski, Arsenii Nikolaevich, **48:** 113,n5

Vreeland, Alice May Brown, (Mrs. Williamson Updike), **44:** 55,n2,3

Vreeland, Hamilton, Jr., **43:** 462,n1

Vreeland, Williamson Updike, **44:** 55,n2

Vrooman, Carl Schurz, **41:** 379,n1; **45:** 142-47, 221,n1; **48:** 344

W. H. McElwain Company, **47:** 557n4

W. R. Grace Steamship Company, **48:** 303n2

W. W. Harris and Company of Boston, **46:** 168

Wade, Benjamin Franklin, **43:** 350

Wadsworth, Alice Hay (Mrs. James Wolcott, Jr.), **43:** 250-51, n1,2

Wadsworth, Eliot, **41:** 113,n1,3; **43:** 86,n1,3

Wadsworth, James Wolcott, Jr., **44:** 538,n1; **46:** 205

wage commission (railroad workers), **46:** 446

Wages of Street-Car Men and the Rate of Fare (Taft), **48:** 598n2

Wagner, K., **41:** 508

Wagner, Robert Ferdinand, **42:** 327,n1

Wahle, K. W., **41:** 144,n21

Wainwright, Evelyn Wotherspoon (Mrs. Richard), **47:** 547,n1, 572

Wake Up! (Sullivan), **47:** 40n3

Walcott, Charles Doolittle, **45:** 141,n2, 154,n2,5, 155; **46:** 461-62,n1, 468-69, 502-503, 509; **48:** 222

Walcott, Frederic Collin, **42:** 83n1, 122

Walcott, Frederick, **41:** 113,n1,3

Wald, Lillian D., **40:** 121-22, 163; **41:** 708, 167-69,n1,2, 305n1; **42:** 118, 118-19,n1, 153, 208, 214; **43:** 420-24, 503,n1; **44:** 192-94, 559n1; **45:** 39, 541-42

Waldorf-Astoria Hotel, N.Y., **40:** 35n1; **51:** 142, 145, 315, 316

Waldow, Wilhelm von, **45:** 595,n5

Waldron, John Milton, **42:** 49-51,n1, 98, 321, 321-22, 357-58; **48:** 155-61

Waldron, Laurence Ambrose, **42:** 403,n3

Walker, Allen, **51:** 92,n2

Walker, Amelia Himes (Mrs. Robert), **43:** 201n1, 243-44

Walker, George H., **44:** 276-77

Walker, Harold, **41:** 365-67

Walker, John, **43:** 513

Walker, John Caffery, Jr., **46:** 598,n3

Walker, John Hunter, **44:** 104,n1, 214, 520; **46:** 74, 147; **47:** 116

Walker, Quiller, **49:** 399-400

Walker, Sarah Breedlove (Mrs. Charles J.), **43:** 412,n2

Wall, Bernhardt, **48:** 557,n1

Wall, Louise Herrick, **41:** 185n, 196n, 240n, 260n, 283n, 350n, 518n; **46:** 515n; **51:** 415n, 548n, 605n, 616n

Wall Street, **44:** 366,n1, 416, 469, 473; **45:** 119, 287-88, 326; **46:** 122; **47:** 297

Wall Street Journal, **41:** 407; **43:** 349; **44:** 423n2; **46:** 174n1

Wall Street leak: *see* New York Stock Exchange

Walla Walla, Wash., **48:** 290-91, 291-94, 322; **49:** 79, 80

Wallace, Donald Mackenzie, **42:** 393,n3

Wallace, Henry Cantwell, **46:** 614,n1; **48:** 77,n1, **49:** 78-79,n2

Wallace, Hugh Campbell, **40:** 241, 463; **42:** 158; **43:** 194,n1; **44:** 184; **48:** 143-44; **51:** 341

Wallace, Mildred Fuller (Mrs. Hugh Campbell), **44:** 184

Wallace, Leslie E., **51:** 375,n1

Wallace, Regina, **46:** 520

Wallace's Farmer (Des Moines), **48:** 77n1

Walling, William English, **42:** 148n1, 203-204,n1, 291, 318, 319; **43:** 103-104; **44:** 39; **45:** 153,n1, 162; and Russian Commission, **42:** 166, 197-99, 216, 217, 239, 240, 252, 254n3, 267; and international socialist conference, **42:** 268, 364; memorandum on revolutionary movements, **46:** 310-12, 334, 349-50

Wallraf, Max (Ludwig Theodor Ferdinand Wallraf), **46:** 267,n1

Walls, George H., **45:** 547,n2

Walsh, David Ignatius, **42:** 237n4; **51:** 552,n1, 552-53, 624

Walsh, Elinor Cameron McClements (Mrs. Thomas James), **44:** 64,n1, 102,n1

Walsh, Francis Patrick (Frank), **40:** 154,n1; **46:** 26, 27, 578, **48:** 115n1; **49:** 186,n2, 211, 223n1, 251, 520-22; and National War Labor Board, **47:** 223, 248, 252, 252-53, 272, 283, 464; **51:** 522-23; on F. Ryan's release, **47:** 212, 219; and telegraphers' strike, **48:** 337, 338, 374-75, 394; and inter-urban railways, **48:** 432, 526n1, 567-68, 623-24

Walsh, Thomas James, **40:** 471, 561n2; **41:** 5, 359n3; **42:** 346-47, 561; **43:** 43, 75-76; **44:** 64, 102; **46:** 61,n1; **47:** 573n1; **48:** 220; **49:** 90-91, 449n1, 481; **51:** 116,n1, 138, 213, 589, 612; and water-power legislation, **40:** 287, 424, 522-23, 543; **45:** 172, 301; and woman suffrage, **45:** 279, 338; **48:** 217-18; on aircraft investigation, **47:** 541-42, 580; and I.W.W., **47:** 573-74,n1, 604

Walter Hines Page: The Southerner as American, 1855-1918 (Cooper), **49:** 155n1

Walter Lippman and the American Century (Steel), **45:** 459n1; **49:** 402n3, 434n2

Walters, Alexander, **43:** 359n1

Walthall, Edward Cary, **43:** 369,n2

Walton, Lester Aglar, **48:** 302,n1

Waltz, Millard Fillmore, **44:** 42,n5

Wandycz, Piotr Stefan, **42:** 11n1; **44:** 6n1; **46:** 403n3

Wanted: A Leader (Harvey), **47:** 15,n1

War? (magazine of the Collegiate Anti-Militarism League), **47:** 154n1

War Board Ask 7¢ Jersey Trolley Fare (clipping), **49:** 424,n1

War Board of the Port of New York, **44:** 502

War Cabinet (Great Britain), **44:** 16, 200, 237-38, 369-70, 494; **45:** 68, 149n2, 313, 316, 317, 418, 420; **46:** 577; **47:** 388n1, 564, 565; **48:** 463, 502, 503, 536; **49:** 530, 531, **51:** 288, 289, 290, 327n1, 633; memorandum on submarine situation, **43:** 375-78

War Cabinet (U.S.), **46:** 40n1, 41, 49n1, 54, 63n1, 78-79, 83, 100, 101n1, 103, 204, 217, 257n2, 264n1, 444,n2; **47:** 171-72,n1, 241; **49:** 83, 145, 258, 476n2, 529; **51:** 92, 173, 372, 416, 615; first meeting, **47:** 43,n1; B. Crowell reports on, **47:** 144-47; and industrial mobilization plan, **47:** 296,n1, 299-300; photograph, *illustration section,* 47

War Camp Community Service, **49:** 425-26; **51:** 636

War College: *see* Army War College; Naval War College

War Council of the Red Cross, **42:** 251, 251-52,n2, 258, 280, 282

War Department, **41:** 151-52, 169, 427-28, 512, 550-51; **42:** 40, 49, 118, 322, 412, 445, 559; **43:** 89, 91, 388, 392, 490; **44:** 176, 177, 198, 283, 394n1, 502; **45:** 42, 43, 44, 63-64, 65, 110, 110-11, 168,n1, 177n1, 425, 489; **46:** 16n1, 111, 217, 284; **47:** 66, 478n2, 562; **48:** 87, 558,n3; **49:** 53n1, 242n1; and labor, **45:** 10-11; **47:** 378-79, 463; **49:** 521, 539-40; expenditures and shipping problem, **45:** 424, 532, 533; Chamberlain's charges against and WW's and Baker's defense of, **46:** 40n1, 55, 147n1, 205; and housing crisis, **46:** 171; reorganization of War Industries Board and, **46:**

477, 602-603, 607; and Marshall-Wells-McNab Committee and aircraft investigation, **47:** 41n1, 293, 541, 542, 545; and truck gardens, **47:** 478n1; and Sheriff Wheeler's commission, **47:** 598; and aircraft production, **49:** 349, 350; **51:** 15n1; and military intelligence and YMCA workers' passports, **49:** 387, 390, 395-96; and issue of propaganda abroad, **49:** 447, 449, 487; discrimination charges in, **51:** 170; selection of officer candidates, **51:** 288,n2, 271-72; and absentee voting, **51:** 287,n1; statistics on soldiers sent abroad, **51:** 404-405, 405

War Emergency Finance Corporation (proposed), **45:** 266,n1

War Emergency Fund (WW's), **46:** 479n1; **48:** 137-39, 168, 335n1, 463n1; and employment service, **45:** 162, 183n1; allotment for cost-of-living surveys, **45:** 183n1

War Expenditures, Committee on (proposed): *see* Lever bill

War Finance Corporation, **46:** 442n1, 448; **47:** 580; act creating, **46:** 442,n1, 561, 562; **48:** 598, 612n1; and public utilities, **48:** 597-99, 611, 612,n1; **49:** 118n1, 120, 121-22, 143

War in Siberia (Clarke), **49:** 93n1

War Industries Board, **42:** 498; **44:** 13; **45:** 42, 44, 61, 63, 64, 65, 209n2, 276, 299; **46:** 23n3, 208n1, 299,n3, 238, 438, 523; **47:** 117n1, 255,n1, 463; **48:** 145n3, 169, 188,n1; **49:** 53n1, 61, 71, 277,n2, 435; **51:** 104n4, 114, 367, 407n2, 610n1; appointment suggestions, **43:** 25-26; **46:** 36n1, 91, 91-92, 105-106, 111, 168, 217-18, 259, 269, 448, 491; establishment of, **43:** 148n1, 156n1, 192, 319n1; members of, **43:** 341,n1,2, 515; J. Daniels visits WW with members of, **43:** 341,n2, 373, 380; and price fixing and proposed powers, **43:** 413-14, 489-91; **45:** 233, 234, 244; **46:** 602-603, 603, 607; **47:** 208, 224-25, 225, 255, 494-95; **48:** 9, 474, 487-88; and Purchasing Commission, **44:** 64, 268; and commodity prices, **44:** 64, 222, 223-24; **45:** 342-43, 344; **46:** 58, 59, 336; **51:** 5n1; and F. A. Scott's resignation, **44:** 208, 212, 232-33, 450; D. Willard and, **45:** 71-72, 75, 77-78, 92, 600-601; **46:** 15, 61-62; R. S. Lovett resigns from, **46:** 39,n1, 439, 476, 524; reorganization of, **46:** 205, 215-17, 252, 520-22, 522,n1, 532, 610; B. M. Baruch on purchasing methods of, **46:** 251, 289; and priorities committee, **46:** 477-78, 490-91, 506; **48:** 484-85,n1; Council of National Defense lists six services of, **46:** 427; B. M. Baruch appointed chairman of, **46:** 520, 527; and issue of separation from Council of National Defense, **47:** 114, 143, 527, 533; estimate of expenditures of, **48:** 139, 189; WW signs order mak-

War Industries Board (*cont.*)
  ing separate administrative agency of,
  48: 176n1; and Seattle hydroelectric
  plant, **49:** 119-20, 121-22; and cooperation among agencies, **49:** 424-25; and
  C. A. Lindbergh, **49:** 536n1; **51:** 64-
  65,n2
*War Industries Board: Business-Govern-
  ment Relations During World War I*
  (Cuff), **42:** 168n1; **43:** 25n1, 148n1; **44:**
  238n1
War Labor Administration (proposed),
  51: 369
War Labor Board: *see* National War Labor Board
War Labor Conference Board **46:** 578-80,
  582; **47:** 223,n1,2, 247, 248, 272, 282-
  83, 302, 557; **48:** 337n1, 374, 637n6; **49:**
  135
War Labor Policies Board, **48:** 334; **49:**
  53,n1, 181, 440n1; **51:** 125n1
War Loan Act, April 1917 (bond bill), **42:**
  25, 27, 126, 307, *see also* Liberty Loan
War Memoirs of David Lloyd George, **42:**
  340n6; **45:** 430n3, 487n2
War Message and the Facts Behind It **43:**
  168n2
War Prison Association, **44:** 484n1
war-profits tax, **48:** 127; **49:** 162-63,n1,2,
  163-64; **51:** 219-20
War Relief Fund, **43:** 506
war-risk insurance: bill **42:** 455, 565; **43:**
  6, 93-94, 385n1, 478,n1; **44:** 92, 116-17,
  199, 273-74, 279-80, 292; Act, **44:**
  323,n1; **47:** 211
War Risk Insurance, Bureau of, **41:**
  280,n1, 318n1; **42:** 565; **43:** 94; **46:** 468
War Supplies Board, **43:** 345
War Supplies, Department of (proposed),
  45: 65-67
*War to End All Wars: The American Mil-
  itary Experience in World War I* (Coffman), **51:** 3n1
War Trade Board, **44:** 284-85, 486n3; **45:**
  61, 64, 66, 78, 80, 141n1; **46:** 91, 329,
  380n2, 477, 491, 502, 521, 522,n1; **47:**
  395, 601; **48:** 137, 145n4, 306n1; **49:**
  435,n1, 493; **51:** 88, 104,n4; and Norway, **45:** 74n2; relationship between
  Food Administration and, **45:** 116-
  17,n1; and financial aid for Poland, **45:**
  349-50; T. D. Jones resigns from, **45:**
  350, 367; and commandeering of Dutch
  ships in U.S. ports, **45:** 366; and relief,
  47: 44-45, 555; **48:** 137, 145n4, 306n1;
  49: 435,n1, 493; **51:** 88, 104,n4; *see also*
  Exports Administrative Board
War Trade Committee, **42:** 29,n1, 49,
  117, 118
War Trade Intelligence Department,
  London, **42:** 224, 236
Warburg, Felix Moritz, **47:** 555
Warburg, Max Moritz, **43:** 186,n6
Warburg, Nina J. Loeb (Mrs. Paul Moritz), **43:** 186,n4

Warburg, Paul Moritz, **40:** 76, 77, 112; **42:**
  303; **43:** 185-86; resignation from Fed-
  eral Reserve Board, **48:** 171-73; **49:**
  218,n1, 222, 236
Warburton, Barclay Harding, **49:** 41,n2,
  41-42,n1
Ward, Eugene, **46:** 520
Ward, Joseph George, **42:** 339,n4
Wardwell, Allen, **45:** 543,n4; **46:** 233,n3;
  48: 234; **51:** 4, 18n1
Ware, Mary, **44:** 79
Warfield, Lewis, **49:** 140,n1,2, 141, 174
Warnemünde, Germany, **41:** 240n2
Warner, Charles D., **51:** 579,n2
Warner, Henry Morris, **48:** 311n1
Warner, Langdon, **48:** 458,n3, 459
Warner and Swasey Company, Cleve-
  land, **41:** 530n1; **43:** 25
Warren, Alice Edith Binsse (Mrs. Schuy-
  ler Neilson), **41:** 399,n1, 399-401
Warren, Bentley Wirt, **48:** 297,n1
Warren, Charles, **42:** 490; **43:** 315, 316,
  317, 320-21; **46:** 335
Warren, Francis Emroy, **45:** 332n1
Warren, Whitney, **48:** 482,n3
Warren and Wetmore, **48:** 482n3
Warringer, Robert Douglas, **49:** 11n4
Was Baker Right? (Sullivan), **47:** 40n3
Washburn, Alice Langhorne (Mrs. Stan-
  ley), **43:** 521
Washburn, Stanley, **42:** 164,n1, 284, 285;
  43: 409, 413, 424, 460n1, 521; **45:** 143,
  264, 339, 348
Washington, George, **41:** 181, 302,
  466n3; **42:** 29n1; **43:** 364, 499, 509; **44:**
  178; **45:** 332n1, 371n1; **46:** 41n1, 314,
  368n1; **48:** 514, 515; **51:** 107-108, 131
Washington (state), **42:** 564; **45:** 234; **46:**
  556; **47:** 194; labor problems in, **43:** 200,
  222n1, 266-67, 281, 494; **44:** 14, 17, 50,
  242, 243, 263, 277, 344-45; coal prices
  in, **44:** 3n1; hydroelectric plant near
  Seattle approved, **49:** 119,n2, 119-21,
  121-22, 143, 148, 170, 295-96,n1,2; politics in, **51:** 633
Washington, D.C., **40:** 438, 475, 492; **47:**
  249; and prohibition, **41:** 329, 432; and
  district court appointment in, **43:** 33-
  34; C. A. Lindbergh report on woman
  suffrage demonstrations in, **44:** 108-16;
  housing crisis in, **45:** 336, 337; **46:**
  37n1, 67, 195; **47:** 38,n1,2, 53; **48:**
  150n1, 159-60, 190,n1, 192-93; and alley legislation, **47:** 53, 192-93,n2,
  255,n1; and child-welfare, **47:** 548, 560,
  596, 602-603; **48:** 9; and airmail service, **47:** 615n1; Sunday baseball in, **48:**
  32; WW on Olmsted's contribution to,
  49: 513-14; rules on German aliens in,
  51: 172n1, 270-71
Washington, University of, **46:** 509n1
Washington Bee, **51:** 193n1
*Washington-Berlin 1908/1917: Die Tä-
  tigkeit des Botschafters Johann Heinrich Graf von Bernstorff in Washington*

vor dem Eintritt der Vereinigten Staat-
en von Amerika in den Ersten Welt-
krieg (Doerries), **43:** 217n4
Washington case (Houston riot), **49:** 325-
26, 327-28, 400, 401
Washington Censors (*Springfied*, Mass.,
Republican), **44:** 358,n1
Washington *Evening Star*, **40:** 349n9,
350n13, 353; **41:** 308n2; **42:** 245,n3; **47:**
388,n1,2
Washington Herald, **46:** 101n1
Washington Post, **40:** 20n, 130n2, 188n1,
349n12, 353; **41:** 240n2, 451n1; **42:**
237n1, 281n1, 301n2, 392n, 422n1,
451n1, 498n1, 537n5, 554n1, 567n1;
43: 154,n2, 182-83, 201n1, 205n1,
213n1, 217n5, 344n1, 412n2, 412n4,
509n4; **44:** 107n3, 110n2; **45:** 87, 89,
147n1, 173, 200n1, 238n1, 368n1, 437,
598n1; **46:** 195n1, 355,n4, 525-26,n2,3,
527; **47:** 178, 194n1, 310, 388n3, 411,
414n1, 418n2, 615n1; **48:** 119n2,
356n2, 465,n1; **49:** 5n1, 292n3, 441n9,
512n1; **51:** 168n1, 316, 464
Washington State Federation of Labor,
44: 104n1
Washington State Grange, **49:** 79-80,
232,n2; **51:** 212n2, 249,n2, 257, 310-12;
breakup of meeting leads to investigation of, **48:** 290-91, 291-94, 322
Washington State Grange 1889-1924: A
Romance of Democracy (Crawford), **48:**
293n5, **51:** 249n2
Washington Times, **43:** 318n1, 416n1,
495,n1; **44:** 299, 322; **45:** 320n1; **46:**
102n1; **47:** 587n1
Washington University, St. Louis, **40:**
9,n1,2, 215n1; **48:** 450n2
Washington Wife: Journal of Ellen
Maury Slayden from 1897-1919, **49:**
73n3
Water Power Commission (proposed), **40:**
207
Water Power Committee (House of
Reps.), **51:** 6
water-power legislation, **40:** 206-207,
214, 269, 287, 424, 522-23; **41:** 5, 19-20,
23, 82-83, 319; **48:** 260, 405, 452-53; **49:**
289-92, 304, 316, 317, 329-32, 344, 351,
355-56, 356-57, 357, 406, 425, 499, 505-
506, 515; **51:** 6,n2, 27; comments on, **45:**
168-69, 171-72, 201, 299-301, 302,
335,n1, 379-80, 406, 433,n1; **51:** 6,n2,
20-21, 206; *see also* under names of individual bills such as Ferris water-
power bill
Watertown, N.Y., **42:** 469-70, 490
Watertown, N.Y., *Standard*, **42:** 469,n1
Watkins, John Thomas, **48:** 299-30,n1
Watonwan County, Minn., **47:** 235n3
Watson, Clarence Wayland, **51:** 437,n1,4,
537-38,n3, 540
Watson, James Eli, **48:** 17,n2
Watson, Madeline M. (Mrs. William Upton), **44:** 110,n2

Watson, Richard Lyness, Jr., **43:** 65n1
Watson, Robert, **47:** 58,n1
Watson, Thomas Edward (Tom), **43:**
389,n1; **49:** 115,n2
Watt, Richard Morgan, **46:** 564,n2
Watterson, Henry, **49:** 268n1
Ways and Means Committee (House of
Reps.), **42:** 25, 27; **43:** 491; **46:** 561; **48:**
119n2, 128,n1, 393; **49:** 125, 164, 232,
234; **51:** 108n9, 205, 219
We Shall Be All: A History of the Indus-
trial Workers of the World (Dubofsky),
43: 17n4, 22n1; **44:** 17n1, 50n1, 163n1;
46: 144n1; **47:** 574n5
Weaver, Zebulon, **51:** 207, 214, 482
Webb, Ben, **43:** 253
Webb, Edwin Yates, **41:** 197n1; **42:** 113,
117n1, 245n2, 290n2, 298-99, 343, 369-
70,n1; **43:** 213,n1; **44:** 314; **45:** 242, 243,
277
Webb, Frank C., **40:** 176,n1
Webb, Sidney James, 1st Baron Pass-
field, **46:** 435n3; **47:** 159,n1; **51:** 566
Webb, Ulysses Sigel, **42:** 272,n8; **46:**
72,n5, 73
Webb, Walter Prescott, **49:** 73n3
Webb bill, **40:** 252, 253, 268; **41:** 84, 93;
42: 3
Weber, Victor Edler von Webenau, **51:**
616,n1
Webster, Daniel, **41:** 530
Webster, Edwin Sibley, **43:** 267,n1
Webster, James Edwin, **41:** 354,n2; **45:**
411n2
Webster, Nelson P., **42:** 153-54,n2
Webster, Texas, Presbyterian Church,
40: 516,n1; **41:** 408
Wedgwood, Cicely Veronica, **40:** 361n1
Wedgwood, Josiah Clement, **40:** 359,n1,
361-62,n1, 403; **43:** 364,n1
Wedrowski, Jacek R., **42:** 355n2
Weeks, John Wingate, **43:** 16, 18, 242n1,
348, 461, 515, 517, 534; **46:** 460; and
postwar reconstruction, **51:** 216, 227,
229, 270; and WW's endorsement, **51:**
552, 552-53
Wehle, Louis Brandeis, **45:** 7-11,n1
Weibright, J. F., **47:** 432,n1
Weinberg, Israel, **46:** 69, 70, 71
Weinstein, Aaron, **45:** 572,n2
Weinstein, Edwin Alexander, **43:** 361n1
Weinstein, James, **42:** 148n1
Weizmann, Chaim, **43:** 159n1,2; **45:** 572;
46: 494,n3, 516
Weizmann Commission, **49:** 364, 403
Wekerle, Sander (Alexander), **45:** 57,n3
Welborn, Jesse Floyd, **42:** 459n1
Welland Canal, **41:** 418n1; **42:** 476, 477
Weller, B. Uwe, **43:** 246n1
Welles, Roger, **46:** 67,n2
Wells, Sumner, **40:** 82n1
Welliver, Judson Churchill, **41:** 374,n1
Wells, Edward Hubbard, **47:** 41n2, 328-
32, 545n1; *see also* Marshall-Wells-
McNab Committee

Wells, H. G. (Herbert George), **41:** 83,n2, 113; **45:** 24, 340,n1, 363; **51:** 298,n2
Welsh, Herbert, **47:** 559,n1
Welty, Benjamin Franklin, **45:** 307,n1
Wemyss, Rosslyn Erskine, **48:** 385,n4
Wendt, Christian H., **47:** 216-17,n1
Werner, Commander, **40:** 389n1
Wescott, John Wesley, **49:** 432,n1; **51:** 179
Wesleyan University, **42:** 88; **43:** 85n2
Wessel, Clem, **44:** 242, 277
West, Andrew Fleming, **40:** 567; **42:** 439n1; **44:** 237; **45:** 254; **49:** 257
West, George P., **44:** 470n3, 472
West, Oswald, **48:** 241,n1,2,3
West Coast Lumbermen's Association, **46:** 106n1
West Indies, Danish: *see* Danish West Indies
West Point: *see* United States Military Academy
West Virginia, **47:** 410; and coal problems, **43:** 33,n1, 54, 59, 385; and district attorney appointment in, **43:** 278-79; labor laws, **43:** 418,n1; politics in, **51:** 437n1,2,3,4, 537-38,n3,4, 540,590, 633
Westarp, Kuno Friedrich Viktor, Count von, **40:** 433,n7; **45:** 32,n6; **46:** 188-89,n4, 190-91, **48:** 555n7
Westcott, John Howell, **40:** 347, 355
Westcott, Mary Dunton, **40:** 347,n1, 355
Westenhaver, David Courtney, **41:** 55-56,n2
Western Electric Company, **47:** 400
Western Federation of Miners, **41:** 302n2
Western Pine Association, **45:** 234, 244
Western Union Company, **41:** 322, 323, 324; **48:** 281,n1, 313, 337-40, 349-50, 374-75, 393-94
Westinghouse Electric and Manufacturing Company, **46:** 578n2
Westminster Congregational Chapel, London, **47:** 420n1
Weygand, Maxime, **48:** 367,n1, 388, 396
Whaley, Percival Huntington, **46:** 353,n1
What Happened in the Mooney Case (Hopkins), **42:** 270n2
What Happened to the August *Masses*? (*The Masses*), **43:** 165n2
What Men Four Years Hence Will Lead Nation's Parties? (Creel), **40:** 315n1
What Military Aid May Entente Expect from the United States? (Geneva *Nouvelliste*), **43:** 435n1
What Voice Is Speaking Now? (New York *Sun*), **51:** 331n6
wheat: supply and prices, **44:** 88,n1, 89,n1, 215,n2; **45:** 58-60, 69, 74, 83, 86, 178; **46:** 345-47, 368, 430-32, 505; **47:** 120-21,n1; **48:** 42,n1, 74, 488, 576, 580, 593-94, 595-97, 628,n1; **49:** 391-93; and food conservation proclamation, **46:** 20; grain crisis in, **46:** 213-14, 306, 461, 565, 572; and price fixing, **47:** 88, 95-96, 139; **49:** 49, 104, 278, 352-53, 354,

354n1, 356, 427,n2, 433, 441,n9; H. Hoover on cereal program, **48:** 308; farmers' need for appropriations for, **48:** 629,n2,3; aid to drought-stricken areas, **49:** 91, 99-100
Wheat Export Company, **46:** 461n1
Wheat Growers' Protective Association, **46:** 345-46
Wheeler, Benjamin Ide, **42:** 30, 43, 45
Wheeler, Burton Kendall, **44:** 259n1, 262; **48:** 220n1; **51:** 302
Wheeler, Charles Brewster, **45:** 390n1; **49:** 279,n2; **51:** 35,n4
Wheeler, Harry Andrew, **49:** 314,n1, 455, 457, 541; **51:** 207-208, 229; WW on, **49:** 455,n1
Wheeler, Harry Cornwall, **44:** 135, 479, 517, 520, 523; **45:** 134; and army commission, **46:** 573,n1, 584, 598-99; **47:** 115-16, 187, 347, 597-98
Wheeler, Howard Duryee, **43:** 477,n1
Wheeler, Wayne Bidwell, **43:** 52,n1, 65
Wheeler-Bennett, John Wheeler, **45:** 595n2; **46:** 341n4,5, 471n3
Wheeling, W. Va., **42:** 473
Which? War without a Purpose? Or Armed Neutrality with a Purpose? (Hayes), **41:** 164,n2
Whigham, Henry James, **47:** 16,n3; **48:** 147,n5
Whigham, Robert Dundas, **47:** 371,n4, 374
Whipple, Sherman Leland, **45:** 399; **51:** 407, 439-40, 451, 484, 485
White, Andrew Dickson, **42:** 139-40, 200
White, Edward Douglass, **41:** 310, 327, 430n2, 432, 531; **47:** 425
White, Henry, **41:** 292; **42:** 169, 170; **46:** 429; **48:** 119,n1
White, Henry Middleton, **43:** 266,n1, 267; **44:** 50,n2
White, James C., **47:** 576n2
White, John Albert, **51:** 100n2
White, John Barber, **43:** 50,n2, 260,n1,4
White, John Beaver, **45:** 116,n1
White, John H., **43:** 368
White, John Philip, **40:** 154,n1, 217; **42:** 458, 458-59, 471-73; **46:** 601
White, Ruth, **48:** 303n1
White, Walter Francis, **49:** 88,n3
White, William Alanson, **44:** 559-61,n5; **48:** 129,n1
White Armies of Russia: A Chronicle of Counter-Revolution and Allied Intervention (Stewart), **51:** 102n1
White Mountains National Forest, **47:** 589
White Sulphur Springs, W. Va., **48:** 564
Whitehouse, John Howard, **40:** 4-5,n1,2, 20, 111,n1, 133, 138, 172, 185, 186, 189, 233-34, 276, 305, 465, 558; **41:** 85-86, 555; **42:** 30, 45, 64, 65-69, 80, 379, 381
Whitehouse, Sheldon, **44:** 532,n1; **51:** 18n2
Whitehouse, Vira Boarman (Mrs. Nor-

man de R.), **43:** 462,n1,2; **44:** 61, 62, 79, 335, 384, 440-41, 460-61, 533, 537; **51:** 603,n1

Whitehouse and Company, **43:** 462n1

Whiteway, Mary Bird (Mrs. William Keen), **44:** 159-60

Whiteway, William Keen, **44:** 159

Whitfield, William H, **48:** 569n1

Whitin, Ernest Stagg, **48:** 248n1

Whitlock, Brand, **40:** 530-31, 554; **41:** 214-15,n2, 234; **42:** 20, 427; **43:** 477-78, 493,n1; **44:** 84-85, 450n1

Whitman, Charles Seymour, **44:** 290,n3: **45:** 11n1, 573, 574, 593; **48:** 16; **51:** 144,n1; on H. A. Garfield's coal order, **46:** 19, 24

Whitman, Walt, **40:** 42

Whitmarsh, Theodore Francis, **48:** 484n1

Whitney, Louis Bernard, **43:** 158-59,n1

Whitridge, Frederick Wallingford, **40:** 88-89

Whittier, Edmond A., **48:** 17,n1

Who's Who Against America (Hopkins), **44:** 301-302,n1

Who's Who in America, **42:** 165, 166n3

Why Declare War (*Springfield,* Mass., *Republican*), **41:** 451n2

Why Germany Must Surrender (*Springfield,* Mass., *Republican*), **51:** 267,n2

Why Is Roosevelt Unjailed? (*The Nation*), **51:** 646,n1

'Why' of the Tie-Up (Snyder), **47:** 40n3

Why Woodrow Wilson Will Stand By His Colored Fellow Citizens (New York *Sun*), **43:** 359n1

Wiart, Henri Carton de, **40:** 184,n1

Wickersham, George Woodward, **46:** 566

Wickersham, James, **40:** 291-92,n2

Widenor, William C., **41:** 11n1

Wiegand, Karl H. von, **40:** 133, 375-78; **41:** 79, 127, 134, 149; **44:** 105; **46:** 350,n1

Wiesbaden, S.M.S., **51:** 490

Wiggin, Albert Henry, **48:** 612n1

Wilberforce University, **51:** 193n1

Wilbur, Ray Lyman, **44:** 146,n1

Wilcox, T. B., **44:** 191,n1

Wilder, William Royal, **41:** 180,n1; **42:** 104-105, 134, 491; **44:** 3,n1; **45:** 574-75; on Poland, **46:** 401-402, 403, 404, 405

Wildman, Edwin, **49:** 165,n1

Wiley, Anna Campbell Kelton (Mrs. Harvey Washington), **47:** 547,n1, 572

Wiley, Louis, **43:** 246, 291, 333

Wilfley, Xenophon Pierce, **48:** 115n1; **51:** 374

Wilkins, Clement, **44:** 50n1, 345

Will It Be 'Mr. Justice Brandeis?' (Philadelphia *Public Ledger*), **40:** 315,n1

Will to Believe (James), **48:** 620,n3

Will to Believe and Other Essays in Popular Philosophy (James), **48:** 620n3

Willard, Daniel, **41:** 151, 430n2; **42:** 19, 168n1, 193, 222, 290, 449, 462,n1; **43:** 177, 249, 424; **45:** 265, 276, 299, 570, 600-601; **46:** 3, 92, 93; **47:** 437; **48:** 465; **49:** 78; and War Industries Board, **45:** 71-72, 75, 77-78, 92; **46:** 15, 61-62, 105, 216; on prices in lumber industry, **45:** 233-34, 244; on steel prices, **45:** 342-43, 344

Willard, Joseph Edward, **40:** 304, 404-405; **41:** 35; **46:** 50n1, 67

Willcox, William Russell, **40:** 359,n1; **41:** 164-65, 501; **44:** 326, 502,n2; **45:** 340-41; **46:** 60; **47:** 557

Wille, Ulrich, **40:** 460,n5, 462

Willert, Arthur, **40:** 262n1; **47:** 401n1

William II (of Germany), **40:** 21n1, 65, 131, 137, 142, 144, 204, 357, 389, 390, 409, 411, 434, 486, 516, 527, 554, 555; **41:** 24, 26n1, 59n1, 533; **42:** 355, 389,n4, 425, 456, 520, 521-22; **43:** 185,n1,2, 405n2, 498; **44:** 320, 548n2; **45:** 30-31, 36,n14, 238n1, 255, 394, 418, 595n3; **46:** 173, 253, 483, 488; **47:** 25, 202, 296, 462, 500,n1, 522, 524n1; **48:** 160, 171, 213n8, 239, 240, 555n7; **49:** 399; **51:** 96, 253n2, 267,n3, 277n6,7, 320, 330n1, 331n4,6, 403, 415, 528, 541n1, 560; on rejection of his peace offer, **40:** 487,n5; meets with Charles I, **48:** 114,n2

William Filene's Sons Company, Boston, **47:** 557n4

William P. Frye, S.S.: see Frye case

Williams, Albert Rhys, **48:** 143,n9,10

Williams, Charles Turner, **48:** 477-79, 493

Williams, Cora Bell Brewer (Mrs. Homer B.), **44:** 23

Williams, Dixon C., **47:** 226,n1, 235-37

Williams, Edward Thomas, **41:** 38-39; **42:** 53, 53-54; **43:** 458,n1 **45:** 96, 97-100; **46:** 301, 302-303, 303-304, 500-501; **48:** 518,n2

Williams, Harold, **46:** 411,n1; **48:** 187n4; **49:** 93n1

Williams, John Elias, **45:** 96,n1, 356

Williams, John Sharp, **40:** 168, 190, 201, 318, 344; **41:** 55n1, 107-108, 250; **42:** 5, 213, 227, 281n1; **43:** 455; **44:** 117-18, 155-56; **46:** 104,n1, 104, 257, 369-70; **47:** 561; **51:** 331,n5; and Young-Dockery affair, **43:** 4,n1, 78, 79, 118; on not seeking reelection, **43:** 344, 368-69; and woman suffrage, **45:** 279, 338, 339; **46:** 61; **48:** 400-401; answers G. M. Hitchcock on Chamberlain bills, **46:** 257,n2 287-88; advocates "watchful waiting" in Russian situation, **46:** 287; death of daughter, **48:** 557-58,n1; on soldiers and absentee voting, **48:** 558,n1

Williams, John Skelton, **40:** 181-82, 202,n2, 214; **42:** 303, 401, 411; **43:** 11; **49:** 72; on railroads, **44:** 400-405, 406-407, 422-23, 428, 430; **45:** 306,n1; **47:** 241, 405-11, 418-19, 488; and Seattle hydroelectric plant, **49:** 143, 148

Williams, Richard H., **42:** 462,n2
Williams, William Appleman, **46:** 232n1
Williams College, **40:** 238; **43:** 25
Williamson, John Grant, **45:** 32n4
Williamstown, Mass., **40:** 572-73, 573, 576; **42:** 151; **44:** 55
Willis, Irene Cooper, **42:** 422,n2
Willoughby, William Franklin, **40:** 443n1, 497-99, 549
Willoughby, Woodbury, **46:** 442n1
Wilm, Émil Carl, **47:** 518-20,n1
Wilmington, Del., **45:** 132
Wilmington, N.C., **42:** 203,n1; **43:** 115; centennial celebration of First Presbyterian Church in, **42:** 86-89
Wilson, Afred McCalmont, **48:** 451,n1
Wilson, Alice, niece of WW, **45:** 346; marriage of, **49:** 292,n3, 319
Wilson, Cedric Frederick, **43:** 540,n2
Wilson, Charles Stetson, **41:** 35,n2; **46:** 67,n1
Wilson, Clarence True, **41:** 311-12,n1
Wilson, Edith Bolling Galt (Mrs. Woodrow), **40:** 30, 84, 94, 96, 113, 127, 128, 129n2, 164, 201, 221, 240, 289, 338, 374, 403, 408, 413, 483, 576; **41:** 29, 88, 172, 317, 328, 331, 341, 357, 364, 367, 368, 380, 449, 451, 452, 455, 473, 483, 496, 498, 515, 528, 529, 531, 557; **42:** 13, 31, 69, 125, 127, 158, 161, 168, 171, 210n1, 232, 560; **43:** 100, 183, 235n1, 238, 240, 247, 317, 318, 338, 390; **44:** 56, 65, 107, 175, 184, 203, 365, 378, 380, 390, 439, 448, 455, 536, 571; **45:** 186, 237, 318, 335, 346, 381, 459, 598, 600, 601; **46:** 51, 100, 114, 115, 167, 264n1, 290, 314, 327, 328, 336, 343, 371, 407, 435, 445, 485, 489, 496; **47:** 59, 84, 86, 117, 137, 154, 185, 217n1, 309, 324, 350, 380, 393, 401,n2, 454, 476, 502, 506, 534n1, 604; **48:** 45, 50, 51, 57n1, 61, 62, 63, 69, 70, 79, 121, 169, 173, 174-75, 310, 311, 391, 440, 564, 578; **49:** 96, 164, 167, 216, 219 267, 275, 276, 292, 292n3, 294, 318, 351,n2, 397, 398, 529n1; **51:** 77, 83, 110, 144, 152, 255, 279, 315, 316, 341; on Grayson promotion, **40:** 463; H. Bones on, **40:** 574; death of sister, **41:** 288,n1; on W. G. McAdoo, **41:** 318; accompanies WW on business call to cabinet members, **41:** 466, 473-74; helps WW with paperwork, **41:** 549-50; and Pocahontas, **42:** 58,n1; and WW's last will and testament, **42:** 426; ill with grippe, **44:** 242, 244-45, 246, 266, 328; and Fourteen Points Address, **45:** 555; on film *Hearts of the World,* **48:** 313-14,n1; chooses Gobelin tapestry, **49:** 156-57; and launching of *Quistconck,* **49:** 433,n4; on WW's appeal to voters, **51:** 390, photographs, *illustration sections,* **41; 49**
Wilson, Edmund Beecher, **41:** 230,n1, 235
Wilson, Ellen Louise Axson (Mrs. Woodrow), **40:** 565; **42:** 292n2, 426; **47:**

193n2, 454n1; letters to Jessie (1906-14), **40:** 566-72; on Princeton's club-quad controversy of 1907, **40:** 567-69, 570; monument for grave of, **44:** 340, 347; photograph, *illustration section,* **44**
Wilson, Frederick J., **46:** 380,n1
Wilson, Henry Braid, **43:** 178,n2
Wilson, Sir Henry Hughes, **45:** 48,n1, 112; **46:** 241, 453; **47:** 238; **51:** 373, 385, 386, 396, 429, 580
Wilson, Hugh Robert, **45:** 384-85,n1, 415n1, 415-17,n5; **46:** 235n1, 352-53; **47:** 64n2,4; **49:** 187-93, 382; on G. Hertling's and O. Czernin's speeches, **46:** 172-73; on Herron-Lammasch negotiations and Austria-Hungary's peace talk, **46:** 198-200, 241, 253-54, 261-63, 388, 412-13, 510, 615,n1, 616; on rumor of German peace talk, **46:** 428; on Swiss President's offer, **46:** 592-94
Wilson, James Clifton, **45:** 307,n1
Wilson, Janet Woodrow (Mrs. Joseph Ruggles), mother of WW: WW on, **44:** 199
Wilson, John, uncle of WW, **40:** 170n1
Wilson, John Adams, cousin of WW, **48:** 451n1
Wilson, Joseph Ruggles, father of WW, **42:** 87, 89, 203; **43:** 155; **45:** 237, 282; **46:** 469; **48:** 578
Wilson, Joseph R., Jr., brother of WW, **40:** 62, 90, 238; **43:** 247-48; **45:** 77, 346; **47:** 6, 33, 37; **49:** 292n3
Wilson, Kate Wilson (Mrs. Joseph R., Jr.), **45:** 346
Wilson, Luther Barton, **42:** 259,n1
Wilson, Margaret Woodrow, daughter of WW and EAW, **40:** 94, 128, 336, 403, 542, 566, 568, 570, 573, 575; **41:** 328, 529, 531; **43:** 241, 248, 318, 338; **44:** 55, 266; **45:** 582; **46:** 317,n3, 327, 328, 371; **47:** 453n1; **48:** 7, 313n1; **49:** 167; **51:** 144; WW's birthday greetings to, **42:** 77; and WW's last will and testament, **42:** 426; and H. Froelicher, **47:** 454, 536, 537; on a singing tour, **47:** 502-503; distressed over father's burned hand, **48:** 60-61
Wilson, Philip Whitwell, **47:** 297-99,n1
Wilson, Samuel, **49:** 137-38,n1
Wilson, Smith W., **43:** 540,n1
Wilson, Thomas Edward, **45:** 179n2; **48:** 77,n1
Wilson, William Bauchop, **40:** 7, 173, 175, 188n1; **41:** 123, 299, 518, 541; **42:** 153-54,n1,3, 266n1, 448; **43:** 3, 4, 26, 61, 94, 177, 237, 336, 437, 486, 512; **44:** 219, 497, 501, 523, 526, 552; **45:** 8, 46, 60, 94, 95, 103-104, 129, 134, 148n1, 322n1, 331, 355, 370, 448, 555; **46:** 26, 15,n2, 212, 297n1, 482, 508n2, 509-10, 582; **47:** 153, 221, 222n2, **48:** 7, 219-20, 248, 261, 337-38,n1, 432, 434, 439, 444; **49:** 3, 24, 25-26, 53-54, 71n1, 72, 85, 104-105, 105, 147-48, 148, 166, 211, 394, 520-22; **51:** 280, 367, 616; on rail-

roads, **40:** 97-100; **41:** 402, 412-13, 413, 425, 430n2, 437; **44:** 22-23; on Porto Rico bill, **40:** 295-97; and Industrial Arbitration Commission, **41:** 253-55, 258, 262; advocates war entry, **41:** 441-42; offers resignation and WW declines, **41:** 446-47, 450; suggestions for Russian Commission, **42:** 165-66, 197, 240, 252, 262, 263, 267, 291; and Council of National Defense, **42:** 279,n1, 471-73; **43:** 511,n1; on labor's right to organize, **42:** 473-74; **43:** 292-93; on labor situation in Arizona mines, **42:** 562, 562-64; **44:** 173n1, 223, 424-25, 429, 478, 483, 515-16, 516-20; on British seamen who desert in U.S. ports, **42:** 566-67; on labor problems in western states, **43:** 16-18, 98, 104, 266-67; and various strikes, **43:** 368, 506, **44:** 15, 80, 144n1, 163n1, 225, 276-77, 277-78; **45:** 95-96; **47:** 189-91, 272-74, 292; **48:** 281, 393-94, 546, n1; **49:** 132-34, 181, 519-20; **51:** 24n1; and President's Mediation Commission, **44:** 103-104, 120, 191, 213-14, 214, 216, 241, 257n1, 424-25, 478, 515-16, 523; **45:** 126-27; **46:** 127-47, 149-50; and Shipbuilding Labor Adjustment Board, **44:** 257,n1, 268; on Mooney case, **44:** 290-91; **46:** 68-74, 74, 84; **47:** 467n1; report on Bisbee deportations,

44: 515-16, 516-20; and war emergency service appropriation, **45:** 130; on lumber industry, **45:** 234, 244, 295; **46:** 106-108, 218, 508-509, 509; on housing, **46:** 151, 171, 179; **48:** 150, 594; on settlement of Texas and Louisiana oil dispute, **46:** 170, 179; on War Labor Conference Board and National War Labor Board, **46:** 578-80, 582; **47:** 247, 248, 272, 557-58; **48:** 43; and H. C. Wheeler's army commission, **47:** 115; on protection of children, **47:** 180, 188; on difficulty of assuring steady employment, **47:** 291-92; and proposed appointment of Director General of Labor, **47:** 377, 391, 425; refutes Woolley's and Hale's statements, **47:** 461-65, 537-38; on education campaign by Labor Department, **48:** 222-25; on Maryland's compulsory work law, **48:** 270,n1; on creating labor newspaper in Mexico, **49:** 89-90; on wage discrepancy issue, **49:** 181, 186, 206-207, 251, 367, 464; immigration resolution of, **49:** 310n1; and N.J. public utilities, **49:** 424, 463-64; and wages, **51:** 32, 260-61, 361-62, 369, 423, 593; on postwar reconstruction, **51:** 270; and peace notes, **51:** 412, 414, 415; photograph, *illustration section*, **46**

WOODROW WILSON

I

APPEARANCE, 297
FAMILY AND PERSONAL LIFE, 297
HEALTH, 298
OPINIONS, 298
RECREATION, 299
RELIGION, 299
WRITINGS, 299

II

GENERAL, 300
INAUGURATION, 301
APPOINTMENTS AND RESIGNATIONS, 301
CAZINET, 302
FOREIGN POLICY: *see under the names of individual countries*
PRESIDENTIAL CAMPAIGN: *see under* Democratic Presidential Campaign of 1916

APPEARANCE

41: 70, 88, 89; **47:** 154, 297-98; F. K. Lane's picture of during stormy cabinet session, **41:** 282-83; I could almost feel the President stiffen as if to resist and see his powerful jaw set, **41:** 443; President Wilson is of a very Anglo-Saxon type—lean, with a long and bony face, eyes calm and piercing behind his pince-nez, measured in his gestures, precise as a lawyer in his words, only rarely allowing the inner flame that animates him to appear in his language, **42:** 175; E. Hovelaque on, **42:** 210n1; weary, war-worn, **45:** 128; W. Wiseman on, **46:** 85; R. Bridges on J. S. Sargent portrait of, **46:** 219,n6; J. W. Johnson on, **46:** 385n1; E. M.

House on, **46:** 485; Many of his portraits do him an injustice. Not only are his eyes direct and kindly, but his smile is singularly open and engaging, nor is the firmness of his mouth on which so much has been written nearly as prominent as we have been led to believe by photographers and caricaturists, **47:** 297-98; photographs: *illustration sections*, **41**; **42**; **43**; **44**; **45**; **46**; **47**; **48**; **49**; **51**

FAMILY AND PERSONAL LIFE

43: 240-42; and niece Annie Cothran, **40:** 93-94, 108, 127; **43:** 236, 241, 317, 318; enjoyed *Uncle Remus Tales* as a child, **40:** 169; continues to support Clara Böhm, **40:** 174, 177; spends Christmas

Woodrow Wilson, Family and Personal Life, cont.

with family, **40:** 336; birthday greetings, **40:** 338, 347; **45:** 369, 380, 380-81, 381, 389, 395-96; and Ruth Preble Hall, **40:** 551-52; **41:** 15; spends Thanksgiving, 1914, in Williamstown, **40:** 572-73, 573; small talk in presence of family, **40:** 575; some views on child-rearing, **40:** 575-76; renews subscription to *Living Age,* **41:** 133; cousin and nephew offer moral and physical help in time of world crisis, **41:** 157, 172, 180, 210; Aunt Felie distraught over WW's and country's crisis, **41:** 157; and settlement of sister's estate, **41:** 259-60, 457-58, 469; death of sister-in-law, Mrs. Maury, **41:** 288,n1; activities and mood between cabinet meeting and signing proclamation for extra session of Congress, **41:** 448-49; deducts income tax from his salary, **41:** 449; thriftiness of, **41:** 449; and his sons-in-law, **41:** 474-75, 549; **42:** 5; **43:** 391; how he likes his eggs, **41:** 474; and haircuts, **41:** 474; peevish while composing war message, **41:** 515; sends birthday greetings to Margaret, **42:** 77; unassuming qualities of, **42:** 88; blacks uncle's boots, **42:** 88-89; reaction to Jessie's fears for her children's safety, **42:** 151-52; last will and testament, **42:** 426; Sayres spend weekend with, **42:** 551,n1; arrangements to have mature man look after Jessie and children, **42:** 556-57, 559, 560; writes letter of introduction for son-in-law F. B. Sayre, **42:** 559,n1; has no time to write article for *Outlook,* **42:** 570-71; sends good-bye telegram to F. B. Sayre, **43:** 53,n1; story of his trip to church in Pohick, Va., **43:** 142; nephew J. Wilson Howe gets a new job, **43:** 242-43,n2; invites brother to White House, **43:** 247-48,n1; and cousin Jessie Brower, **43:** 338; A. S. Hulbert's difficulties and WW aid to, **43:** 502; **44:** 82-83; sends birthday greetings to Jessie, **44:** 64-65; on his mother, **44:** 199; concern over wife's case of grippe, **44:** 242, 244-45, 266, 328; sends roses to former landlady, **44:** 268,n1; E. P. Davis' poems for and WW's thanks, **44:** 285-86, 287, 310; **49:** 462; and monument for EAW's grave, **44:** 340, 347; WW contributes to his church, **45:** 46; upset about not sending get-well wishes to S. H. Thompson, Jr., **45:** 163; on death of Charlie Mitchell, **45:** 404,n1, 423; and investments, **46:** 168; Harper and Brothers' request for exclusive rights to WW's work, **46:** 259-60; a rapid dresser, **46:** 290; condolences to W. L. Chambers, **46:** 325; thanks Mrs. Davis for eggs and butter, **46:** 336; sends news and health reports of family to Cousin Lucy, **46:** 371; at-

Woodrow Wilson, Family and Personal Life, cont.

tempts to aid sister-in-law in getting her poems published, **46:** 371,n1; thanks Mrs. Foley for turkey, **46:** 407; and loan to Mrs. Petty, **46:** 449,n1; on essay written by Edith Reid, **46:** 596; Jessie keeps WW up to date on news of her family, **47:** 392-93; refuses to reveal his personal subscription to Liberty Loan campaign, **47:** 436-37,n1; note to his insurance company about his burned hand and payment received, **47:** 479,n1; **48:** 280; E. M. House on W. G. McAdoo's possible resignation and, **47:** 498, 499; will not appear in public on Sundays, **48:** 119,n1; Aunt Felie on news of her grandsons and WW's reply, **48:** 203, 231; and H. Morgenthau's forthcoming book, **48:** 284, 311; thanks Mme. Bochkareva for image of Ste. Anne, **48:** 475; Mrs. Beach asks for position abroad for her husband, **49:** 257, 318; lucky number of, **49:** 266; to become grandfather again, **49:** 292; cannot make draft exemption for friend's son, **49:** 305-306; concern over Jessie's situation, **49:** 318-19; W. Wiseman's observations of, **49:** 397-99; misses college life, **49:** 399; and Stockton Axson, **49:** 543

HEALTH

40: 30n3, 62, 63, 74, 93, 566, 567-68, 569-70, 571-72, 574, 576; **41:** 359, 364, 364-65, 381, 382, 388, 403, 411, 418, 423, 424, 452, 482, 515; **44:** 395, 406, 490; **47:** 154, 297; **49:** 286, 294; must escape madness of Washington aboard *Mayflower,* **43:** 238, 240; I am surprisingly well, by all the tests that the doctor can apply, though *very* tired all the time. I am very thankful. I do not see how any but a well man could safely be trusted to decide anything in the present circumstances, **43:** 241; need for rest, **44:** 33, 65, 121, 185; **45:** 128, 399, 459; **46:** 485, 508, 532; has massage, **44:** 380; cold, **46:** 105, 114, 117, 150, 174n1, 193n1; burns left hand, **47:** 383,n1, 391, 401, 418, 479, 502, 534, 546, 578; **48:** 7, 60, 201, 280; tired but well, **48:** 550

OPINIONS

on American flag, **43:** 429-30
Bible, **43:** 244
on censorship, **42:** 129
on conservation, **46:** 17; **48:** 643,n1
on Constitution, **40:** 196
on death, **45:** 423
on democracy, **40:** 195; **41:** 525; **42:** 297; **44:** 32
discouragement of, **41:** 11
on duty, **48:** 53, 55

Woodrow Wilson, Opinions, cont.
and education, **42:** 439, 569; **46:** 29
on elections, **40:** 193-94; **41:** 403; **46:** 583-84; **48:** 558
farmers, farming, **42:** 73; **46:** 177-78
force, **47:** 270
on freedom, **46:** 279, 297, 324; **47:** 288
freedom of the seas, **41:** 286, 286-87, 335
Germany, German people, German art, **42:** 8-9, 371; **43:** 429, 430; **44:** 35, 59; **47:** 268-69, 270; **49:** 360; **51:** 129
on history, **42:** 504; **49:** 390
on industry, productivity, **42:** 73; **45:** 14-15
justice, **45:** 539; **46:** 239, 268, 497
law, lawlessness, **40:** 196; **45:** 16-17; **49:** 98
league of nations, **47:** 105, 258-59, 526; **48:** 29-30; **51:** 129
on leaks, **40:** 130
on lies, **49:** 351
on lynching and mob violence, **49:** 97-98
on his mother, **44:** 199
movies, **47:** 388,n3; **48:** 311
on his Mexican policy, **47:** 288-89
on neutrality, **41:** 523
and pacifists, **45:** 41
on patriotism, **40:** 197; **42:** 75; **45:** 238; **48:** 456
peace, peace terms, **40:** 67-70, 72, 73, 120, 195, 536; **41:** 112,n1; **42:** 366-67; **44:** 33-36, 57-59, 120-21, 146, 279; **45:** 15, 202, 536; **46:** 276, 278, 293, 296-97, 320, 321, 323, 497; **47:** 84, 287, 289; **48:** 258; **51:** 224
on the press, **40:** 471-72, 474-75; **42:** 68; **47:** 359
prices, profits, **43:** 151, 153; **48:** 164; **49:** 164
principle, **45:** 238; **47:** 394
on prudence, **43:** 430
responsibility and, **41:** 543; **42:** 325, 423; **44:** 65; **45:** 240, 535
Russia, Russian people, **45:** 199; **46:** 257; **48:** 550, 624-27; **49:** 204
on selective service, **42:** 97-98
on making speeches, **46:** 582-83
submarine warfare; **41:** 520
taxation, **48:** 163; **49:** 164
unity of purpose, **41:** 121, 285, 335; **42:** 283, 367; **44:** 142, 525; **49:** 415; **51:** 382, 344
on universal military training, **46:** 103; **49:** 203, 359
on volunteers, **42:** 452
war: conduct of, **42:** 283, 301n2, 325, 537; **46:** 432; **48:** 10; **51:** 169; objectives, **42:** 370-71; **44:** 34, 58; **48:** 455, 456, 516-17; **49:** 99; **51:** 75, 146-47; U.S. entry into, **41:** 286, 521, 526, 527; **43:** 153-54; **45:** 12; **51:** 128
woman suffrage, women, **40:** 427; **42:** 241, 293; **43:** 251n2, 436; **44:** 441-43; **45:** 545; **46:** 573; **47:** 577-78; **48:** 303-304, 371; **51:** 159, 160
on his writing, **41:** 22,n1; **42:** 162

Woodrow Wilson, Recreation, cont.
RECREATION

plays golf, **40:** 96, 405, 572, 574; **41:** 88, 341, 431, 449, 473, 515, 528, 531; **42:** 13, 31; **43:** 338; **45:** 236-37, 558; **47:** 122, 604; **48:** 7, 643,n1; **49:** 275, 293, 397-98; horseback riding, **40:** 566; **42:** 560; singing, **40:** 574; attends theater, **41:** 445, 483,n1, 550; **42:** 13, 64, 158; **44:** 427,n1; **45:** 317; **46:** 264,n1, 314,n1, 485, 490, 519-20; **47:** 308, 414,n1, 476,n5, 604; **48:** 52-53,n3, 356n2; **51:** 110; takes motor ride, **41:** 448; **43:** 338; **44:** 185; **46:** 437-38; **49:** 268, 398; tells stories, **41:** 455; views film *Patria*, **41:** 483,n1; plays games, **41:** 498; **47:** 409; reading, **42:** 161,n5; **44:** 82,n1, 287,n1; **45:** 558; spends a week aboard *Mayflower*, **44:** 182,n2; invited to attend theater at Camp Meade but declines, **47:** 220,n1, 222; D. Fairbanks offers WW movie projector, **51:** 485,n1

RELIGION

and Wilmington, N.C., Presbyterian Church's Centennial, **42:** 86-88; C. A. Spring Rice sends verse from Isaiah, **42:** 112-13; But the wise heart never questions the dealings of Providence, **42:** 451; on reading the Bible, **43:** 244; Thanksgiving Proclamation, **44:** 525-26; contributes to his church, **45:** 46; The hand of God is laid upon the nations, **45:** 202; on reunion of northern and southern Presbyterian churches, **45:** 286; statement on Sabbath observance by troops, **46:** 41-42,n1; attends church, **46:** 435; proclaims a day of prayer, **47:** 598-99; on Sunday School, **49:** 317, 422

WRITINGS

42: 69,n2; *The State*, **40:** 567; **44:** 487-88; *Constitutional Government*, **41:** 22,n1; on future writing, **42:** 161-62; **46:** 285, 448-49; last will and testament, **42:** 426; has no time to write article for *Outlook*, **42:** 570-71; preface to W. N. Rice's book, **43:** 85; A. Shaw editor of *President Wilson's State Papers and Addresses*, **44:** 273,n1; and Muller edition of *Presidential Messages and State Papers*, **45:** 249-50,n2; on request for some of his speeches to be translated into Latin, **46:** 119-20,n1,2; republication of *An Old Master*, **46:** 259-60, 285, 449; **49:** 128-29, 184; on transferring publishing rights to *Mere Literature* and *Congressional Government*, **46:** 448-49, 605; **47:** 41; on request for an article on how WW acquired his writing skills, **46:** 460, 469; limited edition of *History of the American People* to profit Red Cross, **46:** 570; **47:** 302, 336;

Woodrow Wilson, Writings, cont.
    48: 479, 482-83; *The New Freedom,* **46:**
    589; and *Congressional Government,*
    47: 385; **51:** 621; *George Washington*
    translated into French, **47:** 421,n1;
    against republication of article "Proper
    Perspective of American History," **49:**
    165,n1; WW against making film of
    History of the American People, **51:** 14-
    15,n1, 172-73; and E. G. Elliott and re-
    visions of *The State,* **51:** 535-36,n1,2

GENERAL

talk of 1920 election, **40:** 185; and illumi-
    nation of Statue of Liberty, **40:** 35,n1,2,
    119, 119-20; receives framed parch-
    ment from Armenian Catholic Church,
    40: 105-106,n3; attends memorial serv-
    ice for Francis Joseph, **40:** 113-14; com-
    mutes sentences of labor organizers,
    40: 217,n1; does not wish to have inau-
    gural ball, **40:** 163; on his typewriter,
    40: 335; declines to speak at same func-
    tion as H. C. Lodge, **40:** 354; on not
    making statement on his peace note,
    40: 412, 413; club-quad controversy of
    1907, **40:** 567-69, 570; alleged assassi-
    nation plot against, **41:** 127,n1; denies
    clemency in Diggs-Caminetti case, **41:**
    261, 453-54, 454; on film *Patria,* **41:**
    483,n1; **42:** 447, 467,n1, 527; **43:** 431-
    32, 501-502; **44:** 231-32,n1, 287,n1;
    congratulations on his election, **41:**
    495; and dedication of Tagore book, **41:**
    502,n3, 554-55; **42:** 21; signs war reso-
    lution, **41:** 557; forms for acknowledge-
    ments help keep abreast of correspond-
    ence, **42:** 13; meetings with T. Roo-
    sevelt, **42:** 31-32,n1; McCosh story, **42:**
    67-68; appeal to American people, **42:**
    71-75; and J. S. Sargent portrait, **42:**
    390-91, 403-404, 545; **43:** 191, 203, 243;
    44: 360, 383, 439; **45:** 400; **46:** 219,n6,
    239; R. S. Bridges (poet laureate) sends
    WW verses, **42:** 392; reply to Pope's
    peace appeal and comments on reply,
    44: 33-36, 40-41, 49-50, 57-59, 83-84,
    94, 103, 105, 105-106, 119, 130-31, 149,
    155, 157, 158, 169-70, 181, 295-96, 390-
    91, 393-94, 468, 469; message to sol-
    diers in U.S. Army, **44:** 142; the Gray-
    sons reveal WW's private views of sub-
    marine situation, **44:** 173-75; form
    letter for refusing public speaking re-
    quests, **44:** 207; hymn dedicated to, **44:**
    266,n1; praises 65th Congress, **44:** 317;
    proclamations for Days of Prayer, **44:**
    399-400; **47:** 598-99; mention of upcom-
    ing message to Congress, **44:** 438, 454;
    W. E. Rappard on voluntary isolation
    of, **44:** 484-85; motion picture of, **44:**
    494; Thanksgiving Proclamation
    (1917), **44:** 525-26; on canceling Army-
    Navy game, **44:** 535, 571; H. Morgen-
    thau dedicates book to, **45:** 128n1; Les-

Woodrow Wilson, General, cont.
    sons of the War (statement), **45:** 187;
    and *Chronicles of America,* **45:** 352,
    362-63, 453, 540-41; railroad procla-
    mation, **45:** 358-61; presented with
    sculpture of Robert Emmet, **45:** 559-61;
    speeches translated into Latin, **46:**
    119-20,n1,2; and W. S. Sims as honor-
    ary member of British Admiralty, **46:**
    203; on *Peter Ibbetson,* **46:** 264,n1; rec-
    ommends F. Janeway for naval chap-
    laincy, **46:** 286; and clemency for Hous-
    ton rioters, **46:** 385,n1; on cultivating
    war gardens, **46:** 439; Smithsonian In-
    stitution requests typewriter of, **46:**
    461-62, 468; editor offers to send roy-
    alties from autographing books to fa-
    vorite charity of, **46:** 570; declines to
    speak at fiftieth anniversary of his
    church, **46:** 582-83; and inquiry into
    authorized biography of, **46:** 589; mes-
    sage to Fourth Congress of All-Russia
    Soviets, **46:** 598; recommends Joffre as
    member of American Philosophical So-
    ciety, **47:** 4; cannot spare time for
    D. Lawrence's article on, **47:** 4-5, 39-40;
    tries to get G. F. Close a higher paying
    job, **47:** 5; on Monticello, **47:** 38; invites
    members to first War Cabinet meeting,
    47: 43,n1; refuses honorary member-
    ship in Britain's Institution of Naval
    Architects, **47:** 67; Russia's reply to
    message of, **47:** 79,n2; letter to N.J.
    Democrats and editorial comments on,
    47: 82-84, 253-54; receives honorary
    degree from Cambridge University, **47:**
    85,n1, 264, 396; **48:** 249,n1, 250; re-
    ceives honorary degree from Univer-
    sity of Bologna, **47:** 85,n2; discourages
    preparation of biography, **47:** 139;
    against naming Muscle Shoals dam
    after himself, **47:** 191,n1; on badge of
    mourning, **47:** 217-18; **48:** 117; com-
    mutes F. M. Ryan's sentence, **47:**
    232,n1,2; on a patriotic German Amer-
    ican, **47:** 275,n2; proclamation estab-
    lishing National War Labor Board, **47:**
    282-84; thanks Mary Pickford for
    roses, **47:** 301-302; declines Mrs.
    Stokes' offer of a summer White House,
    47: 350,n1; declines W. Irvine's invita-
    tion from Mercersburg Academy, **47:**
    450,n1; and Red Cross Week Procla-
    mation, **47:** 515-16; on Hans Froe-
    licher, **47:** 536, 537; on one of the most
    touching letters ever received, **47:** 578-
    79; on use of his war emergency funds,
    47: 600-602; **48:** 137-39, 168, 335n1,
    463n1; on not delivering speeches in
    large auditoriums, **48:** 6; elected to the
    Académie des Sciences Morales et Po-
    litiques of the Institut de France, **48:**
    27n1; presented with N. D. Baker's in-
    scribed *Frontiers of Freedom,* **48:**
    30,n2; parades on behalf of Red Cross,
    48: 53n1, 59; makes contribution to

Woodrow Wilson, General, cont.

Red Cross, **48:** 78; message to various ethnic societies, **48:** 117; waives royalties on *History of the American People* on behalf of Italian-American Union, **48:** 120; receives map from Foch, **48:** 178,n1; contributes proceeds from White House wool to Red Cross, **48:** 191,n3, 475; on Gen. L. Wood, **48:** 192, 242; on not endorsing congressional candidates, **48:** 229-30; on Mooney case, **48:** 237; rejects idea of button bearing his picture, **48:** 311,n1; appeal to industry and labor to use U.S. Employment Service, **48:** 333-34; avoids private interviews, **48:** 381; refuses interview for *Ladies' Home Journal*, **48:** 382-83; message to teachers, **48:** 455-56,n1; veto message on increase in working hours for governmental employees, **48:** 471; sent special edition of *History of the American People*, **48:** 479, 482-83; thanks J. J. Jusserand for gift of his inscribed book, **48:** 491,n1,2; on etching of himself in uniform, **48:** 557; and honorary degree from University of Paris, **48:** 575-76, 579; veto message on governmental takeover of all interurban railroads, **48:** 589-91; veto of agricultural appropriations bill because of wheat section, **48:** 595-97; recommends C. L. Swem for Aviation Corps, **48:** 628; Swem's replacement and, **49:** 4,n2; bridge in Lyon, France named for, **49:** 37,n1; on George V's message on naval cooperation, **49:** 69, 70; statement on lynching and mob violence, **49:** 97-98, 151; rejects idea of J. S. Sargent painting picture of war, **49:** 101; does not want Democratic club named after him, **49:** 103; declines being godfather to English boy, **49:** 123; G. F. Peabody's praise of Fourth of July Address at Mt. Vernon, **49:** 125; street in Philadelphia named for, **49:** 165; on mineworkers, **49:** 216; personal coal conservation of, **49:** 240; talk of third term, **49:** 275-76, 286, 444-45, 488; E. M. House on need for WW to delegate work, **49:** 294; intervenes in behalf of Mexican exchange tutor, **49:** 305; to become grandfather again, **49:** 318-19; knowledge of England impresses W. Wiseman, **49:** 398; and concern for safety of, **49:** 445-46, 451, 512; wants to have propaganda matters in his own hands, **49:** 447, 449, 487; on not permitting his correspondents to publish extracts of his letters, **49:** 450; and England's Poet Laureate, **49:** 462-63; Covenant of league of nations, **49:** 467-71; decides against making Liberty Loan tour, **49:** 490; on woman suffrage, **51:** 58, 59, 158-61, 161, 190; on Liberty Loan campaign, **51:** 80-81; on taxation of his salary, **51:** 108-109,n9; votes in

Woodrow Wilson, General, cont.

primaries in Princeton, **51:** 110; sympathy for his German gardener, **51:** 172,n1, 270-71; note to Germany, Oct. 8, 1918, **51:** 263-64, 264-65; drafts of appeal to voters for a Democratic Congress, **51:** 317-18, 343-44, 353-55, 380-81; draft of note to Germany, Oct. 14, 1918, **51:** 333-34,n1; appeal to voters for a Democratic Congress, **51:** 381-82, 389, 390-91, 392-93; note to Allies on German-U.S. correspondence, **51:** 416-17; note to Germany, Oct, 23, 1918, **51:** 417-19; on election (1918) results, **51:** 620; on gubernatorial nomination (1910), **51:** 649

INAUGURATION

second inaugural address **41:** 63-64, 304, 317, 329, 332, 332-35, 340, 344, 344-45, 345, 354, 358, 380; inaugural ceremonies, **41:** 327-29, 331, 357-58, 400; suffragists picket during, **41:** 329-30, 400; observes fireworks inauguration night, **41:** 341; thanks his carriage driver, **41:** 451; E. P. Davis poem on the occasion of, **41:** 452,n1

APPOINTMENTS AND RESIGNATIONS

postmasterships, **40:** 74,n1; **41:** 208,n1; minister to The Netherlands, **40:** 113; J. G. Coolidge refuses Colombian position, **40:** 116; and Tariff Commission, **40:** 173-74, 305, 343, 347-48; **41:** 24, 65, 93, 379-80; WW on embarrassment of personally seeing candidates, **40:** 190, 201; and W. H. Page, **40:** 240-41, 463; **41:** 70,n1, 128-29, 137, 497; and Interstate Commerce Commission, **40:** 255; **45:** 265n1; **46:** 238,n2; W. H. Page's suggestions, **40:** 369-70; E. M. House and WW on foreign service, **40:** 408, 409, 463; for Federal Trade Commission, **40:** 413, 417, 419-20, 427-28, 490, 493; **41:** 45-47, 93, 206,n1,2, 209, 255-56; **42:** 217, 221, 347,n2; **46:** 492-93, 518; **49:** 431; B. Long as Third Assistant Secretary of State, **40:** 425, 548; **41:** 70; W. Phillips named Assistant Secretary of State **40:** 457; and Ambassador to Argentina, **40:** 463,n2; B. N. Baker resigns from Shipping Board, **41:** 16,n1, 21; on judgeships, **41:** 55-56; **43:** 146-47, 162; C. H. Dodge and, **41:** 133, 170-72; talk of E. M. House replacing W. H. Page, **41:** 341; suggestions for ambassador to Japan, **41:** 374, 510; **42:** 347,n1; **43:** 333-34, 347,n1; and Philippines, **41:** 417-18, 505; **44:** 8-9,n1; and House's suggestion to replace secretaries of war and navy, **41:** 483; suggestions for Russian Commission, **42:** 36-37, 43-44, 45-46, 58, 80-81, 95, 124-25, 143-44,n1, 152, 154, 164-65, 165-66, 166-67, 194-95, 204,

Woodrow Wilson, Appointments and Resignations, cont.
215-16, 216-17, 240, 259, 262, 263; and chief of Committee on Public Information, **42:** 59; and district attorneyship of New York, **42:** 244,n1,2; suggestions for special envoy to Far East, **42:** 244-45; and Red Cross War Council, **42:** 251-52,n2; and head of publicity office in Russia, **42:** 252,n1,3, 258, 284-85, 289, 377, 388; WW on, **42:** 260-61; and International Boundary Commission, **42:** 260-61,n2; and Food Administration, **42:** 345, 522-23; in Montana, **42:** 346-47; W. Phillips suggests replacing minister to Switzerland, **42:** 454-55; and proposed mission to Brazil, **43:** 11-12,n1; N. D. Baker's suggestions for War Industries Board, **43:** 25-26; on reasons for not appointing S. H. Thompson, Jr., to district court, **43:** 33-34; and V. C. McCormick and Export Council, **43:** 34-35; and G. W. P. Hunt as labor mediator, **43:** 53, 72, 87, 104, 127, 131; and Central Purchasing Commission, **43:** 76, 137, 189; Denman-Goethals controversy resolved by resignations, **43:** 233-34, 257-60, 261, 272; E. N. Hurley to head Shipping Board, **43:** 260, 270-71, 286, 291; W. L. Capps to replace W. Goethals, **43:** 260n2, 271; B. Colby to serve on Shipping Board, **43:** 260, 310; WW accepts T. Brent's resignation, **43:** 272; S. Gompers against G. I. Neal as district attorney in West Virginia, **43:** 278-80; resignation of D. F. Malone, **43:** 290-91,n1; and **44:** 169, 190, 200; T. D. Jones to serve on War Trade Board, **43:** 291, 325; and Alaska, **42:** 385,n1; House's suggestions for Interstate Commerce Commission, **43:** 425; talk of asking for R. Lansing's resignation, **44:** 176-77; on Catholics and, **44:** 177; Collector of Port of New York, **44:** 208-209,n1; and President's Mediation Commission, **44:** 214; new Chief of Staff, **44:** 232,n1; resignations due to Section 3 of Lever Act, **44:** 238,n1; F. A. Scott resigns from War Industries Board, **44:** 450, 464; D. Willard and War Industries Board chairmanship, **45:** 71-72, 75, 77-78, 92, 600-601; **46:** 15, 61-62; W. L. Capps resigns from Emergency Fleet Corporation, **45:** 103, 117; T. D. Jones resigns from War Trade Board, **45:** 350, 367; suggestions for War Industries Board, **46:** 17, 91-92, 105-106, 111-12, 215, 217-18, 259, 269, 448, 491; R. S. Lovett resigns from War Industries Board, **46:** 39,n1, 52; and recall of naval attaché in Madrid, **46:** 49-50,n1, 67; J. K. Vardaman's suggestions for Mississippi, **46:** 104,n1; E. M. House and WW on peace commission delegates, **46:** 115-16, 316; WW on military attaché in Russia, **46:** 179,n1; suggestions for Aircraft Board,

Woodrow Wilson, Appointments and Resignations, cont.
46: 229-30; recommends F. Janeway for chaplaincy, **46:** 286; W. J. Harris resigns from Federal Trade Commission, **46:** 330, 335; W. G. McAdoo's suggestions for War Finance Corporation Board, **46:** 442-43; B. M. Baruch appointed chairman of War Industries Board, **46:** 520-22, 527; J. E. Davies resigns from Federal Trade Commission, **46:** 609; **47:** 52-53; and National War Labor Board, **47:** 283; and E. R. Stettinius, **47:** 321; H. Coffin resigns from Aircraft Board, **47:** 361-62, 383; and C. M. Schwab, **47:** 385,n6, 437; and J. D. Ryan, **47:** 436, 437, 501; and H. B. Thayer's resignation from Aircraft Board, **47:** 400,n1, 414, 415; suggestions for minister to Denmark, **48:** 143-44; and P. M. Warburg, **48:** 171-73; **49:** 218,n1, 222; women press for more responsible governmental positions, **48:** 198-99, 221, 250, 345-46,n1; B. M. Baruch's suggestions for price-fixing committee of War Industries Board, **48:** 607; W. H. Page's resignation and replacement, **49:** 155,n1, 275, 346, 348,n1, 350, 423, 424; **51:** 22, 107, 276; and Assistant Surgeon General, **49:** 235,n1; and reorganization of Aircraft Production Board, **49:** 349; suggestions for members of labor commission to Porto Rico, **49:** 394; and proposed Russian relief commission, **49:** 407-408; and C. A. Lindbergh, **49:** 536,n1; **51:** 64-65,n2; and Permanent Court of Arbitration, **49:** 540,n1, 540-41; suggestion that women be appointed to National War Labor Board, **51:** 522-23

CABINET
40: 239-40, 241; **41:** 67, 317, 327, 329; **42:** 343, 374; **43:** 100, 389, 486, 512; **44:** 49, 80-81, 107, 263, 370-71, 392, 452, 495; **45:** 74,n2, 95, 147, 176, 207, 237, 271-72, 341-42, 448, 573, 601-602; **46:** 33, 79, 212-13, 297, 468, 508-509, 553-54, 581-82, 620-21; **47:** 82, 206, 219, 334, 353; **48:** 221, 331, 432, 448; **49:** 90; and decision for break with Germany, **41:** 88,n1, 94,n1, 123-24; F. K. Lane on meetings of, **41:** 183-84, 239, 260-61, 282-83, 517-18; **51:** 413, 548; decision to send troops to Cuba, **41:** 298-99; and Zimmermann telegram, **41:** 325; and railroad crisis, **41:** 424-25; war resolution meeting of, **41:** 436-44, 444-45, 445; Composure is a marked characteristic of the President. Nothing ruffles the calmness of his manner or address. It has a sobering effect on all who sit with him in council. Excitement would seem very much out of place at the Cabinet table with Woodrow Wilson

Woodrow Wilson, Cabinet, cont.
presiding. **41:** 437; news article implies WW should replace some members, **41:** 446,n1; W. B. Wilson offers resignation, **41:** 446-47; on keeping intact, **41:** 450; and decision to call Congress on April 2, **41:** 454-55; J. Daniels on meetings, **41:** 461, 484; **49:** 69, 137, 246, 431; **51:** 275, 344, 604; E. M. House recommends some replacements, **41:** 483; WW on R. Lansing as Secretary of State, **41:** 497; and WW's war message, **41:** 506, 507, 528, 529; and Council of National Defense, **42:** 48; and War Trade Committee, **42:** 118; pays for trip made by W. B. Wilson and F. K. Lane to avert railroad strike, **42:** 153-54,n1; WW on coordination of secret work among departments, **43:** 154-55; R. L.

Woodrow Wilson, Cabinet, cont.
Owen on war expenditures and, **43:** 348-49; W. G. McAdoo on, **43:** 390; **49:** 489; and difficulty of having a son-in-law in, **43:** 391; and WW's reply to Pope's appeal, **44:** 157; and Fourteen Points address, **45:** 555; WW and House discuss, **42:** 162; **45:** 555-56; **46:** 116-17; discusses proposed Japanese intervention in Siberia, **46:** 515; and War Industries Board, **46:** 522,n1; House on reorganization of, **48:** 69-70; and women's resolution on more government positions for women, **48:** 250, 345-46,n1; and Russian situation, **48:** 433, 434, 444; discusses German notes, **51:** 275, 412, 413, 414; policy on members' speechmaking, **51:** 301-302, 302; *see also* War Cabinet (U.S.)

End of Woodrow Wilson entry

Wilson Administration and Civil Liberties 1917-1921 (Scheiber), **48:** 146n3
Wilson and Company, **46:** 28, 462n3; **48:** 77,n1, 108-109, 508
Wilson Backs Amendment for Woman Suffrage (*New York Times*), **45:** 545n1
Wilson: Campaigns for Progressivism and Peace, 1916-1917 (Link), **40:** 19n1, 76n1, 349n11, 383n1, 529n1; **41:** 11n1, 59n1, 88n1, 94n1, 149n2, 280n1, 318n1, 349n2, 352n1, 393n1, 418n1, 425n1, 430n2
Wilson Dam, **47:** 191,n3
Wilson Era: Years of Peace 1910-1917 (Daniels), **42:** 526n3
Wilson Era: Years of War and After, 1917-1923 (Daniels), **43:** 463n1; **44:** 346n1; **46:** 297n3; **47:** 347n1
Wilson Hands Off in Georgia Fight (Holloman), **47:** 382n1
Wilson in Germany (Harden), **40:** 376,n3
Wilson Lifted 'Nation' Ban (*New York Times*), **51:** 55n1
Wilson Receives Aircraft Report (New York *World*), **47:** 335,n1
Wilson: The New Freedom (Link), **42:** 526n1; **46:** 589
Wilson: The Struggle for Neutrality (Link), **40:** 82n1, 137n3
Wilson Upholds Goethals in Row over Steel Ships (*New York Times*), **42:** 567n1
Wilson With League? (Portland *Oregon Voter*), **47:** 352,n2
Wilsonians As War Managers: Coal and the 1917-18 Winter Crisis (Johnson), **46:** 12n1
Wilson's Attitude Toward Russia Big in Peace Portent (Swope), **46:** 22n1
Wilton, Robert, **48:** 187,n5
Win the War for Permanent Peace: Addresses made at the National Convention of the League to Enforce Peace, in

the City of Philadelphia, May 16th and 17th 1918, **48:** 29n
Windom, Minn., **47:** 235
Windsor, R. H., **49:** 391,n1
Winslow, Erving, **46:** 257,n1, 287, 369-70,n1
Winslow, Lanier, **41:** 149; **44:** 433
Winslow, Rose, **44:** 559-61,n4
Winston, George Tayloe, **43:** 174,n1
Winter, William, **40:** 335-36,n1
Wintersteen, Abram Heebner, **40:** 108n1, 128; **41:** 259, 260, 458, 469
wire-control legislation, **48:** 556,n1,2, 591-92, 623,n1, 628-29; *see also* telegraph system
Wisconsin, **41:** 360; **43:** 512n1; **44:** 365n1; **46:** 478; **47:** 439; **49:** 441n7; senatorial campaign (1918) in, **46:** 566,n5, 609; **47:** 40-41,n1, 58, 120, 129, 137, 148, 326,n1; and issue of WW's participation in campaign in, **47:** 388-90,n1; politics in, **51:** 633
Wisconsin, University of, **42:** 254; **47:** 427n2; **48:** 570; **49:** 440; patriotism controversy at, **45:** 142-47, 221,n1; supports Fourteen Points, **45:** 586-87, 593
Wisconsin German Press Association, **44:** 318n1
Wisconsin Idea (McCarthy), **49:** 440n1
Wisconsin State Journal, **45:** 142,n1,2, 221n1; **46:** 119n1
Wise, Stephen Samuel, **41:** 180-81, 209; **42:** 41-42, 44-45, 124-25, 152; **45:** 369-70, 567, 572,n1; **46:** 516-17; **49:** 363-64,n1, 403; **51:** 331,n5
Wiseman, Sir William George Eden, **40:** 262,n1, 294, 307n1, 464-65, 493-94, 527-28, 558; **41:** 3, 17, 26,n1, 39-40, 87, 95, 149, 196, 466n1, 544, 554; **42:** 18, 120, 142n1, 143, 169, 456, 461, 543-45; **43:** 20, 38-39, 44, 97, 124, 147, 195, 278n2, 364-65, 451, 452, 453; **44:** 56-57, 80, 140,n2, 150, 164, 186, 200, 284, 325,

Wiseman, Sir William (*cont.*)
342, 380, 381, 382, 391, 392; **45:** 70-71,
175n4, 311-13, 322-23, 323; **46:** 181,
183, 215, 220-21, 221,n2, 328, 419, 429,
438, 467, 487, 488-89, 490; **47:** 72n4,
131, 156-57, 158, 170, 203, 227-28, 239,
239-41, 303, 436, 444; **48:** 62, 152, 231,
310, 391, 430; **49:** 267, 280, 294, 302,
303, 452-55, 466, 548-49; **51:** 6-10, 64,
146, 188, 246, 290-91, 295-96, 313, 326,
327, 352, 511n1, 595
on Allied reply to WW's peace note of
Dec. 18, 1916, **40:** 503-504; on Anglo-
American relations, **41:** 346-48; and
Northcliffe, **42:** 487-88; and plan to
send special agent to Russia, **42:** 527,
529-30, 551-52; E. M. House on, **43:** 24,
183; **47:** 251; on meetings with WW, **43:**
172-74; **46:** 85-88, 247-50; **51:** 347-52;
on Britain and U.S. and shipbuilding
program, **43:** 209-10; and A. J. Balfour
and exchange crisis, **43:** 356-57; and
Ireland, **43:** 361, 365, 451-52; **47:** 266-
67, 442, 443, 444, 465-66; on Polish
Army, **43:** 426-27; on Pope Benedict's
peace appeal and reply to, **43:** 453; **44:**
30, 31, 33; on situation in U.S., **44:** 230;
on U.S. representation on three Allied
councils, **44:** 353-56, 373-75; on U.S.
recognition of Poland, **44:** 278; on German peace offer through Spain, **44:**
311; on embargo, **44:** 396,n1; to return
to U.S., **45:** 324, 332; on proposed Japanese intervention in Siberia, **46:** 213,
214, 248-49, 250, 530-31, 553, 561-62,
576, 590-91; **47:** 35-36, 503-505; on
WW's view on sending U.S. troops to
join British, **46:** 231-32, 247-48, 272-
73; on WW and Bolsheviks, **46:** 333-34,
389, 485; on Charles I's message to
WW, **46:** 464, 507-508; to go to Europe,
47: 102, 256, 307; on WW's attitude toward crisis of spring 1918, **47:** 184-85;
and proposed cable from Lloyd George
acknowledging U.S. help, **47:** 206; ar-
rives in England, **47:** 313, 391; reports
to E. M. House on political and military
situation, **47:** 433-35, 442-43, 443-44;
to attend Supreme War Council meeting, **47:** 471; on Abbeville agreement
and J. J. Pershing, **47:** 616, 616-20; on
U.S. views on intervention in Russia,
48: 203-206, 315-16, 470, 523-24; on
proposed Board of American Commissioners in Europe, **48:** 331; on Reading
as ambassador to U.S., **48:** 381, 524-25;
on K. Ishii's meeting with House, **48:**
577-78; and Phillimore Report, **48:**
647,n1; on league of nations, **49:** 11-14,
265, 273-74; on WW's Mexican policy,
49: 299-300; on WW's views on Germany and Britain's economic measures, **49:** 300-301; on WW's position on
Czechs in Siberia, **49:** 345; on WW's
view on proposed war declaration
against Bulgaria and Hungary, **49:**

365, 537-38; on proposed commission to
Russia, **49:** 366; on week spent with
E. M. House and WW, **49:** 397-99; on
proposed visit of W. M. Hughes, **49:**
408, 409; on strained relations between
Britain and the U.S., **49:** 453-55; on
W. Lippmann, **51:** 9; on WW's reply to
Bulgaria, **51:** 145; on U.S. in Russia,
51: 188; on WW's slight to Britain in
his woman suffrage speech, **51:** 208-
209; on publication of Sisson Docu-
ments, **51:** 252; on T. H. Bliss' cable on
proposed Allied peace terms, **51:** 291-
92; on WW's moves regarding German
note, **51:** 328; photograph, *illustration
section,* **43**
Wissell, Rudolf Karl, **47:** 75,n2
Wister, Owen, **47:** 16,n3
Withers, Robert G., **51:** 453,n1
Withycombe, James, **44:** 81,n1; **47:** 194,
195
Wittelsbach, Rupprecht von, Crown
Prince of Bavaria: *see* Rupprecht,
Maria Luitpold Ferdinand von Wittelsbach
Wodehouse, P. G. (Pelham Grenville), **51:**
314n1
Wolcott, Josiah Oliver, **47:** 577-78; **48:**
370; and woman suffrage, **45:** 278,n1,
279, 338, 339; **51:** 133, 171, 177
Wolf, Simon, **42:** 506-507
Wolff, Theodor, **43:** 411-12; **46:** 163
Wolff News Agency, **41:** 261, 276, 326; **44:**
457
*Woman Citizen: The Woman's Journal,
Official Organ of the National American Woman Suffrage Association,* **43:**
244n1; **48:** 303n1
woman suffrage, **40:** 173; **41:** 399-401; **42:**
215-16, 237,n1,4, 293, 474-75, 497; **43:**
71,n1, 214-15,n1, 284-85, 432n1; **44:**
12,n1, 144-45, 523,n1, 551,n1, 556n3;
45: 40n1, 169,n1, 242-43, 542, 545, 565;
49: 264-65; **51:** 82-83, 155-57, 281, 294,
304, 337, 375, 404, 452; WW on, **40:**
196, 473; **41:** 13, 299; **43:** 273; **44:** 62,
144-45, 372, 441-43, 537; **46:** 79-81; **47:**
577-78; **49:** 139-40, 304-305
meeting with WW and decision to
picket White House, **40:** 379,n1,2,3,4,
420-21, 426; WW's speech to representatives of, **40:** 427; North Dakota and Illinois grant, **40:** 549,n2; **41:** 13; pickets
on Inauguration Day, **41:** 329-30, 400;
and Maryland, **42:** 124,n1, 138-39; establishment of committee in House of
Representatives, **42:** 241, 269-70, 320-
21,n1; demonstration before Russian
mission, **42:** 560,n1; T. J. Heflin on, **43:**
36; picket crisis and comments on pardon of arrested suffragists, **43:** 201-
202,n1, 213, 235, 243-44,n1, 250-51,
436-37; poll on suffrage amendment,
43: 212, 213, 214; **45:** 121,n1, 129, 306-
307, 338-39; **46:** 59-61; D. F. Malone
and, **43:** 283,n1, 290; **44:** 167-69, 185,

200; activity in New York State, **43:** 462,n1,2; **44:** 61, 62, 79, 335, 384, 391, 440-41, 460-61, 523,n1, 532-33,n1, 533, 556n2; H. N. Hall on demonstration at White House, **43:** 476-77,n1; C. A. Lindbergh report on Washington riots and, **44:** 108-16; W. G. Gardiner report on hunger strikes, **44:** 559-61; fear of defeat by early House vote, **45:** 277; opposition requests WW to deny he secretly favors, **45:** 345-46; N. O'Shaughnessy on, **45:** 518,n1; amendment on, **45:** 545n1, 565n3; J. P. Tumulty on, **46:** 608,n1; **47:** 34-35,n2, 547, 571-72; in Texas, **47:** 42, 104, 144,n2; and Rhode Island, **47:** 399,n1; Mrs. E. T. Kent on, **47:** 572; J.C.W. Beckham on, **47:** 580-81; B. R. Tillman on, **47:** 597; A. Pomerene on, **47:** 608-609; **51:** 176-77; D. U. Fletcher on, **47:** 609; suggestions that WW make public statement on, **48:** 24-27, 233-34, 263-64, 271-72; comments from senators opposed to, **43:** 43-44, 110, 427; WW and suffragists attempt to get senators to support, **48:** 110-11, 116, 217-18, 237,n2, 279, 370, 371, 400-401, 404, 427, 440; and Louisiana, **48:** 237,n1,2, 352; **51:** 537; WW's public statement to French Union for Woman Suffrage, **48:** 303-304, 340-41; WW approves of early vote on, **48:** 365; D. Baird on, **49:** 182-83; and Kansas, **49:** 309; and senatorial appointment from Kentucky, **49:** 381, 388, 481, 486, 529; K. Pittman on, **51:** 30-31; and C. Benet's vote, **51:** 49, 58, 59, 110, 122-23, 123, 167-68, 294; and R. L. Owen, **51:** 76, 83; mentioned as war issue, **51:** 117-18, 156; and P. Trammell, **51:** 123, 165; WW appeals to J. O. Wolcott, **51:** 133, 171, 177; WW's address to Senate on amendment passage as war measure, **51:** 158-61, 161; suffragists thank WW for his efforts, **51:** 189; amendment defeated in Senate, **51:** 189n1; WW's remarks to suffragists, **51:** 190; W. Wiseman on slight to Britain in WW's speech on, **51:** 208-209; and Governor Stanley and Kentucky, **51:** 288, 294; and Oklahoma, **51:** 444,n1,2

Woman Suffrage, Committee on (House of Reps.): establishment of, **43:** 71n1

Woman Suffrage, Committee on (Senate), **43:** 213n1; **44:** 168; **48:** 363, 364; **49:** 264n2

Woman Suffrage Movement in Texas (Taylor), **47:** 144n2

Woman's College of Baltimore (Goucher College), **45:** 158n1; and Froelicher affair, **47:** 453,n1,2, 454, 536, 537,n1

Woman's Committee (of Council of National Defense), **48:** 57-58,n1, 169-70, 174-75; and mourning badge, **48:** 28,n1, 46, 111, 117; requests more governmental board positions for women, **48:** 198-99, 221, 345-46,n1; and religious discrimination by YWCA, **48:** 208,n1; comments on importance of, **48:** 321-22, 357-58

Woman's Dining Club of Kansas City, **48:** 422

Woman's Foreign Missionary Society, **45:** 158

Woman's party: *see* National Woman's party

Woman's Peace party, **41:** 231; **43:** 395; **45:** 586, 593

Woman's Peace party of New York, **40:** 418

women, **48:** 24n1, 169-70; and eight-hour law, **40:** 7-8, 152; proposal for international congress, **41:** 113n1; in Russia, **42:** 215, 241; and dedication of Red Cross Building, **42:** 281,n1, 283; and Food Administration and conservation, **42:** 437n1, 485-86; **46:** 21, 109n1; Helen Todd on women's faith in WW, **43:** 536-38; and labor force, **44:** 337-38, 359, 564, 565, 568; **45:** 132n2, 133, 334; **47:** 251; role in war, **44:** 440-41, 442; **47:** 614; **49:** 546n1; and Pacific Telephone and Telegraph Company dispute, **46:** 136-37; and housing of governmental employees, **47:** 38, 58; and alien enemy law, **47:** 364,n3, 381; and Woman's Committee of Council of National Defense, **47:** 476; WW on, **48:** 56, 382-83; F. P. Walsh on National War Labor Board and, **51:** 522-23

Women's Auxiliary Army Corps, **47:** 614

Women's Battalion of Death (Russian), **48:** 469n1

Women's Christian Temperance Union, **44:** 144n1

Women's Defense Work, Committee on, **47:** 114

Women's Volunteer Aid Corps, **42:** 281,n1

Wood, Leonard, **40:** 35, 267n1, 455-56, 464; **41:** 114, 455,n2, 461,n1, 470, 486, 501; **42:** 120, 158, 522; **43:** 115; **45:** 111,n12, 332n1; **46:** 249, 259, 297,n3, 452, 488n1; **47:** 234, 303, 308, 616; **49:** 74n1; health of, **41:** 481,n3; controversy over keeping him at home, **48:** 173,n1, 189, 192, 193-94, 242; photograph, *illustration section,* **49**

Wood, Levi Hollingsworth, **42:** 420; **44:** 266-67,n3

Wood, Stephen B., **49:** 23n1

Wood, William Robert, **40:** 349n11

Woodbridge, Janie Wilson Woodrow (Mrs. Samuel Isett), cousin of WW, **44:** 7n1

Woodbridge, Samuel Isett, **44:** 7-8,n1

Wooden Ship Controversy (*Springfield, Mass., Republican*), **42:** 556n3

wooden ships, **45:** 314; *see also* shipbuilding program

Woodrow, Felexiana Shepherd Baker (Mrs. James) (Aunt Felie), **40:** 62, 91;

Woodrow, Felexiana Shepherd Baker (*cont.*) **41:** 157,n1, 180; **45:** 381, 404; **48:** 203, 231

Woodrow, James, cousin of WW, **41:** 157, 180

Woodrow Wilson (*The Independent*), **46:** 14n1

Woodrow Wilson: A Medical and Psychological Biography (Weinstein), **43:** 361n1

Woodrow Wilson and the World's Peace (Herron), **40:** 542n1,2; **44:** 287n2; **45:** 256,n1

Woodrow Wilson As I Know Him (Tumulty), **41:** 541n1; **42:** 29n1

Woodrow Wilson: Life and Letters (Baker), **43:** 41n1; **45:** 93n3; **46:** 147n2, 194n1; **48:** 347n1

Woodrow Wilson, Man of Letters (Harper), **45:** 334-35,n2

Woodrow Wilson, Politician (*The Nation*), **51:** 646,n1

Woodrow Wilson, President, March 5, 1917 (poem, Davis), **41:** 452,n1

Woodrow Wilson: The Academic Years (Bragdon), **46:** 508n1

Woodrow Wilson's China Policy, 1913-1917 (Li), **41:** 394n1

Woods, Edwin Augustus, **48:** 78; **51:** 639

Woods, Hiram, **40:** 344; **41:** 354,n2; **45:** 404, 411,n2

Woodward, Comer Vann, **43:** 389n1

Woodward, David R., **45:** 487n2

Woodward, Ernest Llewellyn, **44:** 501n2

Woodward and Dickerson, Phila., **51:** 179n3

wool: R. S. Brookings on prices of, **47:** 383-84, 444-45, 495; **49:** 70, 277-78; WW on, **47:** 395, 450

Wool Growers' Association, **47:** 384

Wooledge, G. S., **48:** 628n1

Woolley, Clarence Mott, **46:** 91,n1, 229; **48:** 484,n1; **51:** 407,n1

Woolley, Robert Wickliffe, **40:** 413; **42:** 158; **43:** 197-98, 425; **44:** 430; **47:** 312, 408; **49:** 237; **51:** 113-16, 173, 248,n5, 409-10; on assuring full-time employment, **47:** 210-12, 291, 291-92; on standardizing labor policies, **47:** 376-79; on appointment of Director General of Labor, **47:** 391,n1, 425-26, 449, 467; W. B. Wilson refutes ideas of, **47:** 461, 465, 537-38

Woolsey, Lester Hood, **41:** 120, 124, 125; **45:** 177n1

Wooster, College of, **41:** 321n1

Worden, Beverly Lyon, **42:** 477,n2; **47:** 223,n2, 248, 252, 283

Words That Won the War: The Story of the Committee on Public Information, 1917-1919 (Mock and Larson), **43:** 168n2

Wordsworth, William, **45:** 558

Working Class Union, **44:** 294,n1

workmen's compensation bill, **44:** 313-14

Works, John Downey, **43:** 216; **44:** 79

World Conflict in Its Relation to American Democracy (Lippmann), **43:** 454n1

World Politics (Princeton, N.J.), **42:** 317n3

World Tomorrow (N.Y.), **51:** 12,n1, 77

World War: *United States neutrality and rights of neutrals during*: **40:** 5, 10, 11, 13, 14, 17-18, 22-23, 36n3, 46-48, 63, 65, 70-71, 198, 200, 222-23, 227, 260, 306,n1, 307,n1, 409, 546-47,n2; **41:** 4, 75-79, 94, 101-102, 109-10, 114, 116, 135, 165-67, 183-84, 249-50, 263-66, 283-87, 338, 348, 390, 434, 451n2, 467-68, 489, 521; R. Lansing and WW discuss, **41:** 120-21, 437; WW and armed neutrality, **41:** 283-87, 487-88, 488-89, 498-500; M. Eastman on, **41:** 306-308; H. Bergson on, **41:** 315n2; trainloads of pacifists to arrive in Washington, **41:** 515; and WW's declaration to Switzerland, **44:** 489n5

preparedness: U.S. preparations for entry into war, **41:** 385, 460, 462; N. D. Baker on steps taken in present emergency, **41:** 151-52; and arming of merchant ships, **41:** 187-88, 189-90, 232, 233, 263-66, 279-81,n1, 283-87, 341-44, 360-61, 363-64, 364, 369-72, 372, 377-79, 381, 387, 387-88, 395-98, 403, 430, 431, 432,n1, 461-62, 492, 534-35; H. Hoover on steps to be taken if U.S. enters war, **41:** 227-29; F. K. Lane on mobilization of industries and resources, **41:** 239; WW indicates war is inevitable, **41:** 304n3; comments advocating entry, **41:** 353-54, 425-27, 429-30, 461,n1, 468, 503-505, 514, 516-17; WW calls extra session of Congress, **41:** 367,n1; railroad crisis and, **41:** 410-11; cabinet endorses war resolution, **41:** 436-44; and increase in number of military departments, **41:** 455,n1; J. P. Tumulty on being masters of our own destiny, **41:** 462-64; and Congress' power to declare war, **41:** 471-72; and question of Cuba and Panama, **41:** 472-73; Polish-American's offer of 500 officers, **41:** 507-509, 511-12; war message to Congress, **41:** 519-27; Civil Service Commission's recommendations for precautions in hiring, **41:** 546-48; WW's statement on raising army forces, **41:** 550-51

atrocities and war crimes: **40:** 440, 482-85; **44:** 159, 452; **49:** 199; R. Lansing on German submarines and, **41:** 97; and Belgium, **41:** 217; treatment of U.S. consuls' wives in Germany, **41:** 240,n2, 282; A. J. Balfour on Germans, **42:** 342; B. Whitlock on, **42:** 427-28; **44:** 450,n1; sinking of various vessels, **44:** 532,n1; **45:** 238,n2; **46:** 433n2; **51:** 326,n2; H. Morgenthau on, **45:** 124; **48:** 284; explosion in Halifax harbor, **45:** 230,n1; question of chemical warfare, **46:** 263,n2, 395-97; W. S. Sims on British

World War, cont.

and German losses, **47:** 161-62; in Paris, **47:** 231; Jusserand on Allied declaration condemning Germany, **49:** 497-98; the Red Terror, **51:** 61-62, 62-63, 78,n2; by retreating Germans in France and Belgium, **51:** 135, 215, 216, 256-57, 265, 268, 330, 333-34, 576, 577; captured aviators in Austria-Hungary, **51:** 174-75; and *S. S. Leinster,* **51:** 326,n2; *see also* Belgian deportations

general impact on United States: and civil service precautions, **41:** 546-48; WW signs joint resolution declaring state of war with Germany, **41:** 557; **42:** 3; coordination of secret service work, **42:** 16-17; Cuba enters, **42:** 41,n1, 51,n1; and Guatemala, **42:** 46-47; and contraband list, **42:** 101-102, 106; and German ships in U.S. ports, **42:** 133-34, 292; and mail censorship, **42:** 163, 195-96; idea of educational program for populace on, **42:** 394, 395; Brazil enters, **42:** 439-40,n1; WW on how Germany forced U.S. into, and U.S. purpose in, **42:** 499-504; loss of British tonnage creates critical need, **43:** 9-11, 18-19, 45-46; and French army mutiny, **43:** 31,n5; A.R.E. Pinchot on opposition to entry into, **43:** 277-78; and public health issues, **45:** 26-28, 108-109; public opinion on, **45:** 123, 128, 315; U.S. declares war on Austria-Hungary, **45:** 224,n1; how war started, **45:** 255, 267; Bolsheviks to lead Russia out of, **45:** 288-91; and Creel on war progress, **45:** 407-10, 422, 435,n1,2; rumor of German plot to destroy U.S. shipping by explosives, **46:** 3-4, 17-18; and plan for international commission to China, **46:** 499, 500-501; messages on first anniversary of U.S. entry into, **47:** 172, 257, 258, 263-64, 265-66, 277-78, 278; and Liberia, **47:** 315-17; and Mexico, **47:** 351n1; anniversary of Italian entry into, **47:** 525-26, 553, 554, 600; L. Marshall on relief for Jews, **47:** 555-56; casualties, **48:** 477; N. D. Baker on numbers of German, French and British soldiers on western front, **48:** 483; submarine scare of 1918, **49:** 167,n1; WW on question of declaring war on Bulgaria, **49:** 447; T. Bliss on various aspects of, **51:** 34-49; and tonnage issue, **51:** 94-95; WW on issues of, **51:** 128

economic impact on United States: **40:** 19-20,n1, 76, 227; **41:** 6, 499; Federal Reserve Board on purchase of Allied notes, **40:** 76-80, 87-88, 136-37,n2; **41:** 256-57, 349,n2; and cost-of-living, **40:** 102-104, 519-21; **45:** 183; and foreign securities held by national banks, **40:** 181-82,n1, 202; inflation and, **40:** 244-46; **42:** 401-402, 411; gold and, **40:** 476,n4; **43:** 227; German-Americans'

World War, cont.

fear of confiscation of savings, **41:** 132, 157-58; WW statements on various issues, **41:** 283-84, 522; **42:** 71-75; **43:** 122-23, 151-54; **44:** 212; **48:** 137-39, 333-34; **51:** 476-77; W. H. Page on Anglo-French financial crisis, **41:** 336-37; and steel industry, **41:** 407, 556,n2; **43:** 155-56; and Allied need for supplies, **41:** 428-29; and raising revenue for preparedness and war, **41:** 448,n1,2; H. A. Garfield on, **41:** 487-88; and Liberty bonds, **42:** 25-27, 294-95, 401,n1; **49:** 99,n1; **51:** 80-81, 146-47; and shipbuilding program, **42:** 32, 233-34, 235-36, 248-49, 249, 285-87, 475-80; **43:** 72-73; and food, **42:** 73-74, 108-109; and labor, **42:** 135-38, 205-208, 564; **47:** 272, 273-74, 292; and export restrictions, **42:** 224,n2; **43:** 14-15; and Central Purchasing Agency (or Commission), **42:** 256-57, 397, 411-13, 414-17, 424, 447-49, 538-39, 540-41; **43:** 77-78, 136-38,n1,2; and Red Cross appeal, **42:** 282; and priority shipments, **42:** 289-90; Lever bills, **42:** 294,n1,2, 344-46; and prices and price control, **42:** 298, 301,n2, 372,n2, 374, 411-13, 414-17, 419-20, 424, 447-49, 534; **43:** 6,n1, 33n1, 41,n1, 90-92, 151-54, 251-53, 366, 373, 397-99,n1, 489-91; **46:** 58-59; and proposed amendments to Federal Reserve Act, **42:** 302,n1,2; and Britain, **42:** 379-80; **43:** 34, 38-39, 44, 66, 67-69, 139-40,n2,3, 194, 195, 196-97, 223-30, 326-33, 335-36, 347, 356n1; cost of building cantonments, **42:** 406-407; and Food Administration, **42:** 481-85, 528-29, 531-32; opinions of H. C. Hoover, **43:** 117-18; **44:** 191-92; **46:** 126n1, 304-309; **48:** 484; W. G. McAdoo on loans, **43:** 203-204; and building railroad cars and locomotives, **43:** 296-97; war financing and taxation, **43:** 350n2; **46:** 15n1; **48:** 19-21; **49:** 162-63,n1, 163-64; **51:** 29-30; U.S. sends wheat to France, **43:** 358; cost of war, **43:** 460n1, 478-79; and oversight committee, **44:** 117-18, 147, 155-56, 159; inter-Allied council and, **44:** 197; and Treasury withdrawals for YMCA, **44:** 270,n1; and housing for war contract workers, **44:** 279,n1; **46:** 37,n1, 67, 98-99, 151; S. Bertron on, **44:** 335-37, 359; suggestions for U.S. commercial policy, **44:** 455-57; L. Wehle on war production and adjustment of labor disputes, **45:** 7-11; and grain situation, **45:** 58-60; **46:** 213-14, 345-47, 368, 565,n1, 572-73; and Chamber of Commerce's proposals, **45:** 61-67; effect of drought in Texas on, **45:** 76-77; and brewing industry, **45:** 83-85, 228; and need for national employment service, **45:** 130-32, 182-83; and government takeover of railroads, **45:** 225-28, 358-61, 448-51; and War

World War, cont.

Emergency Finance Corporation, **45:** 266,n1; and war expenditures and treasury situation, **45:** 424-25, 532, 533, 588-92; possible postwar economic boycott of Germany, **46:** 6-7,n2, 7-8, 14-15, 417-18; **48:** 506,n1; and Garfield's fuel conservation order, **46:** 12,n1, 16, 18, 19; and Hoover's food conservation proclamation, **46:** 19-21; advantage of Britain and U.S., **46:** 87; and lumber industry, **46:** 107-108; plea for aid from Polish National Committee, **46:** 120-23; and livestock industry, **46:** 125-26; and report of President's Mediation Commission, **46:** 128-47; and farmers, **46:** 174-78, 279-81; **49:** 232-34, 241; and postwar reconstruction, **46:** 353; **51:** 465-67; McAdoo rejects "white list" financial blockade, **46:** 423n1; and propaganda campaign in Russia, **46:** 479,n1; and relief to Poland and Turkey, **47:** 44-45; appropriations considerations in Congress, **47:** 72, 85; and creation of National War Labor Board, **47:** 247-53, 282-84; and industrial manpower mobilization resolution, **47:** 296,n1; McAdoo on revenue legislation, **47:** 561-62; **48:** 121-27; **49:** 85-87; **51:** 204-206; WW on use of his war fund, **47:** 600-602; WW's address to Congress on urgent need for revenue legislation, **48:** 162-65; and loan to China, **48:** 371-74; and report on war industries profiteering, **48:** 487,n1; and public utilities, **48:** 597-99; **49:** 159-62, 252-53, 458-59; and nonwar industries, **49:** 6-8, 61, 70-71; and WW's policy toward Germany differs from Britain's, **49:** 300-301; and interest rates, **49:** 471,n1, 472, 503-504; wage and hour issues, **51:** 363-70; B. Baruch on equality of economic opportunity, **51:** 419-20; Republican peace demands and, **51:** 424; McAdoo on questions to be considered at peace conference, **51:** 468-70; F. I. Cobb on Britain and freedom of the seas, **51:** 613-14; and United War Work campaign, **51:** 636-37; *see also* Liberty Loan; prices and price fixing; war revenue bill of 1917

strategic plans and military operations: **44:** 480; U.S. to send destroyers abroad, **42:** 121, 121-22; N. D. Baker on, **42:** 192; expeditionary force to be sent to France, **42:** 186-91, 194, 202, 391-92; WW on navy and, **42:** 220; A. J. Balfour on, **42:** 264,n2, 398-400; **49:** 58-59; antisubmarine warfare, **42:** 348,n1, 358, 449,n1, 457, 546-47; **43:** 26, 47-48, 65-66, 71,n1, 180-81, 305-10, 375-78, 463-64; **44:** 464-66, 477-78; and idea of an all-Polish army, **42:** 352-53, 431-32, 491-94; G. G. Moore on defensive and offensive warfare, **42:** 373-74; J. J. Per-

World War, cont.

shing receives his command, **42:** 404-405; T. Bliss on training troops, **42:** 408-10; Britain on counter-propaganda campaign in Russia, **42:** 463-65; and aircraft program, **42:** 530-31, 549-50, 552; and comments on convoy system, **43:** 65, 87, 88-89, 112, 116, 172, 178-79, 463; arrival of first American troop transports in France, **43:** 79n1; WW on ineffectiveness of British navy, **43:** 79-80; and Allied war conference in Paris, **43:** 94-95, 150, 208-209, 236,n1, 255, 269; W. S. Sims on naval, **43:** 179-82; and proposed Allied shipping conference in London, **43:** 302, 304; D. Lloyd George on, **44:** 16,n1, 125-30, 362-63; W. H. Page on, **44:** 132, 134, 330; Graysons reveal WW's private views on, **44:** 173-75; H. H. Sargent on, **44:** 239,n1; British drive into Flanders, **44:** 332-33,n1; and Supreme War Council, **44:** 355; P. D. Lochridge on, **44:** 361,n1; advances into Italy, **44:** 506-509; report on Liberty Engine, **44:** 538-41; C. E. Russell on Russia and, **44:** 557-58; N. D. Baker on H. H. Sargent memorandum, **45:** 4-6; Winston Churchill (American) on, **45:** 19-24; J. Grew on German invasion of Italy, **45:** 37-38; and Turkey, **45:** 52-53, 72-73; sending Chinese troops to Europe, **45:** 308; and French and British request for U.S. troops, **45:** 328, 372-73; H. R. Wilson on, **45:** 384-85; Britain recommends Allied policy in Russia, **45:** 417-19; J. J. Pershing on troop disposition, **45:** 439-40; **47:** 611-12; and Inquiry Memorandum, **45:** 459-68; and resolution of issue of U.S. troops serving abroad, **46:** 8-11,n1, 11-12, 162, 196-98, 211-12, 220, 237-38, 240-41, 337-38; and Inter-Allied General Reserve, **46:** 241, 558-60; request for transfer of division from Italian to western front, **47:** 107,n1, 129-30, 468; need for and deployment of U.S. troops on western front, **47:** 130-31, 157, 158, 170, 260-61, 271; **48:** 243-45; comments on F. Foch's appointment as Supreme Commander, **47:** 160,n1, 181-82, 209, 237-38; W. S. Sims on British military situation, **47:** 161-62; Baker on French situation and Supreme War Council's resolution on U.S. troops, **47:** 166, 174-76, 261-62; Lloyd George on troop crisis and, **47:** 181-83, 203-205, 229-30, 338-41; W. Wiseman on, **47:** 433-35, 443, 617-20; and agreements among Pershing, Milner, Haig, and Foch for U.S. troop transport, **47:** 456-58; **48:** 227; H. Frazier on Gen. Studd's plan not being implemented, **47:** 505; and Abbeville agreement, **47:** 497-98, 512-14, 517-18, 615-16; **48:** 32-34; T. Bliss on conference with Foch and Pershing, **47:**

World War, cont.

563-64; and question of a U.S declaration of war against Turkey and Bulgaria, **47:** 568-71; House on problems of command and coordination, **48:** 232-33; Allied intervention in Russia, **48:** 236, 378-79; **49:** 170-72; **51:** 25-26, 33, 139; J. Joffre on situation in France, **48:** 332-33; Bliss on, **48:** 383-90; **49:** 258-61, 276-77, 336-44; **51:** 34-49; deployment on Western front, **48:** 386-87, 415, 483, 568n1; **49:** 260-61; A. Konovalov on Allied policy in Russia and, **48:** 406-10; Baker's monthly statistics on troops sent abroad, **48:** 476-77; Balfour on Foch's responsibilities, **48:** 595; WW on, **48:** 624-25, 639-43; **49:** 111-12, 112-13; E. Geddes on, **49:** 410-13; and Italian front, **49:** 136-37, 369; Norway and, **49:** 312,n1; note to Supreme War Council on conduct of the war in 1918 and 1919, **51:** 195-203; Germany's recognition of facing defeat, **51:** 384-85; Baker on reasons for slow progress on Pershing's front, **51:** 385-86; issue of sending troops to Italy, **51:** 386-87, 387-88; and proposed Japanese intervention in Siberia: *see* Russia—Siberia, intervention in; Czech troops in Russia

peace moves: **43:** 268,n1; **44:** 10,n1, 18-22, 184n3; comments on, **40:** 4-6,n1, 12-13, 20, 21, 23-24, 29, 30n1, 39, 75n1, 111,n1, 124n3, 125-27, 134-35, 137-39, 172, 178-80, 186,n1, 189, 229,n1; **41:** 17-18, 23n1, 26n1, 36, 40, 83,n1, 85-86, 135, 149-51; J. Grew on German situation and, **40:** 21,n1, 160-61, 428-36; and Switzerland, **40:** 22-23, 42-46; **46:** 592-94; N. M. Butler on, **40:** 24n1; WW on terms for a lasting peace, **40:** 67-70, 70-74, 84-85, 110-11, 197-200, 209-11, 222-25, 226-29, 256-59, 259-62; and conference of neutrals, **40:** 81n1; Germany's peace proposal, comments on, and U.S. reply, **40:** 231-32, 241,n1, 242-43, 249, 250; WW's peace note, comments on, and Germany's reply, **40:** 273-76,n1,2, 307n1, 311, 314, 317, 318, 324-25, 325-26, 326-27, 330n1, 331, 339, 343, 355-58, 361-62, 370-71, 373, 418, 446n2,3, 453-55, 489, 530; R. Lansing's "verge of war" and subsequent statements, **40:** 306n1, 307,n1; WW's secret negotiations with Britain and Germany, **40:** 362-65, 403-404, 477, 504n1, 516-17, 525-26; Spain's reply, **40:** 378-79; **41:** 35; German reaction to Allied reply to German peace offer, **40:** 383-84,n1; peace note leak, **40:** 421-23; Anglo-French reply and A. J. Balfour's addendum, **40:** 439-41,n1, 470, 500-503; WW's Peace without Victory speech and comments on, **40:** 462-63, 491, 533-39, 539, 558,n1, 559, 559-60, 560, 561; WW looks to Carnegie Endowment for support, **41:** 55; Germa-

World War, cont.

ny's decision not to state terms, **41:** 59-63; E. M. House and J. Bernstorff meet on, **41:** 3, 24-26,n1, 49-52; J. W. Gerard on Germany's terms, **41:** 138; and Austria-Hungary, **41:** 158-59, 185, 211-12, 297-98; **45:** 56-57; **51:** 282-83, 505-506, 526-27, 576,n1; and Bases of Peace, **41:** 160-64, 173-75; WW hopes to maintain Austrian-American relations, **41:** 158-59; and proposed neutral conference in Washington, **41:** 200; and Swiss efforts to restore German-American relations, **41:** 201-203, 273-77; negotiations involving Austria-Hungary and the Entente, **41:** 211-14, 260, 267-68, 270-73, 297-98, 312, 313, 398-99, 421-22; **44:** 513-14; **46:** 577; **47:** 11, 122-23; and Belgium, **41:** 217; G. Kirchwey and, **41:** 242-46; Mexico's and Ecuador's proposal, **41:** 249-50,n1, 258,n1, 352, 404-406; WW meets with leading peace society delegates, **41:** 303-304,n3, 305-308; and Socialist party's attempt at international conference, **42:** 199,n10; T. H. Price's dream of peace commission, **42:** 255-56; and H. Morgenthau's mission, **42:** 315-17,n3; **43:** 159,n1,2,3, 172, 183-84, 206; and Britain's agreements with Allied powers, **42:** 327,n1; Argentina proposes conference of American nations, **42:** 359-60; J. P. Tumulty urges WW to warn of evils of separate peace, **42:** 360-63; Reichstag passes peace resolution, **43:** 185,n1,2; and proposal for an editorial forum in a German and an American newspaper, **43:** 219-20, 220-21, 237-38; N. Angell's memorandum on Allied diplomatic strategy, **43:** 401-409; F. Frankfurter on sending U.S. representatives to Allied conferences, **43:** 447-48; and R. M. LaFollette's and W. H. King's peace resolutions, **43:** 455n1; Pope Benedict's appeal to the belligerents, replies to and comments on, **43:** 482-85, 487-88, 520, 521,n1; **44:** 30, 31, 33-36, 40-41, 49-50, 57-59, 83-84, 93, 94, 103, 105, 105-106, 120, 130-31, 146, 149, 157, 158, 169-70, 180-81, 295-96, 390-91, 393-94, 468, 469; W. Lippmann on, **43:** 534; German Americans desire unofficially to inform German people of the situation, **44:** 154-55; C. W. Eliot on a conference of the belligerents, **44:** 185,n4; E. M. House on missed opportunity for peace, **44:** 201-202; WW on inopportune time for, **44:** 279, 299n1; and German peace offer to Britain through Spain, **44:** 311, 318-20, 325; House to represent U.S. at inter-Allied council, **44:** 427, 437-39; Milner on, **44:** 548-49; and Russia, **45:** 73, 119-20; Britain on separate peace with Turkey, **45:** 148-49; and Brest-Litovsk negotiations, **45:** 384-85,n2; Ger-

World War, cont.

many's attempt to involve U.S. and Allies in, **45**: 432n1; pressures on Allies to respond to German-Austrian proposals, **45**: 436-37; F. Taussig on, **45**: 440-41; WW on answering German, **45**: 486; House and WW discuss peace commission, **46**: 115-16; H. R. Wilson on, **46**: 172-73; suggestions for actions by WW, **46**: 183-85, 207, 268; and Bulgaria, **46**: 235,n1; **51**: 134, 141-42, 154-55; and G. D. Herron's role, **46**: 198-200, 235,n1, 241, 242-47, 253-54, 261, 353, 357, 388, 428, 473, 483, 510, 580, 580n1, 589, 615, 616; **47**: 24-26, 64-65,n1,2,4, 128; **48**: 210-17, 473-74, 538-40, 552-55,n6, 592; **49**: 187-93, 228-30, 231-32, 436,n1, 447; **51**: 9-10, 229-46, 387-88, 565; O. Czernin and, **46**: 271-72; K. von Wiegand on, **46**: 350n1; and WW's Four Points address, **46**: 318-24; and Italy and Vatican, **46**: 365-66; and Charles I's message to WW and reply, **46**: 397-99,n1, 400, 411-12, 424, 432, 440-42, 464, 486-87, 507-508, 508, 551-53; A. J. Balfour on Austria-Hungary, **46**: 473, 483-84; and draft of WW's reply to G. Hertling's address, **46**: 496-98; C. W. Ackerman on, **46**: 557; **47**: 524; and Netherlands' proposal, **46**: 615-17; Vatican suggests Easter armistice, **47**: 63,n1; A. Philips and WW discuss, **47**: 133-34, 142-43; W. H. Page on Charles I's attempts, **47**: 176-77; and France and Austria-Hungary and the Sixtus letter, **47**: 589,n1; WW on Germany's, **49**: 274; R. Kühlmann's attempt at talks between Britain and Germany, **48**: 555n7; R. de Fiori and Herron talks, **48**: 552-55,n6; **49**: 228, 229-30, 231, 436n1; **51**: 230-46; House and WW on The Inquiry, **49**: 281; and Sweden, **49**: 437; and Holland and Germany, **49**: 548n1; and Austria-Hungary's notes, **51**: 10-11,n3, 23-24, 106-107,n7, 258-59, 263; T. H. Bliss on, **51**: 46-47, 571; H. Sulzer's alleged mission from WW, **51**: 76-77,n1; R. Lansing on Central Powers and, **51**: 93-94; German note of Oct. 6, 1918, and U.S. reply, **51**: 253,n2, 255-57, 263, 264-65, 268-69; German note of Oct. 12 and U.S. reply, **51**: 316,n6, 333-34; Germany to evacuate from Belgium and return political prisoners, **51**: 370-71,n2, 371-72n1; talk of Allies taking negotiations out of WW's hands, **51**: 504, 505; House on progress of, **51**: 534, 541; Howard on press censorship and, **51**: 538-39; *see also* postwar organization and security; league of nations

preparations for peace conference: **44**: 217-19, 226, 275,n1, 309, 426, 549-51; House and WW discuss, **49**: 266, 267, 286, 301, 428, 429; suggestions for commissioners, **51**: 109, 314, 315, 316-17, 341; H. F. Hollis on, **51**: 182, 183, 298-

World War, cont.

99; and Balkan settlement, **51**: 187; House on, **51**: 406-408, 606-607; McAdoo on financial questions to be considered at, **51**: 468-70; site suggestions, **51**: 473, 516, 550-51, 617; F. I. Cobb on, **51**: 590-91

peace terms: ideas of and discussions between WW, A. J. Balfour, and E. M. House, **42**: 120, 128-29, 142-43, 155-57, 171-73, 288-89, 332, 385, 425, 433; R. Lansing on Germany and, **42**: 163; House meets with E. Drummond on, **42**: 354-55; and socialists, **42**: 364, 364-65,n1; **47**: 74-75; R. Swing on, **42**: 388-90; R. Cecil on, **42**: 389,n4; and Turkey, **42**: 403; **51**: 455,n1, 456; Russia on, **42**: 418; **43**: 407n4; **45**: 105; Union of Democratic Control on Russia's, **42**: 420-22; R. L. Owen's resolution, **42**: 444,n1; G. Sosnowski on, **42**: 492, 493; House on challenging Germany to state, **42**: 523; WW advises Russian Commission not to discuss, **43**: 15,n2; D. Lloyd George on British war aims, **43**: 291,n1; **45**: 487,n2, 488-89, 556-57; W. R. Hearst on, **43**: 318n1; H. Caine on, **43**: 351-52,n2; and Asia Minor, **43**: 388; and Pope Benedict's appeal and comments on, **43**: 438-39, 472, 484-85, 488, 508, 534; **44**: 20-22, 22, 23-24, 24-26, 26, 43-46, 76, 84,n1, 120; and La Follette resolution, **43**: 455n1; Baron Moncheur on Belgium and, **43**: 465-69; G. Michaelis on, **43**: 498,n1; H. Todd on, **43**: 536-38; restatement of America's aims, **44**: 98; WW asks House to find out what Allies want, **44**: 120-21; T. P. Gore on, **44**: 121n1; W. H. Page on, **44**: 329-31; Vatican on Germany's reply to Pope's appeal, **44**: 349-50; and suggestions regarding commercial policy of U.S., **44**: 454-57; F. C. Howe on, **44**: 474-77; Milner on, **44**: 546-49; **51**: 373; and Inquiry Memorandum, **44**: 549-51; **45**: 17-18, 468-72; Lansdowne's letter and, **45**: 173n1, 174-75; WW on, **45**: 176, 197, 199; **51**: 129-33, 473; and negotiations at Brest Litovsk, **45**: 216-18,n4, 384n2, 411-14, 433-35; J. Meinl on, **45**: 415-17,n5; and secret negotiations between Britain and Austria-Hungary, **45**: 430-31; **46**: 577; American editorials on German-Austrian proposals, **45**: 436-37; WW's Fourteen Points address, **45**: 476-86, 493-517, 534-39; **46**: 497; and J. H. Lewis resolution, **45**: 601,n1; Lansing on Italy and Adriatic question, **46**: 96-97; Germany is not stating, **46**: 110; Charles I and F. Foerster discuss, **46**: 198n2; comparison of G. Hertling's and O. Czernin's, **46**: 222-29; W. Wiseman on WW's, **46**: 249; **49**: 365; WW's outline, draft of, and Four Points address, **46**: 273-74, 274-79, 318-24; and Rumania, **46**: 373-75; **47**: 450,n3; and It-

World War, cont.

aly, **46:** 376; R. Ogden on threat of post-war economic boycott as means to Germany stating, **46:** 418; G. Hertling on, **46:** 428; House on proposed embargo law and, **46:** 490; W. C. Bullitt on Germany's and Austria-Hungary's, **46:** 568-70; T. W. Lamont on Russia and, **46:** 585,n2; and Supreme War Council's declaration on Poland, **46:** 587-88,n1; The Netherlands and B. Jong and, **47:** 64,n4; Austria-Hungary objects to annexation desires of Italy and France, **47:** 239-41; S. Gotō and R. S. Morris discuss, **47:** 430; and Balkans, **47:** 451,n3; **51:** 142-44, 145, 155, 162-63, 163-64, 169, 170, 187; and A. L. Lowell, **48:** 152, 153,n1; and Australia's concerns, **48:** 228; and Poland, **48:** 312, 437n2; P. C. March on Russia and, **48:** 420; G. Herron and R. de Fiori and, **48:** 552, 552-55,n1,6; **51:** 231-46; and Lithuania, **48:** 630,n1; Bavaria's plan, **49:** 229-30; WW's concern over Russia and, **49:** 231-32; and league of nations, **49:** 266; **51:** 513; W. G. Sharp on France and, **51:** 21n1; T. H. Bliss on Britain and, **51:** 47-48; S. Sonnino on, **51:** 119; H. C. Lodge on, **51:** 156,n2, 277n7; German note of Oct. 6, 1918, and WW's reply, **51:** 253,n2, 256, 263-64, 264-65, 268-69,n1, 276-78; Allies' joint opinion on, **51:** 261-62, 272, 272-75, 291-92, 307-309, 428-30; and Prince Max's inaugural speech, **51:** 269,n1; Senate debate on WW's peace terms, **51:** 277n7; importance of military consultation before terms are fixed, **51:** 289,n1; need for U.S. representative in Europe, **51:** 290; Germany accepts WW's terms, and comments on acceptance, **51:** 316,

World War, cont.

n6, 320-24, 324-25, 329-32; draft of U.S. note to Germany, Oct. 14, 1918, and German reply of Oct. 20, **51:** 333-34, 400n1, 403; Great Britain on, **51:** 335-36; and sentiment in Senate on, **51:** 339-40; Viscount Milner and Gen. H. Wilson on, **51:** 373; reply to Austria-Hungary, **51:** 383; Hoover on Belgian relief and, **51:** 399; drafts of and U.S. reply to German note of Oct. 20, **51:** 400-401, 401-402, 413, 417-19; WW answers Republican attacks, **51:** 405; Balfour on not accepting German reply of Oct. 20, **51:** 411-12; Cabinet and War Council discuss, **51:** 413-15, 416; WW's note to Allies, **51:** 416-17; Baruch on equality of economic opportunity, **51:** 419-20; G. M. Hitchcock on Republican demands, **51:** 423-24; T. H. Bliss on, **51:** 425-33, 434-36, 584-85; J. Pershing and, **51:** 454-55, 470-72, 524-25, 596-98; T. Roosevelt on, **51:** 455n1; F. Foch on, **51:** 463-64; naval terms, **51:** 474-75, 486-95, 575; Cobb-Lippmann memorandum on WW's Fourteen Points, **51:** 495-504; and Austria-Hungary's note of Oct. 29, **51:** 505-506, 506-508; House discusses with Allied leaders, **51:** 511-13, 514-17, 568-70; and Germany's amendments to her Constitution, **51:** 518-20; Italy on danger of separate peace with Austria-Hungary, **51:** 529-30, 562; and Yugoslavia, **51:** 562-63,n1; House on Allies' accepting WW's terms with qualifications, **51:** 580-82; celebration in Italy regarding, **51:** 601; and false armistice, **51:** 621n1, 641
legislation concerning: *see* under names of individual bills, such as Lever bill, selective service bill

End of World War entry

World Zionist Organization, **45:** 572n2
World's Work, **40:** 388, 463; **43:** 465, 493; **45:** 128n1; **48:** 284n1, 311
Would Help Both Races (*Atlanta Constitution*), **40:** 153n1
Wright, Albert D., **49:** 327-28, 400
Wright, Carroll D., **47:** 574
Wright, Curtis J., **42:** 116
Wright, Edward H., **43:** 392,n1, 507,n1
Wright, J. George, **47:** 10,n2
Wright, Joshua Butler, **45:** 543,n3; **48:** 202, 274
Wright, Orville, **45:** 357n2
Wright, Theodore, **40:** 35,n1
Wright, Mrs. Theodore, **40:** 35
Wright, William Mason, **45:** 390,n2,4
Wu T'ing-fang, **41:** 175,n3
Württemberg, Germany, **46:** 245
Wyatt, Ethel Morgan Lyle (Mrs. Harvey), **49:** 123,n1
Wyatt, Woodrow Lyle, **49:** 123,n2
Wyatt, Ca., **44:** 242, 277

Wykoff, Leah Lucile Ehrich (Mrs. Walter Augustus), **40:** 570,n4
Wylie, Laura Isabelle Moore (Mrs. Hart) (Loolie Belle), **40:** 169,n1
Wyoming, **41:** 292; **43:** 73-74; politics in, **51:** 590, 633
Wyoming, University of, **47:** 311n1

YMCA: *see* Young Men's Christian Association
Yager, Arthur, **40:** 57-58, 90, 148; **41:** 278, 407n1, 515-16; **47:** 543-44,n1, 577; **48:** 3, 15-16, 17-18, 35-37, 48, 49, 74-75; **49:** 236,n1, 252; S. Gompers drops charges against, **48:** 637,n4
Yakovlev, Nikolai Nikolaevich: *see* Iakovlev, Nikolai Nikolaevich
Yale, William, **42:** 317n3
Yale University, **40:** 444; **42:** 322n1, 323n2; **45:** 352,n1
Yale University Press, **45:** 352,n1, 362, 453

Yalu, Manchuria: *see* Chalantun
Yamagata, Aritomo, **48:** 461,n3
Yangco, Teodoro, **41:** 345
Yaphank strike, **45:** 10
Year as a Government Agent (White-house), **51:** 603n1
Yellow Curtains of Rome (B. Bolling), **46:** 371n1
yellow dog contract, **46:** 297n1
Yiddish language, **51:** 626
York, Archbishop of: *see* Lang, Cosmo Gordon
Yorke, Peter Christopher, **43:** 216,n1, 217
Yoshihito, Emperor of Japan (1912-1926), **41:** 382, 403; **47:** 427
Yoshimoto (Japanese merchant killed in Manchuria), **43:** 83n3
Young, Allyn Abbott, **45:** 141,n1,2
Young, Arthur, **48:** 146,n1, 147; **49:** 208, 306
Young, Charles, **43:** 4,n3, 16, 78,n1, 118, 119, 132
Young, George, **41:** 56n5
Young, George Morley, **44:** 36n1
Young, Harry F., **43:** 246n1
Young, Hugh Hampton, **45:** 108n2
Young, Michael J., **40:** 176,n1; **43:** 513n1,2; **47:** 179n3
Young, Owen D., **49:** 407
Young, Rose, **48:** 303n1
Young, Samuel Baldwin Marks, **41:** 470,n1
Young, William Elmore, **41:** 55-56,n1
Young Men's Christian Association, **41:** 113n3, 527, 556; **42:** 536, 556, 557,n2; **43:** 264, 529; **44:** 68, 69, 85, 270n1, 551-52; **45:** 142, 143,n3, 146, 194, 597; **46:** 479n2,3, 604n1; **47:** 304-305,n1, 540, 613-14; **48:** 78n2, 143, 150-51, 221, 573; and issue of passports and security clearance, **49:** 359-60, 387, 390, 395-96; and fund drive, **49:** 425-26
Young Men's Christian Association's National War Work Council, **48:** 230n1; **49:** 40, 78, 128, 179n1; **51:** 598, 618, 621, 636
Young Men's Hebrew Association, **44:** 552
Young Turk movement, **43:** 298-99
Young Women's Christian Association, **47:** 502,n1, 614; **48:** 6,n1; **49:** 425-26; **51:** 636; religious discrimination by, **48:** 208,n1, 209, 221-22,n1, 230
Younger, Maud, **40:** 379,n4
Ypres, Belgium, **44:** 332; **47:** 498
Ypres, Battle of, **42:** 373; **44:** 333n1
Yüan Shih-K'ai, **42:** 466n1
Yugoslavia and Yugoslavs, **40:** 250; **48:** 96-97, 436, 437,n2,3, 464, 530-31, 545, 591; **49:** 287-88; **51:** 47, 118-19, 156n2, 348, 374, 383, 501, 502, 505, 541, 562-63,n1
Yugoslav National Committee, **51:** 562,n1

Zabel, Winfred C., **47:** 439,n2

Zamoyski, Count Maurice, **42:** 356,n1; **44:** 187
Zangwill, Israel, **45:** 369,n1
Zapata, Emiliano, **49:** 31
Zapatistas, **40:** 110,n4
Zatko, James J., **40:** 407n2
Zayas, Alfredo, **41:** 268n1
Zeebrugge, **43:** 180
Zeit, Die (Berlin), **42:** 389n1
Zeman, Z. A. B., **48:** 398n1
zemstvo(s), **44:** 496-97,n5; **47:** 242, 398, 594; **48:** 39, 105; **49:** 63
Zemstvos and the Red Cross in Russia (Sack), **43:** 455n3
Zemstvos Union: *see* All-Russia Union of Zemstvos
Zeppelin in Combat: A History of the German Naval Airship Division 1912-1918 (Robinson), **40:** 145n2
Zeppelin warfare, **40:** 145-46
Ziegfeld Follies of 1918, **51:** 117n1
Zimmermann, Arthur, **40:** 161,n1, 173, 184, 185, 331, 411, 431, 434, 461, 463n1, 532, 554, 555; **41:** 50n3, 79, 89, 183, 430; instructions to J. H. Bernstorff on reply to WW's peace note of Dec. 18, 1916, **40:** 504n1; meets with J. W. Gerard and reveals peace terms, **41:** 137-38; acknowledges telegram, **41:** 325-26
Zimmermann telegram, **41:** 304n3, 308,n1, 325-26, 405, 459, 462, 513, 525; **42:** 141, 332; **44:** 140,n1, 164, 181, 253; **47:** 164; WW on, **41:** 288; E. M. House on, **41:** 296-97; U.S. thanks Britain for information on, **41:** 297; R. Lansing memorandum on, **41:** 321-27; publication of in U.S., **41:** 324; V. Carranza and, **41:** 392,n1
Zimmerwald, Switzerland, **46:** 456n3
Zimmerwalder Bewegung: Protokolle und Korrespondenz (Lademacher, ed.), **46:** 457n3
zinc, **46:** 336
Zinkhan, Louis F., **44:** 559-60,n6
Zionism, Zionist movement, **42:** 234-35; **43:** 159n2; **44:** 150, 165, 186, 299n2, 323-24, 371, 390, 391, 546-47; **45:** 149,n2, 286, 572,n2; **46:** 333, 493-95, 516-17; **49:** 363-64,n1,2, 403
Zionist Committee, **46:** 493
Zita, Princess of Bourbon and Parma, Empress of Austria and Queen of Hungary, **44:** 26,n2, 43; **46:** 242, 243; **47:** 589n1
Zlatopolsky, Hillel, **45:** 572,n2
Znamiecki, Alexander, **42:** 352
Zowski (Zwierzchowski), Stanislaus Jan, **46:** 404,n6
Zrinyi, S.M.S., **51:** 492
Zubáran Capmany, Rafael, **49:** 33
Zurich, University of, **47:** 454n1
Zurich *Wissen und Leben*, **48:** 213n8
Zwiedinek, Baron Erich, **40:** 113-14; **42:** 23
Zycktinski, K., **41:** 508